PUBLIC AND PRIVATE FAMILIES

PUBLIC AND PRIVATE FAMILIES: A READER

Andrew J. Cherlin

Johns Hopkins University

Boston, Massachusetts   Burr Ridge, Illinois   Dubuque, Iowa
Madison, Wisconsin   New York, New York   San Francisco, California   St. Louis, Missouri

McGraw-Hill

A Division of The McGraw·Hill Companies

PUBLIC AND PRIVATE FAMILIES: A READER

This book is printed on acid-free paper.

2 3 4 5 6 7 8 9 0 DOC/DOC 9 0 9 8 7

ISBN 0-07-011929-5

Editorial director: *Phillip A. Butcher*
Sponsoring editor: *Jill Gordon*
Developmental editor: *Katherine Blake*
Marketing manager: *Sally Constable*
Project manager: *Christina Thornton-Villagomez*
Production supervisor: *Karen Thigpen*
Designer: *Kiera Cunningham*
Compositor: *Shepherd, Incorporated*
Typeface: *10.5/12 Times Roman*
Printer: *R. R. Donnelley*

Library of Congress Cataloging-in-Publication Data

Public and private families : a reader / [selected by] Andrew J.
    Cherlin.
        p.   cm.
    ISBN 0-07-011929-5
    1. Family—United States.   2. Family policy—United States.
I. Cherlin, Andrew J., 1948–
HQ536.P83   1997
306.85′0973—dc21   97–1314

http://www.mhcollege.com

CONTENTS

v

PREFACE

This volume consists of readings that are keyed to the 16 chapters in a textbook I wrote for courses in the sociology of the family, *Public and Private Families: An Introduction* (1996, McGraw-Hill). Nevertheless, it can be used with other textbooks or no textbook at all. I tried to cast a broad net while trawling for the articles and book excerpts presented here. Many pieces describe the stories of real families; for instance, Susan Sheehan's eye-opening report on the struggles of a working-class family, "There Ain't No Middle Class," from *The New Yorker;* and Alex Kotlowitz's riveting portrait of Pharoah Rivers from his best-selling book, *There Are No Children Here: The Story of Two Boys Growing Up in the Other America.* Others, such as Janet Z. Giele's essay on conservative, liberal, and feminist views on family policy, reflect debate and controversy within sociology about the future of the family. Still others are drawn from the current classics of the gender-studies approach to the sociology of the family, such as Arlie Hochschild's already famous portrayal of Nancy and Evan Holt from *The Second Shift: Working Parents and the Revolution at Home.*

From outside of sociology, I have included insightful pieces by psychologists (Jamie K. Keshet's analysis of remarried couples), legal scholars (David Chambers's discussion of the lack of legal recognition of stepparents), and, in one case, a psychologist *and* a legal scholar (an analysis of joint custody by Eleanor Maccoby and Robert Mnookin). I also have imported a few book excerpts from the large literature on family history: Stephanie Coontz's look at family diversity in past times, Elaine Tyler May's discussion of the 1950s, and Ellen K. Rothman's description of the great changes in courtship during the twentieth century in the United States. And I have included some interdisciplinary work, such as an analysis of a recent, national survey on sexual behavior.

In 1996, Congress enacted a welfare reform bill that constitutes the greatest change in social policy toward poor families since the Great Depression. It is too recent to be analyzed in existing textbooks. I have therefore written a background article especially for this volume that I hope will help students understand the implications of the new law for low-income families. In addition, I have included Mark Rank's report on his intensive studies of the family lives of welfare recipients, from *Living on the Edge: The Realities of Welfare in America*.

The metaphor of public and private families in the title of this reader reflects my sense that families matter in two senses. First, they perform activities of great importance to the public interest—most notably raising the next generation and caring for the frail elderly. Second, as the main site of our personal lives, they provide the private satisfactions of love, intimacy, and companionship. Many textbooks and readers focus more on the private family; they mainly describe how people manage their personal relationships as they proceed through the life course. I include this perspective, too, but I attempt to balance it with a consideration of the important public issues raised by the great recent changes in family life. Indeed, hardly a week goes by without some family issue—no-fault divorce, gay marriage, teenage childbearing, welfare reform, child care, deadbeat dads, domestic violence, and so forth—appearing on the front page of the newspapers. Consequently, it is crucial that students studying the sociology of the family encounter not just studies of the individual life course but also of the ways that family life affects our society. I have attempted to provide both the public and private perspectives on the family in this reader.

I would like to thank several people who reviewed the preliminary draft of this reader: Sandra L. Caron, University of Maine; Patricia McManus, Indiana University; Joan Toms Olson, Mary Washington College; William W. Pendleton, Emory University; Stacy Rogers, University of Nebraska-Lincoln; Linda Stephens, Clemson University; and Stephen Wieting, University of Iowa.

Andrew J. Cherlin

ABOUT THE AUTHOR

Andrew J. Cherlin is Benjamin H. Griswold III Professor of Public Policy in the Department of Sociology at Johns Hopkins University. He received a B.S. from Yale University in 1970 and a Ph.D. in sociology from the University of California at Los Angeles in 1976. Author of the McGraw-Hill textbook *Public and Private Families: An Introduction* (1996), his other books include *Marriage, Divorce, Remarriage* (revised and enlarged edition, 1992); *Divided Families: What Happens to Children When Parents Part* (with Frank F. Furstenberg, Jr., 1991); *The Changing American Family and the Public Policy* (1988); and *The New American Grandparent: A Place in the Family, A Life Apart* (with Frank F. Furstenberg, Jr., 1986). In 1989–1990 he was Chair of the Family Section, and in 1995–1996 he was Chair of the Population, Section of the American Sociological Association.

Professor Cherlin is a recipient of a MERIT (Method to Extend Research in Time) Award from the National Institutes of Health for his research on the effects of divorce on children. He was a member of both the Panel on Child Care Policy and the Committee on Child Development Research and Public Policy of the National Academy of Sciences. His recent articles include "Stepfamilies in the United States: A Reconsideration," in the *Annual Review of Sociology;* "Nostalgia as Family Policy," in *The Public Interest;* "Longitudinal Studies of the Effects of Divorce on Children," in *Science;* and "Recent Changes in American Fertility, Marriage, and Divorce," in the *Annals of the American Academy of Political and Social Science.* He also has written many short articles for the *New York Times, The Washington Post, Newsweek,* and other periodicals. He has been interviewed on *ABC News Nightline,* the *Today Show,* the *CBS Evening News,* National Public Radio's *All Things Considered,* and other news programs and documentaries.

PUBLIC AND PRIVATE FAMILIES

PART ONE

INTRODUCTION

CHAPTER 1

Public and Private Families

The state of the American family—indeed, the state of the family in all industrialized nations—is a controversial issue, much debated by social commentators, politicians, and academic experts. A half-century ago, few observers seemed concerned. But since the 1960s, family life has changed greatly. Many users of this reader will have experienced these changes in their own families. Divorce is much more common; at current rates, about one in two marriages would end in divorce. Young adults are postponing marriage and often living with a partner prior to marrying. A growing number of children—currently about 30 percent—are born to mothers who are not married. And many more married women are working outside the home.

These trends aren't necessarily negative. For instance, married women's jobs often give them an improved sense of self-worth and boost their families' standards of living. Young adults may use living with a partner as a way to search for a more compatible spouse. In fact, some commentators hail the decline of the 1950s middle-class family in which wives usually stayed home and specialized in housework and child care. These breadwinner-homemaker families, it is alleged, restricted the lives of women and supported the continuation of conflict-ridden marriages that may have been worse for children than a parental divorce would have been. But the overall tone of the public commentary on family change has been one of concern.

In order to develop your own views on the subject, you first need to know the basic facts about changes in American families over the past several decades. In the first selection, demographers Sara McLanahan and Lynne Casper present an overview of four important demographic trends: the weakening role of marriage in family life; the increase in divorce; the changes in births to married and unmarried women; and the movement of mothers into the work force. All of these aspects have changed dramatically over the past half-century. The numbers and charts they present are the starting point for interpreting the controversy and debate that will be found in subsequent chapters. McLanahan and Casper also make the point that the United States has not been alone in experiencing these trends; rather, most Western European nations have experienced similar trends. This information suggests that the causes of the changes in family life are probably not narrow events in the United States but rather broad changes in the economy and in culture in the industrialized nations of Europe and North America.

Confronted with these great changes, some observers long for the good old days of large, close, extended families. But Stephanie Coontz argues in an excerpt from her book, *The Way We Never Were: American Families and the Nostalgia Trap,* that the good old days are a myth. Coontz makes the point that there was great diversity in the family lives of Americans in previous centuries. Moreover, death disrupted families nearly as much as divorce does now. Emotional closeness and romantic love between spouses weren't seen as very important. Perhaps Coontz occasionally goes too far in her zeal at stripping away the myths of the past. She is more optimistic about the state of contemporary marriage than are most other commentators. The demographic trends chronicled by McLanahan and Casper suggest an erosion in the role of marriage. More than at any other time in the nation's history, people are living with partners outside of marriage, divorcing their spouses, and having children outside of marriages. Even without romanticizing the past, these are major changes.

READING 1-1

Growing Diversity and Inequality in the American Family

Sara McLanahan and Lynne Casper

Dramatic changes have occurred in the American family over the last four decades, as reflected in popular television shows. In the 1950s the typical family portrayed in most situation comedies consisted of a breadwinner-husband, a homemaker-wife, and two or more children. This "ideal" American family was depicted in such shows as "Father Knows Best," "Leave It to Beaver," and "Ozzie and Harriet." The Nelson family—Ozzie, Harriet, and their children David and Ricky—has recently received renewed fame in the press and has come to symbolize the typical American family of the 1950s. It now serves as a baseline against which to compare current family arrangements. Although the Nelson family was more of an ideal than a reality for many people, even in the 1950s, Americans did share a common image of what a family should look like and how parents and children should behave, which reinforced the importance of the family and strengthened the institution of marriage. No such common understanding exists today, for better or for worse.

Since the 1950s, families like the Nelsons have become increasingly rare, as young men and women have delayed marriage and childbearing, as wives and mothers have entered the labor force in greater numbers, and as divorce rates have soared. This does not mean that families are becoming extinct, but rather that they are taking on different forms. Along with the decline of families like the Nelsons, new types

Sara McLanahan and Lynne Casper, "Growing Diversity and Inequality in the American Family" in Reynolds Farley, ed., *State of the Union: America in the 1990s, Volume 2: Social Trends,* pp. 1–16. Copyright © 1996 by Russell Sage Foundation. Reprinted with the permission of the publishers.

of families and living arrangements have become more dominant, including childless couples with two careers, one-parent families, and cohabiting couples with children. Nonfamily households—defined as households containing a single individual or people unrelated by either blood or marriage—have also become more prominent. Today, successful television shows, such as "thirtysomething," "LA Law," and "Murphy Brown," feature divorced and never-married characters, employed mothers, and single mothers (defined as divorced, separated, never-married, or widowed mothers raising children alone), reflecting the diversity of families that is characteristic of the 1990s. These "new families" indicate that Americans have more choices today than they did in the past about how to organize their private lives and intimate relationships (Goldscheider & Waite, 1991).

At the same time, greater diversity has meant greater economic inequality across households. Some of the new, nontraditional families, such as dual-earner couples, are doing very well; others, such as single-mother families, are doing poorly. In 1991, the typical dual-earner couple with children had an annual income of $46,629.[1] In contrast, the typical mother-only family had an income of only $13,012. Families like that of Ozzie and Harriet (working-husband, homemaker-wife, children) had an annual income of $33,961. The increase in single-mother families and dual-earner families during the 1970s and 1980s has led to increased inequality across households and to a feminization of poverty, with more and more of the poor being concentrated in families headed by unmarried mothers (Pearce, 1978). In 1960, 24 percent of poor families were headed by unmarried mothers; in 1990, the number was 53 percent. The diversity of families has also exacerbated racial and ethnic differences in economic well-being. Whereas the fastest growing white families are dual-earner families, a relatively advantaged group, the fastest growing black families are mother-only families, a relatively disadvantaged group.

Many people are concerned about what these changes mean for children and what government can (and should) do to help families and children adjust to change. Since women are spending more of their time working outside the home, their children are spending less time with them; and mothers are confronted with conflicting demands from the workplace and family. Despite the problems encountered by working mothers, today very few people believe that mothers' employment per se is harmful to children, except perhaps during the first year of life. And yet we used to think so, 40 years ago. Today, the policy debate about mothers' employment is primarily a debate over what constitutes quality childcare, how to make quality care accessible and affordable to families, and how to design parental leave policies to suit the needs of parents as well as employers (Da Vanzo, Rahman, & Wadhwa, 1994).

The public is much less sanguine about the future implications of marital disruption and single motherhood. When mothers work outside the home, children may spend less time with their parents, but the family also gains income. In contrast, when parents live in separate households, children experience a loss of parental time (typically the father's time) as well as a loss of income. Because the total loss of resources is substantial for children who live with single mothers, many people fear that this type of arrangement may be harmful to children. And indeed the empirical evidence supports their fears. Children who grow up with only one of their parents are less successful in adulthood, on average, than children who grow up with both parents. They are more likely to drop out of high school, to become teenage and single mothers, and to have trouble finding and keeping a steady job in young adulthood, even after adjusting for differences in parents' socioeconomic background (McLanahan & Sandefur, 1994). About half of the disadvantages associated with single parenthood are due to lower incomes. Most of the rest are due to too little

parental involvement and supervision and too much residential mobility. Given the public concern about the growth as well as the consequences of single motherhood, the policy debate in this area is not just about how to help children adapt to family change, it is about how to reverse change. We use the word single in this chapter to refer to adults who are not currently married and living with a spouse. Many of these people were married in the past or will be in the future.

The idea that government should try to prevent single-mother families from forming is a hotly contested issue. It raises questions about the causes underlying the decline in marriage and the causes of single motherhood. Those who want government to limit the growth of single-mother families often claim that government is responsible for the growth of such families. They argue that the rise in welfare benefits during the sixties and early seventies sent the message to young men and women that if they had children and did not marry, the government would take care of the mothers and children. Thus, fewer couples married and more young women became single mothers. Charles Murray, a leading proponent of this view, argues that the only way to save families is to eliminate welfare entirely, forcing poor young women either to stop having children or to place their newborns with adoption agencies (Murray, 1984, 1993).

At the other end of the political spectrum are those who believe that the decline in marriage is due to the decline in job opportunities for poor young men—jobs that would enable them to support a family (Wilson & Neckerman, 1986). They argue that young men with the least education and the fewest skills were the hardest hit during the 1970s and 1980s by the loss of jobs from central cities and the restructuring of the workplaces that occurred. With no visible means of support and with bleak prospects for the future, these young men are not seen as potential marriage partners by the young women they are dating, even when the women become pregnant. Nor are the parents of the girl likely to try to arrange a "shotgun marriage" as they might have done in the 1950s, when the likelihood of finding steady work was much greater for low-skilled men. In short, marriage has declined because the pool of marriageable men has declined.

These two theories tell us something about why marriage might have declined among women from disadvantaged backgrounds during the past few decades, but they do not explain why the trend also occurred among young women from more advantaged backgrounds. To fully understand what has happened to American families, we must look farther than welfare benefits and the loss of jobs for low-skilled men.

Another theory with considerable merit is that marriage declined because women became more economically independent; increased education, job opportunities, and hourly wages during the past three decades reduced the gains from marriage and gave women an alternative source of income outside marriage (Becker, 1981). This allowed them to be more selective in choosing mates and it encouraged them to leave bad marriages. The women's independence theory incorporates the two previous arguments. Welfare benefits, like earnings, provide less-educated women with an alternative source of income outside marriage. Similarly, the decline in good jobs for low-skilled men makes marriage less attractive for these women, especially if the level of welfare benefits remains constant.

Finally, some people blame the decline in marriage and increase in single motherhood on changes in American culture (Bellah et al., 1985; Lesthaeghe and Surkyn, 1988). The cultural argument has many different facets. Some people see the sexual revolution in the 1960s as the principal engine of change. Changes in attitudes about premarital sex made it easier for young men and women to live together without being married and destigmatized single mother-

hood. And improved and accessible birth control methods and more widely available abortions facilitated intimate relationships without the responsibilities and commitments they once entailed.

Other analysts focus on the shift in values that has taken place throughout the twentieth century, especially after 1960. The shift in values from those favoring family commitment and self-sacrifice to those favoring individual growth and personal freedom has given rise to the so-called "me generation." Many of the characters in recent television shows, such as "Northern Exposure," "Seinfeld," and "thirtysomething," show young people struggling with the tension arising from making permanent commitments to others while remaining true to their own ideals and personal growth.

The debate over the causes of family change has important policy implications. If welfare benefits are the major reason for the decline in marriage and the increase in single motherhood, reducing benefits or redesigning welfare incentives to be more marriage-neutral may have merit. If the decline in men's opportunities, the increase in women's employment opportunities, or value changes are the problem, eliminating welfare is not likely to have much effect on marriage, and it will definitely make poor children worse off economically. Ironically, if the increase in women's economic independence is a major cause of single motherhood, then encouraging welfare mothers to enter the labor force, which is a principal thrust of recent efforts to reform welfare, may actually exacerbate the trend in single motherhood, since it will increase the economic independence of women in the long run.

In this chapter we examine the changes that have made the prototypical Ozzie and Harriet family increasingly rare in the latter half of the 20th century. We begin by focusing on four major demographic trends: the decline in marriage, the rise in marital disruption, the changes in marital and nonmarital childbearing, and the increase in mothers' labor force participation. Certain of these trends, such as the rising divorce rate, are extensions of long-term patterns that have been reshaping family life since the turn of the century. Others, such as the employment of mothers with young children, are more recent and represent a break with the past.

We also examine demographic changes in other Western industrialized countries in order to place the U.S. experience in the broadest possible context. The cross-national comparisons help us think about the causes underlying the changes in the American family, and how we might minimize the cost of change for children. Too often, commentators and political pundits in the United States speak as though the changes affecting the American family were unique to this country. As noted above, the growth of single-mother families is often attributed to the increase in welfare benefits during the 1960s and early 1970s. As we shall see, however, the United States is not unique with respect to divorce, nonmarital childbearing, and women's employment. Nor is there a simple 1:1 relationship between the prevalence of single parenthood and the level of welfare benefits across different countries. Many European countries, such as France, Great Britain, and Sweden, are much more generous toward single mothers, and yet they have less single motherhood than we do.

In the second part of the chapter, we examine family diversity and its implications for the economic well-being of American women. Census data allow us to compare the characteristics of several different types of "new families," including single-mother families, single-father families, and cohabiting couples. They also allow us to examine the prevalence of different work and family roles among American women and the standard of living commensurate with these statuses. As in the previous section, we compare the U.S. case with other industrialized countries. We find that married-couple families in which the wife is employed have the lowest poverty rates in nearly all the countries examined,

whereas families headed by nonemployed single mothers have the highest poverty rates. We also find that single mothers are much worse off in the United States, relative to other families with children, than in most other countries.

The final part of the chapter directly addresses the question of why marriage has declined during the past two decades. Here we present new evidence based on our own empirical analysis of marriage market characteristics in different metropolitan areas of the United States. We find that marriage is more common in areas where women's employment opportunities and earnings are low, where welfare benefits are low, and where men's employment opportunities and earnings are high. We also find that increases in women's employment opportunities can account for a good deal of the decline in marriage between 1970 and 1990 among white women but not among blacks. Our results do not support the argument that increases in welfare benefits or declines in men's employment opportunities have led to large declines in marriage.

FOUR DEMOGRAPHIC TRENDS

Four demographic changes have profoundly affected the American family in the past 40 years: the decline in marriage, the increase in marital instability, the change in marital and nonmarital fertility, and the increase in mothers' labor force participation. To understand what has happened to the family, we must understand what has happened in each of these domains (Da Vanzo & Rahman, 1994).

The Delay in Marriage

Throughout the 1950s, the typical young woman married when she was about 20 years old and the typical young man when he was about 23. This situation prevailed throughout the 1950s. By 1990, however, the median age at first marriage—the age at which half of the population has married for the first time—was 24 for women and 26 for men. In just three decades, the median age at first marriage in-

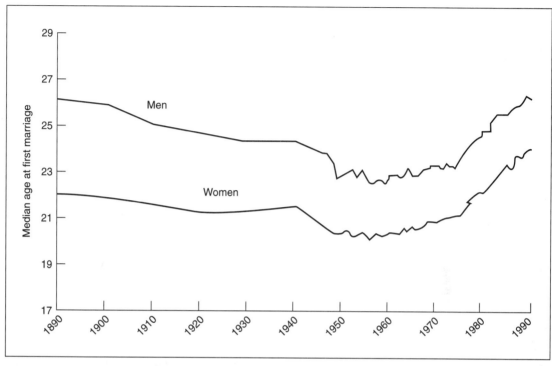

FIGURE 1   Median Age at First Marriage, by Sex and Year.
(*Source:* U.S. Bureau of the Census. 1991. *Current Population Reports.* "Marital Status and Living Arrangements: March 1990." Series P–20, No. 450.)
Note: Data points after 1947 are plotted for single years.

creased by four years among women and by three years among men (see Figure 1).

The postponement of marriage that took place after 1960 led to a substantial increase in the percentage of never-married young adults. In 1970, about 6 percent of women and 9 percent of men aged 30–34 had never married. By 1990, the figures were 16 percent and 27 percent, respectively.[2] In one sense, the rise in the age at first marriage was not as unusual as it might at first appear. Marital patterns in the 1950s and early 1960s were unique (Cherlin, 1992). Never before in this century had so many people married, and never before had they married so young. Thus, using 1950 or 1960 as a benchmark against which to evaluate recent behavior makes the current situation appear much more unusual than it actually is. Had we used 1900 as

our baseline, for example, we would have found a much smaller increase in the median age at first marriage—no change among men and only a two-year increase among women.

Yet, certain aspects of the relatively high age at first marriage today differ from those at the turn of the century. In 1900 most young adults lived with their parents or other relatives until they married; today they are more likely to leave home and establish independent households. Thus, the increase in the age at first marriage after the 1960s led to a substantial increase in nonfamily households—households containing a single person or several unrelated adults. This further undermined the institution of marriage, since it provided young people with an alternative way of establishing their independence from their families of origin.

Living away from home prior to marriage was especially pronounced throughout the 1960s and 1970s as the baby boom generation came of age, as contraception techniques improved, and as young men and women became active in the civil rights and women's liberation movements. During the 1980s, the trend reversed as economic conditions worsened for young people, who found it harder to find jobs and become self-supporting. Even so, the proportion of unmarried adults living on their own or with unrelated adults was substantially higher in 1990 than it was in 1970.

The increasing median age at first marriage and the rising percentage of never-married adults has coincided with an increase in cohabitation—two persons of the opposite sex living together in a marriagelike relationship. In 1960 and 1970, the earliest years for which cohabitation data are available, about 2 percent of unmarried adults were cohabiting.[3] After 1970, the percentage increased rapidly. Between 1980 and 1990, it grew from 5.3 percent to 7.9 percent among unmarried men and from 4.3 to 6.6 percent among unmarried women. The increase in cohabitation occurred among all age groups (except people over 65), but it was greatest among men and women in their late 20s and early 30s.

Although some analysts argue that cohabitation reinforces the institution of marriage by allowing people to "try out" potential marriage partners, thereby choosing their mates more carefully, there are several reasons for believing otherwise.[4] First, cohabiting unions are less stable than legal marriages and of much shorter duration (Bumpass, Sweet, & Cherlin, 1991). Second, a sizable proportion of cohabitors (10 percent) intend to continue living together, but do not intend to marry their current partner (Casper, 1992). For these couples, cohabitation is clearly an alternative rather than a precursor to marriage. There is another subset of cohabitors (7 percent) who plan to marry eventually but who do not plan to marry the person they are currently living with (Sweet & Bumpass, 1992). And finally, regardless of how people view their

relationship, the rights and obligations that go with legal marriage are much more difficult to enforce among cohabiting couples than among married couples. To take just one example: an unmarried woman who becomes a mother has a much weaker claim on the resources of the child's father than a woman who is married to the father. Only about 30 percent of children born outside marriage have a legally designated father (Garfinkel, 1992). Although the courts have been moving in the direction of extending "marital rights and obligations" to cohabiting couples, there continues to be a large disparity between these two types of partnerships.

The Increase in Marital Instability

A second major factor affecting families is the increase in divorce. Whereas in 1950, most people married once and remained married until they (or their spouses) died, as Ozzie and Harriet did, today over half of all couples end their marriages voluntarily. The divorce rate—the number of divorces each year per 1,000 married women—rose steadily during the first half of the 20th century and increased dramatically after 1960. Over half of all marriages contracted in the mid-1980s were projected to end in divorce (Castro-Martin & Bumpass, 1989). The divorce rate leveled off during the 1980s but this was not necessarily a sign of greater marital stability. We would have expected such a leveling off, given the increase in cohabitation (which means that the couples who do marry are likely to be the most committed), given the increase in the average age at first marriage, and given the fact that the large baby boom cohorts have reached middle age and passed through the period of their lives when they were most likely to divorce (Bumpass & Sweet 1989a).

The increase in divorce and the delay/decline in marriage led to a rise in the ratio of divorced to married people (Figure 2). In 1960, there were 35 divorced men and women for every 1,000 married adults; by 1990, there were 140. The ratio of divorced to married people is nearly twice as

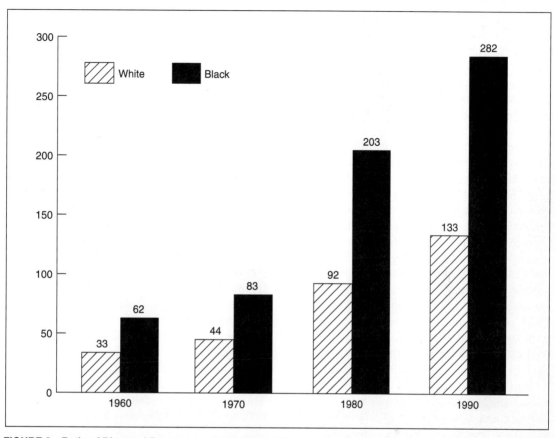

FIGURE 2 Ratio of Divorced Persons per 1,000 Married Persons, by Race and Year.
(*Source:* U.S. Bureau of the Census. 1991. *Current Population Reports.* "Marital Status and Living Arrangements: March 1990." Series P–20, No. 450.)

large for blacks as for whites, and this was true throughout the period from 1960 to 1990. In just three decades, the ratio of divorced to married adults grew over fourfold! Although the ratio was higher for blacks than for whites, the percentage increase over time was the same for both races. The increase in the divorce ratio is likely to have a feedback effect on marriage. By increasing the chance that married and single people will interact with people who have ended their marriages through divorce, a high divorce ratio makes divorce more acceptable and marriage more uncertain. In addition, legal changes since the 1950s have made divorce easier and more accessible. For example, until the 1960s, divorce was per-

missible in New York State only if one partner proved the other had committed adultery.

The Shift in Marital and Nonmarital Fertility

A third change affecting the American family is the shift in marital and nonmarital fertility rates. Between 1960 and 1990, marital fertility rates—births to married women between the ages of 15 and 44—declined sharply, while nonmarital fertility rates—births to unmarried women of similar ages—increased gradually. Together, these two trends represented a reduction in overall fertility while increasing the proportion of children born outside of marriage.

The rapid rise in the illegitimacy ratio—the proportion of all births each year occurring to unmarried women—has recently attracted considerable attention, as the public has become increasingly concerned about the economic and social costs of nonmarital childbearing for children, mothers, and the country at large.[5] What is often missing from such discussions, however, is the recognition that marital fertility has a significant effect on the trend in the illegitimacy ratio. Since married women account for a much larger proportion of all births than do unmarried women, a change in the fertility behavior of married women can have a large impact on this measure. In addition, an increase in the proportion of women who are single can also have a large effect on the proportion of children born outside marriage.[6] To understand why the illegitimacy ratio has gone up so fast in recent years, we must understand what is happening to both the marital and nonmarital birthrates as well as to the changing marital status composition of women, that is, the proportions of women who are married and unmarried.

The 1950s were an unusual decade. Not only did men and women marry at relatively young ages, they also became parents when they were quite young, and they gave birth to more children than in the previous decade. This increase in marital fertility caused what demographers called a baby boom from the mid-1940s to the early 1960s.

However, married women began to change their behavior in the early 1960s. Marital fertility rates declined by more than 40 percent between 1960 and 1975, from 157 births per 1,000 married women to 92 births per 1,000 married women. During this same period, nonmarital fertility hovered around 22–24 births per 1,000 unmarried women. The increase in the illegitimacy ratio between 1960 and 1975 was due to two factors: the decline in the fertility of married women and the delaying of marriage. But not to an increasing birthrate of unmarried women.

Beginning in the mid-1970s, marital fertility rates stopped declining, nonmarital fertility rates begin to rise, and the age at first marriage

continued to rise. After 1975, the rise in the illegitimacy ratio was due to increases in nonmarital fertility as well as to increases in the number of women at risk of having a nonmarital birth (see Figure 3).

The distinctions between the different forces underlying the rises in the illegitimacy ratio are crucial for understanding the recent debate over the causes of out-of-wedlock childbearing. In this debate, policymakers and political pundits often point to the rise in the illegitimacy ratio as evidence that increases in welfare benefits were responsible for the increases in nonmarital childbearing. But their explanations do not fit the data. During the period when welfare benefits were going up—from 1960 to 1975—the rise in the illegitimacy ratio was driven primarily by the *decline* in marital birthrates and *delays* in marriage. Birthrates of unmarried women rose only 13 percent during this period. Not until the late 1970s and 1980s was the rise in the illegitimacy ratio driven by an actual increase in nonmarital fertility, and by that time, welfare benefits had started to decline in value. This does not mean that welfare has no impact on unmarried childbearing, but it does suggest that the relationship is much weaker and more complex than many people think. Clearly, the rise in the percentage of births occurring to unmarried women is not the simple consequence of more welfare benefits. And curtailing welfare benefits now will probably not reduce the illegitimacy ratio.

Changes in marital and nonmarital fertility altered family life in two major ways: they reduced the prevalence of parenthood overall, and they increased the proportion of families headed by single mothers. In 1960, 44 percent of American households contained a married couple with a minor child. Recall that a household includes all the persons who share a dwelling unit, while a family includes two or more persons who share a dwelling unit *and* are related to each other by blood, marriage, or adoption. A person living alone is counted as a household but not a family. An additional 4 percent of

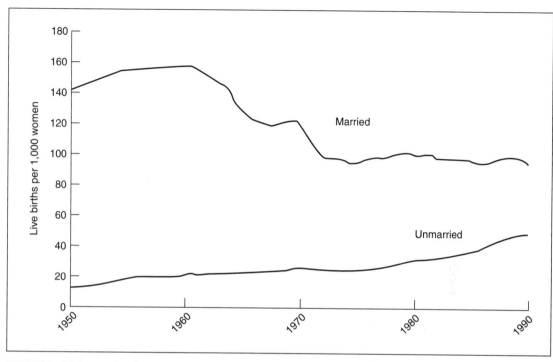

FIGURE 3   Birthrates for Women Aged 15–44, by Marital Status: 1950–1991.
(*Sources:* National Center for Health Statistics, *Vital Statistics of the U.S. 1988,* Vol. 1, Natality; National Center for Health Statistics, *Advance Report of Natality Statistics, 1993,* Vol. 41, No. 9.)

households contained a child and either a single parent or neither parent (Wetzel, 1990). Thus, nearly half of all households included children, and nearly 90 percent of the households with children contained two parents. But by 1990, only about 35 percent of all households contained children, and an increasing proportion of households with children did not contain two parents. Between 1960 and 1990, the proportion of children living in single-parent families grew from 9 percent to 25 percent.[7] And this number understates the proportion of children that will ever experience single parenthood. Demographers estimate that over half of all children born in the late 1970s will live in a single-parent family at some point before reaching age 18 (Bumpass & Sweet, 1989a).

The growth of single-parent families is covered in more detail in the next section. For now, we simply note that single-parent families are very different from two-parent families in terms of their economic status, and this difference has important implications for the future well-being of children.

The Increase in Mothers' Employment

The final, and perhaps most fundamental, change affecting the American family is the increase in mothers' employment. Women's labor force participation—the percentage of women who are working or looking for work—has been going up since the beginning of the 20th century. In the early part of the century the increase occurred primarily among young unmarried women. After 1940, married women began entering the labor force in greater numbers, and after 1960, married mothers with children at home followed suit.

In the early 1950s, only about 30 percent of married mothers with school-aged children were

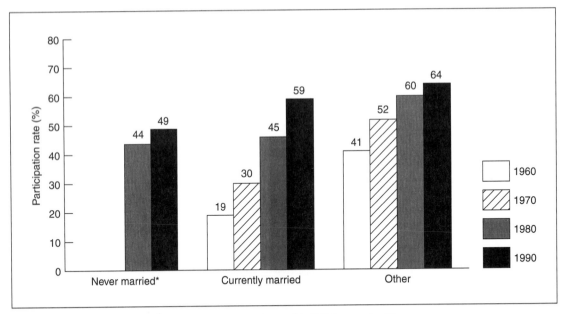

FIGURE 4 Labor Force Participation Rates for Mothers with Children under Six.
(*Source:* Statistical Abstract of the United States, 1993.)
Notes: *Not available for 1960 and 1970.
"Other" includes widowed, divorced, and separated mothers.

working outside the home. By 1990, this number had risen to over 73 percent. In just four short decades, a behavior that once described only a minority of mothers now fit a large majority of mothers, and this was true of mothers of all marital statuses. The figures for mothers with preschool children (under age six) are even more dramatic. In 1960, only 19 percent of married mothers with preschool children were in the labor force, whereas by 1990, 59 percent were employed (Figure 4). By 1990, currently married mothers were nearly as likely to be in the labor force as formerly married single mothers (64 percent), and they were more likely to be employed than never-married mothers (49 percent).[8]

Race Differences

Racial and ethnic groups differed considerably in 1990 with respect to the prevalence of marriage, parenthood, and employment among mothers. The trends, however, were consistent for all of the groups we examined. White women were the most likely to be married in 1990; black women the least likely; and Hispanic women fell in between. All three groups experienced a decline in the prevalence of marriage between 1980 and 1990.

The pattern for single parenthood was just the opposite. Black women were four times as likely as white women to be single mothers—28 percent versus 7 percent—and Hispanic women, again, were in the middle. Single includes women who reported they had never married or were divorced, separated, or widowed at the time of the census. The prevalence of single motherhood, as a percentage of all women, did not increase among white women during the 1980s, and increased by only 2 and 1 percentage points among blacks and Hispanics, respectively. (Single motherhood grew much more rapidly in the 1960s and 1970s than in the 1980s.) With respect to mothers' employment, all three racial and ethnic groups experienced an increase in mothers' labor force participation (mothers

TABLE 1

INTERNATIONAL COMPARISONS: DIVORCE RATES, ILLEGITIMACY RATIOS, SINGLE PARENTS AND EMPLOYED WOMEN

	Divorce rate[a]		Illegitimacy ratio[b]		Single parents[c]		Employed women[d]	
	1960[e]	1990[f]	1960	1990	1960	1988	1970[g]	1988
United States	9	21	5	28	9	23	45	73
Canada	2	12	4	24	9	15	41	75
Denmark	6	13	8	46	17	20	NA	90
France	3	8	6	30	9	12	52	75
Germany[h]	4	8	6	11	8	14	48	62
Italy	1	2	2	6	NA	NA	44	61
Netherlands	2	8	1	11	9	15	24	55
Sweden	5	12	11	47	9	13	61	89
United Kingdom	2	12	5	28	6	13	43	66

NA = Not available.
[a]Divorce rate per 1,000 married women.
[b]Percentage of all births born to unmarried women.
[c]Percentage of all family households that are single-parent. 1971 and 1986 for Canada. 1976 and 1988 for Denmark. 1968 and 1988 for France. 1972 and 1988 for Germany. 1961 and 1985 for Netherlands. 1960 and 1985 for Sweden. 1961 and 1987 for the United Kingdom. Age restrictions for children differ by country.
[d]Percentage of women aged 25–34 (25–39 in Italy) in the labor force.
[e]1970 for Italy.
[f]1989 for France; 1988 for United Kingdom.
[g]1977 for Italy.
[h]For former West Germany.
Sources: U.S. Bureau of the Census, Statistical Abstract of the United States, 1993; Sorrentino, 1990.

working at least 20 hours per week) between 1980 and 1990. White mothers were the most likely to be working outside the home in 1990, and Hispanic mothers were the least likely.

Cross-National Comparisons

The United States is not the only country to have experienced significant demographic changes during the past three decades. Declines in marriage, increases in divorce, growth in the proportion of children born outside marriage, and increases in the labor force participation of women have affected family life in most European countries as well as in Canada and the United States. The average age at marriage has risen since the beginning of the 1970s in most Western countries as it has in the United States. Europeans who were born in the 1950s and who came of age during the "free-love generation" of the 1960s initiated the retreat from marriage

characterized by both later and less frequent marriage (Sorrentino, 1990). Indeed, the age at first marriage is actually lower in the United States than in most of the European countries.

Divorce rates have also increased throughout the Western world. While the United States had by far the highest rate of divorce in 1990, the increase over the past several decades was dramatic in nearly all of the Western countries (see Table 1). In Canada and the United Kingdom, the divorce rate grew from about 2 divorces per 1,000 married women in 1960 to 12 per 1,000 in 1990; in France it grew from 3 to 8 per 1,000 married women; and in the Netherlands from 2 to 8 per 1,000. Italy was the only European country that did not experience a sharp rise in divorce between 1960 and the mid-1980s.

The illegitimacy ratio also rose dramatically in nearly all of the Western countries. Sweden and Denmark experienced the largest percentage point increases (from 11 to 47 percent and from 8 to 46 percent for these two countries, respectively). While some countries had much higher illegitimacy ratios than the United States, they did not have a higher percentage of single-mother families. Nearly 23 percent of all families with children in the United States were headed by a single mother in the late 1980s, whereas the percentages were 20 and 13 percent in Denmark and Sweden, respectively. The higher prevalence of single motherhood in the United States is due in part to the fact that divorce is more common in the United States than in other countries and in part because children born outside of marriage are less likely to live with both parents in the United States than in other countries. In the United States about 25 percent of nonmarital births during the 1970s and 1980s were to cohabiting couples, whereas in Denmark and Sweden nearly all nonmarital births were to cohabiting couples (Bumpass & Sweet, 1989; Sorrentino, 1990).

Finally, women's labor force participation rates have been going up in nearly all the countries. In the late 1980s, Denmark and Sweden had the highest percentage of employed women, followed by Canada, France, and the United States. The increase in employment was greatest among women in the Netherlands. The labor force participation rates of Dutch women more than doubled, increasing from 24 percent to 55 percent! Canadian women also experienced relatively large increases in employment, from 41 percent in 1970 to 75 percent in 1988.

The labor force participation rate of mothers was lower than the rate of all women in the late 1980s, but a majority of mothers were working outside the home in most countries. Germany and Italy were the only countries in which less than half of mothers were in the labor force in the mid-1980s. Comparable numbers for the Netherlands are not available, but our own estimates indicate that Holland has one of the lowest labor force participation rates for mothers of all the Western European countries (McLanahan, Casper, & Sørensen, forthcoming).

ENDNOTES

1. U.S. Bureau of the Census (1992). "Money Income of Households, Families, and Persons in the United States: 1991."
2. U.S. Bureau of the Census (1991). "Marital Status and Living Arrangements: March 1990."
3. Percentages calculated from U.S. Bureau of the Census (1960). "Marital Status and Family Status: March 1970" (1981); "Marital Status and Living Arrangements: March 1980" (1991); and "Marital Status and Living Arrangements: Unpublished Tabulations."
4. Lynne Casper (1992). Also see Rindfuss, R. R., Vandenheuvel, A. (1990). Cohabitation: precursor to marriage or alternative to being single? *Population and Development Review, **16,** 103–126.
5. The term illegitimacy is a technical term used by demographers and is not intended to be judgmental.
6. For more information on the decomposition of the illegitimacy ratio see Smith, H. L., and Cutright, C. (1988). Thinking about change in illegitimacy ratios: United States: 1963–1983. *Demography, **25,** 235–247.
7. U.S. Bureau of the Census (1991). "Household and Family Characteristics: March 1990 and 1989" (1991); and "Marital Status and Living Arrangements: March 1990."
8. U.S. Bureau of the Census (1991). Statistical Abstract of the United States, 1993.

REFERENCES

Becker, G. S. (1981). *A Treatise on the Family.* Cambridge, MA: Harvard University Press.

Bellah, R., Madsen, R., Swidler, A., Sullivan, W., & Tipton, S. (1985). *Habits of the Heart: Individualism and Commitment in American Life.* Berkeley, CA: University of California Press.

Bumpass, L. L., & Sweet, J. A. (1989). Children's experience in single-parent families: implications of cohabitation and marital transitions. *Family Planning Perspectives, **21,** 256–260.

Bumpass, L. L., Sweet, J. A., & Cherlin, A. J. (1991). The role of cohabitation in declining rates of marriage. *Journal of Marriage and the Family, **53,** 913–927.

Casper, L. M. (1992). Community norms and cohabitation: effects of level and degree of consensus. Paper presented at the annual meeting of the Population Association of America, Denver, CO.

Castro-Martin, T., & Bumpass, L. L. (1989). Recent trends and differentials in marital disruption. *Demography, 26,* 37–51.

Cherlin, A. J. (1992). *Marriage, Divorce, Remarriage.* Cambridge, MA: Harvard University Press.

Da Vanzo, J., & Rahman, O. (1994). American families: trends and correlates. *Population Index, 59,* 350–386.

Da Vanzo, J., Rahman, O., & Wadhwa, K. T. (1994). American families: policy issues. *Population Index, 59,* 547–566.

Garfinkel, I. (1992). *Assuring Child Support.* New York: Russell Sage Foundation.

Goldscheider, F. K. & Waite, L. J. (1991). *New Families, No Families?* Berkeley, CA: University of California Press.

Lesthaeghe, R., & Surkyn, J. (1988). Cultural dynamics and economic theories of fertility change. *Population and Development Review, 14,* 1–45.

McLanahan, S. & Sandefur, G. D. (1994). *Growing Up with a Single Parent.* Cambridge, MA: Harvard University Press.

Murray, C. (1984). *Losing Ground: American Social Policy, 1950–1980.* New York: Basic Books.

Murray, C. (1993). The coming white underclass. *The Wall Street Journal,* October 12, p. A13.

Pearce, Diana. (1978). The feminization of poverty: women, work, and welfare. *Urban and Social Change Review:* 28–36.

Sorrentino, C. (1990). The changing family in international perspective. *Monthly Labor Review, 113,* 41–58.

Sweet, J. A., & Bumpass, L. L. (1992). Young adults' views of marriage, cohabitation, and family. In S. South & S. Tolnay (Eds.), *The Changing American Family: Sociological and Demographic Perspectives* (pp. 143–170). Boulder, CO: Westview Press.

U.S. Bureau of the Census. *Statistical Abstract of the United States,* 1993. Washington, DC: U.S. Government Printing Office.

U.S. Bureau of the Census. (1991). *Current Population Reports,* Series P–20, no. 450, marital status and living arrangements. Washington, DC: U.S. Government Printing Office.

U.S. National Center for Health Statistics. (1988). *Vital Statistics of the U.S., 1988.* Vol. 1: Natality. Washington, DC: U.S. Government Printing Office.

U.S. National Center for Health Statistics. (1993). *Advance Report of Natality Statistics,* vol. 41, no. 9. Washington, DC: U.S. Government Printing Office.

Wetzel, J. R. (1990). American families: 25 years of change. *Monthly Labor Review, 113,* 4–13.

Wilson, W. J., & Neckerman, K. (1986). Poverty and family structure: the widening gap between evidence and public policy issues. In S. H. Danziger & D. H. Weinberg (Eds.), *Fighting Poverty: What Works and What Doesn't* (pp. 232–259). Cambridge, MA: Harvard University Press.

READING 1-2

The Way We Wish We Were: Defining the Family Crisis

Stephanie Coontz

When I begin teaching a course on family history, I often ask my students to write down ideas that spring to mind when they think of the "traditional family." Their lists always include several images. One is of extended families in which all members worked together, grandparents were an integral part of family life, children learned responsibility and the work ethic from their elders, and there were clear lines of authority based on respect for age. Another is of nuclear families in which nurturing mothers sheltered children from premature exposure to sex, financial worries, or other adult concerns, while fathers taught adolescents not to sacrifice their education by going to work too early. Still another image gives pride of place to the couple relationship. In traditional families, my students write—half derisively, half wistfully—men and women remained chaste until marriage, at which time they extricated themselves from competing obligations to kin and neighbors and committed themselves wholly to the marital relationship, experiencing an all-encompassing intimacy that our more crowded modern life seems to preclude. As one freshman wrote: "They truly respected the marriage vowels"; I assume she meant *I-O-U.*

Such visions of past family life exert a powerful emotional pull on most Americans, and with good reason, given the fragility of many modern commitments. The problem is not only that these visions bear a suspicious resemblance to reruns of old television series, but also that the scripts of different shows have been mixed up: June Cleaver suddenly has a Grandpa Walton dispensing advice in her kitchen; Donna Stone, vacuuming the living room in her inevitable pearls and high heels, is no longer married to a busy modern pediatrician but to a small-town sheriff who, like Andy Taylor of "The Andy Griffith Show," solves community problems through informal, old-fashioned common sense.

Like most visions of a "golden age," the "traditional family" my students describe evaporates on closer examination. It is an ahistorical amalgam of structures, values, and behaviors that never coexisted in the same time and place. The notion that traditional families fostered intense intimacy between husbands and wives while creating mothers who were totally available to their children, for example, is an idea that combines some characteristics of the white, middle-class family in the mid-19th century and some of a rival family ideal first articulated in the 1920s. The first family revolved emotionally around the mother-child axis, leaving the husband-wife relationship stilted and formal. The second focused on an eroticized couple relationship, demanding that mothers curb emotional "overinvestment" in their children. The hybrid idea that a woman can be fully absorbed with her youngsters while simultaneously maintaining passionate sexual excitement with her husband was a 1950s invention that drove thousands of women to therapists, tranquilizers, or alcohol when they actually tried to live up to it.

Similarly, an extended family in which all members work together under the top-down authority of the household elder operates very differently from a nuclear family in which husband and wife are envisioned as friends who patiently devise ways to let the children learn by trial and error. Children who worked in family enterprises seldom had time for the extracurricular activities that Wally and the Beaver recounted to their parents over the dinner table; often, they did not even go to school full-time. Mothers who did home production generally relegated child care to older children or servants; they did not suspend work to savor a baby's first steps or discuss with their husband how to facilitate a grade-schooler's "self-esteem." Such families emphasized formality, obedience to authority, and "the way it's always been" in their child rearing.

Nuclear families, by contrast, have tended to pride themselves on the "modernity" of parent-child relations, diluting the authority of grandparents, denigrating "old-fashioned" ideas about child raising, and resisting the "interference" of relatives. It is difficult to imagine the Cleavers or the college-educated title figure of "Father Knows Best" letting grandparents, maiden aunts, or in-laws have a major voice in child-rearing decisions. Indeed, the kind of family exemplified by the Cleavers . . . represented a conscious *rejection* of the Waltons' model.

THE ELUSIVE TRADITIONAL FAMILY

Whenever people propose that we go back to the traditional family, I always suggest that they pick a ballpark date for the family they have in mind. Once pinned down, they are invariably unwilling to accept the package deal that comes with their chosen model. Some people, for example, admire the discipline of colonial families, which were certainly not much troubled by divorce or fragmenting individualism. But colonial families were hardly stable: High mortality rates meant that the average length of marriage was less than a dozen years. One-third to one-half of all children lost at least one parent before the age of 21; in the South, more than half of all children aged 13 or under had lost at least one parent.[1]

While there are a few modern Americans who would like to return to the strict patriarchal authority of colonial days, in which disobedience by women and children was considered a small form of treason, these individuals would doubtless be horrified by other aspects of colonial families, such as their failure to protect children from knowledge of sexuality. Eighteenth-century spelling and grammar books routinely used *fornication* as an example of a four-syllable word, and preachers detailed sexual offenses in astonishingly explicit terms. Sexual conversations between men and women, even in front of children, were remarkably frank. It is worth contrasting this colonial candor to the climate in 1991, when the Department of Health and Human Services was forced to cancel a proposed survey of teenagers' sexual practices after some groups charged that such knowledge might "inadvertently" encourage more sex.[2]

Other people searching for an ideal traditional family might pick the more sentimental and gentle Victorian family, which arose in the 1830s and 1840s as household production gave way to wage work and professional occupations outside the home. A new division of labor by age and sex emerged among the middle class. Women's roles were redefined in terms of domesticity rather than production, men were labeled "breadwinners" (a masculine identity unheard of in colonial days), children were said to need time to play, and gentle maternal guidance supplanted the patriarchal authoritarianism of the past.

But the middle-class Victorian family depended for its existence on the multiplication of other families who were too poor and powerless to retreat into their own little oases and who therefore had to provision the oases of others. Childhood was prolonged for the 19th-century middle class only because it was drastically fore-shortened for other sectors of the population. The spread of textile mills, for example, freed middle-class women from the most time-consuming of their former chores, making cloth. But the raw materials for these mills were produced by slave labor. Slave children were not exempt from field labor unless they were infants, and even then their mothers were not allowed time off to nurture them. Frederick Douglass could not remember seeing his mother until he was seven.[3]

Domesticity was also not an option for the white families who worked 12 hours a day in Northern factories and workshops transforming slave-picked cotton into ready-made clothing. By 1820, "half the workers in many factories were boys and girls who had not reached their eleventh birthday." Rhode Island investigators found "little half-clothed children" making their way to the textile mills before dawn. In 1845, shoemaking families and makers of artificial flowers worked 15 to 18 hours a day, according to the New York *Daily Tribune*.[4]

Within the home, prior to the diffusion of household technology at the end of the century, house cleaning and food preparation remained mammoth tasks. Middle-class women were able to shift more time into child rearing in this period only by hiring domestic help. Between 1800 and 1850, the proportion of servants to white households doubled, to about one in nine. Some servants were poverty-stricken mothers who had to board or bind out their own children. Employers found such workers tended to be "distracted," however; they usually preferred young girls. In his study of Buffalo, New York, in the 1850s, historian Lawrence Glasco found that Irish and German girls often went into service at the age of 11 or 12.[5]

For every 19th-century middle-class family that protected its wife and child within the family circle, then, there was an Irish or a German girl scrubbing floors in that middle-class home, a Welsh boy mining coal to keep the home-baked goodies warm, a black girl doing the family laundry, a black mother and child picking cotton to be made into clothes for the family, and a Jewish or an Italian daughter in a sweatshop making "ladies" dresses or artificial flowers for the family to purchase.

Furthermore, people who lived in these periods were seldom as enamored of their family arrangements as modern nostalgia might suggest. Colonial Americans lamented "the great neglect in many parents and masters in training up their children" and expressed the "greatest trouble and grief about the rising generation." No sooner did Victorian middle-class families begin to withdraw their children from the work world than observers began to worry that children were becoming *too* sheltered. By 1851, the Reverend Horace Bushnell spoke for many in bemoaning the passing of the traditional days of household production, when the whole family was "harnessed, all together, into the producing process, young and old, male and female, from the boy who rode the plough-horse to the grandmother knitting under her spectacles.[6]

The late 19th century saw a modest but significant growth of extended families and a substantial increase in the number of families who were "harnessed" together in household production. Extended families have never been the norm in America; the highest figure for extended-family households ever recorded in American history is 20 percent. Contrary to the popular myth that industrialization destroyed "traditional" extended families, this high point occurred between 1850 and 1885, during the most intensive period of early industrialization. Many of these extended families, and most "producing" families of the time, depended on the labor of children; they were held together by dire necessity and sometimes by brute force.[7]

There was a significant increase in child labor during the last third of the 19th century. Some children worked at home in crowded tenement sweatshops that produced cigars or women's clothing. Reformer Helen Campbell found one house where "nearly thirty children

of all ages and sizes, babies predominating, rolled in the tobacco which covered the floor and was piled in every direction."[8] Many producing households resembled the one described by Mary Van Kleeck of the Russell Sage Foundation in 1913:

> In a tenement on MacDougal Street lives a family of seven—grandmother, father, mother and four children aged four years, three years, two years and one month respectively. All excepting the father and the two babies make violets. The three year old girl picks apart the petals; her sister, aged four years, separates the stems, dipping an end of each into paste spread on a piece of board on the kitchen table; and the mother and grandmother slip the petals up the stems.[9]

Where children worked outside the home, conditions were no better. In 1900, 120,000 children worked in Pennsylvania mines and factories; most of them had started work by age 11. In Scranton, a third of the girls between the ages of 13 and 16 worked in the silk mills in 1904. In New York, Boston, and Chicago, teenagers worked long hours in textile factories and frequently died in fires or industrial accidents. Children made up 23.7 percent of the 36,415 workers in southern textile mills around the turn of the century. When reformer Marie Van Vorse took a job at one in 1903, she found children as young as six or seven working 12-hour shifts. At the end of the day, she reported: "They are usually beyond speech. They fall asleep at the tables, on the stairs; they are carried to bed and there laid down as they are, unwashed, undressed; and the inanimate bundles of rags so lie until the mill summons them with its imperious cry before sunrise."[10]

By the end of the 19th century, shocked by the conditions in urban tenements and by the sight of young children working full-time at home or earning money out on the streets, middle-class reformers put aside nostalgia for "harnessed" family production and elevated the antebellum model once more, blaming immigrants for introducing such "un-American" family values as child labor. Reformers advocated adoption of a "true American" family—a restricted, exclusive nuclear unit in which women and children were divorced from the world of work.

In the late 1920s and early 1930s, however, the wheel turned yet again, as social theorists noted the independence and isolation of the nuclear family with renewed anxiety. The influential Chicago School of sociology believed that immigration and urbanization had weakened the traditional family by destroying kinship and community networks. Although sociologists welcomed the increased democracy of "companionate marriage," they worried about the rootlessness of nuclear families and the breakdown of older solidarities. By the time of the Great Depression, some observers even saw a silver lining in economic hardship, since it revived the economic functions and social importance of kin and family ties. With housing starts down by more than 90 percent, approximately one-sixth of urban families had to double up in apartments. The incidence of three-generation households increased, while recreational interactions outside the home were cut back or confined to the kinship network. One newspaper opined: "Many a family that has lost its car has found its soul."[11]

Depression families evoke nostalgia in some contemporary observers, because they tended to create "dependability and domestic inclination" among girls and "maturity in the management of money" among boys. But, in many cases, such responsibility was inseparable from "a corrosive and disabling poverty that shattered the hopes and dreams of . . . young parents and twisted the lives of those who were 'stuck together' in it." Men withdrew from family life or turned violent; women exhausted themselves trying to take up the slack both financially and emotionally, or they belittled their husbands as failures; and children gave up their dreams of education to work at dead-end jobs.[12]

From the hardships of the Great Depression and the Second World War and the euphoria of the postwar economic recovery came a new kind of family ideal that still enters our homes in "Leave It to Beaver" and "Donna Reed" reruns. . . . [T]he 1950s were no more a golden age of the family than any other period in American history. For now, I will argue that our recurring search for a traditional family model denies the diversity of family life, both past and present, and leads to false generalizations about the past as well as wildly exaggerated claims about the present and the future.

THE COMPLEXITIES OF ASSESSING FAMILY TRENDS

If it is hard to find a satisfactory model of the traditional family, it is also hard to make global judgments about how families have changed and whether they are getting better or worse. Some generalizations about the past are pure myth. Whatever the merit of recurring complaints about the rootlessness of modern life, for instance, families are *not* more mobile and transient than they used to be. In most nineteenth-century cities, both large and small, more than 50 percent—and often up to 75 percent—of the residents in any given year were no longer there 10 years later. People born in the 20th century are much more likely to live near their birthplace than were people born in the 19th century.[13]

This is not to say, of course, that mobility did not have different effects then than it does now. In the 19th century, claims historian Thomas Bender, people moved from community to community, taking advantage . . . of nonfamilial networks and institutions that integrated them into new work and social relations. In the late twentieth century, people move from job to job, following a career path that shuffles them from one single-family home to another and does not link them to neighborly networks beyond the family. But this change is in our community ties, not in our family ones.[14]

A related myth is that modern Americans have lost touch with extended-kinship networks or have let parent-child bonds lapse. In fact, more Americans than ever before have grandparents alive, and there is good evidence that ties between grandparents and grandchildren have become stronger over the past 50 years. In the late 1970s, researchers returned to the "Middletown" studied by sociologists Robert and Helen Lynd in the 1920s and found that most people there maintained closer extended-family networks than in earlier times. There had been some decline in the family's control over the daily lives of youth, especially females, but "the expressive/emotional function of the family" was "more important for Middletown students of 1977 than it was in 1924." More recent research shows that visits with relatives did *not* decline between the 1950s and the late 1980s.[15]

Today 54 percent of adults see a parent, and 68 percent talk on the phone with a parent, at least once a week. Fully 90 percent of Americans describe their relationship with their mother as close, and 78 percent say their relationship with their grandparents is close. And for all the family disruption of divorce, most modern children live with at least *one* parent. As late as 1940, 10 percent of American children did not live with either parent, compared to only 1 in 25 today.[16]

What about the supposed eclipse of marriage? Neither the rising age of those who marry nor the frequency of divorce necessarily means that marriage is becoming a less prominent institution than it was in earlier days. Ninety percent of men and women eventually marry, more than 70 percent of divorced men and women remarry, and fewer people remain single for their entire lives today than at the turn of the century. One author even suggests that the availability of divorce in the second half of the 20th century has allowed some women to try marriage who would formerly have remained single all their lives. Others argue that the rate of hidden marital separation in the late 19th century was not much less than the rate of visible separation today.[17]

Studies of marital satisfaction reveal that more couples reported their marriages to be happy in the late 1970s than did so in 1957, while couples in their second marriages believe them to be much happier than their first ones. Some commentators conclude that marriage is becoming less permanent but more satisfying. Others wonder, however, whether there is a vicious circle in our country, where no one even tries to sustain a relationship. Between the late 1970s and late 1980s, moreover, reported marital happiness did decline slightly in the United States. Some authors see this as reflecting our decreasing appreciation of marriage, although others suggest that it reflects unrealistically high expectations of love in a culture that denies people safe, culturally approved ways of getting used to marriage or cultivating other relationships to meet some of the needs that we currently load onto the couple alone.[18]

Part of the problem in making simple generalizations about what is happening to marriage is that there has been a polarization of experiences. Marriages are much more likely to be ended by divorce today, but marriages that do last are described by their participants as happier than those in the past and are far more likely to confer such happiness over many years. It is important to remember that the 50 percent divorce rate estimates are calculated in terms of a 40-year period and that many marriages in the past were terminated well before that date by the death of one partner. Historian Lawrence Stone suggests that divorce has become "a functional substitute for death" in the modern world. At the end of the 1970s, the rise in divorce rates seemed to overtake the fall in death rates, but the slight decline in divorce rates since then means that "a couple marrying today is more likely to celebrate a fortieth wedding anniversary than were couples around the turn of the century."[19]

A similar polarization allows some observers to argue that fathers are deserting their children, while others celebrate the new commitment of fathers to childrearing. Both viewpoints are right. Sociologist Frank Furstenberg comments on the emergence of a "good dad–bad dad complex": Many fathers spend more time with their children than ever before and feel more free to be affectionate with them; others, however, feel more free simply to walk out on their families. According to 1981 statistics, 42 percent of the children whose father had left the marriage had not seen him in the past year. Yet studies show steadily increasing involvement of fathers with their children as long as they are in the home.[20]

These kinds of ambiguities should make us leery of hard-and-fast pronouncements about what's happening to the American family. In many cases, we simply don't know precisely what our figures actually mean. For example, the proportion of youngsters receiving psychological assistance rose by 80 percent between 1981 and 1988. Does that mean they are getting more sick or receiving more help, or is it some complex combination of the two? Child abuse reports increased by 225 percent between 1976 and 1987. Does this represent an actual increase in rates of abuse or a heightened consciousness about the problem? During the same period, parents' self-reports about very severe violence toward their children declined 47 percent. Does this represent a real improvement in their behavior or a decreasing willingness to admit to such acts?[21]

Assessing the direction of family change is further complicated because many contemporary trends represent a reversal of developments that were themselves rather recent. The expectation that the family should be the main source of personal fulfillment, for example, was not traditional in the eighteenth and nineteenth centuries . . . Prior to the 1900s, the family festivities that now fill us with such nostalgia for the good old days (and cause such heartbreak when they go poorly) were "relatively undeveloped." Civic festivals and Fourth-of-July parades were more important occasions for celebration and strong emotion than family holidays, such as Thanksgiving. Christmas "seems to have been more a time for attending parties and dances than for celebrating family solidarity." Only in the 20th century did the family come to be the center of festive attention and emotional intensity.[22]

Today, such emotional investment in the family may be waning again. This could be interpreted as a reestablishment of balance between family life and other social ties; on the other hand, such a trend may have different results today than in earlier times, because in many cases the extrafamilial institutions and customs that used to socialize individuals and provide them with a range of emotional alternatives to family life no longer exist.

In other cases, close analysis of statistics showing a deterioration in family well-being supposedly caused by abandonment of tradition suggests a more complicated train of events. Children's health, for example, improved dramatically in the 1960s and 1970s, a period of extensive family transformation. It ceased to improve, and even slid backward, in the 1980s, when innovative social programs designed to relieve families of some traditional responsibilities were repealed. While infant mortality rates fell by 4.7 percent a year during the 1970s, the rate of decline decreased in the 1980s, and in both 1988 and 1989, infant mortality rates did not show a statistically significant decline. Similarly, the proportion of low-birth-weight babies fell during the 1970s but stayed steady during the 1980s and had even increased slightly as of 1988. Child poverty is lower today than it was in the traditional 1950s but much higher than it was in the nontraditional late 1960s.[23]

WILD CLAIMS AND PHONY FORECASTS

Lack of perspective on where families have come from and how their evolution connects to other social trends tends to encourage contradictory claims and wild exaggerations about where families are going. One category of generalizations seems to be a product of wishful thinking. As of 1988, nearly half of all families with children had both parents in the work force. The two-parent family in which only the father worked for wages represented just 25 percent of all families with children, down from 44 percent in 1975. For people overwhelmed by the difficulties of adjusting work and schools to the realities of working moms, it has been tempting to discern a "return to tradition" and hope the problems will go away. Thus in 1991, we saw a flurry of media reports that the number of women in the work force was headed down: "More Choose to Stay Home with Children" proclaimed the headlines; "More Women Opting for Chance to Watch Their Children Grow."[24]

The cause of all this commotion? The percentage of women aged 25 to 34 who were employed dropped from 74 percent to 72.8 percent between January 1990 and January 1991. However, there was an exactly equal decline in the percentage of men in the work force during the same period, and for both sexes the explanation was the same. "The dip is the recession," explained Judy Waldrop, research editor at *American Demographics* magazine, to anyone who bothered to listen. In fact, the proportion of *mothers* who worked increased slightly during the same period.[25]

This is not to say that parents, especially mothers, are happy with the pressures of balancing work and family life. Poll after poll reveals that both men and women feel starved for time. The percentage of women who say they would prefer to stay home with their children if they could afford to do so rose from 33 percent in 1986 to 56 percent in 1990. Other polls show that even larger majorities of women would trade a day's pay for an extra day off. But, above all, what these polls reveal is women's growing dissatisfaction with the failure of employers, schools, and government to pioneer arrangements that make it possible to combine work and family life. They do not suggest that women are actually going to stop working, or

that this would be women's preferred solution to their stresses. The polls did not ask, for example, how *long* women would like to take off work, and failed to take account of the large majority of mothers who report that they would miss their work if they did manage to take time off. Working mothers are here to stay, and we will not meet the challenge this poses for family life by inventing an imaginary trend to define the problem out of existence.

At another extreme is the kind of generalization that taps into our worst fears. One example of this is found in the almost daily reporting of cases of child molestation or kidnapping by sexual predators. The highlighting of such cases, drawn from every corner of the country, helps disguise how rare these cases actually are when compared to crimes committed within the family.

A well-publicized instance of the cataclysmic predictions that get made when family trends are taken out of historical context is the famous *Newsweek* contention that a single woman of 40 has a better chance of being killed by a terrorist than of finding a husband. It is true that the proportion of never-married women under age 40 has increased substantially since the 1950s, but it is also true that the proportion has *decreased* dramatically among women over that age. A woman over 35 has a *better* chance to marry today than she did in the 1950s. In the past 12 years, first-time marriages have increased almost 40 percent for women aged 35 to 39. A single woman aged 40 to 44 still has a 24 percent probability of marriage, while 15 percent of women in their late 40s will marry. These figures would undoubtedly be higher if many women over 40 did not simply pass up opportunities that a more desperate generation might have snatched.[26]

Yet another example of the exaggeration that pervades many analyses of modern families is the widely quoted contention that "parents today spend 40 percent less time with their children than did parents in 1965." Again, of course, part of the problem is where researchers are measuring from. A comparative study of Muncie, Indiana, for example, found that parents spent much more time with their children in the mid-1970s than did parents in the mid-1920s. But another problem is keeping the categories consistent. Trying to track down the source of the 40 percent decline figure, I called demographer John P. Robinson, whose studies on time formed the basis of this claim. Robinson's data, however, show that parents today spend about the same amount of time caring for children as they did in 1965. If the total amount of time devoted to children is less, he suggested, I might want to check how many fewer children there are today. In 1970, the average family had 1.34 children under the age of eighteen; in 1990, the average family had only .96 children under age eighteen—a decrease of 28.4 percent. In other words, most of the decline in the total amount of time parents spend with children is because of the decline in the number of children they have to spend time with![27]

Now I am not trying to say that the residual amount of decrease is not serious, or that it may not become worse, given the trends in women's employment. Robinson's data show that working mothers spend substantially less time in primary child-care activities than do nonemployed mothers (though they also tend to have fewer children); more than 40 percent of working mothers report feeling trapped by their daily routines; many routinely sacrifice sleep in order to meet the demands of work and family. Even so, a majority believe they are *not* giving enough time to their children. It is also true that children may benefit merely from having their parents available, even though the parents may not be spending time with them.

But there is no reason to assume the worst. Americans have actually gained free time since 1965, despite an increase in work hours, largely as a result of a decline in housework and an increasing tendency to fit some personal requirements and errands into the work day. And according to a recent Gallup poll, most modern mothers think they are doing a better job of communicating with their children (though a worse job of house cleaning) than did their own mothers and that they put a higher value on spending time with their family than did their mothers.[28]

NEGOTIATING THROUGH THE EXTREMES

Most people react to these conflicting claims and contradictory trends with understandable confusion. They know that family ties remain central to their own lives, but they are constantly hearing about people who seem to have *no* family feeling. Thus, at the same time as Americans report high levels of satisfaction with their *own* families, they express a pervasive fear that other people's families are falling apart. In a typical recent poll, for example, 71 percent of respondents said they were "very satisfied" with their own family life, but more than half rated the overall quality of family life as negative: "I'm okay; you're not."[29]

This seemingly schizophrenic approach does not reflect an essentially intolerant attitude. People worry about families, and to the extent that they associate modern social ills with changes in family life, they are ambivalent about innovations. Voters often defeat measures to grant unmarried couples, whether heterosexual or homosexual, the same rights as married ones. In polls, however, most Americans support tolerance for gay and lesbian relationships. Although two-thirds of respondents to one national poll said they wanted "more traditional standards of family life," the same percentage rejected the idea that "women should return to their traditional role." Still larger majorities support women's right to work, including their right to use child care, even when they worry about relying on day-care centers too much. In a 1990 *Newsweek* poll, 42 percent predicted that the family would be worse in 10 years and exactly the same percentage predicted that it would be better.

Although 87 percent of people polled in 1987 said they had "old-fashioned ideas about family and marriage," only 22 percent of the people polled in 1989 defined a family solely in terms of blood, marriage, or adoption. Seventy-four percent declared, instead, that family is any group whose members love and care for one another.[30]

These conflicted responses do not mean that people are hopelessly confused. Instead, they reflect people's gut-level understanding that the "crisis of the family" is more complex than is often asserted by political demagogues or others with an ax to grind. In popular commentary, the received wisdom is to "keep it simple." I know one television reporter who refuses to air an interview with anyone who uses the phrase "on the other hand." But my experience in discussing these issues with both the general public and specialists in the field is that people are hungry to get beyond oversimplifications. They don't want to be told that everything is fine in families or that if the economy improved and the government mandated parental leave, everything would be fine. But they don't believe that every hard-won victory for women's rights and personal liberty has been destructive of social bonds and that the only way to find a sense of community is to go back to some sketchily defined traditional family that clearly involves denying the validity of any alternative familial and personal choices.

Americans understand that along with welcome changes have come difficult new problems; uneasy with simplistic answers, they are willing to consider more nuanced analyses of family gains and losses during the past few decades. Indeed, argues political reporter E. J. Dionne, they are *desperate* to engage in such analyses.[31] Few Americans are satisfied with liberal and feminist accounts that blame all modern family dilemmas on structural inequalities, ignoring the moral crisis of commitment and obligation in our society. Yet neither are they convinced that "in the final analysis," as

David Blankenhorn of the Institute for American Values puts it, "the problem is not the system. The problem is us."[32]

Despite humane intentions, an overemphasis on personal responsibility for strengthening family values encourages a way of thinking that leads to moralizing rather than mobilizing for concrete reforms. While values are important to Americans, most do not support the sort of scapegoating that occurs when all family problems are blamed on bad values. Most of us are painfully aware that there is no clear way of separating family values from the system. Our values may make a difference in the way we respond to the challenges posed by economic and political institutions, but those institutions also reinforce certain values and extinguish others. The problem is not to berate people for abandoning past family values, nor to exhort them to adopt better values in the future—the problem is to build the institutions and social support networks that allow people to act on their best values rather than on their worst ones. We need to get past abstract nostalgia for traditional family values and develop a clearer sense of how past families actually worked and what the different consequences of various family behaviors and values have been. Good history and responsible social policy should help people incorporate the full complexity and the trade-offs of family change into their analyses and thus into action. Mythmaking does not accomplish this end.

ENDNOTES

1. Philip Greven, *Four Generations: Population, Land, and Family in Colonial Andover, Massachusetts* (Ithaca, N.Y.: Cornell University Press, 1970); Vivian Fox and Martin Quit, *Loving, Parenting, and Dying: The Family Cycle in England and America, Past and Present* (New York: Psychohistory Press, 1980), p. 401.
2. John Demos, *A Little Commonwealth: Family Life in Plymouth Colony* (New York: Oxford University Press, 1970), p. 108; Mary Ryan, *Cradle of the Middle Class: The Family in Oneida*

County, New York, 1790–1865 (New York: Cambridge University Press, 1981), pp. 33, 38–39; Carroll Smith-Rosenberg, *Disorderly Conduct: Visions of Gender in Victorian America* (New York: Oxford University Press, 1985), p. 24.

3. Frederick Douglass, *My Bondage and My Freedom* (New York: Dover, 1968), p. 48.

4. David Roediger and Philip Foner, *Our Own Time: A History of American Labor and the Working Day* (London: Greenwood, 1989), p. 9; Norman Ware, *The Industrial Worker, 1840–1860* (New York: Quadrangle, 1964), p. 5; Barbara Wertheimer, *We Were There: The Story of Working Women in America* (New York: Pantheon, 1977), p. 91; Sean Wilentz, *Chants Democratic: New York City and the Rise of the Working Class, 1788–1850* (New York: Oxford University Press, 1984), p. 126.

5. Faye Dudden, *Serving Women: Household Service in Nineteenth-Century America* (Middletown, Conn.: Wesleyan University Press, 1983), p. 206; Susan Strasser, *Never Done: A History of American Housework* (New York: Pantheon, 1982); Lawrence Glasco, "The Life Cycles and Household Structure of American Ethnic Groups," in *A Heritage of Her Own: Toward a New Social History of American Women,* ed. Nancy Cott and Elizabeth Pleck (New York: Simon & Schuster, 1979), pp. 281, 285.

6. Robert Bremner et al., eds., *Children and Youth in America: A Documentary History* (Cambridge: Harvard University Press, 1970), vol. 1, p. 39; Barbara Cross, *Horace Bushnell: Minister to a Changing America* (Chicago: University of Chicago Press, 1958); Ann Douglas, *The Feminization of American Culture* (New York: Knopf, 1977), p. 52.

7. Peter Laslett, "Characteristics of the Western Family Over Time," in *Family Life and Illicit Love in Earlier Generations,* ed. Peter Laslett (New York: Cambridge University Press, 1977); William Goode, *World Revolution and Family Patterns* (New York: Free Press, 1963); Michael Anderson, *Family Structure in Nineteenth-Century Lancashire* (Cambridge, England: Cambridge University Press, 1971); Tamara Hareven, ed., *Transitions: The Family and the Life Course in Historical Perspective* (New York: Academic Press, 1978); Tamara Hareven, "The Dynamics

of Kin in an Industrial Community," in *Turning Points: Historical and Sociological Essays on the Family,* ed. John Demos and S. S. Boocock (Chicago: University of Chicago Press, 1978); Linda Gordon, *Heroes of Their Own Lives: The Politics and History of Family Violence, 1880–1960* (New York: Viking, 1988).

8. Helen Campbell, *Prisoners of Poverty: Women Wage Workers, Their Trades and Their Lives* (Westport, Conn.: Greenwood Press, 1970), p. 206.

9. Rosalyn Baxandall, Linda Gordon, and Susan Reverby, eds., *America's Working Women* (New York: Random House, 1976), p. 162.

10. Rose Schneiderman, *All For One* (New York: P. S. Eriksson, 1967); John Bodnar, "Socialization and Adaption: Immigrant Families in Scranton," in *Growing Up in America: Historical Experiences,* ed. Harvey Graff (Detroit: Wayne State Press, 1987), pp. 391–92; Robert and Helen Lynd, *Middletown: A Study in Modern American Culture* (New York: Harcourt Brace Jovanovich, 1956), p. 31; Barbara Wertheimer, *We Were There: The Story of Working Women in America* (New York: Pantheon, 1977), pp. 336–43; Francesco Cordasco, *Jacob Riis Revisited: Poverty and the Slum in Another Era* (Garden City, N.Y.: Doubleday, 1968); Campbell, *Prisoners of Poverty and Women Wage-Earners* (Boston: Arnoff, 1893); Lynn Weiner, *From Working Girl to Working Mother: The Female Labor Force in the United States, 1829–1980* (Chapel Hill: University of North Carolina Press, 1985), p. 92.

11. For examples of the analysis of the Chicago School, see Ernest Burgess and Harvey Locke, *The Family: From Institution to Companionship* (New York: American Book Company, 1945); Ernest Mowrer, *The Family: Its Organization and Disorganization* (Chicago: University of Chicago Press, 1932); W. I. Thomas and F. Znaniecki, *The Polish Peasant in Europe and America,* 5 vols. (Boston: Dover Publications, 1918–20). On families in the Depression, see Steven Mintz and Susan Kellogg, *Domestic Revolutions: A Social History of American Family Life* (New York: Free Press, 1988), pp. 133–49, quote on p. 136.

12. Glen Elder, Jr., *Children of the Great Depression: Social Change in Life Experience* (Chicago:

University of Chicago Press, 1974), pp. 64–82; Lillian Rubin, *Worlds of Pain: Life in the Working-Class Family* (New York: Basic Books, 1976), p. 23; Edward Robb Ellis, *A Nation in Torment: The Great American Depression, 1929–1939* (New York: Coward McCann, 1970); Ruth Milkman, "Women's Work and the Economic Crisis," in *A Heritage of Her Own: Toward a New Social History of American Women,* ed. Nancy Cott and Elizabeth Pleck (New York: Simon & Schuster, 1979), pp. 507–41.

13. Rudy Ray Seward, *The American Family: A Demographic History* (Beverly Hills: Sage, 1978); Kenneth Winkle, *The Politics of Community: Migration and Politics in Antebellum Ohio* (New York: Cambridge University Press, 1988); Michael Weber, *Social Change in an Industrial Town: Pattern of Progress in Warren, Pennsylvania, from the Civil War to World War I* (University Park: Pennsylvania State University Press, 1976), pp. 138–48. Stephen Thernstrom, *Poverty and Progress* (Cambridge: Harvard University Press, 1964).

14. Thomas Bender, *Community and Social Change in America* (New Brunswick: Rutgers University Press, 1978).

15. Edward Kain, *The Myth of Family Decline: Understanding Families in a World of Rapid Social Change* (Lexington, Mass.: D. C. Heath, 1990), pp. 10, 37; Theodore Caplow, "The Sociological Myth of Family Decline," *The Tocqueville Review* 3 (1981): 366; Howard Bahr, "Changes in Family Life in Middletown, 1924–77," *Public Opinion Quarterly* 44 (1980): 51.

16. *American Demographics,* February 1990; Dennis Orthner, "The Family in Transition," in *Rebuilding the Nest: A New Commitment to the American Family,* ed. David Blankenhorn, Steven Bayme, and Jean Bethke Elshtain (Milwaukee: Family Service America, 1990), pp. 95–97; Sar Levitan and Richard Belous, *What's Happening to the American Family?* (Baltimore: Johns Hopkins University Press, 1981), p. 63.

17. Daniel Kallgren, "Women Out of Marriage: Work and Residence Patterns of Never Married American Women, 1900–1980" (Paper presented at the Social Science History Association Conference, Minneapolis, Minn., November 1990), p. 8; Richard Sennett, *Families Against the City: Middle Income Homes in Industrial Chicago, 1872–1890* (Cambridge: Harvard University Press, 1984), pp. 114–15.

18. Mary Jo Bane, *Here to Stay: American Families in the Twentieth Century* (New York: Basic Books, 1976); Stephen Nock, *Sociology of the Family* (Englewood Cliffs, N.J.: Prentice Hall, 1987); Kain, *Myth of Family Development,* pp. 71, 74–75; Joseph Veroff, Elizabeth Douvan, and Richard Kulk, *Inner American: A Self Portrait from 1957 to 1976* (New York: Basic Books, 1981); Norval Glenn, "The Recent Trend in Marital Success in the United States," *Journal of Marriage and the Family 53* (1991); Tracy Cabot, *Marrying Later, Marrying Smarter* (New York: McGraw-Hill, 1990); Judith Brown *Sanctions and Sanctuary: Cultural Perspectives on the Beating of Wives* (Boulder, Colo.: Westview Press, 1991); Maxine Baca Zinn and Stanley Eitzen *Diversity in American Families* (New York: Harper & Row, 1987).

19. Dorrian Apple Sweetser, "Broken Homes: Stable Risk, Changing Person, Changing Forms," *Journal of Marriage and the Family* (August 1985); Lawrence Stone, "The Road to Polygamy," *New York Review of Books,* March 1989, p. 13; Arlene Skolnick, *Embattled Paradise: The American Family in an Age of Uncertainty* (New York: Basic Books, 1991), p. 156.

20. Frank Furstenberg, Jr., "Good Dads–Bad Dads: Two Faces of Fatherhood," in *The Changing American Family and Public Policy,* ed. Andrew Cherlin (Washington, D.C.: Urban Institute Press, 1988); Joseph Pleck, "The Contemporary Man," in *Handbook of Counseling and Psychotherapy,* ed. Murray Scher et al. (Beverly Hills: Sage, 1987).

21. National Commission on Children, *Beyond Rhetoric: A New Agenda for Children and Families* (Washington, D.C.: GPO, 1991), p. 34; Richard Gelles and Jon Conte, "Domestic Violence and Sexual Abuse of Children," in *Contemporary Families: Looking Forward, Looking Back,* ed. Alan Booth (Minneapolis: National Council on Family Relations, 1991), p. 328.

22. Arlene Skolnick, "The American Family: The Paradox of Perfection," *The Wilson Quarterly* (Summer 1980); Barbara Laslett, "Family Membership: Past and Present," *Social Problems* 25

(1978); Theodore Caplow et al., *Middletown Families: Fifty Years of Change and Continuity* (Minneapolis: University of Minnesota Press, 1982), p. 225.

23. *The State of America's Children, 1991* (Washington, D.C.: Children's Defense Fund, 1991), pp. 55–63; *Seattle Post-Intelligencer,* 19 April 1991; National Commission on Children, *Beyond Rhetoric,* p. 32; *Washington Post National Weekly Edition,* 13–19 May 1991; James Wetzel, *American Youth: A Statistical Snapshot* (Washington, D.C.: William T. Grant Foundation, August 1989), pp. 12–14.

24. *USA Today,* 12 May 1991, p. 1A; Richard Morin, "Myth of the Drop Out Mom," *Washington Post,* 14 July 1991; Christine Reinhardt, "Trend Check," *Working Woman,* October 1991, p. 34; Howard Hayghe, "Family Members in the Work Force," *Monthly Labor Review* 113 (1990).

25. Morin, "Myth of the Drop Out Mom"; Reinhardt, "Trend Check," p. 34.

26. "Too Late for Prince Charming," *Newsweek,* 2 June 1986, p. 55; John Modell, *Into One's Own: From Youth to Adulthood in the United States, 1920–1975* (Berkeley: University of California Press, 1989), p. 249; Barbara Lovenheim, *Beating the Marriage Odds: When You Are Smart, Single, and Over 35* (New York: William Morrow, 1990), pp. 26–27; *U.S. News & World Report,* 29 January 1990, p. 50; *New York Times,* 7 June 1991.

27. William Mattox, Jr., "The Parent Trap," *Policy Review* (Winter 1991): 6, 8; Sylvia Ann Hewlett,

"Running Hard Just to Keep Up," *Time* (Fall 1990), and *When the Bough Breaks: The Cost of Neglecting Our Children* (New York: Basic Books, 1991), p. 73; Richard Whitmore, "Education Decline Linked with Erosion of Family," *The Olympian,* 1 October 1991; John Robinson, "Caring for Kids," *American Demographics,* July 1989, p. 52; "Household and Family Characteristics: March 1990 and 1989," *Current Population Reports,* series P–20, no. 447, table A-1. I am indebted to George Hough, Executive Policy Analyst, Office of Financial Management, Washington State, for finding these figures and helping me with the calculations.

28. John Robinson, "Time for Work," *American Demographics,* April 1989, p. 68, and "Time's Up," *American Demographics,* July 1989, p. 34; Trish Hall, "Time on Your Hands? You May Have More Than You Think," *New York Times,* 3 July 1991, pp. C1, C7; Gannett News Service Wire Report, 27 August 1991.

29. *New York Times,* 10 October 1989, p. A18.

30. E. J. Dionne, Jr., *Why Americans Hate Politics* (New York: Simon & Schuster, 1991), pp. 110, 115, 325; *The Olympian,* 11 October 1989; *New York Times,* 10 October 1989; *Time,* 20 November 1989; *Seattle Post-Intelligencer,* 12 October 1990; Jerold Footlick, "What Happened to the Family?" *Newsweek Special Issue,* Winter/Spring 1990, p. 18.

31. Dionne, *Why Americans Hate Politics.*

32. David Blankenhorn, "Does Grandmother Know Best?" *Family Affairs* 3 (1990): 13, 16.

CHAPTER 2

The History of the Family

Looking back on the 20th century, we can see that the most unusual and distinctive decade for family life was the 1950s.[1] In the period from the end of World War II to the early 1960s, many of the century-long trends turned around. Birth rates rose sharply, creating the "baby boom." The age at which the typical person married dropped to a century-long low. Although the divorce rate continued to rise, it did so at a slower rate than in most other decades. Compared with any other decade, a larger proportion of children—slightly more than half—were being raised in a "breadwinner-homemaker family" consisting of a father who was employed outside the home and a mother who remained at home to care for the children and do the housework.

Observers at that time, and scholars now, speak of a more family oriented value system in the 1950s. Perhaps it would be more accurate to call it marriage-centered because attitudes toward marriage were more positive in the 1950s than in subsequent decades. Some intriguing testimony is reported in *Homeward Bound: American Families in the Cold War Era,* by historian Elaine Tyler May, who studied a set of 300 interviews that had been conducted with white, middle-class couples in 1955. The interviews show the high value women and men placed on home, children, and marriage. Nearly everyone cited the benefits of children, home, and marriage in their personal lives. Few had seriously considered divorce. By and large, they told the interviewers that the sacrifices they had to make for the sake of their home lives were worthwhile.

Nevertheless, as you will see, the sacrifices were not evenly distributed between husbands and wives. It was wives who were asked to make the greater sacrifice by forgoing employment outside the home. Bowing to the ideology, the vast majority of wives refrained from working outside the home at least until their youngest children were in school. Some did not wish to work for pay and therefore sacrificed little; others gave up dreams. You will read about Ida Butler, who said she would have liked to have been a doctor but that now marriage was her career.

---

[1]*Public and Private Families: An Introduction,* pp. 60–63.

May's insights into the 1950s are just the tip of the iceberg of family history. Since the 1960s, historians have produced so much research that family history has become a booming subfield. Because of their efforts, we know much more about families in past times than was the case a few decades ago. You might ask why this historical material is relevant to a course on contemporary families. The answer is that the historical record can give us great insight into the meaning of the kinds of changes in families that we see today. In the second excerpt in this chapter, Arland Thornton, a sociologist who has read widely in family history, interprets for us the contemporary lessons that we can draw from family history. Thornton restricts himself to the Western nations, by which he means primarily Western Europe and the overseas English-speaking countries of the United States and Canada. A question you might want to keep in mind while reading Thornton's article is as follows: In what ways were Western families different in the past than they are today, and in what ways were they similar? Thornton argues that historical research shows a pattern of both continuity and change in Western families. (Thornton sometimes uses the sociological term *dyad,* meaning a two-person group, in referring to husbands and wives. He also uses the term *proscribe,* which means prohibit.)

READING 2-1

Cold War, Warm Hearth

Elaine Tyler May

In summer of 1959, a young couple married and spent their honeymoon in a bomb shelter. *Life* magazine featured the "sheltered honeymoon" with a photograph of the duo smiling on their lawn, surrounded by dozens of canned goods and supplies. Another photograph showed them descending 12 feet underground into the 22-ton steel and concrete 8-by-11-foot shelter where they would spend the next two weeks. The article quipped that "fallout can be fun," and described the newlyweds' adventure—with obvious erotic undertones—as fourteen days of "unbroken togetherness."[1] As the couple embarked on family life, all they had to enhance their honeymoon were some consumer goods, their sexuality, and privacy. This is a powerful image of the nuclear family in the nuclear age: isolated, sexually charged, cushioned by abundance, and protected against impending doom by the wonders of modern technology.

The stunt was little more than a publicity device; yet, in retrospect it takes on symbolic significance. For in the early years of the cold war, amid a world of uncertainties brought about by World War II and its aftermath, the home seemed to offer a secure private nest removed from the dangers of the outside world. The message was ambivalent, however, for the family also seemed particularly vulnerable. It needed heavy protection against the intrusions of forces outside itself. The self-contained home held out the promise of security in an insecure world. It also offered a vision of abundance and fulfill-ment. As the cold war began, young postwar Americans were homeward bound.

Demographic indicators show that in this period, Americans were more eager than ever to establish families. The bomb-shelter honeymooners were part of a cohort of Americans who lowered the age at marriage for both men and women, and quickly brought the birthrate to a twentieth-century high after more than a hundred years of steady decline, producing the "baby boom." These young adults established a trend of early marriage and relatively large families that lasted for more than two decades. From the 1940s through the early 1960s, Americans married at a higher rate and at a younger age than did their European counterparts . . .

To gain insight into this unique historical era, I have drawn on a wide range of sources, including evidence from the popular culture, especially movies, mass-circulation periodicals, and newspapers; the writings of professionals in numerous fields; and the papers and statements of those who influenced and formulated public policies. In addition, I have utilized a remarkable data collection—the Kelly Longitudinal Study (KLS)—which consists of several surveys of 600 white middle-class men and women who formed families during these years.[2] E. Lowell Kelly, a psychologist at the University of Michigan, was interested in long-term personality development among married persons. The 300 couples who participated in the study were contacted through announcements of engagements in the late 1930s in New England local newspapers. Kelly sent questionnaires to them every few years and took his most detailed and extensive surveys in 1955. By that time, most of the respondents had been married for at least a decade and were rearing their baby-boom children in suburban homes.

The KLS questionnaires are a valuable source for finding out why middle-class Americans adhered so strongly to a normative and quite specifically defined notion of family life at the time. Many respondents filled pages with their detailed testimonies, often attaching extra sheets to explain their answers more fully. They wrote about their lives, the decisions they made concerning their careers and children, the quality of their marriages, their family values, their sexual relationships, their physical and emotional health, and their major hopes and worries. They also reflected on their marriages, what they felt they had sacrificed, and what they had gained. In these open-ended responses, freed from Kelly's categories and concerns, they poured out their stories.[3]

The respondents to the KLS were among the cohort of Americans who began their families during the early 1940s, establishing the patterns and setting the trends that were to take hold of the nation for the next two decades. Their hopes for happy and stable marriages took shape during the depression, when many of their parents' generation struggled with disruption and hardship. They entered marriage when World War II thrust the nation into another major crisis, wreaking further havoc on families. They raised children as the cold war took shape, with its cloud of international tension and impending doom.

Yet, these women and men were hopeful that family life in the postwar era would be secure and liberated from the hardships of the past. They believed that affluence, consumer goods, satisfying sex, and children would strengthen their families, enabling them to steer clear of potential disruptions. In pursuing their quest for the "good life," they adhered to traditional gender roles and prized marital stability; few of them divorced. They represent a segment of the predominantly Protestant white population who were relatively well educated and who generally lived comfortable middle-class lives. In other words, they were among those Americans who would be most likely to live out the postwar American dream. Their poignant testimonies, however, reveal a strong undercurrent of discontent; their hopes for domestic happiness often remained unfulfilled.

Since the KLS sample was all white and predominantly Protestant, it is important to keep in mind who was *not* included. Black Americans, as a result of institutionalized racism and widespread poverty, existed on the fringes of the middle-class family ideal. Suburbia was not part of the black experience, since blacks were systematically excluded from postwar suburbs. In segregated neighborhoods, black people created rich and thriving subcultures, rooted in unique historical traditions. Nevertheless, blacks as well as whites participated in the same postwar demographic trends. The fertility rates of blacks peaked in the late 1950s, as did those of whites, and the divorce rate among blacks and whites followed similar patterns.[4]

Although all groups contributed to the baby boom, it was the values of the white middle class that shaped the dominant political and economic institutions that affected all Americans. Those who did not conform to them were likely to be marginalized, stigmatized, and disadvantaged as a result. So although the KLS sample included only a few individuals from other ethnic or socioeconomic backgrounds, it was made up of men and women who wholeheartedly and self-consciously attempted to enact cultural norms. These norms represented the ideal toward which upwardly mobile Americans strove, and reflected the standard against which nonconforming individuals were judged. It is all the more important, then, to understand the standards of appropriate behavior established by the middle class. During the postwar years, there were no groups in the United States for whom these norms were irrelevant.

These white middle-class Americans were among the first to establish families according to the new domestic ideology. Relatively affluent, more highly educated than the average, they were among those Americans who were best able to take advantage of the postwar prosperity. They looked toward the home, rather than the public world, for personal fulfillment. No wonder that when they were asked what they thought they had sacrificed by marrying and raising a family, an overwhelming majority of them replied, "Nothing."

One of the striking characteristics of the KLS respondents was their apparent willingness to give up autonomy and independence for the sake of marriage and a family. Although the 1950s marked the beginning of the glamorization of bachelorhood, most of the men expressed a remarkable lack of nostalgia for the unencumbered freedom of a single life. Typical responses to the question, "What did you have to sacrifice or give up because of your marriage?" were "nothing but bad habits" and "the empty, aimless, lonely life of a bachelor." One who gave up only "a few fishing and hunting trips" claimed that "the time was better . . . spent at home." Many of these men had been married for over a decade and had their share of troubles. The comment for one man was especially poignant. Although he described his wife as addicted to alcohol and "sexually frigid," he claimed that "aside from the natural adjustment, I have given up only some of my personal independence. But I have gained so much more: children, home, etc. that I ought to answer . . . 'nothing at all.' "[5]

Women were equally quick to dismiss any sacrifices they may have made when they married. Few expressed regrets for devoting themselves to the homemaker role—a choice that effectively ruled out other life-long occupational avenues. Although 13 percent mentioned a "career" as something sacrificed, most claimed that they gained rather than lost in the bargain. One wife indicated how her early marriage affected the development of her adult identity: "Marriage has opened up far more avenues of interest than I ever would have had without it . . . I was at a very young and formative age when we were married and I think I have changed greatly over the years . . . I cannot conceive of life without him."[6]

Many wives who said they abandoned a career were quick to minimize its importance and

to state that they "preferred marriage," which suggests that the pursuit of both was not viable. Many defined their domestic role as a career in itself. One woman defended her decision to give up her career: "I think I have probably contributed more to the world in the life I have lived." Another mentioned her sacrifices of "financial independence [and] freedom to choose a career. However, these have been replaced by the experience of being a mother and a help to other parents and children. Therefore the new career is equally as good or better than the old." Both men and women mentioned the responsibilities of married life as sources of personal fulfillment rather than sacrifice.[7]

Further evidence of the enormous commitment to family life appears in responses to the question, "What has marriage brought you that you could not have gained without your marriage?" Although the most common answers of men and women included family, children, love, and companionship, other typical answers were a sense of purpose, success, and security. It is interesting to note that respondents claimed that these elements of life would not have been possible without marriage. Women indicated that marriage gave them "a sense of responsibility I wouldn't have had had I remained single" or a feeling of "usefulness . . . for others dear to me." One said marriage gave her a "happy, full, complete life; children; a feeling of serving some purpose in life other than making money." Another remarked, "I'm not the 'career girl' type. I like being home and having a family. . . Working with my husband for our home and family brings a satisfaction that working alone could not."[8]

Men were equally emphatic about the satisfactions brought about by family responsibility. Nearly one-fourth claimed that marriage gave them a sense of purpose in life and a reason for striving. Aside from love and children, no other single reward of marriage was mentioned by so many of the husbands. Included in the gains they listed were "the incentive to succeed and save for the future of my family," "a purpose in the scheme of life," and "a motivation for intensive effort that would otherwise have been lacking." One man confessed, "Being somewhat lazy to begin with, the family and my wife's ambition have made me more eager to succeed business-wise and financially." A contented husband wrote of the "million treasures" contained in his family; another said that marriage offered "freedom from the boredom and futility of bachelorhood."

Others linked family life to civic virtues by claiming that marriage strengthened their patriotism and morals, instilling them with "responsibility, community spirit, respect for children and family life, reverence for a Supreme Being, humility, love of country." Summing up the feelings of many in his generation, one husband said that marriage

> increased my horizons, defined my goals and purposes in life, strengthened my convictions, raised my intellectual standards and stimulated my incentive to provide moral, spiritual, and material support; it has rewarded me with a realistic sense of family and security I never experienced during the first 24 years of my life.[9]

The respondents expressed a strong commitment to a new and expanded vision of family life, focused inwardly on parents and children and bolstered by affluence and sex. They claimed to have found their personal identities and achieved their individual goals largely through their families. Yet, the superlatives ring hollow, as if these women and men were trying to convince themselves that the families they had created fulfilled all their deepest wishes. For as their extensive responses to other questions in the survey will show, they experienced disappointments, dashed hopes, and lowered expectations. Many who gave their marriages high ratings had actually resigned themselves to a great deal of misery. As postwar Americans endeavored to live in tune with the prevailing domestic ideology, they found that the dividends required a heavy investment of self. For some, the costs were well

worth the benefits; for others, the costs were too high.

Ida and George Butler were among those who felt the costs of marriage were worth the benefits. After more than a decade together, they both claimed that they were satisfied with the life they had built. When they first embarked on married life, they brought high hopes to their union. Ida wrote that George "very nearly measures up to my ideal Prince Charming." George, in turn, noted Ida's attractiveness, common sense, and similar ideas on home life and sex. He was glad she was not the "high stepping" type, but had "experience in cooking and housekeeping." For this down-to-earth couple, the home contained their sexuality, her career ambitions, his drive for success, and their desires for material and emotional comforts.

Yet, like all things worth a struggle, it did not come easy. Ida's choices reflect the constraints that faced postwar women. She sacrificed her plans for "a professional career—I would [have] liked to have been a doctor—but we both agreed that I should finish college, which I did." Following her marriage, there were "obstacles" to her continuing to pursue a career in medicine. It was difficult to combine a professional life with a family. For one thing, the children were primarily her responsibility. She explained:

> My husband works very hard in his business and has many hobbies and friends. The care and problems of children seem to overwhelm him and he admits being an "only" child ill prepared him for the pull and tug of family life. We work closely together on discipline and policies, but he is serious minded and great joy and fun with the children [are] lacking.

If Prince Charming's shining armor tarnished a bit with the years, Ida was not one to complain. She had reasons for feeling contented with the family she helped build:

> I think a *stability* which runs through my life is important. I cannot recall any divorce or separation in my immediate family. We are a rural

close-to-the-soil group and I was brought up to take the "bitter with the sweet"–"you made your own bed, now lie in it" philosophy, so it would not occur to me to "run home to mother."

Although marriage was not Ida's first career choice, it eventually became her central occupation: "Marriage is my career. I chose it and now it is up to me to see that I do the job successfully in spite of the stresses and strains of life." She felt that the sacrifices she made were outweighed by the gains—"children, a nice home, companionship, sex, many friends." George also claimed to be "completely satisfied" with the marriage. He wrote that it brought him an "understanding of other people's problems, 'give and take,' love and devotion." He felt that he sacrificed "nothing but so-called personal freedom." Her medical career and his so-called personal freedom seemed to be small prices to pay for the stable family life they created together.[10]

For couples like the Butlers, the gains were worth the sacrifices. But their claims of satisfaction carried a note of resignation. Combining a profession with a family seemed an unrealistic goal for Ida; combining personal freedom with the role of provider seemed equally out of reach for George. They both thought they faced an either/or situation, and they opted for their family roles. At first glance, this case appears unremarkable: two people who made a commitment to marriage and made the best of it. But the Butlers' choices and priorities take on a larger significance because they were typical of their generation, which was unique in its commitment to family life. The costs and benefits articulated by the Butlers—and their willingness to settle for less than they bargained for—were conditions they shared with their middle-class peers.

Unlike the Butlers, Joseph and Emily Burns emphasized the costs of family life. Haunted by the legacy of the Great Depression and World War II, Joseph expected marriage to yield the "model home" described by Nixon, where affluence, intimacy, and security would prevail. But the worrisome state of the world was inescapable for him, even in the family. Nevertheless, he articulated the way in which the world situation contributed to the intense familism of the postwar years.

At the time of his engagement, Joseph Burns had high expectations for his future marriage. He had chosen his fiancee because he could trust and respect her, her "past life has been admirable," she did not drink or smoke, and "she is pleasing to the eye." If anything made him uneasy about their prospects for future happiness, it was the fear of another depression: "If the stock market takes another drop . . . business will be all shot." The depression had already made him wary, but his disillusionment would be complete by the end of World War II.

Looking back over his life from the vantage point of the 1950s, Joseph Burns reflected:

> As I review the thoughts that were mine at the time of my marriage and as they are now, I would like to give an explanation that should be considered . . . A young couple, much in love, are looking forward to a happy life in a world that has been held up to them by elders as a beautiful world. Children are brought up by their parents to love God and other children, honesty is a must, obedience to the Ten Commandments and to the golden rule is necessary.
>
> With such training, I started out my life only to find out the whole thing is a farce. Blundering politicians lusting for power and self-glory have defiled what is clean and right, honesty is just a word in the dictionary, love of God—who really believes in God? Love of neighbor . . . get him before he gets you.
>
> I agree it does sound cynical, but let us face the facts. Mankind has been slowly degenerating, especially since 1914, and today, what do we have to look forward to? Civil defense tests, compulsory military training, cold wars, fear of the atomic bomb, the diseases that plague man, the mental case outlook? . . . I submit these things to show how a marriage can be vitally affected as was ours and, therefore, many of my ideals, desires, and, most of all, my goal.

Joseph's cynicism toward the wider world made him place even higher hopes on the family to be a buffer. When world events intruded into that private world, he was devastated: "On December 7, 1941, the question burned in my mind, How can so-called Christian nations tear each other apart again?" Joseph resolved his personal anguish in a unique manner: he became a Jehovah's Witness. But he continued to cling to the family as security in a chaotic world. Although he claimed that the world situation had dashed his ideals, he still rated his marriage happier than average and said it gave him "the opportunity to think and reason." As far as what he sacrificed for his marriage, he wrote, "Whatever [I gave] up, which probably would have been material possessions, has been offset by the things [I] gained." Joseph's rage at the world was tempered by the benefits of having a family. He believed that the family provided him with security and satisfaction, and fulfilled at least some of the hopes he originally brought to it.

Emily Burns had a different view of their marriage, and found little comfort in her life with Joseph. Although his religious conversion was at the center of her dissatisfaction, her responses raise other issues as well. Emily complained about her husband's pessimism, coldness, aloofness, and lack of a love of beauty. She emphasized that her husband's change of religion had affected his whole life—"[his] attitude toward wife, children, home, friends, and world. Unless I become absorbed in [his religion], we [will come] to a parting of the ways, since I'm an outsider in my own home."

In addition to the major rift over her husband's conversion, Emily enumerated her sacrifices as follows:

1. A way of life (an easy one).
2. All friends of long duration; close relationships.
3. Independence and personal freedom.
4. What seemed to contribute to my personality.
5. Financial independence.

6. Goals in this life.
7. Idea as to size of family.
8. Personal achievements—type changed.
9. Close relationship with brother and mother and grandmother.

Her complaints add up to much more than religious incompatibility. They suggest some of the costs of adhering to the domestic ideology of the postwar era: an emphasis on the nuclear family at the expense of other relatives and friends, loss of personal freedom, financial independence, "goals" and "personal achievements." For Emily, like Ida Butler and others of their generation, marriage and family life led to a narrowing of options and activities. But it was a bargain she accepted because it appeared to be the best route toward achieving other goals in life. Although she would not have married the same person if she had to do it over again, she never considered divorce. The benefits she gained in marriage offset her discontent with her spouse. Her list of benefits reveals why she chose the domestic path:

1. The desire to give up all for the love of one.
2. The placing of self last.
3. A harmonious relationship until religion . . . changed this.
4. Two ideal children even though the boy is cold and indifferent like his father. (They have strong religious ties in common.)
5. A comfortable home independent of others.
6. Personal satisfaction if all turns out well.
7. Personal satisfaction in establishing a home.

In this list, Emily mentioned practically all the major subjective compensations that made marriage such an important commitment for so many women at the time. Yet, it was a qualified list. Her dissatisfaction was obvious even in her enumeration of her gains. So she struggled to improve her situation as best she could. While her husband used the last space in the questionnaire to brood over the world situation and explain his turn toward religion, Emily used it to reaffirm her faith in the potential for happiness in marriage. She wrote to Kelly and his research team: "Honestly wish this survey will help future generations to maintain happiness throughout marriage and that your book will become more than cold facts and figures. We have enough such now!"

Emily revealed a submerged feminist impulse that also surfaced in numerous testimonies of her peers. To help her formulate these ideas and influence her husband, she turned to experts:

> Have tried to arouse interest in the woman's point of view by reading parts of Dr. Marie Carmichael Stopes' works pertaining to marriage, to my husband. He says, "Oh, she is just a woman, what does she know about it?" and "How can such things (marriage relationship) be learned from a book?" I have ideas on marriage and when I see the same ideas expressed in print by a person of authority, at least I can see that I am not the only woman or person who thinks "such and such."

Recognizing that her husband was not sympathetic to her rebellion against female subordination, she predicted, "Because of a developing hard, slightly independent attitude on my part, I believe my husband's report on me will be anything but favorable."

Joseph and Emily Burns, in spite of their numerous complaints, stayed together. Through all their disillusionment and anger, they never waivered in their commitment to their imperfect relationship and insisted that their marriage was worth the struggle. Emily chafed against the limits to her freedom and turned to experts to bolster her status within the family. Joseph turned to the home to provide solace from the miseries that surrounded him in the public world. Both had invested a great deal of their personal identities in their domestic roles and were not willing to abandon them. Even if the home did not fulfill their dreams of an emancipated, fulfilling life, it still provided more satisfaction and security than they were likely to find elsewhere. For all their struggles and strains,

Joseph and Emily Burns had created something together that met their needs. In 1980, they were still married to each other.[11]

Like the Butlers, the Burnses demonstrate the powerful determination and the considerable sacrifice that went into the creation of the postwar family. Even if the result did not fully live up to their expectations, these husbands and wives never seriously considered bailing out. It is important to consider the limited options and alternatives that these men and women faced. It was not a perfect life, but it was secure and predictable. Forging an independent life outside marriage carried enormous risks of emotional and economic bankruptcy, along with social ostracism. As these couples sealed the psychological boundaries around the family, they also sealed their fates within it.

ENDNOTES

1. "Their Sheltered Honeymoon," *Life,* 10 August 1959, pp. 51–52.
2. This research used the *Kelly Longitudinal Study, 1935–1955* data set [made accessible in 1979, raw and machine-readable data files]. These data were collected by E. L. Kelly and donated to the archive of the Henry A. Murray Research Center of Radcliffe College, Cambridge, Massachusetts (Producer and Distributor). The data set is hereafter referred to as the KLS, in the text and notes. Two articles from the study were published: Charles F. Westoff, Elliot G. Meshler, and E. Lowell Kelly, "Preferences in Size of Family and Eventual Fertility Twenty Years After," *American Journal of Sociology* 62 (March 1957), pp. 491–97; and E. Lowell Kelly "Constancy of the Adult Personality," *American Psychologist* 10 (1955), pp. 659–81. An earlier article, based on a different data base, suggests the direction of Kelly's research in the early years of the study: Kelly, "Marital Compatibility as Related to Personality Traits of Husbands and Wives as Rated by Self and Spouse, *Journal of Social Psychology* 13 (1941), pp. 193–98. Kelly spent years gathering, organizing, coding, and entering into machine-readable form an enormous amount of

data. He then became involved in other projects without publishing a major work summarizing the findings of his study. Quotes from the KLS in the text have been edited slightly to correct spelling and punctuation, and occasionally grammar, since responses were often written in haste. Also, all names used are fictitious.

3. Kelly's data are a social historian's dream, but they are also something of a nightmare. Kelly devised his questionnaires for his purposes, not mine. As one among a growing number of social scientists who were interested in the scientific determinants of marital compatibility, he hoped to identify long-term patterns of marital adjustment that could be used as predictors of successful marriage in the future. His assumptions were implicitly ahistorical, since his study was based on the premise that personality characteristics are as likely to surface in one generation as another, regardless of historical circumstances. Accordingly, he believed that marriage is an institution grounded in personality adjustment, not social or cultural change. My assumptions are the opposite.

The questions Kelly asked locate his study in its era, in spite of the survey's presumed timeless objectivity. Kelly assumed, for example, that distinct domestic gender roles were universally endorsed. Thus, he asked women to rate their adequacy as "cooks" and "homemakers" and men to rate themselves as "handymen" and "providers." In addition to these value judgments, the questionnaires focused exclusively on personal life. There were literally hundreds of questions concerning the respondents' sex lives, but—remarkably—not one item about their political views, not even party affiliation. Kelly and his data, then, were raw material for this study, for they provide evidence of certain assumptions prevalent at the time. It is nevertheless frustrating to draw on a collection of data so rich in some areas and so silent in others. The problem is unavoidable, since my intention is to break down the traditional disciplinary division between public and private lives—a division that

provided the guiding assumptions for scholars such as Kelly.

4. Ronald R. Rindfuss and James A. Sweet, *Postwar Fertility Trends and Differentials in the United States* (New York: Academic Press, 1977), p. 191. On the similarities and differences of the demographic patterns of blacks and whites, see Cherlin, *Marriage, Divorce, Remarriage,* pp. 93–112. On the hardships blacks experienced during the Depression, see Jacqueline Jones, *Labor of Love, Labor of Sorrow: Black Women, Work and the Family from Slavery to the Present* (New York: Basic Books, 1985), chap. 6. For distinctive patterns of black family life, see, for example, Herbert Gutman, *The Black Family in Slavery and Freedom, 1750–1925* (New York: Pantheon, 1976); and Carol Stack, *All Our Kin* (New York: Harper & Row, 1974). On the exclusion of blacks from the suburbs, see Kenneth T. Jackson, *Crabgrass Frontier: The Suburbanization of the United States* (New York: Oxford University Press, 1985).

5. For a discussion of the rebellion against the breadwinner role, the glorification of bachelorhood, and the rise of the *Playboy* culture, see Barbara Ehrenreich, *The Hearts of Men* (Garden City, N.Y.: Doubleday & Co., 1983). Quotes are in responses to open-ended question #B.V.7., 1955 survey, KLS, "Looking back over your life, what did you have to sacrifice or give up because of your marriage?

6. Responses to #B.V.7, 1955 survey, KLS.

7. Ibid.

8. Responses to open-ended question #B.V.8., 1955 survey, KLS, "Looking back over your life, what has marriage brought you that you could not have gained without your marriage?"

9. Ibid.

10. Case 158, KLS. All names are fictitious; the KLS respondents were identified in the survey only by number.

11. Case 290, KLS.

READING 2-2

Comparative and Historical Perspectives on Marriage, Divorce, and Family Life

Arland Thornton

FIVE HUNDRED YEARS OF EUROPEAN DISCOVERY

It has now been five centuries since Europeans discovered the land they named America. The discovery of America by Christopher Columbus five hundred years ago capped one era of European exploration and discovery and opened up a second round of discovery, exploration, and conquest. For the next few centuries, Europeans were to circle the globe, making innumerable discoveries in Australia, Asia, Africa, America, and the islands of the seas.

While our history books primarily chronicle the discoveries and conquests of these European explorers in physical and geographical terms—by listing the various lands, rivers, and seas that they discovered—there were numerous social and cultural discoveries as well. For example, as they expanded their exploratory horizons, the Europeans found numerous groups, each with their own histories, cultures, and customs. In the subsequent five centuries, the centers of European population were inundated by the reports of numerous explorers, missionaries, travelers, colonial administrators, and scholars concerning the customs of the many peoples with whom they came into contact.

In the beginning of this reading, I document some of the central findings of northwestern

European scholars concerning marriage and family life around the globe. I also discuss some of the central conclusions which they derived from their discoveries.[1] As scholars from northwestern Europe began to assimilate, understand, and systematize the information they gleaned from societies around the world, several things became clear. First, they found that family ties and kinship relations were central social structures in all of the populations they encountered. Large fractions of the activities of individual human beings took place within family units. Individuals were born into families, socialized by family members, protected by kinsmen, and organized into economic production units along kinship lines.[2]

Second, these scholars discovered that the human species has been enormously innovative in creating a nearly infinite variety[3] of different family forms and structures.[4] The different forms of family life and marriage were so varied that it was difficult, if not impossible, to construct universally applicable definitions for such concepts as "family" and "marriage." While each culture had similar concepts, the differences were of such magnitude that the concepts and meanings could not easily be translated across cultures and languages. This problem still plagues social scientists today.[5]

Third, northwestern European scholars found that while the family structures of their own cultures shared much in common with those of many other peoples, a cluster of features made northwest Europe unique in many respects. Of central importance in this regard were the marriage, family, and household formation systems of northwestern Europe.[6] Unlike many other societies, households in several northwestern European countries were generally nuclear rather than extended. Instead of multiple generations of married couples living and working together in the same household and economic unit, households generally consisted of only one married couple and their children. Since marriage between northwestern Europeans generally involved the establishment of a separate household and economic unit, it could not usually be contracted until such units were available to the couple desirous of marriage. This marriage system was also characterized by relatively late marriage, with many women postponing marriage until their mid-20s, and many men not marrying until their late 20s. Furthermore, many men and women never married.[7] Yet, although many people never married, marriage was still preferred over remaining single because of the status, opportunity, and stability advantages associated with marriage.

Many of the countries of northwestern Europe also had a system of "lifecourse servanthood," in which a young man or woman would leave the parental home at a relatively young age—sometimes before reaching the teenage years—to live and work in the households of others.[8] This institution of servanthood was not limited to poor children living and working in wealthy households but involved a wide range of families as both receivers and senders of young people. As a result, large fractions of young people in northwestern Europe lived and worked away from their parental families during the young adult years before marriage, often for extended periods of time.[9]

Young people in northwestern Europe undoubtedly received extensive direction and supervision from their parents and other adults as they matured into adulthood. Nevertheless, when compared with their peers in numerous other societies, these young people also enjoyed a remarkable amount of latitude in their behavior and relationships.[10] In particular, northwestern European marriages, unlike those in many other settings, generally were not arranged by parents. Instead, spouses generally were chosen by young people through a courtship and selection system which they managed themselves. While economic, property, and status considerations were undoubtedly important components in this mate selection system, romance was also a central

feature. Young people married for love as well as for money.

Sex, pregnancy, and childbearing before marriage were strongly discouraged in northwestern European societies.[11] However, these activities could not be controlled as effectively as they were in those societies where parents exercised strong parental control over children and where marriages were early and arranged. As a result, the courtship system of northwestern Europe resulted in numerous couples having sex before marriage, many brides being pregnant at marriage, and some children being born outside of wedlock.[12]

Northwestern European populations, like those in most other parts of the world, experienced a high rate of marital dissolution. Since divorce was relatively infrequent in the northwestern European past, however, these marital dissolutions were primarily the result of mortality due to the precarious health conditions of the time.[13] Nevertheless, the result was the creation of significant numbers of single-parent families. Even worse, some children experienced the death of both parents.

As I have documented in detail elsewhere, scholars of the 18th, 19th, and early 20th centuries were unable to accept the enormous differences that they observed among societies as simply representing cross-cultural variations in family structure and form.[14] Instead, they interpreted the cross-cultural variation within an overarching framework of developmental and historical change.[15] Using a biological analogy, these scholars assumed that all societies experienced the same developmental or historical trajectory, with some societies developing at faster rates than others.[16] These scholars also assumed that their own societies were the most advanced and that other societies were situated at various lower positions on the developmental ladder.[17] Using this model of developmental change, these scholars believed they could describe the history of family change by comparing family structure and relationships in their own societies with those observed in other parts of the world.[18] They did so by assuming that the family forms they observed contemporaneously in other parts of the world had existed in northwestern Europe's past.[19]

Given this last assumption, these scholars concluded that northwestern Europe had once had the family structures and processes so prevalent in other parts of the world.[20] They believed that their own societies had once been characterized by extended family households, young and universal marriage, arranged marriage, a lack of romance in the courtship process, and strong parental control over children. Furthermore, these observers concluded that the key features of the northwestern European family and marriage systems—including nuclear family households, marriage at a relatively older age, many people never marrying, love marriages, and extensive autonomy in young adulthood—were the result of recent social and economic development.

It was only in the 1960s that scholars began to examine the records of the past to verify these historical conclusions. Unfortunately, for long periods of the historical past there were no survey research organizations that collected systematic data about courtship, marriage, romance, and family relationships. Consequently, the data we have to work with are scarce and subject to extensive error. Nevertheless, numerous historical studies now document that the basic and unique features of the northwestern European family system described above were *not* the result of recent historical change but instead had existed for centuries.[21] In fact, it now appears that these unique family and marriage characteristics have existed for at least as long as half a millennium—which is as far back as reliable systematic historical evidence goes.[22] As a result, the conclusions of earlier scholars about extended households, arranged marriage, the lack of affection, and young and universal marriage in the northwestern European past are now frequently referred to as myths.

RELEVANT FAMILY CHANGES IN WESTERN SOCIETIES

The documentation of family change in Western societies since the European discovery of America is hampered greatly by shortcomings in the time series of available empirical data. Nevertheless, the available historical record does suggest that family change since the European discovery of America involves an interesting mixture of continuity and change.

One of the most important changes in Western societies during recent centuries has been the proliferation of social organizations and institutions that are not based upon kinship relations. With the creation and expansion of factories, schools, medical and public health organizations, police, commercialized leisure, the mass media, and other nonfamilial organizations, the lives of individuals increasingly have been conducted within, and organized by, nonfamilial institutions. While families, of course, continued to be important organizations for individuals, numerous other institutions began to organize and influence their lives as well.[23]

Of particular importance to this change was the separation of many of the activities of individuals from the family and home. With the rise of industrialization and paid employment, the work activities of men and unmarried women increasingly shifted away from the home to bureaucratic production institutions such as factories and offices.[24] As industrialization and paid employment shifted many of the productive activities of society from the home and farm to the factory and office, married women became increasingly segregated from activities that brought in money and instead concentrated their time and energies on caring for the home and their children. In the last several decades, however, there has been a return of married women to income-producing activities, but that activity now occurs primarily outside the home. With the separation of home and work in recent decades for both mothers and fathers, the combination of employment and parenting has become a particularly difficult concern for both individual families and the larger society.[25] The growth of school systems has also transferred children away from activities within the home to activities in the schools for many of their growing-up years.

The leaving-home process in Western societies continues to be complex, but the nature of that complexity has shifted in the past two centuries.[26] The shift of the workplace from the home to factories and offices terminated the institution of servanthood, where young people left their own families to work and live in the homes of others. Servanthood was replaced during the years of industrialization and urbanization by the practice of boarding and lodging. Young people would migrate from rural agricultural areas to cities to work in factories and offices and to live in factory-owned dormitories or in private rooming houses. More recently, as Western society has become almost completely urbanized, boarding and lodging has nearly disappeared, having been replaced by young people living in their own apartments or houses, either by themselves or with unrelated roommates.

The history of marriage in northwestern European countries reveals important swings in the timing and propensity of marriage but few long-term secular trends in these marital dimensions. Eighteenth-century England experienced an important increase in the propensity to marry, with both the age at marriage and the number of people never marrying declining sharply. These changes helped to initiate two centuries of population growth in that country.[27] Most countries of northwestern Europe as well as the European immigrant populations in North America and Australia also experienced an important marriage boom following World War II, with marriage rates increasing, age at marriage falling, and the fraction of the population never marrying declining.[28] During the 1970s and 1980s, marriage rates declined rapidly in most of these

populations.[29] In the United States, the prevalence of marriage at the end of the 1980s was slightly lower than that observed at the beginning of the 20th century.

However, the decline in marriage in the 1970s and 1980s was not due to abandonment of intimate coresidential male-female relationships. Nonmarital cohabitation was increasing sharply at exactly the same time that the prevalence of marriage was declining. In fact, unmarried cohabitation has increased so much in recent years that it has become a part of the life course for a large fraction of young people in many Western populations. Furthermore, the increase in cohabitation has been so pervasive that the fraction of young people who have never experienced a coresidential union—either marriage or cohabitation—is only slightly lower in the United States today than it was at the height of the post-World War II marriage boom.[30]

In some respects, the increase in unmarried cohabitation in this country is part of a larger increase in sexual relationships outside of marriage. Numerous studies have revealed a high and increasing rate of premarital sex among young unmarried Americans, with the great majority experiencing sexual relations before marriage.[31] One result of this rise in premarital sex has been the large increase in premarital pregnancy and childbearing among young unmarried women. In fact, this increase in out-of-wedlock childbearing has become so significant that more than one child in four is now born outside of marriage.[32] Additionally, the growing prevalence of premarital pregnancy has contributed to the increased number of abortions performed in Western societies.[33]

Of course, the increasing divorce rate has been one of the most important and well-publicized family trends in recent years. While divorce has been increasing in most Western countries, including the United States, for well over a century, the pace of that increase quickened sharply in the 1960s and 1970s. By the end of the 1970s, the upward expansion of divorce did come to an end. Nevertheless, it is now projected that more than one-half of all marriages in the United States will end in divorce.[34]

Less well appreciated than the rising divorce rate, however, is the equally dramatic decline in marital dissolutions produced by the death of a husband or wife—a phenomenon that has been occurring for long periods of Western history. In fact, the decline in human mortality has been so substantial that the overall rate of marital dissolution from both divorce and mortality in the United States is now only somewhat higher than it was a century ago.[35] Of course, with the switch of marital dissolution from mortality to divorce, the meaning of marital dissolution and remarriage in the lives of both children and adults has changed dramatically. People now must deal with the realities and difficulties associated with voluntary marital dissolution and adjust to blended and reconstituted families. In many instances, these blended families can be very complex and include multiple households involving both a divorced father and mother. Such complexities can be sources of both support and strain in the lives of parents and their children.

The changes in family behavior occurring in the United States after 1960 were accompanied by significant trends in attitudes, norms, and values. During the years following 1960, there were fundamental changes in views concerning marriage, divorce, childbearing, gender roles, premarital sex, cohabitation, abortion, and out-of-wedlock childbearing.[36] One important general phenomenon of this period was the relaxing of social prescriptions for family behavior and the expanding range of choices available to individuals. There was an important weakening of the normative pressure to get married, to stay married, to postpone sexual relations until marriage, to have children, to wait until marriage to have children, to *not* have an abortion, and to have a strict segregation of labor between men and women. It has thus become more acceptable in recent decades to go through life without

marrying, to get a divorce, to have sexual relations before marriage, to cohabitate without being married, to bear children outside of marriage, to obtain an abortion, and for women to pursue careers outside the home. As a result, many important behaviors that were previously restricted by prevailing norms have become both relatively common and accepted by significant fractions of Americans.

These shifts in values and norms have also been institutionalized in the law. Whereas morality and the public regulation of intimate behavior were previously important components of legal philosophy, such matters now receive little emphasis. Instead, there is now a focus on the right of privacy and the non-involvement of the larger community in the private lives of individuals.[37] Examples of this legal trend are the universal adoption of no-fault divorce laws in America and the extension of the right of privacy to cover abortion (although the latter is now under serious attack).

These widespread changes in marital behavior, attitudes, values, norms, and laws suggest a major restructuring of the institution of marriage in Western societies in recent decades. The meaning of, rights in, and obligations associated with marriage may now be different from what they were in the past, and the future may hold additional changes. Marriage today is much less of a lifetime commitment than it was in previous decades. Also of crucial importance is the fact that the institution of marriage, as legitimated and regulated by the church and state, is much less of a regulator of human behavior than it was in the past. Legal marriage as sanctioned by religion, government, and the local community is less important today than in past decades as an institution for legitimizing sexual relations and co-residence. Furthermore, with the increase in out-of-wedlock childbearing and divorce, marriage has become substantially separated from parenthood and child rearing. With such changes, it seems likely that young people will now approach marriage with a significant amount of uncertainty and ambivalence about its centrality and meaning in their lives.

While it is difficult to underestimate the importance of the trends toward acceptance of previously prohibited behaviors, we should observe that these trends do not necessarily represent an endorsement of behaviors that were previously proscribed.[38] For example, the shift toward tolerance of sex among unmarried people, unmarried cohabitation, unmarried childbearing, abortion, never marrying, getting divorced, and remaining childless does not mean that there is now widespread endorsement of these same behaviors. That is, while these previously proscribed behaviors have become increasingly accepted, there is no evidence suggesting that they have become positive goals to be achieved. The vast majority of Americans continues to value family life, plans to marry and have children, and is optimistic about achieving success in marriage.

Increasing acceptance of these previously proscribed behaviors also should not be interpreted as a simple rejection of historical values and the adoption of a permissive approach to life. While attitudes about such things as remaining single, divorce, cohabitation, out-of-wedlock childbearing, and premarital sex were becoming more accepting, attitudes toward extramarital sex were becoming less tolerant.[39] This suggests that fidelity within relationships may have become more, rather than less, valued in recent years. Once a marital relationship is contracted, norms against intimate involvement outside of that relationship may now be stronger among young people than they were in previous decades. There is also recent evidence suggesting that the extent of marital infidelity is not particularly great.[40]

The increased emphasis in America on individual freedom and privacy, coupled with a decreased emphasis on conformity to a set of rules and standards concerning family life, has been accompanied by important value shifts in many other domains of American life, including religion, socialization values, civil liberties, and politics.[41] Childrearing values have changed over most of the past century, with Americans now placing less importance on children being obedient, conforming, and loyal to the church. The values of tolerance, autonomy, and thinking for yourself now receive substantially more support than in the past.[42]

There also have been substantial changes in religious values, practice, and authority in recent decades. These changes include declines in the authority of religious leaders and institutions, the value of the Bible as a guide to personal decisions, and confidence in religious answers to the problems of life.[43] Although church membership and attendance increased in the United States before 1960, there were declines after 1960 in membership in religious institutions, the number of people identifying with religion, the perceived importance of religion, the frequency of prayer, and attendance at religious services.[44] Parents also became more willing to permit their children to make their own religious decisions, and they have provided less religious training and less encouragement for their children to pray.[45] These changes have generally been more marked for Catholics than for Protestants.[46]

There is also evidence that the structure of religious experience has been changing. The pluralistic nature of American religion is now generally recognized, and Americans increasingly accept the authenticity of the beliefs and faith of other religions while at the same time believing less that their own religion and morals are necessarily applicable to others.[47] Furthermore, just as family and intimate behavior have been privatized, so has religion, with faith and morals being largely shifted from the community arena to the individual.[48] Consequently, religion today is less compulsory, more voluntaristic, and less condemning and punitive towards those who deviate from its religious teachings.[49] In fact, it now appears that a norm of tolerance has emerged to replace the norm of conformity regarding many dimensions of religious teaching. As a result, most religions now permit more freedom of individual choice and exhibit less intolerance and censorship of the behavior of those who do not follow the teachings of the church.

The expanding power of the norm of tolerance also extends to politics. In the years following World War II, there were substantial increases in support of free speech for atheists, communists, and socialists. There have also been recent increases of independent thinking in politics, with political party identification declining.[50]

SOME IMPLICATIONS FOR PUBLIC POLICY FORMULATIONS

I noted at the beginning of this chapter that the age of European exploration revealed some central facts about the nature of human lifestyles around the world. One of the most important conclusions emanating from these explorations was the discovery of the universal importance of family institutions. Family and kinship relations historically have been central principles of social organization throughout the world. Kinship structures have been central features of virtually every society studied by several generations of explorers and scholars.

It is also true that one of the most important historical trends of the last two centuries in many societies, including our own, has been the dramatic differentiation of society, which has increased the number and importance of nonfamily institutions. Whereas our society in the past was primarily organized around kinship relations, today there are many nonfamilial units that organize people's time, determine their well-being, and exercise authority over them.

One of the most interesting and powerful accounts of the differentiation of society into many specialized nonfamilial units was provided a century ago by Emile Durkheim, a scholar still revered in sociology and anthropology today.[51] Durkheim went so far as to postu-

late a "law of contraction," in which the family would continuously decline in importance over time until it would finally disappear as a vital means of social organization.[52] This decline of the family theme has been echoed by others over the intervening years of the 20th century.[53]

The only thing we can say for certain about Durkheim's prediction about the disappearance of families is that it is currently far from being fulfilled. Scholarly literature contains many studies showing the continuing importance of family units in organizing the activities and well-being of individual human beings.[54] In fact, family and kinship relationships continue to be so important to life in America that it is difficult to imagine social life without them. While humility requires us to be careful about dogmatic assertions about the future, it is difficult to imagine this fundamental fact about the centrality of family life changing in the foreseeable future. This suggests that family relationships will continue to be of central importance in shaping the well-being and activities of individuals and their social milieu well into the future.

The continuing importance of family relationships indicates that the nature of family life should be an important concern for people interested in the quality of contemporary and future well-being in the United States. While policy makers should not ignore the potential roles that government, business, schools, and other bureaucratic organizations can play in enriching the lives of individuals, they should not lose sight of the fact that families are important producers and distributors of the necessities and luxuries of life.

A key discovery of the age of exploration was the enormous diversity of family forms found around the world. The human species has been very innovative in creating a substantial number of marriage types and family forms to solve the basic problems of human existence. This fundamental fact has been recognized by scholars who have tried to create definitions of marriage and family that transcend specific cultural forms and arrangements. This definitional problem, as mentioned earlier, has been so profound and difficult to solve that it has seriously impeded comparative research across international boundaries.

The rapid social changes of the last two centuries in the United States and elsewhere have created similar problems of definition within our own cultural tradition. As marriage and family patterns have changed, it has become increasingly difficult to specify exactly what is meant by such universally used words as *family* and *marriage*. This problem continuously plagues policymakers in their attempt to find solutions to perceived problems in marriage and family life.

As I have already indicated, the tremendous array of family diversity found around the world has both marveled and puzzled several generations of social scientists and has provided the raw material for some of the most complex and intricate accounts of historical change ever created by the human mind. Central to this entire scholarly endeavor was the simple and powerfully ethnocentric assumption that the family systems existing in northwestern Europe were in some way better and more advanced than those existing elsewhere around the world. With this assumption, scholars created a powerful account of the evolution of family types in human history. Included within this historical story was a picture of family life in the northwestern European past.

Despite its elegance in describing and explaining the history of contemporary northwestern European family life, this story of family evolution was eventually discredited because of one simple but fatal flaw: it did not fit the facts. The ethnocentric assumption of the superiority of one type of family over another turned out to be a faulty foundation for scientific and historical description and explanation.

This scientific critique brings me to a key observation about the current policy debate regarding the family: ethnocentric assumptions about the relative merit of various family types may be as deleterious to public policy discussions as to scientific discourse. While I recognize that by necessity the public policy debate brings into the picture many factors, including preferences and values which are appropriately excluded from scientific discourse, it is also true that ethnocentric assumptions about the relative merits of family organization may also damage the appropriateness of public policies.

My point here is *not* to say that all forms of human organization are equally beneficial. Rather, I want to say that the history of human experience has demonstrated that many forms of family organization work well, and that it is easy to make value judgments about the various forms of family life that are greatly influenced by upbringing or personal preference. We should, therefore, proceed very cautiously and carefully when making public statements about the relative merits of different kinds of personal and family arrangements. This, of course, is not a call for silence concerning our evaluations and values but an invitation for a strong awareness and appreciation of the range of acceptable alternatives created throughout the history of human experience.

There is also some hope that the historical and comparative record can provide useful insights into the criteria we might use in distinguishing among the various alternative approaches today. By looking broadly across the range of human experience, we may be more effective in identifying those features of family life that are effectively built into the systems of many cultures. This may enable us to move beyond the immediate contingencies of form and structure and identify the principles that would allow us to choose more effectively among alternatives.

While such an undertaking is clearly beyond both my current capabilities and the scope of this paper, there are some dimensions of family life that seem to be universal enough to merit serious consideration for this purpose. As previously noted, social organization throughout the world has been characterized by multiple kinsmen being organized into small communities called families where individual relatives intertwine their energy and resources to accomplish individual and group goals. These family members share energy, space, resources, and social organization to meet the numerous goals of life. Thus, the family has been the central primary unit that provides the resources and social support needed to navigate life. This means that family members are supposed to care about each other and be committed to shared interests. Of course, as in all communities, relationships within families are and always have been characterized by conflict as well as cooperation, by hate as well as love.

It is also useful to note that while family units have sometimes been as small as two individuals, families more typically have included additional members. In fact, most family systems have recognized substantial numbers of relatives and relationships. This suggests that many of the tasks of human existence can frequently be handled more effectively and pleasantly in families with multiple dyads than in those consisting of a single dyad. This observation may be relevant when considering family groups involving a single parent with children. While one-parent families may be able to handle the numerous tasks of life, multiple adults can probably take care of those tasks more efficiently and productively. This consideration, of course, should be only one of the factors taken into account as individuals and the larger society consider and contemplate such issues as marriage, out-of-wedlock childbearing, divorce, and single parenthood.[55]

Another feature of family life commonly found around the world is stability and permanence. Although the ways in which permanence has been achieved vary across cultural boundaries, the continuity of family units has been an important feature of virtually all family systems. For example, in Chinese society, the ancestral chain permanently linking together the living

with their ancestors and their future unborn children provides an identification with a stable family unit that permeates Chinese life.[56] In a somewhat different way, the indissolubility of marriage in the Western world in the past gave the nuclear family unit a sense of stability.

Of course, the termination of a marriage by the death of a parent was particularly disruptive in Western societies. The rise in divorce in recent decades represents a new and in some ways more powerful form of family impermanence. The actual and perceived fragility of family life in the United States today undoubtedly has significant ramifications for the ways in which people conduct their lives. Accordingly, the issue of permanence and stability should be given clear prominence among the myriad of considerations that individuals and the larger society take into account when they consider issues of family formation and dissolution.

The final commonality I would like to draw from the cross-cultural and historical record is the significant extent to which family and marriage have been embedded within the sacred. Historically, the scope and meaning of marriage and family relationships have not been limited to the biological or social but have also extended to the cosmological. For example, the key feature of the Chinese cosmos was the ancestral chain that linked together ancestors with the living and the as yet unborn.[57] Marriage and childbearing thus took on eternal significance as key acts in the continuation of the ancestral chain. Similarly, in many Western societies, marriage was considered to be a sacrament undertaken with the blessing of deity and the church. This blending of the mundane with the sacred in the institutions of marriage and family undoubtedly gave marital and family relationships favored status in these communities. As such, these relationships could call forth loyalty and sacrifice unavailable to many nonfamilial relationships.

Unfortunately, I am unaware of any data indicating the extent to which family relationships today are intertwined with the sacred. The evidence discussed earlier about recent changes in religious orientation, however, suggests that the sacred underpinnings of family relationships today may be less extensive than in the past. This hypothesis, if correct, has ramifications for many dimensions of family life today.

CONCLUSION

It should be clear that I have not presented anything resembling a public policy agenda for marriage, family life, or personal relationships in the United States. Rather, I have tried to draw some principles and cautionary notes from international and historical family experience. If these observations and concerns make some small contribution to the continuing debate about the American family, I will judge my time in presenting them well spent.

ENDNOTES

1. In order to facilitate communication, I use the term *northwestern Europe* and its population and scholars to refer not only to the geographical area of northwestern Europe, but also to the migrant populations from northwestern Europe to North America, Australia, and New Zealand.
2. See generally Peter Laslett, *The World We Have Lost* (New York: Charles Scribner, 1965) for a discussion of English society before and after industrial revolution; Arland Thornton and Thomas E. Fricke, "Social Change and the Family: Comparative Perspectives from the West, China, and South Asia," *Sociological Forum* 2 (1987): 746–79, for an examination of the effects of social and economic transformations upon the family.
3. Included within the many family and marriage forms of humanity are the following: cross-cousin marriages, polygyny, polyandry, bride service, bride price, matrilineality, patrilineality, extended households, nuclear households, arranged marriages, love matches, adoption, child fosterage, lifecourse servanthood, patrilocal residence, matrilocal residence, neolocal residence, child

marriage, universal marriage, extensive celibacy, marriage alliances, exogenous marriage, and exogamous marriage.
4. For discussions of the diverse family and marriage structures from various societies, see Myron L. Cohen, *House United, House Divided* (New York: Columbia University Press, 1976), studying family organization in Yen-Liao, Taiwan; Thomas E. Fricke, *Himalayan Households: Tamang Demography and Domestic Processes* (Ann Arbor, MI: UMI Research Press, 1986), studying "the demography and household process of an agro-pastoral people of North Central Nepal"; Hildred Geertz, *The Javanese Family* (New York: The Free Press, 1961), examining kinship and socialization in Java, Indonesia; Nancy E. Levine, *The Dynamics of Polyandry* (Chicago: University of Chicago Press, 1988), discussing polyandry as practiced among Nyinba, Tibetan residents of northwestern Nepal; Alan MacFarlane, *Marriage and Love in England: Modes of Reproduction 1300–1840* (Oxford, England: Basil Blackwell, 1986), discussing the history of Malthusian family system and its effects on economic growth in England; Arthur P. Wolf and Chieh-Shan Huang, *Marriage and Adoption in China, 1845–1945* (Stanford, CA: Stanford University Press, 1980), studying marriage and adoption practices in northern Taiwan and concluding Chinese marriages and adoptions were complex reflections of various sources that shaped family organization; John Hajnal, "Two Kinds of Preindustrial Household Formation System," *Population and Development Review* 8 (1982): 449–94, contrasting preindustrial northwest European household formation systems with those of other populations; Hilary J. Page, "Childrearing versus Childbearing: Coresidence of Mother and child in Sub-Saharan Africa," in *Reproduction and Social Organization in Sub-Saharan Africa,* ed. Ron J. Lesthaeghe (Berkeley, CA: University of California Press, 1989), pp. 401–41, discussing the nature of family systems in Africa.
5. See E. Kathleen Gough, "The Nayars and the Definition of Marriage," *Journal of the Royal Anthropological Inst.* 89 (1959): 23–34, stating that anthropologists have had difficulty satisfactorily defining "marriage"; Sylvia J. Yanagisako,

"Family and Household: The Analysis of Domestic Groups," *Annual Review of Anthropology* 8 (1979): 196–200, arguing against ability to reduce "family" to one universal definition.

6. MacFarlane, *Marriage and Love in England*, pp. 35–48; John Hajnal, "European Marriage Patterns in Perspective," in *Population in History*, ed. D. V. Glass and D. E. C. Eversley (Chicago: Aldine, 1965), 101; Hajnal, "Two Kinds of Household Formation," 452–59. See generally Laslett, *The World We Have Lost*, arguing that marriage at young age was rare in nineteenth-century England.

7. In some societies, up to 20 percent of the adult population remained unmarried. See Hajnal, "European Marriage Patterns in Perspective," pp. 101–4.

8. Ann Kussmaul, *Servants in Husbandry in Early Modern England* (Cambridge, England: Cambridge University Press, 1981), 3; Hajnal, "Two Kinds of Household Formation," pp. 470–73.

9. Kussmaul, *Servants in Husbandry*, 3; Hajnal, "Two Kinds of Household Formation," p. 471.

10. See MacFarlane, *Marriage and Love in England*, 87–96; Alan MacFarlane, *The Origins of English Individualism: The Family, Property, and Social Transition* (Cambridge, England: Cambridge University Press, 1978), pp. 197–98, arguing that romantic love basis for marriage has predominated in England since at least 1300; Thornton and Fricke, "Social Change and the Family," pp. 753–55.

11. Edward Shorter, *The Making of the Modern Family* (New York: Basic Books, 1975), p. 51.

12. See Edward Shorter et al., "The Decline of Non-Marital Fertility in Europe, 1880–1940," *Population Studies* 25 (1971): 375, 376–78; Daniel S. Smith and Michael S. Hindus, "Premarital Pregnancy in America 1640–1971: An Overview and Interpretation," *Journal of Interdisciplinary History* 5 (1975): 537, 548.

13. Arland Thornton and Deborah Freedman, "The Changing American Family," *Population Bulletin* 38 (1983): 1, 10.

14. Arland Thornton, "Reading History Sideways: The Negative Effect of the Developmental Paradigm on Family and Demographic Research" (Ann Arbor: Institute for Social Research, University of Michigan, 1992).

15. Ibid., pp. 21–33; see also Robert A. Nisbet, *Social Change and History* (New York: Oxford University Press, 1969), pp. 166–88; Anthony D. Smith, *The Concept of Social Change* (London: Routledge and Kegan Paul, 1973), pp. 26–28.

16. Nisbet, *Social Change and History*, 166–88; Smith, *The Concept of Social Change*, pp. 26–28; Thornton, "Reading History Sideways," 21–33.

17. George W. Stocking, Jr., *Victorian Anthropology* (New York: The Free Press, 1987), 235; Edward B. Tylor, *Primitive Culture* (London: John Murray, Albermarle Street, 1871), pp. 23–24; Thornton, "Reading History Sideways," pp. 25–31.

18. Edward A. Westermarck, *The History of Human Marriage* (London: Macmillan and Co., 1891), pp. 1–2; Thornton, "Reading History Sideways," pp. 25–31.

19. Westermarck, *The History of Human Marriage*, pp. 1–2; Thornton, "Reading History Sideways," pp. 25–31.

20. Tylor, *Primitive Culture*, 23–24; Westermarck, *The History of Human Marriage*, pp. 1–2; Thornton, "Reading History Sideways," 25–31.

21. See William J. Goode, *The Family* (Englewood Cliffs, NJ: Prentice-Hall, 1964), 193–94; William J. Goode, *World Revolution and Family Patterns* (New York: The Free Press, 1963), pp. 6–7; Laslett, *The World We Have Lost*, pp. 90–91; Steven Ruggles, *Prolonged Connections: The Rise of the Extended Family in Nineteenth-Century England and America* (Madison, WI: University of Wisconsin Press, 1987), pp. 3–4; Thornton, "Reading History Sideways," pp. 1–7.

22. Laslett, *The World We Have Lost*, pp. 3–4; Macfarlane, *Marriage and Love in England*, pp. 35–48; Hajnal, "Two Kinds of Household Formation," pp. 452–59.

23. Thornton and Fricke, "Social Change and the Family," pp. 755–69.

24. Ibid., pp. 758–62.

25. Kingsley Davis, "Wives and Work: The Sex Role Revolution and Its Consequences," *Population and Development Review* 10 (1984): 397, 413.

26. Frances K. Goldscheider and Julie DaVanzo, "Living Arrangements and the Transition to Adulthood," *Demography* 22 (1985): 545–63; Frances E. Kobrin, "The Fall in Household Size and the Rise of the Primary Individual in the

United States," *Demography* 13 (1976): 127, 128, 134–36; John Modell and Tamara K. Hareven, "Urbanization and the Malleable Household: An Examination of Boarding and Lodging in American Families," *Journal of Marriage and the Family* 35 (1973): 467, 478.

27. E. A. Wrigley and R. S. Schofield, *The Population History of England 1541–1871: A Reconstruction* (Cambridge, MA: Harvard University Press, 1981), pp. 174–75, 257–69.

28. Susan C. Watkins, "Regional Patterns of Nuptiality in Europe 1870–1960," *Population Studies* 35 (1981): 199–215.

29. Andrew J. Cherlin, *Marriage, Divorce, Remarriage* (Cambridge, MA: Harvard University Press, 1992), pp. 2, 6–7, 67.

30. Ibid., 11–13; Larry L. Bumpass et al., "The Role of Cohabitation in Declining Rates of Marriage," *Journal of Marriage and the Family* 53 (1991): 913–18; Larry L. Bumpass and James A. Sweet, "National Estimates of Cohabitation," *Demography* 26 (1989): 615–21; Kathryn A. London, "Cohabitation, Marriage, Marital Dissolution, and Remarriage: United States, 1988," in *Advance Data from Vital and Health Statistics,* ed. National Center for Health Statistics (1991), pp. 1–4.

31. Shorter, *Making of Modern Family,* pp. 79–85, 163–65; Jacqueline D. Forrest and Susheela Singh, "The Sexual and Reproductive Behavior of American Women, 1982–1988," *Family Planning Perspectives* 22 (1990): 206–9; Freya L. Sonenstein et al., "Levels of Sexual Activity Among Adolescent Males in the United States," *Family Planning Perspectives* 23 (1991): 162; Melvin Zelnik and John F. Kantner, "Sexual Activity, Contraceptive Use and Pregnancy Among Metropolitan-Area Teenagers: 1971–1979," *Family Planning Perspectives* 12 (1980): 230–33.

32. See National Center for Health Statistics, Public Health Service, *Monthly Vital Statistics Report 39, Advance Report of Final Natality Statistics, 1988,* no. 4 (Washington, DC: Department of Health and Human Services, 1990).

33. Forrest and Singh, "Sexual and Reproductive Behavior," 213; Zelnik and Kantner, "Sexual Activity, Contraceptive Use," pp. 233–34.

34. Cherlin, *Marriage, Divorce, Remarriage,* 24; Larry L. Bumpass, "What's Happening to the Family? Interactions Between Demographic and Institutional Change," 1990 Presidential Address before the Population Association of America, in *Demography* 27 (1990): 483, 485.

35. Thornton and Freedman, "The Changing American Family," pp. 7–8.

36. Arland Thornton, "Changing Attitudes Toward Family Issues in the United States," *Journal of Marriage and the Family* 51 (1989): 873, 887.

37. Carl E. Schneider, "Moral Discourse and the Transformation of American Family Law," *Michigan Law Review* 83 (1985): 1803, 1833–46.

38. Thornton, "Changing Attitudes Toward Family Issues," pp. 887–91.

39. Ibid., pp. 885–87.

40. Andrew M. Greeley et al., "Americans and Their Sexual Partners," *Sociology* (July–August 1990): 36–38; Tom W. Smith, "Adult Sexual Behavior in 1989: Number of Partners, Frequency of Intercourse and Risk of AIDS," *Family Planning Perspectives* 23 (1991): 102, 104.

41. Thornton, "Changing Attitudes Toward Family Issues," pp. 887–91.

42. Duane F. Alwin, "Changes in Qualities Valued in Children in the United States, 1964–1984," *Social Science Research* 18 (1989): 195, 203–14; Duane F. Alwin, "From Obedience to Autonomy: Changes in Traits Desired in Children, 1924–1978," *Public Opinion Quarterly* 52 (1988): 33, 41–44; Duane F. Alwin, "Religion and Parental Childrearing Orientations: Evidence of a Catholic-Protestant Convergence," *American Journal of Sociology* 92 (1986): 412–13; Duane F. Alwin, "Trends in Parental Socialization Values: Detroit, 1958–1983," *American Journal of Sociology* 90 (1984): 359, 366–79.

43. Theodore Caplow et al., *All Faithful People* (Minneapolis, MN: University of Minnesota Press, 1983), pp. 87–108, 147–49; Andrew M. Greeley et al., *Catholic Schools in a Declining Church* (Kansas City, MO: Sheed and Ward, 1976), pp. 29–36; Andrew M. Greeley, *Religious Change in America* (Cambridge, MA: Harvard University Press, 1976), pp. 16, 20, 57–66; Norval D. Glenn, "Social Trends in the United States," *Public Opinion Quarterly* 51 (1987): S109, S115–17; Michael Hout and Andrew M. Greeley, "The Center Doesn't Hold: Church

Attendance in the United States, 1940–1984," *American Sociological Review* (1987): 325–37.

44. Greely, *Religious Change in America,* 37–40, 55–66; Glenn, "Social Trends in the U.S.," pp. S115–17.

45. Duane F. Alwin, "Religion in Detroit, 1958–1988" (unpublished paper, Institute for Social Research, University of Michigan, Ann Arbor, 1988), p. 14.

46. Greely, *Religious Change in America,* pp. 16–20, 57–66; Hout and Greeley, "The Center Doesn't Hold," pp. 326–27.

47. Robert N. Bellah et al., *Habits of the Heart* (Berkeley, CA: University of California Press, 1985), pp. 225–27; Caplow et al., *All Faithful People,* pp. 98–99, 166–69; Wade C. Roof and William McKinney, *American Mainline Religion* (New Brunswick, NJ: Rutgers University Press, 1987), pp. 40–45, 50–57, 244–49.

48. Roof and McKinney, *American Mainline Religion,* pp. 40–57.

49. Ibid.

50. Clyde Z. Nunn et al., *Tolerance for Non-conformity* (San Francisco: Jossey-Bass, 1978), pp. 69, 167–78; Glenn, "Social Trends in the U.S.," S112–15. See generally John Mueller, "Trends in Political Tolerance," *Public Opinion Quarterly* 52 (1988): 1, 12–17, discussing trends in tolerance of political groups.

51. Emile Durkheim, "The Conjugal Family," in *Emile Durkheim on Institutional Analysis,* trans. and ed. Mark Traugott (Chicago: University of Chicago Press, 1978), pp. 229–39. See generally Emile Durkheim, *The Division of Labor in Society,* trans. W. D. Halls (New York: The Free Press, 1984) explaining consequences of complex systems of division of labor on cohesion and solidarity of society.

52. Durkheim, "The Conjugal Family," pp. 232–33.

53. See, e.g., Jan E. Dizard and Howard Gadlin, *The Minimal Family* (Amherst, MA: University of Massachusetts Press, 1990), pp. 199–221, describing rise in public familialism; David Popenoe, *Disturbing the Nest: Family Change and Decline in Modern Societies* (Hawthorne, NY: Aldine De Gruyter, 1988), pp. 43, 51–54, discussing decline of family within societies.

54. See e.g., Ronald Fletcher, *The Family and Marriage in Britain,* 3d ed. (London: Penguin Books, 1973), pp. 203–33, concluding that family is a central figure in a broad array of human activities; Donald J. Hernandez, *America's Children: Resources from Family, Government and the Economy* (New York: Russell Sage, 1993), pp. 417–46, studying consequences to children's lives of changing family structures; Alice S. Rossi and Peter H. Rossi, *Of Human Bonding: Parent-Child Relations Across the Life Course* (Hawthorne, NY: Aldine De Gruyter, 1990), pp. 455–58, exploring extent to which family ties remain a support system across the life course.

55. For a discussion of the effects of single parents on children, see Sara McLanahan and Gary Sandefur, *Growing Up with a Single Parent: What Hurts, What Helps* (Cambridge, MA: Harvard University Press, 1994).

56. See Arland Thornton and Hui-Sheng Lin, *Social Change and the Family in Taiwan* (Chicago: University of Chicago Press, 1994).

57. Ibid.

CHAPTER 3

Gender and Families

In Western culture, there are two genders, woman and man. This is a social reality we take for granted. Yet in some other cultures, such as many American Indian Societies, a third, in-between gender has been possible. Named the *berdache* by French colonists, the American Indian in-between gender provides a fascinating example of how a reality we see as natural—two genders—can be socially constructed in a different way.[1] And if the gender distinctions of American Indians are socially constructed, must not ours be socially constructed as well? This would seem to be the lesson of the saga of the berdache, as described by Walter L. Williams in *The Spirit and the Flesh: Sexual Diversity in American Indian Culture*. Yet there also are hints in Williams's account that American Indian parents looked for inherent characteristics of children that made parents more likely to raise them as berdaches. The lesson of the berdache may not be that gender is entirely a social construction but rather that social construc-

tion and inherent tendencies interact to create gender identities. In any case, the story of the berdache is a fascinating counterpoint to the taken-for-granted gender identities in the United States today. (Williams uses the phrase *morphological male* to mean biological male; and he uses the word *androgyny* to mean combining masculine and feminine dress and behavior.)

Perhaps no male identity has been as powerful and pervasive in this century as the image of the man who should earn enough to support his family. Is is an image that Jessie Bernard calls forth in the following article, "The Good Provider Role: Its Rise and Fall." Bernard, who died in 1996, was a pioneer in the study of gender and family; her work was not fully appreciated until a younger generation of sociologists began to study gender in the 1970s. In this widely cited article, Bernard details the rise and fall of the good-provider role. It turns out that men have not always been expected to support their families by themselves. The peak of the role, we learn, occurred in the middle of the 20th century. But even before then, it was important as a cultural ideal. Working-class families

---

[1]*Public and Private Families: An Introduction,* pp. 67–72.

attempted, mostly unsuccessfully, to attain it. It gave men great prestige and responsibility in the world outside the home.

The good-provider role also saddled them with a financial responsibility that was not easy to meet. Bernard describes the factors that have led to its downfall since the 1950s. Yet although fewer married couples have just one earner, the financial responsibility still falls more heavily, for most couples, on the husband. And it is still the case that about one-fourth of all children are being brought up in a family with two parents, only one of whom is employed. The good-provider role has weakened, but it has not disappeared.[2]

[2]Donald J. Hernandez, *America's Children: Resources from the Family, Government, and the Economy* (New York: Russell Sage Foundation, 1993).

READING 3-1

Family Matters: The Economic and Social Position of the Berdache

Walter L. Williams

Because it is such a powerful force in the world today, the Western Judeo-Christian tradition is often accepted as the arbiter of "natural" behavior of humans. If Europeans and their descendant nations of North America accept something as normal, then anything different is seen as abnormal. Such a view ignores the great diversity of human existence.

This is the case for the study of gender. How many genders are there? To a modern Anglo-American, nothing might seem more definite than the answer that there are two: men and women. But not all societies around the world agree with Western culture's view that all humans are either women or men. The commonly accepted notion of "the opposite sex," based on anatomy, it itself an artifact of our society's rigid sex roles.

Among many cultures, there have existed different alternatives to "man" or "woman." An alternative role in many American Indian societies is referred to by anthropologists as *berdache*. This reading will take an anthropological and historical approach to understand this topic. The role varied from one Native American culture to another, which is a reflection of the vast diversity of aboriginal New World societies. Small bands of hunter-gatherers existed in some areas, with advanced civilizations of farming peoples in other areas. With hundreds of different languages, economies, religions, and social patterns existing in North America alone, every

generalization about a cultural tradition must acknowledge many exceptions.

Briefly, a berdache can be defined as a morphological male who does not fill a society's standard man's role, who has a nonmasculine character. This type of person is often stereotyped as effeminate, but a more accurate characterization is androgyny. Such a person has a clearly recognized and accepted social status, often based on a secure place in the tribal mythology. Berdaches have special ceremonial roles in many Native American religions, and important economic roles in their families. They will do at least some women's work, and mix together much of the behavior, dress, and social roles of women and men. Berdaches gain social prestige by their spiritual, intellectual, or craftwork/artistic contributions, and by their reputation for hard work and generosity. They serve a mediating function between women and men, precisely because their character is seen as distinct from either sex. They are not seen as men, yet they are not seen as women either. They occupy an alternative gender role that is a mixture of diverse elements.

In their erotic behavior berdaches also generally (but not always) take a nonmasculine role, either being asexual or becoming the passive partner in sex with men. In some cultures the berdache might become a wife to a man. This male-male sexual behavior became the focus of an attack on berdaches as "sodomites" by the Europeans who, early on, came into contact with them. From the first Spanish conquistadors to the Western frontiersmen and the Christian missionaries and government officials, Western culture has had a considerable impact on the berdache tradition. In the last two decades, the most recent impact on the tradition is the adaptation of a modern Western gay identity.

Societies often bestow power upon that which does not neatly fit into the usual. Since no cultural system can explain everything, a common way that many cultures deal with these inconsistencies is to imbue them with negative

Walter Williams, "Family Matters: The Economic and Social Position of the Berdache" from *The Spirit and the Flesh: Sexual Diversity in American Indian Culture,* pp. 1–6, 44–51, and 54–57. Copyright © 1986 by Walter Williams. Reprinted with the permission of Beacon Press.

power, as taboo, pollution, witchcraft, or sin. That which is not understood is seen as a threat. But an alternative method of dealing with such things, or people, is to take them out of the realm of threat and to sanctify them.[1] The berdaches' role as mediator is thus not just between women and men, but also between the physical and the spiritual. American Indian cultures have taken what Western culture calls negative, and made it a positive; they have successfully utilized the different skills and insights of a class of people that Western culture has stigmatized and whose spiritual powers have been wasted.

Many Native Americans understood that gender roles have to do with more than just biological sex. The standard Western view that one's sex is always a certainty, and that one's gender identity and sex role always conform to one's morphological sex is a view that dies hard. Western thought is typified by such dichotomies of groups perceived to be mutually exclusive: male and female, black and white, right and wrong, good and evil. Clearly, the world is not so simple; such clear divisions are not always realistic. Most American Indian worldviews generally are much more accepting of the ambiguities of life. Acceptance of gender variation in the berdache tradition is typical of many native cultures' approach to life in general. . .

A French explorer in the upper Mississippi Valley in the 1680s described berdaches as male Indians who are "Batchelours to their dying day, and never appear either at hunting or in warlike expeditions, as being either lunatick or sickly: But at the same time they are as much esteem'd as the bravest and hailest men in the country."[2] How is it that berdaches could be so highly esteemed without fulfilling a man's role? How could they fit into the family structure while remaining bachelors? Why might they be seen as "lunatick or sickly" and still be respected?

While the spiritual explanation of berdachism provides an important justification for acceptability, a supportive family structure allows berdaches to be raised as proud and productive members of society. American Indian societies are kin-based, so most of a berdache's personal interactions take place with relatives. The extended family and the clan serve many of the functions that governmental institutions provide in a society that is state-based. Because of the way berdaches are raised and the economic role they fulfill, many kinship systems provide a secure place for them.

The major factor affecting the role of the berdache within the family is the notion that the berdache is taking the role because of spiritual guidance. According to a Lakota traditionalist, it is because of directions from a spirit that "*Winktes* had to assume the role, because if they did not, something bad would happen to them or their family or their tribe."[3] This belief effectively restrained parents from trying to change a child who was showing berdachelike behavior.

On the other hand, a family might try to encourage one of their youngsters to take on a berdache role. In some cultures berdaches are known to be from specific prominent clans. A few societies supposedly restricted berdache status to such clans.[4] More commonly, berdaches may come from any family, but it is sometimes said that a certain family will have a tradition of having several berdaches in their family line.[5] A Lakota berdache remembers that when he was about 20 years old his grandparents told him that one male in every generation of the family was a *winkte,* so they accepted it on those terms. The elders told him stories about several *winktes* in his family history who were chosen to do ceremonials in association with a shaman.[6] A family might have a special reputation for having gifted children, one of whom might be a berdache. For example, a famous Omaha *mexoga* had a brother who was a shaman. People told me about both of them: "That whole family was classified." When I asked what they meant, they explained that the family was prominent in the tribe and had special respected roles.[7] Having a berdache for a child is similar to having a shaman in the family; both are sacred.

ASSIGNED GENDER IN CHILDHOOD

It is unclear to what extent parents choose to raise a boy as a berdache. In some cases there does appear to be parental direction. Among the Aleut and Kodiak Islanders in southern Alaska, for example, a Russian explorer in 1812 described berdaches, called *shopan* or *achnucek,* as respected shamans: "A Koniag who has an Achnucek instead of a wife is regarded as lucky. A father or a mother design a son for an Achnucek from his infancy, if he seems to them to resemble a girl."[8] Kodiak parents would select their most handsome and promising boy to raise as feminine. His hair was styled like a woman's, he was dressed in women's clothing, and any facial hair was carefully plucked out. At the age of 10 to 15 years, he would be married to a wealthy man. The husband regarded his boy-wife as a major social accomplishment, and the boy's family benefited from association with their new wealthy in-law. Since the boy was treated with great respect, this practice seemed to provide a no-lose situation for easy social mobility among Aleut and Kodiak families. It is thus not surprising that early observers reported the pride of the parents in having such a son, and the frequent appearance of berdaches.[9]

Likewise, a Spanish explorer among the Lache Indians of Colombia, South America, reported:

> It was a law among them that if a woman bore five consecutive male children, without giving birth to a female, they could make a female of one of the sons when he reached the age of twelve— that is to say, they could rear him as a woman and teach him the habits of a woman, bringing him up in that wise. In their bodily form and manners they appeared so perfectly to be women that no one who beheld them could distinguish them from the others, and these were known as *cusmos* and they performed womanly tasks with the strength of men, as a result of which, when they had attained the proper age, they were given in wedlock as women. And indeed the Laches preferred them to true women, whereby it follows that the abomination of sodomy was freely permitted.[10]

In California, Spanish priests writing in the 1820s implied that a similar practice existed among the Luiseño and Gabrielino Indians. One wrote that the chiefs greatly valued berdaches as auxiliary wives. While still young, berdaches "were selected and instructed as they increased in years in all the duties of the women—in their mode of dress, of walking, and dancing; so that in almost every particular, they resembled females."[11]

What is interesting in these references is the implication for gender flexibility. But we should not let these sources imply that berdache status would be imposed on any young boy against his will. Indian children generally have wide latitude to live where they are comfortable, and in a manner that is compatible with their inclinations. I have observed instances, in several tribes, where a child decides to live in a different household. Their wishes are respected, and no one tries to coerce them. Children are allowed to live where and how they wish.

If children feel manipulated, in a direction other than the one they are inclined to take, they refuse to cooperate. Refusal is interpreted as a reflection of the child's "spirit." The more likely pattern with the youngsters is that such boys as are "chosen" by families to be raised as berdaches would already have evidenced an inclination for nonmasculine behavior. A Tewa boy nicknamed Missy was allowed to develop in this role beginning when he was nine years old. Yet, even before then, according to older people in his pueblo, "There had never been any doubt in anyone's mind, who remembered him at six years old, as to where he would be heading." He had by that age begun to act nonmasculinely, and his mother let him wear his sister's dresses when he asked for them.[12]

In a reference that may denote a similar practice, a pueblo male now in his 60s remembers that when he was six years old his family told him that he would become a "substitute woman," and that they were not going to raise him as an ordinary man but as someone special. They stated this simply and as a matter of fact, based on their observations of his character. The boy accepted it in the same spirit. He feels special, as an especially chosen one. He values his specialness, and is happy in his secure position in the Pueblo traditional community.[13]

AVERSION TO MASCULINITY

The variation of the family origins of berdachism is evidenced by a Lakota man's statement: "*Winktes* come from families where they are raised with lots of sisters and no brothers. They come from different ways—it could be how they are brought up."[14] Perhaps, it has been suggested, berdachism is related to cultural expectations of masculinity. Some anthropologists see berdaches as boys who in childhood have a strong aversion to the ultramasculine male role. Many Indian societies, especially those of the 19th-century Plains, placed extreme pressure on males to achieve individual prestige through warfare. Boys had to be prepared for the warrior role from early childhood, to learn toughness and physical endurance. They were expected to take life-threatening chances. The mechanism in Plains culture for conditioning boys to face pain and death was through extremely rough team games. Even young boys were prepared for warfare through the "Fire-throwing Game," in which boys struck each other with burning sticks. A variation on the game involved throwing at each other mud balls with live coals in the middle. The object for another such game, called "Swing-kicking," was kicking those on the other team in the face until they bled.[15]

It was not only on the Plains that extreme demands were placed on boys to compete in brutal games of physical competition. By the time they reached their late teens boys were participating in both the hunt and the fight. Mohave males, for example, were expected to be exceptionally warlike and to participate in raids. Cowards were despised. Mohave men, like men in many tribes, prized bravery above most other virtues.

Yet despite these values, no demands for demonstrations of bravery were placed on berdaches. *Alyha* were known as "rather peaceful persons" and were respected as such. While bravery was valued, power obtained in a dream was even more highly prized. The Mohave explanation was spiritual; berdaches, after all, had received their instructions from a vision.

Taking a Western perspective, ethnographer George Devereux considered the possibility that such aggressive masculinity pressures might have had something to do with the inclination of a "faint-hearted boy" to opt out of the system by becoming a berdache.[16] The problem with this interpretation is that it is not sufficient in itself. It might have prompted some boys in warlike cultures of the Plains, but if this interpretation is correct, why do we not find berdaches in all warlike tribes? Among tribes that value some of the most aggressive male roles, like the Comanche or the Iroquois, references to berdaches are notably absent. And, more important, why does a berdache tradition exist in native cultures that are not warlike? There is no simple correlation between aggressive male roles and berdachism.[17]

Another problem is that this explanation lends itself to a theory of causation by "overmothering." Using Freudian terminology, Donald Forgey concluded that "Overmothering produced a child neurotically anxious about his own masculinity. . . . A 'mama's boy'—when finally confronted with the period in which he is expected to adopt the ultramasculine, aggressively individualistic and often dangerous role of the adult male—might instead identify with the principal source of his childhood dependency and protection—his mother." Forgey's view that berdachism is a "flight from masculinity," and his use of terms like "neurotically anxious" are merely Freudian value judgments.[18] Berdaches seem anything but neurotic, and their peaceful inclinations would be honored in many gentler cultures. Furthermore, a boy's relation with his mother has been shown not to be the determining factor in gender variance in Anglo-American society. The basic propositions of the thesis have been rejected by most psychologists.[19]

INBORN CHARACTER AND CHILDHOOD ACTIVITIES

Rather than being seen as due to outside causes like overmothering or a "flight" from masculinity, the main emphasis of American Indian explanations is that berdachism is a reflection of the child's individual character. This recognition of an inborn character is at the heart of the Indian spiritual explanation. For example, among the Navajos, a people who place great value on individual freedom, becoming a *nadle* is considered to be solely a reflection of the basic nature of the individual child. Parents would not try to impose such a role on a child, without the child's initiative.[20]

The Zapotec Indians of Oaxaca, Mexico, would never consider that the berdache has chosen to live as he does, because the idea that someone could freely choose her or his character is as ludicrous to the Zapotecs as the idea that someone could freely choose eye color. They defend the right of *ira' muxe* to their different gender and sexual roles simply because "God made them that way." Both characteristics are accepted as integral to the character of berdaches.[21] It is this emphasis on a person's character, or "spirit," that is one of the most important elements of berdachism.

Indians claim that such a future role is easily observed by families. A Lakota traditionalist says, "It is obvious from infancy that one is a *winkte*. He is a beautiful boy, and the sound of his voice is effeminate. It is inborn. The mother realizes this soon, and allows the boy to do feminine things (how to prepare meat and other foods). They all end up being homosexual."[22] Tewa Indians claim that a *kwih-doh* child's nature of doing things in his own special way nearly always begins to show by about age three to five. Only after then will such a child be sin-

gled out as special.[23] A Hupa berdache recalls, "I was real feminine as a child, from as early as I can remember. Noticing how I liked to do cooking and cleaning, my grandmother said I would grow up as a woman. Within the family, Indians believe you can be whatever you choose."[24]

Descriptions by anthropologists of preberdache children support this viewpoint. Margaret Mead, writing about a boy who later became a berdache, said that even as a small boy he showed "marked feminine physical traits."[25] In the 1910s Elsie Clews Parsons knew three adult berdaches at Zuni, but also a six-year-old boy whom she felt was likely to become a berdache. She wrote about him, "His features are unusually fine and delicate. . . . Whenever I saw him playing about he was with a girl."[26]

Among the Crows in the 1850s Edwin Denig remarked about the numerous "berdeches" who, as young children, "cannot be brought to join in any of the work or play of the boys, but on the contrary associate entirely with the girls. . . . When arrived at the age of 12 or 14, and his habits are formed, the parents clothe him in a girl's dress."[27] Half a century later, S. C. Simms met a Crow berdache who was "almost gigantic in stature, but was decidedly effeminate in voice and manner. I was told that, when very young, these persons manifested a decided preference for things pertaining to female duties." Even if parents tried to invite such children to take a standard male role, they invariably resisted.[28] It was more a matter of the family adjusting to the child than vice versa.

The consistency of reports from various culture areas over the centuries is amazing. Even as early as 1702, a French explorer who lived for four years among the Illinois Indians noted that berdaches were known "from their childhood, when they are seen frequently picking up the spade, the spindle, the axe [women's tools], but making no use of the bow and arrows, as all the other small boys do."[29] Among groups like the Papagos, who designed a brushfire test for a berdache, it was only after a family noticed that "a boy liked female pursuits" that he was put through the test.[30] A modern Indian of the Southwest in the 1970s indicated that throughout his life he had "no interest in being a male, in taking over aspects of male roles, or in daydreaming of pleasurably masculine experiences." He remembered that he preferred playing with girls and in games played only by girls. While schoolteachers had forced him to participate in boys' games, he did this unwillingly. He was interested in girls' roles from his earliest memories.[31] Faced with masculinizing pressures, it is not surprising that some boys who were nonmasculine in their disposition would avoid rough and brutal play, and might instead seek the gentler play of girls. It is this characteristic that is most commonly noted about the childhood of berdaches.

While the published literature does not suggest it, my own interviewing turned up a pattern that is more individual and unique than strictly feminine. A Lakota *winkte* remembers his childhood, being raised by his grandparents on the reservation, as unlike other children's:

> I was different. I never played with the boys. I played with the girls a little, or off in my own little world. There were other things I had to do besides play. I did drawings and things. I hung around my grandparents a lot. My grandfather taught me the traditions, and my grandmother taught me how to sew and cook. I was the only child there and they basically responded to my interests. I loved things like beadwork. I was mostly involved in doing artistic things. It isolated me from the other kids, so I took a liking to it. I did all the isolating things. You do beadwork and you're not bothered with other kids.[32]

Likewise, a Hupa berdache remembers, "I was always into something else, things that were never expected of me. I did what I wanted to do, and I liked that."[33]

BERDACHES AS FAMILY MEMBERS, TEACHERS, AND PARENTS

The family of a berdache is more interested in accepting the contribution the child can offer to the family than in finding a supposed cause. Not being stigmatized and alienated, a berdache can offer positive advantages to a family. I stayed with an elderly berdache on the Omaha reservation, in his scrupulously clean house. Even though he lives by himself, he often has members of his extended family over for dinner. They bring their children, who appreciate the care and attention he shows to them. He has provided a home for most of his teenage nephews when their parents' house has gotten too crowded, and he has assisted various relatives financially with school expenses and helped them get established in a new job.

Jerry Baldy, a berdache on the Hupa reservation, says, "You live your life around your family. My aunt says, 'I'm counting on you.' What she means is that someone like me has a special responsibility to help care for the elders."[34] Likewise, a Navajo woman whose uncle was a well respected *nadle* healer says:

> They are seen as very compassionate people, who care for their family a lot and help people. That's why they are healers. *Nadles* are also seen as being great with children, real Pied Pipers. Children love *nadles,* so parents are pleased if a *nadle* takes an interest in their child. One that I know is now a principal of a school on the reservation. . . . *Nadle* are not seen as an abstract group, like 'gay people,' but as a specific person, like 'my relative so-and-so.' People who help their family a lot are considered valuable members of the community."[35]

Thus it is in the context of individual family relations that much of the high status of berdaches must be evaluated. When family members know that one of their relatives is this type of person, and when they have positive cultural reinforcements that account for such individuals, then barriers are not placed inside the family. Without interference from outside religious groups claiming that there is something wrong with parents who raise such a child, unprejudiced family love can exert itself.

Berdaches are recognized as having a special talent in educating children. Part of this recognition is due to the berdache's reputation for high intelligence. A Kwakiutl chief in the 1930s said that a berdache he knew was the wisest man in the community: "All the stories from the beginning of the world he knows, and he makes songs."[36] Upon visiting the Yuki and Pomo reservation at Round Valley, California, in 1871–72, Stephen Powers met a Yuki *i-wa-musp* ("man-woman") and a Pomo *dass:* "They are set apart as a kind of order of priests or teachers . . . [They] devote themselves to the instruction of the young by the narration of legends and moral tales . . . spending the whole time in rehearsing the tribal history in a sing-song monotone to all who choose to listen."[37]

Berdaches in the 20th century have continued to be reputed as effective teachers of the young. In the 1930s ethnographer Ruth Landes met a Potawatomi young man who was a teacher in the primary school on the Kansas reservation. He was admired by the other Indians because "he loved to care for the children, to advise their parents, and to scrub the schoolhouse till it shone."[38] Landes's description could be used word for word to describe a *winkte* I met in 1982. He is recognized as the best teacher in the elementary school on his reservation. A very spiritual person, active in traditional Lakota religion, his great interest is his teaching. He loves children, and seems more animated when discussing his students than any other topic. He wants to have his own children someday. That will undoubtedly be possible through adoption.

A berdache can easily take a parental role, since adoption of children is commonly accepted in most American Indian societies. Adoption may involve orphaned children or children from overcrowded families. The ease with which children above their fifth year move from one household to another, often to distant kin and on their own initiative, is remarkable.

When children were captured in warfare they were almost always adopted as a family member by someone related to their captor. It was very seldom that children would be left to

starve if their parents were killed. Believing that the essence of a person is the spiritual character rather than the physical body, Indian shamans of many tribes commonly invoked a ceremony that incorporated the spirit of a departed relative into the body of the captured child. By this means adopted individuals were accepted into the family as a full-fledged member, without any stigma that they were alien or not "really" a member of the family. This ease of adoption is also extended to non-Indians, which is why so many white captive children on the frontier became socialized as Indians and refused to return to white society if later recaptured.[39] In this context it was quite common for berdaches to adopt older children and adolescents, either as orphans or as captives.[40]

Even today berdaches are known to be very good with children. Terry Calling Eagle, a Lakota berdache, states, "I love children, and I used to worry that I would be alone without children. The Spirit said he would provide some. Later, some kids of drunks who did not care for them were brought to me by neighbors. The kids began spending more and more time here, so finally the parents asked me to adopt them."[41] After those children were raised, Terry was asked to adopt others. In all, he has raised seven orphan children, one of whom was living with him when I was there. This boy, a typical masculine 17-year-old, interacts comfortably with his *winkte* parent. After having been physically abused as a young child by alcoholic parents, he feels grateful for the stable, supportive atmosphere in his adoptive home. The two of them live in a close extended family household, along with Terry's mother, sister, and nephew. A male cousin also lives with them off and on, when he does not have an off-reservation job, and his grandmother's sister stays there part of the time. During the summer I was living there, various other relatives were coming and going in a rather bewildering pattern of changing residence. In this Lakota family at least, people seem almost as nomadic as they were in their days on horseback. In the midst of all this hubbub, however, Terry and his mother are the central persons of the household, looked up to by all.

Thus, an individual who in Western culture would be considered a misfit, an embarrassment to his family who would likely be thrown out of the household, is instead made central to the family. Since other relatives do not feel threatened, family disunity and conflict are avoided. The berdache is not expected to suppress his tendency for feminine behavior. Neither does he internalize a low self-image. He thus avoids the tendency of those considered deviant in Western culture to engage in self-destructive behavior. Berdaches who value their traditions do not tend to be alcoholic or suicidal, even in tribes where such problems are common. They are too valued by their families. In Native American lifestyles, seldom is anything thrown away unused—including people.[42] A Crow traditionalist says, "We don't waste people, the way white society does. Every person has their gift."[43]

ENDNOTES

1. Mary Douglas, *Purity and Danger* (Baltimore: Penguin, 1966), p. 52. I am grateful to Theda Perdue for convincing me that Douglas's ideas apply to berdachism. For an application of Douglas's thesis to berdaches, see James Thayer, "The Berdache of the Northern Plains: A Socioreligious Perspective," *Journal of Anthropological Research* 36 (1980): 292–93.
2. Louis Armand de Lom d'Arce de Lahontan, *New Voyages to North America,* ed. Reuben Gold Thwaites (Chicago: McClurg, 1905), vol. 2, p. 462.
3. Calvin Jumping Bull, Lakota informant 1, July 1982.
4. Alfred Bowers, *Mandan Social and Ceremonial Organization* (Chicago: University of Chicago Press, 1950), p. 168; Alfred Bowers, "Hidatsa Social and Ceremonial Organization," *Bureau of American Ethnology Bulletin* 194 (1965): 502; William Whitman, "The Oto," *Columbia University Contributions to Anthropology* 28 (1969): 50; Frederica de Laguna, "Tlingit Ideas about the Indian," *Southwestern Journal of Anthropology* 10 (1954): 178.
5. Lakota enthnographer Luis Kemnitzer, personal communication, 3 June 1982.
6. Michael One Feather, Lakota informant 14, April 1985.
7. Richard White, Omaha informant 2, June 1982.
8. Quoted in Ales Hrdlicka, *The Anthropology of Kodiak Island* (New York: AMS Press, 1975), p. 79.
9. Georg Langsdorff, *Voyages and Travels in Various Parts of the World during the Years 1803–1807* (Carlisle, Pa.: George Philips, 1817), pp. 345, 64; Martin Sauer, *An Account of a Geographical and Astronomical Expedition to the Northern Parts of Russia . . . 1785–1794* (London, 1802), pp. 160, 176; Hubert Bancroft, "The Koniagas," in *The Native Races of the Pacific States of North America* (New York: Appleton, 1875), vol. 1, p. 82; Havelock Ellis, *Studies in the Psychology of Sex* (New York: Random House, 1910, 1936), vol. 2, pt. 2, pp. 16–17.
10. Fernandez de Piedrahita, quoted in Antonio Requena, "Noticias y Consideraciones Sobre las Anormalidades Sexuales de los Aborígenes Americanos: Sodomía," *Acta Venezolana* 1 (July–September 1945): 16. An English translation of this article, titled "Sodomy among Native American Peoples," appears in *Gay Sunshine* nos. 38–39 (Winter 1979): 37–39.
11. Father Gerónimo Boscana, "Indians at the Missionary Establishment of St. Juan Capistrano, Alta California" (c. 1826), trans. in Jonathan Katz, *Gay American History* (New York: Crowell, 1976), p. 614. See another translation in Gerónimo Boscana, *Chinigchinich* (Banning, Calif.: Malki Museum Press, 1978), p. 54.
12. Harry Hay, personal communication, 1 September 1985.
13. Edmund White, *States of Desire: Travels in Gay America* (New York: E. P. Dutton, 1980), pp. 99–101.
14. Calvin Jumping Bull, Lakota informant 1, July 1982.
15. Royal Hassrick, *The Sioux: Life and Customs of a Warrior Society* (Norman: University of Oklahoma Press, 1964), pp. 133–34, 144–45.
16. George Devereux, "Institutionalized Homosexuality of the Mohave Indians," *Human Biology* 9 (1937): 517.

17. Charles Callender and Lee Kochems, "The North American Berdache," *Current Anthropology* 24 (1983): 443–70.

18. Donald Forgey, "The Institution of Berdache among the North American Plains Indians," *Journal of Sex Research* 11 (1975): 12. This interpretation is also put forth by Hassrick, *Sioux,* pp. 133–34.

19. Alan Bell, Martin Weinberg, and Sue Hammersmith, *Sexual Preference: Its Development in Men and Women* (Bloomington: Indiana University Press, 1981).

20. Jennie Joe, Navajo informant 1, November 1984.

21. Beverly Chiñas, "Isthmus Zapotec 'Berdaches,'" *Newsletter of the Anthropological Research Group on Homosexuality* 7, pt. 2 (May 1985): 1–4.

22. Ronnie Loud Hawk, Lakota informant 4, July 1982.

23. Harry Hay, personal communication, 1 September 1985.

24. Jerry Baldy, Hupa informant 1, September 1985.

25. Margaret Mead, *Sex and Temperament in Three Primitive Societies* (New York: Morrow Quill, 1935, 1963), p. 294.

26. Elsie Clews Parsons, "The Zuni La' Mana," *American Anthropologist* 18 (1916): 521–22.

27. Edward Thompson Denig, *Five Indian Tribes of the Upper Missouri,* ed. John Ewers (Norman: University of Oklahoma Press, 1961), pp. 187–88.

28. S. C. Simms, "Crow Indian Hermaphrodites," *American Anthropologist* 5 (1903): 580–81.

29. Pierre Liette, "Memoir of Pierre Liette on the Illinois Country," in *The Western Country in the Seventeenth Century,* ed. Milo Quaife (New York: Citadel, 1962), pp. 112–13; quoted in Katz, *Gay American History,* p. 228.

30. Ruth Underhill, *Social Organization of the Papago Indians* (New York: Columbia University Press, 1938), p. 186. It is improper to assume, as some theorists on berdachism have, that a ceremonial or visionary origin of berdachism is in opposition to childhood character. Both are reflections of the child's spirit.

31. Robert Stoller, "Two Feminized Male American Indians," *Archives of Sexual Behavior* 5 (1976): 530.

32. Michael One Feather, Lakota informant 14, April 1985. What is interesting in this description is the similarity of this life history to that of gay North American men. Weinberg, Bell, and Hammersmith (*Sexual Preference*) found this same pattern of gender variance in childhood to be about the only factor with which they could find a correlation to adult homosexuality. What is notable is that the focus of Western research is usually on sexual preference, while the emphasis of many Indians is clearly on the character of the person.

33. Jerry Baldy, Hupa informant 1, September 1985.

34. Jerry Baldy, Hupa informant 1, September 1985.

35. Jennie Joe, Navaho informant 1, October 1982.

36. Clellan Ford, *Smoke From Their Fires: The Life of a Kwakiutl Chief* (New Haven: Yale University Press, 1941), p. 130.

37. Stephen Powers, *Tribes of California,* ed. Robert Heizer (originally published 1877; reprint Berkeley: University of California Press, 1976), p. 132.

38. Ruth Landes, *The Prairie Potawatomi* (Madison: University of Wisconsin Press, 1970), p. 197.

39. Irving Hallowell, "American Indians White and Black: The Phenomenon of Transculturation," *Current Anthropology* 4 (1963): 519–31.

40. Bowers, "Hidatsa Organization," p. 167.

41. Lakota informant 5, July 1982.

42. I am grateful to Maurice Kenny, Mohawk poet, for this insight. Personal communication, 22 November 1982.

43. Joe Medicine Crow, Crow informant 2, August 1982.

The Good-Provider Role—
Its Rise and Fall

Jessie Bernard

The Lord is my shepherd, I shall not want. He sets a table for me in the very sight of my enemies; my cup runs over (23rd Psalm). And when the Israelites were complaining about how hungry they were on their way from Egypt to Canaan, God told Moses to rest assured: There would be meat for dinner and bread for breakfast the next morning. And, indeed, there were quails that very night, enough to cover the camp, and in the morning the ground was covered with dew that proved to be bread (Exodus 16:12–13). In fact, in this role of good provider, God is sometimes almost synonymous with Providence. Many people, like Micawber, still wait for him, or Providence, to provide.

Granted, then, that the first great provider for the human species was God the Father, surely the second great provider for the human species was Mother, the gatherer, planter, and general factotum. Boulding (1976), citing Lee and de-Vore, tells us that in hunting and gathering societies, males contribute about one-fifth of the food of the clan, females the other four-fifths (p. 96). She also concludes that by 12,000 B.C. in the early agricultural villages, females provided four-fifths of human subsistence (p. 97). Not until large trading towns arose did the female contribution to human subsistence decline to equality with that of the male. And with the beginning of true cities, the provisioning work of women tended to become invisible. Still, in today's world it remains substantial.

Jessie Bernard, "The Good Provider Role: Its Rise and Fall" from *American Psychologist* 36 (1981). Copyright © 1981 by the American Psychological Association. Reprinted with the permission of Dorothy Jackson and the American Psychological Association.

Whatever the date of the virtuous woman described in the Old Testament (Proverbs 31: 10–27), she was the very model of a good provider. She was, in fact, a highly productive conglomerate. She woke up in the middle of the night to tend to her business; she oversaw a multiple-industry household; *her* candles did not go out at night; there was a ready market for the high-quality linen girdles she made and sold to the merchants in town; and she kept track of the real estate market and bought good land when it became available, cultivating vineyards quite profitably. All this time her husband sat at the gates talking with his cronies.

A recent counterpart to the virtuous woman was the busy and industrious shtetl woman:

> The earning of a livelihood is sexless, and the large majority of women . . . participate in some gainful occupation if they do not carry the chief burden of support. The wife of a "perennial student" is very apt to be the sole support of the family. The problem of managing both a business and a home is so common that no one recognizes it as special . . . To bustle about in search of a livelihood is merely another form of bustling about managing a home; both are aspects of . . . health and livelihood. (Zborowski & Herzog, 1952, p. 131)

In a subsistence economy in which husbands and wives ran farms, shops, or businesses together, a man might be a good, steady worker, but the idea that he was *the* provider would hardly ring true. Even the youth in the folk song who listed all the gifts he would bestow on his love if she would marry him—a golden comb, a paper of pins, and all the rest—was not necessarily promising to be a good provider.

I have not searched the literature to determine when the concept of the good provider entered our thinking. The term *provider* entered the English language in 1532, but was not yet male sex typed, as the older term *purveyor* already was in 1442. Webster's second edition defines the good provider as "one who provides, especially, colloq., one who provides food, clothing, etc. for his family; as, he is a good or an adequate provider." More simply, he could be defined as a man whose wife did not have to enter the labor force. The counterpart to the good provider was the housewife. However the term is defined, the role itself delineated relationships within a marriage and family in a way that added to the legal, religious, and other advantages men had over women.

Thus, under the common law, although the husband was legally head of the household and as such had the responsibility of providing for his wife and children, this provision was often made with help from the wife's personal property and earnings, to which he was entitled:

> He owned his wife's and children's services, and had the sole right to collect wages for their work outside the home. He owned his wife's personal property outright, and had the right to manage and control all of his wife's real property during marriage, which included the right to use or lease property, and to keep any rents and profits from it. (Babcock, Freedman, Norton, & Ross, 1975, p. 561)

So even when she was the actual provider, the legal recognition was granted the husband. Therefore, whatever the husband's legal responsibilities for support may have been, he was not necessarily a good provider in the way the term came to be understood. The wife may have been performing that role.

In our country in Colonial times women were still viewed as performing a providing role, and they pursued a variety of occupations. Abigail Adams managed the family estate, which provided the wherewithal for John to spend so much time in Philadelphia. In the 18th century "many women were active in business and professional pursuits. They ran inns and taverns; they managed a wide variety of stores and shops; and, at least occasionally, they worked in careers like publishing, journalism and medicine" (Demos, 1974, p. 430). Women sometimes even "joined the menfolk for work in the fields" (p. 430). Like the household of the proverbial virtuous woman, the Colonial household was a little factory that produced clothing, furniture, bedding, candles, and other accessories, and again, as in the case of the virtuous woman, the female role was central. It was taken for granted that women provided for the family along with men.

The good provider as a specialized male role seems to have arisen in the transition from subsistence to market—especially money—economies that accelerated with the industrial revolution. The good-provider role for males emerged in this country roughly, say, from the 1830s, when de Tocqueville was observing it, to the late 1970s, when the 1980 census declared that a male was not automatically to be assumed to be head of the household. This gives the role a life span of about a century and a half. Although relatively short-lived, while it lasted the role was a seemingly rocklike feature of the national landscape.

As a psychological and sociological phenomenon, the good-provider role had wide ramifications for all of our thinking about families. It marked a new kind of marriage. It did not have good effects on women: The role deprived them of many chips by placing them in a peculiarly vulnerable position. Because she was not reimbursed for her contribution to the family in either products or services, a wife was stripped to a considerable extent of her access to cash-mediated markets. By discouraging labor force participation, it deprived many women, especially affluent ones, of opportunities to achieve strength and competence. It deterred young women from acquiring productive skills. They dedicated themselves instead to winning a good provider who would "take care of" them. The wife of a more successful provider became for all intents and purposes a parasite, with little to do except indulge or pamper herself. The psychology of such dependence could become all but crippling. There were other concomitants of the good-provider role.

EXPRESSIVITY AND THE GOOD-PROVIDER ROLE

The new industrial order that produced the good provider changed not so much the division of labor between the sexes as it did the site of the work they engaged in. Only two of the concomitants of this change in work site are selected for comment here, namely, (a) the identification of gender with work site as well as with work itself and (b) the reduction of time for personal interaction and intimacy within the family.

It is not so much the specific kinds of work men and women do—they have always varied from time to time and place to place—but the simple fact that the sexes do different kinds of work, whatever it is, which is in and of itself important. The division of labor by sex means that the work group becomes also a sex group. The very nature of maleness and femaleness becomes embedded in the sexual division of labor. One's sex and one's work are part of one another. One's work defines one's gender.

Any division of labor implies that people doing different kinds of work will occupy different work sites. When the division is based on sex, men and women will necessarily have different work sites. Even within the home itself, men and women had different work spaces. The woman's spinning wheel occupied a different area from the man's anvil. When the factory took over much of the work formerly done in the house, the separation of work space became especially marked. Not only did the separation of the sexes become spatially extended, but it came to relate work and gender in a special way. The work site as well as the work itself became associated with gender; each sex had its own turf. This sexual "territoriality" has had complicating effects on efforts to change any sexual division of labor. The good provider worked primarily in the outside male world of business and industry. The homemaker worked primarily in the home.

Spatial separation of the sexes not only identifies gender with work site and work but also reduces the amount of time available for spontaneous emotional give-and-take between husbands and wives. When men and women work in an economy based in the home, there are frequent occasions for interaction. (Consider, for example, the suggestive allusions made today to the rise in the birth rate nine months after a blackout.) When men and women are in close proximity, there is always the possibility of reassuring glances, the comfort of simple physical presence. But when the division of labor removes the man from the family dwelling for most of the day, intimate relationships become less feasible. De Tocqueville was one of the first to call our attention to this. In 1840 he noted that

> almost all men in democracies are engaged in public or professional life; and . . . the limited extent of common income obliges a wife to confine herself to the house, in order to watch in person and very closely over the details of domestic economy. All these distinct and compulsory occupations are so many natural barriers, which, by keeping the two sexes asunder, render the solicitations of the one less frequent and less ardent—the resistance of the other more easy. (de Tocqueville, 1840, p. 212)

Not directly related to the spatial constraints on emotional expression by men, but nevertheless a concomitant of the new industrial order with the same effect, was the enormous drive for achievement, for success, for "making it" that escalated the provider role into the good-provider role. De Tocqueville (1840) is again our source:

> The tumultuous and constantly harassed life which equality makes men lead [becoming good providers] not only distracts them from the passions of love, by denying them time to indulge in it, but it diverts them from it by another more secret but more certain road. All men who live in democratic ages more or less contract ways of thinking of the manufacturing and trading classes. (p. 221)

As a result of this male concentration on jobs and careers, much abnegation and "a constant sacrifice of her pleasures to her duties" (de Tocqueville, 1840, p. 212) were demanded of the American woman. The good-provider role, as it came to be shaped by this ambience, was thus restricted in what it was called upon to provide. Emotional expressivity was not included in the role. One of the things a parent might say about a man to persuade a daughter to marry him, or a daughter might say to explain to her parents why she wanted to, was not that he was a gentle, loving, or tender man but that he was a good provider. He might have many other qualities, good or bad, but if a man was a good provider, everything else was either gravy or the price one had to pay for a good provider.

Lack of expressivity did not imply neglect of the family. The good provider was a "family man." He set a good table, provided a decent home, paid the mortgage, bought the shoes, and kept his children warmly clothed. He might, with the help of the children's part-time jobs, have been able to finance their educations through high school and, sometimes, even college. There might even have been a little left over for an occasional celebration in most families. The good provider made a decent contribution to the church. His work might have been demanding, but he expected it to be. If in addition to being a good provider, a man was kind, gentle, generous, and not a heavy drinker or gambler, that was all frosting on the cake. Loving attention and emotional involvement in the family were not part of a woman's implicit bargain with the good provider.

By the time de Tocqueville published his observations in 1840, the general outlines of the good-provider role had taken shape. It called for a hardworking man who spent most of his time at his work. In the traditional conception of the role, a man's chief responsibility is his job, so that "by definition any family behaviors must be subordinate to it in terms of significance and [the job] has priority in the event of a clash"

(Scanzoni, 1975, p. 38). This was the classic form of the good-provider role, which remained a powerful component of our societal structure until well into the present century.

COSTS AND REWARDS OF THE GOOD-PROVIDER ROLE FOR MEN

There were both costs and rewards for those men attached to the good-provider role. The most serious cost was perhaps the identification of maleness not only with the work site but especially with success in the role. "The American male looks to his breadwinning role to confirm his manliness" (Brenton, 1966, p. 194).[1] To be a man one had to be not only a provider but a *good* provider. Success in the good-provider role came in time to define masculinity itself. The good provider had to achieve, to win, to succeed, to dominate. He was a bread*winner*. He had to show "strength, cunning, inventiveness, endurance—a whole range of traits henceforth defined as exclusively 'masculine'" (Demos, 1974, p. 436). Men were judged as men by the level of living they provided. They were judged by the myth "that endows a moneymaking man with sexiness and virility, and is based on man's dominance, strength, and ability to provide for and care for 'his' woman" (Gould, 1974, p. 97). The good provider became a player in the male competitive macho game. What one man provided for his family in the way of luxury and display had to be equaled or topped by what another could provide. Families became display cases for the success of the good provider.

The psychic costs could be high:

> By depending so heavily on his breadwinning role to validate his sense of himself as a man, instead

---

[1] Rainwater and Yancey (1967), critiquing current welfare policies, note that they "have robbed men of their manhood, women of their husbands, and children of their fathers. To create a stable monogamous family we need to provide men with the opportunity to be men, and that involves enabling them to perform occupationally" (p. 235).

of also letting his roles as husband, father, and citizen of the community count as validating sources, the American male treads on psychically dangerous ground. It's always dangerous to put all of one's psychic eggs into one basket. (Brenton, 1966, p. 194)

The good-provider role not only put all of a man's gender-identifying eggs into one psychic basket, but it also put all the family-providing eggs into one basket. One individual became responsible for the support of the whole family. Countless stories portrayed the humiliation families underwent to keep wives and especially mothers out of the labor force, a circumstance that would admit to the world the male head's failure in the good-provider role. If a married woman had to enter the labor force at all, that was bad enough. If she made a good salary, however, she was "co-opting the man's passport to masculinity" (Gould, 1974, p. 98) and he was effectively castrated. A wife's earning capacity diminished a man's position as head of the household (Gould, 1974, p. 99).

Failure in the role of good provider, which employment of wives evidenced, could produce deep frustration. As Komarovsky (1940, p. 20) explains, this is "because in his own estimation he is failing to fulfill what is the central duty of his life, the very touchstone of his manhood—the role of family provider."

But just as there was punishment for failure in the good-provider role, so also were there rewards for successful performance. A man "derived strength from his role as provider" (Komarovsky, 1940, p. 205). He achieved a good deal of satisfaction from his ability to support his family. It won kudos. Being a good provider led to status in both the family and the community. Within the family it gave him the power of the purse and the right to decide about expenditures, standards of living, and what constituted good providing. "Every purchase of the family—the radio, his wife's new hat, the children's skates, the meals set before him—all were symbols of their dependence upon him" (Ko-

marovsky, 1940, pp. 74–75). Such dependence gave him a "profound sense of stability" (p. 74). It was a strong counterpoise vis-à-vis a wife with a stronger personality. "Whether he had considerable authority within the family and was recognized as its head, or whether the wife's stronger personality . . . dominated the family, he nevertheless derived strength from his role as a provider" (Komarovsky, 1940, p. 75). As recently as 1975, in a sample of 3,100 husbands and wives in 10 cities, Scanzoni found that despite increasing egalitarian norms, the good provider still had "considerable power in ultimate decision-making" and as "unique provider" had the right "to organize his life and the lives of other family members around his occupation" (p. 38).

A man who was successful in the good-provider role might be freed from other obligations to the family. But the flip side of this dispensation was that he could not make up for poor performance by excellence in other family roles. Since everything depended on his success as provider, everything was at stake. The good provider played an all-or-nothing game.

DIFFERENT WAYS OF PERFORMING THE GOOD-PROVIDER ROLE

Although the legal specifications for the role were laid out in the common law, in legislation, in legal precedents, in court decisions, and, most importantly, in custom and convention, in real-life situations the social and social-psychological specifications were set by the husband or, perhaps more accurately, by the community, alias the Joneses, and there were many ways to perform it.

Some men resented the burdens the role forced them to bear. A man could easily vent such resentment toward his family by keeping complete control over all expenditures, dispensing the money for household maintenance, and complaining about bills as though it were his wife's fault that shoes cost so much. He could, in effect, punish his family for his having to perform the role. Since the money he earned belonged to him—was "his"—he could do with it what he pleased. Through extreme parsimony he could dole out his money in a mean, humiliating way, forcing his wife to come begging for pennies. By his reluctance and resentment he could make his family pay emotionally for the provisioning he supplied.

At the other extreme were the highly competitive men who were so involved in outdoing the Joneses that the fur coat became more important than the affectionate hug. They "bought off" their families. They sometimes succeeded so well in their extravagance that they sacrificed the family they were presumably providing for to the achievements that made it possible (Keniston, 1965).[2]

The Depression of the 1930s revealed in harsh detail what the loss of the role could mean both to the good provider and to his family, not only in the loss of income itself—which could be supplied by welfare agencies or even by other family members, including wives—but also and especially in the loss of face.

The Great Depression did not mark the demise of the good-provider role. But it did teach us what a slender thread the family hung on. It stimulated a whole array of programs designed to strengthen that thread, to ensure that it would never again be similarly threatened. Unemployment insurance was incorporated into the Social Security Act of 1935, for example, and a Full Employment Act was passed in 1946. But there

---

[2]Several years ago I presented a critique of what I called "extreme sex role specialization," including "work-intoxicated fathers." I noted that making success in the provider role the only test for real manliness was putting a lot of eggs into one basket. At both the blue-collar and the managerial levels, it was dysfunctional for families. I referred to the several attempts being made even then to correct the excesses of extreme sex role specialization: rural and urban communes, leaving jobs to take up small-scale enterprises that allowed more contact with families, and a rebellion against overtime in industry (Bernard, 1975, pp. 217–239).

proved to be many other ways in which the good-provider role could be subverted.

ROLE REJECTORS AND ROLE OVERPERFORMERS

Recent research in psychology, anthropology, and sociology has familiarized us with the tremendous power of roles. But we also know that one of the fundamental principles of role behavior is that conformity to role norms is not universal. Not everyone lives up to the specifications of roles, either in the psychological or in the sociological definition of the concept. Two extremes have attracted research attention: (a) the men who could not live up to the norms of the good-provider role or did not want to, at one extreme, and (b) the men who overperformed the role, at the other. For the wide range in between, from blue-collar workers to professionals, there was fairly consistent acceptance of the role, however well or poorly, however grumblingly or willingly, performed.

First the nonconformists. Even in Colonial times, desertion and divorce occurred:

> Women may have deserted because, say, their husbands beat them; husbands, on the other hand, may have deserted because they were unable or unwilling to provide for their usually large families in the face of the wives' demands to do so. These demands were, of course, backed by community norms making the husband's financial support a sacred duty. (Scanzoni, 1979, pp. 24–25)

Fiedler (1962) has traced the theme of male escape from domestic responsibilities in the American novel from the time of Rip Van Winkle to the present:

> The figure of Rip Van Winkle presides over the birth of the American imagination; and it is fitting that our first successful home-grown legend should memorialize, however playfully, the flight of the dreamer from the shrew—into the mountains and out of time, away from the drab duties

of home . . . anywhere to avoid . . . marriage and responsibility. One of the factors that determine theme and form in our great books is this strategy of evasion, this retreat to nature and childhood which makes our literature (and life) so charmingly and infuriatingly "boyish." (pp. xx–xxi)

Among the men who pulled up stakes and departed for the West or went down to the sea in ships, there must have been a certain proportion who, like their mythic prototype, were simply fleeing the good-provider role.

The work of Demos (1974), a historian, offers considerable support for Fiedler's thesis. He tells us that the burdens thrust on men in the 19th century by the new patterns of work began to show their effects in the family. When "the [spatial] separation of the work lives of husbands and wives made communication so problematic," he asks, "what was the likelihood of meaningful communication?" (Demos, 1974, p. 438). The answer is, relatively little. Divorce and separation increased, either formally or by tacit consent—or simply by default, as in the case of a variety of defaulters—tramps, bums, hoboes—among them.

In this connection, "the development of the notorious 'tramp' phenomenon is worth noticing," Demos (1974, p. 438) tells us. The tramp was a man who just gave up, who dropped out of the role entirely. He preferred not to work, but he would do small chores or other small-scale work for a handout if he had to. He was not above begging the housewife for a meal, hoping she would not find work for him to do in repayment. Demos (1974) describes the type:

Demoralized and destitute wanderers, their numbers mounting into the hundreds of thousands, tramps can be fairly characterized as men who had run away from their wives. . . . Their presence was mute testimony to the strains that tugged at the very core of American family life . . . Many observers noted that the tramps had created a virtual society of their own [a kind of counterculture] based on a principle of single-sex companionship. (p. 438)

A considerable number of them came to be described as "homeless men" and, as the country became more urbanized, landed ultimately on skid row. A large part of the task of social workers for almost a century was the care of the "evaded" women they left behind.[3] When the tramp became wholly demoralized, a chronic alcoholic, almost unreachable, he fell into a category of his own—he was a bum.

Quite a different kettle of fish was the hobo, the migratory worker who spent several months harvesting wheat and other large crops and the rest of the year in cities. Many were the so-called Wobblies, or Industrial Workers of the World, who repudiated the good-provider role on principle. They had contempt for the men who accepted it and could be called conscientious objectors to the role. "In some IWW circles, wives were regarded as the 'ball and chain.' In the West, IWW literature proclaimed that the migratory worker, usually a young, unmarried male, was 'the finest specimen of American manhood . . . the leaven of the revolutionary labor movement'" (Foner, 1979, p. 400). Exemplars of the Wobblies were the nomadic workers of the West. They were free men.

[3]In one department of a south Carolina cotton mill early in the century, "every worker was a grass widow" (Smuts, 1959, p. 54). Many women worked "because their husbands refused to provide for their families. There is no reason to think that husbands abandoned their duties more often than today, but the woman who was burdened by an irresponsible husband in 1890 usually had no recourse save taking on his responsibilities herself. If he deserted, the law-enforcement agencies of the time afforded little chance of finding and compelling him to provide support" (Smuts, 1959, p. 54). The situation is not greatly improved today. In divorce child support is allotted in only a small number of cases and enforced in even fewer. "Roughly half of all families with an absent parent don't have awards at all . . . Where awards do exist they are usually for small amounts, typically ranging from $7 to $18 per week per child" (Jones, 1976, abstract). A summary of all the studies available concludes that "approximately 20 percent of all divorced and separated mothers receive child support regularly, with an additional 7 percent receiving it 'sometimes'; 8 percent of all divorced and separated women receive alimony regularly or sometimes" (Jones, 1976, p. 23).

The migratory worker, "unlike the factory slave of the Atlantic seaboard and the central states, . . . was most emphatically 'not afraid of losing his job.' No wife and family cumbered him. The worker of the East, oppressed by the fear of want for wife and babies, dared not venture much" (Foner, 1979, p. 400). The reference to fear of loss of job was well taken; employers preferred married men, disciplined into the good-provider role, who had given hostages to fortune and were therefore more tractable.

Just on the verge between the area of conformity to the good-provider role—at whatever level—and the area of complete nonconformity to it was the non-good provider, the marginal group of workers usually made up of "the under-educated, the under-trained, the under-employed, or part-time employed, as well as the under-paid, and of course the unemployed" (Snyder, 1979, p. 597). These included men who wanted—sometimes desperately—to perform the good-provider role but who for one reason or another were unable to do so. Liebow (1966) has discussed the ramifications of failure among the black men of Tally's corner: The black man is

> under legal and social constraints to provide for them [their families], to be a husband to his wife and a father to his children. The chances are, however, that he is failing to provide for them, and failure in this primary function contaminates his performance as father in other respects as well. (p. 86)

In some cases, leaving the family entirely was the best substitute a man could supply. The community was left to take over.[4]

At the other extreme was the overperformer. De Tocqueville, quoted earlier, was already de-

scribing him as he manifested in the 1830s. And as late as 1955 Warner and Ableggen were adding to the considerable literature on industrial leaders and tycoons, referring to their "driving concentration" on their careers and their "intense focusing" of interests, energies, and skills on these careers, "even limiting their sexual activity" (pp. 48–49). They came to be known as workaholics or work-intoxicated men. Their preoccupation with their work even at the expense of their families was, as I have already noted, quite acceptable in our society.

Poorly or well performed, the good-provider role lingered on. World War II initiated a challenge, this time in the form of attracting more and more married women into the labor force, but the challenge was papered over in the 1950s with an "age of togetherness" that all but apotheosized the good provider, his house in the suburbs, his homebody wife, and his third, fourth, even fifth, child. As late as the 1960s most housewives (87 percent) still saw breadwinning as their husband's primary role (Lopata, 1971, p. 91).[5]

INTRINSIC CONFLICT IN THE GOOD-PROVIDER ROLE

Since the good-provider role involved both family and work roles, most people believed that there was no incompatibility between them or at least that there should not be. But in the 1960s and 1970s evidence began to mount that maybe something was amiss.

De Tocqueville had documented the implicit conflict in the American businessman's devotion to his work at the expense of his family in the early years of the 19th century; the Industrial Workers of the World had proclaimed that the

[4]Even though the annals of social work agencies are filled with cases of runaway husbands, in 1976 only 12.6 percent of all women were in the status of divorce and separation, and at least some of them were still being "provided for." Most men were at least trying to fulfill the good-provider role.

[5]Although all the women in Lopata's (1971) sample saw breadwinning as important, fewer employed women (54 percent) than either nonemployed urban (63%) or suburban (64 percent) women assigned it first place (p. 91).

good-provider role which tied a man to his family was an impediment to the great revolution at the beginning of the 20th century; Fiedler (1962) had noted that throughout our history, in the male fantasy world, there was freedom from the responsibilities of this role; about 50 years ago Freud (1930/1958) had analyzed the intrinsic conflict between the demands of women and the family on one side and the demands of men's work on the other:

> Women represent the interests of the family and sexual life; the work of civilization has become more and more men's business; it confronts them with ever harder tasks, compels them to sublimitations of instinct which women are not easily able to achieve. Since man has not an unlimited amount of mental energy at his disposal, he must accomplish his tasks by distributing his libido to the best advantage. What he employs for cultural [occupational] purposes he withdraws to a great extent from women, and his sexual life; his constant association with men and his dependence on his relations with them even estrange him from his duties as husband and father. Woman finds herself thus forced into the background by the claims of culture [work] and she adapts an inimical attitude towards it. (pp. 50–51)

In the last two decades, researchers have been raising questions relevant to Freud's statement of the problem. They have been asking people about the relative satisfactions they derive from these conflicting values—family and work. Among the earliest studies comparing family–work values was a Gallup poll in 1940 in which both men and women chose a happy home over an interesting job or wealth as a major life value. Since then there have been a number of such polls, and a considerable body of results has now accumulated. Pleck and Lang (1979) and Hesselbart (Note 1) have summarized the findings of these surveys. All agree that there is a clear bias in the direction of the family. Pleck and Lang conclude that "men's family role is far more psychologically significant to them than is their work role" (p. 29), and

Hesselbart—however critical she is of the studies she summarizes—believes they should not be dismissed lightly and concludes that they certainly "challenge the idea that family is a 'secondary' valued role" (p. 14).[6] Douvan (Note 2) also found in a 1976 replication of a 1957 survey that family values retained priority over work: "Family roles almost uniformly rate higher in value production than the job role does" (p. 16).[7]

The very fact that researchers have asked such questions is itself interesting. Somehow or other both the researchers and the informants seem to be saying that all this complaining about the male neglect of the family, about the lack of family involvement by men, just is not warranted. Neither de Tocqueville nor Freud was right. Men do value family life more than they value their work. They do derive their major life satisfactions from their families rather than from their work.

It may well be true that men derive the greatest satisfaction from their family roles,

---

[6]Pleck and Lang (1979) found only one serious study contradicting their own conclusions: "Using data from the 1973 NORC [National Opinion Research Center] General Social Survey, Harry analyzed the bivariate relationship of job and family satisfaction to life happiness in men classified by family life cycle stage. In three of the five groups of husbands . . . job satisfaction had a stronger association than family satisfaction to life happiness" (pp. 5–6).

[7]In 1978, a Yankelovich survey on "The New Work Psychology" suggested that leisure is now becoming a strict competitor for both family and work as a source of life satisfactions: "Family and work have grown less important than leisure; a majority of 60 percent say that although they enjoy their work, it is not their major source of satisfaction" (p. 46). A 1977 survey of Swedish men aged 18 to 35 found that the proportion saying the family was the main source of meaning in their lives declined from 45 percent in 1955 to 41 percent in 1977; the proportion indicating work as the main source of satisfaction dropped from 33 percent to 17 percent. The earlier tendency for men to identify themselves through their work is less marked these days. In the new value system, the individual says, in effect, "I am more than my role. I am myself" (Yankelovich, 1978). Is the increasing concern with leisure a way to escape the dissatisfaction with both the alienating relations found on the work site and the demands for increased involvement with the family?

but this does not necessarily mean they are willing to pay for this benefit. In any event, great attitudinal changes took place in the 1960s and 1970s.

Douvan (Note 2), on the basis of surveys in 1957 and 1976, found, for example, a considerable increase in the proportion of both men and women who found marriage and parenthood burdensome and restrictive. Almost three fifths (57 percent) of both married men and married women in 1976 saw marriage as "all burdens and restrictions," as compared with only 42 percent and 47 percent, respectively, in 1957. And almost half (45 percent) also viewed children as "all burdens and restrictions" in 1976, as compared with only 28 percent and 33 percent for married men and married woman, respectively, in 1957. The proportion of working men with a positive attitude toward marriage dropped drastically over this period, from 68 percent to 39 percent. Working women, who made up a fairly small number of all married women in 1957, hardly changed attitudes at all, dropping only from 43 percent to 42 percent. The proportion of working men who found marriage and children burdensome and restrictive more than doubled, from 25 percent to 56 percent and from 25 percent to 58 percent, respectively. Although some of these changes reflected greater willingness in 1976 than in 1957 to admit negative attitudes toward marriage and parenthood—itself significant—profound changes were clearly in process. More and more men and women were experiencing disaffection with family life.[8]

---

[8]Men seem to be having problems with both work and family roles. Veroff (Note 3), for example, reports an increased "sense of dissatisfaction with the social relations in the work setting" and a "dissatisfaction with the affiliative nature of work" (p. 47). This dissatisfaction may be one of the factors that leads men to seek affiliative-need satisfaction in marriage, just as in the 19th century they looked to the home as shelter from the jungle of the outside world.

"ALL BURDENS AND RESTRICTIONS"

Apparently, the benefits of the good-provider role were greater than the costs for most men. Despite the legend of the flight of the American male (Fiedler, 1962), despite the defectors and dropouts, despite the tavern habitué's "ball and chain" cliché, men seemed to know that the good-provider role, if they could succeed in it, was good for them. But Douvan's (Note 2) findings suggest that recently their complaints have become serious, bone-deep. The family they have been providing for is not the same family it was in the past.

Smith (1979) calls the great trek of married women into the labor force a subtle revolution— revolutionary not in the sense of one class overthrowing a status quo and substituting its own regime, but revolutionary in its impact on both the family and the work roles of men and women. It diluted the prerogatives of the good-provider role. It increased the demands made on the good provider, especially in the form of more emotional investment in the family, more sharing of household responsibilities. The role became even more burdensome.

However men may now feel about the burdens and restrictions imposed on them by the good-provider role, most have, at least ostensibly, accepted them. The tramp and the bum had "voted with their feet" against the role; the hobo or Wobbly had rejected it on the basis of a revolutionary ideology that saw it as enslaving men to the corporation; tavern humor had glossed the resentment habitués felt against its demands. Now the "burdens-and-restrictions" motif has surfaced both in research reports and, more blatantly, in the male liberation movement. From time to time it has also appeared in the clinicians' notes.

Sometimes the resentment of the good provider takes the form of simply wanting more appreciation for the life-style he provides. All he does for his family seems to be taken for granted. Thus, for example, Goldberg (1976), a psychiatrist, recounts the case of a successful businessman:

> He's feeling a deepening sense of bitterness and frustration about his wife and family. He doesn't feel appreciated. It angers him the way they seem to take the things his earnings purchase for granted. They've come to expect it as their due. It particularly enrages him when his children put him down for his "materialistic middle-class trip." He'd like to tell them to get someone else to support them but he holds himself back. (p. 124)

Brenton (1966) quotes a social worker who describes an upper-middle-class woman: She has "gotten hold of a man who'll drive himself like mad to get money, and [is] denigrating him for being too interested in money, and not interested in music, or the arts, or in spending time with the children. But at the same time she's subtly driving him—and doesn't know it" (p. 226). What seems significant about such cases is not that men feel resentful about the lack of appreciation but that they are willing to justify their resentment. They are no longer willing to grin and bear it.

Sometimes there is even more than expressed resentment; there is an actual repudiation of the role. In the past, only a few men like the hobo or Wobbly were likely to give up. Today, Goldberg (1976) believes, more are ready to renounce the role, not on theoretical revolutionary grounds, however, but on purely selfish ones:

> Male growth will stem from openly avowed, unashamed, self-oriented motivations . . . Guilt-oriented "should" behavior will be rejected because it is always at the price of a hidden build-up of resentment and frustration and alienation from others and is, therefore, counterproductive. (p. 184)

The disaffection of the good provider is directed to both sides of his role. With respect to work, Lefkowitz (1979) has described men among whom the good-provider role is neither being completely rejected nor repudiated, but diluted. These men began their working lives in the conventional style, hopeful and ambitious. They found a job, married, raised a family, and "achieved a measure of economic security and earned the respect of . . . colleagues and neighbors" (Lefkowitz, 1979, p. 31). In brief, they successfully performed the good-provider role. But unlike their historical predecessors, they in time became disillusioned with their jobs—not jobs on assembly lines, not jobs usually characterized as alienating, but fairly prestigious jobs such as aeronautics engineer and government economist. They daydreamed about other interests. "The common theme which surfaced again and again in their histories, was the need to find a new social connection—to reassert control over their lives, to gain some sense of freedom" (Lefkowitz, 1979, p. 31). These men felt "entitled to freedom and independence." Middle-class, educated, self-assured, articulate, and for the most part white, they knew they could talk themselves into a job if they had to. Most of them did not want to desert their families. Indeed, most of them "wanted to rejoin the intimate circle they felt they had neglected in their years of work" (p. 31).

Though some of the men Lefkowitz studied sought closer ties with their families, in the case of those studied by Sarason (1977), a psychologist, career changes involved lower income and had a negative impact on families. Sarason's subjects were also men in high-level professions, the very men least likely to find marriage and parenthood burdensome and restrictive. Still, since career change often involved a reduction in pay, some wives were unwilling to accept it, with the result that the marriage deteriorated (p. 178). Sometimes it looked like a no-win game. The husband's earlier career brought him feelings of emptiness and alienation, but it also brought financial rewards for the family. Greater work satisfaction for him in lower paying work meant reduced satisfaction with lifestyle. These findings lead Sarason to raise a number of points with respect to the good-provider role. "How much," he asks, "does an individual or a family need in order to maintain a satisfactory existence? Is an individual being responsible to himself or his family if he provides them with little more than the bare essentials of living?" (p. 178). These are questions about the good-provider role that few men raised in the past.

Lefkowitz (1979) wonders how his downwardly mobile men lived when they left their jobs. "They put together a basic economic package which consisted of government assistance, contributions from family members who had not worked before and some bartering of goods and services" (p. 31). Especially interesting in this list of income sources are the "contributions from family members who had not worked before" (p. 31). Surely not mothers and sisters. Who, of course, but wives?

WOMEN AND THE PROVIDER ROLE

The present discussion began with the woman's part in the provider role. We saw how as more and more of the provisioning of the family came to be by way of monetary exchange, the woman's part shrank. A woman could still provide services, but could furnish little in the way of food, clothing, and shelter. But now that she is entering the labor force in large numbers, she can once more resume her ancient role, this time, like her male counterpart the provider, by way of a monetary contribution. More and more women are doing just this.

The assault on the good-provider role in the Depression was traumatic. But a modified version began to appear in the 1970s as a single income became inadequate for more and more families. Husbands have remained the major providers, but in an increasing number of cases the wife has begun to share this role. Thus, the proportion of married women aged 15 to 54 (living with their husbands) in the labor force more than doubled between 1950 and 1978, from 25.2 percent to 55.4 percent. The proportion for 1990 is estimated to reach 66.7 percent

(Smith, 1979, p. 14). Fewer women are now fulltime housewives.

For some men the relief from the strain of sole responsibility for the provider role has been welcome. But for others the feeling of degradation resembles the feelings reported 40 years earlier in the Great Depression. It is not that they are no longer providing for the family but that the role-sharing wife now feels justified in making demands on them. The good-provider role with all its prerogatives and perquisites has undergone profound changes. It will never be the same again.[9] Its death knell was sounded when, as noted above, the 1980 census no longer automatically assumed that the male member of the household was its head.

THE CURRENT SCENE

Among the new demands being made on the good-provider role, two deserve special consideration, namely, (a) more intimacy, expressivity, and nurturance—specifications never included in it as it originally took shape—and (b) more sharing of household responsibility and child care.

As the pampered wife in an affluent household came often to be an economic parasite, so also the good provider was often, in a way, a kind of emotional parasite. Implicit in the definition of the role was that he provided goods and material things. Tender loving care was not one of the requirements. Emotional ministrations from the family were his right; providing them was not a corresponding obligation. Therefore, as de Tocqueville had already noted by 1840, women suffered a kind of emotional deprivation

---

[9]Among the indices of the waning of the good-provider role are the increasing number of married women in the labor force; the growth in the number of female-headed families; the growing trend toward egalitarian norms in marriage; the need for two earners in so many middle-class families; and the recognition of these trends in the abandonment of the identification of head of household as a male.

labeled by Robert Weiss "relational deficit" (cited in Bernard, 1976). Only recently has this male rejection of emotional expression come to be challenged. Today, even blue-collar women are imposing "a host of new role expectations upon their husbands or lovers . . . A new role set asks the blue-collar male to strive for . . . deep-coursing intimacy" (Shostak, Note 4, p. 75). It was not only vis-à-vis his family that the good provider was lacking in expressivity. This lack was built into the whole male role script. Today not only women but also men are beginning to protest the repudiation of expressivity prescribed in male roles (David & Brannon, 1976; Farrell, 1974; Fasteau, 1974; Pleck & Sawyer, 1974).

Is there any relationship between the "imposing" on men of "deep-coursing intimacy" by women on one side and the increasing proportion of men who find marriage burdensome and restrictive on the other? Are men seeing the new emotional involvements being asked of them as "all burdens and restrictions"? Are they responding to the new involvements under duress? Are they feeling oppressed by them? Fearful of them?

From the standpoint of high-level pure-science research there may be something bizarre, if not even slightly absurd, in the growing corpus of serious research on how much or how little husbands of employed wives contribute to household chores and child care. Yet it is serious enough that all over the industrialized world such research is going on. Time studies in a dozen countries—communist as well as capitalist—trace the slow and bungling process by which marriage accommodates to changing conditions and by which women struggle to mold the changing conditions in their behalf. For everywhere the same picture shows up in the research: an image of women sharing the provider role and at the same time retaining responsibility for the household. Until recently such a topic would have been judged unworthy of serious attention. It was a subject that might be worth a good laugh, for instance, as when an all-thumbs man

in a cartoon burns the potatoes or finds himself bumbling awkwardly over a diaper, demonstrating his—proud—male ineptness at such female work. But it is no longer funny.

The "politics of housework" (Mainardi, 1970) proves to be more profound than originally believed. It has to do not only with tasks but also with gender—and perhaps more with the site of the tasks than with their intrinsic nature. A man can cook magnificently if he does it on a hunting or fishing trip; he can wield a skillful needle if he does it mending a tent or a fishing net; he can even feed and clean a toddler on a camping trip. Few of the skills of the homemaker are beyond his reach so long as they are practiced in a suitably male environment. It is not only women's work in and of itself that is degrading but any work on female turf. It may be true, as Brenton (1966) says, that "the secure man can wash a dish, diaper a baby, and throw the dirty clothes into the washing machine—or do anything else women used to do exclusively—without thinking twice about it" (p. 211), but not all men are that secure. To a great many men such chores are demasculinizing. The apron is shameful on a man in the kitchen; it is all right at the carpenter's bench.

The male world may look upon the man who shares household responsibilities as, in effect, a scab. One informant tells the interviewer about a conversation on the job: "What, are you crazy?" his hard-hat fellow workers ask him when he speaks of helping his wife. "The guys want to kill me. 'You son of a bitch! You are getting us in trouble' . . . The men get really mad" (Lein, 1979, p. 492). Something more than persiflage is involved here. We are fairly familiar with the trauma associated with the invasion by women of the male work turf, the hazing women can be subjected to, and the male resentment of admitting them except into their own segregated areas. The corresponding entrance of men into the traditional turf of women—the kitchen or the nursery—has analogous but not identical concomitants.

Pleck and Lang (1979) tell us that men are now beginning to change in the direction of greater involvement in family life. "Men's family behavior is beginning to change, becoming increasingly congruent with the long-standing psychological significance of the family in their lives" (p. 1). They measure this greater involvement by way of the help they offer with homemaking chores. Scanzoni (1975), on the basis of a survey of over 3,000 husbands and wives, concludes that at least in households in which wives are in the labor force, there is the "possibility of a different pattern in which responsibility for households would unequivocally fall equally on husbands as well as wives" (p. 38). A brave new world indeed. Still, when we look at the reality around us, the pace seems intolerably slow. The responsibilities of the old good-provider role have attenuated far faster than have its prerogatives and privileges.

A considerable amount of thought has been devoted to studying the effects of the large influx of women into the work force. An equally interesting question is what the effect will be if a large number of men actually do increase their participation in the family and the household. Will men find the apron shameful? What if we were to ask fathers to alternate with mothers in being in the home when youngsters come home from school? Would fighting adolescent drug abuse be more successful if fathers and mothers were equally engaged in it? If the school could confer with fathers as often as with mothers? If the father accompanied children when they went shopping for clothes? If fathers spent as much time with children as do mothers?

Even as husbands, let alone as fathers, the new pattern is not without trauma. Hall and Hall (1979), in their study of two-career couples, report that the most serious fights among such couples occur not in the bedroom, but in the kitchen, between couples who profess a commitment to equality but who find actually implementing it difficult. A young professional reports that he is philosophically committed to

egalitarianism in marriage and tries hard to practice it, but it does not work. He even feels guilty about this. The stresses involved in reworking roles may have an impact on health. A study of engineers and accountants finds poorer health among those with employed wives than among those with nonemployed wives (Burke & Wier, 1976). The processes involved in role change have been compared with those involved in deprogramming a cult member. Are they part of the increasing sense of marriage and parenthood as "all burdens and restrictions"?

The demise of the good-provider role also calls for consideration of other questions: What does the demotion of the good provider to the status of senior provider or even mere co-provider do to him? To marriage? To gender identity? What does expanding the role of housewife to that of junior provider or even co-provider do to her? To marriage? To gender identity? Much will of course depend on the social and psychological ambience in which changes take place.

A PARABLE

I began this essay with a proverbial woman. I close it with a modern parable by William H. Chafe (Note 5), a historian who also keeps his eye on the current scene. Jack and Jill, both planning professional careers, he as doctor, she as lawyer, marry at age 24. She works to put him through medical school in the expectation that he will then finance her through law school. A child is born during the husband's internship, as planned. But in order for him to support her through professional training as planned, he will have to take time out from his career. After two years, they decide that both will continue their training on a part-time basis, sharing household responsibilities and using day-care services. Both find part-time positions and work out flexible work schedules that leave both of them time for child care and companionship with one another. They live happily ever after.

That's the end? you ask incredulously. Well, not exactly. For, as Chafe (Note 5) points out, as usual the personal is also political:

Obviously such a scenario presumes a radical transformation of the personal values that today's young people bring to their relationships as well as a readiness on the part of social and economic institutions to encourage, or at least make possible, the development of equality between men and women. (p. 28)

The good-provider role may be on its way out, but its legitimate successor has not yet appeared on the scene.

REFERENCE NOTES

1. Hesselbart, S. *Some underemphasized issues about men, women, and work.* Unpublished manuscript, 1978.
2. Douvan, E. *Family roles in a twenty-year perspective.* Paper presented at the Radcliffe Pre-Centennial Conference, Cambridge, Massachusetts, April 2–4, 1978.
3. Veroff, J. *Psychological orientations to the work role: 1957–1976.* Unpublished manuscript, 1978.
4. Shostak, A. *Working class Americans at home: changing expectations of manhood.* Unpublished manuscript, 1973.
5. Chafe, W. *The challenge of sex equality: A new culture or old values revisited?* Paper presented at the Radcliffe Pre-Centennial Conference, Cambridge, Massachusetts, April 2–4, 1978.

REFERENCES

Babcock, B., Freedman, A. E., Norton, E. H., & Ross, S. C. *Sex discrimination and the law: Causes and remedies.* Boston: Little, Brown, 1975.

Bernard, J. *Women, wives, mothers.* Chicago: Aldine, 1975.

Bernard, J. Homosociality and female depression. *Journal of Social Issues,* 1976, *32,* 207–224.

Boulding, E. Familial constraints on women's work roles. *SIGNS: Journal of Women in Culture and Society,* 1976, *1,* 95–118.

Brenton, M. *The American male.* New York: Coward-McCann, 1966.

Burke, R., & Wier, T. Relationship of wives' employment status to husband, wife and pair satisfaction and performance. *Journal of Marriage and the Family,* 1976, *38,* 279–287.

David, D. S., & Brannon, R. (Eds.). *The forty-nine percent majority: The male sex role.* Reading, Mass.: Addison-Wesley, 1976.

Demos, J. The American family in past time. *American Scholar,* 1974, *43,* 422–446.

Farrell, W. *The liberated man.* New York: Random House, 1974.

Fasteau, M. F. *The male machine.* New York: McGraw-Hill, 1974.

Fiedler, L. *Love and death in the American novel.* New York: Meredith, 1962.

Foner, P. S. *Women and the American labor movement.* New York: Free Press, 1979.

Freud, S. *Civilization and its discontents.* New York: Doubleday-Anchor, 1958. (Originally published, 1930.)

Goldberg, H. *The hazards of being male.* New York: New American Library, 1976.

Gould, R. E. Measuring masculinity by the size of a paycheck. In J. E. Pleck & J. Sawyer (Eds.), *Men and masculinity.* Englewood Cliffs, N.J.: Prentice-Hall, 1974. (Also published in *Ms.,* June 1973, pp. 18ff.)

Hall, D., & Hall, F. *The two-career couple.* Reading, Mass.: Addison-Wesley, 1979.

Jones, C. A. *A review of child support payment performance.* Washington, D.C.: Urban Institute, 1976.

Keniston, K. *The uncommitted: Alienated youth in American society.* New York: Harcourt, Brace & World, 1965.

Komarovsky, M. *The unemployed man and his family.* New York: Dryden Press, 1940.

Lefkowitz, B. Life without work. *Newsweek,* May 14, 1979, p. 31.

Lein, L. Responsibility in the allocation of tasks. *Family Coordinator,* 1979, *28,* 489–496.

Liebow, E. *Tally's corner.* Boston: Little, Brown, 1966.

Lopata, H. *Occupation housewife.* New York: Oxford University Press, 1971.

Mainardi, P. The politics of housework. In R. Morgan (Ed.), *Sisterhood is powerful.* New York: Vintage Books, 1970.

Pleck, J. H., & Lang, L. Men's family work: Three perspectives and some new data. *Family Coordinator,* 1979, *28,* 481–488.

Pleck, J. H., & Sawyer, J. (Eds.). *Men and masculinity.* Englewood Cliffs, N.J.: Prentice-Hall, 1974.

Rainwater, L., & Yancey, W. L. *The Moynihan report and the politics of controversy.* Cambridge, Mass.: M.I.T. Press, 1967.

Sarason, S. B. *Work, aging, and social change.* New York: Free Press, 1977.

Scanzoni, J. H. *Sex roles, life styles, and childbearing: Changing patterns in marriage and the family.* New York: Free Press, 1975.

Scanzoni, J. H. An historical perspective on husband-wife bargaining power and marital dissolution. In G. Levinger & O. Moles (Eds.), *Divorce and separation in America.* New York: Basic Books, 1979.

Smith, R. E. (Ed.). *The subtle revolution.* Washington, D.C.: Urban Institute, 1979.

Smuts, R. W. *Women and work in America.* New York: Columbia University Press, 1959.

Snyder, L. The deserting, non-supporting father: Scapegoat of family non-policy. *Family Coordinator,* 1979, *38,* 594–598.

Tocqueville, A. de. *Democracy in America.* New York: J. & H. G. Langley, 1840.

Warner, W. L., & Ablegglen, J. O. *Big business leaders in America.* New York: Harper, 1955.

Yankelovich, D. The new psychological contracts at work. *Psychology Today,* May 1978, pp. 46–47; 49–50.

Zborowski, M., & Herzog, E. *Life is with people.* New York: Schocken Books, 1952.

PART TWO

RACE, ETHNICITY, CLASS, AND THE STATE

CHAPTER 4

Social Class and Families

In the 1950s and 1960s, the American economy was strong and wages were rising. In fact, the average income of full-time workers, adjusted for inflation, doubled. Most workers without college educations could find jobs in the expanding factories of the nation. But the 1973 decision by oil-producing countries to sharply raise the price of oil sent the U.S. economy into a tailspin, and wages have been stagnant ever since for workers without college degrees. Even after the United States adjusted to the oil price shock, it became clear that our employment base in manufacturing was not growing the way it had in the past. Corporations moved production overseas in order to take advantage of the lower wages paid to workers in the developing world. Computers and other technologies allowed employers to replace some workers with machines, such as the robots on automobile assembly lines.

Consequently, adults without college educations have found it harder to obtain jobs with adequate wages, as I discuss in my textbook.[1] These reduced prospects have hurt working-class families in two ways. First, young men who are unemployed, or who are employed but earn low wages, are often reluctant to marry because they don't think that they earn enough to help support a family. Young women realize the difficulty of finding a spouse who is a reliable earner, which may make them less likely to wait until marriage to have children. Thus, the stagnant wages may be related to the postponement of marriage and the growth of childbearing outside of marriage during the last two decades or so. Second, the marriages that do exist face more strain because of inadequate incomes. Most generations of Americans have expected to do better economically than their parents' generation. Now, a significant number of working-class families find that those expectations are not being met.

One such family, the Mertens of Des Moines, Iowa, was profiled in *The New Yorker* magazine in 1995 by Susan Sheehan, Her article, presented in its entirety, is the only selection in this chapter. It is a story worth studying for what it says about working-class families in the United

---

[1]*Public and Private Families: An Introduction,* pp. 106–11.

States today. Kenny Merten earned $7 an hour at his first job after marrying Bonita in 1972; his pay rose to $8.95 before he lost that job. Two decades later, working for a highway barricade company, he makes $7.30 an hour. During the two decades, the cost of consumer goods more than tripled because of inflation. Consequently, Kenny would have to be earning over $24 an hour to match the buying power he had in 1972. Instead, his buying power has declined by 70 percent. "There ain't no middle class no more," said Kenny, who had hoped to join it, "there's only rich and poor."

As you read the article, you might ask yourself what is responsible for the constant money troubles the Mertens have. Is it an inability to control spending? An advertising industry that pushes consumption? An economy that doesn't pay adequate wages? "I know I'll never be able to earn $11.80 an hour again," Kenny said. "The most I can hope for is a seven-dollar-an-hour job that doesn't involve swinging sandbags. Maybe if I come home less tired at the end of the day, I can handle an evening job."

READING 4-1

Ain't No Middle Class

Susan Sheehan

At 10 o'clock on a Tuesday night in September, Bonita Merten gets home from her job as a nursing-home aide on the evening shift at the Luther Park Health Center, in Des Moines, Iowa. Home is a two-story, three-bedroom house in the predominantly working-class East Side section of the city. The house, drab on the outside, was built in 1905 for factory and railroad workers. It has aluminum siding painted an off-shade of green, with white and dark-brown trim. Usually, Bonita's sons—Christopher, who is 16 and David, who is 20 and still in high school (a slow learner, he was found to be suffering from autism when he was eight)—are awake when she comes home, but tonight they are asleep. Bonita's husband, Kenny, who has picked her up at the nursing home—"Driving makes Mama nervous," Kenny often says— loses no time in going to bed himself. Bonita is wearing her nursing-home uniform, which consists of a short-sleeved navy-blue polyester top with "Luther Park" inscribed in white, matching navy slacks, and white shoes. She takes off her work shoes, which she describes as "any kind I can pick up for 10 or 12 dollars," puts on a pair of black boots and a pair of gloves, and goes out to the garage to get a pitchfork.

In the spring, Bonita planted a garden. She and David, who loves plants and flowers, have been picking strawberries, raspberries, tomatoes, and zucchini since June. Bonita's mother, who lives in Washington, Iowa, a small town about a hundred miles from Des Moines, has always had a large garden—this summer, she

gave the Mertens dozens of tomatoes from her 32 tomato plants—but her row of potato plants, which had been bountiful in the past, didn't yield a single potato. This is the first year that Bonita has put potato plants in her own garden. A frost has been predicted, and she is afraid her potatoes (if there are any) will die, so instead of plunking herself down in front of the television set, as she customarily does after work, she goes out to tend her small potato strip alongside the house.

The night is cool and moonless. The only light in the back yard, which is a block from the round-the-clock thrum of Interstate 235, is provided by a tall mercury-arc lamp next to the garage. Traffic is steady on the freeway, but Bonita is used to the noise of the cars and trucks and doesn't hear a thing as she digs contentedly in the yellowy darkness. Bonita takes pleasure in the little things in life, and she excavates for potatoes with cheerful curiosity—"like I was digging for gold." Her pitchfork stabs and dents a large potato. Then, as she turns over the loosened dirt, she finds a second baking-size potato, says "Uh-huh!" to herself, and comes up with three smaller ones before calling it quits for the night.

"Twenty-two years ago, when Kenny and me got married, I agreed to marry him for richer or poorer," Bonita, who is 49, says. "I don't have no regrets, but I didn't have no idea for how much poorer. Nineteen-ninety-five has been a hard year in a pretty hard life. We had our water shut off in July *and* in August, and we ain't never had it turned off even once before, so I look on those five potatoes as a sign of hope. Maybe our luck will change."

When Bonita told Kenny she was going out to dig up her potatoes, he remembers thinking, Let her have fun. If she got the ambition, great. I'm kinda out of hope and I'm tired.

Kenny Merten is almost always tired when he gets home, after 5 P.M., from his job at Bonnie's Barricades—a small company, started 10 years ago by a woman named Bonnie Ruggless,

Susan Sheehan, "Ain't No Middle Class" from *The New Yorker* (December 11, 1995): 82–93. Copyright © 1995 by Susan Sheehan. Reprinted with the permission of Lescher & Lescher, Ltd.

that puts up barriers, sandbags, and signs to protect construction crews at road sites. Some days, he drives a truck a hundred and fifty miles to rural counties across the state to set up roadblocks. Other days, he does a lot of heavy lifting. "The heaviest sandbags weigh between 35 and 40 pounds dry," he says. "Wet, they weigh 50 or 60 pounds, depending on how soaked they are. Sand holds a lot of water." Hauling the sandbags is not easy for Kenny, who contracted polio when he was 18 months old and wore a brace on his left leg until he was almost 20. He is now 51, walks with a pronounced limp, and twists his left ankle easily. "Bonnie's got a big heart and hires people who are down on their luck," he says.

Kenny went to work at Bonnie's Barricades two years ago, and after two raises he earns seven dollars and thirty cents an hour. "It's a small living—too small for me, on account of all the debts I got," he says. "I'd like to quit working when I'm 65, but Bonnie doesn't offer a retirement plan, so there's no way I can quit then, with 28 years left to pay on the house mortgage, plus a car loan and etceteras. So I'm looking around for something easier—maybe driving a forklift in a warehouse. Something with better raises and fringe benefits."

On a summer afternoon after work, Kenny sits down in a rose-colored La-Z-Boy recliner in the Merten's living room/dining room, turns on the TV—a 19-inch Sylvania color set he bought secondhand nine years ago for a hundred dollars—and watches local and national news until six-thirty, occasionally dozing off. After the newscasts, he gets out of his work uniform—navy-blue pants and a short-sleeved orange shirt with the word "Ken" over one shirt pocket and "Bonnie's Barricades" over the other—and takes a bath. The house has one bathroom, with a tub but no shower. Last Christmas, Bonita's mother and her three younger brothers gave the Mertens a shower for their basement, but it has yet to be hooked up—by Kenny, who, with the help of a friend, can do the work for much less than a licensed plumber.

Kenny's philosophy is: Never do today what can be put off until tomorrow—unless he really wants to do it. Not that he is physically lazy. If the Mertens' lawn needs mowing, he'll mow it, and the lawn of their elderly next-door neighbor, Eunice, as well. Sometimes he gets up at 4:30 A.M.—an hour earlier than necessary—if Larry, his half uncle, needs a ride to work. Larry, who lives in a rented apartment two miles from the Mertens and drives an old clunker that breaks down regularly, has been married and divorced several times and has paid a lot of money for child support over the years. He is a security guard at a tire company and makes five dollars an hour. "If he doesn't get to work, he'll lose his job," Kenny says. In addition, Kenny helps his half brother Bob, who is also divorced and paying child support, with lifts to work and with loans.

Around 7:30 P.M., Kenny, who has changed into a clean T-shirt and a pair of old jeans, fixes dinner for himself and his two sons. Dinner is often macaroni and cheese, or spaghetti with store-bought sauce or stewed tomatoes from Bonita's mother's garden. He doesn't prepare salad or a separate vegetable ("Sauce or stewed tomatoes *is* the vegetable," he says); dessert, which tends to be an Iowa brand of ice cream, Anderson Erickson, is a rare luxury. Kenny takes the boys out for Subway sandwiches whenever he gets "a hankering" for one. Once a week— most likely on Friday, when he gets paid—he takes them out for dinner, usually to McDonald's. "It's easier than cooking," Kenny says.

Because Bonita works the evening shift, Kenny spends more time with his sons than most fathers do; because she doesn't drive, he spends more time behind the wheel. Christopher, a short, trim, cute boy with hazel eyes and brown hair, is one badge away from becoming an Eagle Scout, and Kenny drives him to many Scouting activities. This summer, Kenny drove Eunice, who is 85, to the hospital to visit her 90-year-old husband, Tony, who had become seriously ill in August. After Tony's death, on September 12th,

Kenny arranged for the funeral—choosing the casket and the flowers, buying a new shirt for Tony, and chauffeuring the boys to the private viewing at the funeral home. "Everyone was real appreciative," he says.

At around eight-thirty on evenings free from special transportation duties, Kenny unwinds by watching more television, playing solitaire, dozing again, and drinking his third Pepsi of the day. (He is a self-described "Pepsiholic.") Around nine-fifty, he drives two miles to the Luther Park nursing home for Bonita.

Bonita Merten leaves the house before 1 P.M., carrying a 16-ounce bottle of Pepsi (she, too, is a Pepsiholic), and catches the bus to work. She is dressed in her navy-blue uniform and white shoes. Since the uniforms cost 33 dollars, Bonita considers herself lucky to have been given a used one by a nurse's aide who quit, and she bought another, secondhand, for 10 dollars. Luther Park recently announced a mandatory change to forest-green uniforms, and Bonita does not look forward to having to shell out for new attire.

Bonita clocks in before one-forty-five, puts her Pepsi in the break-room refrigerator, and, with the other evening aides, makes rounds with the day aides. She and another aide are assigned to a wing with 20 long-term residents. "The residents have just been laid down on top of their beds before we get there," Bonita says. "First, I change water pitchers and give the residents ice—got to remember which ones don't want ice, just want plain water. We pass out snacks—shakes fortified with protein and vitamins, in strawberry, vanilla, or chocolate. They need the shakes, because they ordinarily don't want to eat their meals. While I'm doing that, the other aide has to pass out the gowns, washrags, and towels, and the Chux—great big absorbent pads—and Dri-Prides. They're adult snap pants with liners that fit inside them. We don't call them diapers because they're not actually diapers, and because residents got their pride to be considered."

At three-thirty, Bonita takes a 10-minute break and drinks some Pepsi. "We start getting the residents up and giving showers before our break and continue after," Bonita says. "Each resident gets two showers a week, and it works out so's I have to shower three patients a day."

One aide eats from four-thirty to five, the other from five to five-thirty. Until August 1st, Bonita bought a two-dollar meal ticket if she liked what was being offered in the employees' dining room. When the meal didn't appeal to her—she wouldn't spend the two dollars for, say, a turkey sandwich and a bowl of cream-of-mushroom soup ("I don't like it at all")—she either bought a bag of Chee-tos from a vending machine or skipped eating altogether. On August 1st, the nursing home reduced meal tickets to a dollar. "Even a turkey sandwich is worth that much," she says.

The residents eat at five-thirty, in their dining room. "We pass trays and help feed people who can't feed themselves," Bonita says. "Sometimes we feed them like a baby or encourage them to do as much as they can." At six-thirty, Bonita charts their meals—"what percent they ate, how much they drank. They don't eat a whole lot, because they don't get a lot of exercise, either. We clear out the dining room and walk them or wheel them to their rooms. We lay them down, and we've got to wash them and position them. I always lay them on their side, because I like lying on my side. I put a pillow behind their back and a blanket between their legs. We take the false teeth out of those with false teeth, and put the dentures into a denture cup for those that will let us. A lot of them have mouthwash, and we're supposed to rinse their mouth. We're supposed to brush their teeth if they have them. After everyone is down, we chart. We check off that we positioned them and if we changed their liners. I'm supposed to get a 10-minute evening break, but I hardly ever take it. Charting, I'm off my feet, and there's just too much to do. Often we're short—I'll be alone on a hall for a few hours. The last thing we do is make rounds with the shift coming in. I clock out by nine-forty-five. Ninety-nine percent of the time, Kenny picks me up. When I had different hours and he'd be bowling, his half brother Bob picked me up, or I took a cab for five dollars. The bus is one dollar, but it stops running by seven o'clock."

Bonita has worked all three shifts at Luther Park. The evening shift currently pays 50 cents an hour more than the day shift and 50 cents less than the night shift, but days and nights involve more lifting. (In moving her patients, Bonita has injured her back more times than she can remember, and she now wears a wide black belt with straps which goes around her sacroiliac; she also uses a mechanical device to help carry heavy residents between their wheelchairs and their beds.) Bonita's 1994 earnings from Luther park were only 869 dollars higher than her 1993 earnings, reflecting an hourly increase in wages from six dollars and fifty cents to six-sixty-five and some overtime hours and holidays, for which she is paid time and a half. This July 1st, she received the grandest raise that she has ever had in her life—75 cents an hour—but she believes there is a hold-down on overtime, so she doesn't expect to earn substantially more in 1995. Luther Park gives her a ham for Easter, a turkey for Thanksgiving, 10 dollars for her birthday, and 20 dollars for Christmas.

Bonita rarely complains about working at the nursing home. "I don't mind emptying bedpans or cleaning up the residents' messes," she says. She regards her job, with its time clocks, uniforms, tedious chores, low wages, penny-ante raises, and Dickensian holiday rewards, as "a means to a life."

Bonita and Kenny Merten and their two sons live in a statistical land above the lowly welfare poor but far beneath the exalted rich. In 1994, they earned $31,216 between them. Kenny made $17,239 working for Bonnie's Barricades; Bonita made $13,977 at Luther Park. With an additional $1,212 income from other sources, including some money that Kenny withdrew from the retirement plan of a previous employer, the Mertens' gross income was $32,428. Last year, as in most other years of their marriage, the Mertens spent more than they earned.

The Mertens' story is distinctive, but it is also representative of what has happened to the working poor of their generation. In 1974, Kenny Merten was making roughly the same hourly wage that he is today, and was able to buy a new Chevrolet Nova for less than 4,000 dollars; a similar vehicle today would cost 15,000 dollars—a sum that even Kenny, who is far more prone than Bonita to take on debt, might hesitate to finance. And though Kenny has brought on some of his own troubles by not always practicing thrift and by not always following principles of sound money management, his situation also reflects changing times.

In the 1960s, jobs for high-school graduates were plentiful. Young men could easily get work from one day to the next which paid a living wage, and that's what Kenny did at the time. By the mid-80s, many of these jobs were gone. In Des Moines, the Rock Island Motor Transit Company (part of the Chicago, Rock Island & Pacific Railroad) went belly up. Borden moved out of the city, and so did a division of the Ford Motor Company. Utility companies also began downsizing, and many factory jobs were replaced by service-industry jobs, which paid less. Although there is a chronic shortage of nurse's aides at Luther Park, those who stay are not rewarded. After 15 years of almost continuous employment, Bonita is paid 7 dollars and 40 cents an hour—55 cents an hour more than new aides coming onto the job.

Working for one employer, as men like Kenny's father-in-law used to do, is a novelty now. Des Moines has become one of the largest insurance cities in the United States, but the Mertens don't qualify for white-collar positions. Civil-service jobs, formerly held by high-school graduates, have become harder to obtain because of competition from college graduates, who face diminishing job opportunities themselves. Bonita's 37-year-old brother, Eugene, studied mechanical engineering at the Univer-

sity of Iowa, but after graduation he wasn't offered a position in his field. He went to work for
a box company and later took the United States
Postal Service exam. He passed. When Bonita
and Kenny took the exam, they scored too low
to be hired by the Post Office.

Although 31 percent of America's four-
person families earned less in 1994 than the
Mertens did, Kenny and Bonita do not feel like
members of the middle class, as they did years
ago. "There ain't no middle class no more,"
Kenny says. "There's only rich and poor."

This is where the $32,428 that the Mertens
grossed last year went. They paid $2,481 in fed-
eral income taxes. Their Iowa income-tax bill was
$1,142, and $2,388 was withheld from their paychecks for Social Security and Medicare. These
items reduced their disposable income to $26,417.
In 1994, Bonita had $9.64 withheld from her bi-
weekly paycheck for medical insurance, and
$14.21 for dental insurance—a $620.10 annual
cost. The insurance brought their disposable income down to $25,797.

The highest expenditures in the Mertens'
budget were for food and household supplies,
for which they spent approximately $110 a
week at various stores and farmers' markets, for
a yearly total of $5,720. They tried to econo-
mize by buying hamburger and chicken and by
limiting their treats. (All four Mertens like
potato chips.) Kenny spent about eight dollars
per working day on breakfast (two doughnuts
and a Pepsi), lunch (a double cheeseburger or a
chicken sandwich), and sodas on the road—an
additional $2,000 annually. His weekly dinner
out at McDonald's with his sons cost between
11 and 12 dollars—600 dollars a year more.
Bonita's meals or snacks at work added up to
about 300 dollars. Kenny sometimes went out
to breakfast on Saturday—alone or with the
boys—and the meals he and his sons ate at Mc-
Donald's or Subway and the dinners that all
four Mertens ate at restaurants like Bonanza
and Denny's probably came to another 600 dollars annually. David and Christopher's school

lunches cost a dollar-fifty a day; they received
allowances of 10 dollars a week each, and that
provided them with an extra 2 dollars and
50 cents to spend. The money the boys paid for
food outside the house came to 500 dollars a
year. The family spent a total of about $9,720
last year on dining in and out; on paper products
and cleaning supplies; and on caring for their
cats (they have two). This left them with $16,077.

The Mertens' next-highest expenditure in
1994 was $3,980 in property taxes and pay-
ments they made on a fixed-rate, 30-year,
32,000-dollar mortgage, on which they paid an
interest rate of 8.75 percent. This left them with
$12,097.

In April of 1994, Kenny's 1979 Oldsmobile,
with 279,000 miles on it, was no longer worth
repairing, so he bought a 1988 Grand Am from
Bonita's brother Eugene for 3,000 dollars, on
which he made four payments of 200 dollars a
month. The Grand Am was damaged in an accident in September, whereupon he traded up to
an 11,000-dollar 1991 Chevy Blazer, and his
car-loan payments increased to $285 a month.
Bonita has reproached Kenny for what she regards as a nonessential purchase. "A man's got
his ego," he replies. "The Blazer is also safer—
it has four-wheel drive." The insurance on
Kenny's cars cost a total of $798, and he spent
500 dollars on replacement parts. Kenny figures
that he spends about 20 dollars a week on gas,
or about $1,040 for the year. After car expenses
of $2,338 and after payments on the car loans of
$1,655, the Mertens had $8,104 left to spend. A
10-day driving vacation in August of last year,
highlighted by stops at the Indianapolis Motor
Speedway, Mammoth Cave, in Kentucky, and
the Hard Rock Cafe in Nashville, cost 1,500
dollars and left them with $6,604.

The Mertens' phone bill was approximately
25 dollars a month: the only long-distance calls
Bonita made were to her mother and to her
youngest brother, Todd, a 33-year-old aerospace
engineer living in Seattle. She kept the calls
short. "Most of our calls are incoming, and most

of them are for Christopher," Bonita says. The Mertens' water-and-sewage bill was about 50 dollars a month; their gas-and-electric bill was about 150 dollars a month. "I have a hard time paying them bills now that the gas and electric companies have consolidated," Kenny says. "Before, if the gas was 75 dollars and the electric was 75 dollars, I could afford to pay one when I got paid. My take-home pay is too low to pay the two together." After paying approximately 2,700 dollars for utilities, including late charges, the Mertens had a disposable income of $3,904.

Much of that went toward making payments to a finance company on two of Kenny's loans. To help pay for the family's 1994 vacation, Kenny borrowed 1,100 dollars, incurring payments of about 75 dollars a month for two years and three months, at an interest rate of roughly 25 percent. Kenny was more reluctant to discuss the second loan, saying only that it consisted of previous loans he'd "consolidated" at a rate of about 25 percent, and that it cost him 175 dollars a month in payments. Also in 1994 he borrowed "a small sum" for "Christmas and odds and ends" from the credit union at Bonnie's Barricades; 25 dollars a week was deducted from his paycheck for that loan. Payments on the three loans—about 4,300 dollars last year—left the Merten family with a budget deficit even before their numerous other expenses were taken into account.

Except in a few small instances (according to their 1994 Iowa income-tax return, Bonita and Kenny paid H & R Block 102 dollars to prepare their 1993 return, and they gave 125 dollars to charity), it isn't possible to determine precisely what the rest of the Mertens' expenditures were in 1994. Several years ago, Kenny bounced a lot of checks, and he has not had a checking account since. Kenny exceeded the limits on both of their MasterCards a few years ago, and the cards were cancelled. Bonita has a J. C. Penney charge card but says, "I seldom dust if off." Now and then, Bonita went to a downtown outlet store, and if a

dress caught her fancy she might put it on layaway. On special occasions, she bought inexpensive outfits for herself and for Kenny. Before last year's summer holiday, she spent seven dollars on a top and a pair of shorts, and during the trip Kenny bought a 75 dollar denim jacket for himself and about 50 dollars' worth of T-shirts for the whole family at the Hard Rock Cafe. One consequence of Kenny's having had polio as a child is that his left foot is a size 5½ and his right foot a size 7. If he wants a comfortable pair of shoes, he has to buy two pairs or order a pair consisting of a 5½ and a 7. Often he compromises, buying sneakers in size 6½. David wears T-shirts and jeans as long as they are black, the color worn by Garth Brooks, his favorite country singer. Christopher is partial to name brands, and Bonita couldn't say no to a pair of 89 dollar Nikes he coveted last year. The Mertens spent about 700 dollars last year on clothing, and tried to economize on dry cleaning. "I dry-clean our winter coats and one or two dresses, but I avoid buying anything with a 'Dry-clean only' label," Bonita says.

The Mertens' entertainment expenses usually come to a thousand dollars a year, but that amount was exceeded in 1994 when Kenny bought a mountain bike for every member of the family. The bikes (Bonita has yet to ride hers out of the driveway) cost 259 dollars apiece, and Kenny made the final payments on them earlier this year. This July, David rode Kenny's bike to a hardware store, and it was stolen while he was inside. Kenny yelled at David; Bonita told Kenny he was being too hard on him, and Kenny calmed down.

Bonita and Kenny don't buy books or magazines, and they don't subscribe to newspapers. (They routinely borrowed Eunice and Tony's Des Moines *Register* until Tony's death, when Eunice cancelled it.) They rarely go to the movies—"Too expensive," Kenny says—but regularly rent movies and video games, usually at Blockbuster. For amusement, they often go to malls, just to browse, but when they get a serious urge to buy they go to antique stores. Kenny believes in "collectibles." His most treasured possession is an assortment of Currier & Ives dishes and glasses.

The Mertens have never paid to send a fax, or to send a package via Federal Express, and they aren't on-line: they have no computer. They even avoid spending money on postage: Kenny pays his bills in person. Bonita used to send out a lot of Christmas cards, but, she says, "I didn't get a whole lot back, so I quit that, too." They spend little on gifts, except to members of Bonita's family.

Kenny knows how much Bonita loves red roses. Twenty-two years ago, he gave her one red rose after they had been married one month, two after they had been married two months, and continued until he reached 12 red roses on their first anniversary. He also gave her a dozen red roses when she had a miscarriage, in 1973, "to make her feel better." To celebrate the birth of David and of Christopher, he gave her a dozen red roses and one yellow one for each boy. And Kenny gives Bonita a glass rose every Christmas.

On a Sunday evening this summer, the four Mertens went to Dahl's, their supermarket of choice in Des Moines. They bought four rolls of toilet paper (69 cents); a toothbrush (99 cents); a box of Rice Krispies (on sale for $1.99); eight 16-ounce bottles of Pepsi ($1.67); a gallon of 2-percent milk ($2.07); a large package of the least expensive dishwasher detergent ($2.19), the Mertens having acquired their first dishwasher in 1993, for 125 dollars; two jars of Prego spaghetti sauce ($3); a box of Shake 'n Bake ($1.99); two rolls of film ($10.38), one for Kenny, who owns a Canon T50 he bought for 125 dollars at a pawnshop, and one for Christopher to take to Boy Scout camp in Colorado; a battery ($2.99) for Christopher's flashlight, also for camp; a pound of carrots (65 cents); a green pepper (79 cents); some Ziploc bags ($1.89); a Stain Stick ($1.89); a box of 2000 Flushes ($2.89); a package of shredded mozzarella ($1.39) to add to some pizza the Mertens already had in the freezer; and 12 cans

of cat food ($3). Bonita bought one treat for herself—a box of toaster pastries with raspberry filling ($2.05). Christopher asked for a Reese's peanut-butter cup (25 cents), a bottle of Crystal Light (75 cents), and a package of Pounce cat treats ($1.05). All three purchases were O.K.'d.

David, who is enchanted by electrical fixtures, was content to spend his time in the store browsing in the light-bulb section. He was born with a cataract in his left eye, and the Mertens were instructed to put drops in that eye and a patch over his "good" right eye for a few years, so that the left eye wouldn't become lazy. Sometimes when they put the drops in, they told David to look up at a light. Today, David's main obsession, which apparently dates back to the eyedrops, is light. "We'd go someplace with David, and if there was a light with a bulb out he'd say, 'Light out,'" Bonita recalls. "We'd tell him, 'Don't worry about that,' and pretty soon he was saying, 'Light out, don't worry about that.'"

At 20, David looks 15. A lanky young man with coppercolored hair, hearing aids in both ears, and eye-glasses with thick lenses, he attends Ruby Van Meter, a special public high school for the city's mentally challenged. He reads at a fifth-grade level, and he doesn't read much. For years, the Mertens have been applying—without success—for Supplemental Security Income for David. In June of this year, when his application for S.S.I. was once again turned down, the Mertens hired a lawyer to appeal the decision. David has held a series of jobs set aside for slow learners (working, for instance, as a busboy in the Iowa statehouse cafeteria and in the laundry room of the local Marriott hotel), but he says that his "mood was off" when he was interviewed for several possible jobs this summer, and he drifted quietly through his school vacation. He will not be permitted to remain in school past the age of 21. If David could receive monthly S.S.I. checks and Medicaid, the Mertens would worry less about what will happen to him after they are gone. They have never regarded David as a burden, and although he has always been in special-education classes, they have treated him as much as possible the way they treat Christopher. Say "special ed" to Bonita, and she will say, "Both my boys are very special."

The Dahl's bill came to $44.75. When Kenny failed to take money out of his pocket at the cash register, Bonita, looking upset, pulled out her checkbook. She had expected Kenny to pay for the groceries, and she had hoped that the bill would be 40 dollars or less. But Kenny was short of money. "Aargh," Bonita said, softly.

Bonita didn't want to write checks for groceries, because she has other ideas about where her biweekly paychecks—about 400 dollars take-home—should go. Most of her first check of the month goes toward the mortgage—$331.68 when she pays it before the 17th of the month, $344.26 when she doesn't. Bonita likes to put aside the second check for the two most important events in her year—the family's summer vacation and Christmas. In theory, Kenny is supposed to pay most of the other family expenses and to stick to a budget—a theory to which he sometimes has difficulty subscribing. "I don't like to work off a budget," he says. "I think it restricts you. My way is to see who we have to pay this week and go from there. I rob Peter to pay Paul and try to pay Peter back." In practice, Kenny rarely pays Peter back. With his take-home pay averaging about 235 dollars a week, he can't.

When a consumer counsellor, who does not know the Mertens, was questioned about the family's current financial predicament—specifically, their 1994 income and expenditures—she made numerous recommendations. Among her suggestions for major savings was that the Mertens cut their food bills dramatically, to 5,400 dollars a year. She proposed stretching the Mertens' food dollars by drastically curtailing their eating out and by buying in bulk from the supermarket. She said that Kenny should get rid of his high-interest loans, and use the money he was spending on

usurious interest to convert his mortgage from 30 years to 15. The way Kenny and Bonita were going, the counsellor pointed out, they would not finish paying off their current mortgage until they were 79 and 77 years old, respectively. The Mertens' principal asset is 8,000 dollars in equity they have in their house. If the Mertens wanted to retire at 65, they would need more than what they could expect to receive from Social Security.

The counsellor had many minor suggestions for economizing at the grocery store. The Mertens should buy powdered milk and mix it with one-percent milk instead of buying two-percent milk. They should cut down even further on buying meat; beans and lentils, the counsellor observed, are a nutritious and less costly form of protein. She recommended buying raisins rather than potato chips, which she characterized as "high-caloric, high-fat, and high-cost."

The counsellor had one word for the amount—between 1,500 and 2,500 dollars—that the Mertens spent on vacations: "outlandish." Their vacations, she said, should cost a maximum of 500 dollars a year. She recommended renting a cabin with another family at a nearby state park or a lake. She urged the Mertens to visit local museums and free festivals, and go on picnics, including "no-ant picnics"—on a blanket in their living room.

Kenny and Bonita were resistant to most of the suggestions that were passed on to them from the counsellor, who is funded mainly by creditors to dispense advice to those with bill-paying problems. According to Kenny, buying a dozen doughnuts at the supermarket and then taking breakfast to work would be "boring." Bonita says she tried powdered milk in the mid-80s, when Kenny was unemployed, and the kids wouldn't drink it. She does buy raisins, but the boys don't really like them. Bonita and Kenny both laugh at the prospect of a no-ant picnic. "Sitting on the living-room carpet don't seem like a picnic to me," Bonita says.

Bonita surmises that the counsellor hasn't experienced much of blue-collar life and therefore underestimates the necessity for vacations and other forms of having fun. "We couldn't afford vacations in the 80s, and if we don't take them now the kids will be grown," she says. Kenny reacted angrily to the idea of the boys' eating dried beans and other processed foods. "I lived on powdered milk, dried beans, surplus yellow cheese, and that kind of stuff for two years when I was a kid," he says. "I want better for my boys."

Kenny acknowledges that he tried to confine his responses to the consumer counsellor's minor suggestions, because he realizes that her major recommendations are sound. He also realizes that he isn't in a position to act on them. He dreams of being free of debt. He has tried a number of times to get a 15-year mortgage, and has been turned down each time. "We both work hard, we're not on welfare, and we just can't seem to do anything that will make a real difference in our lives," he says. "So I save 10 dollars a bowling season by not getting a locker at the alley to store my ball and shoes, and have to carry them back and forth. So I save 25 dollars by changing my own oil instead of going to Jiffy Lube. So what? Going out to dinner is as necessary to me as paying water bills."

Kenneth Deane Merten was born poor and illegitimate to Ruby Merten in her mother's home, outside Des Moines, on October 5, 1944; his maternal relatives declined to reveal his father's name, and he never met his father. Ruby Merten went on to marry a soldier and had another son, Robert. She divorced Bob's father, and later married Don Summers, a frequently unemployed laborer, with whom she had three more children. "Mr. Summers was so mean he made me stand up all night in the bed when I was eight years old," Kenny recalls. He has never hit his own sons, because "I know what it done to my life and I don't want it to get passed down." The family often moved in haste when the rent was due. Kenny attended eight or ten

schools, some of them twice, before he completed sixth grade.

Kenny's mother died of cancer at 27, when he was 14. The three younger children stayed with Don Summers and a woman he married a month later. Kenny and Bob went to live with their maternal grandparents, and their lives became more stable. Even so, Kenny's school grades were low. "I had a hard time with math and science," he says. "Coulda been because of all the early moving around. I ain't stupid." He spent his high-school years at Des Moines Technical High School and graduated in 1964, when he was almost 20.

Two days later, he found a job as a shipping clerk for *Look* magazine. He kept the job until 1969, and left only when it became apparent that the magazine was cutting back its operations. He drove a cab from 1969 to 1972, drank too much, and did what he calls "some rowdy rambling." He had put much of that behind him when he got a job as a factory worker at EMCO Industries, a manufacturer of muffler parts and machinery bolts, in the fall of 1972, shortly before he met Bonita.

Bonita Anne Crooks was born on October 7, 1946, in Harper, Iowa. Her father, Cloyce Crooks, was employed all his working life by the Natural Gas Pipeline Company; his wife, Pauline, stayed home to take care of Bonita and her three younger brothers. Bonita was required to do chores, for which she was paid, and to deposit those earnings in a bank. She took tap-dancing lessons, wore braces on her teeth, and often went with her family on vacation to places like California and Texas. "Kenny's growing up was a lot worse than mine," she says. In 1965, Bonita graduated from a Catholic high school and became a nurse's aide, while living at home and continuing to bank her money. In 1971, she moved to Des Moines, and the following year she got a job as a keypunch operator for a large insurance company. Keypunching, however, proved too difficult for her (she couldn't combine accuracy with high speed), and she soon transferred within the company to a lower-paying position—that of a file clerk.

Bonita met Kenny in October 1972 on a blind date that had been arranged by a friend of hers. "I had been jilted by a younger man, and I knew Kenny was meant for me on our first date, when he told me he was born on October 5, 1944—exactly two years and two days earlier than me," Bonita says. She and Kenny fell in love quickly and were married in a traditional ceremony at a Catholic church in Harper on June 30, 1973. The newlyweds set off for Colorado on their honeymoon, but Kenny's car, a secondhand 1966 Pontiac Bonneville convertible, broke down, and the couple ended up in the Black Hills of South Dakota. When they were courting, Kenny had asked Bonita what sort of engagement ring she wanted. She had declined a "chunky" diamond, and said that matching wedding bands would suffice. "I suspected Kenny had debts," Bonita says. "I just didn't know how many he had until we got home."

The couple moved into a modest two-bedroom house. Bonita kept her file-clerk job after David's birth, in April 1975, but when she became pregnant with Christopher, who was born in November 1979, her doctor ordered her to bed. From the window of her bedroom, Bonita could see the Luther Park nursing home being built "kinda like next to my back yard." She didn't return to the insurance company, because her pay couldn't cover the cost of daytime care for two children. Kenny was working days at EMCO, so in June 1980 Bonita took a job on the 3-to-11 P.M. shift at Luther Park. She earned more there than she had as a file clerk. On some nights, Kenny drove a cab. He needed two jobs, because he regularly spent more than he and Bonita earned, just as he had overspent his own pay when he was single. Every year or two, he bought a new car. "I shouldn't have bought those new cars, but life with Don Summers made me feel completely insecure," he says. "Driving new cars gave me a sense of self-worth."

Kenny lost his job at EMCO at the end of 1983. He says that he had asked his supervisor for permission to take some discarded aluminum parts, and that permission was granted. But as he was driving off EMCO's premises with the parts in the bed of his pickup he was accused of stealing them. His supervisor then denied having given Kenny permission to take the parts. A demoralized Kenny didn't seek a new job for a year. He had already stopped driving the cab—after being robbed twice—and had started mowing lawns part time in the spring and summer, and doing cleanup work and shovelling snow in the fall and winter. Kenny's business failed—"There were too many unemployed guys like me out there." Many of his prized belongings were repossessed, among them a Curtis-Mathes stereo console. For two weeks in the summer of 1984, the Mertens were without gas or electricity or telephone service. They went on food stamps. Bonita felt guilty about going to work in air-conditioned surroundings while her husband and children were at home in the heat. Kenny felt humiliated when Bonita's parents visited their dark, sweltering house over the Fourth of July weekend. While Kenny has done better financially than most of his side of the family, it pains him that he hasn't done as well as Bonita's brothers, and that they regard him as a spendthrift and an inadequate provider. "When they get down on Kenny, I feel like I'm caught between a rock and a crevice," Bonita says.

Kenny's starting salary at EMCO had been seven dollars an hour. By the time he was terminated, it was eight-ninety-five an hour. In 1985, he found several jobs he liked, but none paid more than seven dollars an hour. One such job was with Bob Allen Sportswear, and he kept it until 1987, when he was let go during the off-season. He occasionally filed unemployment claims, and the family qualified for food stamps and received some groceries from food banks. During the rocky period between 1984 and 1988, Kenny tried to continue making payments on bills that he owed, in order to avoid having to declare bankruptcy, but his debts grew to the point where they exceeded his assets by "I think 12 or 13 thousand dollars"; his creditors—mostly finance companies—got fed up with him, and then he had no choice. The Mertens were able to keep their house and their '79 Olds. Going on food stamps didn't embarrass them—the boys had to eat, and they went off food stamps whenever Kenny had a new job—but the bankruptcy filing was published in the newspaper and made Bonita feel ashamed.

In 1989, after seeing an ad on television, Kenny enrolled in electronics courses at a local vocational school and borrowed 7,200 dollars to pay for his studies. His deficiency in math came back to haunt him, and he eventually dropped out. While at school, he had heard of an opening as a janitor at Ryko Manufacturing, an Iowa manufacturer of car washes. He eventually moved up to a factory job, working full time at Ryko in the early 90s for three years. Those years were happy ones. He got regular raises, and during the April-to-December busy season he earned a lot of overtime. In the summer of 1991, the Mertens flew to Seattle to visit Bonita's brother Todd. They had just enough money to cover one plane fare, and asked Bonita's brother Eugene to lend them the money for the three other tickets. Bonita took three months off that year; by then, she had worked full time at Luther Park for 11 straight years and needed a break. Kenny was proud to be the family's main provider, and wanted Bonita to stay home and take it easy.

In February 1993 Ryko fired Kenny Merten. His supervisors said that the work he did on the assembly line was neither fast enough nor of a sufficiently high quality. He was earning 11 dollars and 80 cents an hour—almost 30,000 dollars a year including overtime—when he was terminated. "In today's job market, first-rate companies like Ryko can afford to be selective," he says. "They want to hire young men."

Around the same time, Luther Park announced that it intended to expand. The nursing home offered the Mertens 39,000 dollars for the house they had lived in for 18 years. Kenny and Bonita accepted the offer, and were allowed to stay on, free of charge, for six months while they went house hunting. After they sold their house, it became apparent that they had been using it to supplement their income. The house they had bought for 14,800 dollars had appreciated handsomely in value, but they had kept remortgaging, and now they owed 29,000 dollars on it. As a result, they netted only 10,000 dollars from the sale. The purchase price of the Mertens' new home was 40,000 dollars. They spent 2,000 dollars from the sale of the old house on improvements to their new home, and this reduced the amount of the down payment they were able to afford to 8,000 dollars.

Kenny attempted to return to work at several of the companies where he had previously been employed, but they weren't hiring. It took him five months to find his current job with Bonnie's Barricades—far more arduous work, at lower wages than he had been paid at EMCO more than 20 years earlier. "I know I'll never be able to earn 11.80 an hour again," he says. "The most I can hope for is a seven-dollar-an-hour job that doesn't involve swinging sandbags. Maybe if I come home less tired at the end of the day, I can handle an evening job."

This year did not get off to a good start for Kenny. In January, he hocked two rings that Bonita had given him for a hundred dollars, in order to pay a utility bill. Then, three months later, true to form, Kenny spotted two rings at a local pawnshop that he wanted Bonita to have—a 199-dollar opal ring and a 399-dollar diamond-cluster ring. He asked the pawnshop owner to take the two rings out of the showcase and agreed to make periodic 20 dollar payments on them until they were paid off.

Kenny was not worried about how he would pay for the rings, or how he would pay for the family's annual summer vacation. In September of last year, a few days after the Mertens returned from that summer's driving trip, his Grand Am was rear-ended. After the collision, in which Kenny hurt his back, he hired a lawyer on a contingency basis. The young man who had caused the accident had adequate insurance, and Kenny expected to be reimbursed for medical bills and lost wages. (He hadn't been permitted to lift heavy objects for several weeks.) He also expected the insurance company to pay a sizable sum—10 or 15 thousand dollars—for pain and suffering. Kenny's lawyer told him that he could expect the insurance company to settle with him by March. When the insurance money failed to arrive that month, Kenny's lawyer told him to expect an offer in April, then in May, and then in June. In early July, the lawyer said that he could get Kenny 6,500 dollars by the end of the month—just in time to save the Mertens' summer vacation. The insurance payment and the annual vacation had been the focus of Bonita's attention for seven months. "If you don't go on vacation, a year has gone by with nothing to show for it," she says.

Bonita wanted the family to travel to Seattle to visit Todd because he had a new home and she was eager to see it. The Mertens made meticulous plans for a driving trip to the state of Washington. They decided they would get up at 4 A.M. on Saturday, August 5th, and drive to Rapid City, South Dakota. They would visit Mt. Rushmore, and Kenny, who has an eye for landscapes, would take photographs of the Devils Tower, in Wyoming, at sunrise and sunset. They would arrive at Todd's home on Wednesday, August 9th, spend a few days there, and return to Des Moines, by way of the Mall of America, in Bloomington, Minnesota, on August 19th. Both Bonita and Kenny had arranged with their employers to take one week off with pay and one without.

Six days before their departure, however, their lawyer called with crushing news; the insurance payment would not be arriving until September. The following evening, Bonita in-

jured her shoulder lifting a patient at the nursing home, but she was still determined to have her vacation. Although Kenny was behind on almost all his bills—he had just borrowed 75 dollars from David to pay a water bill—he went to a bank and to his credit union on August 2nd to borrow 2,500 dollars to cover the cost of the vacation, figuring he would pay off this newest loan from the insurance money in September. On the evening of August 2nd, Bonita reinjured her shoulder while helping another aide transfer a resident from her wheelchair to her bed.

Both the bank and the credit union turned Kenny down. Not only did he have too much outstanding debt of his own but he had also co-signed a loan on his half brother Bob's car. Without being able to borrow, the Mertens could not go on vacation. To make matters worse, Luther Park had sent Bonita to a doctor, and he informed her that she would require physical therapy three times a week for the next two weeks. The vacation would have to be cancelled. "When Kenny told me he'd been turned down for the loan, his jaw dropped about two inches," Bonita recalls. "Kenny was so shocked and disappointed for me that I couldn't be disappointed for myself."

The Mertens have had their share of disappointments, but they don't stay down long. On the morning they had set aside to pack for their trip, Bonita baked banana bread. That evening, after she finished work, Kenny took the whole family out to dinner. From there they drove to Blockbuster and bought two videos—"Sister Act 2" (David had loved the original) and a Beatles movie. They also rented two movies, and a video game that Christopher wanted. The boys spent the following week at their grandmother's. During the second vacation week, Bonita took David to the Iowa State Fair, in town. "Me and David really had fun together," she says.

Both Mertens spent a little money during the two weeks that they didn't go out West. Bonita made a payment to Fingerhut on a shelf that she had bought for David's room and on a game that she had bought him, and she finished paying Home Interiors for some mirrors, sconces, and a gold shelf that she had bought for her bedroom. "When I buy this stuff, I can see Kenny getting a little perturbed, but he doesn't say anything," she says. Later in August, the front brakes on Kenny's Blazer failed, and replacement parts cost about a hundred dollars. The labor would have cost him twice that much, but Eunice, the next-door neighbor, gave him some furniture that she no longer needed, and he bartered the furniture with a friend who is an auto mechanic. Kenny and Bonita agreed that driving with faulty brakes through the mountains on their way West would have been dangerous, so it was a blessing in disguise that they had been forced to remain at home.

On Friday, September 22nd, Kenny, feeling unusually fatigued, decided to take the day off from work. After lunch, he drove Bonita to their lawyer's office. The insurance company had agreed to pay Kenny 7,200 dollars. The lawyer would get a third—2,400 dollars—and Kenny owed 1,200 dollars in medical bills, so he would net 3,600 dollars. He had wanted more—to pay off more of his debts and bills—but this was three days after Bonita's lucky potato strike, and she was feeling optimistic. She persuaded Kenny to put the agony of waiting behind them and to accept the offer.

The next day, Kenny drove Bonita, David, and Christopher to the pawnshop. The proprietor, Doug Schlegel, was expecting them. At the cash register, Doug handed Kenny a small manila envelope with the opal ring inside. "Hey, Kiddo!" Kenny called out to Bonita as he removed the ring from the envelope. "Come here!"

Bonita tried to kiss Kenny, but he quickly moved away. "I love you," she said. After Bonita finished working the opal ring down the third finger of her left hand, checking to see whether it fitted properly, Doug told her, "You don't want to let it sit in the sun or put it in hot water."

"I know," Bonita said. "Opals are soft and touchy. They're my birthstone. I have one I bought for myself, but this is lots prettier."

Once the Mertens were back in the Blazer, Bonita asked Kenny, "Is the opal my birthday present?" Her 49th birthday was coming up in two weeks.

"It's a prebirthday present," Kenny replied. He didn't mention his plan to give her the more expensive ring—the one with the diamond cluster—for Christmas, provided he could make the payments in time.

"Thank you, Kenny. I love you," Bonita said.

"Sure," Kenny said. "You love to pick on me and drive me crazy."

Bonita touched Kenny's hand. "Leave me alone, I'm driving," he told her.

When Kenny stopped at a red light, Bonita said, "You're not driving now." But the light suddenly turned green.

Throughout the fall, Kenny Merten refused to fret over the very real possibility that he would have to file for bankruptcy again if he didn't get his financial house in order. He was thinking only as far ahead as Christmas—imagining himself putting the box that held the diamond-cluster ring for Bonita under the tree in their living room and marking it "Open this one last." Kenny predicts that when his brothers-in-law see the ring they will surely disapprove, but he doesn't care. "The rings shouldn't be in the budget, but they are," he says.

Kenny's mother's short life left him with a determination to marry once and to make that marriage succeed—something that few of his relatives have done. Bonita has often said that one reason she loves Kenny is that he surprises her every once in a while.

"Diamonds are a girl's best friend, next to her husband," Kenny says. "And Bonita's worth that ring, every bit of it. After all, she puts up with me."

CHAPTER 5

Race, Ethnicity, and Families

In 1903 the great African-American sociologist W. E. B. DuBois wrote in his book, *The Souls of Black Folk,* that "the problem of the 20th century is the problem of the color line—the relation of the darker to the lighter races of men in Asia and Africa, in America and the islands of the sea." Nearly a century later, the "problem" of color still looms large in discussions of American society, including family life. DuBois was referring to the difference between African Americans and Americans of European descent. Although that black/white distinction is still a central part of American life, there are other "colors" now. The largest of the newer groups is comprised of people who speak Spanish and mostly trace their ancestry through Latin America. In the American political discourse they are increasingly lumped together as "Hispanics," even though there are great differences among the major Hispanic groups.

It's well known that the family patterns of African Americans, non-Hispanic whites, and Hispanic groups such as Mexican Americans or Puerto Ricans differ. One difference is in the prevalence of single-parent families and childbearing outside of marriage. In the following article, Mercer Sullivan examines how young men in three neighborhoods in New York—African American, non-Hispanic white, and Puerto Rican—respond to the pregnancies of their girlfriends. Do they marry? Do they deny responsibility? Do they urge abortion? Sullivan conducted ethnographic studies—meaning that, like an anthropologist on a South Pacific island, he spent a great deal of time in the neighborhoods, getting to know the young people he would later write about.

Sullivan finds distinctive patterns in each neighborhood. He ascribes the differences to three factors. The first is cultural differences among the groups. You will notice that at the start of the article he feels he has to justify including culture. He is defensive about culture because many liberal commentators in the 1970s and 1980s charged that invoking cultural reasons for the prevalence of single-parent families in black or Hispanic neighborhoods was like "blaming the victim." Sullivan's other two factors are the overall economic situation of the New York region (e.g., the long-term decline in skilled blue-collar jobs) and what he calls the *social ecology* of particular neighborhoods. By the latter term he means the ways in which young men in each neighborhood are encouraged to go about entering the work force.

Sullivan's findings suggest that part—although by no means all—of the differences in the family lives of racial and ethnic groups are really a reflection of the class differences among them. But because racial and ethnic group membership is easier to see than class membership, our public discussions often focus on race and ethnicity more than class. In fact, the public dialog about race has, if anything, become more intense in recent years. Lillian B. Rubin explored the reasons for the focus on race in the thinking of working-class families in her book, *Families on the Fault Line.* She ar-

gues, in part, that white working-class men and women, who often are struggling to get by in an unfriendly economy, find it easy to blame the groups below them—African Americans and immigrants—for their economic troubles. Twenty years earlier, Rubin had interviewed families for her critique of working-class family life, *Worlds of Pain.* In the early 1990s, she reinterviewed many of these families and interviewed some new families. In this excerpt, she recounts her last visits to two of the families, one African American and one Mexican American. Their comments provoked her to speculate on why race and ethnicity are still such major factors in the lives of working-class families.

READING 5-1

Absent Fathers in the Inner City

Mercer L. Sullivan

The long-standing and increasing relationship between officially female-headed households and poverty has prompted much recent speculation that absent fathers are a major cause of concentrated and persistent poverty in the inner cities. Child support enforcement is now widely touted as a major solution to the emerging formation of a so-called underclass. As part of this strategy for reducing poverty, many proponents of reform do recognize the need for addressing the employment, education, and training difficulties of young men. Yet current welfare-reform proposals are more emphatic about the need to collect child support payments from young men than they are about the need to improve their economic opportunities. Meanwhile, knowledge of the economic circumstances of young, unmarried, officially absent fathers and of their relationships to the households in which their children live is sadly lacking. Official statistics do not convey an accurate picture of the extent to which officially absent fathers are really absent from the households and lives of their children or of the extent to which these men are actually able to support families.

Explanations of the relationship between family form and poverty have long been controversial in social science and in discussions of public policy. Although the association between poverty and female headship of households has been apparent for some time, the direction of causal relationships between the two has been hotly debated. Because poverty and female-headed households both occur at high rates among members of cultural minority groups in the United States, there has also been much controversy about the role that culture plays in the processes that produce both female-headed households and poverty. The culture-of-poverty theories of the late 1960s drew harsh criticism because they seemed to imply that cultural values concerning the control of sexual activity and the value of marriage were the causes rather than the results of poverty.

These theories provoked such heated reactions that research on family patterns among the poor was virtually suspended during the 1970s. During that decade, however, the proportions of female-headed households increased across society and soared among minority residents of inner-city areas. The associations between female headship of households, welfare dependency, and concentrated and persistent poverty became stronger than ever, eventually prompting social scientists and leaders of minority groups to pay renewed attention to family patterns among the poor. Fortunately, much of the recent research on these questions has maintained a steady focus on structural causes of both poverty and family disruption. Recent work by William Julius Wilson has sharpened this focus on structural factors by linking economic changes to powerful demographic shifts that have concentrated poor blacks in certain central-city areas while upwardly mobile blacks have left these areas.[1]

Unfortunately, the role of culture in these social changes remains as neglected as it has been since the days when overly vague notions of the culture of poverty brought disrepute to the culture concept as a tool for understanding the effects of the concentration of poverty among cultural minorities. This neglect of culture is unfortunate because it leaves us in the dark as to

Mercer L. Sullivan, "Absent Fathers in the Inner City" from *Annals of the American Academy of Political and Social Science* 501 (1989): 48–58. Copyright © 1989 by the AAPSS. Reprinted with the permission of Sage Publications, Inc.

NOTE: The research reported here could not have been carried out without the sensitive and dedicated work of three field research assistants: Carl Cesvette, for Projectville; Richard Curtis, for Hamilton Park; and Adalberto Mauras, for La Barriada. Our research on the role of young males in teenage pregnancy and parenting has been supported by the Ford Foundation and the W. T. Grant Foundation.

how people deal collectively with economic disadvantage, prejudice, and the dilemmas of procreating and raising families under such conditions. Lacking such an understanding, we are left with two sorts of explanatory framework, structural and individual, both of which beg crucial questions of how people in real communities devise collective responses to their problems. Too extreme an emphasis on individual causation ignores growing evidence of the proliferation of low-wage jobs and increasing joblessness in inner-city labor markets. Too much emphasis on structural causation ignores evidence that postponing childbearing leads to greater occupational success even within inner-city populations.

The neglect of culture stems both from a lack of ethnographic research, which alone can portray culture, and from theoretical confusion concerning the ways in which individual action, culture, and social structure are interrelated. The comparative ethnographic research on young fathers in three inner-city neighborhoods reported here attempts to resolve some of these issues, first by providing data on cultural processes and, second, by relating these cultural processes both upward to the structural constraints of the political economy and downward to the choices and strategies of particular individuals, which vary even within these neighborhoods.

A key to the theoretical approach employed here is the concept of social ecology, the idea that each neighborhood we studied is distinctive not just because of primordial cultural values that may have been retained from a distant past but, perhaps more important, because each neighborhood occupies a distinctive ecological niche in relation to the regional economy, the educational system, and other institutions of the larger society. Though even the early culture-of-poverty theorists maintained that culture is adaptive to structure,[2] their tendency to portray pathology and not adaptation led to the unfortunate current tendency either to dismiss culture or to reify it as a set of mysterious and immutable values. By focusing on social ecology, the pre-

sent comparison of the adaptive strategies of young people in three different inner-city communities attempts to portray cultural process in a more complex way, as the collective adaptations of different groups of people with different group histories to similar yet distinctive difficulties in obtaining a living income, procreating, and supporting and raising children.

THREE NEIGHBORHOODS AND A RESEARCH PROJECT

The three neighborhoods we have studied are in Brooklyn, New York. In order to maintain the confidentiality of the very detailed and personal data we have gathered, we refer to these places using the pseudonyms Hamilton Park, Projectville, and La Barriada. The three neighborhoods are all relatively low income, yet they differ in class and in culture. Hamilton Park is a predominantly white, Catholic area many of whose adult residents are third- and fourth-generation descendants of immigrants from Italy and Poland. Though census figures show this neighborhood to have some of the lowest income levels among predominantly white, non-Hispanic neighborhoods in New York City, median income levels are still significantly higher than those in the two minority neighborhoods. Less than 12 percent of families are below the poverty level and less than 10 percent of households receive Aid to Families with Dependent Children (AFDC). Projectville is a predominantly black neighborhood whose adult residents are first- or second-generation immigrants from the southern United States. La Barriada is a predominantly Hispanic area in which all of the families we have contacted are headed by first- or second-generation immigrants from Puerto Rico. Family poverty levels and household AFDC enrollment levels are around 50 percent in both these areas.

We began research in these areas in 1979 in a study of the relationships between schooling, employment, and crime in the careers of young males. In that study, we described distinctive career patterns in each neighborhood and related these patterns to the distinctive social ecology of each neighborhood.[3] In 1984, we began to look at young men who had become fathers at an early age and how their responses with respect to marriage, child support, and household and family formation related to the career patterns we had already been studying.[4] At that time, we recontacted some of the young males who had become fathers during our study a few years earlier; we also were introduced by them to younger males in their neighborhoods whose sexual partners had become pregnant. Some of the similarities and differences within and between these neighborhood-based groups of young men in how they became fathers and what they did about these critical life-cycle transitions are reported and compared here.

In order to assess the influences of both culture and economic opportunity on the ways in which young men become fathers and how they react, the three neighborhoods are compared in terms of (1) the careers of young males; (2) patterns of teenage sexual activity; and (3) responses to pregnancy, including whether abortions are sought, whether marriage and coresidence are entered into, and how the children of young mothers are supported. The data are reported for 16 young males from Projectville, 17 from La Barriada, and 15 from Hamilton Park. These are not random samples but were recruited by ethnographic snowballing techniques. In addition, there is considerable variation within each sample. Each includes about a third who are nonfathers and each includes fathers who have been more and less effective in providing support for their children. Nonetheless, variation within each neighborhood sample falls within a distinctive range that reflects both community values and the resources available within that community.

All of those referred to as fathers fathered children by teenage mothers. Many of the fathers, however, were one or two years older and

not themselves teenagers at the time they became fathers.

THE CAREERS OF YOUNG MALES

The higher employment rates and median family incomes of Hamilton Park residents are associated with more employment for young males and better wages when they are employed. Although work can also be scarce for them, they enjoy much better access to jobs, both while they are still of school age and subsequently, than their minority counterparts. The jobs that they do find are located almost entirely through neighborhood-based and family-based personal networks. While they are still of school age, this work is almost entirely off the books, yet it usually pays better than minimum wage. As they get older, some find their way into relatively well-paying and secure unionized blue-collar jobs. Education plays very little role in their access to work. Most have attended a public vocational high school, but only about a third of them have obtained any sort of diploma.

Young males from the two minority neighborhoods fare much worse. They suffer more from lack of employment, and they earn very low wages when they do work, both as teenagers and as young adults. Yet the career patterns differ between these two minority neighborhoods in distinctive ways that are related to the neighborhoods' social ecology. La Barriada's young males leave school earlier than their peers in the other two neighborhoods. They tend to work in unskilled manual jobs in nearby factories and warehouses when they do work. Projectville's young males stay in school longer than their counterparts in La Barriada or in Hamilton Park. Nearly half of our sample from Projectville had either completed a diploma or were still working toward one. As a result of their prolonged participation in schooling, they tend to enter the labor market somewhat later than the others. They then tend to move into clerical and service-sector jobs in downtown business districts. Many of these jobs require a high school diploma. As a result, though they enter the labor market somewhat later than young males in La Barriada, they have better prospects for upward mobility. Yet they still tend to earn less than their less educated counterparts in Hamilton Park.

In our earlier study of crime and employment, we found that, although many young males in each of these neighborhoods are involved in exploratory economic crimes, the blocked access to employment among the minority youths leads to more sustained and prevalent involvement in intensive criminal activities and to periods of probation and incarceration. Census and police statistics generally support our findings concerning the relative involvements of those in the three neighborhoods in schooling, work, and crime.

These career patterns are described as background for understanding the different ranges of responses to early pregnancy within each of the neighborhoods.

SEXUAL ACTIVITY

Before looking at how young males in the three neighborhoods respond to early pregnancy and whether or not they become absent fathers, it is necessary to compare their patterns of early sexual activity and contraceptive use. If we had found substantial differences, we might conclude that differences in becoming fathers at an early age were due to later or less frequent sexual activity or, alternatively, to greater use of contraceptives. In fact, our data show relatively few such differences between the neighborhood groups, although we do find such differences within each group. Almost all those in each group had experienced intercourse by the age of 15, and few had used contraceptives in their first acts of intercourse.

These findings differ somewhat from survey findings that indicate a greater likelihood of early intercourse among blacks than among whites,[5] although Hamilton Park's whites are much poorer than the middle-class whites often sampled in these surveys. In fact, we found in each neighborhood that, from their early teens on, males are almost entirely outside of adult supervision, except when they are in school, as they frequently are not. They also are encouraged to prove their manhood by sexual adventures and receive little consistent encouragement or instruction in the use of contraceptives.

What our data do suggest, however, is variations within each neighborhood in the use of contraceptives. We first sought out young fathers in each place and subsequently interviewed four or five friends of the fathers who were not themselves fathers. The nonfathers generally began sexual activity as early and heedlessly as the fathers. Some seemed to have avoided becoming fathers through chance, but others reported developing contraceptive practices that prevented their becoming fathers. These practices included some use of condoms but more often involved careful use of withdrawal or a long-term relationship with a partner who used birth-control pills.

RESPONSES TO PREGNANCY

In contract to this relative lack of difference between the neighborhoods in patterns of early sexual activity and contraception, the ranges of response to early pregnancy differed between the neighborhoods in quite distinctive ways that can be related to differences in culture, class, and social ecology. After the discovery that the partners of these young males had become pregnant, those involved in each community faced a number of choices. The first choice was whether or not the young female should seek an abortion. If not, then it had to be decided whether the young couple should get married and/or establish coresidence and what extent and manner of support and care the young father should be expected to provide for his child. These choices usually involved not just the conceiving young couple but also their parents and even extended families. In this way, individual choices became embedded in the context of the wider neighborhood community and its values and resources.

In all these choices, we found distinctive neighborhood patterns, although a range of choices was apparent within each neighborhood group. These patterns are described separately for each neighborhood. We begin with Projectville, which fits many of the stereotypes of underclass neighborhoods with high rates of out-of-wedlock childbearing by teenage mothers and related high rates of absent fatherhood. We then compare these patterns with Hamilton Park in order to assess the effects of different levels of economic opportunity. Finally, we examine La Barriada, an area that is similar to Projectville in class but different in culture and social ecology.

In Projectville, we found very ambivalent attitudes and behavior concerning the decision to seek abortions or not. Most of the young males reported extreme disapproval of abortion, often calling it murder and saying that they had urged their partners not to abort. Yet the same individuals would often say that their mothers might support abortions for their sisters. Three of them reported that they had been involved in pregnancies that terminated in abortions. In two of these cases, the decision was made by the female and her family, and the males were not involved. In the other case, the abortion was of a second pregnancy. Health statistics, which cover a fairly homogeneous area in this neighborhood, indicate that more than half of all teen pregnancies in Projectville end in abortion.

Attitudes toward marriage as a response to early pregnancy, however, were more uniform. Projectville residents generally did not encourage immediate marriage or coresidence for young parents. Two couples eventually did marry, though not until over a year after the birth, during which time the father's employment status had improved, in one case because the father had joined the military and had completed basic training. Another marriage occurred when a young mother married another male, not the father of her first child. The other fathers would be classified officially as absent. They neither married, nor, in most cases, did they establish coresidence.

Yet the absence of marriage and coresidence did not mean that they had no further relationships with the mothers and children. Although romantic commitments to the mothers tended to be volatile, most of the fathers reported strong commitments to their children. Their paternity was recognized within the neighborhood. Most eventually also established legal paternity. Further, most provided some measure of care and support, to the extent that they were able. They contributed money, some from employment, usually part-time and/or low-wage, others from criminal activities. Some continued with education and training for a time after the birth, unlike their counterparts in the other neighborhoods. In these cases, the mothers' families saw the young fathers' continued education as being in the best long-term interests of the children. These unmarried young fathers also visited regularly and frequently took the children to their own homes, for weekends or even longer periods of time. Many reported providing direct child care when they were with their children, to a greater extent than fathers in either of the other two neighborhoods.

The only ones who provided no care or support at all for some period of time were those who became heavily involved in crime or drug use and underwent incarceration, including 6 of the 16 at some point. Even these were involved with their children before or after incarceration.

These data were, of course, collected from a self-selected sample of young fathers who were willing to talk with researchers. All also reported that they knew of fathers who had "stepped off," as they put it, from their children. They attributed stepping off in some of these cases to the young fathers' inability to make contributions. Despite the self-selected nature of our sample, however, participation by young, unmarried fathers in informal systems of care and support for their children does seem to be quite common in this neighborhood. Other studies have shown that poor, black, officially absent fathers actually have more contact with and provide more informal support for their children than middle-class, white absent fathers.[6]

In Hamilton Park, we found quite different patterns of abortion, marriage, coresidence, and support. None of the young males we interviewed expressed strong condemnations of abortion, and several openly supported abortions in cases where the couple was not ready to get married. One of those who had not become a father as a teenager had avoided doing so by encouraging an abortion. Another nonfather said he would "slip her the two hundred dollars" if his partner became pregnant. Even one of the young fathers and his partner had aborted a first pregnancy and then married after a second pregnancy and before the birth.

Marriage was also more common in this group. Over half the fathers in this group married after conception and before the birth. One married before conception, he being the only one whose child was planned. Marriage also entailed setting up coresidence in apartments of their own. This pattern of family formation has deep roots in working-class tradition. Early sexual activity is a recognized form of risk taking that is often understood to lead to marriage if a pregnancy occurs.

This pattern of family formation is also strongly linked to the traditional working-class career patterns that are still maintained in this neighborhood, despite the recent pressures of economic change that threaten this way of life. Decent jobs are available, through neighborhood and family contacts, that do not depend on educational credentials and that allow young males to establish independent households and support their families. Those who got married found both work and housing through these local channels. These early unions were often

troubled, and household arrangements did shift over time. Significantly, the only case of court-ordered child support we encountered in any of the three neighborhoods was among this group of relatively economically advantaged youths.

The relatively well-paying, blue-collar jobs that have sustained this neighborhood are disappearing from the regional economy, however, and the effects of this economic erosion are evident throughout the neighborhood. Many young people leave the area for the suburbs or western states. Others become heavily involved in drugs and hang out on the streets, working irregularly. The differences in career and family-formation patterns between the neighborhoods are not absolute but matters of degree. Two of the nonmarrying fathers in Hamilton Park, for example, resembled some of their peers in Projectville, working irregularly and making regular contributions and visits but not marrying. The other nonmarrying fathers were all heavy drug users who made poor marriage prospects. One of them did not learn that he had become a father until two years later. Their children and the mothers of their children were among the AFDC recipients who, though less heavily concentrated than in the minority neighborhoods, still accounted for about 10 percent of the households in Hamilton Park.

In La Barriada, young males whose partners became pregnant also faced disappointing economic opportunities. Like their peers in Projectville and unlike some of their peers in Hamilton Park, they had relatively poor chances of being able to find jobs that would allow them to marry and provide full support for their children. Yet culture and social ecology led them to a different set of responses to their predicament.

Their attitudes toward abortion were even more negative than those we discovered in Projectville, yet some of them also had been involved in abortions. One of the nonfathers reported an abortion. In addition, three of the fathers reported abortions of second pregnancies. They said that they still disapproved of abortions but simply could not afford a second child right away. Health statistics for La Barriada and Hamilton Park were not readily comparable to those for Projectville, but statistics for the city as a whole did show the same patterns that we found: among pregnant teens, whites had the highest rate of abortions, followed by blacks and then by Hispanics.[7]

Though even less likely than those in Projectville to see abortions as a solution, the young males in La Barriada were far more likely to pursue marriage and coresidence, despite formidable obstacles in the way of their being able to support families. Only 5 of 11 fathers did not marry legally, but 3 of these described themselves as being in common-law marriages and had established coresidence. Common-law partners openly referred to themselves as "husband" and "wife," unlike the unmarried but still involved couples in Projectville.

One father, a highly religious Pentecostal, married as a virgin at 18, indicating the relatively young age at which even so-called normal marriage and parenting can occur in this group. The others married after conception, either before or after the birth. Marriage entailed coresidence, though usually in the household of one of the young couple's parents. Most coresident couples lived with the father's parents, a distinctive pattern not found in the other neighborhoods and tied to cultural expectations that the father and his family are responsible for the child and mother.

Despite their willingness to marry and establish coresidence, however, these fathers' prospects for finding jobs that paid enough and were steady enough to allow them to support families remained poor. As a result, they entered the labor market somewhat earlier than those in Projectville, yet with fewer prospects for advancement. All the young fathers ceased attending school after they became fathers, though some later returned to school or training programs. None of them remained in school continuously, as did some of the Projectville fathers.

Structural circumstances also discouraged marriage for some in La Barriada. The mothers and children in the common-law marriages, for example, all received AFDC. Refraining from marriage concealed their unions from scrutiny by the AFDC program.

Even though the young fathers from La Barriada were more likely to marry, their own family backgrounds suggested that the future of these marriages was highly doubtful. Most of them came from families in which the parents had been married, by ceremony or common-law arrangement, yet almost all their own fathers had left the households when they were young children. The departure of their own fathers was usually related to employment difficulties and led to household AFDC enrollment.

Crime and drugs also were involved in the inability of some of these young fathers to support their families. Two were incarcerated at some point and five others had some history of heavy drug use.

None of the officially absent fathers from La Barriada or Projectville had ever been involved in legal child support proceedings. Local child support agencies assigned a low priority to young fathers and especially to young, unemployed fathers. Young fathers who themselves lived with families on AFDC were automatically excluded from child support actions.

CONCLUSION

These comparisons of young males in three neighborhoods demonstrate the interrelated influences of structural economic factors, culture, and social ecology in shaping processes of family and household formation. The high rates of female-headed and AFDC-receiving households in the two minority neighborhoods are clearly related not only to an overall lack in this region of jobs paying wages that could allow men to assume traditional breadwinning roles but also to social-ecological factors that link the different neighborhoods to the regional labor market in quite different ways. The distinctive range of responses to early pregnancy in each community depends heavily on the resources that are available within that community.

Culture also plays a role in shaping local responses to teenage pregnancy. When cultural values are seen in relation to social ecology, however, they appear not as unchanging, primordial entities but rather as collective responses of people with distinctive group histories to different and changing structural positions in society. Hamilton Park's residents most closely adhere to a long-standing working-class tradition, in which teenage sexual activity is understood to be a risk-taking enterprise that should lead to marriage when pregnancy results. The erosion of well-paying entry-level jobs that have made this way of life possible, however, threatens these understandings as more young men, unable to find such jobs, turn to drugs and away from marriage.

Projectville's residents have known the link between lack of jobs and lack of marriage longer and live with much greater concentrations of joblessness and dependency, yet they have well-defined attitudes toward how to cope with these problems. They put great faith in education, despite its frequently disappointing payoffs in the job market, and they have developed complex ways of supporting children in kin-based networks.[8] Young males play important roles in these networks, which are highly flexible and adaptive to shifting circumstances.

La Barriada's residents are the most recent immigrants and cling tenaciously to a traditional culture even as its assumptions about a male's role in the family clash harshly with the realities of the low-wage labor market and the welfare system.

The influences of structural economic factors, culture, and social ecology on the actions of young men demonstrated in this analysis are not intended as disavowals of individual potential; nor are they intended as claims for an absolute cultural relativism, which would imply that processes of family formation in these neighborhoods, though different from those in the mainstream, are entirely satisfactory for local residents. To the contrary, the relationships between early pregnancy, absent fatherhood, and persistent poverty are quite evident to the residents of these communities. Some individuals in these communities do manage to escape these and other hazards of life in the inner cities. These struggles are particularly evident among Projectville residents, for example, as seen in their perseverance with education and their ambivalence toward abortion.

In none of these communities is any honor given to fathers who do not at least try to support their children. All the accounts we have heard indicate that failure to support one's children is experienced as a loss of manhood. The standards for judging individual fathers are clear within each neighborhood but differ somewhat between the neighborhoods in terms of relative emphasis on immediate cash contributions, continued education, marriage, and the provisions of child care. The higher rate at which young men in the two minority neighborhoods fail to meet such standards is a function neither of the random occurrence of high rates of pathological individuals in these areas nor of the content of ethnic culture but rather of blocked access to decent jobs.

Social policy that hopes to deal effectively with persistent poverty must move beyond assumptions that uncontrolled sexuality and an undeveloped work ethic are at the root of the problem. Policies and programs must recognize not only the powerful structural economic factors that concentrate poverty and dependency in the inner cites but also the unique ways in which individual communities attempt to reconcile their lack of access to jobs and their universal, human desire to reproduce.

At present, young males in these areas are particularly ill served by the job market, the schools, and the social welfare system. Males must be redefined as important parts of the solution and not merely as the sources of the problem. Some recent innovative efforts have been undertaken. Programs for the prevention of unwanted early pregnancy have begun to include males in their services. Some discussion has also begun concerning ways to alter the child support enforcement system to provide incentives for young fathers to acknowledge paternity. Such incentives could include connecting them to job-training and employment programs, encouraging continued education, recognizing in-kind contributions and not just cash payments, and expanding the amount they could contribute to AFDC households without having their contributions deducted from that household's AFDC budget. In order to be effective, these efforts will need to be part of an overall program of intensive and comprehensive services for inner-city children and adolescents.

ENDNOTES

1. William Julius Wilson, *The Truly Disadvantaged: The Inner City, the Underclass, and Public Policy* (Chicago: University of Chicago Press, 1987).
2. Oscar Lewis, *La Vida: A Puerto Rican Family in the Culture of Poverty—San Juan and New York* (New York: Vintage Books, 1965), p. xliv.
3. Mercer L. Sullivan, *Getting Paid: Economy, Culture, and Youth Crime in the Inner City* (Ithaca, NY: Cornell University Press, forthcoming).
4. Mercer L. Sullivan, "Teen Fathers in the Inner City: An Exploratory Ethnographic Study," mimeographed (New York: Vera Institute of Justice, 1985).
5. Freya A. Sonenstein, "Risking Paternity: Sex and Contraception among Adolescent Males," in *Adolescent Fatherhood,* ed. Arthur B. Elster and Michael E. Lamb (Hillsdale, NJ: Lawrence Erlbaum, 1986), pp. 31–54.
6. Ron Haskins et al., "Estimates of National Child Support Collections Potential and Income Security of Female-Headed Families: Final Report to the Office of Child Support Administration, Social Security Administration" (Bush Institute for Child and Family Policy, Frank Porter Graham Child Development Center, University of North Carolina, 1985).
7. Adolescent Pregnancy Interagency Council, *A Coordinated Strategy on the Issues of Adolescent Pregnancy and Parenting* (New York: Mayor's Office of Adolescent Pregnancy and Parenting Services, 1986), p. 10.
8. Carol B. Stack, *All Our Kin: Strategies for Survival in a Black Community* (New York: Harper & Row, 1974).

READING 5-2

Families on the Fault Line

Lillian B. Rubin

THE TOMALSONS

When I last met the Tomalsons, Gwen was working as a clerk in the office of a large Manhattan company and was also a student at a local college where she was studying nursing. George Tomalson, who had worked for three years in a furniture factory, where he laminated plastic to wooden frames, had been thrown out of a job when the company went bankrupt. He seemed a gentle man then, unhappy over the turn his life had taken but still wanting to believe that it would come out all right.

Now, as he sits before me in the still nearly bare apartment, George is angry. "If you're a black man in this country, you don't have a chance, that's all, not a chance. It's like no matter how hard you try, you're nothing but trash. I've been looking for work for over two years now, and there's nothing. White people are complaining all the time that black folks are getting a break. Yeah, well, I don't know who those people are, because it's not me or anybody else I know. People see a black man coming, they run the other way, that's what I know."

"You haven't found any work at all for two years?" I ask.

"Some temporary jobs, a few weeks sometimes, a couple of months once, mostly doing shit work for peanuts. Nothing I could count on."

"If you could do any kind of work you want, what would you do?"

He smiles, "That's easy; I'd be a carpenter. I'm good with my hands, and I know a lot about it," he says, holding his hands out, palms up, and looking at them proudly. But his mood shifts quickly; the smile disappears; his voice turns harsh. "But that's not going to happen. I tried to get into the union, but there's no room there for a black guy. And in this city, without being in the union, you don't have a chance at a construction job. They've got it all locked up, and they're making sure they keep it for themselves."

When I talk with Gwen later, she worries about the intensity of her husband's resentment. "It's not like George; he's always been a real even guy. But he's moody now, and he's so angry, I sometimes wonder what he might do. This place is a hell hole," she says, referring to the housing project they live in. "It's getting worse all the time; kids with guns, all the drugs, grown men out of work all around. I'll bet there's hardly a man in this whole place who's got a job, leave alone a good one."

"Just what is it you worry about?"

She hesitates, clearly wondering whether to speak, how much to tell me about her fears, then says with a shrug, "I don't know, everything, I guess. There's so much crime and drugs and stuff out there. You can't help wondering whether he'll get tempted." She stops herself, looks at me intently, and says, "Look, don't get me wrong; I know it's crazy to think like that. He's not that kind of person. But when you live in times like these, you can't help worrying about everything.

"We both worry a lot about the kids at school. Every time I hear about another kid shot while they're at school, I get like a raving lunatic. What's going on in this world that kids are killing kids? Doesn't anybody care that so many black kids are dying like that? It's like a black child's life doesn't count for anything. How do they expect our kids to grow up to be good citizens when nobody cares about them?

"It's one of the things that drives George crazy, worrying about the kids. There's no way you can keep them safe around here. Sometimes I wonder why we send them to school. They're not getting much of an education there. Michelle just started, but Julia's in the fifth grade, and believe me, she's not learning much.

"We sit over her every night to make sure she does her homework and gets it right. But what good is it if the people at school aren't doing their job. Most of the teachers there don't give a damn. They just want the paycheck and the hell with the kids. Everybody knows it's not like that in the white schools; white people wouldn't stand for it.

"I keep thinking we've got to get out of here for the sake of the kids. I'd love to move someplace, anyplace out of the city where the schools aren't such a cesspool. But," she says dejectedly, "we'll never get out if George can't find a decent job. I'm just beginning my nursing career, and I know I've got a future now. But still, no matter what I do or how long I work at it, I can't make enough for that by myself."

George, too, has dreams of moving away, somewhere far from the city streets, away from the grime and the crime. "Look at this place," he says, his sweeping gesture taking in the whole landscape. "Is this any place to raise kids? Do you know what my little girls see every day they walk out the door? Filth, drugs, guys hanging on the corner waiting for trouble.

"If I could get any kind of a decent job, anything, we'd be out of here, far away, someplace outside the city where the kids could breathe clean and see a different life. It's so bad here, I take them over to my mother's a lot after school; it's a better neighborhood. Then we stay over there and eat sometimes. Mom likes it; she's lonely, and it helps us out. Not that she's got that much, but there's a little pension my father left.

"What about Gwen's family? Do they help out, too?"

"Her mother doesn't have anything to help with since her father died. He's long gone; he was killed by the cops when Gwen was a teenager," he says as calmly as if reporting the time of day.

"Killed by the cops!" The words leap out at me and jangle my brain. But why do they startle me so? Surely with all the discussion of police violence in the black community in recent years, I can't be surprised to hear that a black man was "killed by the cops."

It's the calmness with which the news is relayed that gets to me. And it's the realization once again of the distance between the lives and experiences of blacks and others, even poor others. Not one white person in this study reported a violent death in the family. Nor did any of the Latino and Asian families, although the Latinos spoke of a difficult and often antagonistic relationship with Anglo authorities, especially the police. But four black families (13 percent) told of relatives who had been murdered, one of the families with two victims—a teenage son and a 22-year-old daughter, both killed in violent street crimes.

But I'm also struck by the fact that Gwen never told me how her father died. True, I didn't ask. But I wonder now why she didn't offer the information. "Gwen didn't tell me," I say, as if trying to explain my surprise.

"She doesn't like to talk about it. Would you?" he replies somewhat curtly.

It's a moment or two before I can collect myself to speak again. Then I comment, "You talk about all this so calmly."

He leans forward, looks directly at me, and shakes his head. When he finally speaks, his voice is tight with the effort to control his rage. "What do you want? Should I rant and rave? You want me to say I want to go out and kill those mothers? Well, yeah, I do. They killed a good man just because he was black. He wasn't a criminal; he was a hard-working guy who just happened to be in the wrong place when the cops were looking for someone to shoot," he says, then sits back and stares stonily at the wall in front of him.

We both sit locked in silence until finally I break it. "How did it happen?"

He rouses himself at the sound of my voice. "They were after some dude who robbed a liquor store, and when they saw Gwen's dad, they didn't ask questions; they shot. The bastards. Then they said it was self-defense, that they saw a gun in his hand. That man never held a gun in his life, and nobody ever found one either. But nothing happens to them; it's no big deal, just another dead nigger," he concludes, his eyes blazing.

It's quiet again for a few moments, then, with a sardonic half smile, he says, "What would a nice, white middle-class lady like you know about any of that? You got all those degrees, writing books and all that. How are you going to write about people like us?"

"I was poor like you once, very poor," I say somewhat defensively.

He looks surprised, then retorts, "Poor and white; it's a big difference."

Thirty years before the beginning of the Civil War, Alexis de Tocqueville wrote: "If ever America undergoes great revolutions, they will be brought about by the presence of the black race on the soil of the United States; that is to say they will owe their origin, not to the equality, but to the "inequality of condition."[1] One hundred and sixty years later, relations between blacks and whites remain one of the great unresolved issues in American life, and "the inequality of condition" that de Tocqueville observed is still a primary part of the experience of black Americans.

I thought about de Tocqueville's words as I listened to George Tomalson and about how the years of unemployment had changed him from, as Gwen said, "a real even guy" to an angry and embittered one. And I was reminded, too, of de Tocqueville's observation that "the danger of conflict between the white and black inhabitants perpetually haunts the imagination of the [white] Americans, like a painful dream."[2] Fifteen generations later we're still paying the cost of those years when Americans held slaves—whites still living in fear, blacks in rage. "People see a black man coming, they run the other way," says George Tomalson.

Yet however deep the cancer our racial history has left on the body of the nation, most Americans, including many blacks, believe that things are better today than they were a few decades ago—a belief that's both true and not true.[3] There's no doubt that in ending the legal basis for discrimination and segregation, the nation took an important step toward fulfilling the promise of equality for all Americans. As more people meet as equals in the workplace, stereotypes begin to fall away and caricatures are transformed into real people. But it's also true that the economic problems of recent decades have raised the level of anxiety in American life to a new high. So although virtually all whites today give verbal assent to the need for racial justice and equality, they also find ways to resist the implementation of the belief when it seems to threaten their own status or economic well-being.

Our schizophrenia about race, our capacity to believe one thing and do another, is not new. Indeed, it is perhaps epitomized by Thomas Jefferson, the great liberator. For surely, as Gordon Wood writes in an essay in the *New York Review of Books,* "there is no greater irony in American history than the fact that America's supreme spokesman for liberty and equality was a lifelong aristocratic owner of slaves."[4]

Jefferson spoke compellingly about the evils of slavery, but he bought, sold, bred, and flogged slaves. He wrote eloquently about equality but

he was convinced that blacks were an inferior race and endorsed the racial stereotypes that have characterized African Americans since their earliest days on this continent. He believed passionately in individual liberty, but he couldn't imagine free blacks living in America, maintaining instead that if the nation considered emancipating the slaves, it must also prepare for their expulsion.

No one talks seriously about expulsion anymore. Nor do many use the kind of language to describe African Americans that was so common in Jefferson's day. But the duality he embodied—his belief in justice, liberty, and equality alongside his conviction of black inferiority—still lives.

THE RIVERAS

Once again Ana Rivera and I sit at the table in her bright and cheerful kitchen. She's sipping coffee; I'm drinking some bubbly water while we make small talk and get reacquainted. After a while, we begin to talk about the years since we last met. "I'm a grandmother now," she says, her face wreathed in a smile. "My daughter Karen got married and had a baby, and he's the sweetest little boy, smart, too. He's only two and a half, but you should hear him. He sounds like five."

"When I talked to her the last time I was here, Karen was planning to go to college. What happened?" I ask.

She flushes uncomfortably. "She got pregnant, so she had to get married. I was heartbroken at first. She was only 19, and I wanted her to get an education so bad. It was awful; she had been working for a whole year to save money for college, then she got pregnant and couldn't go."

"You say she had to get married. Did she ever consider an abortion?"

"I don't know; we never talked about it. We're Catholic," she says by way of explanation. "I mean, I don't believe in abortion." She hesitates, seeming uncertain about what more she wants to say, then adds, "I have to admit, at a time like that, you have to ask yourself what you really believe. I don't think anybody's got the right to take a child's life. But when I thought about what having that baby would do to Karen's life, I couldn't help thinking, *What if . . . ?*" She stops, unable to bring herself to finish the sentence.

"Did you ever say that to Karen?"

"No, I would *never* do that. I didn't even tell my husband I thought such things. But, you know," she adds, her voice dropping to nearly a whisper, "if she had done it, I don't think I would have said a word."

"What about the rest of the kids?"

"Paul's going to be 19 soon; he's a problem," she sighs. "I mean, he's got a good head, but he won't use it. I don't know what's the matter with kids these days; it's like they want everything but they're not willing to work for anything. He hardly finished high school, so you can't talk to him about going to college. But what's he going to do? These days if you don't have a good education, you don't have a chance. No matter what we say, he doesn't listen, just goes on his smart-alecky way, hanging around the neighborhood with a bunch of no-good kids looking for trouble.

"Rick's so mad, he wants to throw him out of the house. But I say no, we can't do that because then what'll become of him? So we fight about that a lot, and I don't know what's going to happen."

"Does Paul work at all?"

"Sometimes, but mostly not. I'm afraid to think about where he gets money from. His father won't give him a dime. He borrows from me sometimes, but I don't have much to give him. And anyway, Rick would kill me if he knew."

I remember Paul as a gangly, shy 16-year-old, no macho posturing, none of the rage that shook his older brother, not a boy I would have thought would be heading for trouble. But

then, Karen, too, had seemed so determined to grasp at a life that was different from the one her parents were living. What happens to these kids?

When I talk with Rick about these years, he, too, asks in bewilderment: What happened? "I don't know; we tried so hard to give the kids everything they needed. I mean, sure, we're not rich, and there's a lot of things we couldn't give them. But we were always here for them; we listened; we talked. What happened? First my daughter gets pregnant and has to get married; now my son is becoming a bum."

"Roberto—that's what we have to call him now," explains Rick, "he says it's what happens when people don't feel they've got respect. He says we'll keep losing our kids until they really believe they really have an equal chance. I don't know; I knew I had to *make* the Anglos respect me, and I had to make my chance. Why don't my kids see it like that?" he asks wearily, his shoulders seeming to sag lower with each sentence he speaks.

"I guess it's really different today, isn't it?" he sighs. "When I was coming up, you could still make your chance. I mean, I only went to high school, but I got a job and worked myself up. You can't do that anymore. Now you need to have some kind of special skills just to get a job that pays more than the minimum wage.

"And the schools, they don't teach kids anything anymore. I went to the same public schools my kids went to, but what a difference. It's like nobody cares anymore."

"How is Roberto doing?" I ask, remembering the hostile eighteen-year-old I interviewed several years earlier.

"He's still mad; he's always talking about injustice and things like that. But he's different than Paul. Roberto always had some goals. I used to worry about him because he's so angry all the time. But I see now that his anger helps him. He wants to fight for his people, to make things better for everybody. Paul, he's like the wind; nothing matters to him.

"Right now, Roberto has a job as an electrician's helper, learning the trade. He's been working there for a couple of years; he's pretty good at it. But I think—I hope—he's going to go to college. He heard that they're trying to get Chicano students to go to the university, so he applied. If he gets some aid, I think he'll go," Rick says, his face radiant at the thought that at least one of his children will fulfill his dream. "Ana and me, we tell him even if he doesn't get aid, he should go. We can't do a lot because we have to help Ana's parents and that takes a big hunk every month. But we'll help him, and he could work to make up the rest. I know it's hard to work and go to school, but people do it all the time, and he's smart; he could do it."

His gaze turns inward; then, as if talking to himself, he says, "I never thought I'd say this but I think Roberto's right. We've got something to learn from some of these kids. I told that to Roberto just the other day. He says Ana and me have been trying to pretend we're one of them all of our lives. I told him, 'I think you're right.' I kept thinking if I did everything right, I wouldn't be a 'greaser.' But after all these years, I'm still a 'greaser' in their eyes. It took my son to make me see it. Now I know. If I weren't I'd be head of the shipping department by now, not just one of the supervisors, and maybe Paul wouldn't be wasting his life on the corner."

We keep saying that family matters, that with a stable family and two caring parents children will grow to a satisfactory adulthood. But I've rarely met a family that's more constant or more concerned than the Riveras. Or one where both parents are so involved with their children. Ana was a full-time homemaker until Paul, their youngest, was 12. Rick has been with the same company for more than 25 years, having worked his way up from clerk to shift supervisor in its shipping department. Whatever the conflicts in their marriage, theirs is clearly a warm, respectful, and caring relationship. Yet their daughter got pregnant and gave up her plans for college,

and a son is idling his youth away on a street corner.

Obviously, then, something more than family matters. Growing up in a world where opportunities are available makes a difference. As does being able to afford to take advantage of an opportunity when it comes by. Getting an education that broadens horizons and prepares a child for a productive adulthood makes a difference. As does being able to find work that nourishes self-respect and pays a living wage. Living in a world that doesn't judge you by the color of your skin makes a difference. As does feeling the respect of the people around you.

This is not to suggest that there aren't also real problems inside American families that deserve our serious and sustained attention. But the constant focus on the failure of family life as the locus of both our personal and social difficulties has become a mindless litany, a dangerous diversion from the economic and social realities that make family life so difficult today and that so often destroy it.

Two decades ago, when I began the research for *Worlds of Pain,* we were living in the immediate aftermath of the civil rights revolution that had convulsed the nation since the mid-1950s. Significant gains had been won. And despite the tenacity with which this headway had been resisted by some, most white Americans were feeling good about themselves. No one expected the nation's racial problems and conflicts to dissolve easily or quickly. But there was also a sense that we were moving in the right direction, that there was a national commitment to redressing at least some of the worst aspects of black–white inequality.

In the intervening years, however, the national economy buckled under the weight of three recessions, while the nation's industrial base was undergoing a massive restructuring. At the same time, government policies requiring preferential treatment were enabling African-Americans and other minorities to make small but visible inroads into what had been, until then, largely white terrain. The sense of scarcity, always a part of American life but intensified sharply by the history of these economic upheavals, made minority gains seem particularly threatening to white working-class families.

It isn't, of course, just working-class whites who feel threatened by minority progress. Wherever racial minorities make inroads into formerly all-white territory, tensions increase. But it's working-class families who feel the fluctuations in the economy most quickly and most keenly. For them, these last decades have been like a bumpy roller coaster ride. "Every time we think we might be able to get ahead, it seems like we get knocked down again," declares Tom Ahmundsen, a 42-year-old white construction worker. "Things look a little better; there's a little more work; then all of a sudden, boom, the economy falls apart and it's gone. You can't count on anything; it really gets you down."

This is the story I heard repeatedly: Each small climb was followed by a fall, each glimmer of hope replaced by despair. As the economic vise tightened, despair turned to anger. But partly because we have so little concept of class resentment and conflict in America, this anger isn't directed so much at those above as at those below. And when whites at or near the bottom of the ladder look down in this nation, they generally see blacks and other minorities.

True, during all of the 1980s and into the 1990s, white ire was fostered by national administrations that fanned racial discord as a way of fending off white discontent—of diverting anger about the state of the economy and the declining quality of urban life to the foreigners and racial others in our midst. But our history of racial animosity coupled with our lack of class consciousness made this easier to accomplish than it might otherwise have been.

The difficult realities of white working-class life not withstanding, however, their whiteness has accorded them significant advantages—both materially and psychologically—over people of color. Racial discrimination and segregation in the workplace have kept competition for the best jobs at a minimum. They do, obviously, have to compete with each other for the resources available. But that's different. It's a competition among equals; they're all white. They don't think such things consciously, of course; they don't have to. It's understood, rooted in the culture and supported by the social contract that says they are the superior ones, the worthy ones. Indeed, this is precisely why, when the courts or the legislatures act in ways that seem to contravene that belief, whites experience themselves as victims.

From the earliest days of the republic, whiteness has been the ideal, and freedom and independence have been linked to being white. "Republicanism," writes labor historian David Roediger, "had long emphasized that the strength, virtue and resolve of a people guarded them from enslavement."[5] And it was whites who had these qualities in abundance, as was evident, in the peculiarly circuitous reasoning of the time, in the fact that they were not slaves.

By this logic, the enslavement of blacks could be seen as stemming from their "slavishness" rather than from the institution of slavery. Slavery is gone now, but the reasoning lingers on in white America, which still insists that the lowly estate of people of color is due to their deficits, whether personal or cultural, rather than to the prejudice, discrimination, and institutionalized racism that has barred them from full participation in the society.

This is not to say that culture is irrelevant, whether among black Americans or any other group in our society. The lifeways of a people develop out of their experiences—out of the daily events, large and small, that define their lives; out of the resources that are available to them to meet both individual and group needs; out of the place in the social, cultural, and political systems within which group life is embedded. In the case of a significant proportion of blacks in America's inner cities, centuries of racism and economic discrimination have produced a subculture that is both personally and socially destructive. But to fault culture or the failure of individual responsibility without understanding the larger context within which such behaviors occur is to miss a vital piece of the picture. Nor does acknowledging the existence of certain destructive subcultural forms among some African-Americans disavow or diminish the causal connections between the structural inequalities at the social, political, and economic levels and the serious social problems at the community level.

In his study of "working-class lads" in Birmingham, England, for example, Paul Willis observes that their very acts of resistance to middle-class norms—the defiance with which these young men express their anger at class inequalities—help to reinforce the class structure by further entrenching them in their working-class status.[6] The same can be said for some of the young men in the African-American community, whose active rejection of white norms and "in your face" behavior consigns them to the bottom of the American economic order.

To understand this doesn't make such behavior, whether in England or the United States, any more palatable. But it helps to explain the structural sources of cultural forms and to apprehend the social processes that undergird them. Like Willis's white "working-class lads," the hip-hoppers and rappers in the black community who are so determinedly "not white" are not just making a statement about black culture. They're also expressing their rage at white society for offering a promise of equality, then refusing to fulfill it. In the process, they're finding their own way to some accommodation and to a place in the world they can call their own, albeit one that ultimately reinforces their outsider status.

But, some might argue, white immigrants also suffered prejudice and discrimination in the years after they first arrived, but they found more socially acceptable ways to accommodate.

It's true—and so do most of today's people of color, both immigrant and native born. Nevertheless, there's another truth as well. For wrenching as their early experiences were for white ethnics, they had an out. Writing about the Irish, for example, Roediger shows how they were able to insist upon their whiteness and to prove it by adopting the racist attitudes and behaviors of other whites, in the process often becoming leaders in the assault against blacks. With time and their growing political power, they won the prize they sought—recognition as whites. "The imperative to define themselves as white," writes Roediger, "came from the particular 'public and psychological wages' whiteness offered to a desperate rural and often preindustrial Irish population coming to labor in industrializing American cities."[7]

Thus does whiteness bestow its psychological as well as material blessings on even the most demeaned. For no matter how far down the socioeconomic ladder whites may fall, the one thing they can't lose is their whiteness. No small matter because, as W. E. B. DuBois observed decades ago, the compensation of white workers includes a psychological wage, a bonus that enables them to believe in their inherent superiority over nonwhites.[8]

It's also true, however, that this same psychological bonus that white workers prize so highly has cost them dearly. For along with the importation of an immigrant population, the separation of black and white workers has given American capital a reserve labor force to call upon whenever white workers seemed to them to get too "uppity." Thus, while racist ideology enables white workers to maintain the belief in their superiority, they have paid for that conviction by becoming far more vulnerable in the struggle for decent wages and working conditions than they might otherwise have been.

Politically and economically, the ideology of white supremacy disables white workers from making the kind of interracial alliances that would benefit all of the working class. Psychologically, it leaves them exposed to the double-edged sword of which I spoke earlier. On one side, their belief in the superiority of whiteness helps to reassure them that they're not at the bottom of the social hierarchy. But their insistence that their achievements are based on their special capacities and virtues, that it's only incompetence that keeps others from grabbing a piece of the American dream, threatens their precarious sense of self-esteem. For if they're the superior ones, the deserving ones, the ones who earned their place solely through hard work and merit, there's nothing left but to blame themselves for their inadequacies when hard times strike.

In the opening sentences of *Worlds of Pain* I wrote that America was choking on its differences. If we were choking then, we're being asphyxiated now. As the economy continues to falter, and local, state, and federal governments keep cutting services, there are more and more acrimonious debates about who will share in the shrinking pie. Racial and ethnic groups, each in their own corners, square off as they ready themselves for what seems to be the fight of their lives. Meanwhile, the quality of life for all but the wealthiest Americans is spiraling downward—a plunge that's felt most deeply by those at the lower end of the class spectrum, regardless of color.[9]

As more and more mothers of young children work full-time outside the home, the question of who will raise the children comes center stage. Decent, affordable child care is scandalously scarce, with no government intervention in sight for this crucial need. In poor and working-class families, therefore, child care often is uncertain and inadequate, leaving parents apprehensive and children at risk. To deal with their fears, substantial numbers of couples now work different shifts, a solution to the child-care problem that puts its own particular strains on family life.

In families with two working parents, time has become their most precious commodity—time to attend to the necessary tasks of family life; time to nurture the relationships between wife and husband, between parents and children; time for oneself, time for others; time for solitude, time for a social life.[10] Today more than ever before, family life has become impoverished for want of time, adding another threat to the already fragile bonds that hold families together.

While women's presence in the labor force has given them a measure of independence unknown before, most also are stuck with doing two days' work in one—one on the job, the other when they get home at night. Unlike their counterparts in the earlier era, today's women are openly resentful about the burdens they carry, which makes for another dimension of conflict between wives and husbands.

Although the men generally say they've never heard of Robert Bly or any of the other modern-day gurus of manhood, the idea of men as victims has captured their imagination.[11] Given the enormous amount of publicity these men's advocates have garnered in the last few years, it's likely that some of their ideas have filtered into the awareness of the men in this study, even if they don't know how they got there. But their belief in their victimization is also a response to the politics of our time, when so many different groups—women, gays, racial minorities, the handicapped—have demanded special privileges and entitlements on the basis of past victimization. And once the language of victimization enters the political discourse, it becomes a useful tool for anyone wanting to resist the claims of others or to stake one of their own.

As the men see it, then, if their wives are victims because of the special burdens of women, the husbands, who bear their own particular hardships, can make the claim as well. If African-American men are victims because of past discrimination, then the effort to redress their grievances turns white men into victims of present discrimination.

To those who have been victimized by centuries of racism, sexism, homophobia, and the like, the idea that straight white men are victims, too, seems ludicrous. Yet it's not wholly unreal, at least not for the men in this study who have so little control over their fate and who so often feel unheard and invisible, like little more than shadows shouting into the wind.

Whether inside the family or in the larger world outside, white men keep hearing that they're the privileged ones, words that seem to them like a bad joke. How can they be advantaged when their inner experience is that they're perched precariously on the edge of a chasm that seems to have opened up in the earth around them? It's this sense of vulnerability, coupled with the conviction that their hardships go unseen and their pain unattended, that nourishes their claim to victimhood.

Some analysts of family and social life undoubtedly will argue that the picture I've presented here is too grim, that it gives insufficient weight to both the positive changes in family life and the gains in race relations over these past decades. It's true that the social and cultural changes we've witnessed have created families that, in some ways at least, are more responsive to the needs of their members, more democratic than any we have known before.[12] But it's also true that without the economic stability they need, even the most positive changes will not be enough to hold families together.

Certainly, too, alongside the racial and ethnic divisions that are so prominent a part of American life today is the reality that many more members of these warring groups than ever before are living peaceably together in our schools, our factories, our shops, our corporations, and our neighborhoods. And, except for black–white marriages, many more are marrying and raising children together than would have seemed possible a few decades ago.

At the same time, there's reason to fear. The rise of ethnicity and the growing racial separation also means an escalating level of conflict that sometimes seems to threaten to fragment the nation. In this situation, ethnic entrepreneurs like Al Sharpton in New York and David Duke in Louisiana rise to power and prominence by fanning ethnic and racial discord. A tactic that works so well precisely because the economic pressures are felt so keenly on all sides of the racial fissures, because both whites and people of color now feel so deeply that "it's not fair."

As I reflect on the differences in family and social life in the last two decades, it seems to me that we were living then in a more innocent age—a time, difficult though it was for the working-class families of our nation, when we could believe anything was possible. Whether about the economy, race relations, or life inside the family, most Americans believed that the future promised progress, that the solution to the social problems and inequities of the age were within our grasp, that sacrifice today would pay off tomorrow. This is perhaps the biggest change in the last 20 years: The innocence is gone.

But is this a cause for mourning? Perhaps only when innocence is gone and our eyes unveiled will we be able to grasp fully the depth of our conflicts and the sources from which they spring.

We live in difficult and dangerous times, in a country deeply divided by class, race, and social philosophy. The pain with which so many American families are living today, and the anger they feel, won't be alleviated by a retreat to false optimism and easy assurances. Only when we are willing to see and reckon with the magnitude of our nation's problems and our people's suffering, only when we take in the full measure of that reality, will we be able to find the path to change. Until then, all our attempts at solutions will fail. And this, ultimately, will be the real cause for mourning. For without substantial change in both our public and our private worlds, it is not just the future of the family that is imperiled but the very life of the nation itself.

ENDNOTES

1. Alexis de Tocqueville, *Democracy in America,* George Lawrence, trans., J. P. Mayer, ed. (New York: Anchor Books, 1969), p. 639.
2. Ibid.
3. For a longitudinal study of racial attitudes among both African Americans and whites, see Robert Blauner, *Black Lives, White Lives* (Berkeley: University of California Press, 1989).
4. *New York Review of Books,* May 13, 1993.
5. David R. Roediger, *Wages of Whiteness: Race & the Making of the American Working Class,* p. 35. (Pub by Verso UK 1991).
6. Paul Willis, *Learning to Labour* (New York: Columbia University Press, 1977).
7. David R. Roediger, *Wages of Whiteness: Race & the Making of the American Working Class,* p. 137. (Pub by Verso UK 1991). For a full discussion of this issue, see chapter 7, pp. 133–163, "Irish-American Workers and White Racial Formation in the Antebellum United States."
8. W. E. B. DuBois, *Black Reconstruction in the United States, 1860–1880* (New York: Harcourt Brace, 1935).
9. When adjusted for inflation, the average after-tax income of the one hundred million Americans who make up the bottom two-fifths of the income spectrum has fallen sharply since 1977. The average of the middle fifth of households has edged up 2–4 percent. But the average after-tax income of upper middle-income households has climbed more than 10 percent. And among the wealthiest 5 percent of taxpayers—those with incomes of $91,750 and more—after-tax income rose more than 60 percent during this period (Robert Greenstein, "The Kindest Cut," *The American Prospect* [Fall 1991]: 49–57.
10. Juliet Schor, *The Overworked American: The Unexpected Decline of Leisure* (New York: Basic) shows that Americans now work 140 hours a year more than they did 20 years ago. Partly at least this is because most people need every dollar they can earn, so they're reluctant to give up any part of their income for leisure. In fact, large numbers of working-class people forgo taking their vacation time off and take the money instead while continuing to work, thereby earning double wages for the vacation period.
11. Robert Bly, *Iron John* (Reading, Mass.: Addison-Wesley, 1990). See also Sam Keen, *Fire in the Belly* (New York: Bantam Books, 1991).
12. See, for example, Judith Stacey, *Brave New Families* (New York: Basic Books, 1990); Stephanie Coontz, *The Way We Never Were;* and Arlene Skolnick, *Embattled Paradise.*

CHAPTER 6

The Family, the State, and Social Policy

In 1996, the U.S. Congress passed the most sweeping changes since the Great Depression in the program that provides cash assistance to poor families with children. President Bill Clinton, who had promised in his 1992 campaign to "end welfare as we know it," overcame misgivings about the bill and signed it. With the stroke of his pen, "welfare," as the program is commonly called, was transformed from an open-ended source of income to a program that required work and limited the amount of time that families could spend on the rolls. The debates over the new bill and its consequences reflect many of the main themes of the broader policy debates between liberals and conservatives over family issues.[1]

The legislation is so new that there are few good articles that provide the background to its passage, explain its main provisions, and discuss its consequences for children and families. So I decided to write the following article, "How Will the 1996 Welfare Reform Law Affect Poor Fami-

lies?" for this volume. I hope it will help the reader make sense of this momentous change in public policy toward poor families.

Notably absent from the debates about welfare during this period were the voices of the recipients themselves. They are assumed by many Americans to be malingerers who have many children at government expense and whose family ties have broken down. Mark Rank intensively studied 50 welfare families selected randomly from a Wisconsin county for his book, *Life on the Edge: The Realities of Welfare in America.* He also analyzed the case records of nearly 3,000 welfare recipients from the same county. Rank found that their family lives did not resemble the stereotypes. They did not have lots of children, and they had close ties to kin— older parents, sisters, aunts, cousins, and others who helped them out. He did find that marriage seemed weaker among this group; there was less marriage and more separation and divorce than among the general population. His chapter on the family dynamics of the welfare recipients is excerpted here.

---

[1]See *Public and Private Families: An Introduction,* pp. 167–174.

READING 6-1

How Will the 1996 Welfare Reform Law Affect Poor Families?*

Andrew J. Cherlin

When Bill Clinton promised during the 1992 presidential election campaign that he would "end welfare as we know it," he didn't realize how sweeping his promise would prove. In August 1996, he signed into law a striking bill that has the potential to thoroughly transform the welfare system. According to its supporters, it will help poor families by restoring their motivation to work and making them self-sufficient. According to its detractors, it will cause untold suffering and misery for poor families by cutting off their financial support. In truth, neither group knows for sure what the results of the new legislation will be for poor families. It is a great experiment with the lives of millions of parents and children.

POOR LAWS IN THE PAST

There is nothing particularly new about public assistance to the poor; it has been part of Western society for several hundred years. Before working for wages was common, most poor people were attached to the land, either farming their own plot or farming someone else's fields and keeping part of the harvest. Although there were plenty of poor families, they were not very visible. But as working for wages became common and cities began to grow, many people migrated to urban areas in search of paid work. Those who could not find or keep steady jobs formed a dispossessed group that often was reduced to begging. Faced with this suddenly visi-

ble problem, societies began to formulate ways to reduce the worst of the misery they saw.

The early "poor laws" were based on principles that still characterize public assistance to the poor today. The principles were aimed, above all, at enforcing work among the poor. First, a distinction was made between the *deserving* and *undeserving* poor. Infants, the elderly, and the chronically ill were held incapable of working and therefore deserving of public assistance. But older children and able-bodied adults were held to be capable of working and therefore undeserving of assistance. Second, the amount of assistance was kept lower than the prevailing wage in the area so that public aid would be less attractive than working. Third, assistance to the poor was administered by local authorities rather than national authorities, on the theory that they knew best the local labor market conditions and need for workers. Thus, the early laws were designed to provide a bare minimum of assistance to persons deemed incapable of working and almost no assistance to persons deemed capable of working.

In the United States, these principles characterized assistance to the poor throughout the 1800s and the first few decades of the 1900s (Katz, 1996). Assistance to the poor was carried out by a mixture of local government agencies and private charities. There was no national program of assistance to the poor, although many states instituted pensions for widowed mothers in the early 1900s (Skocpol, 1992). But in the 1930s, the old system was overwhelmed by the demands of the huge number of people who were unable to find work during the Great Depression. After winning the 1932 election, Franklin D. Roosevelt expanded federal relief efforts and convinced Congress to pass landmark social legislation that greatly expanded the federal government's role in assisting the poor, the unemployed, and the elderly.

FEDERAL WELFARE POLICY, 1935–1996

The major piece of legislation, the Social Security Act of 1935, began the modern era of gov-

---

Andrew J. Cherlin, "How Will the 1996 Welfare Reform Laws Affect Poor Families" (original article). Copyright © 1997 by Andrew J. Cherlin. Reprinted with the permission of the author.

*I wish to thank Mark Rank and Estelle Young for comments on an earlier version of this article.

ernment assistance to the poor. It established Social Security (the nation's system of retirement benefits), unemployment compensation for workers who lose their jobs, and Aid to Families with Dependent Children (AFDC), the program of cash assistance to low-income, single parents and their children.[1] It is the AFDC program that has come to be known informally as "welfare." All three programs were established as entitlements, meaning that if a person qualified for a benefit (as by retiring or being laid off from work), the government had to provide it. But whereas Social Security was a national program in which the federal government merely issued checks, the AFDC program followed many of the old principles, reflecting the continuing ambivalence about providing cash assistance to the poor. AFDC was administered at the state rather than the national level, with each state free to set the amount of its benefit. In general, states with lower wages set their benefit rates lower. After the state established its benefit level, the federal government agreed to pay about half of the cost of the program. AFDC also excluded two-parent families because men were viewed as capable of working and supporting their families.

Most of the families that received AFDC in the 1930s were headed by widowed mothers, who were judged to be deserving of assistance. This assistance allowed them to stay home and raise their children. Because the rates of divorce and childbearing outside of marriage were far lower than today, no one expected that large numbers of separated, divorced, and never-married mothers would be applying for assistance. But by the 1960s, changes in the American family had greatly altered the characteristics of the typical welfare-receiving parent. Due to increases in the divorce rate, declines in the death rate, and increases in the proportion of births to unmarried mothers, the vast majority of adult recipients were not widowed but separated, divorced, or never-married. Although it was just as hard for divorced single parents to raise children as for widowed single parents,

some Americans viewed them as less deserving for having chosen to divorce or to have children outside of marriage.

During the 1960s, the welfare rolls expanded sharply as states eased their eligibility requirements and advocates for the poor urged families to apply. Several factors underlay the increase. First, the civil rights movement raised public consciousness to the plight of the poor. Second, the expanding American economy provided a larger pie from which to give the poor a slice. Third, African Americans rioted in several cities, scaring and troubling politicians (Piven and Cloward, 1993). The expansion brought more minority families onto the rolls, many of whom were visibly concentrated in central city ghettos. (In 1993, about 39 percent of AFDC recipients were African American, and 21 percent were Hispanics, who could be of any race [U.S. Bureau of the Census, 1996].)

As long as the economy was strong, few people seemed concerned about the expansion, but as the boom era ended in the 1970s, public sentiment against AFDC grew. Critics charged that the system discouraged work and instead encouraged people to become dependent on government support. The white majority's misperception that the typical welfare family was black eroded their empathy for the families on the rolls (Quadagno, 1994). Another common complaint was that welfare was imposing too much of a tax burden on workers, even though AFDC cost far less than several other government social programs.[2]

Another underlying factor was that the work lives of women had changed greatly since the passage of the Social Security Act of 1935. In the second half of the 20th century, millions of married and unmarried mothers entered the paid labor force. By the 1990s, a majority of married mothers with children under 18—and even a majority of mothers with preschool-age children—were working outside the home (Cherlin, 1992). Because of this social change, it became more difficult to argue that poor mothers deserved assistance so they could stay home and raise their children. Gradually, the status of poor mothers shifted in public opinion from the deserving to the undeserving poor.

Liberal defenders of AFDC argued that the number of recipients had increased because of a shortage of jobs for unskilled workers that paid enough to sustain a family. Therefore, according to this view, blaming poor families for receiving welfare amounted to blaming the victims of social inequality (Handler, 1995). Supporters of the program, however, were unable to prevent a series of changes to AFDC in the 1970s and 1980s that imposed ever-tougher work requirements for adult recipients.

By the late 1980s, even liberals seemed willing to concede that it was fair to ask poor mothers to work for pay if they were provided with adequate support. The new liberal sentiment was typified by David Ellwood, a poverty scholar who wrote a book proposing an overhaul of the welfare system (Ellwood, 1988). Although he acknowledged that it was often difficult for a welfare mother to find and keep a job, Ellwood recommended limiting the payment of cash assistance under AFDC to five years. During that period, recipients would be given extensive assistance in job training, job search, and education. The government would also make a greater effort to collect unpaid child support payments from absent fathers of AFDC families, and would guarantee a minimum level of child support to poor, single mothers. It would provide greater tax relief to the working poor, and it would provide health insurance to the millions of low-income families without it. If, at the end of the five years cash assistance, an AFDC parent still did not have a job, she would be provided with a public-service job at the minimum wage.

TOWARD RADICAL WELFARE REFORM

Essentially, Ellwood proposed a carrot-and-stick reform, with the carrot of greater support in obtaining work and the stick of just five years of

cash payments. It was in this context that Clinton, influenced by welfare experts such as Ellwood, made his famous 1992 promise. But after his election, he chose to delay proposing changes to the welfare system while he attempted to convince Congress to enact legislation providing for universal health insurance coverage. Clinton failed, however, to convince Congress to pass his health insurance plan, and in the 1994 mid-term elections, the Republicans took control of Congress. After the 1994 election, the Republicans developed their own welfare reform plan. Their view harkened back to the pre-1935 tradition of public assistance. The sponsors of the bill and their conservative supporters argued that the main problem of families receiving AFDC was not a lack of jobs but a lack of work discipline.

The welfare system, conservatives argued, reduced poor people's initiative by providing them with unending cash benefits (Mead, 1986). Moreover, they argued, the combination of AFDC payments, food stamps, medical coverage, and other benefits provided a standard of living that low-wage work could never match. It was rational, they argued, for mothers to stay on welfare rather than look for paid work (Murray, 1984). Finally, some conservative thinkers argued that welfare programs worked better when private religious and charitable organizations played a major role, as had been the case prior to 1935. Therefore, they urged that government's role in helping the poor be minimized (Olasky, 1992).

The Republican majority introduced a bill that was much tougher than Clinton's version of welfare reform. First, it ended the entitlement to cash assistance. Instead of a commitment to provide welfare to all eligible families, the federal government would give a fixed amount of money to each state and allow the states to deny aid to eligible families if they exhausted their welfare funds. The federal contribution will not increase until 2003 at the earliest. Second, it limited cash assistance to a maximum of five years (states were free to set shorter time limits), but unlike the Ellwood plan, it provided no federal money for public service jobs for families that reached the time limit. Third, after two years, adults in most welfare families would be required to work at least part-time or their benefits would be cut off. The bill also provided far less in the way of job training, education, and tax benefits than did the liberal approach. In a sense, the Republican plan kept the stick of Clinton's program but threw away most of the carrots.

Twice the Republicans passed a welfare reform bill and twice Clinton, responding to pleas from liberal supporters, vetoed it. Then, in the summer of 1996, just before the start of the presidential election campaign, the Republicans softened their bill a bit and passed it again. Clinton's welfare advisers urged another veto, but his political advisers, noting his 1992 promise and the unpopularity of welfare with the voters, urged him to sign it. In August he signed it. Afterward, several of his top federal advisers resigned in protest from their posts in the Administration.[3]

The new law carries the somewhat grandiose title of "The Personal Responsibility and Work Opportunity Reconciliation Act of 1996." It abolishes AFDC and replaces it with Temporary Assistance to Needy Families (TANF). States are now given a fixed amount of money—a so-called TANF block grant, and they are required to maintain their own spending at 75 percent (or more) of their previous levels. However, they have great flexibility in deciding how to spend their TANF funds. They may use the block grant to assist their poor residents in any reasonable way they choose. They may choose time limits shorter than five years (several have chosen time limits of two years or less). Overall, states have much greater control over their programs than before.

THE CONSEQUENCES FOR MARRIAGE AND CHILDBEARING

The entire package—no entitlement, fixed federal payments, work requirement after two years,

five-year lifetime limit, and other changes—is breathtaking in scope compared to previous rounds of welfare reform. As recently as the 1980s, no president—not even a conservative Republican such as Ronald Reagan—would have been able to push such a tough program through Congress. Its supporters claim that if recipients are forced to take responsibility for themselves by looking for work and taking any job they can get, they will be better off in the long run. They will have more self-esteem, it is said; their ability to be good parents will improve, and some will eventually move up the job ladder to better-paying work. The opponents of the 1996 legislation call it cruel and heartless. They argue that in today's economy there are not enough jobs for people with little in the way of skills or education. They warn of destitute families, of increases in homelessness, and of more children placed into the expensive and troubled foster care system.

It is commonly believed that the pre-1996 welfare system discouraged marriage, encouraged divorce, and encouraged childbearing outside of marriage among the poor. The reason is that, with few exceptions, it was difficult for two-parent families to obtain assistance. In the 1960s, the AFDC program was expanded to cover two-parent families, but only under restrictions so severe that few such families could qualify. As a result, most couples who had children could receive welfare payments only if they didn't marry or live together. And, for the most part, a married couple could receive welfare payments only if they separated or divorced. Despite the plausibility of the idea that these rules discouraged marriage and encouraged the formation of single-parent families, the social scientific evidence suggests that the effects of welfare on family structure are of moderate size, at most, although they may have been increasing in the 1980s (Moffitt, 1992). Currently, under TANF many states are allowing more poor two-parent families to apply for benefits; it remains to be seen whether this change will increase marital stability.

Before 1996, a recipient's benefits were increased if she had another child while on the rolls. During the deliberations on the welfare law, some members of Congress proposed a "family cap," under which a mother who is already receiving welfare benefits and who has another child would not receive an increase in benefits. Their reasoning was that the increase in benefits serves as an incentive for welfare recipients to have more children. Critics responded that the modest size of the increases makes them a minor factor in a woman's decision about having children. The family cap provision was deleted from the federal bill before its passage, but the law does allow states to institute family caps if they wish, and many are in the process of doing so. Initial evidence on whether these family caps diminish childbearing among welfare recipients is inconclusive.

One reason why the effects of welfare on marriage and childbearing may be smaller than commonly thought is that the value of the average AFDC benefit declined sharply between the 1970s and the 1990s. The decline occurred because most state legislatures refused to increase the benefit level even though inflation had eroded its purchasing power. Adjusted for inflation and measured in 1994 dollars, the average state paid $792 per month in 1970 for a family of four and only $435 per month in 1994 for a similar family (Blank, 1997). If welfare benefits were a strong influence on marriage and fertility, one would expect that this drop in welfare benefits would have made marriage more attractive and childbearing outside of marriage less attractive. Yet divorce, cohabitation, and the percentage of births that occurred outside of marriage all increased during this period.

It is possible, nevertheless, that by the 1970s, welfare benefit levels had reached a high enough level so that, even with some erosion, they sustained family behaviors that weakened the place

of marriage. But other influential changes also were occurring in American society. Since the early 1970s, the earning power of young men without college educations has lessened because of falling wages in the manufacturing sector of the economy. This trend might have made young men reluctant to marry, and it might have made young women skeptical of finding a partner with enough earning power to help sustain a family. A poor young woman who sees little prospect of finding a suitable husband is probably more likely to go ahead and have a child without marrying. In addition, a broad cultural shift away from marriage and toward individual fulfillment was occurring among all social classes.

THE CONSEQUENCES FOR CHILDREN

We know even less about how the new law will affect poor children. Consider the possible consequences for children of limiting their mother's time on welfare and requiring them to work outside the home. Ronald Haskins, a developmental psychologist and congressional staff member who was one of the architects of the 1996 law, speculated that the following consequences could occur (Haskins, 1995). On the negative side:

- Children's families could have lower incomes if mothers leave the welfare program for work at very low wages. In some states, the combination of cash welfare, food stamps, and other benefits can exceed the income from minimum wage jobs. Moreover, low-wage jobs impose new costs (transportation, child care, clothes) and often do not include health insurance.
- Children could be placed in low-quality day care (e.g., too many children per caregiver) while their mothers work. This could hurt their cognitive and emotional development.
- Mothers may be less-effective parents because of the increased responsibilities of combining paid work and childrearing. They will be

available to their children for fewer hours. They may be more harried and pressed for time, and this may make them more irritable, neglectful, and impatient with their children.

On the positive side, Haskins listed:

- Mothers may be better parents because paid work will give them more self-esteem and satisfaction with their lives. It will improve the mood of those who were depressed because of their dependence on welfare. Consequently, mothers will be less harsh, angry, and punitive in their interactions with their children.
- Paid work imposes a daily routine—a set time to wake up, get to work, cook and eat dinner—that could increase order in the household. Without a daily adult routine, it is harder for a parent to make sure that children get to school on time, keep doctors' appointments, and so forth.
- Employed parents may make better role models. Children will see parents who are attached to the world of work and may be more confident that they, too, will be able to find employment as adults. They may be more likely to stay in school and to postpone early, nonmarital childbearing.

We don't know which of these effects will dominate or if other important effects will emerge. Haskins concluded, "although claims of promoting child welfare will be tossed about by all sides during the debate, there is embarrassingly little good evidence about the impact of the welfare, intervention, and work strategies on children's long-term prospects" (1995, p. 267).

THE CONSEQUENCES FOR IMMIGRANT FAMILIES

The 1996 law also contained sharp restrictions on the receipt of other government benefits. These provisions have little to do with welfare reform itself, but they do provide much of the budgetary savings of the bill. A complex series of provisions drastically reduces the benefits that immigrants can legally receive in the United States (Primus, 1996). (Illegal immigrants already were ineligible for nearly all benefits and services except emergency medical care and public schools for their children.) Almost all new immigrants who enter the country are now ineligible for TANF, food stamps, and most other federally funded benefits until they become citizens (which takes a minimum of five years). Even most legal immigrants who were already in the United States prior to the passage of the law will have food stamps and other benefits taken away, although states can choose to keep them eligible for TANF.

Concern about public assistance to immigrants resulted from news reports about legal immigrants who brought their elderly parents to the United States and then had them apply for Supplemental Security Income (SSI), a program of cash assistance to the blind, the disabled, and the elderly poor. Studies confirmed that noncitizens were using SSI at a higher rate than citizens (Primus, 1996). Yet the same studies showed that noncitizens didn't have significantly higher rates of usage of other public assistance programs. Nevertheless, some supporters of these restrictions argued that generous U.S. public assistance programs attract excessive numbers of poor immigrants with negative consequences for the economy. Others argued that immigrants, like poor U.S.-born citizens, would be better served by low-wage work than by welfare.[4] (A small proportion of immigrants who are officially classified as political "refugees," such as many Southeast Asians from countries involved in the Vietnam War [Rumbaut, 1989], will remain eligible for all benefits.) Critics of the immigrant provisions predicted that hundreds of thousands of immigrant families will be pushed into poverty.

CONCLUSION

The Personal Responsibility and Work Opportunity Reconciliation Act of 1996 may be the most important piece of poverty-policy legislation since the Great Depression. It repeals basic principles of assistance that were established in the Social Security Act of 1935: an entitlement to benefits among all families that qualify for them and a commitment to providing benefits for as long as a family still qualifies. It represents a return to an even older principle of assistance to the poor: that reliance on public assistance for more than a brief period saps people's initiative and self-reliance. According to this line of reasoning, the biggest problem that poor people face is not a low income but rather dependence on the support of others. Supporters hail the 1996 law for the support of "personal responsibility" and the creation (through work requirements and time limits on benefits) of "work opportunities" that are in its title.

Critics argue that it may make the lives of many poor families even worse by limiting the assistance they can receive. According to the critics, the basic problem that poor families face is that there are not enough jobs for people without college educations at wages that can sustain a family (Wilson, 1996). They predict widespread hardship, more homelessness, and more domestic violence. They believe that poor children will suffer rather than benefit from the new lives their parents are forced to lead.

Frances Fox Piven and Richard A. Cloward, two longtime critics of the welfare system, maintain that the expansion of the rolls in the 1960s and the contraction in the 1990s reflect the same underlying motivation: the use of welfare as a way to control and discipline labor (Piven and Cloward, 1993). They state that governments historically have increased the welfare rolls when poor people protest, organize, or riot, as was the case in the 1960s. When the pressure from poor people subsides, they argue, governments tend to scale back the welfare system in order to motivate poor people to take low-wage jobs. They view the ever-tougher work requirements and benefit restrictions of the 1980s and 1990s as part of this cycle of expansion and contraction.

In between the critics and supporters are the opinions of some veteran welfare-watchers (e.g., Blank, 1997) who have observed several unsuccessful attempts to enforce work through changes in the welfare laws. They argue that the 1996 bill, like previous versions of welfare reform, will produce less change than its supporters wish and than its critics dread. Welfare bureaucrats who sympathize with their clients will find ways to work around the regulations; states will petition Congress for changes when they realize how difficult it is to move large numbers of long-term welfare recipients into the work force. Perhaps so, but the previous attempts at reform have not been this bold and this comprehensive. The 1996 law may prove to be the one that finally produces substantial changes in the lives of poor American families. Whether those changes will match the hopes of its defenders or the fears of its critics, we cannot yet say.

ENDNOTES

1. The original program was named "Aid to Dependent Children," or ADC; the word "families" was added later.
2. For example, in 1994, total federal and state expenditures for AFDC, job training for AFDC recipients, and child care for AFDC recipients and ex-recipients were $28.5 billion. In contrast, Social Security benefits for 1994 cost $316.8 billion. Medicaid, the program of health insurance benefits for the nonaged poor and for the elderly in nursing homes cost $143.6 billion. Food benefits, including food stamps and programs such as school breakfasts and lunches, cost $38.1 billion. (U.S. Bureau of the Census, 1996.)
3. One of those officials, Peter Edelman, subsequently described his objections in detail (Edelman, 1997). Ellwood, who returned to academia in 1994, well before the passage of the law, also wrote an article about his experiences (Ellwood, 1996).

4. See Espenshade et al., 1996, for a summary of these arguments.

REFERENCES

Blank, Rebecca M. (1997). "The 1996 Welfare Reform" *Journal of Economic Perspectives, 11,* 169–177.

Cherlin, Andrew J. (1992). *Marriage, Divorce, Remarriage.* Revised and Enlarged Edition. Cambridge: Harvard University Press.

Edelman, Peter (1997). "The Worst Thing Bill Clinton Has Done." *The Atlantic Monthly,* March, pp. 43–56.

Ellwood, David T. (1988). *Poor Support: Poverty in the American Family.* New York: Basic Books.

———. (1996). "Welfare Reform as I Knew It." *The American Prospect,* no. 26 (May/June), pp. 22–29.

Espenshade, Thomas J., Fix, Michael, Zimmerman, Wendy, & Corbett, Thomas. (1996). "Immigration and Social Policy: New Interest in an Old Issue." *Focus, 18*: 1–10.

Handler, Joel F. (1995). *The Poverty of Welfare Reform.* New Haven: Yale University Press.

Katz, Michael B. (1996). *In the Shadow of the Poorhouse: A Social History of Welfare in America.* Tenth anniversary edition, revised and updated. New York: Basic Books.

Mead, Lawrence M. (1986). *Beyond Entitlement: The Social Obligations of Citizenship.* New York: Free Press.

Murray, Charles (1984). *Losing Ground: American Social Policy, 1950–1980.* New York: Basic Books.

Olasky, Marvin (1992). *The Tragedy of American Compassion.* Washington, DC: Regnery.

Piven, Francis Fox, & Cloward, Richard A. (1993). *Regulating the Poor: The Functions of Public Welfare.* Updated Edition. New York: Vintage Books.

Primus, Wendell (1996). "Immigration Provisions in the New Welfare Law." *Focus, 18,* 14–19.

Quadagno, Jill S. (1994). *The Color of Welfare: How Racism Undermined the War on Poverty.* New York: Oxford University Press.

Rumbaut, Rubén G. (1989). "The Structure of Refuge: Southeast Asian Refugees in the United States, 1975–1985." *International Review of Comparative Public Policy, 1,* 97–129.

Skocpol, Theda (1992). *Protecting Mothers and Soldiers: The Political Origins of Social Policy in the United States.* Cambridge, MA: The Belknap Press of Harvard University Press.

U.S. Bureau of the Census. 1996. *Statistical Abstract of the United States: 1996.* Washington, DC: U.S. Government Printing Office.

Wilson, William J. (1996). *When Work Disappears: The World of the New Urban Poor.* New York: Alfred A. Knopf.

READING 6–2

Family Dynamics

Mark Robert Rank

> *That was one of my dreams when I was in school. Just being married and raising a family totally the opposite of what I grew up in. It became an obsession with me to do that. And I guess I overlooked a lotta things. That's why I was married so many times and it didn't work out. I stayed with my last two children's father as long as I did trying to hold on to that family structure. And willing to accept different things, just to keep that family structure. Just to keep them with their father, to keep the two of us together, which was a fight.*
>
> —Twice-divorced mother of three children

From childhood and adolescence, through marriage and raising children, and finally into old age, family relationships play significant roles in our lives. This reading focuses on four different family experiences among welfare recipients: first, recollections of family background and upbringing; second, current family relationships; third, the likelihood and determinants of women giving birth while on welfare; and, finally, the probability of and causes related to marriage and divorce among welfare recipients.

GROWING UP

We begin by exploring recollections of family background and upbringing.[1] Most of the recipients interviewed reported growing up in or around the Ridgeton area, the exception being black families, who often had been raised in Chicago or the South. The economic status of these households can best be described as working class. That is, families were able to keep afloat, but without much left over. Fathers tended to work in manual, blue-collar occupations, often holding down several jobs at once. Typical jobs included factory work, construction, and so on. Mothers often worked as well, especially when the children were in school, to provide extra income for the family.

An example comes from Colleen Bennett. Colleen and her husband, Ron, had gone on public assistance two months prior to our interview. She was asked about the kind of work her parents did when she was growing up.

Colleen: We were lucky. My dad was a drunk, but he could work two jobs. And so financially we were always . . . fine, or borderline. You know, we always had enough.

Q: What kind of work did he do?

Colleen: Construction. Road construction. He worked in warehousing, driving forklifts, or both. Or a combination of a gas attendant with one of the other jobs.

Q: And your mom worked also?

Colleen: Yeah. She works. She started working when I was three months old at the DNR [Department of Natural Resources]. And she's been there for 21 years.

A common response among recipients was that, although they seldom went hungry, there was not much extra. Hand-me-down clothes, furniture on its last legs, and leftovers stretched for days were often the norm. Yet few of these families received public assistance. Of the households we interviewed, only 18 percent recalled that their parents had collected any kind of welfare assistance.[2]

Many recipients also reported the presence of serious family problems during their childhood: alcoholism among parents, child and spouse abuse, family breakup, and so on. One-third of interviewees under the age of 65 revealed that one or both parents had suffered from serious alcohol problems. An example comes from Joyce Mills, who had recently separated from her husband as a result of physical abuse.

> My mom and dad used to fight a lot. My dad was, I guess you could call him an alcoholic. He used to drink a lot. And from the very beginning, I cannot remember a moment where my mom and dad were not fighting. I would see pictures in the album of when they were dating. But yet it didn't look like mom and dad because they weren't fighting. But that was why my mom and dad divorced. Back then I didn't even know what was going on. But when she got back together with him again it was just so that my sister and I could have a father. And when I think back on it, that was the worst thing she could have done. Because things didn't improve. They were just as harsh as they were before she left.

Another example of severe family problems occurring during childhood comes from Nancy Jordon, who was quoted at the beginning of this reading.

Nancy: I was born in St. Louis. We moved from there when I was four to East Moline. My mother remarried. It was a very horrible childhood. I felt that I was robbed of my childhood, from the point where we left St. Louis when my mother remarried. I was robbed of my childhood, and I was robbed of being a teenager. We've had a very abused home. I come from . . . a nightmare. And it took a long time for me to understand it. I don't know if I've yet to understand it.

Q: Can you tell me a little bit more? Are you talking about alcoholism, physical abuse, sexual abuse, emotional abuse?

Nancy: Physical abuse, sexual abuse.

Q: On the part of your stepfather, or other people like that?

Nancy: My stepfather and my mother. My older sister, her mind was halfway destroyed. And she still has got some loose balls up there now. But you know, it was just [*long pause*] very horrible [*sighs, near tears*]. And back then I would run away from home. And all the agency would do was send me back. They chose to believe the parents. Or they chose not to deal with the problem, and just write it off. That's how I felt about it, they just chose to write it off [*spoken in a very depressed tone*].

When coupled with the tight economic conditions that most of their families faced, the childhoods of our interviewed sample can best be described as formidable. Perhaps, then, it is not surprising that many female heads and married couples reported having a child at an early age and/or marrying early, whether to escape family problems, because of a shortage of information, or for lack of alternatives. Typical ages for women at first birth were the late teens and early 20s. Often, pregnancies were accidental but nevertheless carried to term. Couples also tended to marry young, usually no later than their early 20s.

A young age at childbirth, together with constrained economic resources, foreclosed the possibilities of higher education for most recipients with children. For those without children, the likelihood of going on and completing college was slim given the lack of financial support from families. As a result, many began working full-time at an early age, typically 16, 17, or 18.

The childhood experiences of our sampled recipients closely resemble the recollections of the working-class families portrayed in Lillian Rubin's book *Worlds of Pain* (1976). Rubin writes,

> Thus, whether settled- or hard-living, most of the working-class adults I spoke with recall childhoods where, at best, "things were tight" financially. They recall parents who worked hard, yet never quite made it; homes that were overcrowded; siblings or selves who got into "trouble"; a preoccupation with the daily struggle for survival that precluded planning for a future. Whether they recall angry, discontented, drunken parents, or quiet, steady, "always-there" parents, the dominant theme is struggle and trouble. (p. 48)

In short, these are childhoods in which life chances and options have been substantially reduced. The odds simply are stacked against such kids. Although some may become bankers or lawyers, most will not. The resources and support necessary to take such paths are largely unavailable. With few exceptions, these children will revisit as adults many of the struggles that their parents grappled with. While many will leave the welfare system relatively quickly, they are likely to remain on a financial tightrope, one step away from public assistance. This process of class reproduction has been detailed in numerous studies, including Whyte (1943), Liebow (1967), Rubin (1976), and MacLeod (1987)[3].

FAMILY TIES

There is a Spanish proverb that says, "An ounce of blood is worth more than a pound of friendship." Certainly this saying holds true among welfare recipients. In spite of the problems and difficulties of childhood, family ties are nevertheless an important source of strength and support.

I focus on three aspects of family ties. First, the demographic characteristics of households. Second, the care and raising of children. And, finally, the support available from the extended family.

Family Demographic Characteristics

The overall household composition of families on welfare is slightly different from the composition of households entering the welfare system. Female-headed families and the elderly tend to remain on public assistance longer than do married couples or singles. Consequently, a random sample of all recipients at any given

TABLE I

HOUSEHOLD AND FAMILY CHARACTERISTIC PERCENTAGES BY HOUSEHOLD TYPE

Household characteristics	Household type			
	Female heads	Married heads	Single heads	Elderly heads
Household size				
1	2.6	0.2	79.8	93.8
2	34.9	9.0	7.9	4.8
3	29.8	22.1	3.6	0.7
4	16.3	26.1	2.8	0.5
5	8.1	19.2	2.4	0.0
6 or more	8.4	23.4	3.6	0.2
Average	3.2	4.5	1.5	1.1
Living arrangement				
Home	99.6	99.4	78.1	18.8
Nursing home	0.0	0.2	20.0	81.2
Other	0.4	0.4	2.0	0.0
Marital status				
Never married	39.7	—	73.8	13.8
Married	—	100.0	—	3.9
Separated	27.2	—	8.2	16.6
Divorced	31.4	—	12.1	4.2
Widowed	1.7	—	5.8	61.5
Number of generations in household				
1	3.8	9.6	97.2	98.0
2	94.7	88.8	2.8	1.8
3	1.6	1.6	—	0.2
Number of children				
0	3.9	11.6	100.0	98.7
1	41.8	23.2	—	1.2
2	29.5	26.9	—	0.0
3	14.2	19.0	—	0.0
4 or more	10.7	19.2	—	0.2
Average	1.9	2.3	—	—
Ages of children				
Less than 6	40.2	36.3	—	—
6–17	56.3	59.1	—	—
18 or more	3.3	4.6	—	—

time will tend to comprise more female-headed and elderly households as a percentage of the total. In Table 1, 41 percent of the caseload sample of welfare households were female headed, 19 percent were headed by married couples, 18 percent by singles, and 22 percent by the elderly (less than 1 percent were male-headed families).

Family characteristics by these household types are shown in Table 1.[4] Single and elderly households are quite small—79.8 percent of single heads and 93.8 percent of elderly heads have a household size of one. Household size for female-headed and married households is larger, averaging 3.2 and 4.5 individuals, respectively.

Not all households live in a home or apartment. This is most true for the elderly, where 81.2 percent reside in nursing homes. Twenty percent of singles are also institutionalized.

Turning to marital status, approximately 40 percent of female heads have never been married, while the bulk of the remainder are either separated or divorced. Roughly three out of four single heads have never been married, while 61.5 percent of the elderly are widowed.

Most female heads have one or two children in the household, while married couples have a slightly higher number of children. In both cases, approximately 40 percent of children in the household are under the age of six, and slightly less than 60 percent are between the ages of 6 and 17. Very few children living in the household are over the age of 17.

The table does not support the theory that large, extended families live together on welfare. Female-headed households average 3.2 individuals, and only 1.6 percent include three generations. However, as we will see, other family members do often live in the immediate vicinity.

Married households are somewhat larger, averaging 4.5 members; again, only 1.6 percent include three generations. Single and elderly headed households generally contain only themselves.

Raising Children

Welfare recipients share much the same frustrations and joys as other parents. Those interviewed spoke of the way their children have enriched their lives, mentioned disciplinary problems and other worries about their sons or daughters, and described their efforts to do what is best for their offspring together with their pride in their children's accomplishments. But along with these and many other topics relevant to parenting in general, welfare parents repeatedly raised several issues that appeared to be related to the experience of living in poverty.

Many parents discussed their frustrations over not being able to meet fully the physical needs of their children. These ranged from not having enough food on the table to not being able to keep up with the status symbols that other parents were able to provide for their children. The example of Marta Green is typical.

> Like the kids at school, they wear Nike tennis shoes. Name-brand tennis shoes. And then I go and buy them a five-dollar pair of tennis shoes. And they say, "Mom, no. We want the Nike shoes because my girlfriend, Emily, has them." And I say, "No, because for 13 dollars I can buy shoes for both of you." And they get angry and they don't understand. But I try to talk to them. They are very good kids. They get upset for a little while and sometimes they cry, but after they get over it, I just talk to them and say, "Listen, this is the situation that we are going through. But we'll get over this. And in a couple of years, Mommy's going to buy you some nicer stuff. But right now we have to take it like it is."

Perhaps as a result, most recipients reported stressing to their children the importance of developing strong, independent lives of their own, particularly, of never having to rely on public assistance. This is reflected in the words of Donna Anderson, a 43-year-old separated mother of nine:

> I want them number one to be independent. And I want them to be honest. That's the main thing I demand from them. I can't stand dishonesty. Because I like to be able to say, "My kid's telling the truth." And I want them to be achievers. I want them to have certain things that they know they need to do in life. Instead of making up excuses why they can't do it. Like I tell them all the time, you *have* [with emphasis] to go to school. There's no way of getting out of that. You have to learn. This is the only way you're gonna learn. So that's basically all I want of them, is honesty, and to be independent one day. To work toward being independent and to be able to take care of themselves.

Parents emphasized to their children the importance of education as the means to achieving a strong, independent life. Ruth Miller, a 38-year-old female head of household with five children, explains:

> I teach them that education is the best thing these days. As far as trying to drop out of school, we don't need that. 'Cause we're going to need the education in order to get us a good job. And they say they understand. They love going to school. My kids don't have a real problem with mischief. Sometimes they get out of hand, and we'll have a grade argument or whatever. But other than that, they understand that it's best to go to school. It's better than out on the streets, where you've got nothing to do, and you get lonely. You got no education. Can't get no good job. You gotta just take whatever they give you. They [*referring to her children*] don't want to be like that. They want to go to school, get a good education, and be assured they're going to get a job. And if they want to go to college, if I can see fit, I can send them to a college. So that's the way it is.

The dilemma facing many of these parents, as undoubtedly it was for their own parents, is the difficulty of promoting such goals for their children given their economic constraints. Like most families, the parents in my sample want what is best for their children. Their frustration comes from not being able to provide it.

Kinship Networks

Extended family ties are often an important source of strength and support for these households. Yet as we might expect, the amount of economic support that other family members can provide is rather limited given their own financial constraints. Furthermore, some family members are hostile to the idea of their kin receiving public assistance. Nevertheless, recipients reported a fairly high degree of contact with relatives and a modest amount of shared resources.

Extended family contact was either face to face or by telephone. Often parents, siblings, and/or grown-up children lived in the immediate vicinity. Recipients reported being in touch with

a relative an average of once a week; for some, this average was two to three times a week.

Valerie Jones is a 30-year-old never-married mother of two who has been on and off the welfare system for nine years. When interviewed, she was working as a cook in a fraternity house, while still qualifying for public assistance. How did she deal with troubles paying the bills? "Well, I have two sisters and two brothers here. So if they can help, they will. And then my aunt, she's in a good enough position and her husband. I kinda depend on my family if I need help. 'Cause if they need help, I'll do the same for them."

What about if she runs out of food? "If I don't have any food in my house, especially if the kids are here, my aunt will bring something. Or if I can get to my sister's house, I will raid their refrigerator [*laugh*]." For Valerie, such help was often the difference between getting by and a serious emergency.

The importance of family ties was also evident for Colleen Bennett and her husband. They lived in a rural area north of Ridgeton in a ranch-style house owned by Colleen's parents. She was asked about her family.

> We're all very close. We take care of each other if anybody has a problem. My husband and I have had financial problems on and off for years. And my brother recently lost his job. So when we have something where we can help them, we go ahead and give them a couple of dollars for gas in their car so they can find a job. 'Cause we know what it feels like when you don't have it. And then when we're low, they'll give to us. And nobody asks anybody to pay it back. It's like a running loan company.

These types of reciprocal exchanges are fairly common among the poor. As Carol Stack (1974) noted in her classic work on kinship networks in a low-income black neighborhood, they are an adaptive strategy for dealing with the uncertainties inherent in poverty. Being able to count on family members for support during troubled times helps people weather such spells.

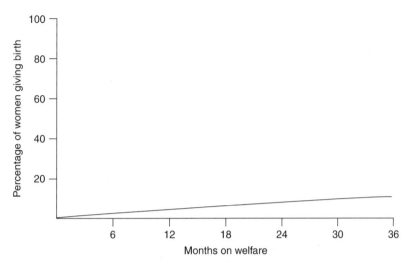

FIGURE 1   Cumulative percentage of women giving birth by months on welfare.

BIRTHRATES

Policymakers and the general public tend to assume that women on welfare have large numbers of children. In addition, many contend that because benefits increase with the size of a household, women on welfare have a financial incentive to bear more children.[5] For example, President Reagan's Working Group on the Family, headed by Gary Bauer, observed, "Does the welfare system, particularly AFDC, give some women incentives to bear children? Statistical evidence does not prove those suppositions; and yet, even the most casual observer of public assistance programs understands that there is indeed some relationship between the availability of welfare and the inclination of many young women to bear fatherless children" (1986, p. 35). Several states have frozen or are considering freezing benefits to women who have a child while on welfare for precisely these reasons. Yet what does the evidence tell us? The longitudinal caseload data yields some surprising answers.[6]

Incidence and Determinants

Three separate questions are addressed with the numerical data. First, what is the percentage and rate of women giving birth while receiving welfare? Second, how do these rates compare with those for the general population? And, third, what factors increase or decrease the likelihood of childbearing among welfare recipients?

The Likelihood of Childbearing   Figure 1 graphically represents the percentage of women on welfare (age 18 to 44) giving birth over the course of three years. The proportion of women giving birth during any six-month interval is relatively stable at approximately 2 percent. After one year on welfare, 4.58 percent of women will have given birth, while 11.49 percent will bear children during a three-year spell on welfare. The one-year overall fertility rate for women on public assistance is therefore 45.8 per 1,000 women on welfare.[7] The lower overall birthrates among women receiving public assistance programs are therefore not an artifact of a more favorable demographic structure.

Determinants of Fertility   What factors increase or decrease the probability of women on welfare bearing children? In order to address this, I have calculated what is known as a *logistic* *regression model* to examine how individual characteristics increase or decrease the probability of giving birth during any given six-month period. Several variables significantly affect the likelihood of childbearing among women on welfare: education, race, age, having a child under the age of four in the household, and length of welfare use. Women with less education, non-white women, older women, and women having a child under the age of four all have a greater probability of giving birth while on welfare.

Perhaps most interesting is the effect of the length of welfare use on fertility. The longer a woman remains on welfare, the less likely she is to give birth. Each additional year on welfare lowers the probability of giving birth by .62 to 1. Thus, controlling for confounding factors, rather than encouraging women to give birth, being on public assistance for longer periods of time actually reduces the rate of fertility.[8]

Reasons

Why is the rate of fertility among women on welfare relatively low? To shed some light on the potential reasons, I asked women about their experiences and their attitudes toward pregnancy and childbirth.

Twenty-nine of the 50 interviews were with a female household head or wife between the ages of 18 and 44, with most women being in their 20s or 30s. Two women were pregnant at the time of the interview. The majority of women had borne one or two children.

None of the 27 nonpregnant women were contemplating having a child in the near future, and only a handful were considering having more children in the long term. They clearly wished to avoid childbearing at this particular time in their lives. Several examples illustrate the underlying reasons behind this.

Marta Green, who had discussed the frustrations of trying to provide for her children, was asked whether she thought she would ever want to have any more children. She responded, "No. No. I don't think that I *ever* want to have an-

other child. I think that will stop me from doing things that I want to do. And it won't be fair to me. It won't be fair for the new child. And it won't be fair at all for the two that I have."

Jennifer Smith, a never-married woman in her early 30s, commented, "It's hardest to get by with one, let alone have another one just me by myself, ya' know. Tryin' to raise two."

Jill Nelson, a 19-year-old woman with one child, when asked if she had considered having any more children, replied, "Not quite yet [*laughter*]. I kinda thought about, you know, the age difference. I don't want it to be real far, but I'm not quite ready for another kid, financially or . . . or mentally. I don't think I could handle two kids. [*Laughter.*]"

Finally, Cindy Franklin . . . was asked why she was planning not to have a third child. She answered, "I suppose mostly, it has to do with me. Depression is a factor. I just don't know that I can handle more than this. And also, I want to get on preparing for my own career. And I don't want to have to go back to square one and raise a child, and stay home with it again."

These examples illustrate several of the predominant feelings and attitudes of the women that were interviewed. The economic, social, and psychological situations in which women on welfare find themselves is simply not conducive to desiring more children. Such women would appear to be motivated by cost-benefit considerations, but it is the costs that outweigh the benefits, not the reverse. Becoming pregnant and having a child are perceived as making the situation worse, not better. In addition, virtually all of the interviewed women expressed a desire to get off public assistance. Having an additional child was perceived as severely hampering that desire.

Denise Turner has four children, ages 14, 12, 10, and 8. When asked whether the availability of welfare had had anything to do with her having children, she quickly responded,

Nothing. I've read a lot of studies about that, and they're not true. No. It had nothing to do with it.

You know . . . having a child is very traumatic. It's a very beautiful experience, but it's also very traumatic. And I suppose there are some women that just might have additional children to get an increase in money, but I would say that that's less than a very small percentage. Because you're committing yourself to anywhere from 15 to 20 years of your life to that individual. You're taking nine months from the very beginning and doing all kinds of traumatic things to your body. So, no. That was not a consideration in having additional children.

Many of the pregnancies and births occurring to the interviewed women while on welfare had been accidental rather than planned. Education and race are significant factors affecting the likelihood of childbearing, and both have also been shown in previous research to be highly correlated with an increased likelihood of unplanned births (Pratt et al., 1984). Angela Lewis, a never-married women in her mid-20s, was asked about her three pregnancies after her first child and whether she had wanted to have another. "Never. After that first time, my mom kept drilling into me about school and the importance of education and all. So that stuck with me all those years. And I always got pregnant through carelessness, you know. I kept saying, 'Well when I get married one day and settle down, and make sure my life is secure, then I'll have the children.' So that's why I always got the abortions."

The belief that women on welfare have a high fertility rate, so often implicitly accepted by social and policy analysts (e.g., Working Group on the Family, 1986), is simply not supported by this analysis. In fact, women on welfare have a relatively low rate of fertility, with that rate dropping with years of recipiency.

MARRIAGE AND DISSOLUTION

Policymakers have also been concerned about the effects of the welfare system on family structure. Some have argued that the welfare system encourages the formation of female-headed families (Bahr, 1979; Murray, 1984). Others have suggested that female-headed families create the need for welfare (Draper, 1981; Darity & Meyers, 1984). In this section, I examine the incidence of marriage and separation/divorce in the welfare population and the factors associated with these family compositional changes.

Overall Patterns of Marriage and Dissolution

Figure 2 charts the marriages and dissolutions of female heads of households and married couples over six half-year intervals. Slightly over 2 percent of female heads are likely to marry during any given six-month interval on welfare. The marriage rate for female heads during their first year on welfare is 5.49 percent, or 54.9 marriages per 1,000 women. This is below the national marriage rate of 102.6 per 1,000 unmarried women age 18 to 44, and 61.4 per 1,000 unmarried women age 15 and over during this period (U.S. Bureau of the Census, 1991). Over the course of the three years examined, 13 percent of female heads of households married.

Approximately 3 to 5 percent of married couples dissolve their marriages during any given six-month spell on public assistance. The first year divorce/separation rate is 8.94 percent, or 89.4 divorces/separations per 1,000 marriages. This is substantially higher than the divorce rate of 22.6 per 1,000 married women age 15 and over in the general population during this period (U.S. Bureau of the Census, 1991).[9] Finally, over the course of three years on welfare, an estimated 21 percent of couples will end their marriages.

As this figure makes plain, the likelihood of a separation or divorce occurring among married couples in the welfare population is substantially greater than that of a female head marrying. Furthermore, the divorce/separation rate of married couples is much higher than the divorce rate for the general population, while the marriage rate for women on welfare is lower than their counterparts in the general population.

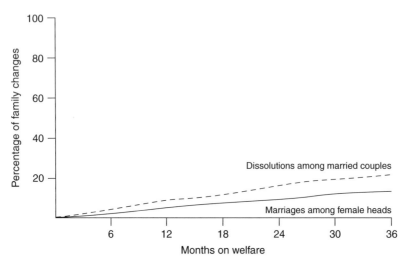

FIGURE 2 Cumulative percentage of marriages and dissolutions by months on welfare.

These findings make sense in light of the uncertain and stressful conditions in which individuals in poverty find themselves.

Clarissa and John Williams had been married for only three months but were already experiencing severe strains when I interviewed them in their upstairs flat in a poor neighborhood of Ridgeton . . . John and Clarissa often sell their blood plasma to tide themselves through the month. Clarissa was asked about the problems they faced: "We don't have the money. It makes us frustrated or mad with each other. We run out of things. We take that out on each other. 'Cause it makes you frustrated when you don't know where your next dollar's coming from. You just start in on money and it just brings on an argument." Later in the interview they elaborated:

John: When I'm out there, she's here. She don't know what I'm doing. And I'm trying to tell her that, and she's goin' on, "You're not doing this, you're not doing that." And that just makes me mad because I know what I'm doing.

Clarissa: Now that's our biggest problem. Money and that job. Him not having a job. Makes me frustrated. I'm paying all the bills. Taking care of everything. Even though he's on my grant.

Which is nothing because they cut it. It just seems like I be doin' everything. That's a problem.

John: It frustrates me because I'm not working. I'm used to working.

This example illustrates the strains that many married couples in poverty experience every day. Such stress puts additional pressure on the relationship, which increases the likelihood of a separation or divorce. Indeed, a U.S. Census Bureau report indicates that poor two-parent families are approximately twice as likely to break up as are two-parent families that aren't poor. The report notes that the "stresses arising from low income and poverty may have contributed substantially to discontinuation rates for two-parent families" (1992c, pp. 29–30).

On the other hand, an example of a female head of household being unlikely to marry was Denise Turner. A 37-year-old never-married mother of four, Denise has been on and off welfare for the past 14 years, often working as well. She was asked if she would like to be in a permanent relationship at some point in the future.

Sometimes yes, sometimes no. Sometimes I think about it and I say it would really be nice to have somebody that I could relate to. Somebody I could talk to and laugh with and share things with. And then it makes me sad that I don't. And then sometimes I look at it, and I say well I really don't have the time . . .

You know, I think that if I had been more career minded when I was younger, I would not be in the position that I'm in today. So, at this point that's really what I'm moving to. I want a career! I want a job! I want to make some good money! The hell with everybody else! I will see you all later. I will find a man . . . on the other end. If not, that's just too bad. And I think that's what I'm moving towards. And I think I'm doing that out of survival reasons.

Again, it would appear that the conditions of poverty limit the options for such women. This is not to say that female heads on welfare do not marry. Indeed they do, as shown in Figure 2. Nevertheless, poor women face very real constraints on their opportunities to cultivate the kinds of relationships that lead to marriage.

Factors Related to the Process of Marriage and Divorce

As in the earlier analysis of fertility, I used logistic regression equations to model and acquire odds ratios related to the processes of marriage and separation/divorce among welfare recipients. Three sets of characteristics are examined— demographic, children, and welfare variables.[10]

[As for marriage,] of the variables examined, only race is significantly related to marriage for female heads. Being white increases the odds of marriage by 60 percent over the odds for nonwhites. This finding is consistent with previous research demonstrating that the marriage market for black women is problematic. As Wilson (1987) has argued, black women, especially young black women, have access to a shrinking pool of "marriageable" (that is, economically stable) men. White women have not had to face this problem to the same extent.

Neither employment nor age are significantly correlated with marriage. Likewise, the number and age of children present in the household have no effect on predicting the likelihood of marriage.

As to the third set of variables, lowered welfare benefits resulting from the Reagan administration's cutbacks are insignificantly related to the likelihood of marriage. Likewise, female heads receiving all three programs (AFDC, Food Stamps, and Medicaid) are as likely to marry as their counterparts who receive public assistance through one or two programs. Finally, there is no evidence that being on welfare for an extended period of time significantly reduces or increases the odds of getting married. In short, the effect of welfare variation on the probability of marriage is negligible.

[As for separation and divorce,] two factors are significantly correlated with a change in family composition. A wife's employment increases the odds of a dissolution by 89 percent, a finding consistent with previous research (Adams, 1986; Cherlin, 1992). Employment may serve as a means for a woman to leave an unsatisfactory marriage. It may also reduce a husband's reluctance to end a marriage, knowing that his wife will be able to partially support herself. Or it may create further stress for a husband steeped in the traditional ideology of the male as the family breadwinner.

The second factor statistically correlated with separation/divorce is the presence of a young child in the household, which significantly increases the likelihood of a marital breakup. This finding differs from analyses of divorce in the general population, which have shown that children at preschool ages deter divorce (Waite and Lillard, 1991).

For married couples as for female heads, variation in welfare use does not significantly increase or decrease the risk of a change in family composition. Lowered welfare benefits, the number of programs received, and the length of time on welfare are all nonsignificant.[11]

In the analyses for both female heads and married couples, it would appear reasonable to argue that the conditions of poverty are more influential in affecting family formation than are the specific welfare programs per se. People in low-income families experience considerable tension and stress. These factors undoubtedly create problems in their lives. For married couples, these problems may lead to separation or divorce. For female heads, they may result in difficulties and constraints in finding a spouse. In either case, poverty, rather than welfare, is the more likely factor influencing the observed changes in family composition.

The issue of family dynamics among welfare recipients has been debated long and hard among policymakers. There is often an underlying fear that welfare contributes to the breakdown of the family: specifically that it encourages families to dissolve, women to have more children, extended families to crumble, children to follow in their parent's footsteps of welfare dependency, female heads not to marry, and so on (see Working Group on the Family, 1986). The results presented in this chapter flatly contradict these assumptions.[12] For the vast majority of families, welfare does not appear to influence family dynamics (see Bane & Jargowsky, 1988, Duncan, Hill, & Hoffman, 1988, Duncan & Hoffman, 1988, and Moffitt 1992 for a review of the literature and a similar conclusion).[13]

What does appear to be of utmost importance is the condition of living and growing up in poverty and hardship. In each of the familial experiences examined in this chapter, economic hardship has played a significant role.

To a large extent, welfare recipients follow in their parents' economic footsteps; however, this is not because children learn from their parents the easy life of welfare (indeed, most recipients' parents did not receive assistance). Rather, their educational and occupational opportunities have been severely limited as a result of parental financial constraints. Their scripts are too often written early on, resulting in formidable odds later in life.

This process is perhaps most cogently described in Elliot Liebow's study of street-corner men in Washington, D.C.:

Each generation does provide role models for each succeeding one. Of much greater importance for the possibilities of change, however, is the fact that many similarities between the lower-class Negro father and son (or mother and daughter) do not result from "cultural transmission" but from the fact that the son goes out and independently experiences the same failures, in the same areas, and for much the same reasons as his father. What appears as a dynamic, self-sustaining cultural process is, in part at least, a relatively simple piece of social machinery which turns out, in rather mechanical fashion, independently produced look-alikes. The problem is how to change the conditions which, by guaranteeing failure, cause the son to be made in the image of the father. (1967, p. 223)

Like their parents before them, these children are constrained in what they can offer to their own offspring. During our interviews, parents repeatedly stressed their belief in the importance of education for their children and the desire that their children be independent. A better life is what they want for their kids. Yet their children's opportunities are likely to be as limited as theirs were. As this chapter has demonstrated, the key to understanding this and other dynamics within the family is not the influence of welfare but rather the conditions of poverty.

ENDNOTES

1. Social scientists know that people's recollections of past events and attitudes are liable to be distorted (see Sudman and Bradburn 1982). This is particularly true for experiences in the distant past, such as childhood. And yet without retrospective questions, multidecade longitudinal studies would be the only source of information about these experiences. Even taking into account the potential inaccuracies, I believe the interviews yielded several generalities that are both valid and revealing.

2. Of course, this is the type of information that can become distorted with time or may simply be kept from children. It should therefore be interpreted cautiously. However, it does correspond roughly with percentages in other data sets. For

example, the National Survey of Households and Families is a national random sample of approximately thirteen thousand households interviewed in 1987 and 1988. In an analysis of intergenerational welfare use, I found that 76 percent of respondents who had received welfare during the previous year reported that their parents had never used welfare when they were growing up, 15 percent reported that their parents used welfare sometimes, and 9 percent said their parents used welfare frequently. For those who reported some amount of welfare use during one or more of the six years prior to the interview, the percentages were identical (Rank, Cheng, and Cox 1992).

3. Certainly, this process is not common to all families. Indeed, Greg Duncan (1984) has demonstrated that a fair amount of income mobility occurred among households during the ten-year period he studied. However, most of these fluctuations were from one income quintile to an adjacent one.

4. The data for this table are taken from the first month of the longitudinal sample and can be seen as a representative cross-section of the welfare population at a given time.

5. This argument goes back hundreds of years. For example, England's Poor Law Report of 1834 argued that allowing every man with a family the amount necessary to purchase bread at the price of "five quarten loaves per week, with two quarten loaves added for each number of his family" was leading to an increase in family size (Galper 1970).

6. The two standard age brackets used for estimating fertility rates are fifteen to forty-four and eighteen to forty-four. The analysis is confined to the second bracket, since very few women aged fifteen to seventeen head households on welfare. However, using either age bracket would allow a comparison of welfare fertility rates with the overall national and state rates.

The analysis pools married and unmarried women together. This is standard procedure for calculating and reporting overall fertility rates of women. However, marital status is also taken into account in the aggregate comparisons, as well as in the multivariate analysis.

The event being modeled in the life table and logistic regression analyses found in appendix B is the first observed spell of childbearing. Once a birth has occurred, women are no longer included in later time intervals. The numbers of women

experiencing a birth are extremely small, which prevents a detailed analysis of the occurrence and determinants of a second observed birth. In addition, when analyzing repeatable events, a number of statistical questions are raised (see Allison 1984). I did, however, include such women in the total sample in a separate analysis. No significant differences from the results presented here were found.

Once women exit from the welfare rolls, they are no longer included in the analysis even if they subsequently reenter the welfare system, because this would distort the representativeness of the sample. However, I did conduct separate analyses including such women and found no significant differences from the results presented here.

Finally, I include in the analysis all women who have been on welfare for at least nine months, since some women enter the welfare system because of an upcoming birth. In these cases, cause and effect is reversed—a forthcoming birth leading to welfare use, rather than welfare use leading to birth. Including only women who have been receiving welfare for at least nine months eliminates this bias.

7. The average fertility rate over the three-year period was 38.3. However, the one-year rate of 45.8 was used for comparison purposes because using the three-year average would distort the representativeness of the sampled welfare population (e.g., longer-term cases would be overrepresented).

8. Caution is warranted in the interpretation of the length of welfare variable on fertility. Without a control group of poor women not receiving public assistance, it is difficult to determine whether the welfare programs themselves or some other factor(s) were lowering the fertility rate over time.

9. Of course, this compares two slightly different events—the divorce/separation rate for welfare recipients and the divorce rate only for the overall population. State and national data for a combined divorce/separation rate (which would undoubtedly be somewhat higher) were not available.

10. The variable definitions and contrasts are as follows: employment (employed, not employed); race (white, nonwhite); current age of recipient; number of children present in recipient's household; age of youngest child (child under age four in the household, no child under age four in the household); number of programs received (all three

programs—AFDC, Food Stamps, Medicaid—received, one or two programs received); changes in
regulations (before OBRA, after OBRA); length of
time on welfare, in exact years and months, since
the beginning of the current spell, a date that could
precede the beginning of the study.

11. It should be noted that in this study, as is true for
the country as a whole (by 1994), married couples
are able to qualify for AFDC. As a result, the possibility of married couples splitting up to qualify
for cash assistance is not particularly germane.

12. The tendency to use welfare as a causal factor in
explaining family dynamics is a classic example
of misinterpreting a correlational relationship as a
causal relationship. As Arthur Okun has noted, a
naive person seeing an automobile with a flat tire
will assume that the hole in the tire must be at the
bottom, since that is where the tire is flat (see
Solow 1990, for further examples of such logic
with regard to the poor). A similar type of logic
is often used regarding welfare recipients; that is,
if a family is receiving welfare and experiences
high family disruption, welfare must be causing
the family disruption. Such causal reasoning is
simply spurious.

13. An interesting parallel is found in many Western
European countries, where low birthrates and the
fear of labor shortages have led to relatively generous financial policies designed to increase fertility rates. Overall these policies have appeared
to have had little effect on raising birthrates.

REFERENCES

Adams, B. (1986). *The family: A sociological interpretation.* San Diego, CA: Harcourt Brace Jovanovich.

Bahr, S. J. (1979). The effects of welfare on marital stability and remarriage. *Journal of Marriage and the
Family, 41,* 553–560.

Banc, M. J., & Jargowsky, P. A. (1988). The links
between government policy and family structure: What
matters and what doesn't. In A. J. Cherlin (Ed.),
The changing American family and public policy
(pp. 219–261). Washington, DC: The Urban Institute
Press.

Cherlin, A. J. (1992). Marriage, divorce, remarriage.
Cambridge: Harvard University Press.

Darity, W. A., Jr. & Meyers, S. L., Jr. (1984). Does welfare dependency cause female headship? The case of

the black family. *Journal of Marriage and the Family, 46,* 765–779.

Draper, T. W. (1981). On the relationship between welfare and marital stability: A research note. *Journal of
Marriage and the Family, 43,* 293–299.

Duncan, G. J., Hill, M. S., & Hoffman, S. D. (1988).
Welfare dependence within and across generations.
Science, 239, 467–471.

Duncan, G. J., & Hoffman, S. D. (1988). The use and
effects of welfare: A survey of recent evidence. *Social Service Review, 62,* 238–257.

Liebow, E. (1967). *Tally's corner: A study of negro
streetcorner men.* Boston: Little, Brown.

MacLeod, J. (1987). *Ain't no makin' it: Leveled aspirations in a low-income neighborhood.* Boulder, CO:
Westview Press.

Moffitt, R. (1992). Incentive effects of the U.S. welfare system: A review. *Journal of Economic Literature, 30,*
1–61.

Murray, C. (1984). *Losing ground: American social policy 1950–1980.* New York: Basic Books.

Pratt, W. F., Mosher, W. D., Bachrach, C. A., & Haun,
M. C. (1984). Understanding U.S. fertility: Findings
from the national survey of family growth, cycle III.
Population Bulletin, 38, 1–43.

Rubin, L. B. (1976). *Worlds of pain: Life in the working-
class family.* New York: Basic Books.

Stack, C. B. (1974). *All Our Kin: Strategies for Survival
in a Black Community.* New York: Harper & Row.

U.S. Bureau of the Census. (1991). *Statistical Abstract
of the United States,* 1991. Washington, DC: U.S.
Government Printing Office.

U.S. Bureau of the Census. (1992). Poverty in the
United States. *Current Population Reports,* series
P-60, no. 181. Washington, DC: U.S. Government
Printing Office.

Waite, L. J., & Lillard, L. (1991). Children and marital
disruption. *American Journal of Sociology, 96,*
930–953.

Whyte, W. F. (1943). *Street Corner Society: The Social
Structure of an Italian Slum.* Chicago: University of
Chicago Press.

Wilson, W. J. (1987). *The Truly Disadvantaged: The
Inner City, The Underclass, and Public Policy.*
Chicago: University of Chicago Press.

Working Group on the Family. (1986). *The Family: Preserving America's Future.* Washington, DC: U.S. Department of Education, Office of the Under Secretary.

PART THREE

SEXUALITY, PARTNERSHIP, AND MARRIAGE

CHAPTER 7

Sexuality and Love

Sociology is here to tell you that sexual behavior, our most private activity, and romantic love, our most personal emotion, are heavily influenced by society. That might be obvious in a society where unmarried women's chastity is closely protected and parents choose their children's spouses. It might even be obvious were we to look back at the United States in the 1950s, when many young men and a majority of young women had first sexual intercourse with the person they chose to marry. But the claim is that although social influences are weaker now, sex and love are still structured in large part by society.

That is certainly the message of social scientists from the University of Chicago, who in 1992 conducted the first comprehensive national survey of sexual behavior and attitudes. They published a long, scholarly work full of tables, *The Social Organization of Sexuality.*[1] A shorter, less-technical version, *Sex in America: A Defini-*

tive Survey, from which the following excerpt is taken, was written in collaboration with science writer Gina Kolata. The authors argue that although sex may seem personal, it is also influenced by the social attitudes of family members and friends, by laws, and by customs. They demonstrate this by analyzing the responses of people in the study to nine statements about sexuality (for example, "premarital sex is always wrong"). They found that, based on responses to these statements, people can be classified into a few groups that differ sharply in their social characteristics. The authors attempt to draw lessons from these group differences about why debates over sexual issues are so heated.

In recent years, one of the most heated debates has occurred over whether homosexual couples, gay male or lesbian, should be able to marry. The laws of the federal government and every state give certain rights and responsibilities to married couples, and all states currently require that the couple consist of a woman and a man. But as the meaning of marriage has changed, and as gay and lesbian activists have pursued an equal-rights agenda, pressure has mounted for states to recognize same-sex

---

[1]Edward O. Laumann, John H. Gagnon, Robert T. Michael, and Stuart Michaels. *The Social Organization of Sexuality: Sexual Practices in the United States* (Chicago: University of Chicago Press, 1994).

143

couples. Many localities recognize same-sex "domestic partnerships," in which unmarried couples, gay or heterosexual, have certain rights (such as the ability to cover your partner under your employer's health insurance plan). But some couples have pushed for full recognition as married partners. In 1997 or 1998, the Hawaii Supreme Court will rule on whether gay and lesbian couples can be granted marriage licenses. The prospect of gay marriage in Hawaii caused many states, and the U.S. Congress, to pass legislation in 1996 allowing a state not to recognize gay marriages registered in other states.

In the following essay, a gay-male writer whose long-time partner has died of AIDS steps back from this debate and asks searching questions. Should gay men and lesbians aspire to be married? Isn't marriage an outmoded form of partnership that is based on male dominance over women, that has existed to assure that economically dependent women who are raising children will be supported by their children's fathers, and that has attempted to control sexual behavior? What is the meaning of marriage these days, and what is its value to society? What role should the government have in regulating intimate partnerships? These are questions on which reasonable people, of whatever sexual orientation, can, and do, disagree.

READING 7-1

Sex and Society

Robert T. Michael, John H. Gagnon, Edward O. Laumann, and Gina Kolata

In private and in public, within our families and among our friends, most of us are living the sexual lives that society has urged upon us. Social networks match up couples, sexual preferences are learned or mimicked within networks, social forces push Americans toward marriage and so richly reward wedded couples that marriage turns out to be the best way to have regular sex and the best way to have a happy sex life.

But there is more to social forces than social networks, social scripts, and a widespread conviction that marriage is the ultimate goal for nearly everyone. There also are social attitudes and beliefs, the very beliefs that show up in many of the contradictory messages that we all hear about the power and the pleasure—and the shame—of sexuality.

These attitudes and beliefs underlie some of the bitter social debates of our day. Should there be limits on a woman's right to an abortion? Should sex education be taught in schools? Should we treat homosexuality as just another lifestyle or should we consider it a sin or abnormality?

One way to look at the roots of these arguments is to ask whether there is any relationship between sexual behavior and deep-seated feelings about sexual morality. And if there is a relationship between behavior and beliefs, who is likely to hold which attitudes? Are highly educated people more likely to be libertarians? Do religious people have fewer sexual partners? Do people who view sex as a form of recreation do different

Robert T. Michael, John G. Gagnon, Edward P. Laumann, and Gina Kolata, "Sex and Society" from *Sex in America: A Definitive Survey,* pp. 230–246. Copyright © 1994 by CGS Enterprises, Inc., Edward P. Laumann, Robert T. Michael, and Gina Kolata. Reprinted with the permission of Little, Brown and Company.

things in bed than people who say their sexual behavior is guided by their religious beliefs?

In a broader sense, looking for such a relationship tests our entire thesis that sexual behavior is a social behavior, determined, shaped, and molded by society like other more visible behaviors—religious practices or recreational habits, for example. If sexual behavior were a completely independent force, not subject to conscious thoughts but controlled instead by hormones, or whipped up by drives, then it should matter little what a person's attitudes are.

We asked our respondents about their attitudes and beliefs about sexual behavior, and, separately, we asked them what appealed to them sexually and what they did. This enabled us to put the pieces together. We found that there is a strong, robust link between attitudes and sexual behavior, and that it suggests why so many social issues related to sex are so contentious. Not only do people's underlying attitudes about questions of sexual morality predict what sort of sex they have in the privacy of their bedrooms, but they even predict how often people *think* about sex.

From the different attitudes and, correspondingly, different behavior of men and women, of older and younger people, and of people of different religions, we can suggest why it is that there is a war between the sexes, why it is that many women complain that men will not commit themselves to marriage, and why it is that many older people are dismayed by the sexual practices of the young.

To learn about attitudes and beliefs, we asked several questions about opinions regarding sexual behavior and other related topics, nine of which we discuss below. For example, we asked respondents to tell us how they felt about premarital sex. Was it always wrong, almost always wrong, sometimes wrong, or not wrong at all? We asked about sex between people of the same gender. Was it always, almost always, sometimes, or never wrong? We asked respondents if their religious beliefs guided their behavior.

Then, with the replies to nine such questions in hand, we used a method called cluster analysis to divide the population into groups according to their opinions about those nine issues. Although people in each group varied, overall they had a general set of similar beliefs about key issues.

Cluster analysis is a frequently used tool of social scientists who often need to find patterns in masses of data and are not aided by strong theory in their quest. In our case, we did not know ahead of time how people would sort themselves out by their answers to these questions and we knew, at the outset, that there were a large number of possible combinations of answers to our nine questions. Since each person answered all nine questions about his or her attitudes and beliefs, and since we are focusing here on whether the respondents agreed or disagreed with each statement, there are a total of 2^9 or 512 ways to answer the set of nine questions. But, we reasoned, if there are logical or belief-driven patterns to the answers, there should be certain clusters of replies among all these possibilities. A man, for example, who says his religious convictions guide his views toward sexuality might also say that sex outside of marriage is always wrong, that teenage sex is always wrong, that extramarital sex is always wrong, and that abortions should be prohibited.

Cluster analysis underlies many studies in which people are categorized according to their replies to an array of questions rather than a single one. For example, a cluster analysis looking for voting patterns might group people according to their replies to such questions as: Should capital punishment be abolished? Should all companies be required to practice affirmative action? Should handguns be outlawed? Should women have the right to an abortion for any reason? Should states provide vouchers for parents who choose to send their children to private schools? People in each group would have similar answers to the questions. While no one question characterizes a person's political views, and while each person in a cluster will not give ex-

actly the same answers as every other person in the cluster, the pattern of their replies could be a good indication of their political leanings.

In this particular analysis, we divided the respondents into three broad categories on the basis of their attitudes. First is the *traditional* category, which includes about one-third of our sample. These people say that their religious beliefs always guide their sexual behavior. In addition, they say that homosexuality is always wrong, that there should be restrictions on legal abortions, that premarital sex, teenage sex, and extramarital sex are wrong.

Second is what we called the *relational* category, whose members believe that sex should be part of a loving relationship, but that it need not always be reserved for marriage. These people, who make up nearly half of our sample, disagree with the statement that premarital sex is always wrong, for example. Most, however, say that marital infidelity is always wrong and that they would not have sex with someone they did not love. The third group is the *recreational* category, who constitute a little more than a quarter of the sample. Their defining feature is their view that sex need not have anything to do with love. In addition, most of those in this third group oppose laws to prohibit the sale of pornography to adults.

Within each of these categories, however, people varied in their attitudes, and so we subdivided the categories to further characterize our respondents. A man would be part of the relational group, for example, if he thinks extramarital sex is always wrong and that he would not have sex with anyone unless he loved her. But he might also say that same-gender sex is always wrong. A woman who is in a different group in that category might agree with him about extra-marital sex and sex with a partner she loved, but disagree about same-gender sex being wrong.

Table 1 shows how the groups are categorized, according to people's replies to the nine questions on attitudes.

TABLE 1

DESCRIPTION OF SEVEN NORMATIVE ORIENTATIONS TOWARD SEXUALITY

	Traditional			Relational		Recreational		Total sample
	Conservative	Pro-choice	Religious	Conventional	Contemporary religious	Pro-life	Libertarian	
1. Premarital sex is always wrong	100.0*	23.6	0.0	0.4	0.8	6.5	0.0	19.7
2. Premarital sex among teenagers is always wrong	99.5	90.3	78.6	29.1	33.6	65.7	19.7	60.8
3. Extramarital sex is always wrong	98.2	91.0	92.1	94.2	52.1	59.3	32.0	76.7
4. Same-gender sex is always wrong	96.4	94.4	81.9	65.4	6.4	85.9	9.0	64.8
5. There should be laws against the sale of pornography to adults	70.6	47.2	53.1	12.2	11.7	14.9	6.4	33.6
6. I would not have sex with someone unless I was in love with them	87.5	66.0	98.0	83.8	65.3	10.1	19.5	65.7
7. My religious beliefs have guided my sexual behavior	91.3	72.9	74.7	8.7	100.0	25.0	0.0	52.3
8. A woman should be able to obtain a legal abortion if she was raped	56.3	98.6	82.3	99.1	99.3	84.3	99.8	88.0
9. A woman should be able to obtain a legal abortion if she wants it for any reason	0.5	100.0	0.0	87.4	84.9	9.3	88.6	52.4
N = 2,843	15.4%	15.2%	19.1%	15.9%	9.3%	8.7%	16.4%	100.0%

Oversample was excluded from analysis, as were respondents who had missing values for one or more items. Clusters were derived by minimizing the squared Euclidean distance between members within each cluster. All items were dichotomized before clustering. Column percentages.
*Indicates the percentage of persons in the "Conservative Traditional" cluster who believe that premarital sex is always wrong.

TABLE 2

DISTRIBUTION OF NORMATIVE ORIENTATIONS WITHIN DEMOGRAPHIC GROUPS

Social characteristics	Normative orientation		
	Traditional	Relational	Recreational
Gender			
Men	26.9%	40.1%	33.0%
Women	33.7	47.6	18.7
Age			
Men			
18–24	17.4	46.9	35.7
25–29	21.0	46.2	32.9
30–39	26.2	38.6	35.2
40–49	31.2	38.2	30.5
50–59	40.1	31.3	28.6
Women			
18–24	23.0	51.8	25.3
25–29	27.5	54.6	17.9
30–39	34.6	46.6	18.8
40–49	34.5	44.9	20.6
50–59	47.0	43.4	9.6
Marital/Residential Status			
Men			
Noncohabiting	18.4	39.7	42.0
Cohabiting	8.6	48.4	43.0
Married	36.4	39.0	24.5
Women			
Noncohabiting	31.9	46.8	21.3
Cohabiting	23.9	50.4	25.6
Married	36.2	48.1	15.8

The columns show the percentages of our population who agree with the statements in the column on the left. We divided the traditional category into "conservative" and "pro-choice" groups essentially according to their opinions on abortion. Although people in this category nearly all believe that premarital sex among teenagers, same-gender sex, and extramarital sex are always wrong, they split on whether a women should be able to have an abortion.

The relational category breaks down into three groups, which we have labeled as religious, conventional, and contemporary religious. Those in the religious group said that religious beliefs shape their sexual behavior and tended to say that they oppose sex between people of the same gender and they oppose abortions. The conventional group is more tolerant than the religious group toward teenage sex, pornography, and abortion and are far less likely to say they are influenced by religious beliefs. But most think that same-gender sex and extramarital sex are always wrong. The contemporary religious group is much more tolerant of homosexuality but people in this group say that they are guided by their religious beliefs.

In the recreational category, there are two groups. One, which we call pro-life, consists of people who oppose both homosexuality and abortion for any reason but who are more accepting of teenage sex, extramarital sex, and pornog-

TABLE 2 (continued)

DISTRIBUTION OF NORMATIVE ORIENTATIONS WITHIN DEMOGRAPHIC GROUPS

Social characteristics	Normative orientation		
	Traditional	Relational	Recreational
Education			
Men			
Less than high school	31.6	39.5	28.8
High school graduate or equivalent	28.3	40.9	30.8
Any college	25.0	39.8	35.2
Women			
Less than high school	36.6	47.6	15.9
High school graduate or equivalent	38.3	46.0	15.7
Any college	30.4	48.7	20.9
Religion			
Men			
None	11.7	39.1	49.2
Mainline Protestant	24.2	43.8	32.0
Conservative Protestant	44.5	30.1	25.3
Catholic	17.8	49.6	32.6
Women			
None	10.4	44.4	45.2
Mainline Protestant	30.9	51.4	17.7
Conservative Protestant	50.5	38.4	11.2
Catholic	22.2	58.0	19.8
Race/Ethnicity			
Men			
White	26.1	41.6	32.3
Black	32.4	25.4	42.3
Hispanic	25.3	45.1	29.7
Women			
White	30.5	48.3	21.2
Black	45.3	45.8	8.9
Hispanic	40.7	43.2	16.1

Note: Percentages in rows total 100 percent.

raphy. The second group is the libertarian group. They have the most accepting position on all the items. None of this libertarian group considers religion as a guide to their sexual behavior.

Just dividing the respondents into these groupings on the basis of their opinions, however, tells only part of the story. We also want to know how the groups differ by social characteristics. Men and women gravitate to different groups, as seen in Table 2. So do older and younger people and so do blacks and whites. The distribution of people into groups reveals why the formation of so-

cial policy regarding sexual issues is so contentious and so complex.

The top rows of Table 2 tell us that women are more likely to have the opinions we labeled "traditional" and are much less likely to have the views we called "recreational." By age, we see that the older men and women are disproportionately "traditional" and much less likely to hold the "recreational" views.

With distributions like this, it is no wonder that the battle between the sexes rages. Lance Morrow, a columnist for *Time* magazine, bemoaned men's fate. Women, he complained, have a particularly pejorative view of hapless men, thinking and saying something like "Men-are-animals-I-don't-care-if-they're-not-doing-anything-at-the-moment-they're-thinking-about-it-and-they-will-when-they-have-a-chance." Some women, on the other hand, have sniped that men are not so blameless, pointing out that many men still leer at women when they walk down the street, and some men act like they have to be dragged kicking and screaming into marriage, behaving as if marriage is a ball and chain.

The distribution of men and women in the attitude clusters tells us, at least, that many more women than men are looking for love and consider marriage to be a prerequisite for sex. When women bitterly complain that the men they meet are not interested in long-term commitments, their laments have a ring of truth. Many more men than women are looking for sexual play and pleasure, with marriage or even love not necessarily a part of it. After all, men in the recreational category may be unlikely to feel that linking sex with marriage is high on their list of priorities. When men note that their girlfriends are always trying to lure them into a making a commitment to exclusivity or that their relationships seem to end with an ultimatum—marry me or get out—there is a good reason for it.

The conflicting goals of men and women—and particularly young men and young women—are played out in the lines the men may use when they meet women. And at no time is this more true than in adolescence and young adulthood, the very time that men are most likely to be part of all-male groups who have recreational attitudes toward sex.

Elijah Anderson, a sociologist at the University of Pennsylvania, tells how black teenagers in an inner-city neighborhood take on these roles: "The lore of the streets says there is a contest going on between the boy and girl before they even meet. To the young man, the woman becomes, in the most profound sense, a sexual object. Her body and mind are the object of a sexual game, to be won for his personal aggrandizement." And to win a young woman, Anderson says, the young man devises a rap, "whose object is to inspire sexual interest."*

The young women, on the other hand, want "a boyfriend, a fiancé, a husband, and the fairy-tale prospect of living happily ever after with one's children in a good house in a nice neighborhood," Anderson says. So the young man, trying to have sex with a woman, "shows her the side of himself that he knows she wants to see, that represents what she wants in a man." He may take the young woman to church, visit her family, help her with chores. But after the young man has sex with the young woman, he often leaves her for a new conquest.

The teenage woman "may know she is being played but given the effectiveness of his rap, his presentation of self, his looks, his age, his wit, his dancing ability, and his general popularity, infatuation often rules," Anderson notes.

Put differently, we see in this typical script the competitive marketplace for sexual partners. The young man is emphasizing those of his attributes that he thinks will attract the young woman. He engages in negotiations and interchanges designed, with all his strategic skills, to persuade her that a friendship that includes sex will be to her liking. She, similarly, emphasizes her attributes that she thinks might attract the most appealing guy. She carefully calibrates her encouragement and insists on behavior that wraps sex into the bundle of activities that she desires.

Whether the outcome is a single sex episode or a more steady dating relationship or even a longer-term sexual partnership, each of these young people offers and withholds, explores and considers, and reaches agreement about the sex.

---

*Elijah Anderson, *Streetwise: Race, Class, and Change in an Urban Community* (Chicago: University of Chicago Press, 1990).

The strategic behavior by each, designed to attract the partner and achieve the objective that each seeks, embeds the individual's endeavor in a social context that typically involves competition.

The table also shows us that the married men and women are least likely to hold the recreational view of sexuality, while the not-married men are far more likely to hold that set of views. The cohabiting men and women, on the other hand, are least likely to hold the traditional views of sexuality. Of course, these unmarried men and women are also likely to be younger than those who are married, so the pattern by marital status partly just mirrors the pattern we noted above that older (and married) people hold more traditional views while the younger (unmarried) people are more likely to be in the recreational category. This contributes to the battle of the generations. Older people, often the parents of teenagers or of people in their 20s, tend to have a very different view of the purpose of sex.

The age distribution also suggests the possibility that people change their attitudes over the years (though our data cannot confirm this), moving from times, in their youth, when they thought love need have nothing to do with sex to times, when they grow older, when loving relationships became more central to sexuality. People seem to move along the spectrum from libertarian toward conservative as they age. This could be one reason why 58 percent of our respondents who said premarital sex is always wrong also told us that they themselves had had sex before they were married. And it could explain why 26 percent of our respondents who told us that teenage sex is always wrong also said that they had had sex when they were teenagers. These differences by age might, on the other hand, reflect lifelong held differences of opinion of those born in the 1930s, the 1940s, and so on, but we speculate that these opinions change with age.

When we look at the relationship between race, religion, and education and attitudes about sex, we can see why people tend to feel more comfortable when they choose partners like themselves. The table shows, for example, that few who are not religious are part of the traditional category, but 48 percent of conservative Protestants are traditionalists. People with no religion are most likely to be part of the recreational category—nearly half are found here.

Our findings also show that the clichéd strife between black men and black women may, in fact, reflect fundamentally different attitudes about sex. Black women are more likely than white or Hispanic women to be traditionalists and are noticeably less likely than other women to be in the recreational category—fewer than 10 percent of black women have recreational views toward sex. But black men are noticeably more likely than other men to be in the recreational group—more than 40 percent have recreational views.

The pattern seen in Table 2 by education level is not dramatic, but it is quite systematic. Those with less than a high school level of education are more likely to hold traditional views about sexuality and less likely to hold recreational views; those with college education are just the opposite: they are more likely to hold the recreational views and least likely to hold the traditional views.

We did not have strong expectations or theories about how people's views of sexuality might be related to their social characteristics. But our findings seem to confirm the notion that people's beliefs about sexual morality are part of a much broader social and religious outlook that helps define who they are. Their orientations are reinforced by their friends and family and others in their social networks.

The next question is whether what people believe about sexual behavior is linked to what they actually do sexually. It is one thing to have a certain set of attitudes, but it is another thing to have those attitudes determine your most private acts, wishes, and thoughts. Yet that is what we find, as seen in Table 3. Membership in a

TABLE 3

SELECTED SEXUAL BEHAVIORS WITHIN NORMATIVE GROUPS

Panel A: Men

Sexual behaviors	Normative orientation		
	Traditional	Relational	Recreational
Partners last year: Noncohabiting			
None	40.6%	22.4%	12.8%
One	30.2	41.0	27.9
Two or more	29.2	36.6	59.4
Partners last year: Married			
Zero or one	97.0	96.0	84.9
Two or more	3.0	4.0	15.1
Last year sex frequency			
None	12.5	8.8	8.4
Three times a month or less	31.4	34.2	35.9
Once a week or more	56.1	57.1	55.7
Think about sex			
Twice a month or less	13.4	14.1	7.1
Twice a week or less	40.8	35.3	27.0
Daily or more	45.8	50.6	65.9
Masturbate			
Never	50.2	35.5	25.6
Three times a month or less	32.1	38.5	39.4
Once a week or more	17.7	26.0	35.0
Had oral sex (active or passive) with primary partner in last year			
Yes	56.4	78.2	80.7
Had anal sex during lifetime			
Yes	18.7	23.1	32.3
Ever had same-gender partner since age 18			
Yes	2.6	4.5	7.8

particular attitudinal group is closely associated with what their sexual practices are. It is even correlated with how often people think about sex and how often they have sex.

The top portion of both panels of Table 3 shows the number of sex partners in the past year for the men and women who are not living with a partner. We see there that those who have traditional views about sexuality mostly have zero or one partner and only a relatively small percentage had two or more sex partners in the past year: about 30 percent of the men and about 14 percent of the women have that many. But of those who held recreational views of sexuality, about 60 percent of the men and nearly 50 percent of the women had two or more sex partners in the past year. Their attitudes and opinions, as characterized by the three categories of traditional, relational, and recreational, do in fact distinguish these unmarried and non-cohabiting respondents quite effectively in terms of their number of sex partners in the past year.

| TABLE 3 (continued) |

SELECTED SEXUAL BEHAVIORS WITHIN NORMATIVE GROUPS

Panel B: Women

Sexual behaviors	Normative orientation		
	Traditional	Relational	Recreational
Partners last year: Noncohabiting			
None	46.7	25.2	14.6
One	39.1	52.6	36.6
Two or more	14.1	22.2	48.8
Partners last year: Married			
Zero or one	98.0	98.5	92.5
Two or more	2.0	1.5	7.5
Last year sex frequency			
None	18.5	10.8	8.0
Three times a month or less	31.5	34.0	39.6
Once a week or more	50.0	55.1	52.4
Think about sex			
Twice a month or less	45.0	36.8	30.1
Twice a week or less	40.6	44.0	39.0
Daily or more	14.3	19.2	30.8
Masturbate			
Never	69.0	56.6	37.5
Three times a month or less	26.0	35.4	50.2
Once a week or more	5.0	8.1	12.3
Had oral sex (active or passive) with primary partner in last year			
Yes	55.9	73.9	83.6
Had anal sex during lifetime			
Yes	13.2	19.5	37.5
Ever had same-gender partner since age 18			
Yes	0.8	3.0	8.6

Note: Percentages in columns total 100 percent within the categories; the "no" percentages are omitted in the last three.

To be sure, there are a few of those with a traditionalist view who have several sex partners, and a few of those with a recreationalist's view who have no sex partner or one partner, but in the main, the views they held are very consistent with the number of partners they had in the past year.

The same is true of those who are married, as seen in the second set of rows in Table 3. For the men who were traditionalists or relational-ists, only 3 or 4 percent had more than one sex partner in the past year, but as many as 15 percent of those who were recreationalists had more than one. The same pattern is seen for the married women where only 1 or 2 percent of the traditionalists and relationalists had more than one partner but more than 7 percent of the recreationalists had more than one. The tremendous influence of marital status on the number of sex partners is seen here, with a vast majority of the married men and women having zero or one sex partner in the past year, and the unmarried much more likely to have several, but within both marital statuses the influence of these opinions shines through.

In contrast, people's views about sex had little bearing on how often they had sex. Roughly half of those in each of the three categories report having sex once a week or more. Although somewhat fewer recreationalists said they did not have sex at all last year, the difference between them and those in other groups was not very great. We suspect it reflects the fact that people in the recreational group are more likely to be young and may not have yet found a sexual partner, however much they may want to.

Whether they are actually having sex or not, people who are recreationalists are much more likely than traditionalists to think about sex every day and are much more likely to masturbate. Those in the recreational group are twice as likely as those in the traditionalist group to report that they masturbated once a week or more.

Oral and anal sex and sex with someone of the same gender follow the same patterns, as is seen in the bottom three rows of Table 3. Recreationalists are more likely than traditionalists to have had oral sex in the last year with their partner. They also are more likely to have had anal sex. And they are more likely to have had same-gender sex. In fact, as we move along the scale from traditionalist to recreationalist, the frequency of oral sex, anal sex, and same-gender sex increases.

Overall, people's sexual opinions and their behavior mesh quite closely. We cannot tell whether the opinions prompted the behavior or whether the behavior prompted the opinions, or both, but the relationship is clear.

From these findings on attitudes, beliefs, and sexual behavior along with our findings on sexual networks and choices of sexual partners, we can start to see why America has such heated social policy debates about sexual issues such as abortion, public nudity, gay rights, and pornography.

As Table 2 showed, opinions and social characteristics seem to go hand in hand. The young have one set of opinions about sexuality while older adults have another; conservative Protestants have one set of views while those without religious affiliations have another; the less educated tend to have different views than the well educated. Table 3 showed that people's attitudes are reflected in their behavior, so different groups really do act differently.

We see that we have probably paired off with someone who has many of our own opinions about sexuality. That is, in fact, probably a key reason why we choose partners from our own social group. Of course, opinions also may shift and become more similar as the partnership continues, but when that happens, it only makes the partnership stronger. It can be very difficult to maintain a sexual relationship with someone who strongly disagrees with you about such matters as whether abortion or extramarital sex is always wrong or whether religious beliefs always guide sexual behavior.

Our friends and families, the members of our social networks, also tend to be like us in social characteristics, and so they are likely to share many of our opinions about sexual behavior. Consequently, when we have discussions with our friends we tend to be speaking to people who are like us and who agree with us about sex. So we tend to get reinforcement for our views. That is probably one of the main reasons why our opinions are so internally consistent and so well reflected in our sexual behavior.

But all this reinforcement and consistency make it very threatening to change our views, to become convinced by an outside argument or to change an opinion about one aspect of sexual behavior, such as whether extramarital sex is always wrong, without changing any other opinions. Our opinions, behavior, and social networks all tend to encourage us to hold to those views that help tie all these opinions, beliefs, and behavior together. And when we see these sets of behaviors as woven together by our religious beliefs and our ethical principles, we are, quite understandably, reluctant to give ground. So the national debates on so many of these sexual issues become heated and all sides become entrenched. No wonder we are a nation that is deeply conflicted about sexual matters and that the disputes seem to go on forever, with no compromises in sight.

And with this we have traveled full circle, going from an investigation of what people do and who they are to who they are and what they do and what they believe about sex. We began our study by asking whether sexual behavior could be studied in the same way as other social behaviors and, if so, whether it followed any social rules. We asked whether the privateness of sexual behavior and the powerful myths put it in a class apart from other social behaviors or whether, when we drew back the curtain and looked at what really happens, sexual behavior would turn out to be not so mysterious after all.

In every instance, our data have shown that social forces are powerful and persistent in determining sexual behavior. We have found that our society constrains us, nudging us toward partners who are like ourselves. But, at the same time, it frees us, putting us together with people who have the same sorts of general understandings about sex that we do and so easing our way into sexual intimacies and revelations. We also found that although America may not be as sexy a place as it is often portrayed, most people are satisfied with the sexual lives they have chosen or that were imposed upon them.

America is not the golden land of eroticism where everybody who is young and beautiful has a hot sex life. Nor is it a land where vast hordes of miserable people, kicked out of the sexual banquet, lick their wounds in silence and resentment. Instead, it is a nation that uses social forces to encourage sexual norms and whose sexual behavior is, in large measure, socially determined. It is a nation of people who are for the most part content, or at least not highly dissatisfied, with the sexual lots they have drawn.

And, for those who feel the status quo is far from ideal, we have found that the costs of breaching the social pressures may be high, and the rewards of going along may be great. But by seeing where and how the pressures are brought to bear, we can break away from the myths and magical thinking that have captured us in the past. With unclouded eyes, we can ask whether we really want changes in sexual behavior and, if so, what the benefits and costs of these changes might be.

READING 7–2

Wedded to an Illusion: Do Gays and Lesbians Really Want the Right to Marry?

Fenton Johnson

Last summer, when American politicians underwent yet another of their periodic convulsions over the status of gays and lesbians, I found myself pondering the evolving history of marriage. In response to the possible recognition of same-gender marriages by the state of Hawaii, Congress overwhelmingly passed the Defense of Marriage Act, which reserves federal benefits and rights for male-female couples and permits states not to recognize same-gender marriages performed in other states. Sponsored in the House of Representatives by Bob Barr (three marriages) and endorsed by then Senator Bob Dole (two marriages), the bill was called "gay baiting" by the White House and "unnecessary" by President Clinton (he of the colorful personal

---

Fenton Johnson, "Wedded to an Illusion: Do Gays and Lesbians Really Want the Right to Marry?" from *Harper's* (November 1996): 41–50. Copyright © 1986 by *Harper's* magazine. Reprinted with the permission of *Harper's*. All rights reserved.

life), who signed it nonetheless in late September. The law might appear to be only so much election-year positioning and counterpositioning, but long after this year's political season is forgotten, we will be agonizing over the questions implicit in the legislation. As a married, straight friend cracked to me, "If marriage needs Congress to defend it, then we know we're in trouble."

Marriage. What does it mean these days? Peau de soie, illusion veil, old, new, borrowed, blue? Can it mean the same thing to a heterosexual couple, raised to consider it the pinnacle of emotional fulfillment, as to a same-gender couple, the most conventional of whom must find the label "married" awkward? Can it mean the same thing to a young lesbian—out since her teens, occasionally bisexual, wanting a child, planning a career—as to me, a forty-plus shell-shocked AIDS widower? And in an era of no-fault divorce, can it mean to any of us what it meant to our parents?

The unacceptability of gay marriages may have bloomed with sudden propitiousness on the agendas of Clinton and Dole, but the issue has been steadily moving into the legal conversation across the last 25 years. In 1991 three Hawaiian couples—two lesbian, one gay-male—sued the state over the denial of their applications for marriage licenses; on principle, a heterosexual ACLU attorney took the case. Two years later, to everyone's amazement, the Hawaii Supreme Court ruled, in *Baehr* v. *Lewin,* that the state's denial of licenses violated the Hawaii constitution's equal-rights protections. The court took care to note that the sexual orientation of the plaintiffs was irrelevant. At issue instead was discrimination based on gender: the state discriminates by offering benefits (including income tax, worker's compensation, retirement, welfare, and spousal support) to married men and women that it denies to exclusively male or female couples.

This is no minor point. What the court ruled on in Hawaii was not *gay* marriage but simply *marriage*: whether the union of two people of the same gender qualifies for the benefits the state offers to mixed-gender couples, no matter if the spouses marry for love or children or Social Security benefits, no matter if they are gay or straight or celibate—in other words, all those reasons, good and bad, for which men and women now marry.

The Hawaii justices remanded the case to a lower court, challenging the attorney general to justify gender discrimination in marriage benefits. The plaintiff's attorneys currently expect the State Supreme Court to allow the issuance of marriage licenses to same-gender couples by late 1997, though more litigation seems as likely, given the determination and financing of the opposition. If the state court acts as the plaintiffs anticipate, the matter will surely reach the federal level. Contrary to widespread reporting and rhetoric, Article IV of the U.S. Constitution does not necessarily require states to recognize marriages performed in other states; interstate recognition of marriage remains largely unexplored legal terrain.[1] If a couple marries in Hawaii, then moves to New York or Georgia, can those states refuse to recognize the marriage? Under the Defense of Marriage Act, the answer is yes, though some legal experts argue that states already have this right, while other experts contend that the act is unconstitutional. Either way the issue invokes a resonant precedent: as recently as 1967, 16 states refused to recognize mixed-race marriages legally performed elsewhere. Those antimiscegenation laws were struck down that same year by the U.S. Supreme Court in *Loving* v. *Virginia,* a landmark case that the Hawaii court cited at length in *Baehr* v. *Lewin.*

At stake first and foremost are the rights of gays and lesbians to assume the state-conferred benefits of marriage. The assumption of these rights is controversial enough, but *Baehr* has still larger implications for an institution that has historically served as the foundation of a male-dominated society. It's instructive to recall that in the late 1970s Phyllis Schlafly and her anti-Equal Rights Amendment (ERA) allies predicted that the codification of the equality of women and men, as embodied in a federal ERA, would lead to gay marriage, presumably because they felt that to codify the equality of women and men would undermine the values upon which traditional marriage rests. The federal amendment failed, but Hawaii (along with several other states) adopted its own ERA; and here we are, just as Schlafly predicted—right in the place, I argue, where we ought to be. For this is the profound and scary and exhilarating fact: to assume the equality of women and men is to demand rethinking the institution that more than any other defines how men and women relate.

Marriage has always been an evolving institution, bent and shaped by the historical moment and the needs and demands of its participants. The Romans recognized the phenomenon we call "falling in love," but they considered it a hindrance to the establishment of stable households. Marriages certified by the state had their foundations not in religion or romance but in pragmatics—e.g., the joining of socially prominent households. Divorce was acceptable, and women were generally powerless to influence its outcome; the early Catholic Church restricted divorce partly as a means of protecting women and children from easy abandonment.

At the beginning of the 13th century, facing schisms and heresies, and seeking to consolidate its power, the Catholic Church institutionalized marriage, confirming it as a sacrament and requiring that a priest officiate—a crucial step in the intrusion of organized religion into what had previously been a private transaction. Several centuries later, the conception of "family" began to be transformed from an extended feudal unit that often included cousins, servants, and even neighbors to a tightly knit nuclear unit composed of parents and children and headed by a man. With marriage as its cornerstone, this idealized unit forms the foundation for virtually all American legislation concerning the family.

Throughout these developments, one aspect of marriage remained consistent: even as women were idealized, they were widely regarded as chattel—part of the husband's personal property; marriage was state certification of that ownership. With the women's suffrage movement came a growing acceptance of the equality of women and men, along with the principle that the individual's happiness is of equal or greater importance than the honoring of social norms, including the marriage contract. Divorce became both common and accepted, to the point that even the woman who marries into wealth gains little economic security (absent a good lawyer or a prenuptial agreement).

Women have arguably gotten the worst of both worlds: Men may more easily leave their wives, but women are nowhere near achieving earning parity, so that now they must cope with economic insecurity as well as the fear of being dumped. For every woman who revels in freedom and the income from a fulfilling career, many more face supporting themselves and often their children on welfare or at a low salary with few benefits and no job security, dependent on child support or alimony often in arrears. No wonder that almost a third of babies are now born out of wedlock, a figure that has risen consistently since the 1950s. Some of these mothers (more than a few of them lesbians) are building matriarchal families, but many are giving birth to unplanned and probably unwanted children. Whether by design or by happenstance, these unmarried women are the primary force in changing the profile of the family; any discussion about contemporary marriage that excludes them is pointless.

Both our culture and its couples are searching for some new thinking, informed by the understanding that what is at stake is our perception of the marriage contract and women's role in defining it. Understandably, advocates of same-gender marriage have shied away from territory so daunting, focusing on the narrower civil-rights issues—the need to extend, as required by our American commitment to equal treatment before the law, the invitation to another class of people to participate in the same troubled ritual, with one tangible result being a bonanza for attorneys specializing in gay divorce.

That fight is important, but in the long run the exclusive focus on civil rights minimizes the positive implications of the social transformation lesbians and gays are helping to bring about. For centuries gay and lesbian couples, along with significant numbers of unmarried heterosexuals, have formed and maintained relationships outside legislative and social approval that have endured persecution and duress for this simple reason: love. This is not to downplay the importance of the marriage license, which comes with rights and responsibilities without which gays and lesbians will never be considered full signatories to the social contract; nor is it to imply that these relationships are perfect. It is rather to point out the nature of gay couples' particular gift, the reward of those lucky enough to be given the wits and courage to survive in the face of adversity. Many of us know as much or more about partnering than those who have fallen into it as a given, who may live unaware of the degree to which their partnerships depend on the support of conventions—including the woman's acceptance of the man's primacy.

Baehr v. *Lewin* represents the logical culmination of generations of challenge, by feminists joined later by gay and lesbian activists, to an institution once almost exclusively shaped by gender roles and organized religion. As such, it presents an historic opportunity to reexamine the performance and practice of the institution on which so many of our hopes, rituals, and assumptions are based; to reconsider what we are institutionalizing and why.

Seeking to provide a legally defensible justification for limiting benefits to mixed-gender marriages, the Hawaii attorney general, after years of research, has thus far only confirmed this insurmountable reality: if one subscribes to the principles that government should not serve specific religious agendas and that it should not discriminate on the basis of gender, there is no logical reason to limit marriage benefits to mixed-gender couples. Opponents of same-gender marriage argue that it contradicts the essential purpose of the institution, which is procreation; but the state does not ask prospective mixed-gender spouses if they intend to have children, and the law grants a childless married couple the same rights and benefits as their most prolific married neighbors. Invoking the nation's Judeo-Christian heritage is no help; even if one believes that Christians and Jews should dictate government policy, a few of the more liberal denominations have already endorsed same-gender marriage, and the issue is under serious debate in mainstream churches.[2] How may the state take sides in a theological debate, especially when the parties to the debate are so internally divided? In 1978, the Supreme Court established in *Zablocki* v. *Redhail* that a citizen's right to marry is so fundamental that it cannot be denied even to individuals who have demonstrated that they are inadequate to the task. Given that the law guarantees the right of deadbeat dads and most prison inmates to marry, what could be the logic for denying that right to two men or two women who are maintaining a stable, responsible household?

The strongest argument against same-gender marriage is not logical but arbitrary: society must have unambiguous definitions to which it turns when faced with conflicts between the desires of its citizens and the interests of its larger community. Marriage is a union between a man and a woman because that is how most people define the word, however unjust this may be for same-gender couples who wish to avail themselves of its rights.

Advocates of same-gender marriage respond that "the interests of the larger community" is an evolving concept. That an institution embodies social norms does not render it immune to change—slavery was once socially accepted, just as mixed-race marriages were widely forbidden and divorce an irreparable stigma. The rebuttal is accurate, but it evades the question of where the state draws the line in balancing individual needs and desires against the maintenance of community norms. Why should the state endorse same-gender couples but not (as opponents of same-gender marriage argue will result) polygamists or child spouses? The question is now more pressing because of the prevailing sense of accelerated cultural breakdown, wherein nothing seems secure, not even the definition of . . . well, marriage.

Surely the triumph of Reaganomics and corporate bottom-line thinking is more responsible for this breakdown of the social contract than the efforts of an ostracized minority to stabilize its communities. In any case marriage and the family began their transformation long before the gay civil-rights movement. By 1975, only six years after the Stonewall rebellion that marked the first widespread public emergence of lesbians and gays, half of all marriages ended in divorce. But in uncertain times people search for scapegoats, and unless gays and lesbians can make a convincing case for the positive impact of our relationships, we are not likely to persuade any but the already converted.

Tellingly enough, male writers have been more passionate than women in their attachment to traditional marriage forms. Among gay male writers, Andrew Sullivan (*Virtually Normal*) and William Eskridge Jr. (*The Case for Same-Sex Marriage*) have written excellent supporting arguments.[3] Both consider legalization of same-gender marriage a means toward encouraging same-gender couples to model themselves on heterosexual marriage.

Sullivan makes an eloquent case for gay marriage but gives only a nod to the high failure rate of heterosexual marriages. Eskridge is sensitive to the women's issues inherent in marriage, but like Sullivan he endorses the institution as it exists, albeit alongside other options for partner-

ing. Along the way he endorses the myth that marriage conveys the means to control extramarital sexual behavior to men (or women) otherwise unlikely to achieve such control, as well as the myth that gay men are more promiscuous than their straight counterparts.[4] More discouraging is Eskridge's acceptance of the assumption that sexual desire is the beast lurking in our social jungle, whose containment is a prerequisite for a moral civilization (he subtitles his book *From Sexual Liberty to Civilized Commitment*, epitomizing in a phrase the puritanical impulse to make bachelorhood equivalent to moral lassitude, where all sexual expression outside wedlock is morally tainted).

That sexuality and morality are intimately linked I take as a given; one loses sight of this connection at the risk of one's self-respect and, by extension, one's ability to love others. We are surrounded by evidence of that loss of respect, particularly in television and advertising, whose relentless promotion of amoral heterosexual sex is surely the greatest factor in breaking down public and private morality. But to presume that morality follows on marriage is to ignore centuries of evidence that each is very much possible without the other.

Among heterosexual male writers, even the most intelligent dwell in fantasy logic; when they arrive at a difficult point they invoke God (an unanswering authority), or homophobic bombast, or both. James Q. Wilson, management and public policy professor at UCLA, is among the more reasonable, but even he attacks (with no apparent irony) the "overeducated," whom he accuses of "mounting a utilitarian assault on the family." As the ninth of nine children of a rural, blue-collar family whose parents (married 47 years) sacrificed a great deal to educate their children, I note that the only "overeducated" people I have met are those who take as gospel the rules they have been taught rather than open their eyes to the reality in which they live, who witness love and yet deny its full expression.

Not all men and women fall into marriage unconscious of role models, of course. But it's hard work to avoid a form shouted at all of us daily in a million ways, whereas for same-gender partnerships to fall into that form requires deliberate denial. For same-gender relationships to endure, the partners have to figure out that we are required to make them up as we go along. This does not mean that we are always adequate to the task, which is why my friend Frederick Hertz, an Oakland attorney specializing in same-gender partnerships, originally opposed same-gender marriage. "Marriage as it exists imposes a legal partnership on people that is seldom in sync with how they think about their relationship," he tells me. "Marriage is designed to take care of dependent spouses, people who stay home to take care of the children, as well as to compensate for economic inequalities between genders. The idea of supporting a spouse for the rest of his or her life is totally contrary to the way most people nowadays think." Hertz (a partner in a 14-year relationship) resists the "couple-ism" that he perceives arising among gays and lesbians because he believes it imitates a heterosexual world in which women whose partners die or abandon them are left with almost no social support. "I talk to straight divorced women in their 40s and 50s" he says. "They have a lack of self-worth that's devastating. My single gay friends have a hard enough time—imagine what things would be like for them if marriage were the norm."

Then the realities of working with gay and lesbian couples struggling without social approval brought Hertz to an uneasy support of the battle for same-gender marriage rights. Unlike most advocates, however, he qualifies his endorsement by adding that "while we're working for gay-marriage rights we should also be talking about issues of economic and emotional dependency among couples . . . A partner can contribute emotional support to a relationship that is as valuable to its sustenance as an economic contribution. We need to find legal ways to protect those dependent spouses." To that end Hertz argues for a variety of state-endorsed domestic-partnership arrangements in addition to marriage, noting that although such categories may create a kind of second-class relationship, they're a step toward the state offering options that reflect contemporary life. "I want to go to the marriage bureau and have options among ways of getting married," he says. "I want the social acceptance of marriage but with options that are more appropriate for the range of couples' experiences—including same-gender childless couples."

In other words, rather than attempt to conform same-gender couplings to an institution so deeply rooted in sexism, why not consider ways of incorporating stability and egalitarianism into new models of marriage? Rather than consider the control of sexual behavior as a primary goal of marriage, why not leave issues of monogamy to the individuals and focus instead on marriage as the primary (though not the only) means whereby two people help each other and their dependents through life?

Invoking the feminist writer Martha Fineman, American University law professor Nancy Polikoff argues that organizing society around sexually connected people is wrong; the more central units are dependents and their caretakers. Extrapolating from this thinking, one can imagine the state requiring that couples, regardless of gender, take steps toward attaining the benefits currently attached to marriage. Under this model the state might restrict the most significant of marriage's current benefits to those couples who demonstrate stability. The government might then get out of the marriage-certification business altogether; Hawaii governor Ben Cayetano, among others, has suggested as much. Government-conferred benefits currently reserved for married couples would instead be allocated as rewards for behavior that contributes to social stability. Tax breaks would be awarded, regardless of marital status, to stable lower- and middle-income households financially responsible for children, the elderly, or the handicapped. Other state- or federally conferred privileges—such as residency for foreign spouses, veteran's benefits, tax-free transfer of property, and the right to joint adoption—would be reserved for couples who had demonstrated the ability to sustain a household over two to five years. The decision to assume the label "marriage" would be left to the individuals involved, who might or might not seek ratification of their decision by a priest or minister or rabbi. The motivation behind such changes would be not to eliminate marriage but to encourage and sustain stable households, while leaving the definition and sustenance of marriage to the partners involved, along with their community of relatives, friends, and—if they so choose—churches.

In the most profound relationship I have known, my partner and I followed a pattern typical of an enduring gay male relationship. We wrangled over monogamy, ultimately deciding to permit safe sex outside the relationship. In fact, he never acted on that permission; I acted on it exactly once, in an incident we discussed the next day. We were bound not by sexual exclusivity but by trust, mutual support, and fidelity—in a word, love, only one manifestation of which is monogamy.

Polikoff tells of another model, unconventional by the standards of the larger culture but common among gay and lesbian communities: A friend died of breast cancer; her blood family arrived for the funeral. "They were astounded to discover that their daughter had a group of people who were a family—somebody had organized a schedule, somebody brought food every night," she says. "In some ways it was the absence of marriage as a dominant institution that created space for the development of a family defined in much broader ways." I find it difficult to imagine either of these relationships—mine or that described by Polikoff—developing in the presence of marriage as practiced by most of our forebears; easier to imagine our experiences influencing the evolution of marriage to a more encompassing, compassionate place.

Earlier I called myself an "AIDS widower," but I was playing fast and loose with words; I can't be a widower, since my partner and I were never married. He was the only child of Holocaust survivors, and he taught me, an HIV-negative man preoccupied with the future, the lessons his parents had taught him: the value of living fully in the present and the power of love.

He fell ill while we were traveling in France, during what we knew would be our last vacation. After checking him into a Paris hospital, I had to sneak past the staff to be at his side; each time they ordered me out, until finally they told me they would call the police. Faced with the threat of violence, I left the room. He died alone as I paced the hall outside his door, frantic to be at his side but with no recourse—I was, after all, only his friend.

At a dinner party not long ago I asked a mix of gay and heterosexual guests to name ways society might better support the survival of gay and lesbian relationships. A beat of silence followed, then someone piped up: "You mean, the survival of *any* relationships." Everyone agreed that all relationships are under stress, that their dissolution had become an accepted, possibly assumed part of the status quo.

The question is not, as opponents would have us believe, will marriage survive the legalization of same-gender partnerships? Instead, the questions are how do society and the state support stable households in a world where the composition of families is changing, and how might same-gender relationships contribute to that end?

Denied access to marriage, lesbians and gays inevitably idealize it, but given the abuse the dominant culture has heaped on the institution, maybe it could use a little glamour. In my more hopeful moments, I think gays and lesbians might help revitalize and reconceptualize marriage by popularizing the concept of rich, whole, productive couplings based less on the regulation of sexual behavior and the maintenance of gender roles than on the formation of mutually respectful partnerships. *Baehr* v.

Lewin presents us with a chance to conceive of a different way of coupling, but only if we recognize and act on its implications. Otherwise the extension (if achieved) to same-gender couples of the marital status quo will represent a landmark civil-rights victory but a subcultural defeat in its failure to incorporate into the culture at large lessons learned by generations of women and men—lesbian or gay or straight—who built and sustained and fought for partnerships outside the bounds of conventional gender roles.

In *Word Is Out,* a 1977 documentary portraying lesbian and gay lives, comedienne Pat Bond described butch and femme role-playing among lesbians in the 1950s, roles as unvarying as those of Ozzie and Harriet. "Relationships that lasted 20 or 30 years were role-playing," she says. "At least in that role-playing you knew the rules, you at least knew your mother and father and you knew what they did and you tried to do the same thing . . . Now you say, 'Okay, I'm not butch or femme, I'm just me.' Well, who the hell is me? What do I do? How am I to behave?"

To heterosexuals who feel as if the marriage debate is pulling the rug of certainty from beneath them, I say, Welcome to the club. Gays' and lesbians' construction of community—which is to say, identity—is the logical culmination of the American democratic experiment, which provides its citizens with an open playing field on which each of us has a responsibility to define and then respect his or her boundaries and rules. Human nature being what it is, the American scene abounds with stories of people unable, unwilling, or uninterested in meeting that challenge—people who fare better within a package of predetermined rules and boundaries. For those people (so long as they are straight), traditional marriage and roles remain. But for the questioning mind and heart, the debate surrounding marriage is only the latest intrusion of ambiguity into the artificially ordered world of Western thinking.

And Western culture has never tolerated ambiguity. The Romans placed their faith in the state; the Christians, in God; the rationalists, in reason and science. But in marked contrast to Eastern religions and philosophy, all have in common their search for a constant governing structure, a kind of unified field theory for the workings of the heart. The emergence of gays and lesbians from the closet (a movement born of Western religious and rationalist thinking) is only one among many developments that reveal the futility of that search—how it inevitably arrives at the enigma that lies at the heart of being.

But the rules are so comforting and comfortable! And it is easier to oppress some so that others might live in certainty, ignoring the reality that the mystery of love and life and death is really grander and more glorious than human beings can grasp, much less legislate.

ENDNOTES

1. States have always established their own standards for the recognition of marriage; no consistent, nationwide definition of marriage has ever existed. Currently, a few states (e.g., Pennsylvania) still recognize common-law marriages, though for such marriages to be recognized in a noncommon-law state, participants must usually submit to some official procedure. Some states allow first cousins to marry, some do not, and the minimum age for legal marriage varies from state to state, as does the recognition of such contracts across state lines.

2. Many gay Protestant congregations, Reform Jews, Unitarians, and a number of Quaker congregations have endorsed and/or performed same-gender marriage. Presbyterians recently passed a resolution urging the national office to explore the feasibility of filing friend-of-the-court briefs "in favor of giving civil rights to same-sex partners," and the Episcopal Church is studying the blessing of same-sex unions. In addition, Hawaii's Buddhist bishops have announced their support of same-gender marriage.

3. By contrast, *Virtual Equality,* lesbian activist Urvashi Vaid's 440-page treatment of gay and lesbian civil rights, mentions same-gender marriage

only glancingly, by way of offering a generalized endorsement.

4. Since great numbers of gay men remain partly or wholly in the closet, there's no accurate way to measure or compare gay male and straight male experiences. But generalizations about gay male life based on behavior in bars and sex clubs are surely no more accurate than generalizations about heterosexual male behavior drawn from visiting America's red-light districts.

CHAPTER 8

Paths to Family Formation

The 20th century has been a time of great change in the way in which most young people associate with age mates of the opposite sex, begin romantic attachments, initiate sexual activity, live with partners, and marry. At the beginning of the century, this process was less private, more closely supervised by parents, and more directly tied to marriage. The now-quaint term *courtship* was used by experts who observed the process. In my textbook, I defined courtship as a publicly visible process with rules and restrictions through which young men and women find a partner to marry.[1] At the start of the 20th century, the process *was* public, it had many restrictions, and it was seen by all parties as leading to marriage. However, courtship, in this sense, hardly exists anymore. Historian Ellen K. Rothman tells the story of this transformation in the following excerpt from her book, *Hands and Hearts: A History of Courtship in America.* You will learn how and when dating and courtship evolved between 1920 and 1980.

At that point, Rothman's book ends. She notes the great rise in divorce in the 1960s and 1970s but concludes that the increase in divorce doesn't really threaten the institution of marriage. She cites social scientists (I was one of them) who reported that most divorced people remarried fairly quickly. But since 1980, rates of remarriage have declined; and cohabitation among previously married adults has increased greatly.[2] Most demographers would no longer be so quick to conclude that the institution of marriage has been unharmed by frequent divorce.

With the rise in premarital sex and the post-1960 increases in age at marriage has come the teenage pregnancy problem. There's nothing new about teenage pregnancy and childbearing, but until the 1960s most of it occurred to teenage women who were married. It is the decline in marriage, coupled with increasing sexual activity of the young and unmarried, that has caused public concern about unmarried teenagers having children.[3] Yet among social scientists of late,

---

[1]*Public and Private Families: An Introduction*, p. 229.

[2]Ibid., pp. 243–44.
[3]Ibid., pp. 250–53.

there is disagreement over just how much of a problem teenage childbearing is.[4] Some researchers have claimed recently that the problems of poor teenage mothers occur because they are poor, not because they are mothers. Even if these teenagers were to postpone childbearing, so this argument goes, their life prospects would not improve much. Other researchers claim that there are additional disadvantages to having a baby as a teenager—and that the baby is likely to be disadvantaged as well. In the following article, Kristin Luker attempts to untangle the strands of the teenage pregnancy problem in America.

---

[4]Ibid., pp. 253–56.

READING 8–1

In Our Own Time, 1920–1980

Ellen K. Rothman

. . . Until the Second World War, Americans continued to marry at the age and rate characteristic of the 19th century. The median age at first marriage in 1900 was 21.9 for women and 25.9 for men; after "a slow and measured decline" in the first four decades of the 20th century, the figure in 1940 was 21.5 for women and 24.3 for men. The rate of marriage dipped in the early 1930s, but by 1939, it had returned to the 19th-century level. The 1940s brought a sudden interruption in this remarkable stability. The marriage rate rose and the median age at marriage fell, both dramatically. According to demographer Donald Bogue, during that one decade "the proportion of persons never married and the median age at first marriage declined by as much as they had during the entire preceding half-century." In the late 1940s, more than half of all women were married by the age of 21.[1]

The immediate dislocations of wartime may have accounted for the outbreak of what one commentator called "the war disease," but the epidemic did not subside after V–J Day. Young Americans continued to marry at an age that would, at any other time, have been considered dangerously young. In 1956, the median age at first marriage reached an all-time low (20.1 for women, 22.5 for men); and a year later, the birth rate reached its peak. Beginning about 1960, the median age at first marriage began a gradual rise. By the late 1970s, it had attained its prewar level. The children of the couples who had participated in the 1940s "marriage marathon" and

produced the 1950s "baby boom" returned to patterns of family formation that their parents had broken.[2]

Thus the 20th century has been a time of demographic continuity. Except for the 1940s and 1950s, the transition to marriage appears as a steady line on the nation's statistical record. But when we turn from demographic trends to other forms of behavior, a different pattern emerges: a period of rapid change at the beginning (roughly 1910 to 1930); then more gradual, evolutionary change during the middle decades (1930 to about 1965); followed by another period of heightened change since the mid-1960s. The shifts of the last two decades can be gauged, at least indirectly, in the rise of cohabitation and teenage pregnancy; the discontinuity that marked the first quarter of the century is much harder to measure.

The subject of public consternation and celebration at the time, and of literary legend and historical debate ever since, "a first-class revolt against the accepted American order" took place among American youth in the 1920s. The "shock troops of the rebellion," as Frederick Lewis Allen called the fomenters of this "revolution in manners and morals," were not the first to breach the barricades. The assault on "the moral code of the country" had begun well before the battles along the Somme. What happened in the 1920s was that ideas and behavior which had once marked the outermost limits of acceptability moved to the center of middle-class youth culture. The sound of jazz, the smell of cigarette smoke, the discussions of Freud emanated not just from Greenwich Village but from Main Street and Fraternity Row. This was not a sudden eruption but rather a series of seismic tremors that occurred with increasing intensity and frequency though the 1910s and 1920s. The automobile, the moving picture, the close dance had all appeared before the First World War; but in the 1920s, they dominated and liberated American youth to an unprecedented extent. By 1930, the terrain through which young

Americans passed en route to marriage would be almost unrecognizable to their parents.[3]

The men and women who courted circa 1900 and their children coming of age in the 1920s were separated by as wide a gulf as that between any two American generations. Standards for behavior had undergone change before, of course, but never so radically in such a short time. It was understandable that people who had ridden their wheels around town, danced the two-step at the bandstand, and kissed goodnight on the front porch would be alarmed to see their children go off on joy rides in closed cars, to "petting parties," or to "pictures with hot lovemaking in them."[4] In 1900, middle-class courtship was more carefully supervised and more formal than it had been at any time since the Revolution; by 1930, the supervision and formality had given way, like a poorly designed dam, and many of the familiar landmarks were swept aside. While the result may have looked like chaos and disarray, a new system, created and regulated by young people themselves, was in place almost as soon as the old one was abandoned. The youths of the 1920s, in the words of historian Paula Fass, "elaborated two basic rituals of social interaction—dating and petting."[5] Separately and together, these two rituals would define the experience of courtship for the next half-century.

The young women and men of the 1920s did not invent paired-off social behavior—couples had been "keeping company" for 200 years; nor were they the first to discover sexual pleasure.[6] What they did was to develop a systematic, peer-controlled approach to the social and sexual relationships of late adolescence and early adulthood. The date, one historian has recently observed, "had a compelling logic quite distinct from that of prior forms: it was a step in an ongoing negotiation with rules defined and deviations punished by age-peers." Dating provided a way to manage the social demands of the peer society. It was an alternative to group activities, on the one hand, and to serious, marriage-oriented courtship, on the other. In a world where "press accounts of high school club dances [were] careful to emphasize the escort of each girl attending," the dating system ensured that a girl need not have a suitor in order to attend a dance.[7] Indeed, the fact that dating could operate independently of mate selection caused some observers to condemn it.

The sociologist Willard Waller, who studied campus life in the 1930s, concluded that dating "is not true courtship, since it is supposed not to eventuate in marriage; it is a sort of dalliance relationship." The decline of "formal modes of courtship" had, in Waller's view, been replaced by a "rating and dating complex" that rewarded "thrill-seeking" and "exploitative" behavior by young men and women. "Whether we approve or not" (and Waller made it clear that he did not), "courtship practices today allow for a great deal of pure thrill-seeking," he wrote in 1937. "Dancing, petting, necking, the automobile, amusement park, and a whole range of institutions and practices permit or facilitate thrill-seeking behavior." In this system, the goal was prestige rather than mate selection, plural rather than exclusive relationships. Men were rated according to the fraternity they belonged to, the clothes they wore, the amount of money they had to spend, and the skill they showed on the dance floor; what mattered was that they were "smooth" and had a "good line." For women, the important criteria were similar: "good clothes, a smooth line, ability to dance well, and popularity as a date."[8]

The pattern Waller described, based on a study conducted at Pennsylvania State University in the 1930s, was neither as novel nor as predominant as he thought.[9] A system oriented toward pluralistic, if not competitive, dating had evolved simultaneously among high school and college students well before the Crash.[10] The 1920s campus was above all a social scene, and that scene was designed around dating. Social activities rather than academic pursuits were what demanded time and conferred status.

"Study in too enthusiastic a form" was widely considered "bad form . . . Too constant attendance at the Library is likely to lead to derogatory classification," the *Daily Princetonian* warned in 1926. Such misplaced enthusiasm was rare; at Ohio State that year, the average co-ed went on dates four nights a week. Because selection for fraternity and sorority membership "usually had more to do with superficial attractiveness and personality than rigid socio-economic class," "rating and dating" tended to flourish on campuses where the Greek societies were strong. Even there, however, it functioned alongside a more traditional social system. As one sociologist recently concluded, "rating and dating and less exploitive and pluralistic dating appear to have existed simultaneously."[11]

The social scientists saw good data and the journalists good copy in the collegian; but in 1930, less than 15 percent of the country's 18- to 21-year-olds were attending institutions of higher education. And off the campus, "going together" was the norm. The heroine of one 1920s novel described the "thing you called going together":

> You went with a boy. He was your fellow then and you were his girl. When you were old enough you got engaged and married . . . Going together was beautiful. You had fun then; all the fun there was. You were not an odd girl. You were not left out . . . You could belong to a crowd. You had somebody to walk home with you, pay for your ticket at shows, send you valentines, candy at Christmas.[12]

Whether they were dating many different people or "going together" with one special person (and most young people in and out of college probably experimented with both modes), middle-class youths organized their social lives around dating beginning well before 1930.

One of the chief characteristics—and attractions—of a date was that it took place away from home. In his survey of undergraduate life in the late 1920s, Robert Angell explained, "In seeking means of diversion together there seem to be two principal aims, to have as much privacy and at the same time as much excitement as possible." Angell realized that "the former has probably been present from time immemorial," but he thought that the latter had been "enormously developed in the past years by the automobile and other means of exciting recreation." The middle-class home was, by definition, neither private nor exciting. "Unless couples are engaged, they are rarely content to spend the afternoon or evening conversing in the parlor or even strolling together along shady walks." The same rule applied off the campus as well. In the Indiana town that the sociologists Robert and Helen Lynd called Middletown, in the 1920s, " a 'date' at home [was] 'slow' compared with motoring, a new film, or a dance in a near-by town." Half the boys and girls queried on the subject reported that they were home fewer than four evenings out of the week.[13]

The most popular pastime for both high school and college students was dancing. In the early 1920s, many high schools "instituted dances, in an effort of varying success to take the play away from commercial dance halls and road houses."[14] College students could attend dances sponsored by college organizations or patronize local cabarets. By the 1920s, dancing had become an activity for couples rather than groups; it encouraged sensuality rather than sociability. Angell commented on "the slight degree of mingling" at university dances. "Often a man and woman spend practically the whole evening together," he reported. Not only were they together, they were close together. The new dances "fostered an unheard of closeness between partners . . . Couples often held each other very close." There were rules governing proper behavior on the dance floor, but they were "usually treated in a cavalier fashion."[15] In spite of its sexual potential, however, dancing retained a certain innocent quality. Irene and Vernon Castle, who elevated cabaret dancing to respectability in the 1910s, "took the potentially seductive dance and made it 'fun.'" Irene Castle once explained, "If Vernon had ever looked into my eyes with smoldering passion during the tango, we should have both burst out laughing." Dancing, in the Castle style, offered young people "a means to experience physical closeness and erotic excitement, without the dangers of sexuality."[16]

Like the dance hall, the movie theater was another setting that offered young people privacy and excitement, within limits. As movies became an increasingly legitimate form of middle-class entertainment, they also became increasingly popular. Most collegians in the 1920s regularly attended the movies once a week, and high school students were no less devoted followers of Clara Bow and Rudolph Valentino. In Middletown in 1928, there were nine motion-picture theaters offering over 300 performances every week of the year. "Go to a motion picture and let yourself go," the readers of the *Saturday Evening Post* were told, and Americans heeded the call by the millions. In a typical week, one-third of Middletown's high school students attended the movies once; 20 percent went twice.[17]

Some of their teachers believed that movies were "a powerful factor in bringing about the 'early sophistication' of the young and the relaxing of social taboos," and the Lynds agreed that the "constant public watching of love-making on the screen" had a noticeable effect. The woman who happily sent her daughter "because a girl has to learn the ways of the world somehow and the movies are a good safe way" was not necessarily as naïve as she might have appeared to the Lynds. The movies presented both an opportunity and stimulation for sexual intimacy, but they left conventional boundaries in place. Robert Angell considered the excitement to be found at the movies "much milder" than at the dance hall. As historian Elaine Tyler May explains:

> The message of the plot reinforced the need for restraint. Love-struck viewers might hold hands or embrace in the darkened theater; but not much else could happen. They sat in a public place, facing the screen without talking to each other,

watching attractive film idols instruct them in the art of gaining allure without losing virtue.[18]

Of all the new influences on the behavior of young women and men, none was more powerful than the automobile. Here, in the closed cars which were fast replacing open ones, anything *could* happen. Of the 30 girls charged with "sex crimes" in Middletown in 1924, 19 committed the offense in an automobile. In 1923, there were more than 6,000 cars in Middletown, two for every three families. Car ownership had reached the point of being an "accepted essential of normal living" for middle-class people.[19] It had become an "accepted essential of normal" courting for their children as well. The automobile was, however, no less revolutionary for being readily incorporated into normalcy. The Lynds concluded that the automobile had "revolutionized . . . leisure" in general and had specifically caused the "increasing relaxation of some of the traditional prohibitions upon the approaches of boys and girls to each other's persons." Robert Angell concurred. In 1928, he declared:

> To this invention must be assigned much responsibility . . . for the change, amounting to almost a revolution, which has come about during the last 15 years in the conduct of young men and women. The ease with which a couple can secure absolute privacy when in possession of a car and the spirit of reckless abandon which high speed and moonlight drives engender have combined to break down the traditional barriers between the sexes.[20]

Even at slower speeds and in broad daylight, the car allowed a level of intimacy and privacy reminiscent of the early republic. A Rhode Island woman explained in 1923, "You can be so nice and all alone in a machine, just a little one that you can go on crazy roads in and be miles away from anyone but each other." Fifteen years later, when Dorothy Bromley and Florence Britten published their study *Youth and Sex,* it was obvious that the car was "an incredible engine of escape." A boy called for his date, usually just by honking the horn, and the young couple was "off and away, out of reach of parental control. A youth now . . . has a refuge . . . complete privacy. He has taken full advantage of it, not only as a means of going places, but as a place to go where he can take his girl and hold hands, neck, pet, or if it's that kind of an affair, go the limit."[21]

The car provided far more privacy and excitement than either the dance hall or the movie theater, and the result was the spread of petting. In 1928, Robert Angell conceded that "what is vulgarly known as 'petting' is the rule rather than the exception in all classes of society"; and by 1930, Floyd Dell could refer to "the universal convention of petting" with little risk of overstatement.[22] The statistical pattern is clear. A 1924 study of "Certain Aspects of the Sex Life of the Adolescent Girl" found that 92 percent of the respondents (177 college girls) had indulged in "spooning" or "petting." (Spooning was a more old-fashioned term for kissing than petting, which included all forms of erotic behavior short of intercourse.[23]) This limited data was confirmed in the report on *Sexual Behavior in the Human Female* prepared by Alfred Kinsey and his associates in the early 1950s. About 80 percent of the women born just before 1900—in other words those who courted in the 1910s and 1920s—had engaged in some sort of petting, and the proportion increased with every decade. The story for men was similar. Among the older generation (born between 1895 and 1904), 65 percent had petting experience by age 18; while in the younger generation (born between 1917 and 1929), 85 percent had petted by that age.[24]

Much of this petting took place in the quasi-public setting of the "petting party." Petting parties were a regular feature of high school life in the 1920s. When asked if it was true that "nine out of every ten boys and girls of high school age have 'petting parties,'" 50 percent of the Middle-town youths answered yes. Although fewer students themselves admitted to petting, almost half of the boys and more than one-third of the girls

indicated that they had taken part in a petting party. Such parties were not limited to the high school scene; college students indulged as well. In both cases, the petting party was, as Paula Fass points out, "a self-limiting form of experimentation . . . Here sexual activity was manifestly regulated by the group . . . a certain aura of intrigue and 'naughtiness' hovered around this semi-illicit behavior in the twenties."[25]

There was nothing *semi*-illicit about premarital coitus. "To maintain one's position with peers," Fass writes, "petting was permitted but intercourse was not." Only a minority violated the prohibition on premarital sexual intercourse, but their action was considered "an indiscretion and not a moral outrage." Virginity had ceased to be an absolute requirement in a bride, even if most men and women still considered it highly desirable. Although most of the young women in a 1936 study conducted by Phyllis Blanchard and Carlyn Manasses "assumed that it would make no difference to the men who wished to marry them if it was known that they had had previous sex experience," the authors concluded that "many girls draw a distinct line between the exploratory activities of the petting party and complete yielding of sexual favors to men." Blanchard and Manasses found a "decidedly tolerant attitude toward pre-marital sex experiences," and a 1936 effort to measure attitudinal change showed that "a consistent liberalizing of opinion" was taking place in the course of young people's college careers.[26]

While attitudes shifted toward greater tolerance for premarital sexual activities, the tie between love and sex remained strong. Indeed, it was, if anything, affirmed by the "rebels" of the 1920s. "I disapprove of promiscuous relations on moral grounds; not, however, between a man and woman in love," one co-ed told Blanchard and Manasses. In Fass's analysis, "it was emotional commitment above all that legitimized eroticism, for the young were true romantics who believed strongly in love." One college editor described the youth of his generation: "Where the ancient code had touched a vital principle he has hesitated to overstep its bounds." Even as they overthrew the "ancient code," young Americans preserved this principle. The bounds that marked off the sanctity of married love were readjusted, but they were not abandoned. "The revolution in sexual morality went on within the rules of the game," and the rules tied sex securely to love.[27]

Middle-class Americans had long considered love a "necessary condition" for sexual intimacy; what changed now was not the condition but the "point in the courtship process when it is applied." A growing minority of college students "altered the traditional notion of being a virgin when you marry to being a virgin when you reach engagement."[28] The commitment to this new standard is reflected in the fact that the increase in premarital coitus was largely confined to engaged couples. In the Kinsey Report, only a quarter of the women born before 1900 indicated they had had premarital intercourse, while for those born after 1900, the figure was close to 50 percent. However, at least one-half of the women in the 1920s who reported engaging in premarital coitus did so only with a future spouse. (Kinsey found a similar trend among his male respondents.)[29]

From data collected in the 1940s, Alfred Kinsey concluded that the greatest increase in premarital sexual activity occurred in the generation that reached adulthood in the late 1910s and early 1920s, and that "later generations appear to have accepted the new pattern and maintained or extended it." Observers in the 1930s agreed. The young no longer seemed to be diverting the mainstream into new directions, perhaps because the turbulence of the 1920s had already made the channel wide enough to accommodate a range of youthful experimentation. Some commentators even detected "a conservative reaction among the young to the 'Scott Fitzgerald wave'" of the early 1920s, but the retreat was more apparent than real. "The innovations of the 1920s," Fass writes, "had been solidified so that by the 30s the sexual mores begun by the college youth of

the 20s were already a widespread and casual feature of behavior."[30]

When Helen and Robert Lynd returned to Middletown in 1935, they got "a sense of sharp, free behavior between the sexes (patterned on the movies) and of less disguise among the young." The liberalization of attitudes and behavior that had taken place in college in the 1920s now showed up among high school students. One young man, several years out of the Middletown high school, told the Lynds in 1935, "The fellows regard necking as a taken-for-granted part of a date. We fellows used occasionally to get slapped for doing things, but the girls don't do that much any more . . . Our high school students of both sexes . . . know everything and do everything—openly." The girls of Middletown might read in the local paper's advice columns, "A girl should never kiss a boy unless they are engaged," but few heeded such old-fashioned words.[31]

Petting was less notorious but no less popular than it had been in the 1920s. In their 1938 study of 1,300 undergraduates, Bromley and Britten found that, although at some colleges the terms *necking* and *petting* were no longer used, "the custom signified persists . . . on every campus and under many new names." As the novelty of petting wore off, it lost its more extreme, exhibitionistic qualities. Writing in 1937, the sociologist Theodore Newcomb argued that, while there had been "no quantitative decline in premarital sex relations since the alleged excesses" of the 1920s, there had been "changes in manners and morals associated with such behavior." Among the most important changes, Newcomb listed: "more widespread acceptance, particularly by females, of the 'naturalness' of sex intimacies, with or without coitus; less extreme 'petting' on first or early acquaintance; and more 'steady dating' with fewer inhibitions as to sex intimacy following long acquaintance." In June 1936, *Fortune* magazine reported, "As for sex, it is, of course, still with us. But the campus takes it more casually than it did ten years ago. Sex is no longer news."[32]

What was news was the worldwide economic crisis and the mounting threat of war in Europe. As the Depression tightened its grip on America, college enrollments fell, and the size and influence of campus fraternities declined. The Depression cast a long shadow and brought an altogether more somber mood to campus life. For many middle-class youths, college attendance represented a difficult sacrifice. The madcap social whirl of the 1920s was an extravagance few could afford. Academic pursuits and the students who excelled in them were rescued from the margins of college life and given new prestige. At the same time, college students expressed more eagerness for marriage and children than they had in the 1920s. In *Fortune*'s 1936 poll, 60 percent of the women and 50 percent of the men wanted to marry within a year or two of graduation; but when 50 percent to 85 percent of male college students were among the 13 million unemployed, these were dreams to be deferred.[33]

Deferred, but not abandoned. By the time war broke out in Europe, both the marriage rate and the age at marriage had returned to their pre-1930 levels.[34] With people rushing into marriage in response to the threat of separation and perhaps of death during wartime, symptoms of the "war disease" began to appear in ever younger people. From 1940 to 1948, the median age at first marriage fell by a full year, and three-quarters of women born between 1920 and 1924 were married by the age of 24.[35]

The "marriage marathon" was not the only sign of the war's impact on the social life of the middle-class young. At the University of Wisconsin in 1944, there were nine women for every man in the freshman class; and at Ohio State, the ratio was four to one. When a reporter from *Fortune* visited Cornell in 1942, he found Fraternity Row deserted, house parties suspended for the duration, and only meager crowds at the football games. Male students left school early or attended classes year-round and prepared for active duty. Off the campus, most single men over 18 were in uniform and isolated from normal social life. "In comparison with the civilians, men in the armed forces had less spare time, fewer automobiles, and fewer contacts among the female population . . . Most servicemen were concentrated by the tens of thousands in one place or another . . . There were just not enough women to go around."[36] With men largely segregated in the armed forces and women in colleges or the war industries, the normal process and pace of social relationships were disrupted.

For younger groups, however, the social scene remained largely unaffected by the war. Petting was as common as ever. Of the women Kinsey interviewed in the late 1940s, 39 percent of those under 15 and 88 percent of those age 16 to 20 were having petting experience. For men in Kinsey's younger generation, 66 percent had petting experience by the age of 16; 93 percent by the time they were 20. Kinsey concluded that the incidence of petting had increased, and that men were starting to pet at an earlier age. Petting was no longer restricted to the back seat or the "petting party." "On doorsteps and on street corners, and on high school and college campuses . . . [it] may be observed in the daytime as well as in the evening hours," Kinsey wrote in 1948. Calling it "one of the most significant factors in the sexual lives of high school and college males and females," Kinsey hailed petting for the education it offered young people "in making socio-sexual contacts."[37]

Dating was the context within which most youthful petting took place, and it too functioned to educate young women and men about themselves and each other. While some observers still detected, and decried, a "rating and dating" complex at work in the "no strings attached" relationships many young people favored, other commentators recognized that it was precisely the association with freedom that gave dating its appeal. "Dating is a relationship expressing freedom, lack of commitment or public obligation for any sort of future action," wrote sociologist Samuel Lowrie in 1951.[38] At the same time, a contradictory pattern was emerging. Far from avoiding commitment, many young Americans were attaching strings with a vengeance. By the end of the Second World War, going steady had taken root, and the result was to impart "a different color to the social life of the youth. It makes it more serious, less frivolous." Writing in *Harper's* in 1957, Amherst College president George Cole expressed regret at what he saw happening to dating:

> In the twenties and early thirties, when the social pattern was one of multiple or polygamous dating—on the part of both boys and girls—young people did not think nearly so much about marriage as they do today . . . They dated each other for the fun of it, because they enjoyed each other's company, because they liked the same things, or merely because in the competitive social life of their time it was a good thing to have dates—the more, the better. Today young people often play with the idea of marriage as early as the second or third date, and they certainly think about it by the fifth or sixth. By the time they have been going steady for a while they are quite apt to be discussing the number and names of their future children.[39]

Indeed, with the marriage age dropping to an all-time low, large numbers of young people were moving through the dating system directly—and immediately—into marriage. Public policy and family values accounted for "the disappearance of the idea that a man should be able to support a wife before he gets married." New resources were available: The government subsidized mortgages and paid veterans a subsistence allowance—60 dollars if they were single, 75 if married—while they were in school. Working wives and parents supplemented that income. "Nowadays," Cole noted in 1957, "one or both sets of parents are expected to help."[40] Another less easily quantifiable factor was at work here, too. In 1958, *Parents Mag-*

azine explained to its readers "Why They Can't Wait to Wed": "Youngsters want to grasp what little security they can in a world gone frighteningly insecure. The youngsters feel they will cultivate the one security that's possible—their own gardens, their own . . . home and families." That they had begun at an early age to "cultivate . . . security" in steady relationships gave "young people the feeling that they really know members of the opposite sex well enough to choose a marriage partner much earlier in life than people . . . would have dared to do . . . in an earlier day," sociologist David Riesman observed a year later.[41]

While public policy directly, and the political climate indirectly, encouraged early marriage, personal experience was the most important ingredient in the equation. By the 1950s, Americans began to acquire dating and petting experience as young teenagers. Winston Ehrmann found that, except for school, dating was the most time-consuming activity in his subjects' lives, beginning in junior high or even elementary school. Doubtless many parents disapproved of their children's early exposure to heterosexual socializing, but other parents clearly promoted it. In the April 1956 issue of *Good Housekeeping,* Phyllis McGinley bemoaned the fact that

> abetted, indeed pushed and prodded and egged on by their mothers or the PTA or scoutmasters, sixth-grade children are now making dates on the telephone and ineptly jitterbugging together every weekend evening . . . They are coaxed and bullied and enticed into "mingling." There are school dances and church dances and scout dances. There are Coke parties and local "assemblies" and what passes for dances at private homes.[42]

It was certainly true that by the time middle-class children entered junior high school, they were full participants in the first stages of dating ritual. Most began with "group dating": "Everything is done in gangs, although pairing off usually occurs sometimes during the evening," reported one student. Another described the process in greater detail:

> The boys and girls seldom attend the basketball games together, as couples, but prefer instead to drift in with a crowd of their own gender. When the lights are more discreetly lowered after the games, however, the boys tend to seek out their latest interests and pair off for dancing. At the end of such dances a few boys walk their "girls" home, but the majority of the crowd walks in groups of paired couples "en masse" down to the local hangout for a Coke.

For the clique that "set the pace for the others," there were two rituals of importance: the Saturday night date to the movies and "Coke parlor" afterward, and the more occasional private parties ("minus chaperons") at someone's house. The main attractions there were the games of "Spin the Bottle," "Postoffice," and "Spotlight."[43]

When these students went on to high school, they "began to date with real intent and purpose [and] played the field." Susan Allen Toth, who grew up in Ames, Iowa, in the 1950s, remembered that "high school courtship usually was meticulously slow, progressing through inquiry, phone calls, planned encounters in public places, double or triple dates, hand-holding, and finally a good-night kiss." Dates had a predictable form: "Movie, something to eat, and out to park. Movie, something to eat, come home, and perhaps neck there. Movie, home for something to eat, and then perhaps T.V.," a college student recalled. By senior year, the majority of the class was "going steady with someone." Many of those not going on to college married soon after graduation. College-bound students were less likely to marry their high school steadies than were classmates who went directly into the labor force.[44]

College enrollments rose at a slow rate during the years of Depression and war, but after the passage of the G.I. Bill in 1944, they surged ahead. More than twice as many Americans graduated from college in 1950 as had a decade

earlier, and by 1960, 22 percent of the 18- to 24-year-old population was in school.[45] College students might not have talked about "going steady," a phrase with more currency in high school than collegiate circles, but "the institution was as strong in the latter as in the former." In a *Harper's* piece titled "American Youth Goes Monogamous," George Cole declared that "the present pre-marital monogamy of youth . . . is one of the most important phenomena of recent times." Nora Johnson, a 1954 graduate of Smith College, reported that when she was on campus in the early 1950s "everybody [was] doing it." In her view, "the phenomena of pinning, going steady, and being monogamous-minded [were] symptoms of our inclination to play it safe. . . . What a feeling of safety not to have to worry about a date for months ahead!" Johnson believed that the "male wish for dating security" was as strong as the woman's. "Their fraternity pins are burning holes in their lapels," she wryly observed. Getting "pinned" or "engaged to be engaged" was the ritual—and the symbol—for the college version of monogamy.[46]

Going steady or being pinned was not merely a source of social security. Sociologist Ira Reiss perceived that one of the great attractions of steady dating for teenagers was that "sex and affection can be quite easily combined"; and that especially for the girl, sexual behavior was "made respectable by going steady." In Nora Johnson's account, the "perpetual twosome" of the college scene was "often based on sex and convenience." Going steady allowed a woman to be respectable and available at the same time. It reconciled the two, often conflicting, principles by which middle-class girls operated: "One is that anything is all right if you're in love . . . and the other is that a girl must be respected, particularly by the man she wants to marry," as Johnson put it in "Sex and the College Girl." The "ideal girl," she suggested, "has done every possible kind of petting without actually having had intercourse. This gives her savoir-faire, while still maintaining her dignity."[47]

The "ideal girl" was also the typical girl: through the 1940s and 1950s, the increases in premarital sexual activity occurred in petting rather than coitus. By the mid-1950s, more than 90 percent of college-age men and women reported engaging in premarital petting. The incidence of premarital intercourse had remained fairly constant since the 1920s: between one-third and two-thirds of college men and about one-third of women reported that they had coitus before marriage. In one 1958 study, 10 percent of the co-eds had had sexual intercourse while in a dating relationship, 15 percent while going steady, and twice as many (31 percent) during engagement. The researchers concluded that "engagement was very often the prerequisite to a girl having premarital sexual intercourse." If a girl had coitus, it was likely to be with her fiancé, during the year or two before they were married.[48]

The frequency of this behavior reflects the acceptance among middle-class teenagers of what Ira Reiss has labeled "permissiveness with affection." High school couples "feel it is proper to engage in heavy petting if they are going steady, the justification being that they are in love or at least extremely fond of each other," he explained in 1961. Especially among a slightly older age group, similar reasoning supported the decision to have coitus during the late stages of the transition to marriage. One young man gave a typical rationale for why he and his girl friend "indulged in petting, and at times . . . heavy petting . . . [It] was the result of a drive that had something beside pure sex as a motivating factor. We didn't believe in petting because of the sex alone, but because we were very much in love and this was a means of expressing our love to each other." They refrained from sleeping together not because they thought it was wrong, but because they "didn't want to take any unnecessary chances."[49]

This young man and his girl friend agreed on where to draw the limits in their sexual relationship; but, in general, "permissiveness with affection" figured more largely in the female than

in the male code of sexual ethics. Boys may have been more sexually experienced (more than twice as many boys as girls had coitus in their teens), but they were also more conservative, in the sense that they were more likely to embrace the traditional double standard which sanctioned conduct in men that it condemned in women. However, during the 1950s, young men evinced "increased willingness . . . to accept some coitus on the part of females, especially if it occurs when the girl is in love and/or engaged." An even more egalitarian standard, which made premarital intercourse right for both sexes, gained ground among older teenagers, particularly those in college. By 1959, a majority of the men in Ehrmann's study of college students adhered to a single standard; and for most of them, it was a *liberal* single standard.[50]

Ehrmann concluded that, in spite of these attitudinal changes, women were still the arbiters and enforcers of sexual codes. A survey published in the *Ladies' Home Journal* in January 1962 summarized the sentiments of women 16- to 21-years old: "They feel a special responsibility for sex *because* they are women." In their comments, these young women revealed an understanding of the different roles played by men and women in the sexual game. "A woman has much more to lose than a man," one woman said. "Girls especially should have a great deal of self-control, seeing quite a few boys don't," was another's response. One young woman declared, "A man will go as far as a woman will let him," and another agreed, "A girl has to set the standard."[51]

The standard was based on emotion more than on eroticism. For the women in Ehrmann's study, sexual expression was "primarily and profoundly related to being in love and going steady"; while for the men, "sexuality is more indirectly and less exclusively associated with romanticism and intimate relationships." Ehrmann noticed an even more striking difference in the sexual standards of young men and women: "The degree of physical intimacy actually experienced or considered permissible is among males *inversely* related and among females *directly* related to the intensity of and familiarity and affection in the male-female relation." In other words, the more a young woman loved a man, the more permissive she was likely to be; the more a young man loved a woman, the less permissive he was likely to be. Furthermore, where women rarely went beyond the limits set by their codes, men were often prevented by their partners from going "as far sexually as their codes permit."[52]

By the end of the 1950s, the differences between male and female standards were fading. Men were moving away from the traditional double standard toward permissiveness with affection; while women's attitudes were shifting toward the "transitional double standard—coitus is all right for men under any condition, but it is acceptable for women only if they are in love." Investigators detected signs of a related change in the "steady decrease in the tendency to express different standards for members of one's own sex than for members of the opposite sex." By 1968, the double standard had not disappeared, but its decline was noticeable. It was being eroded by an overall liberalization of sexual attitudes. The new ground broken by the youths of the 1950s was not so much in the incidence of premarital coitus as in the wider acceptance of it.[53]

Reflecting on this convergence of sexual attitudes and behavior, Ira Reiss speculated in 1966, "We may well witness soon an increase in many forms of sexual behavior . . . The stage is set for another upward cycle of increasing sexual behavior and sexual acceptance." Reiss was soon proved right. After decades of relative stability, the rate of premarital coitus showed a dramatic increase. The most marked change for men occurred among those in college. Half of the college-bound men in a 1972 survey had had premarital intercourse by the age of 17, more than twice the rate in the Kinsey Report. (Among males not in college, the increase was substantially lower.)[54] The change for women

was even more dramatic. The percentage of women who had first intercourse by the age of 17 doubled between the 1940–49 and 1950–59 birth cohorts. A range of studies yielded higher premarital coital rates among college women in the late 1960s than in the 1950s and early 1960s. Only two studies showed a nonvirgin rate below 30 percent for college women, and most found between 40 percent and 55 percent.[55]

When Ira Reiss described the teenage girl in 1961 as "the guardian of sexual limits," he observed that "she appears increasingly to be a half-willing guardian who more and more seeks her self-satisfaction and strives to achieve sexual equality." By the late 1960s, she was drawing closer to this goal. It was not just the rate of premarital intercourse that increased dramatically in the 1960s; the context changed as well. In a 1968 replication of a 1958 study, Robert Bell and Jay Chaskes found that, in 10 years, the proportion of women having premarital coitus while in dating relationships had gone from 10 percent to 23 percent; for those going steady, the increase was from 15 percent to 28 percent. The rise in the rate of premarital intercourse during engagement was smaller, from 31 percent to 39 percent. The authors concluded that in 1968 women were more likely than a decade before to have their first sexual experience prior to becoming engaged. Furthermore, the young women in the 1968 sample were far more likely than those in the 1958 group to feel comfortable with that decision. The percentage of co-eds who felt they had gone "too far" was cut in half for all three dating levels. Other investigators uncovered a similar pattern: there was a general decline in the proportion of women who reported feeling guilt or remorse after their first coital experience. "What was done by a female in 1925 acting as a rebel and a deviant can be done by a female in 1965 as a conformist," Reiss declared.[56]

While her parents were likely to be more critical than her peers, by the early 1970s older as well as younger Americans were evincing more liberal attitudes toward premarital sex. In a 1969 Gallup Poll, 68 percent of a national sample believed premarital sex was wrong; four years later, only 48 percent agreed. Older respondents remained more conservative than younger ones, but a shift toward permissiveness had taken place among all age groups. "Marriage no longer seemed to occupy its place as the dividing line between socially approved and socially disapproved sexual intimacy," sociologist Robert Sorensen observed. More than half of the teenagers in his 1973 nationwide study thought it was "abnormal or unnatural for a boy not to have sex until he gets married." (That the double standard lingered on is reflected in the fact that only 42 percent of the boys and 27 percent of the girls answered yes when the same question was asked about girls.) The concept of "premarital sex" was fast disappearing. Teenagers assumed "there is nothing wrong with sex without marriage."[57]

Sex without love, on the other hand, was another matter. This generation preserved the rule that had guided their parents: "It's all right for young people to have sex before getting married if they are in love with each other." Behavior patterns suggest that "permissiveness with affection" was still the prevailing standard. In Morton Hunt's 1972 study, twice as many women reported having had premarital coitus as in Kinsey's sample, but the proportion of those whose premarital experience was confined to one partner remained the same. Of the women born between 1948 and 1955 (in other words, those who reached early adulthood in the late 1960s and early 1970s), 53 percent had premarital coitus only with their future husbands. "Today's 'nice' girl is still guiding herself according to romantic and historically rooted values," Hunt concluded in 1974.[58] For the next generation, the teenagers of the 1970s, those values appear to have lost some of their hold. Magazines might remind their young female readers of "Your Right to Say No," but more and more teenage girls were saying yes. In 1979, 50 percent of the teenage girls living in metropolitan areas had had premarital sex, an increase of 20 percent since the start of the decade.[59]

Young people in the 1970s may have been sexually active at a younger age than earlier generations, but most acquired this sexual experience in settings that would have been familiar to their parents and grandparents.[60] There was, however, one important addition: a growing minority of young men and women lived together before marriage. Just as the "sexual revolution" of the first quarter of the 20th century involved the innoculation of mainstream youth with a germ incubated in bohemia, so too the dramatic rise in cohabitation reflects the diffusion of an alternative life style throughout middle-class culture. In the late 1960s, unmarried couples who lived together were described in the pages of the *New York Times* as a "tiny minority" within "the dissident youth subculture—the intellectual, politically liberal to radical, from middle- and upper-middle-class backgrounds, antimaterialistic and anti-Establishment." Between 1970 and 1982, the number of cohabiting couples tripled. While some of these couples were older people, a leading demographer concluded that the increase was "accounted for . . . primarily by *young couples without children.*" During the 1970s, the number of cohabiting couples under 25 with no children increased eightfold.[61]

In spite of the alarms sounded by parents and the press, cohabitation posed little threat to marriage. An unmarried couple told the *Times* in 1969 that the usual sequence was to "slide from dating into shacking up into marriage." As parents saw their children sliding into marriage rather than into a life in the counter culture, fears subsided. A report on the 1980 census remarked that "young Americans are becoming increasingly attracted to this lifestyle, and their parents are becoming less critical of this behavior." An occasional couple found themselves at odds with the law or a censorious landlord, and many young people continued to conceal their living arrangements from their parents; but by the early 1980s, cohabitation had lost its association with the "dissident youth subculture" that had spawned it. A 1981 research team described it as "part of the courtship process rather than a long-term alternative to marriage."[62]

When couples made the transition from living together to marriage, as so many eventually did, they observed the same rituals as their noncohabiting comtemporaries.[63] While a small minority devised "alternative" weddings, most Americans who married in the late 1960s and the 1970s followed a familiar pattern. Three out of four first-time brides received an engagement ring; 85 percent of them wore a formal bridal gown. "We Americans are getting married almost precisely as we did a hundred years ago," Marcia Seligson wrote in 1973:

> We are adorning ourselves in long white romantic gowns, going to church or to a hotel or country club, repeating established vows we have heard at other folks' weddings for years, sipping champagne, cutting cake, dancing, tossing the bouquet, posing for pictures, fleeing through a shower of rice as we head for our Caribbean honeymoon.

This list, which would have served as a guide to American wedding ritual any time between 1920 and 1980, explains the growth of the "wedding industry" in the past 50 years. Americans who married in 1979 and their families spent about $12.5 billion dollars on rings, wedding expenses, home furnishings, and honeymoons; and the wedding market seemed immune to hard times. In May of 1982, the *New York Times* reported on a "return to traditionalism," noting that for "bridal merchants, it's a state of bliss."[64]

Were the objects of all this commercial activity equally blissful? Presumably so, yet at a time when one in every two marriages was likely to end in divorce, couples could not help but approach the altar with some sense that they were taking on a challenge at which many of them would fail. Lorenzo Dow's 1833 reflection on matrimony, "If a man have a farm and don't like it, he can pull it down and build another. But this is for life!" had ceased to describe the American experience. Although the annual divorce rate had been rising steadily for well over a century (with the exception of a drop during the Depression and an upsurge after both world wars), it has increased more sharply in the 1960s and 1970s than ever before. Between 1966 and 1976, the divorce rate doubled and then, in the late 1970s, showed signs of leveling off. The rate of remarriage declined (along with the rate of first marriage) during the 1970s, but Americans had not lost faith in marriage. Four out of every five divorced persons remarried, half of them within three years, and in 1983, two and a half million marriages were recorded.[65]

When a boyhood friend announced his engagement in the fall of 1905, Walter Price sent his congratulations: "The union of a man and a woman in these days where precedents are disregarded & 'Novelty holds sway' is the one old fashioned thing to which people cling. Without it life's a shipwreck."[66] In the perilous world of the 1980s, Americans are no more willing to let go than their grandparents were.

ENDNOTES

1. U.S. Census, Current Population Reports, "Marital Status and Living Arrangements," series P-20, no. 365, March 1980, pp. 1–2; Andrew J. Cherlin, *Marriage Divorce Remarriage* (Cambridge, MA, 1981), Figures 1.1, 1.2; Donald J. Bogue, *The Population of the United States* (Glencoe, IL, 1959), p. 215.

   Related changes that occurred in the 1940s were the increasing independence of the transition to marriage from the transition to labor force participation and from parenthood; and the sharp reduction in the spread of ages at which Americans married. For a detailed examination of these phenomena, see John Modell, Frank Furstenberg, Jr., and Douglas Strong, "The Timing of Marriage in the Transition to Adulthood: Continuity and Change, 1860–1975," in John Demos and

Sarane Spence Boocock, eds. *Turning Points,* supplement to *AJS* 84 (1978): S122–47. Here, and elsewhere in this chapter, the figures apply only to whites. Cherlin discusses the similarities and differences in the demographic patterns of the black and white populations (*Marriage,* chap. 4, passim).

2. Cherlin, *Marriage,* chap. 1, passim.

One important new pattern that appears to be developing in the early 1980s is the increase, among 25- to 29-year-olds, of those who are single. According to the 1980 census, one-fifth of the women in that age group had not yet married, a twofold increase since 1970. There was a 70 percent increase for men, from one-fifth in 1970 to one-third in 1980. One result of this trend was to raise the median age at first marriage; by 1983, Americans were marrying later than at any time since 1890.

3. Frederick Lewis Allen, *Only Yesterday: An Informal History of the 1920s* (New York, 1931; Perennial Library ed. 1964), p. 73. For the classic statement of the changes under way in American life before the First World War, see Henry F. May, *The End of American Innocence* (New York, 1959), pp. 138–39, 266–67.

4. Lynd and Lynd, *Middletown,* p. 139.

5. Paula Fass, *The Damned and the Beautiful: American Youth in the 1920s* (New York, 1977), p. 262. While Fass has a tendency to overgeneralize from the college youth who are the focus of her book, *The Damned and the Beautiful* is an indispensable resource to anyone interested in the experience of young Americans during the 1920s.

6. Alfred Kinsey recognized that older generations had engaged in "flirting, flirtage, courting, bundling, spooning, mugging, smooching, larking, sparking, and other activities which were simply petting under another name." Alfred C. Kinsey, et al., *Sexual Behavior in the Human Female* [hereafter cited as *SBHF*] (Philadelphia, 1953), p. 231.

7. John Modell, "Dating Becomes the Way of American Youth," in *Essays on the Family and Historical Change,* ed. by Leslie Page Moch and Gary D. Stark (College Station, TX, 1983), p. 102; Lynd and Lynd, *Middletown,* p. 138. I am grateful to Professor Modell for sharing this essay with me before publication.

8. Willard Waller, "The Rating and Dating Complex," *ASR* 2 (1937): 729, 728, 730. Christopher Lasch discusses the challenge Waller presented to sociological orthodoxy in the 1920s and 1930s; see *Haven in a Heartless World* (New York, 1977), pp. 50–55.

9. Michael Gordon suggests that Penn State may have been especially well suited to support a "rating and dating complex": it was geographically isolated; it had six males for every female student (as opposed to ratios of three to one at Cornell and two to one at Michigan); and its student body represented the lower rather than the upper reaches of the middle class. Michael Gordon, "Was Waller Ever Right? The Rating and Dating Complex Reconsidered," *JMF,* 43 (February 1981): 69, n. 3.

10. Modell argues persuasively that Fass's account of the development of dating needs to be revised to take into account the importance of peer-group activities, especially dating, on the high school level. He points out that "high schools had almost even sex ratios—a demography far more conducive to widespread dating than that in college" ("Dating," p. 104).

11. Fass, *The Damned,* pp. 175, 200, 153; Gordon, "Was Waller Ever Right?" [11]: 73.

12. Louise Dutton, *Going Together* (Indianapolis, IN, 1923), pp. 20–21.

13. Robert Angell, *The Campus: A Study of Contemporary Undergraduate Life in the American University* (New York, 1928), pp. 165–69; Lynd and Lynd, *Middletown,* p. 134.

This distaste for home dates held true when Susan Allen Toth was growing up in Ames, Iowa, in the 1950s. She recalled that young couples rarely spent time in each other's homes. "We might not have been bothered," Toth explained, "but we really wouldn't have been alone. Cars were our private space, a rolling parlor, the only place we could relax and be ourselves . . . Driving gave us a feeling of freedom." Susan Allen Toth, *Blooming: A Small Town Girlhood* (Boston, 1981), p. 52.

14. Modell, "Dating," p. 106.

15. Lewis Erenberg, *Steppin' Out: New York Nightlife and the Transformation of American Culture, 1890–1930* (Westport, CT, 1981), pp. 154–55; Angell, *Campus,* p. 169; Fass, *The Damned,* p. 196.

16. Elaine Tyler May, *Great Expectations: Marriage and Divorce in Post-Victorian America* (Chicago, 1980), p. 69. Erenberg examines the Castle phenomenon at length in *Steppin' Out,* pp. 146–76.

17. Fass, *The Damned,* p. 206; Lynd and Lynd, *Middletown,* pp. 263–64.

Children unaccompanied by a parent accounted for the largest share of the movie audience in Middletown, prompting the Lynds to wonder about the "decentralizing tendency of the movies upon the family" (p. 265).

18. Lynd and Lynd, *Middletown,* pp. 267, 139, 268; Angell, *Campus,* p. 169; May, *Great Expectations,* p. 69.

The Lynds suggested that the "sex adventure" magazines which were widely read in Middletown had some of the same effects as the movies (pp. 241–42). For a discussion of the evolution of movies as a reflection of and stimulus to middle-class values, see Lary May, *Screening Out the Past: The Birth of Mass Culture and the Motion Picture Industry, 1896–1929* (New York: 1980).

19. Lynd and Lynd, *Middletown,* pp. 258, 253. As the car became a measure of social status, it also became a source of parent-child conflict. In Middletown, "among the high school set, ownership of a car by one's family has become an important criterion of social fitness; a boy almost never takes a girl to a dance except in a car; there are persistent rumors of the buying of a car by local families to help their children's social standing in high school." Ibid., p. 137.

20. Ibid., p. 137; Angell, *Campus,* p. 169.

21. Katharine Merrill to William McCormick, 25 August, 1923, PC; Dorothy Dunbar Bromley and Florence Haxton Britten, *Youth and Sex: A Study of 1300 College Students* (New York, 1938), p. 11.

22. Angell, *Campus,* p. 169; Floyd Dell, *Love in the Machine Age* (New York, 1930), p. 166. According to Modell, petting in the 1920s "was almost universal, in the sense that all daters petted at some time, but not in the sense that all couples petted." ("Dating," p. 100).

23. According to Kinsey, "distinctions between necking and petting, mild and heavy petting, and still other classifications which are current among American youth, appear to differentiate nothing more than various techniques, or the parts of the body which are involved in the contacts, or the level of arousal which is effected." Alfred Kinsey, Wardell B. Pomeroy, and Clyde E. Martin, *Sexual Behavior in the Human Male* [hereafter cited as *SBHM*] (Philadelphia, 1948), p. 228.

24. Geraldine Frances Smith, "Certain Aspects of the Sex Life of the Adolescent Girl," *JAP* (September 1924) 348–49; *SBHF,* pp. 298–301; *SBHM,* p. 406.

25. Lynd and Lynd, *Middletown,* pp. 138–39; Fass, *The Damned,* pp. 266–69.

26. Fass, *The Damned,* pp. 266, 278, 268; Phyllis Blanchard and Carlyn Manasses, *New Girls for Old* (New York, 1930), pp. 69, 73, 75; Walter Buck, "A Measurement of Changes in Attitudes and Interests of University Students over a Ten-Year Period," *JASP* 31 (1936): 14.

27. Blanchard and Manasses, *New Girls,* p. 71; Fass, *The Damned,* pp. 273, 274, 276.

28. Robert R. Bell and Jack V. Buerkle, "Mother and Daughter Attitudes to Premarital Sexual Behavior," *MFL* 23 (1961): 391. This statement was written about the 1950s, but it is an accurate description of a process that began in the 1920s and 1930s.

29. *SBHF,* table 83, figure 50, p. 339; Fass, *The Damned,* p. 455, n. 28; *SBHM,* pp. 410–13.

30. *SBHF* [8], p. 299; Robert S. Lynd and Helen Merrell Lynd, *Middletwon in Transition: A Study in Cultural Conflicts* (New York, 1937), p. 170; Fass, *The Damned,* p. 271.

31. Lynd and Lynd, *Middletown in Transition,* p. 170.

32. Bromley and Britten, *Youth and Sex,* pp. 15–16; Theodore Newcomb, "Recent Changes in Attitudes toward Sex and Marriage," *ASR* 2 (1937): 667, 662; "Youth in College," *Fortune* 13, 3 June 1936, p. 101.

Michael Gordon has tried to explain the apparent contradictions between the views of 1930s campus life offered by Waller and Newcomb; see "Was Waller Ever Right?" pp. 68–69.

33. Fass, *The Damned,* p. 180; "Youth in College," p. 101; Calvin B. Lee, *Campus USA 1900–1970: Changing Styles in Undergraduate Life* (New York, 1970), p. 48.

34. The marriage rate fell from 10.14 per 1,000 in 1929 to 7.9 in 1932 and then started up again, reaching its late 1920s level by 1934 and surpassing it by 1940. Paul Glick and Hugh Carter, *Marriage and Divorce: A Social and Economic Study* (Cambridge, Mass., 1970), p. 41.

35. U.S. Census, Current Population Reports, "Statistical Portrait of Women in the United States: 1978," series P-23, no. 100, p. 24; Cherlin, *Marriage* [3], p. 9.
36. Lee, *Campus USA,* p. 76; "Education for War," *Fortune,* December 1942, p. 146; Winston Ehrmann, *Premarital Dating Behavior* (New York, 1959), p. 76.
37. *SBHF,* p. 234; *SBHM,* pp. 406, 539, 541.

While Kinsey recognized the educational value of petting, he had grave doubts about it on other grounds. He saw petting as the way college groups "attempt to avoid pre-marital intercourse." He was appalled by "the mixture of scientifically supported logic, and of utter illogic, which shapes the petting behavior of most of these youths. . . . They are particularly concerned with the avoidance of genital union. The fact that petting involved erotic contacts which are as effective as genital union . . . does not disturb the youth so much as actual intercourse would." He suggested that the lower incidence of petting among working-class men reflected their lack of respect for the distinction that was all important to the college group. *SBHM,* pp. 541, 543–44.
38. Lowrie, "Dating Theories," p. 337. Lowrie takes a prodating position. He attacks the negative view of dating offered by Waller and others by showing that students themselves emphasized the learning rather than the thrill-seeking aspects of dating behavior.
39. Ira Reiss, "Sexual Codes in Teen-Age Culture," *AAAPSS* (November 1961): 54; Charles W. Cole, "American Youth Goes Monogamous," *Harper's Magazine,* March 1957, p. 32. What Cole missed in the 1950s approach to dating are precisely those elements that Willard Waller found so disturbing in the 1930s.
40. Cole, "American Youth," p. 32.

Co-residence with parents was, however, not a popular strategy. After 1947, the "prevalence of family extension declined abruptly" (Modell, Furstenberg, and Strong, "Timing of Marriage," pp. S136–37).
41. Mildred Gilman, "Why They Can't Wait to Wed," *Parents Magazine,* November 1958, p. 46; David Riesman, "Permissiveness and Sex Roles," *MFL* (August 1959): 21.

Elaine Tyler May has recently suggested that one of the attractions of early marriage in the 1950s was the containment of sexuality which, like communism and atomic war, threatened American stability and order ("Explosive Issues: Sex, Women, and the Bomb in Post-War America," unpublished paper, American Historical Association, December 1982). The couples who married during this period were the "only cohorts in the last hundred years to show a substantial, sustained shortfall in their lifetime levels of divorce": that is, they had a lower rate of divorce than one would expect from the long-term trends (see Cherlin, *Marriage,* p. 25).
42. Ehrmann, *Premarital Dating,* p. 268; Phyllis McGinley, "The Fearful Aspect of Too-Early Dating," *Good Housekeeping,* April 1956, pp. 60–61, 287–88.

Ira Reiss attributed this early socialization to the spread of junior high schools: "The anticipatory socialization of sex games like 'spin the bottle,' . . . begins prior to junior high levels and thus prepares students for dating in junior high" ("Sexual Codes," p. 54, n. 3).
43. Jesse Bernard, Helen E. Buchanan, and William M. Smith, Jr., *Dating, Mating and Marriage* (Cleveland, OH, 1958), pp. 34, 25–28. The Bernard book is unusual among marriage and family texts in that it takes a "documentary case approach." The "informants" are unidentified college students, presumably enrolled in the authors' courses.
44. Ibid., pp. 27–28; Toth, *Blooming,* p. 49.
45. Godfrey Hodgson, *America in Our Time* (New York, 1978), pp. 53–54; *Historical Statistics of the United States from Colonial Times to 1970,* Bicentennial Edition (Washington, D.C., 1975), part I, p. 383.
46. Cole, "American Youth," pp. 30, 33; Nora Johnson, "Sex and the College Girl," *Atlantic,* November 1959, pp. 57–58.

Pinning was "made quite a bit of in the fraternity set" on at least one campus. The couple would announce, after the weekly chapter meeting, that they were about to become pinned; and "then the next weekend the 'fellow' and several of his friends came to the sorority house and there was singing and 'serenading.' After that the pinning was official. Depinning was also a ritual.

Both announced after chapter meetings that they were no longer pinned. It was the custom for no one to ask any questions or even to discuss it." Bernard, Buchanan, and Smith, *Dating,* p. 43.

47. Reiss, "Sexual Codes," pp. 55, 59; Johnson, "College Girl," pp. 57, 59, 60.

48. Ehrmann, *Premarital Dating,* p. 36, tables 1.6, 1.7; Robert R. Bell and Jay B. Chaskes, "Premarital Sexual Experience among Coeds, 1958–1968," *JMF* 32 (February 1970): 83.

Ehrmann pointed out the "curious fact [that] there exist more quantitative data about the incidence rates of coitus, the most taboo of premarital heterosexual activities, than about kissing and hugging, the most socially acceptable" (p. 32).

49. Reiss, "Sexual Codes," 55; Bernard, Buchanan, and Smith, *Dating,* p. 58. Reiss's *Premarital Sexual Standards in America* (Glencoe, IL, 1961) is a detailed inquiry into the values underlying sexual standards in America.

50. Reiss, "Sexual Codes," 59; Ehrmann, *Premarital Dating,* p. 270.

51. "Shaping the 60s . . . Foreshadowing the 70s," *Ladies' Home Journal,* January 1962, pp. 30, 73.

In spite of the fact that "so few they would hardly count supported greater sexual freedom for men and women than our society condones," George Gallup concluded from this poll that these girls were "unconventional in their attitudes toward sex." Ibid., p. 30.

52. Ehrmann, *Premarital Dating,* p. 269. All of these distinctions prompted Ehrmann to suggest that there were "distinct male and female subcultures" in the world of American youth; see pp. 270–77, for his discussion of this idea.

53. Edwin O. Smigel and Rita Seiden, "Decline and Fall of the Double Standard," *AAAPSS* 376 (March 1968): 12; Gilbert R. Kaats and Keith E. Davis, "The Dynamics of Sexual Behavior of College Students," *JMF* 32 (August 1970): 391; Ira Reiss, "The Sexual Renaissance: A Summary and Analysis," *JSI* 22 (1966): 126.

54. Reiss, "Sexual Renaissance," p. 126; Morton Hunt, *Sex in the 70s* (Chicago, 1974), p. 149.

55. J. Richard Udry, Karl E. Bauman, and Naomi M. Morris, "Changes in Premarital Coital Experience of Recent Decade-of-Birth Cohorts of American Women," *JMF* 37 (November 1975): 784; Kenneth L. Cannon and Richard Long, "Premarital Sexual Behavior in the 60s," *JMF* 33 (February 1971): 40; Kaats and Davis, "Dynamics," 391.

56. Reiss, "Sexual Codes," pp. 58–59; Bell and Chaskes, "Premarital Sexual Experience," pp. 82–83; Cannon and Long, "Premarital Sexual Behavior," p. 41; Reiss, "Sexual Renaissance," p. 126.

57. Hunt, *Sex in the 70s,* p. 21; Smigel and Seiden, "Decline and Fall," p. 14; Robert C. Sorensen, *Adolescent Sexuality in Contemporary America* (New York, 1973), pp. 341, 242, 100.

Sorenson suggests that his subjects' lack of interest in marriage was a reflection of the developmental nature of adolescence. Adolescents do not "seek lifelong companionship and financial security in their immediate post-adolescent life. They are moving away from their own family ties, and few seek to replace them with new ones . . . Commitment to the future is not to their liking, and when most adolescents think of marriage, they think of commitment" (p. 345). While this argument is sensible, it fails to explain the phenomenon of teenage pregnancy—and parenthood.

58. Sorenson, *Adolescent Sexuality,* p. 100; Hunt, *Sex in the 70s,* pp. 151–53.

59. Sally Helgesen, "Your Right to Say No," *Seventeen,* August 1981, pp. 284–85; Melvin Zelnik and Jon F. Kantner, "Sexual Activity, Contraceptive Use and Pregnancy among Metropolitan-Area Teenagers," *FPP* 12 (September/October 1980): 230–31.

Virtually all of the growth in coitus between 1976 and 1979 occurred among white teenagers. This increase in teenage sexual activity was accompanied by a steady increase in teenage pregnancy and abortion. In 1979, 16 percent of all teenage women had been premaritally pregnant; 37 percent of these pregnancies were terminated by induced abortion. In spite of "increased and more consistent" use of contraception by teenagers, pregnancy rates were rising, perhaps because many adolescents were substituting withdrawal for more effective methods, such as the pill and the IUD. See Zelnik and Kantner, "Sexual Activity," p. 237.

60. One entirely new setting has recently been introduced to the college social scene. In January 1983, the *New York Times* reported that computer

centers were "to some extent replacing libraries as a focus of student life, both academic and social." *New York Times,* 2 January 1983, p. A:1.

61. Arno Karlen, "Unmarried Marrieds on Campus," *New York Times Magazine,* 26 January 1969, p. 77; U.S. Census, "Marital Status," p. 1; Paul Glick and Graham B. Spanier, "Married and Unmarried Cohabitation in the United States." *JMF* 42 (February 1980): 20–21.

Some of this increase is the result of the absolute increase in the numbers of young adults in the population and of greater frankness in reporting; but all analysts agree that while it may be exaggerated by the statistics, the real magnitude of the change is very great.

62. Karlen, "Unmarrieds," p. 78; Glick and Spanier, "Married and Unmarried Cohabitation," 21; Barbara J. Risman et al., "Living Together in College: Implications for Courtship," *JMF* 43 (February 1981): 82.

63. Risman et al., found some evidence that cohabiting couples were more likely to have smaller and, presumably, less formal weddings than their noncohabiting counterparts ("Living Together," p. 82).

64. "Big Weddings Are Back," *McCall's,* April 1981, pp. 124–34; Marcia Seligson, *The Eternal Bliss Machine: America's Way of Wedding* (New York, 1973), p. 4; *New York Times,* 26 October 1980, p. C:19; *New York Times,* 18 May 1982, p. B:2.

65. Lorenzo Dow, "Reflections on Matrimony," in Peggy Dow, *Vicissitudes in the Wilderness* (Norwich, CT, 1833), p. 156; Cherlin, *Marriage,* pp. 22–23; Arthur J. Norton and Paul C. Glick, "Marital Instability in America: Past, Present, and Future," in *Divorce and Separation,* ed. by George Levinger and Oliver C. Moles (New York, 1979), p. 13.

66. Walter W. Price to James Lee Laidlaw, 8 September 1905, Harriet Burton Laidlaw Papers, SL.

READING 8-2

Dubious Conceptions: The Controversy over Teen Pregnancy

Kristin Luker

The conventional wisdom has it that an epidemic of teen pregnancy is today ruining the lives of young women and their children and perpetuating poverty in America. In polite circles, people speak regretfully of "babies having babies." Other Americans are more blunt. "I don't mind paying to help people in need," one angry radio talk show host told Michael Katz, a historian of poverty, "but I don't want my tax dollars to pay for the sexual pleasure of adolescents who won't use birth control."

By framing the issue in these terms, Americans have imagined that the persistence of poverty and other social problems can be traced to youngsters who are too impulsive or too ignorant to postpone sexual activity, to use contraception, to seek an abortion, or failing all that, especially if they are white, to give their babies up for adoption to "better" parents. Defining the problem this way, many Americans, including those in a position to influence public policy, have come to believe that one attractive avenue to reducing poverty and other social ills is to reduce teen birth rates. Their remedy is to persuade teenagers to postpone childbearing, either by convincing them of the virtues of chastity (a strategy conservatives prefer) or by making abortion, sex education, and contraception more freely available (the strategy liberals prefer).

Reducing teen pregnancy would almost certainly be a good thing. After all, the rate of teen childbearing in the United States is more similar to the rates prevailing in the poor countries of the world than in the modern, industrial nations we think of as our peers. However, neither the problem of teen pregnancy nor the remedies for it are as simple as most people think.

In particular, the link between poverty and teen pregnancy is a complicated one. We do know that teen mothers are poorer than women who wait past their 20th birthday to have a child. But stereotypes to the contrary, it is not clear whether early motherhood causes poverty or the reverse. Worse yet, even if teen pregnancy does have some independent force in making teen parents poorer than they would otherwise be, it remains to be seen whether any policies in effect or under discussion can do much to reduce teen birth rates.

These uncertainties raise questions about our political culture as well as our public choices. How did Americans become convinced that teen pregnancy is a major cause of poverty and that reducing one would reduce the other? The answer is a tale of good intentions, rising cultural anxieties about teen sex and family breakdown, and the uses—and misuses—of social science.

HOW TEEN PREGNANCY BECAME AN ISSUE

Prior to the mid-1970s, few people talked about "teen pregnancy." Pregnancy was defined as a social problem primarily when a woman was unmarried; no one thought anything amiss when an 18- or 19-year-old got married and had children. And concern about pregnancies among unmarried women certainly did not stop when the woman turned 20.

But in 1975, when Congress held the first of many hearings on the issue of adolescent fertility, expert witnesses began to speak of an "epidemic" of a "million pregnant teenagers" a year. Most of these witnesses were drawing on statistics supplied by the Alan Guttmacher Institute, which a year later published the data in an influ-

ential booklet, *Eleven Million Teenagers.* Data from that document were later cited—often down to the decimal point—in most discussions of the teenage pregnancy "epidemic."

Many people hearing these statistics must have assumed that the "million pregnant teenagers" a year were all unmarried. The Guttmacher Institute's figures, however, included married 19-year-olds along with younger, unmarried teenage girls. In fact, almost two-thirds of the "million pregnant teenagers" were 18- and 19-year olds; about 40 percent of them were married, and about two-thirds of the married women were married prior to the pregnancy.

Moreover, despite the language of epidemic, pregnancy rates among teenagers were not dramatically increasing. From the turn of the century until the end of World War II, birth rates among teenagers were reasonably stable at approximately 50 to 60 births per thousand women. Teen birth rates, like all American birth rates, increased dramatically in the period after World War II, doubling in the baby boom years to a peak of about 97 births per thousand teenage women in 1957. Subsequently, teen birth rates declined, and by 1975 they had gone back down to their traditional levels, where, for the most part, they have stayed (see Figure 1).

Were teen births declining in recent decades only because of higher rates of abortion? Here, too, trends are different from what many people suppose. The legalization of abortion in January of 1973 made it possible for the first time to get reliable statistics on abortions for women, teenagers and older. The rate among teenagers rose from about 27.0 to 42.9 abortions per 1,000 women between 1974 and 1980. Since 1980 teen abortion rates have stabilized, and may even have declined somewhat. Moreover, teenagers account for a declining proportion of all abortions: in the years just after *Roe v. Wade,* teenagers obtained almost a third of all abortions in the country; now they obtain about a quarter. A stable teen birth rate and a stabilizing teen abortion rate means that pregnancy rates,

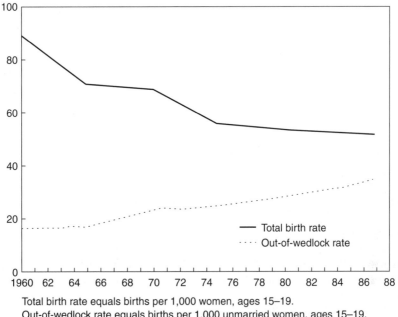

Total birth rate equals births per 1,000 women, ages 15–19.
Out-of-wedlock rate equals births per 1,000 unmarried women, ages 15–19.

FIGURE 8.1 **Trends in Teen Birth Rates**
(Sources: National Center for Health Statistics, *Annual Vital Statistics,* and *Monthly Vital Statistics Reports;* U.S. DHEW, Vital and Health Statistics, "Trends in Illegitimacy, U.S. 1940–1965.")

which rose modestly in the 1970s, have in recent years leveled off.

What has been increasing—and increasing dramatically—is the percentage of teen births that are out-of-wedlock (Figure 1). In 1970 babies born out of wedlock represented about a third of all babies born to teen mothers. By 1980 out-of-wedlock births were about half; and by 1986 almost two-thirds. Beneath these overall figures lie important racial variations. Between 1955 and 1988 the out-of-wedlock rate rose from 6 to 24.8 per thousand unmarried, teenage, white women, while for unmarried, nonwhite teenagers the rate rose from 77.6 to 98.3 per thousand. In other words, while the out-of-wedlock birth rate was rising 25 percent among nonwhite teens, it was actually quadrupling among white teens.

The immediate source for this rise in out-of-wedlock teen pregnancy might seem to be obvious. Since 1970 young women have increasingly postponed marriage without rediscovering the virtues of chastity. Only about 6 percent of teenagers were married in 1984, compared to 12 percent in 1970. And although estimates vary, sexual activity among single teenagers has increased sharply, probably doubling. By 1984 almost half of all American teenage women were both unmarried and sexually active, up from only one in four in 1970.

Yet the growth of out-of-wedlock births has not occurred only among teens; in fact, the increase has been more rapid among older women. In 1970 teens made up almost half of all out-of-wedlock births in America; at present they account for a little less than a third. On the other hand, out-of-wedlock births represent a much larger percentage of births to teens than of births to older women. Perhaps for that reason, teenagers have become the symbol of a problem that, to many Americans, is "out of control."

Whatever misunderstandings may have been encouraged by reports of a "million pregnant teenagers" a year, the new concept of "teen pregnancy" had a remarkable impact. By the mid-1980s, Congress had created a new federal office on adolescent pregnancy and parenting; 23 states had set up task forces; the media had published over 200 articles, including cover stories in both *Time* and *Newsweek;* American philanthropy had moved teen pregnancy into a high priority funding item; and a 1985 Harris poll showed that 80 percent of Americans thought teen pregnancy was a "serious problem" facing the nation, a concern shared across racial, geographic, and economic boundaries.

But while this public consensus has been taking shape, a debate has emerged about many of its premises. A growing number of social scientists have come to question whether teen pregnancy causes the social problems linked to it. Yet these criticisms have at times been interpreted as either an ivory-tower indifference to the fate of teen parents and their babies or a Panglossian optimism that teen childbearing is just one more alternate lifestyle. As a result, clarity on these issues has gotten lost in clouds of ideological mistrust. To straighten out these matters, we need to understand what is known, and not known, about the relation of teen pregnancy to poverty and other social problems.[1]

DISTINGUISHING CAUSES FROM CORRELATIONS

As the Guttmacher Institute's report made clear, numerous studies have documented an association between births to teenagers and a host of bad medical and social outcomes. Compared to women who have babies later in life, teen mothers are in poorer health, have more medically treacherous pregnancies, more stillbirths and newborn deaths, and more low-birth-weight and medically compromised babies.

Later in life, women who have babies as teenagers are also worse off than other women.

By their late 20s, women who gave birth as teenagers are less likely to have finished high school and thus not to have received any subsequent higher education. They are more likely to have routine, unsatisfying, and dead-end jobs, to be on welfare, and to be single parents either because they were never married or their marriage ended in divorce. In short, they often lead what the writer Mike Rose has called "lives on the boundary."

Yet an interesting thing has happened over the last 20 years. A description of the lives of teenage mothers and their children was transmuted into a causal sequence, and the often-blighted lives of young mothers were assumed to flow from their early childbearing. Indeed, this is what the data would show, if the women who gave birth as teenagers were the same in every way as women who give birth later. But they are not.

Although there is little published data on the social origins of teen parents, studies have documented the effects of social disadvantage at every step along the path to teenage motherhood. First, since poor and minority youth tend to become sexually active at an earlier age than more advantaged youngsters, they are "at risk" for a longer period of time, including years when they are less cognitively mature. Young teens are also less likely to use contraceptives than older teenagers. Second, the use of contraception is more common among teens who are white, come from more affluent homes, have higher educational aspirations, and who are doing well in school. And, finally, among youngsters who become pregnant, abortions are more common if they are affluent, white, urban, of higher socio-economic status, get good grades, come from two-parent families, and aspire to higher education. Thus, more advantaged youth get filtered out of the pool of young women at risk of teen parenthood.

Two kinds of background factors influence which teens are likely to become pregnant and give birth outside of marriage. First is inherited disadvantage. Young women from families that are poor, or rural, or from a disadvantaged minority, or headed by a single parent are more likely to be teen mothers than are their counterparts from more privileged backgrounds. Yet young mothers are not just disadvantaged; they are also discouraged. Studies suggest that a young woman who has other troubles—who is not doing well in school, has lower "measured ability," and lacks high aspirations for herself—is also at risk of becoming a teenage mother.

Race plays an independent part in the route to teen motherhood. Within each racial group, according to Linda Waite and her colleagues at the Rand Corporation, teen birth rates are highest for those who have the greatest economic disadvantage and lowest academic ability. The effects of disadvantage, however, vary depending on the group. The Rand study found that among young high-ability, affluent black women from homes with two parents, only about one in a hundred become single, teenage mothers. For comparable whites, the risk was one in a thousand. By contrast, a poor, black teenager from a female-headed household who scores low on standardized tests has an astonishing one in four chance of becoming an unwed mother in her teens. Her white counterpart has 1 chance in 12. Unwed motherhood thus reflects the intersecting influences of race, class, and gender; race and class each has a distinct impact on the life histories of young women.

Since many, if not most, teenage unwed mothers are already both disadvantaged and discouraged before they get pregnant, the poor outcomes of their pregnancies as well as their later difficulties in life are not surprising. Consider the health issues. As the demographer Jane Menken pointed out some time ago (and as many other studies have corroborated), the medical complications associated with teen pregnancy are largely due not to age but to the poverty of young mothers. As poor people, they suffer not from some biological risk due to

youth, but from restricted access to medical care, particularly to prenatal care. (To be fair, some research suggests that there may be special biological risks for the very youngest mothers, those under age 15 when they give birth, who constitute about 2 percent of all teen mothers.)

Or, to take a more complicated example, consider whether bearing a child blocks teenagers from getting an education. In the aggregate, teen mothers do get less education than women who do not have babies at an early age. But teen mothers are different from their childless peers along exactly those dimensions we would expect independently to contribute to reduced schooling. More of them are poor, come from single-parent households, and have lower aspirations for themselves, lowered measured ability, and more problems with school absenteeism and discipline. Given the nature of the available data, it is difficult to sort out the effects of a teen birth apart from the personal and social factors that predispose young women to both teen motherhood and less education. Few would argue that having a baby as a teenager enhances educational opportunities, but the exact effect of teen birth is a matter of debate.

Educational differences between teen mothers and other women may also be declining, at least in terms of graduating from high school. Legislation that took effect in 1975 forbade schools to expel pregnant teens. Contrary to current skepticism about federal intervention, this regulation seems to have worked. According to a study by Dawn Upchurch and James McCarthy, only 18.6 percent of teenagers who had a baby in 1958 subsequently graduated from high school. Graduation rates among teen mothers reached 29.2 percent in 1975; by 1986 they climbed to 55 percent. Teen mothers were still not graduating at a rate equal to other women (as of 1985, about 87 percent of women ages 25 to 29 had a high school diploma or its equivalent). But over the decade prior to 1986, graduation rates had increased more quickly for teen mothers than for other women, suggesting that federal policies tailored to their special circumstances may have made a difference.

Since education is so closely tied to later status, teasing out the relationship between teen pregnancy and schooling is critical. The matter is complicated, however, because young people do many things simultaneously, and sorting out the order is no easy task. In 1984 Peter Morrison of the Rand team reported that between a half and a third of teen mothers in high school and beyond dropped out before they got pregnant. Upchurch and McCarthy, using a different and more recent sample, found that the majority of female dropouts in their study left school before they got pregnant and that teens who got pregnant while still in school were not particularly likely to drop out. On the other hand, those teens who first drop out and then get pregnant are significantly less likely to return to school than other dropouts who do not get pregnant. Thus the conventional causal view that teens get pregnant, drop out of school, and as a result end up educationally and occupationally disadvantaged simply does not match the order of events in many people's lives.

THE SEXUAL ROOTS OF PUBLIC ANXIETY

Teen pregnancy probably would not have "taken off" as a public issue quite so dramatically, were it not for the fact it intersects with other recent social changes in America, particularly the emergence of widespread, anxiety-producing shifts in teen sex. Academics debate whether there has been a genuine "sexual revolution" among adults, but there is no doubt in regard to teenagers. Today, by the time American teenagers reach age 20, an estimated 70 percent of the girls and 80 percent of the boys have had sexual experiences outside of marriage. Virtually all studies confirm that this is a dramatic historical change, particularly for young women. (As usual, much less is known about the historical experiences of young men.) For example, Sandra Hofferth and her colleagues, using nationally representative data from the 1982 National Survey of Family Growth, found that women navigating adolescence in the late 1950s had a 38.9 percent chance of being sexually active before marriage during their teenage years. Women who reached their 20th birthday between 1979 and 1981, in contrast, had a 68.3 percent likelihood.

Yet even these statistics do not capture how profoundly different this teen sexuality is from that of earlier eras. As sources such as the Kinsey Report (1953) suggest, premarital sex for many American women before the 1960s was "engagement" sex. The woman's involvement, at least, was exclusive, and she generally went on to marry her partner in a relatively short period of time. Almost half of the women in the Kinsey data who had premarital sex had it only with their fiancés.

But as the age at first marriage has risen and the age at first intercourse has dropped, teen sexuality has changed. Not surprisingly, what scattered data we have about numbers of partners suggest that as the period of sexual activity before marriage has increased, so has the number of partners. In 1971, for example, almost two-thirds of sexually active teenaged women in metropolitan areas had had only one sexual partner; by 1979 fewer than half did. Data from the 1988 National Survey of Family Growth confirm this pattern for the nation as a whole, where about 60 percent of teens have had two or more partners. Similarly, for metropolitan teens, only a small fraction (about 10 percent) were engaged at the time of their first sexual experience, although about half described themselves as "going steady."

Profound changes in other aspects of American life have complicated the problem. Recent figures suggest that the average age at first marriage has increased to almost 24 years for women and over 25 years for men, the oldest since reliable data have been collected. Moreover, the age of sexual maturity over the last century has decreased by a little under six months each decade owing to nutritional and other changes. Today the average American girl has her first menstrual period at age 12 and a half, although there are wide individual variations. (There is less research on the sexual maturity of young men.) On average, consequently, American girls and their boyfriends face over a decade of their lives when they are sexually mature and single.

As teenagers pass through this reproductive minefield, the instructions they receive on how to conduct themselves sexually are at best mixed. At least according to public opinion polls, most Americans have come, however reluctantly, to accept premarital sex. Yet one suspects that what they approve is something closer to Kinsey-era sex: sexual relations en route to a marriage. Present-day teenage sex, however, starts for many young people not when they move out of the family and into the orbit of what will be a new family or couple, but while they are still defined primarily as children.

When young people, particularly young women, are still living at home (or even at school) under the control, however nominal, of parents, sexual activity raises profound questions for adults. Many Americans feel troubled about "casual" sex, that is, sex which is not intimately tied to the process by which people form couples and settle down. Yet many teenagers are almost by definition disqualified as too young to "get serious." Thus the kinds of sexuality for which they are socially eligible—sex based in pleasure, not procreation, and in short-term relationships rather than as a prelude to marriage—challenge fundamental values about sexuality held by many adults. These ambiguities and uncertainties have given rise to broad anxieties about teen sexuality that have found expression in the recent alarm about teen pregnancy.

RAISING CHILDREN WITHOUT FATHERS

While Americans have had to confront the meaning and purpose of sexuality in the lives of teenagers, a second revolution is forcing them to think about the role—and boundaries—of marriage and family. Increasingly for Americans, childbearing and, more dramatically, childrearing have been severed from marriage. The demographer Larry Bumpass and his colleagues have estimated that under present trends, half or more of all American children will spend at least part of their childhood in a single-parent (mainly mother-only) family, due to the fact that an estimated 60 percent of recent marriages will end in divorce.

At the same time, as I indicated earlier, out-of-wedlock births are on the rise. At present, 26 percent of all births are to single women. If present trends continue, Bumpass and others estimate, almost one out of every six white women and seven out of ten black women will give birth to a child without being married. In short, single childbearing is becoming a common pattern of family formation for all American women, teenagers and older.

This reality intersects with still another fact of American life. The real value of inflation-adjusted wages, which grew 2.5 to 3.0 percent a year from the end of World War II to at least 1973, has now begun to stagnate and for certain groups decline; some recent studies point to greater polarization of economic well-being. Americans increasingly worry about their own standard of living and their taxes, and much of that worry has focused on the "underclass." Along with the elderly and the disabled, single women and their children have been the traditional recipients of public aid in America. In recent years, however, they have become especially visible among the dependent poor for at least two reasons. First, the incomes of the elderly have improved, leaving behind single mothers as a higher percentage of the poor; and second, the number of female-headed households has increased sharply. Between 1960 and 1984, households headed by women went from 9.0 percent to 12.0 percent of all white households, and from 22.0 percent to 43 percent of all black households. The incomes of about half of all families headed by women, as of 1984, fell below federal poverty levels.

Raising children as a single mother presents economic problems for women of all ages, but the problem is especially severe for teenagers with limited education and job experience. Partly for that reason, teenagers became a focus of public concern about the impact of illegitimacy and single parenthood on welfare costs. Data published in the 1970s and replicated in the 1980s suggested that about half of all families supported by Aid to Families with Dependent Children (AFDC) were started while the mother was still a teenager. One estimate calculated that in 1975 the costs for these families of public assistance alone (not including Medicaid or food stamps) amounted to $5 billion; by 1985, that figure increased to $8.3 billion.

Yet other findings—and caveats—have been ignored. For example, while about half of all AFDC cases may be families begun while the woman was still a teenager, teens represent only about 7 percent of the caseload at any one time. Moreover, the studies assessing the welfare costs of families started by teens counted any welfare family as being the result of a teen birth if the woman first had a child when under age 20. But, of course, that same woman—given her prior circumstances—might have been no less likely to draw welfare assistance if, let us say, she had a baby at age 20 instead of 19. Richard Wertheimer and Kristin Moore, the source of much of what we know about this area, have been careful to note that the relevant costs are the marginal costs—namely, how much less in welfare costs society would pay if teen mothers postponed their first births, rather than forgoing them entirely.

It turns out, not surprisingly, that calculated this way, the savings are more modest. Wertheimer and Moore have estimated that if by some miracle we could cut the teen birth rate in half, welfare costs would be reduced by 20 percent, rather than 50 percent, because many of these young women would still need welfare for children born to them when they were no longer teens.

Still other research suggests that most young women spend a transitional period on welfare, while finishing school and entering the job market. Other data also suggest that teen mothers may both enter and leave the welfare ranks earlier than poor women who postpone childbearing. Thus teen births by themselves may have more of an effect on the timing of welfare in the chain of life events than on the extent of welfare dependency. In a study of 300 teen mothers and their children originally interviewed in the mid-1960s, Frank Furstenberg and his colleagues found 17 years later that two-third of those followed up had received no welfare in the previous five years, although some 70 percent of them had received public assistance at some point after the birth of their child. A quarter had achieved middle-class incomes, despite their poverty at the time of the child's birth.

None of this is to deny that teen mothers have a higher probability of being on welfare in the first place than women who begin their families at a later age, or that teen mothers may be disproportionately represented among those who find themselves chronically dependent on welfare. Given the disproportionate number of teen mothers who come from socially disadvantaged origins (and who are less motivated and perhaps less able students), it would be surprising if they were not overrepresented among those needing public assistance, whenever they had their children. Only if we are prepared to argue that these kinds of women should never have children—which is the implicit alternative at the heart of much public debate—could we be confident that they would never enter the AFDC rolls.

RETHINKING TEEN PREGNANCY

The original formulation of the teen pregnancy crisis seductively glossed over some of these hard realities. Teen motherhood is largely the province of those youngsters who are already disadvantaged by their position in our society. The major institutions of American life—families, schools, job markets, the medical system—are not working for them. But by framing the issue as teenage pregnancy, Americans could turn this reality around and ascribe the persistence of poverty and other social ills to the failure of individual teenagers to control their sexual impulses.

Framing the problem as teen pregnancy, curiously enough, also made it appear universal. Everyone is a teenager once. In fact, the rhetoric has sometimes claimed that the risk of teen pregnancy is universal, respecting no boundaries of class or race. But clearly, while teenage pregnancies do occur in virtually all walks of life, they do not occur with equal frequency. The concept of "teen pregnancy" has the advantage, therefore, of appearing neutral and universal while, in fact, being directed at people disadvantaged by class, race, and gender.

If focusing on teen pregnancy cast the problem as deceptively universal, it also cast the solution as deceptively simple. Teens just have to wait. In fact, the tacit subtext of at least some of the debate on teen pregnancy is not that young women should wait until they are past their teens, but until they are "ready." Yet in the terms that many Americans have in mind, large numbers of these youngsters will never be "ready." They have already dropped out of school and will face a marginal future in the labor market whether or not they have a baby. And as William J. Wilson has noted, many young black women in inner-city communities will not have the option of marrying because of the dearth of eligible men their age as a result of high rates of unemployment, underemployment, imprisonment, and early death.

Not long ago, Arline Geronimous, an assistant professor of public health at the University of Michigan, caused a stir when she argued that teens, especially black teens, had little to gain (and perhaps something to lose) in postponing pregnancy. The longer teenagers wait, she noted, the more they risk ill health and infertility, and the less likely their mothers are to be alive and able to help rear a child of theirs. Some observers quickly took Geronimous to mean that teen mothers are "rational," affirmatively choosing their pregnancies.

Yet, as Geronimous herself has emphasized, what sort of choices do these young women have? While teen mothers typically report knowing about contraception (which they often say they have used) and knowing about abortion, they tell researchers that their pregnancies were unplanned. In the 1988 National Survey of Family Growth, for example, a little over 70 percent of the pregnancies to teens were reported as unplanned; the teenagers described the bulk of these pregnancies as wanted, just arriving sooner than they had planned.

Researchers typically layer their own views on these data. Those who see teens as victims point to the data indicating most teen pregnancies are unplanned. Those who see teens as acting rationally look at their decisions not to use contraceptives or seek an abortion. According to Frank Furstenberg, however, the very indecisiveness of these young people is the critical finding. Youngsters often drift into pregnancy and then into parenthood, not because they affirmatively choose pregnancy as a first choice among many options, but rather because they see so few satisfying alternatives. As Laurie Zabin, a Johns Hopkins researcher on teen pregnancy, puts it, "As long as people don't have a vision of the future which having a baby at a very early age will jeopardize, they won't go to all the lengths necessary to prevent pregnancy."

Many people talk about teen pregnancy as if there were an implicit social contract in America. They seem to suggest that if poor women would just postpone having babies until they were past their teens they could have better lives for themselves and their children. But for teenagers already at the margins of American life, this is a contract that American society may be hard put to honor. What if, in fact, they are acting reasonably? What can public policy do about teen pregnancy if many teenagers drift into childbearing as the only vaguely promising option in a life whose options are already constrained by gender, poverty, race, and failure?

The trouble is that there is little reason to think any of the "quick fixes" currently being proposed will resolve the fundamental issues involved. Liberals, for example, argue that the answer is more access to contraception, more readily available abortion, and more sex education. Some combination of these strategies probably has had some effect on teen births, particularly in keeping the teen pregnancy rate from soaring as the number of sexually active teens increased. But the inner logic of this approach is that teens and adults have the same goal: keeping teens from pregnancies they do not want. Some teens, however, do want their pregnancies, while others drift into pregnancy and parenthood without ever actively deciding what they want. Consequently, increased access to contraceptives, sex education, and abortion services are unlikely to have a big impact in reducing their pregnancies.

Conservatives, on the other hand, often long for what they imagine was the traditional nuclear family, where people had children only in marriage, married only when they could prudently afford children, and then continued to provide support for their children if the marriage ended. Although no one fully understands the complex of social, economic, and cultural factors that brought us to the present situation, it is probably safe to predict that we shall not turn the clock back to that vision, which in any event is highly colored by nostalgia.

This is not to say that there is nothing public policy can do. Increased job opportunities for both young men and young women; meaningful job training programs (which do not slot young women into traditional low-paying women's jobs); and child support programs . . . would all serve either to make marriage more feasible for those who wish to marry or to support children whose parents are not married. But older ages at first marriage, high rates of sex outside of marriage, a significant portion of all births out of wedlock, and problems with absent fathers tend to be common patterns in Western, industrialized nations.

In their attempts to undo these patterns, many conservatives propose punitive policies to sanction unmarried parents, especially unmarried mothers, by changing the "incentive structure" young people face. The new welfare reform bill of 1988, for example, made it more difficult for teens to set up their own households, at least in part because legislators were worried about the effects of welfare on the willingness to have a child out of wedlock. Other, more draconian writers have called for the children of unwed teen parents to be forcibly removed and placed into foster care, or for the reduction of welfare benefits for women who have more than one child out of wedlock.

Leave aside, for the moment, that these policies would single out only the most vulnerable in this population. The more troublesome issue is such policies often fall most heavily on the children. Americans, as the legal historian Michael Grossberg has shown, have traditionally and justifiably been leery of policies that regulate adult behavior at children's expense.

The things that public policy could do for these young people are unfortunately neither easy to implement nor inexpensive. However, if teens become parents because they lack options, public policy toward teen pregnancy and teenage childbearing will have to focus on enlarging the array of perceived options these young people face. And these must be changes in their real alternatives. Programs that seek to teach teens "future planning," while doing nothing about the futures they can expect, are probably doomed to failure.

We live in a society that continues to idealize marriage and family as expected lifetime roles for women, even as it adds on the expectation that women will also work and be self-supporting. Planning for the trade-offs entailed in a lifetime of paid employment in the labor market and raising a family taxes the skills of our most advantaged young women. We should not be surprised that women who face discrimination by race and class in addition to that of gender are often even less adept at coping with these large and contradictory demands.

Those who worry about teenagers should probably worry about three different dangers as Americans debate policies on teen pregnancy. First, we should worry that things will continue as they have and that public policy will continue to see teens as unwitting victims, albeit victims who themselves cause a whole host of social ills. The working assumption here will be that teens genuinely do not want the children that they are having, and that the task of public policy is to meet the needs of both society and the women involved by helping them not to have babies. What is good for society, therefore, is good for the individual woman.

This vision, for all the reasons already considered, distorts current reality, and as such, is unlikely to lower the teen birth rate significantly, though it may be effective in keeping the teen birth rate from further increasing. To the extent that it is ineffective, it sets the stage for another risk.

This second risk is that the ineffectiveness of programs to lower teen pregnancy dramatically may inadvertently give legitimacy to those who want more punitive control over teenagers, particularly minority and poor teens. If incentives and persuasion do not lead teenagers to conduct their sexual and reproductive lives in ways that adults would prefer, more coercive remedies may be advocated. The youth of teen mothers may make intrusive social control seem more acceptable than it would for older women.

Finally, the most subtle danger is that the new work on teen pregnancy will be used to argue that because teen pregnancy is not the linchpin that holds together myriad other social ills, it is not a problem at all. Concern about teen pregnancy has at least directed attention and resources to young, poor, and minority women; it has awakened many Americans to their diminished life chances. If measures aimed at reducing teen pregnancy are not the quick fix for much of what ails American society, there is the powerful temptation to forget these young women altogether and allow them to slip back to their traditional invisible place in American public debate.

Teen pregnancy is less about young women and their sex lives than it is about restricted horizons and the boundaries of hope. It is about race and class and how those realities limit opportunities for young people. Most centrally, however, it is typically about being young, female, poor, and nonwhite and about how having a child seems to be one of the few avenues of satisfaction, fulfillment, and self-esteem. It would be a tragedy to stop worrying about these young women—and their partners—because their behavior is the measure rather than the cause of their blighted hopes.

ENDNOTE

1. Teen pregnancy affects both young men and young women, but few data are gathered on young men. The availability of data leads me to speak of "teen mothers" throughout this article, but it is important to realize that this reflects an underlying, gendered definition of the situation.

CHAPTER 9

Spouses and Partners

The expectations that wives and husbands have for their marriages have changed greatly during the 20th century.[1] Ernest Burgess described the evolution of marital relations during the first half of the century as a "transition from an institution to a companionship." The "institutional" marriage was governed by the formal authority of the husband, which was backed by community pressure. There was little emphasis on the emotional side of marriage. Marriage as a "companionship," a form that peaked at midcentury, emphasized romantic love, mutual affection, and friendship. Still, there was a sharp distinction between the ideal roles of wives and husbands—she was the homemaker, he was the breadwinner. Moreover, in the companionship marriage, wives held the main responsibility for maintaining the family's emotional life by expressing feelings and providing emotional support to husbands and children.

The companionship marriage was a partnership in which fulfilling one's roles—being a good homemaker, earning the family's income—provided the highest satisfactions. Much of a person's gratifications, then, occurred through activities external to the self. But after the 1950s, marriages, and the rising numbers of heterosexual and homosexual nonmarital partnerships, came to be defined more in terms of individual growth and development than in terms of fulfilling prescribed roles. Sociologist Francesca Cancian, in the following excerpt from her book, *Love in America: Gender and Self-Development,* calls this a transition "from role to self" in the focus of personal rewards in marriages and partnerships.

Cancian maintains that love itself was "feminized" under the older kinds of marriage because emotion was seen as the domain of women. Now, love is more "androgynous," meaning that both women and men are concerned about expressing love and emotional support. Correspondingly, autonomy and self-development were emphasized more for men, whereas now these goals are put forth for both genders. To provide evidence for her view of the evolution of marriage, she studied articles on marriage in popular magazines between 1900 and 1979. Their shifting content, she argues, demonstrates the shift from role to self.

---

[1]*Public and Private Families: An Introduction,* pp. 260–65.

Married couples often find that the birth of a first child alters their relationship. Most couples expect positive change: a greater closeness as a family, a sense of sharing and mutuality. Few are prepared for the unwanted changes that also frequently occur. Studies show that in the months after a first child is born, the relationship between the mother and father often becomes less satisfying, more conflicted, and more distant. Developmental psychologist Jay Belsky studied 250 couples before and after the birth of their first child. He found that 12 to 13 percent became so divided that the quality of their marriages declined severely. For both partners, feelings of love and communication dropped sharply and feelings of conflict and ambivalence rose. Another 38 percent experienced a more moderate decline in marital quality. Thus, half the couples found that the new child reduced their satisfaction with their marriages. These declines weren't inevitable: 30 percent of the couples experienced little or no change in marital quality and 19 percent reported that the birth brought them closer together.

In the excerpt reprinted here from his book with writer John Kelly, *The Transition to Parenthood: How a First Child Changes a Marriage,* Belsky describes the factors that tend to push spouses apart and the factors that tend to pull them together. He argues, as have others, that the transition to parenthood typically is experienced very differently by women and men.

READING 9-1

From Role to Self: The Emergence of Androgynous Love in the 20th Century

Francesca M. Cancian

In the long run, the social changes that began in the 19th century destroyed Victorian family patterns. The ideal of masculine independence spread to women and the private sphere, undermining people's willingness to be restricted by narrow family and gender roles. Wives became less subordinate and absorbed by mothering, as they had fewer children and increasingly joined the labor force, and many husbands became less consumed by their work as leisure time expanded and jobs became bureaucratized. Through most of the 20th century, there has been a trend towards more fluid, androgynous family roles and more involvement in self-

Francesca M. Cancian, "From Role to Self: The Emergence of Androgynous Love in the Twentieth Century" from *Love in America: Gender and Self-Development*, pp. 30–45. Copyright © 1987 by Cambridge University Press. Reprinted with the permission of the author and Cambridge University Press, North American Branch.

development and personal life. Americans have become more concerned with individual happiness and pleasure, more tolerant of alternative life styles, more committed to equality for women and men, and more prone to divorce.

The trend to androgynous love has been discontinuous. In eras that emphasized personal liberation like the 20s and the late 60s, the trend accelerated, while in the 50s the long-range trend reversed as gender roles became more rigid and tolerance declined. These discontinuities can be used to identify different periods in the social organization of marriage, each dominated by a different family blueprint, or a different mix of blueprints.[1] Each blueprint combines a cultural image of the ideal marriage with expectations for daily life that guide behavior.

Figure 1 presents the major blueprints of marriage since the 19th century. First is the Victorian blueprint of family duty in which love is the woman's responsibility. Then come the three blueprints that dominate contemporary marriage: the more traditional companionship blueprint that first evolved in the 20s, and the newer blueprints of independence and interdependence in which the woman and the man share the obligation to work on their relationship, and the goal of self-development replaces conformity to roles. This chapter gives a general description of

	Who is responsible for love?	What is love?
Feminized love		
Family duty		
(19th century)	woman	fulfill duty to family
Companionship		
(1920–)	woman	intimacy in marriage
Androgynous love		
Independence		
(1970–)	woman and man	individual self-development and intimacy
Interdependence		
(1970–)	woman and man	mutual self-development, intimacy, and support

FIGURE 1 Blueprints of love.

these changes in blueprints of marriage, and then presents quantitative data on the major trends.

THE DECLINE OF THE FAMILY DUTY BLUEPRINT

The family duty blueprint was the first solution to the problem of maintaining family bonds in an increasingly individualistic society. According to this image of family life, as we have seen, the ideal family was a nuclear household consisting of a father who left home every day to make the money to support the family, a loving mother who was the center of family life, and the children. Marriage was forever, and a man had considerable authority over his wife and children. The relation between husband and wife began with falling in love and might develop into companionship, although intimacy and sexual relations between spouses were not central and both spouses had important ties with relatives and friends of their own sex. The key relation was an intense, emotional tie between mothers and children, and raising moral, respectable, and healthy children was a woman's major task.

This ideal dominated in the United States from about 1840 to 1880 and then began to show signs of decline.[2] The divorce rate was increasing at the end of the century, and it doubled between 1900 and 1920. The proportion of women remaining single was rising, and so many affluent women were childless that some social critics raised the spectre of "race suicide" and "race sterility." Others criticized the family as an oppressive institution that deprived Americans of freedom and equality. Feminists attacked the tyranny of husbands over wives; plays like Ibsen's *A Doll's House* attacked the childlike position of women; advocates of free love protested against sexual repression; and sociologists viewed the difficulty of divorce as an unnecessary impediment to self-development.

By the turn of the century there was widespread debate in government, churches, and the mass media on the future of the family, the decline of sexual morality, and especially divorce. Opponents of divorce believed that it would destroy the family, which they saw as the basis of civilization. Divorce was attributed to "dangerous individualism," especially individualism in women, and women were charged with being spoiled, romantic, "jealous of men and usurpers of the male's time-honored functions." But by 1910, the opposition was overwhelmed and divorce was accepted.[3]

The 1920s witnessed the dissolution of Victorian family patterns. Social commentators believed that a "revolution in manners and morals" was sweeping the country, and, according to William Chafe, "almost all agreed that the age was one of unprecedented personal liberation."[4] The historian of the family, Arthur Calhoun, writing in 1917, believed he was witnessing the passing of patriarchy and devotion to the family, as people became more and more individualistic.

In the Roaring Twenties, college students and other young people cast aside Victorian clothes and pursued sexual liberation and exciting personal experiences.[5] The institution of dating developed—the pattern of young men and women seeing each other without chaperones, and without any intention of marriage, to "have a good time." High school students in Muncie, Indiana, in 1924 went to necking and petting parties and only with difficulty could be persuaded to be home for dinner three nights a week. On college campuses, dedication to social reform gave way to social activities organized by sororities and fraternities.[6] Women from respectable families smoked in public, wore short skirts and cosmetics, worked as secretaries before they married, and modeled the new image of a woman with an expensive wardrobe and sex appeal. The response of many older, more conservative Americans to all this was horror at the decline of morality and the sexual orgies (real and imagined) of the young.[7]

The causes of the decline of the family duty blueprint include changes in the sexual division of labor and an increasing value placed on self-fulfillment. Women's daily activities shifted away from motherhood and toward more participation in the public sphere. The ideal of the free, self-made man was spreading, and women were beginning to be seen as similar and equal to men, as persons who should develop themselves. The declining birth rate reduced the burdens of motherhood, although many housewives were busier than ever as standards for a clean and attractive home rose. Employment opportunities for women expanded through the growth of respectable jobs such as being a secretary or a saleswoman. "Nowadays," said suffragist Frances Willard in 1897, "a girl may be anything from a college president down to a seamstress or a cash girl. It depends only upon the girl what rank she shall take in her chosen calling."[8] In fact, most working women were segregated in a few low-paying jobs, and it remained shameful for married women to work, but being a single career woman was becoming a respected way of life.[9]

The Victorian ideal that woman's place was in the home was also challenged by women's participation in the temperance movement and in other social reform movements of the early 20th century. The movement for women's suffrage, which obtained the vote for women in 1920 and involved an estimated two million women, most directly undermined the family duty blueprint.[10] The suffragists used the rhetoric of separate spheres and argued that women needed the vote because they were more moral and altruistic than men, but women's suffrage removed a major barrier to women's participation in public life.[11]

Men's lives also changed as routine white-collar jobs expanded with the growth of large corporations, and the 40-hour work week became more common. Men's work became more sedentary and regimented, and less heroic. According to several social historians, as many men found less validation for their masculinity in work, their personal identification with their jobs diminished and they became more involved with their personal lives, their families, and leisure activities.[12] Work probably continued to be the center of life for men pursuing challenging and prestigious careers, but personal life became increasingly important for men as the 20th century advanced.[13]

The increasing focus on personal life and self-development and decreasing commitment to traditional roles was fueled by several changes. Security—experiencing the world as safe and abundant—seems to promote a concern with self-development, and the average person's sense of security probably rose in the early 20th century because of gradual improvements in the standard of living and the widespread economic boom during the early 20s.[14] The growth of consumerism and advertising also encouraged people to develop new personal needs and try to fulfill them. "The American citizen's first importance to his country," editorialized the Muncie newspaper in the 1920s, is "that of consumer."[15] Valuing self-development and independence over conformity to roles was also encouraged by public education, which expanded enormously for both sexes.[16] In 1924, high-school diplomas were awarded to 213,000 men and 281,000 women, an increase since 1900 of about 500 percent for both sexes, while the population had only increased by 50 percent.[17] Finally, the social reform movements of the Progressive Era challenged traditional roles and political institutions, and the unpopularity of World War I further undermined established authority, leading people to seek direction and meaning in their own personal lives.[18]

THE COMPANIONSHIP BLUEPRINT

As the Victorian blueprint of duty to family roles was disintegrating, a new ideal was being articulated in academia and the mass media: the companionship family. This blueprint identified the family with marriage, not parenthood, and emphasized emotional and sexual intimacy between husband and wife.

Sociologists proposed a new family ideal focused on affection and supporting each other's personalities, now that families had lost their traditional economic and social functions. The modern family was "a unity of interacting personalities" in the famous phrase of sociologist Ernest Burgess, and had evolved "from institution to companionship."[19] The first principles of family life, according to Burgess, are "that the highest personal happiness comes from marriage based on romantic love" and "that love and marriage are essentially personal and private and are, perhaps, even more than other aspects of life to be controlled by the individual himself."[20] Marriage, in this view, is a private arena of self-fulfillment, not duty. With the spread of the companionship blueprint, affective individualism and a more androgynous self became part of mainstream American culture.

For the first time, popular advice books suggested that having children might weaken a family, and in 1931, for the first time, there were more advertisements for cosmetics than for food in the *Ladies' Home Journal.* Being an attractive companion was becoming more important than being a competent homemaker. Dorothy Dix, in her syndicated newspaper column for women, advised: "The old idea used to be that the way for a woman to help her husband was by being thrifty and industrious . . . but a domestic drudge is not a help to her husband, she is a hindrance . . . The woman who cultivates a circle of worth-while people, who belongs to clubs, who makes herself interesting and agreeable . . . is a help to her husband."[21]

The companionship family blueprint emphasized the similarity of husband and wife much more than the family duty blueprint. Both partners were expected to need and to give affection and understanding, and increasingly, both were expected to enjoy sexual intimacy. But love was still feminized, and wives were still expected to

be economically dependent and submissive to their husbands. Marriage was to be all of a woman's life but only part of a man's. There was no column by Dorothy Dix instructing a man on how to be a help to his wife, and the magazines of the period consistently told women that it was their responsibility to create successful marriages.[22] Despite some changes towards androgyny, gender roles remained fairly polarized in the companionship blueprint.

The reality of family life in the 20s, according to Robert and Helen Lynd's study of Muncie, is more similar to the family duty blueprint than to the world of companionship marriage and libertine flappers. In the business class (the top 30 percent of the families), wives did not work, and the social status of the family was a primary concern to both husband and wife. Most couples did not place a very high value on companionship in marriage, and frankness between spouses was not encouraged. Husbands described wives as purer, morally better, and more emotional and impractical than men, and their wives agreed. The motto of one of the women's clubs was "Men are God's trees; Women are his flowers."[23] Social life was organized primarily around couples, although men and women were also active in sex-segregated clubs and friendships were important to the women. Wives were very child-centered, while husbands had little contact with their children beyond meals and family auto trips. Husbands were, however, beginning to share in the housework. In the working class, a substantial minority of the wives worked, but marital relations were even farther from the companionship ideal. Husbands and wives rarely talked, and in the absence of other methods of birth control wives kept away from their husbands sexually. Only the beginnings of the companionship family were observable in Muncie; an intimate emotional and sexual bond between two developing personalities was seldom achieved or even strongly desired. Contrary to what many historians have suggested, marital intimacy was rare, as late as the 20s.

The Great Depression from 1929 to 1941 was probably the major force in reversing the trend towards individual freedom of the 20s. As the economy collapsed, people faced an insecure, hostile environment, and adopted a rigid version of the companionship ideal that emphasized traditional family and gender roles more than personal development. Although domestic politics became more radical in the 30s, with the growing power of labor unions and the social programs of the New Deal, family life became more conservative.

College students in the early 30s expressed less approval of divorce and extramarital sex than in the 20s and there was a rise in the proportion of students who intended to marry and have children.[24] Opposition to women's entering the labor force reappeared as more and more men lost their jobs, and employers increasingly denied married women the right to work. A survey of 1,500 school systems in 1930 reported that 77 percent refused to hire wives and 63 percent fired women teachers if they married. When the Gallup Poll asked Americans in 1936 whether wives should work if their husbands were employed, 82 percent said "no."[25] Women's magazines "urged their readers to return to femininity and constructed an elaborate ideology in support of the home and marriage to facilitate the process," according to historian William Chafe.[26] *The Ladies' Home Journal* told its readers that "the creation and fulfillment of a successful home is a bit of craftsmanship that compares favorably with building a beautiful cathedral," while *McCall's* observed that only as a wife and mother could the American woman "arrive at her true eminence."[27]

The effects of economic insecurity on commitment to traditional family roles is documented by Glen Elder's study of people who grew up during the Depression. Compared with people whose families had not suffered economically, men and women from families that had suffered substantial economic losses in the Depression placed a greater value on family life as opposed to work and leisure, and were more interested in raising children and less interested in husband–wife companionship. The deprived men actually had a larger number of children, on the average, than men from nondeprived backgrounds. Another finding that supports the link between economic deprivation and traditionalism is that working-class people have more traditional attitudes about family and gender than middle-class people.[28]

World War II ended the Depression and interrupted normal life for many families as men went off to war and women to work. Between 1940 and 1944, the proportion of married women in the labor force rose from 17 percent to 20 percent.[29] Although there was an effort to push women workers back into the home after the war, married women continued to enter the work force in growing numbers, radically changing the division of labor between husbands and wives that had persisted since the 19th century.

The postwar decades were a period of extreme commitment to the family and to split gender roles. People married earlier, had more children, and avoided childlessness, causing the famous baby boom. The divorce rate stayed unusually steady,[30] and new suburban tracts provided a setting for a family-centered way of life. There was a resurgence of antifeminism and a revival of the 19th-century theme of separate spheres. Thus the head of one women's college advocated that preparing women for "the task of creating a good home and raising good children" be made the primary purposes of women's colleges.[31] Women's magazines described the joys of femininity and togetherness, and public opinion, which had supported wives working during the war, once again opposed their working if their husbands could support them. Most people also supported a traditional division of labor in which men determined where a family lived and how it spent its money.[32] Yet all the while, more and more wives were working.

The blueprint for family life was a revised version of the companionship family of the 20s and 30s.[33] The companionship ideal of the 50s was based on intimate affection between husband and wife. Although the relation between mother and children was vitally important, a woman was warned not to let motherhood weaken her relation with her husband or to smother her children with too much attention. The couple was expected to lead an active social life but not to have close ties outside the nuclear family. The Victorian ideology of separate spheres was still partly intact; it was the husband's job to support the family, while the wife was the center of home life. But the authority of the husband had declined—he was to be more of a pal to his children and more of a companion to his wife. The concept of family togetherness—of mom, dad, and the kids barbecuing dinner together in the backyard—softened the separation of men's and women's spheres. Marriage began with falling in love and developed into companionship; but if love died, divorce might be the best solution.

This family ideal was endorsed by most intellectuals and social scientists in the postwar era. Talcott Parsons provided a theoretical justification with his argument that a well-functioning family required an instrumental father and an expressive mother. Other sociologists obscured the gender differentiation in the companionship model by emphasizing its equality and flexibility in comparison with the patriarchal Victorian family or the marriages of conservative Americans. Few observers noted that as long as marriage was defined as the wife's responsibility and love was feminized, emphasizing companionship increased her dependency on her husband.[34] The Victorian wife at least had her separate sphere of children and women friends. For the wife in a companionship marriage, her husband was her sphere, and her life was focused on getting the right emotional response from him. The price of companionship marriage was high, especially for the educated, middle-class women who valued their independence the most.[35]

The strong commitment to traditional family roles throughout the 50s and early 60s is somewhat puzzling since many social conditions encouraged androgyny and self-development. A growing number of wives had jobs and became less economically dependent on their husbands. By 1965, 45 percent of married women with school-age children worked, compared with 26 percent in 1948. There was an unprecedented economic prosperity in the postwar era, and a very large expansion of public higher education. One would expect these conditions to accelerate the trend from role to self, but this did not happen until the late 60s, when a wave of protest movements and the Vietnam War produced a counterculture that rejected traditional roles and beliefs, including the companionship family blueprint.[36]

THE DECLINE OF THE COMPANIONSHIP BLUEPRINT

Another period of personal liberation began in the sixties. This time many observers felt that a major boundary of social organization had been crossed—that we had passed from an era in which people's private lives were regulated by the obligations of family roles into a new era of the self.[37] There was a rapid reversal of the familism of the 50s. Divorces accelerated sharply and fertility declined to an all time low. The rate of couples living together without being married doubled between 1970 and 1979, and there was a large increase in the number of persons living alone. Premarital sexual experience, which had been increasing since the 20s, became much more frequent; for example, the percentage of single 17-year-old girls who had experienced sex rose from 27 to 41 percent between 1971 and 1976.[38]

The trend toward wives working for money was probably the underlying cause of the decline of the companionship family. But the immediate cause was the antiestablishment social movements of the 60s and 70s. The 60s began a period of "revolution in manners and morals" similar to the twenties, literally a "counterculture."[39] The civil rights movement, the antiwar movement, and the women's movement involved a large minority of Americans in demonstrations, drug trips, petition campaigns and consciousness-raising groups, all of which undermined the patriotism and devotion to family of the postwar era.

The women's movement, in particular, attacked the companionship family blueprint. Conservative feminists endorsed the "two-career family," in which both husband and wife were equally committed to glamorous careers and to childrearing and homemaking. Radical feminists rejected the family as the preferred living arrangement and developed images of homosexual households or socialist collectives. By the early 70s, ideas about gender equality diffused throughout the nation as the women's movement received a great deal of media coverage and achieved a rapid series of legislative victories supporting expanded opportunities for women in the labor force and in education.[40]

Once again, a strong women's movement had undermined traditional family roles. As long as family blueprints emphasized self-sacrifice and polarized gender roles, women's freedom conflicted with family bonds. Thus Carl Degler concludes his history of women and the family in America by observing that "the great values for which the family stands are at odds . . . with those of the women's movement."[41]

Companionship family roles were also attacked by the human potential movement. Popular psychology books like Gail Sheehy's *Passages* rejected the role of successful provider and cheerful housewife as hypocritical and deadening. They urged people to free themselves from restrictive obligations, get in touch with their feelings, and experience their full potential. New therapies and growth centers sprung up—encounter groups, Esalen, Primal Scream, EST—all of them encouraging adult men and women to develop themselves and re-

ject traditional roles. In contrast to the orthodox therapies of previous decades that had urged patients to adjust to traditional family and gender roles, the new therapies preached androgyny, and urged men and women to reject the expectations of others and develop their own true selves.[42]

The decline of the companionship blueprint was welcomed by some groups and opposed by others. Not surprisingly, women supported the new flexibility in gender roles more than men, especially highly educated professional women.[43] These women valued independence the most and could benefit the most from improved career opportunities. Thus, in the political struggle over abortion, the "pro-choice" activists were mostly well-educated, career-oriented women who placed a high value on individual freedom and self-development. The "pro-life" women were primarily less educated housewives with a deep commitment to religion and to the traditional roles of the loving housewife and the strong husband who provides for her.[44] For these women and for many other Americans, the companionship family continued to be their ideal.

THE NEW BLUEPRINTS: INDEPENDENCE AND INTERDEPENDENCE

By the middle of the 70s, new androgynous images of close relationships were beginning to crystallize. A prolonged economic recession dampened people's aspirations for freedom, and academics and the mass media began to criticize the human potential movement as selfish and narcissistic.[45] The need for intimacy began to seem more pressing than the need to combat oppressive family and gender roles.

The new blueprints emphasize three sets of qualities that I label *self-fulfillment, flexible roles,* and *intimacy and open communication.* First, in the new images of love, both partners are expected to develop a fulfilled and independent self, instead of sacrificing themselves for the other person. Second, family and gender roles are flexible and are continually renegotiated. Third, the relationship centers on intimate communication of needs and feelings, and on openly confronting problems. Self-development and love are integrated in these blueprints, and love is the responsibility of the man as well as the woman. The independence and the interdependence blueprints both emphasize these qualities; they differ on the issue of self-sufficiency and independence versus mutual support and commitment.

The new blueprints of relationships began to emerge in the middle of the 60s, according to a study of women's magazines. Women were advised that they must develop an independent self in order to be loving, and they were told to build a vital, spontaneous relationship without fixed rules, by communicating openly about feelings and working through conflicts. In contrast, in the 50s, "putting aside of self was defined as loving behavior," and women were advised to sacrifice themselves for their families, follow traditional sex roles, and strive for harmony and togetherness.[46]

When Ann Swidler interviewed 60 residents of an affluent California suburb around 1980, she found that most of them emphasized self-fulfillment and accepted the "therepautic ideal" of love promoted by psychologists and the human potential movement. They believed that love is partly expressed by sharing oneself and one's feelings; therefore, a person must develop a somewhat independent self in order to be loving. For example, a young wife explained that she had had problems with her husband, Thomas, because "I was doing things just for him and ignoring things for myself." Now, since her therapy, she feels more independent and self-confident. "The better I feel about myself, I feel I have a whole lot that I can contribute to Thomas."[47]

Good communication is crucial in the new blueprints, both to express one's self, and to negotiate a unique, flexible relationship in the absence of definite family and gender roles. Verbal communication is also part of being intimate and working on the relationship. As a college

man commented, "You have to work at your marriage, it's like a job." A poll conducted for *Playboy* magazine in 1976 indicates the importance of communication to contemporary American men. "Someone to be totally open and honest with" was the most frequently mentioned quality for an ideal lover.[48]

The new blueprints are radically androgynous and anti-institutional. The themes of self-fulfillment and intimate communication resemble the companionship blueprint, and its concern with personality development and marital interaction. But unlike the companionship ideal, the new blueprints do not legitimate predetermined roles or a sexual division of labor; they are blueprints for relationships, not marriages. Both partners are expected to work on the relationship, communicate openly and develop themselves. Wives are advised to cultivate independent interests and goals, while husbands are encouraged to express their feelings. Love is no longer part of women's special sphere.

The independence blueprint adds to these themes a strong emphasis on being self-sufficient and avoiding obligations. Developing an independent self and expressing one's needs and feelings is seen as a precondition to love. In contrast, couples who follow the interdependence blueprint believe that they owe each other mutual support and affection, and that love is a precondition to full self-development.

Sociologists disagree about the relative importance of these two blueprints. Robert Bellah and his associates conclude that independence is becoming the dominant image of love in America. People are increasingly avoiding commitments, they argue and support their interpretation by quoting from Swidler's interviews. For example a counselor commented: "I guess, if there is anyone who needs to owe anybody anything, it is honesty in letting each other know how they feel about each other, and that if feelings change, to be open and receptive, to accept those changes, knowing that people in a relationship are not cement."[49]

In contrast, my study of 133 adults in 1980 indicates that Interdependence, not Independence, is the dominant blueprint of love. The respondents, who came from diverse social backrounds, were asked about the "qualities that are most important for a good marriage or love relationship" . . . Contrary to the argument of Bellah et al., the second most frequently mentioned quality was "support and caring." "Good, open communication" was most frequently mentioned, while "tolerance, flexibility and understanding" was third, "honesty" was fourth, and "commitment" was fifth. Individuals who emphasized "support and caring" usually talked about the obligation to be nurturant and attentive, and many of them connected support and caring with self-development. For example, when a 30-year-old minister in San Diego was asked what he most valued in his wife, he replied:

> I trust her to react in a reaffirming way to me when I share with her . . . I know that she will respond to me in a positive way. She will share the pain or frustration or triumph of the day with me, and I feel like what I have to say about me is very important, because it's me in a sense.

Although there is disagreement about the importance of mutual support and commitment in contemporary relationships, researchers agree on the growing importance of self-fulfillment, flexible roles, and intimate, open communication. With the decline of the companionship blueprint, the trend from role to self accelerated, producing new, more androgynous images of love.

It is possible that another shift back to traditional roles has begun, partly as a result of the continued economic difficulties of the 70s and 80s. The slight drop in the divorce rate and the reversal of feminist gains in affirmative action and abortion rights may be signs of such a shift. But the evidence that would document this change is not yet available.

EVIDENCE FROM POPULAR MAGAZINES

The changes in family blueprints that I have just described are clearly reflected in magazine articles that give advice on how to have a happy marriage. I analyzed a sample of articles from 1900 to 1979 and measured the proportion of articles in each decade that endorsed the traditional family duty and companionship blueprints versus the modern themes of self-fulfillment, flexible roles, and intimacy. The results confirm the long-range trend from role to self during the 20th century, and also show that the 20s and 60s were unusually modern while the 50s were unusually traditional. Studies by other researchers show this same pattern of change.

I examined 128 articles on marriage from high circulation magazines like the *Ladies' Home Journal, McCalls,* and *The Reader's Digest.* The articles are addressed primarily to women, and advise them on how to produce a happy, loving marriage and how to overcome feelings of disappointment and loneliness. For each five-year period, I randomly selected eight articles listed in the *Reader's Guide to Periodicals* under the topic "Marriage." The content of each article was coded according to the dominant message that the article seemed to communicate to readers.[50]

The categories used to analyze the articles focused on self-fulfillment, flexible roles, and intimacy and open communication. One category that measured self-fulfillment was "self-sacrifice versus self-fulfillment." An example of endorsing self-sacrifice is a 1909 editorial in *Harper's Bazaar* that advised: "Marriage means self-discipline. Marriage is *not* for the individual, but for the race . . . Marriage is the slow growth of two persons into one—one person with one pursuit, one mind, one heart, one interest . . . one ideal."[51] In contrast, a *Ladies' Home Journal* article in 1978, illustrating the self-fulfillment theme, warned that it was a myth to believe that marriage should "meet all the emotional needs of both spouses," that it "is an all-encompassing blend of two personalities fused into one. A marriage like this leaves no breathing space for two individuals to retain their own personalities."[52]

A category for measuring flexible roles was "rigid versus flexible female gender role." The traditional side of this category is illustrated by a 1940s article which comments that, compared to men, "women have much less time for action, being absorbed, consciously or unconsciously, by their preoccupation with love and maternity."[53] Intimate communication was measured by the category "avoid conflict, and keep up a front versus communicate openly and confront problems." Illustrating the modern view of communication, an article in the *Reader's Digest* in 1974 asserted that "if spouses are thoughtful toward each other on *all* occasions, they probably have a sick marriage."[54]

Table 1 shows the number of articles in each decade that support traditional versus modern themes in these three categories. The percent of modern themes—combining the three categories—gradually rises, as shown at the bottom of the table. There are also discontinuities; for instance, there are more articles endorsing flexible gender roles in the 1920s than in the next three decades. Thus a 1925 article in *The Ladies' Home Journal* proclaimed: "The woman of today acknowledges no master." Women now regard marriage as "a social partnership, an adventure, an experiment even, but it must always be on a fifty-fifty basis."[55] And in every decade, there is considerable variation in what the magazines are saying, and a substantial number of both traditional and modern themes.

The trend from role to self and the discontinuities in this trend are more clearly displayed in the graph in Figure 2. The graph shows the percent of themes in each decade that support self-fulfillment, flexible roles, and intimate communication, combining eight categories that

include the three already discussed. For example, "flexible roles" is measured by the previously discussed category about the female role, as well as categories about the male role and the acceptability of divorce . . .

The graph shows a trend to modern themes over the 20th century. In the first two decades of the century, about 30 percent of the themes are modern, compared to about 70 percent in the 1970s. There is also a clear up-and-down pattern of change, with modern themes predominating in the 20s and again in the 60s and 70s.

The causes of the trend from role to self, as I have discussed, probably include economic prosperity, increasing leisure and education, and the tendency of women as well as men to work for individual wages. The discontinuities can partly be explained by the same factors; in particular, economic hard times apparently reversed the trend in the 30s. Other researchers have emphasized demographic shifts in explaining discontinuities in American family life, and unpopular wars may also be important.[56]

The intriguing association between the women's movement and images of marriage suggests other explanations of the discontinuities—explanations that point to the great importance of gender roles in understanding the American family. A strong women's movement accompanied or preceded the extreme emphasis on personal freedom and self-fulfillment in the 20s and again in the late 60s. The women's movement, as measured by the amount of coverage of women in the *New York Times* and popular magazines, was strongest between 1905 and 1920. It reached its low point between 1950 and the early 60s, and then rose again in the late sixties . . . The rise and fall of the women's movement thus parallels the rise and fall of modern images of marriage, as shown in Figure 2, except that the highpoint of the movement around 1910 preceded the change in marital images by about a decade.

TABLE 1

TRENDS IN MAGAZINE ARTICLES ON MARRIAGE, 1900–1979: NUMBER OF ARTICLES SUPPORTING TRADITIONAL VERSUS MODERN THEMES.

Traditional [T]		Modern [M]	1900–1909		1910–1919		1920–1929		1930–1939		1940–1949		1950–1959		1960–1969		1970–1979	
			T	M	T	M	T	M	T	M	T	M	T	M	T	M	T	M
1 self-sacrifice compromise	vs.	self-fulfillment individuality	7	1	4	3	5	1	7	2	10	0	11	0	7	7	5	2
2 rigid female role	vs.	flexible female role	10	7	14	4	8	10	11	7	8	9	13	5	8	10	6	13
3 avoid conflict, keep up a front	vs.	communicate openly, confront problems	1	2	2	0	3	2	5	3	4	0	4	6	4	8	3	10
Percent of modern themes			36%		26%		45%		34%		29%		28%		57%		64%	

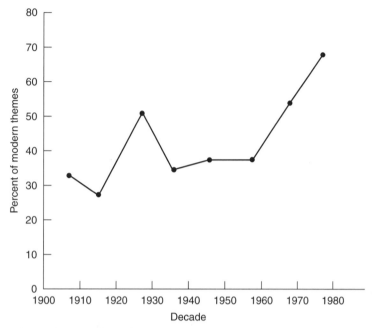

FIGURE 2 Modern themes in magazine articles on marriage, 1900–1979: Percent of themes supporting self-fulfillment, flexible roles, and intimacy.

This relationship between the women's movement and the trend from role to self is not surprising, and has been noted by social historians. The women's movement usually has urged women to avoid self-sacrifice and traditional gender roles, and participating in the movement probably made women more powerful and independent of their families as they acquired new skills and friends, and new ideas about women's proper place.

The conflict between traditional family roles and women's rights may also produce a self-generating cycle of change. When there is a strong commitment to a traditional family blueprint (i.e., the family duty or companionship blueprint), individual freedom and self-development are suppressed, especially for women. But freedom and self-development are highly valued in America, leading to a conflict that eventually undermines the blueprint and produces a period of personal liberation like the 1920s. Greater freedom to develop oneself, especially for women, then threatens people's needs for attachments, creating a readiness to accept a new family blueprint. This cyclic tendency, if it exists, will be weakened by the diffusion of the interdependence blueprint, which combines stable attachments and self-development.

Whatever the causes of the changing images of marriage, two patterns of change emerge clearly from my analysis of magazine articles. There has been a gradual trend towards self-fulfillment, flexible roles, and intimate communication, as well as some major discontinuities.

ENDNOTES

1. Fixing the date of these periods is only approximate, and is based on the sources quoted in this and the previous chapter.
2. The Civil War occurred in the middle of this period, but, surprisingly, most historians do not

attribute great social consequences to it. Eleanor Flexner's history of women is an exception.

3. O'Neil, 1978, pp. 143–44.
4. Chafe, 1972, p. 49.
5. Fass, 1977.
6. Rothman, 1978.
7. Fass, 1977; Newcomb, 1937.
8. Quoted in Rothman, 1978, p. 43.
9. For a poignant description of how respectable but poor married women had to hide the fact that they were working see Rothman, 1978, Chapter 2. Single life was not unattractive, given the close bonds among women, especially for the privileged few with a college education. The women born between 1865 and 1874 "married later and less frequently than any group before or since," and by the turn of the century "nearly one in five married women was childless" (Ryan, 1979, p. 142).
10. Ryan, 1979, p. 140.
11. Many of its supporters and opponents believed that women's winning the vote would change their role in the family and drastically after electoral politics. The large amounts of money spent by the liquor industry and urban political machines to fight women's suffrage are an indication of the importance they attributed to it. On the high hopes of many suffragists about the changes that would occur after women got the vote, see Flexner, 1974; and O'Neil, 1978. O'Neil documents the conservative and occasionally racist rhetoric of the suffrage movement.
12. The eight-hour day became common during World War I and the 40-hour week was mandated by New Deal legislation in the thirties (Harris & Levey, 1975, p. 1, 511). On the declining masculinity of work, see Hantover, 1980, pp. 285–302, and also Filene, 1974.
13. For a supporting argument, see Zaretsky, 1976, and for supporting evidence see Pleck, 1985; and Veroff et al., 1981.
14. On the economic changes, see U.S. Bureau of the Census, 1976, pp. 164–5. On the relation of security and self-development, see Maslow's theory of the hierarchy of needs, 1970.
15. The quotation is from Lynd & Lynd, 1937, p. 80. For a description of this period, also see Chafe, 1972, and Rothman, 1978.
16. Educated people, according to many studies, are more likely to believe that they control their lives

and to question authority and traditional rules. See Kohn, 1969.
17. U.S. Bureau of the Census, 1976, pp. 379 and 380. In 1924 B.A.s or first professional degrees were awarded to 55,000 men and 28,000 women, an increase since 1900 of about 200 percent for men and 500 percent for women.
18. I am indebted to Thomas Kemper for this observation.
19. Quoted in Lasch, 1977, p. 31.
20. These quotes are taken from Rothman, 1978, p. 180.
21. Quoted in Lynd & Lynd, 1937, p. 116.
22. See the thought-provoking analysis of magazines from 1921 to 1940 by Johns-Heine and Gerth, 1949.
23. Lynd & Lynd, 1937, p. 118.
24. Newcomb, 1937. In contrast, the Lynds report that high school students in Muncie became more accepting of premarital sex and women's working between 1924 and 1935. This may be an instance of a lag in changes among working class and provincial people compared to college students.
25. Chafe, 1972, Chapter 4. The proportion of college teachers who were women began to fall in the 30s and continued to decline until the late 50s.
26. Chafe, 1972, p. 105.
27. Quoted in Chafe, 1972, p. 105.
28. Elder, 1974, analyzes the effects of the depression. Virtually all researchers find that middle-class people tend to be more modern. They value companionship between husband and wife more and having children less, and place more emphasis on self-fulfillment, tolerance of diversity, and flexible gender roles. This pattern confirms the hypothesis that economic security, prosperity, and education promote the shift from role to self. The classic study of class and child-rearing values is Melvin Kohn's *Class and Conformity,* 1969. The preference of middle-class people for self-actualization and esteem, and working-class people for belonging and security, is shown in an interesting British study using Abraham Maslow's theory of the hierarchy of needs by Gratton, 1980. Duncan et al., 1973, document the greater importance of job security for working-class people. Also see Gurin et al., 1960; Mason et al., 1976; Gecas, 1979; and Rubin, 1976.
29. U.S. Bureau of the Census, 1976, p. 133.

30. Cherlin, 1981.

31. Chafe, 1972, p. 208.

32. Ibid., p. 178.

33. For a similar interpretation, see Rothman, 1978, p. 218.

34. For an example, see Hicks and Platt's widely quoted and basically sound review of the literature on marital adjustment, published in 1970. Even Komarovsky (1962), usually very sensitive to issues of gender, took for granted the superiority of companionship marriage. She criticized the blue-collar pattern of restricted communication and separate social activities for husbands and wives as a form of "social disorganization," failing to see that the husband's buddies and the wife's close ties with relatives and friends might provide a valuable counterbalance to the tendency of women to be overdependent on their husbands in companionship marriages. Evidence on the role of relatives and friends in limiting wives' dependency on husbands comes from a study of British working-class families by Michael Young and Peter Willmott. They found that wives became more dependent after they moved away from their old community into a suburb.

35. Evidence of the discontent of college educated wives with their marriage is presented in Campbell et al., 1976. Also Pahl & Pahl, 1971.

36. See Cherlin, 1981, for data on changes in women working and an analysis of how the fifties interrupted many long-term demographic and family trends. For quantitative data on the postwar boom, see U.S. Bureau of the Census, 1976, and Lebergott 1976. Generation and politics may explain the unusual familism of the 1950s. Perhaps the generation that raised their families in the 50s had too many frightening memories of depression and war to feel secure, despite their new prosperity. And perhaps American politics of cold war and McCarthyism diminished people's sense of self-direction and the importance of their personal lives by enhancing the significance of government actions and patriotic values.

37. The phrase "from role to self" was suggested to me by Almond's essay (1977) on the transitions from character to role to self since the 19th century. Also see Turner's influential paper (1976).

38. For more detailed information on these trends see Cherlin, 1981, and U.S. Bureau of the Census, 1982. The survey on premarital sex is reported in Zelnik and Kantner, 1980.

39. Several studies document substantial shifts of public opinion towards personal liberation and away from the standards of the companionship family between the middle of the sixties and the middle of the seventies. See, for example, Yankelovich, 1974. Cherlin, 1982, also suggests that the acceptance of divorce accelerated in the late 60s and early 70s.

40. For a history of the women's movement, see Carden, 1974; and Hole and Levine, 1971. Freeman, 1975, gives an excellent account of its legislative victories. For an analysis of media coverage of the movement, see Cancian and Ross, 1981.

41. Degler, 1980, p. 471.

42. See Friedan, 1963, on the conservative message of Freudian and other therapists in the 1950s.

43. See, for example Osmond & Martin, 1975.

44. Luker, 1984.

45. Clecak, 1983, reviews this criticism. Christopher Lasch's book, *The Culture of Narcissism,* 1978, is the critical book that had the greatest impact. On the need for commitment, see Yankelovich, 1981.

46. Kidd, 1974 and 1975. Zube's study (1972) of changing concepts of morality in the *Ladies' Home Journal* from 1948 to 1969 comes up with an interpretation similar to Kidd's. Her quantitative analysis shows a clear shift from values oriented to the future and active "doing," to values oriented to "being" in the present.

47. Bellah *et al.,* 1985, pp. 93 and 100; and Swidler, 1982, pp. 7–8. Similar findings are reported by Quinn, 1982, who did intensive interviews with eleven couples in North Carolina.

48. Harris, 1979.

49. Bellah et al., 1985, p. 101.

50. Here is more detail in the methodology. The high circulation magazines that were included were taken from a list in Kidd, 1975. In the early decades, I also selected articles listed in the *Readers' Guide* from *Harper's* and *Atlantic*. Because of the ease of obtaining articles from *Reader's Digest,* I randomly selected four articles from *Reader's Digest* and four from other magazines, after *Reader's Digest* began publication in the early 1920s. The coding system was originally developed to study changes in magazines

between 1950 and 1970, therefore the categories are progressively less applicable as we move towards the beginning of the century, and the earlier articles receive fewer codes in any of the categories. The categories about gender roles are an exception; every article was coded as traditional or modern on these categories. A few articles contained very contradictory messages and were "double-scored" or counted as both traditional and modern on some categories; however, double-scoring was avoided whenever possible. The category system was refined until I reached a criterion of two coders agreeing on 85 percent of the coding for a particular article. This method of measuring changes in popular images of marriage has several problems. The intended audience of the magazines seems to come from a higher social class in the earlier decades, and the content of the articles partly reflects the policies of editors and advertisers and the attitudes of the writers. None the less, the magazines seem to provide a fairly valid measure, since my findings are consistent with the other sources of data described in this chapter.

51. *Harper's Bazaar,* September 1909.
52. Vahanian & Olds, 1978.
53. Maurois, 1940.
54. Lederer & Jackson, 1974.
55. Miller, 1925.
56. Easterlin, 1980, emphasizes the changing size of birth cohorts. He sees very little change in family blueprints and gender roles since World War II. What has changed, in his view, is young people's income relative to the standard of living they grew up with. When their income was relatively high, they lived according to their family ideals, and wives stayed home and had many children as happened in the 50s. When the baby boom generation (or cohort) reached the labor market in the late 70s wages were relatively low because the cohort was so large that wages were depressed. As a result, they were unable to live according to their ideals and had fewer children. When their children reach the labor market, their income will be relatively high because their cohort is so small, and the cycle will repeat. The relative merits of his theory and mine will be clarified by changes in the family during the recession that began in the 70s. Easterlin

predicts a decline in family attachments as relative income declines. I predict a rise because hard times lower people's aspirations for freedom. See Cherlin, 1981, for an excellent analysis and critique of Easterlin. Although I agree with Easterlin that the changes in gender roles are often exaggerated, he exaggerates the stability. For evidence of major changes in women's goals since the late 60s, see Parelius, 1975; Roper & Labeff, 1977; Duncan et al., 1973; Thornton et al., 1983. Cherlin argues that the pattern of family change is not cyclical; rather there have been gradual changes since 1900 interrupted by the peculiar 50s. Another explanation sociologists have developed is the marriage squeeze argument advanced by Oppenheimer, 1973, and others. They argue that, because women marry men about three years older than themselves, it will be difficult for women to find attractive husbands in historical periods following a rise in fertility, since there will be more younger women on the marriage market than older men. This situation occurred in the 70s, following the baby boom. According to Heer and Grossbard-Shectman's interpretation (1981), the unfavorable marriage market for women in the 70s helps explain why a growing proportion of women did not marry, why they turned to employment instead and became involved in a women's movement to improve their situation at work.

REFERENCES

Almond, Richard (1977). "Character, Role and Self: Evolution in Personality Styles." Unpublished manuscript. Palo Alto, California.

Bellah, Robert, Richard Madsen, William Sullivan, Ann Swidler and Steven Tipton (1985). *Habits of the Heart.* Berkeley: University of California Press.

Burgess, Ernest W. and Harvey J. Locke (1960). *The Family: From Institution to Companionship.* New York: American Book Co.

Calhoun, Arthur W. (1917). A Social History of the American Family. Cleveland: Arthur Clark.

Campbell, Angus, Philip Converse and Willard L. Rodgers (1976). *The Quality of American Life.* New York: Russell Sage.

Cancian, Francesca and Bonnie Ross (1981). "Mass Media and the Women's Movement." *Journal of Applied Behavioral Science* 17:9–26.

Carden, Maren L. (1974). *The New Feminist Movement.* New York: Russell Sage Foundation.

Chafe, William H. (1972). *The American Woman.* New York: Oxford University Press.

Cherlin, Andrew (1981). *Marriage, Divorce, Remarriage.* Cambridge, Massachusetts: Harvard University Press.

Clecak, Peter (1983). *America's Quest for the Ideal Self.* New York: Oxford University Press.

Degler, Carl N.(1980). *At Odds: Women and the Family in America from the Revolution to the Present.* New York: Oxford University Press.

Duncan, Otis Dudley, Howard Schuman and Beverly Duncan (1973). *Social Change in a Metropolitan Community.* New York: Russell Sage.

Easterlin, Richard A. (1980). *Birth and Fortune.* New York: Basic Books.

Elder, Glen (1974). *Children of the Great Depression.* Chicago: University of Chicago Press.

Fass, Paula S. (1977). *The Damned and the Beautiful.* New York: Oxford University Press.

Filene, Peter (1974). *Him/Her/Self: Sex Roles in Modern America.* New York: Harcourt Brace Jovanovich.

Flexner, Eleanor (1974). *Century of Struggle.* New York: Antheneum.

Freeman, Jo (1975). *The Politics of Women's Liberation.* New York: David McKay.

Friedan, Betty (1963). *The Feminine Mystique.* New York: Norton. (1981). *The Second Stage.* New York: Simon Schuster.

Gecas, V. (1979). "The Influence of Social Class on Socialization." In W. Burr *et al.* (eds.) *Contemporary Theories about the Family,* Vol. I. New York: Free Press.

Gratton, Lynda C. (1980). "Analysis of Maslow's Need Hierarchy with Three Social Class Groups." *Social Indicators Research* 7:463–76.

Gurin, Gerald, J. Veroff and S. Feld (1960). Americans View Their Mental Health. New York: Basic Books.

Hantover, Jeffrey P. (1980). "The Boy Scouts and the Validation of Masculinity." In Elizabeth Pleck and Joseph Pleck, *The American Man.* Englewood, New Jersey: Prentice Hall.

Harris, Louis and Associates (1979). *The Playboy Report on American Men.* Playboy Inc.

Harris, William H. and Judith Levy (eds.) (1975). *The New Columbia Encyclopedia.* New York: Columbia University Press.

Heer, David M. and Amyra Grossbard-Shechtman (1981). "The Impact of the Female Marriage Squeeze and the Contraceptive Revolution on Sex Roles and the Women's Liberation Movement in the U.S. 1960–1975." *Journal of Marriage and the Family* February, 43:49-65.

Hicks, Mary W. and Marilyn Platt (1970). "Marital Happiness and Stability: A Review of Research in the Sixties." *Journal of Marriage and the Family* 32:553–74.

Hole, J. and E. Levine (1971). *The Rebirth of Feminism.* New York: Quadrangle.

Johns-Heine, Patrick and Hans Gerth (1949). "Values in Mass Periodical Fiction, 1921–1940." *Public Opinion Quarterly* 13:105–113.

Kidd, Virginia (1974). "Happy Ever After and Other Relationship Styles." Ph.D Dissertation. Department of Speech, University of Minnesota.

Kohn, Melvin (1969). *Class and Conformity: A Study in Values.* Homewood, Illinois: Dorsey Press.

Komarovsky, Mirra (1962). *Blue-Collar Marriage.* New York: Random House. (1976). *Dilemmas of Masculinity.* New York: W.W. Norton.

Lasch, Christopher (1977). *Haven in a Heartless World.* New York: Basic Books.

Lebergott, Stanley (1976). *The American Economy.* Princeton, New Jersey: Princeton University Press.

Lederer, William and Don Jackson (1974). "Do People Really Marry for Love?" *Reader's Digest,* January.

Luker, Kristin (1984). *Abortion and the Politics of Motherhood.* Berkeley: University of California Press.

Lynd, Robert S. and Helen Lynd (1929). *Middletown.* New York: Harcourt, Brace and Co.

Maslow, Abraham (1970). *Motivation and Personality,* Second Edition. New York: Harper and Row.

Mason, Karen, John Czajka and Sara Arber (1976). "Change in U.S. Women's Sex-Role Attitudes, 1969–1974." *American Sociological Review* 41:573–96.

Maurois, Andre (1940). "The Art of Marriage." *Ladies' Home Journal,* April.

Miller, Ruth Scott (1925). "Masterless Wives and Divorce." *Ladies' Home Journal,* January.

Newcomb, Theodore (1937). "Recent Change in Attitudes Toward Sex and Marriage." *American Sociological Review* 1:659–67.

O'Neil, William (1978). "Divorce in the Progressive Era." In M. Gordon (ed.) *The American Family in Social-Historical Perspective.* New York: St Martin's Press, pp. 140-51.

Oppenheimer, Valerie Kincade (1973). "Demographic Influence on Female Employment and the Status of Women." *American Journal of Sociology* 78:946–61.

Osmond, Marie W. and Patricia Y. Martin (1975). "Sex and Sexism." *Journal of Marriage and the Family* 37:744–59.

Pahl, J. M. and R. E. Pahl (1971). *Managers and their Wives.* London: Allen Love and Penguin Press.

Parelius, Ann P. (1975). "Emerging Sex-Role Attitudes, Expectations and Strains among College Women." *Journal of Marriage and the Family* 37:146–54.

Parsons, Talcott and Robert F Bales (1955). *Family, Socialization and Interaction Process.* Glencoe, Illinois: The Free Press.

Pleck, Joseph (1985). *Working Wives, Working Husbands.* New York: Sage Publications.

Quinn, Naomi (1982). "'Commitment' in American Marriage: a Cultural Analysis." *American Ethnologist* 9:775–98.

Roper, Brent S. and Emily Labeff (1977). "Sex Roles and Feminism Revisited: An Intergenerational Attitude Comparison." *Journal of Marriage and the Family* 39:113–20.

Rothman, Sheila M. (1978). *Women's Proper Place: A History of Changing Ideals and Practices 1870 to the Present.* New York: Basic Books.

Ryan, Mary (1979). *Womanhood in America (From Colonial Times to the Present).* Second Edition. New York: New Viewpoints.

Sheehy, Gail (1976). *Passages.* New York: Dutton.

Swidler, Ann (1980). "Love and Adulthood in American Culture." In N. Smelser and E. Erikson (eds.) *Themes of Work and Love in Adulthood.* Cambridge, Massachusetts: Harvard University Press, pp. 120–47.

———. (1982). "Ideologies of Love in Middle Class America." Paper read at Annual Meeting of Pacific Sociological Association, San Diego.

Thornton, Arland, Duane Alwin, and Donald Camburn (1983). "Causes and Consequences of Sex-Role Attitudes and Attitude Change." American Sociological Review 48:211–27.

Turner, Ralph (1976). "The Real Self: From Institution to Impulse." *American Journal of Sociology* 81:789–1,016.

U.S. Bureau of the Census (1976). *The Statistical History of the United States.* New York: Basic Books.

Vahanian, Tilla and Sally Olds (1978). "How Good is Your Marriage." *Ladies' Home Journal,* January.

Veroff, Joseph, Elizabeth Douran and Richard Kulka (1981). *The Inner American: A Self-Portrait from 1957 to 1976.* New York: Basic Books.

Yankelovich, Daniel (1974). *The New Morality.* New York: McGraw-Hill. (1981). *New Rules.* New York: Random House.

Young, Michael and Peter Willmott (1957). *Family and Kinship in East London.* London: Routledge and Kegan Paul.

Zaretsky, Eli (1976). *Capitalism, the Family and Personal Life.* New York: Harper Colophon.

Zelnik, Melvin and John Kantner (1980). "Sexual Activity, Contraceptive Use and Pregnancy." *Family Planning Perspectives,* 12:230–37.

Zube, Margaret (1972). "Changing Concepts of Morality: 1948–1969." *Social Forces* 50:385–96.

READING 9-2

The His and Hers Transition

Jay Belsky and John Kelly

WHAT DIVIDES US

New parents disagree about many things, but when they fight, they usually fight about one of five things: division of labor, money, work, their relationship (who is responsible for the hole that has opened up in it), and social life (are we getting out enough). These five issues are so big, important, and all-pervasive, they might be said to constitute the raw material of

Jay Belsky and John Kelly, "The His and Hers Transition" from *The Transition to Parenthood: How a First Child Changes a Marriage,* pp. 32–50. Copyright © 1994 by Jay Belsky, Ph.D. and John Kelly. Reprinted with the permission of Delacourt Press, a division of the Bantam Doubleday Dell Publishing Group, Inc.

marital change during the transition. Quite simply, couples who manage to resolve these issues in a mutually satisfactory way generally become happier with their marriages, whereas those who do not become unhappier. In order to understand how these five issues operate in a couple's relationship, it will help to know more about the issues themselves and how biology, upbringing, and perhaps evolution have conspired to make men and women see them so differently.

Chores and Division of Labor

On the whole, husbands and wives agree that this is the major stress of the transition. They also agree that while they expected the baby to create a lot more work, that expectation did not prepare them for what they actually encountered. One of our project mothers compared the difference to "watching a tornado on TV and having one actually blow the roof off your house."

Some recent figures explain why the reality of a baby's impact is so much greater than the expectation. Typically nonbaby tasks, such as dishwashing, increase from once or twice a day to four times, laundry from one load a week to four or five, shopping from one expedition per week to three, meal preparation from twice a day to four times, and household cleaning from one a week to usually once a day. Nursing chores add further to the workload. On average a baby needs to be diapered six or seven times and bathed two or three times per day, soothed two or three times per night and often as many as five times per day. His helplessness also transforms once-simple tasks into complex, time-consuming ones. "These days," said one new father, not bothering to hide his exasperation, "going out for ice cream is like planning a moon shot. First I have to check Alex to see if he's wet. Then I have to wrestle him into his clothes, then into the stroller. Next I have to pack an extra diaper in case he wets himself and a bottle in case he starts acting up."

Compared with his 1960s counterpart, a man like this father is notably more involved in baby and household chores. Studies show that, on average, 30 years ago a man devoted 11 hours per week to home and baby, while today he devotes 15 or 16 hours. But this three- to four-hour increase has not significantly alleviated the new mother's burden. Even in a home where a woman works full-time, we found that her contributions to child care, such as diapering, feeding, and bathing, often exceed her husband's by nearly 300 percent. Or to put it another way, for every three diapers he changes, she changes eight. The new mother's contribution to household chores also increases during the transition, usually by about 20 percent.

One of the major changes that has occurred within her transition over the past 15 years is the way women themselves view this division of labor. What was acceptable for earlier generations of new mothers is not acceptable for new mothers of this generation. A combination of factors, including maternal employment, feminism, and egalitarianism, has made today's woman expect and feel entitled to a significant amount of help from a man. By the same token, men have not been untouched by the winds of change either. Men today want to be more involved with home and child, and they also realize that their wives shoulder burdens their own mothers never dreamed of shouldering.

Yet despite these changes, when men and women sit down to discuss who does what, they usually end up sounding like a project couple I interviewed several years ago:

Husband (with some self-congratulation): "My dad is always telling me and my brother he never changed a diaper in his life. I change them all the time, and I think I'm a better parent and a better husband for it."

Wife (after husband left the room): "David knows his father never helped his mother, and since he gives me a little help, he thinks he's

Mother Teresa. The truth is, I do about 80 percent of everything. You know what really burns me up though? The way David acts when his parents visit. Usually he does a little more then, and of course they think he's wonderful. 'Wow,' his dad keeps saying, 'I never did any of that stuff.' Ohhh, when I hear that, I'd like to take the pair of them . . ."

Why do so many new mothers feel that they don't get the help and support they need? Part of the answer lies in several aspects of his transition that make a man perceive his contribution to home and baby differently than his wife. One is that a man uses a different yardstick to measure his contribution to the division of labor. A wife measures what a husband does against what she does. And because what a man does looks small when measured by this yardstick, the woman often ends up as unhappy and disgruntled as the project wife above. The man, on the other hand, usually measures his contribution to chores against what his father did. And because by that yardstick his 15 to 16 hours per week represent a 30 to 40 percent increase over what his father did, he often ends up feeling as good about himself and his contribution to the division of labor as the project father above.

Frequently the man's perception of who does what is also influenced by the fact that, at least temporarily, he becomes the family's sole breadwinner. And because this is a role he has been taught to equate with parenting, fulfilling it not only makes a new father feel like he is already satisfying his parental obligation, it also makes the 20 percent he does at home seem like 200 percent to him. How can his wife not appreciate his contribution? The nature of transition chores can also shape a man's perception of the division-of-labor issue. Because his wife is usually more skilled at baby chores, the man sometimes concludes that his help is really not needed. The new father who hops on this train of thought usually gets off at the same station as the project husband who said to me, "I expected to do more, I really did. But then I started think-

ing. Since Brenda's breast-feeding Jenny, Brenda should get up with Jenny. Then, pretty soon, 'getting up with Jenny is Brenda's job' became 'Jenny is Brenda's job.' "

Sometimes aspects of her transition can also contribute to an unequal division of labor. For example the yardstick a new mother uses to measure a husband's contribution to chores can produce such maternal disgruntlement and withholding that the man does even less because he does not get the gratitude he feels he is entitled to for surpassing his father's. In addition a woman's significant biological investment in the child can make her so critical of her husband's parenting that, without intending to, she drives him away.

I witnessed a dramatic example of this phenomenon at a neighborhood picnic last year. I was talking to another father—a man I'll call Jake—when a scream erupted from a nearby meadow. While we were talking, Jake's two-year-old, Bobby, had wandered off, fallen, and cut his forehead. As Jake comforted him, wife Nora, who had been off getting hot dogs with their older son, appeared. Grabbing Bobby out of Jake's arms, she asked, "What happened?" in a voice full of upset and reproach. Jake told her, then added defensively, "It's only a scratch." Nora, however, was unmollified. "I'm taking Bobby to the nurse," she announced, and proceeded to march off. "Wait," Jake said, running after her, "I'll come with you." "No," said Nora, spinning around. "You stay here. You've already done your work for the day."

As he watched his wife and sons disappear over a hill, I could see Jake struggling with himself. He knew Nora's sharpness was a product of her concern for Bobby, not a personal attack on him. She had simply "lost it" for a moment. Still, the sharpness hurt, and in the end that hurt won out. "Next time let her take the both of them to get a hot dog," Jake said. "I've had it."

Men who find themselves continually criticized for their inadequate diapering, bathing, and dressing skills often end up feeling similarly conflicted. On one level they know that their wives do not really mean to be hurtfully critical; on another level, like Jake, they feel humiliated and often conclude that the best (and safest) policy to adopt vis-à-vis child-care chores is a hands-off policy.

Money Worries

Income among project couples averaged $25,000 per annum (or about $30,000 in current dollars). This is about the national average for new parents, and it explains why finances are also a major transition issue. Twenty-five thousand dollars does not go very far, particularly when, in addition to covering ongoing expenses such as mortgage and car payments, it has to cover the new expenses created by the baby, who despite his small size can be a formidable consumer. For example, the packages of Pampers or Huggies he goes through every three or four days cost $9.50 to $12.50; the Osh-Kosh jeans and shoes he outgrows every few months cost $20 and $30 if he is one year old and $30 and $40 if he is two. On average his new winter coat costs up to $50; his new stroller anywhere from $80 to $250. Depending on where he lives, his visits to the pediatrician can cost between $25 and $75. If his mother continues to work, child-care costs can run as high as $20,000 per year in come cities.

Most of the disagreements new mothers and fathers have about these expenses arise from another difference between members of the his and hers transition: Parenting changes men's and women's self-perceptions in very different ways. When a couple joined the project, one of the first things we asked them to do was play what we called the penny game. We gave the husband and wife 15 pennies each and asked them to allot their money to three roles: spouse, worker, and parent, depending upon how closely they identified with these roles. At the start of the transition, women allotted almost as many pennies as men to the worker role—which is to say that mothers-to-be were almost as likely as

fathers-to-be to identify themselves as workers. But after the baby's birth a divergence developed. Women (including working women) began allotting more and more of their pennies to the parenting role, men relatively more to the worker role.

The different forms of economic logic that new mothers and fathers develop arise from this divergence in self-perception. Many a man's thinking about money issues is dominated by his worker impulse to conserve and enhance financial resources. A new father frequently works longer hours to increase income and begins cutting back on his own consumption. Now he shuts off the lights when he leaves a room and brings a sandwich to work instead of eating lunch out. Many a woman's economic logic is often shaped by her close identification with the parenting role. New mothers also turn out lights and "brown-bag it" to save money. However, because a mother sees herself first and foremost as a nurturer, the woman's chief concern becomes the baby's well-being. And this often produces economic choices that put her in conflict with her conservation-minded husband.

Exhibit A of this phenomenon was project wife Betty van der Hovel's decision to have the living-room windows babyproofed with sliding metal guards two weeks after son Luke's birth. Because husband Ted felt the windows would not pose a hazard until Luke was two or three years old, Betty's decision baffled and annoyed him. "Now on top of everything else I have to find a hundred and fifty dollars to pay for those goddamn guards," he told me one day. "Why couldn't Betty have waited?" But Betty felt that Ted had missed the point entirely. The issue was not money, it was their son's safety. And how could he possibly put economic considerations ahead of that? "Sometimes, you can be such a jerk," I overheard her tell Ted one afternoon during a conversation about the window guards.

Exhibit B of this phenomenon is a disagreement I witnessed one evening at the home of project couple Tom and Maggie Davis. I was sitting in the kitchen with Tom when Maggie arrived home with a bagful of new baby clothes. "Look at these, Tom," she said, pulling a smock, hat, and booties out of the bag in rapid succession. "Won't Alexis look adorable in them?"

In a transition where conservation is an overriding priority, expensive baby clothes make as little economic sense as sliding metal guards, so Tom reacted to this fashion show the way Ted van der Hovel had to the guards. "Jesus, Maggie, how many times do we have to go through this?" he said. "We just bought a house, we're not making much money, we can't afford to keep buying baby clothes. How many dresses does Alexis need, anyway? She doesn't look in a mirror."

Maggie groaned as if to say, "You don't get it, do you?" And from the perspective of her transition, Tom had not gotten it. Often for women new baby clothes represent a sensible economic choice because they advance another of the new mother's priorities: social presentation. This is the name given to her desire to present her baby—her creation—to the larger world of family and friends for admiration and praise. And since a 30-dollar Osh-Kosh outfit and a 40-dollar pair of shoes will make her new creation look even more irresistible to that larger world, frequently the new mother believes them to be a sound investment.

One interesting sidelight of the employed-mother revolution is that it may have enhanced the incidence of clothes and toy buying for baby. When men were providing most of the family's income, a mother often had to curb her buying impulse if a husband said, "Enough," because it was money he earned that she was spending. But now that many new mothers have independent sources of income, they feel (within limits of course) that they have a right to spend their money as they choose.

Relationship Difficulties

It is harder to draw a statistical profile of marital estrangement and drift, but several numbers suggest why it is also an important transition issue. One comes from a recent *Parenting* magazine survey that found that new mothers and fathers are twice as likely to kiss the baby as they are each other. A recent University of Michigan study found that the incidence of sexual intercourse drops 30 to 40 percent in the first year after the baby's arrival.

Fatigue, of course, is partly responsible for these changes, and so is the baby, who attracts attention and affection his parents used to direct at each other. But the principal reason new parents touch less frequently is that they feel less connected, less in tune with each other. It is not accidental that one of the most enduring pieces of transition folklore—one that has been passed down from one generation of new parents to the next—is the story of the couple who, on their first night out alone, run out of things to say within five minutes. The sense of drift, estrangement, and loneliness that produces such tongue-tiedness is as much a feature of the transition in most marriages as are money worries and division-of-labor concerns. But once again, differences in upbringing and biology often make men and women blame these problems on very different things.

For men the chief culprit is maternal preoccupation with the baby. While most new fathers expect the baby to become the main priority in the family, many are stunned at how little wifely attention or affection is left over for them. Our project fathers complained that after the baby's arrival much less interest was shown in their work, hobbies, concerns, or sexual desires. One project husband described a recent sexual encounter with his wife this way: "Last Sunday, while Ellen and I were lying in bed, I reached over and touched her. She'd been half asleep, but as soon as I put my hand on her breast, she bolted upright, pulled a sheet over her and said, 'Don't. Not now. That's for Jonathan.' Believe me, if I ever had any doubts about her priorities, that incident cleared them up in a hurry."

Often adding to the man's sense of estrangement is the coterie of advisers that surrounds the new mother. While men know why this happens, these figures—who include mothers, sisters, aunts, and other female relatives and friends—possess nurturing skills a man often does not. Their sudden importance in a wife's life often makes a husband feel shunted aside and unimportant. A University of Minnesota study found that while in-laws were not among the top five transition complaints of new mothers, they were the number-one complaint of new fathers, many of whom singled out mothers-in-law and sisters-in-law as sources of alienation and estrangement. "Sometimes I wonder if anyone remembers I'm still here," a project father said to me one day.

When women talk about transition-time loneliness and estrangement, their chief culprit is what I call male self-focus. Because of upbringing and perhaps biology as well, a man's emotional energy and attention all too frequently tend to flow inward toward his own concerns and needs. Shared experiences which pull a man outside of himself and force him to concentrate on his partner's needs can sometimes disrupt this flow. But because none of the transition's major events absolutely require male participation—a man does not have to be in the delivery room if he does not want to be, for example—often the new father's focus remains relatively undisrupted. As before the baby's arrival, he continues to be preoccupied with his own wants and needs.

An example of how this self-focus can contribute to maternal estrangement and disaffection is a story a project wife told me about a visit to her husband's parents six weeks after her child's birth. "I'd had a cesarean," the woman said, "so Norman carried Natasha into the house. But he was so concerned about getting to the TV set and the football game that the minute he got through the door, he practically threw her on the floor. He didn't take her out of her baby seat or unwrap her blanket; he didn't ask me what I wanted. He didn't do anything except vanish. Sometimes I wonder whether he realizes the two of us even exist."

An encounter another project wife had with male self-focus left her feeling even more estranged and alienated. One night about three months after daughter Sarah's birth, mother Jill was standing in front of the bedroom mirror in her bra and panties when she happened to catch a glimpse of husband, Michael, examining her from the opposite side of the bedroom. The look on his face so horrified her that Jill rushed to the closet for a bathrobe. When she told one of our female observers about this incident, Jill said it confirmed what she had already begun to suspect about Michael: He was so wrapped up in what he wanted—"a perfect little beauty queen of a wife"—he had no understanding of or sympathy for what she was going through.

The association men make between work and parenting also contributes to maternal loneliness and estrangement. Just at the point when a new mother wants her husband home by her side, this association will often make the husband pull himself out of the family and immerse himself more deeply in his work. "I know Ralph means well," one of our wives told me, "but I don't understand why he only equates parenting with money. It's important, but right now having him here is a lot more important to me than the few extra dollars his overtime brings in."

Career and Work

At the project's start in 1982, 30 percent of our wives were employed in the baby's first year, and most held traditionally female jobs. They were beauticians, nurses, teachers, and clerks. Most also worked for a traditionally female reason: Their families could not get by without their paychecks. At the project's conclusion in 1988, maternal employment stood at 45 percent, and now our employed mothers included more professional women, such as accountants, lawyers, and office managers. An increasing number of our women also looked upon their work, whatever they did, as a career or as the stepping-stone to one. Our data closely mirror national trends, which show that between 1970 and 1990 the number of employed mothers with young children almost doubled, from 30 percent to 53 percent.

This change in maternal employment has fueled another equally momentous change. For reasons of both ideology and need, over the past decade more and more employed mothers have come to embrace the notion of egalitarian role sharing. While today's employed mother expects parity or near parity on division of labor, her adherence to this ideal often leads her to expect something much deeper—marital parity. She expects her partner to share emotional responsibility for their child and family and to share in career sacrifices if they have to be made. Not every woman who goes to work embraces egalitarianism, of course, but enough do to have created another potent source of divisiveness between members of the his and hers transitions.

Some men share their wives' egalitarianism. During the project, we encountered a number of committed male egalitarians, and interestingly the ones most steadfast in their commitment to this ideal tended to be alike . . . For the most part they were low-key, usually nonideological (i.e., they did not have any special intellectual commitment to either egalitarianism or feminism), extremely secure, and often domestically skilled. Also noteworthy, they were all deeply in love with their wives. However, these husbands represented the exception. The norm among project husbands—and I strongly suspect among husbands in general—is a man in transition. This individual also loves his wife and wants to support her, especially when she holds a paying job. But because he has a lingering allegiance to certain aspects of the traditional male role, he is often psychologically and emotionally unprepared to be the full partner his wife wants and expects.

Take chores. The woman's desire for parity or near parity on the division-of-labor issue frequently causes conflict because it bumps into the transitional man's belief that while a hus-

band should contribute, a wife should remain first among equals in the nursery, kitchen, and laundry room. The working mother's belief that emotional responsibility for child and home should be shared also frequently causes conflict. Unlike his father or grandfather, a transitional man will bathe and diaper the baby. But like them he believes, or at least acts as if he believes, that chores that involve assuming emotional responsibility for home and child, such as scheduling pediatrician's visits, overseeing child-care arrangements, and making out shopping lists, are a woman's work—whether she has a job outside the home or not.

Career conflicts are also common between this man and his wife because his view of himself as the family's principal breadwinner (whatever the reality of the situation) produces an expectation that career sacrifices are also his wife's job. One area where this expectation caused a great many problems for project mothers was when they had to work late. Usually if a man's desk was clear at five, he would agree to pick up the baby at the sitter or child-care center. However, if it wasn't—even if there wasn't anything terribly pressing on it—he would generally say, "No, I can't. I have to work too. You'll just have to make other arrangements."

Social Isolation

The weeks immediately following the baby's birth are a whirlwind of social activity. But sometime around the end of the first month the congratulatory calls and visits begin to taper off, and that is when the stress of social isolation really starts to make itself felt. Among project participants, recreational activities in the form of visits to movies, restaurants, and friends' homes declined by 40 percent during the first year of the transition. And several findings from the *Parenting* magazine study suggest that their experience is the rule, not the exception. More than half the survey respondents reported that they did not go out at all during the first six months after the baby's birth unless a relative was able to sit. Even after the first year more than 81 percent had yet to spend a weekend alone, and 91 percent to take a vacation of five or more days alone.

On the whole, new mothers tend to suffer more from isolation than fathers, and new stay-at-home mothers suffer most of all. Said one such mother, "Sometimes it gets so bad, I find myself actually dreading Kate's naps. But when she's up, I spend most of my time wishing I had another adult here to talk to." Work protects men from this kind of desperate isolation. But the lack of date nights, parties, vacations, and extracurricular activities such as Saturday afternoon raquetball takes its toll on them too. In conversations we found men and women equally likely to complain about feeling isolated and cut off. But we also found that like the other major transition stresses, this one is perceived very differently by the two sexes.

Men generally take the position of Mike Evans, one of our project husbands, who felt that the principal reason for his and wife Phoebe's isolation was what he called Phoebe's obsession with the baby. "She won't leave him alone," Mike complained one day. "I know mothers are supposed to be devoted to their babies, but Phoebe's gone way overboard. Every time David hiccups, she makes a federal case out of it. She won't eat unless he's on her lap or leave him if she thinks the slightest thing is wrong. Last week, an hour before we were supposed to go to the movies, Phoebe marched into the living room and announced that she'd just canceled the sitter. She thought David was coming down with a cold and didn't want to leave him. I went ballistic. We've been out exactly three times in the last eight months."

When I talked to Phoebe Evans a few days later, she was still feeling vaguely guilty about this incident. "I know sometimes I overfocus on David," she admitted, "but it's taken me a while to recognize that and also to recognize that it won't change unless I make an effort to change it." But like most women Phoebe also felt that a major factor in the Evans's isolation was her husband's attitude. "Mike's always telling me, 'Come on. Let's go out, let's go out,' and I want to, but I say no because I'm too exhausted. And that's Mike's fault. He barely lifts a finger to help me."

WHAT UNITES US

"One day, when Michela was four months old, I had an incredible experience with her. She'd been crying and I was trying to soothe her, but nothing worked. So finally, out of desperation, I began singing 'Row, Row, Row Your Boat' very softly. All of a sudden the tears stopped, her eyes got shiny and as big as nickels, and her little mouth formed into a perfect 'O.' She was straining every ounce to focus on me. No one had ever looked at me that intently before—as if I were the sun, moon, and stars all wrapped up in one. It made me so happy, I took Michela's little hand in mine and began waltzing her round and round the kitchen."

This story from a project mother indicates what is wrong with the portrait of the transition I've painted over the last 15-odd pages—it leaves out all the good parts. If becoming a parent were an endless conflict about money, chores, work, the relationship, and social activity, babies would be a lot rarer than they are. But of course it is not an endless conflict. Along with the tumult, the exhaustion, the loneliness, and hurt feelings there are also moments of sublime happiness, moments when the new parent literally begins dancing with joy. And for the most part what sets new parents to dancing is the same. Among project husbands and wives there was as much agreement about the transition's gratifications as there was about its stresses. But just as men and women perceive the stresses differently, often they also perceive its gratifications differently.

Take what everyone agrees is the transition's most exquisite gratification: the baby himself. Often when new mothers talk about why he is so wonderful, they speak the language of love. They say the baby has introduced them to a new dimension of this feeling, one they did not know—had not dreamed—existed before. Project mothers tried to explain the uniqueness of this love in many different ways. Some attempted to delineate its parameters in words, and often the words they chose were ones people use when they are trying to describe a profound spiritual awakening. Women talked about being seized by an "all-embracing," "all-encompassing" love. Other mothers employed metaphors to describe the specialness of what they felt. Said one project woman, "Tilly's opened a door in me I didn't even know was there." Still others described the transforming effect of their new feelings. "The love that flows through Adam's eyes when I hold him makes me tingle," said one mother, while another compared her baby's smile to a "magic wand" that "chases my blues away." We also had a fair amount of new mothers who believed that human language had not yet invented words powerful enough to describe what they felt. "I love Cynthia more than words can say," declared one mother when I asked her to describe how she felt about her new baby.

While new fathers are also set to dancing by the baby, they usually dance more slowly and for different reasons. We had a few men who were as swept away by love as any new mother. Representative of this group was the man who said, "I can't fully express the feelings of love I have for Michael. He's a magnificent blessing. He's increased the love I receive and the love I give." But most new fathers are swept away by the baby for more traditional male reasons. Many look upon him as a terrific new playmate. A number of project fathers echoed the sentiment of the man who described his new son as being "more fun than TV." Even more men seem to see the baby as a wonderful new cement that strengthens their feelings toward wife and family. "I feel much more deeply committed to my marriage now," said one new father.

While men and women used different verbal styles to describe their feelings about baby, when they talked about him, I noticed that they both used the same facial expression: They smiled.

Changes in feeling about oneself ranks as the second major transition gratification. At one point or another almost all of our mothers and fathers reported that parenthood had made them feel more mature, more grown-up. But these words meant different things to men and to women. Usually when a man used them, he meant that he felt more responsible about his work. Sometimes this would lead him to devote more hours to it; other times, to begin looking at it in a new way. Instead of seeing it simply as a source of revenue, now the new father would begin to look at his job as part of a larger life plan. As the child grew, the family's income needs would increase; did his job offer an opportunity for advancement? And even more important, his family would need a secure source of income. Did his present job provide that security?

New mothers also equated maturity with responsibility. But when a woman talked about responsibility, usually she meant the responsibility of shaping and molding a new life. Many women reported that motherhood made them behave more sensibly. "I used to be a real speed demon," said one woman. "But not anymore. Since Amy's birth, I don't think I've gone more than 45 miles per hour. My husband can't believe it. But now that she's a part of my life, I don't feel I can afford to take risks anymore." Other women reported that their new sense of responsibility had awakened them to larger concerns. "I never paid much attention to environmental issues," one of our mothers told me one day. "I figured I don't live in Brazil, so why should I worry about the rain forest, and I'm not an Eskimo, so why should I worry about the whales? But Eddie's changed that. These things are a part of the world he's going to live in, and I want to make sure that when he's grown-up, they're still there for him to enjoy."

The new sense of family that the baby creates ranks as a third major transition gratification for most new parents. And interestingly it is one that mothers and fathers experience in the same way. When we asked project participants why the baby enhanced their sense of family, men were as likely as women to cite the same reasons. One was that the new child had given the husband and wife what they had not had before: a biological connection. One project father spoke for many of our study participants when he said, "Since the baby, I feel a lot closer to my wife emotionally and spiritually because she's not just my partner anymore. She's the mother of my child." The need to pull together to meet the demands of the transition can also enhance a couple's sense of being part of the same unit. "Suddenly you realize if you're going to survive this thing intact," said one woman, "the two of you are going to have to learn to work together in a new way, and that creates a tremendous sense of unity." The remark of another project participant hints at a third reason why the baby often enhances a couple's sense of family: "When I was a little girl," she said, "we used to spend every summer on the Jersey shore. Since Jane's birth Everett and I have spent a lot of time talking about the traditions we want to create for our new family."

In interviews project participants singled out one other aspect of the transition as being particularly gratifying: It brought them closer to their own parents. Sometimes this bond arose from empathy. Now that they were parents themselves, participants said they had a better appreciation of what their parents had given them and what they had gone through to give it. Said one man, "Being a dad myself, I realize what a good job my parents did with me and how much I owe them." A project mother added, "It took me 28 years, but I'm finally beginning to understand all the sacrifices my mom and dad made for me."

Other times the new bond with one's own parents was generational. Suddenly the mother and father felt linked in a great family chain that stretched back into some unknown past and now forward into the baby's future. Being part of this chain evoked powerful feelings in a new parent. A particularly dramatic case in point was the project father who ended a five-year dispute with his father after his daughter's birth. The two men had not spoken since having a falling-out over the family business. "I felt my father had behaved very pigheadedly," the man said, "and I was angry at him. But after Natalie's birth I felt it was time to put our dispute aside. We're all part of the same family, and it would be silly to allow a business disagreement to continue disrupting the family. So I gulped hard and called him."

One of the things that became clear early in the project is that couples who are able to focus their attention on what unites them and produces mutual joy usually end up at the end of the transition with a better, happier marriage. I think the reasons for this are fairly self-evident. The transition gives a couple dozens of new and potentially much deeper points of connection. There is the baby and the new biological link he creates between husband and wife; there is the new sense of unity, of family they experience as they join together to nurture him; and there is also the enormous satisfaction of knowing that you and your partner are growing together and growing in the same direction. However, in order to take advantage of these new points of connection, a couple first must learn how to deal with the new differences and divisions the transition also creates.

PART FOUR

POWER, CONFLICT, AND DISRUPTION

CHAPTER 10

Work and Families

No family issue reflects the tensions caused by the movement of married women into the labor force more than the division of labor in the home. In the 1950s, when most married women with children did not work outside the home, housework and child care were seen as their job. Husbands may have helped out a bit, but wives did most of the work. Now, most married women with children are working for pay outside the home. Yet men still do not share equally in domestic work.[1] A series of surveys carried out between 1965 and 1985 showed that women had cut back the number of hours they spent in domestic work and that men had increased their hours by a smaller amount. So, overall, less household work was getting done and men were doing a larger share of it. But women still did over 70 percent of the work.[2] I know of no recent survey that can be compared with the 1965–1985 figures. We do not know, therefore, how much men may have increased their share

since the mid-1980s. Impressionistic evidence suggests that men do somewhat more but that the division is still unequal. Wives work for pay all day and then come home to what Arlie Hochschild called "the second shift."

A major question for sociologists, then, is why this unequal division of labor persists. One answer, favored by social exchange theorists, is that men still have better labor market opportunities than women, which makes married women economically dependent on their husbands. It is said that although wives earn more relative to their husbands than they used to, they still need a husband's earnings to pool with theirs. Thus, with an implied threat of divorce, the middle-class husband can make his wife do more than half of the housework in return for his greater financial contribution.

As valid as the social exchange perspective is, it seems incomplete. Even men whose wives have earnings close to (or more than) theirs often do not share fully in the housework. A number of sociologists, seeking to unravel this puzzle, have turned to the persistence of beliefs about culturally appropriate behavior for women and men. People have "gender ideologies," to use

---

[1]*Public and Private Families: An Introduction,* pp. 295–307.
[2]John F. Robinson, "Who's Doing the Housework?" *American Demographics,* December 1988, pp. 24ff.

Hochschild's term, that stubbornly affect what they do around the house. It is important to the self-image of many men that their wives be seen as the main worker around the house because, they think, men aren't supposed to do much work around the house. Hochschild studied some working-class husbands who did a great deal of domestic work but insisted that they were just helping out their wives.

For women, the inner conflict can be greater. Those who were raised after the feminist revolution of the 1960s typically believe that women should be able to work outside the home and that their husbands should share the housework and child care. But they also may want to prove to their husbands that they are fulfilling the role of a good wife; and this desire may lead them to display how much housework they still do. Or they may want to do more of the housework to support the ego of a husband who is not earning much money and therefore is not fulfilling the culturally prescribed male role. Faced with these tensions, as well as with the grim economic situation of many divorced women, wives may accept an unequal division of labor despite their preferences for greater sharing.

In "Joey's Problem: Nancy and Evan Holt," a chapter reprinted in its entirety from her book, *The Second Shift: Working Parents and the Revolution at Home,* Hochschild tells the story of a married couple who do not share the housework and child care equally even though the wife works full time outside of the home. Nancy struggles to reconcile the reality of the division of labor in her marriage with her ideals. Hochschild provides an insightful account of the tensions in their marriage and how they were resolved.

READING 10-1

Joey's Problem: Nancy and Evan Holt

Arlie Hochschild

Nancy Holt arrives home from work, her son, Joey, in one hand and a bag of groceries in the other. As she puts down the groceries and opens the front door, she sees a spill of mail on the hall floor, Joey's half-eaten piece of cinnamon toast on the hall table, and the phone machine's winking red light: a still-life reminder of the morning's frantic rush to distribute the family to the world outside. Nancy, for seven years a social worker, is a short, lithe blond woman of 30 who talks and moves rapidly. She scoops the mail onto the hall table and heads for the kitchen, unbuttoning her coat as she goes. Joey sticks close behind her, intently explaining to her how dump trucks dump things. Joey is a fat-cheeked, lively four-year-old who chuckles easily at things that please him.

Having parked their red station wagon, Evan, her husband, comes in and hangs up his coat. He has picked her up at work and they've arrived home together. Apparently unready to face the kitchen commotion but not quite entitled to relax with the newspaper in the living room, he slowly studies the mail. Also 30, Evan, a warehouse furniture salesman, has thinning pale blond hair, a stocky build, and a tendency to lean on one foot. In his manner there is something both affable and hesitant.

From the beginning, Nancy describes herself as an "ardent feminist," an egalitarian (she wants a similar balance of spheres and equal power). Nancy began her marriage hoping that she and Evan would base their identities in both their parenthood and their careers, but clearly tilted toward parenthood. Evan felt it was fine for Nancy to have a career, if she could handle the family too.

As I observe in their home on this evening, I notice a small ripple on the surface of family waters. From the commotion of the kitchen, Nancy calls, "Eva-an, will you *please* set the table?" The word *please* is thick with irritation. Scurrying between refrigerator, sink, and oven, with Joey at her feet, Nancy wants Evan to help; she has asked him, but reluctantly. She seems to resent having to ask. (Later she tells me, "I *hate* to ask; why should I ask? It's begging.") Evan looks up from the mail and flashes an irritated glance toward the kitchen, stung, perhaps, to be asked in a way so barren of appreciation and respect. He begins setting out knives and forks, asks if she will need spoons, then answers the doorbell. A neighbor's child. No, Joey can't play right now. The moment of irritation has passed.

Later as I interview Nancy and Evan separately, they describe their family life as unusually happy—except for Joey's "problem." Joey has great difficulty getting to sleep. They start trying to put him to bed at 8:00. Evan tries but Joey rebuffs him; Nancy has better luck. By 8:30 they have him *on* the bed but not *in* it; he crawls and bounds playfully. After 9:00 he still calls out for water or toys, and sneaks out of bed to switch on the light. This continues past 9:30, then 10:00 and 10:30. At about 11:00 Joey complains that his bed is "scary," that he can only go to sleep in his parents' bedroom. Worn down, Nancy accepts this proposition. And it is part of their current arrangement that putting Joey to bed is "Nancy's job." Nancy and Evan can't get into bed until midnight or later, when Evan is tired and Nancy exhausted. She used to enjoy their love-making, Nancy tells me, but now sex seems like "more work." The Holts consider their fatigue and impoverished sex life as results of Joey's problem.

The official history of Joey's problem—the interpretation Nancy and Evan give me—begins with Joey's fierce attachment to Nancy, and Nancy's strong attachment to him. On an afternoon walk through Golden Gate Park, Nancy devotes herself to Joey's every move. Now Joey sees a squirrel; Nancy tells me she must remember to bring nuts next time. Now Joey is going up the slide; she notices that his pants are too short—she must take them down tonight. The two enjoy each other. (Off the official record, neighbors and Joey's baby-sitter say that Nancy is a wonderful mother, but privately they add how much she is "also like a single mother.")

For his part, Evan sees little of Joey. He has his evening routine, working with his tools in the basement, and Joey always seems happy to be with Nancy. In fact, Joey shows little interest in Evan, and Evan hesitates to see that as a problem. "Little kids need their moms more than they need their dads," he explains philosophically; "All boys go through an oedipal phase."

Perfectly normal things happen. After a long day, mother, father, and son sit down to dinner. Evan and Nancy get the first chance all day to talk to each other, but both turn anxiously to Joey, expecting his mood to deteriorate. Nancy asks him if he wants celery with peanut butter on it. Joey says yes. "Are you sure that's how you want it?" "Yes." Then the fidgeting begins. "I don't like the strings on my celery." "Celery is made up of strings." "The celery is too big." Nancy grimly slices the celery. A certain tension mounts. Every time one parent begins a conversation with the other, Joey interrupts. "I don't have anything to drink." Nancy gets him juice. And finally, "Feed me." By the end of the meal, no one has obstructed Joey's victory. He has his mother's reluctant attention and his father is reaching for a beer. But talking about it later, they say, "This is normal when you have kids."

Sometimes when Evan knocks on the baby-sitter's door to pick up Joey, the boy looks past his father, searching for a face behind him: "Where's Mommy?" Sometimes he outright refuses to go home with his father. Eventually Joey even swats at his father, once quite hard, on the face for "no reason at all." This makes it hard to keep imagining Joey's relation to Evan as "perfectly normal." Evan and Nancy begin to talk seriously about a "swatting problem."

Evan decides to seek ways to compensate for his emotional distance from Joey. He brings Joey a surprise every week or so—a Tonka truck, a Tootsie Roll. He turns weekends into father-and-son times. One Saturday, Evan proposes the zoo, and hesitantly, Joey agrees. Father and son have their coats on and are nearing the front door. Suddenly Nancy decides she wants to join them, and as she walks down the steps with Joey in her arms, she explains to Evan, "I want to help things out."

Evan gets few signs of love from Joey and feels helpless to do much about it. "I just don't feel good about me and Joey," he tells me one evening, "that's all I can say." Evan loves Joey. He feels proud of him, this bright, good-looking, happy child. But Evan also seems to feel that being a father is vaguely hurtful and hard to talk about.

The official history of Joey's problem was that Joey felt the "normal" oedipal attachment of a male child to his mother. Joey was having the emotional problems of growing up that any parent can expect. But Evan and Nancy add the point that Joey's problems are exacerbated by Evan's difficulties being an active father, which stem, they feel, from the way Evan's own father, an emotionally remote self-made businessman, had treated him. Evan tells me, "When Joey gets older, we're going to play baseball together and go fishing."

As I recorded this official version of Joey's problem through interviews and observation, I began to feel doubts about it. For one thing, clues to another interpretation appeared in the simple pattern of footsteps on a typical evening. There was the steady pacing of Nancy, preparing dinner in the kitchen, moving in zigzags from counter to refrigerator to counter to stove.

There were the lighter, faster steps of Joey, running in large figure eights through the house, dashing from his Tonka truck to his motorcycle man, reclaiming his sense of belonging in this house, among his things. After dinner, Nancy and Evan mingled footsteps in the kitchen, as they cleaned up. Then Nancy's steps began again: click, click, click, down to the basement for laundry, then thuck, thuck, thuck up the carpeted stairs to the first floor. Then to the bathroom where she runs Joey's bath, then into Joey's room, then back to the bath with Joey. Evan moved less—from the living room chair to Nancy in the kitchen, then back to the living room. He moved to the dining room to eat dinner and to the kitchen to help clean up. After dinner he went down to his hobby shop in the basement to sort out his tools; later he came up for a beer, then went back down. The footsteps suggest what is going on: Nancy was at work on her second shift.

BEHIND THE FOOTSTEPS

Between 8:05 A.M. and 6:05 P.M., both Nancy and Evan are away from home, working a "first shift" at full-time jobs. The rest of the time they deal with the varied tasks of the second shift: shopping, cooking, paying bills; taking care of the car, the garden, and yard; keeping harmony with Evan's mother who drops over quite a bit, "concerned" about Joey, with neighbors, their voluble baby-sitter, and each other. And Nancy's talk reflects a series of second-shift thoughts: "We're out of barbecue sauce . . . Joey needs a Halloween costume . . . The car needs a wash . . ." and so on. She reflects a certain "second-shift sensibility," a continual attunement to the task of striking and restriking the right emotional balance between child, spouse, home, and outside job.

When I first met the Holts, Nancy was absorbing far more of the second shift than Evan. She said she was doing 80 percent of the housework and 90 percent of the childcare. Evan said

she did 60 percent of the housework, 70 percent of the childcare. Joey said, "I vacuum the rug, and fold the dinner napkins," finally concluding, "Mom and I do it all." A neighbor agreed with Joey. Clearly, between Nancy and Evan, there was a "leisure gap": Evan had more than Nancy. I asked both of them, in separate interviews, to explain to me how they had dealt with housework and childcare since their marriage began.

One evening in the fifth year of their marriage, Nancy told me, when Joey was two months old and almost four years before I met the Holts, she first seriously raised the issue with Evan. "I told him: 'Look, Evan, it's not working. I do the housework, I take the major care of Joey, *and* I work a full-time job. I get pissed. This is *your* house too. Joey is *your* child too. It's not all *my* job to care for them.' When I cooled down I put to him, 'Look, how about this: I'll cook Mondays, Wednesdays, and Fridays. You cook Tuesdays, Thursdays, and Saturdays. And we'll share or go out Sundays.' "

According to Nancy, Evan said he didn't like "rigid schedules." He said he didn't necessarily agree with her standards of housekeeping, and didn't like that standard "imposed" on him, especially if she was "sluffing off" tasks on him, which from time to time he felt she was. But he went along with the idea in principle. Nancy said the first week of the new plan went as follows. On Monday, she cooked. For Tuesday, Evan planned a meal that required shopping for a few ingredients, but on his way home he forgot to shop for them. He came home, saw nothing he could use in the refrigerator or in the cupboard, and suggested to Nancy that they go out for Chinese food. On Wednesday, Nancy cooked. On Thursday morning, Nancy reminded Evan, "Tonight it's your turn." That night Evan fixed hamburgers and french fries and Nancy was quick to praise him. On Friday, Nancy cooked. On Saturday, Evan forgot again.

As this pattern continued, Nancy's reminders became sharper. The sharper they became, the more actively Evan forgot—perhaps anticipating even sharper reprimands if he resisted more directly. This cycle of passive refusal followed by disappointment and anger gradually tightened, and before long the struggle had spread to the task of doing the laundry. Nancy said it was only fair that Evan share the laundry. He agreed in principle, but anxious that Evan would not share, Nancy wanted a clear, explicit agreement. "You ought to wash and fold every other load," she had told him. Evan experienced this "plan" as a yoke around his neck. On many weekdays, at this point, a huge pile of laundry sat like a disheveled guest on the living-room couch.

In her frustration, Nancy began to make subtle emotional jabs at Evan. "I don't know *what's* for dinner," she would say with a sigh. Or "I can't cook now, I've got to deal with this pile of laundry." She tensed at the slightest criticism about household disorder; if Evan wouldn't do the housework, he had absolutely *no* right to criticize how she did it. She would burst out angrily at Evan. She recalled telling him: "After work *my* feet are just as tired as *your* feet. I'm just as wound up as you are. I come home. I cook dinner. I wash and I clean. Here we are, planning a second child, and I can't cope with the one we have."

About two years after I first began visiting the Holts, I began to see their problem in a certain light: as a conflict between their two gender ideologies. Nancy wanted to be the sort of woman who was needed and appreciated both at home and at work—like Lacey, she told me, on the television show "Cagney and Lacey." She wanted Evan to appreciate her for being a caring social worker, a committed wife, and a wonderful mother. But she cared just as much that she be able to appreciate *Evan* for what *he* contributed at home, not just for how he supported the family. She would feel proud to explain to women friends that she was married to one of these rare "new men."

A gender ideology is often rooted in early experience, and fueled by motives formed early on and such motives can often be traced to some cautionary tale in early life. So it was for Nancy. Nancy described her mother:

> My mom was wonderful, a real aristocrat, but she was also terribly depressed being a housewife. My dad treated her like a doormat. She didn't have any self-confidence. And growing up, I can remember her being really depressed. I grew up bound and determined not to be like her and not to marry a man like my father. As long as Evan doesn't do the housework, I feel it means he's going to be like my father—coming home, putting his feet up, and hollering at my mom to serve him. That's my biggest fear. I've had *bad* dreams about that.

Nancy thought that women friends her age, also in traditional marriages, had come to similarly bad ends. She described a high school friend: "Martha barely made it through City College. She had no interest in learning anything. She spent nine years trailing around behind her husband [a salesman]. It's a miserable marriage. She hand washes all his shirts. The high point of her life was when she was 18 and the two of us were running around Miami Beach in a Mustang convertible. She's gained seventy pounds and she hates her life." To Nancy, Martha was a younger version of her mother, depressed, lacking in self-esteem, a cautionary tale whose moral was "if you want to be happy, develop a career and get your husband to share at home." Asking Evan to help again and again felt like "hard work" but it was essential to establishing her role as a career woman.

For his own reasons, Evan imagined things very differently. He loved Nancy and if Nancy loved being a social worker, he was happy and proud to support her in it. He knew that because she took her caseload so seriously, it was draining work. But at the same time, he did not see why, just because she chose this demanding career, *he* had to change *his own* life. Why should her personal decision to work outside the home require him to do more inside it? Nancy earned about two-thirds as much as Evan, and her salary was a big help, but as Nancy confided, "If push came to shove, we could do without it." Nancy was a social worker because she loved it. Doing daily chores at home was thankless work, and certainly not something Evan needed her to appreciate about him. Equality in the second shift meant a loss in his standard of living, and despite all the high-flown talk, he felt he hadn't *really* bargained for it. He was happy to help Nancy at home if she needed help; that was fine. That was only decent. But it was too sticky a matter "committing" himself to sharing.

Two other beliefs probably fueled his resistance as well. The first was his suspicion that if he shared the second shift with Nancy, she would "dominate him." Nancy would ask him to do this, ask him to do that. It felt to Evan as if Nancy had won so many small victories that he had to draw the line somewhere. Nancy had a declarative personality; and as Nancy said, "Evan's mother sat me down and told me once that I was too forceful, that Evan needed to take more authority." Both Nancy and Evan agreed that Evan's sense of career and self was in fact shakier than Nancy's. He had been unemployed. She never had. He had had some bouts of drinking in the past. Drinking was foreign to her. Evan thought that sharing housework would upset a certain balance of power that felt culturally "right." He held the purse strings and made the major decisions about large purchases (like their house) because he "knew more about finances" and because he'd chipped in more inheritance than she when they married. His job difficulties had lowered his self-respect, and now as a couple they had achieved some ineffable "balance"—tilted in his favor, she thought—which, if corrected to equalize the burden of chores, would result in his giving in "too much." A certain driving anxiety behind Nancy's strategy of actively renegotiating roles had made Evan see agreement as "giving in." When he wasn't feeling good

about work, he dreaded the idea of being under his wife's thumb at home.

Underneath these feelings, Evan perhaps also feared that Nancy was avoiding taking care of *him*. His own mother, a mild-mannered alcoholic, had by imperceptible steps phased herself out of a mother's role, leaving him very much on his own. Perhaps a personal motive to prevent that happening in his marriage—a guess on my part, and unarticulated on his—underlay his strategy of passive resistance. And he wasn't altogether wrong to fear this. Meanwhile, he felt he was "offering" Nancy the chance to stay home, or cut back her hours, and that she was refusing his "gift," while Nancy felt that, given her feelings about work, this offer was hardly a gift.

In the sixth year of her marriage, when Nancy again intensified her pressure on Evan to commit himself to equal sharing, Evan recalled saying, "Nancy, why don't you cut back to half time, that way you can fit everything in." At first Nancy was baffled: "We've been married all this time, and you *still* don't get it. Work is important to me. I worked *hard* to get my MSW. Why *should* I give it up?" Nancy also explained to Evan and later to me, "I think my degree and my job has been my way of reassuring myself that I won't end up like my mother." Yet she'd received little emotional support in getting her degree from either her parents or in-laws. (Her mother had avoided asking about her thesis, and her in-laws, though invited, did not attend her graduation, later claiming they'd never been invited.)

In addition, Nancy was more excited about seeing her elderly clients in tenderloin hotels than Evan was about selling couches to furniture salesmen with greased-back hair. Why shouldn't Evan make as many compromises with his career ambitions and his leisure as she'd made with hers? She couldn't see it Evan's way, and Evan couldn't see it hers.

In years of alternating struggle and compromise, Nancy had seen only fleeting mirages of cooperation, visions that appeared when she got sick or withdrew, and disappeared when she got better or came forward.

After seven years of loving marriage, Nancy and Evan had finally come to a terrible impasse. Their emotional standard of living had drastically declined: they began to snap at each other, to criticize, to carp. Each felt taken advantage of: Evan, because his offering of a good arrangement was deemed unacceptable, and Nancy, because Evan wouldn't do what she deeply felt was "fair."

This struggle made its way into their sexual life—first through Nancy directly, and then through Joey. Nancy had always disdained any form of feminine wiliness or manipulation. Her family saw her as "a flaming feminist" and that was how she saw herself. As such, she felt above the underhanded ways traditional women used to get around men. She mused, "When I was a teen-ager, I vowed I would *never* use sex to get my way with a man. It is not self-respecting; it's demeaning. But when Evan refused to carry his load at home, I did, I used sex. I said, 'Look, Evan, I would not be this exhausted and asexual every night if I didn't have so much to face every morning.'" She felt reduced to an old "strategy," and her modern ideas made her ashamed of it. At the same time, she'd run out of other, modern ways.

The idea of a separation arose, and they became frightened. Nancy looked at the deteriorating marriages and fresh divorces of couples with young children around them. One unhappy husband they knew had become so uninvolved in family life (they didn't know whether his unhappiness made him uninvolved, or whether his lack of involvement had caused his wife to be unhappy) that his wife left him. In another case, Nancy felt the wife had "nagged" her husband so much that he abandoned her for another woman. In both cases, the couple was less happy after the divorce than before, and both wives took the children and struggled desperately to survive financially. Nancy took stock. She asked herself, "Why wreck a marriage over a dirty frying pan?" Is it really worth it?

UPSTAIRS-DOWNSTAIRS: A FAMILY MYTH AS "SOLUTION"

Not long after this crisis in the Holts' marriage, there was a dramatic lessening of tension over the issue of the second shift. It was as if the issue was closed. Evan had won. Nancy would do the second shift. Evan expressed vague guilt but beyond that he had nothing to say. Nancy had wearied of continually raising the topic, wearied of the lack of resolution. Now in the exhaustion of defeat, she wanted the struggle to be over too. Evan was "so good" in *other* ways, why debilitate their marriage by continual quarreling. Besides, she told me, "Women always adjust more, don't they?"

One day, when I asked Nancy to tell me who did which tasks from a long list of household chores, she interrupted me with a broad wave of her hand and said, "I do the upstairs, Evan does the downstairs." What does that mean? I asked. Matter-of-factly, she explained that the upstairs included the living room, the dining room, the kitchen, two bedrooms, and two baths. The downstairs meant the garage, a place for storage and hobbies—Evan's hobbies. She explained this as a "sharing" arrangement, without humor or irony—just as Evan did later. Both said they had agreed it was the best solution to their dispute. Evan would take care of the car, the garage, and Max, the family dog. As Nancy explained, "the dog is all Evan's problem. I don't have to deal with the dog." Nancy took care of the rest.

For purposes of accommodating the second shift, then, the Holts' garage was elevated to the full moral and practical equivalent of the rest of the house. For Nancy and Evan, "upstairs and downstairs," "inside and outside," was vaguely described like "half and half," a fair division of labor based on a natural division of their house.

The Holts presented their upstairs-downstairs agreement as a perfectly equitable solution to a problem they "once had." This belief is what we might call a "family myth," even a modest delusional system. Why did they believe it? I think they believed it because they needed to believe it, because it solved a terrible problem. It allowed Nancy to continue thinking of herself as the sort of woman whose husband didn't abuse her—a self-conception that mattered a great deal to her. And it avoided the hard truth that, in his stolid, passive way, Evan had refused to share. It avoided the truth, too, that in their showdown, Nancy was more afraid of divorce than Evan was. This outer cover to their family life, this family myth, was jointly devised. It was an attempt to agree that there was no conflict over the second shift, no tension between their versions of manhood and womanhood, and that the powerful crisis that had arisen was temporary and minor.

The wish to avoid such a conflict is natural enough. But their avoidance was tacitly supported by the surrounding culture, especially the image of the woman with the flying hair. After all, this admirable woman also proudly does the "upstairs" each day without a husband's help and without conflict.

After Nancy and Evan reached their upstairs-downstairs agreement, their confrontations ended. They were nearly forgotten. Yet, as she described their daily life months after the agreement, Nancy's resentment still seemed alive and well. For example, she said:

> Evan and I eventually divided the labor so that I do the upstairs and Evan does the downstairs and the dog. So the dog is my husband's problem. But when I was getting the dog outside and getting Joey ready for childcare, and cleaning up the mess of feeding the cat, and getting the lunches together, and having my son wipe his nose on my outfit so I would have to change—then I was pissed! I felt that I was doing *everything*. All Evan was doing was getting up, having coffee, reading the paper, and saying, "Well, I have to go now," and often forgetting the lunch I'd bothered to make.

She also mentioned that she had fallen into the habit of putting Joey to bed in a certain way: he asked to be swung around by the arms, dropped on the bed, nuzzled and hugged, whispered to in his ear. Joey waited for her attention. He didn't go to sleep without it. But, increasingly, when Nancy tried it at eight or nine, the ritual didn't put Joey to sleep. On the contrary, it woke him up. It was then that Joey began to say he could only go to sleep in his parents' bed, that he began to sleep in their bed and to encroach on their sexual life.

Near the end of my visits, it struck me that Nancy was putting Joey to bed in an "exciting" way, later and later at night, in order to tell Evan something important: "You win, I'll go on doing all the work at home, but I'm angry about it and I'll make you pay." Evan had won the battle but lost the war. According to the family myth, all was well: the struggle had been resolved by the upstairs-downstairs agreement. But suppressed in one area of their marriage, this struggle lived on in another—as Joey's problem, and as theirs.

NANCY'S "PROGRAM" TO SUSTAIN THE MYTH

There was a moment, I believe, when Nancy seemed to *decide* to give up on this one. She decided to try not to resent Evan. Whether or not other women face a moment just like this, at the very least they face the need to deal with all the feelings that naturally arise from a clash between a treasured ideal and an incompatible reality. In the age of a stalled revolution, it is a problem a great many women face.

Emotionally, Nancy's compromise from time to time slipped; she would forget and grow resentful again. Her new resolve needed maintenance. Only half aware that she was doing so, Nancy went to extraordinary lengths to maintain it. She could tell me now, a year or so after her "decision," in a matter-of-fact and noncritical way: "Evan likes to come home to a hot meal. He doesn't like to clear the table. He doesn't like to do the dishes. He likes to go watch TV.

He likes to play with his son when he feels like it and not feel like he should be with him more." She seemed resigned.

Everything was "fine." But it had taken an extraordinary amount of complex "emotion work"—the work of *trying* to feel the "right" feeling, the feeling she wanted to feel—to make and keep everything "fine." Across the nation at this particular time in history, this emotion work is often all that stands between the stalled revolution on the one hand, and broken marriages on the other.

It would have been easier for Nancy Holt to do what some other women did: indignantly cling to her goal of sharing the second shift. Or she could have cynically renounced all forms of feminism as misguided, could have cleared away any ideological supports to her indignation, so as to smooth her troubled bond with Evan. Or, like her mother, she could have sunk into quiet depression, disguised perhaps by overbusyness, drinking, overeating. She did none of these things. Instead, she did something more complicated. She became *benignly* accommodating.

How did Nancy manage to accommodate graciously? How did she really live with it? In the most general terms, she had to bring herself to *believe* the myth that the upstairs-downstairs division of housework was fair, and that it had resolved her struggle with Evan. She had to decide to accept an arrangement which in her heart of hearts she had felt was unfair. At the same time, she did not relinquish her deep beliefs about fairness.

Instead, she did something more complicated. Intuitively, Nancy seemed to *avoid* all the mental associations that reminded her of this sore point: the connections between Evan's care of the dog and her care of their child and house, between her share of family work and equality in their marriage; and between equality and love. In short, Nancy refused to consciously recognize the entire chain of associations that made her feel that something was wrong. The maintenance program she designed to avoid thinking about these

things and to avoid the connections between them, was, in one way, a matter of denial. But in another way, it was a matter of intuitive genius.

First, it involved dissociating the inequity in the second shift from the inequity in their marriage, and in marriages in general. Nancy continued to care about sharing the work at home, about having an "equal marriage" and about other people having them too. For reasons that went back to her depressed "doormat" mother, and to her consequent determination to forge an independent identity as an educated, middle-class woman for whom career opportunities had opened up in the early 1980s, Nancy cared about these things. Egalitarianism as an ideology made sense of her biography, her circumstances, and the way she had forged the two. How could she *not* care? But to ensure that her concern for equality did not make her resentful in her marriage to a man remarkably resistant to change, she "rezoned" this anger-inducing territory. She made that territory much smaller: only if Evan did not take care of the dog would she be indignant. Now she wouldn't need to be upset about the double day *in general.* She could still be a feminist, still believe in 50-50 with housework, and still believe that working toward equality was an expression of respect and respect the basis of love. But this chain of associations was now anchored more safely to a more minor matter: how lovingly Evan groomed, fed, and walked the dog.

For Evan, also, the dog came to symbolize the entire second shift: it became a fetish. Other men, I found, had second-shift fetishes too. When I asked one man what he did to share the work of the home, he answered, "I make all the pies we eat." He didn't have to share much responsibility for the home; "pies" did it for him. Another man grilled fish. Another baked bread. In their pies, their fish, and their bread, such men converted a single act into a substitute for a multitude of chores in the second shift, a token. Evan took care of the dog.

Another way in which Nancy encapsulated her anger was to think about her work in a different way. Feeling unable to cope at home, she had with some difficulty finally arranged a half-time schedule with her boss at work. This eased her load, but it did not resolve the more elusive moral problem: within their marriage, her work and her time "mattered less" than Evan's. What Evan did with his time corresponded to what he wanted her to depend on him for, to appreciate him for; what she did with her time did not. To deal with this, she devised the idea of dividing all of her own work in the new schedule into "shifts." As she explained: "I've been resentful, yes. I was feeling mistreated, and I became a bitch to live with. Now that I've gone part-time, I figure that when I'm at the office from eight to one, and when I come home and take care of Joey and make dinner at five—all that time from eight to six is my shift. So I don't mind making dinner every night *since it's on my shift.* Before, I had to make dinner on time I considered to be *after* my shift and I resented always having to do it."

Another plank in Nancy's maintenance program was to suppress any comparison between her hours of leisure and Evan's. In this effort she had Evan's cooperation, for they both clung hard to the notion that they enjoyed an equal marriage. What they did was to deny any connection between this equal marriage and equal access to leisure. They agreed it couldn't be meaningfully claimed that Evan had more leisure than Nancy or that his fatigue mattered more, or that he enjoyed more discretion over his time, or that he lived his life more as he preferred. Such comparisons could suggest that they were both treating Evan as if he were *worth more* than Nancy, and for Nancy, from that point on, it would be a quick fall down a slippery slope to the idea that Evan did not live and honor her as much as she honored and loved him.

For Nancy, the leisure gap between Evan and herself had never seemed to her a simple, practical matter of her greater fatigue. Had it been just that, she would have felt tired but not indignant. Had it been only that, working part time for a while would have been a wonderful solution, as

many other women have said, "the best of both worlds." What troubled Nancy was the matter of her worth. As she told me one day: "It's not that I mind taking care of Joey. I love doing that. I don't even mind cooking or doing laundry. It's that I feel sometimes that Evan thinks his work, his time, is worth more than mine. He'll wait for me to get the phone. It's like his time is more sacred."

As Nancy explained: "Evan and I look for different signs of love. Evan feels loved when we make love. Sexual expression is very important to him. I feel loved when he makes dinner for me or cleans up. He knows I like that, and he does it sometimes." For Nancy, feeling loved was connected to feeling her husband was being considerate of her needs, and honoring her ideal of sharing and equity. To Evan, "fairness" and respect seemed impersonal moral concepts, abstractions rudely imposed on love. He thought he expressed his respect for Nancy by listening carefully to her opinions on the elderly, on welfare, on all sorts of topics, and by consulting her on major purchases. But who did the dishes had to do with a person's role in the family, not with fairness and certainly not with love. In my interviews, a surprising number of women spoke of their fathers helping their mothers "out of love" or consideration. As one woman said, "My dad helped around a lot. He really loved my mom." But in describing their fathers, not one man I interviewed made this link between help at home and love.

SUPPRESSING THE POLITICS OF COMPARISON

In the past, Nancy had compared her responsibilities at home, her identity, and her life to Evan's, and had compared Evan to other men they knew. Now, to avoid resentment, she seemed to compare herself more to *other working mothers*—how organized, energetic, and successful she was compared to them. By this standard, she was doing great: Joey was blooming, her marriage was fine, her job was all she could expect.

Nancy also compared herself to single women who had moved further ahead in their careers, but they fit another mental category. There were two kinds of women, she thought—married and single. "A single woman could move ahead in her career but a married woman has to do a wife's work and mother's work as well." She did not make this distinction for men.

When Nancy decided to stop comparing Evan to men who helped more around the house, she had to suppress an important issue that she had often discussed with Evan: How *unusually* helpful was Evan? How unusually lucky was she? Did he do more or less than men in general? Than middle-class, educated men? What was the "going rate"?

Before she made her decision, Nancy had claimed that Bill Beaumont, who lived two doors down the street, did half the housework without being reminded. Evan gave her Bill Beaumont, but said Bill was an exception. Compared to *most men,* Evan said, he did more. This was true if "most men" meant Evan's old friends. Nancy felt "upwardly mobile" compared to the wives of those men, and she believed that they looked upon Evan as a model for their own husbands, just as she used to look up to women whose husbands did more than Evan. She also noted how much the dangerous "unionizer" she had appeared to a male friend of theirs:

> One of our friends is a traditional Irish cop whose wife doesn't work. But the way they wrote that marriage, even when she had the kid and worked full time, she did everything. He couldn't understand our arrangement where my husband would help out and cook part time and do the dishes once in a while and help out with the laundry [an arrangement that didn't last]. We were *banned* from his house for a while because he told Evan, "Every time your wife comes over and talks to my wife, I get in trouble," I was considered a flaming liberal.

When the wife of Joe Collins, a neighbor on the other side, complained that Joe didn't take equal responsibility, Joe in turn would look down the invisible chain of sharing, half-sharing, and nonsharing males to someone low on his wife's list of helpful husbands and say, "At least I do a hell of a lot more than *he* does." In reply, Joe's wife would name a husband she knew who took fully half the responsibility of caring for the child and the home. Joey would answer that this man was either imaginary or independently wealthy, and then cite the example of another male friend who, though a great humorist and fisherman, did far less at home.

I began to imagine the same evening argument extending down the street of this middle-class Irish neighborhood, across the city to other cities, states, regions . . . wives pointing to husbands who did more, husbands pointing to men who did less. Comparisons like these—between Evan and other men, between Nancy and other women—reflect a semiconscious sense of *the going rates for a desirable attitude or behavior in an available member of the same and opposite sex.* If most of the men in their middle-class circle of friends had been given to drinking heavily, beating their wives, and having affairs, Nancy would have considered herself "lucky" to have Evan, because he didn't do those things. But most of the men they knew weren't like that either, so Nancy didn't consider Evan "above the going rate" in this way. Most of those men only halfheartedly encouraged their wives to advance at work, so Nancy felt lucky to have Evan's enthusiastic encouragement.

This idea of a "going rate" indicated the market value, so to speak, of a man's behavior or attitudes. If a man was really "rare," his wife intuitively felt grateful, or at least both of them felt she ought to. How far the whole culture, and their particular corner of it had gotten through the feminist agenda—criminalizing wife battery, disapproving of a woman's need for her husband's "permission" to work, and so on—became the cultural foundation of the judgment about how rare and desirable a man was.

The "going rate" was a tool in the marital struggle, useful in this case mainly on the male side. If Evan could convince Nancy that he did as much or more than "most men," she couldn't as seriously expect him to do more. Like most other men who didn't share, Evan felt the male "norm" was evidence on his side: men "out there" did less. Nancy was lucky he did as much as he did.

Nancy thought men "out there" did more at home but were embarrassed to say so. Given her view of "men out there," Nancy felt less lucky than seemed right to Evan, given his picture of things. Besides that, Nancy felt that sheer rarity was not the only or best measure. She felt that Evan's share of the work at home should be assessed, not by comparing it to the real inequalities in other people's lives, but by comparing it to the ideal of sharing.

Comparisons between Evan and the going rate of male helpfulness was one basis on which to appraise Evan's offerings to their marriage and the credit and gratitude due him for those offerings. The more rare, the more credit. Their ideals of manhood and womanhood formed another basis. The closer to the ideal, the more credit. And the harder it was to live up to the ideal, the more pride-swallowing it took, or the more effort shown, the more credit. Since Evan and Nancy didn't see this going rate the same way, since they differed in their ideals, and since Evan hadn't actually shown much effort in changing, Nancy had not been as grateful to Evan as he felt she should have been. Not only had she not been grateful, she'd resented him.

But now, under the new "maintenance program" to support the necessary myth of equality in her marriage, Nancy set aside the tangles in the give and take of credit. She thought now in a more "segregated" way. She compared women to women, and men to men, and based her sense of gratitude on that way of thinking. Since the going rate was unfavorable to women, Nancy felt she should feel more grateful for what Evan gave her (because it was so rare in the world) than Evan should feel for what she gave him (which was more common). Nancy did not have

to feel grateful because Evan had compromised his own views on manhood; actually he had made few concessions. But she did feel she owed him gratitude for supporting her work so wholeheartedly; that was unusual.

For his part, Evan didn't talk much about feeling grateful to Nancy. He actually felt she wasn't doing enough around the house. But he said this in a curious way that avoided an Evan-Nancy comparison. He erased the distinction between Nancy and himself: his "I" disappeared into "we," leaving no "me" to compare to "you." For example, when I asked him if he felt that he did enough around the house, he laughed, surprised to be asked point-blank, and replied mildly: "No, I don't think so. No. I would have to admit that we probably could do more." Then using "we" in an apparently different way, he went on: "But I also have to say that I think we could do more in terms of the household chores than we really do. See, we let a lot more slide than we should."

Nancy made no more comparisons to Bill Beaumont, no more unfavorable comparisons to the "going rate." Without these frames of reference, the deal with Evan seemed "fair." This did not mean that Nancy ceased to care about equality between the sexes. On the contrary, she cut out magazine articles about how males rose faster in social welfare than females, and she complained about the condescending way male psychiatrists treat female social workers. She pushed her feminism "out" into the world of work, a safe distance away from the upstairs-downstairs arrangement at home.

Nancy now blamed her fatigue on "everything she had to do." When she occasionally spoke of conflict, it was conflict between her job and Joey, or between Joey and housework. Evan slid out of the equation. As Nancy spoke of him now, he had no part in the conflict.

Since Nancy and Evan no longer conceived of themselves as comparable, Nancy let it pass when Evan spoke of housework in a "male" way, as something he "would do" or "would not do," or something he did when he got around to it. Like most women, when Nancy spoke of housework, she spoke simply of what had to be done. The difference in the way she and Evan talked seemed to emphasize that their viewpoints were "naturally" different and again helped push the problem out of mind.

Many couples traded off tasks as the need arose; whoever came home first started dinner. In the past, Evan had used flexibility in the second shift to camouflage his retreat from it; he hadn't liked "rigid schedules." He had once explained to me: "We don't really keep count of who does what. Whoever gets home first is likely to start dinner. Whoever has the time deals with Joey or cleans up." He had disparaged a female neighbor who kept strict track of tasks as "uptight" and "compulsive." A couple, he had felt, ought to be "open to the flow." Dinner, he had said, could be anytime. The very notion of a leisure gap disappeared into Evan's celebration of happy, spontaneous anarchy. But now that the struggle was over, Evan didn't talk of dinner at "anytime." Dinner was at six.

Nancy's program to keep up her gracious resignation included another tactic: she would focus on the *advantages* of losing the struggle. She wasn't *stuck* with the upstairs. Now, as she talked she seemed to preside over it as her dominion. She would do the housework, but the house would feel like "hers." The new living-room couch, the kitchen cabinet, she referred to as "mine." She took up "supermom-speak" and began referring to *my* kitchen, *my* living-room curtains, and, even in Evan's presence, to *my* son. She talked of machines that helped *her,* and of the work-family conflict itself as *hers.* Why shouldn't she? She felt she'd earned that right. The living room reflected Nancy's preference for beige. The upbringing of Joey reflected Nancy's ideas about fostering creativity by giving a child controlled choice. What remained of the house was Evan's domain. As she remarked: "I never touch the garage, not ever. Evan sweeps it and straightens it and arranges it and plays

with tools and figures out where the equipment goes—in fact, that's one of his hobbies. In the evening, after Joey has settled down, he goes down there and putzes around; he has a TV down there, and he figures out his fishing equipment and he just plays around. The washer and dryer are down there, but that's the only part of the garage that's my domain."

Nancy could see herself as the "winner"—the one who got her way, the one whose kitchen, living room, house, and child these really were. She could see her arrangement with Evan as *more* than fair—from a certain point of view.

As a couple, Nancy and Evan together explained their division of the second shift in ways that disguised their struggle. Now they rationalized that it was a result of their two *personalities.* For Evan, especially, there was no problem of a leisure gap; there was only the continual, fascinating interaction of two personalities. "I'm lazy," he explained. "I like to do what I want to do in my own time. Nancy isn't as lazy as I am. She's compulsive and very well organized." The comparisons of his work to hers, his fatigue to hers, his leisure time to hers—comparisons that used to point to a problem—were melted into freestanding personal characteristics, his laziness, her compulsiveness.

Nancy now agreed with Evan's assessment of her, and described herself as "an energetic person" who was amazingly "well organized." When I asked her whether she felt any conflict between work and family life, she demurred: "I work real well overnight. I pulled overnights all through undergraduate and graduate school, so I'm not too terribly uncomfortable playing with my family all evening, then putting them to bed, making coffee, and staying up all night [to write up reports on her welfare cases] and then working the next day—though I only do that when I'm down to the wire. I go into overdrive. I don't feel any conflict between the job and the child that way at all."

Evan was well organized and energetic on his job. But as Nancy talked of Evan's life at home, he neither had these virtues nor lacked them; they were irrelevant. This double standard of virtue reinforced the idea that men and women cannot be compared, being "naturally" so different.

Evan's orientation to domestic tasks, as they both described it now, had been engraved in childhood, and how could one change a whole childhood? As Nancy often reminded me, "I was brought up to do the housework. Evan wasn't." Many other men, who had also done little housework when they were boys, did not talk so fatalistically about "upbringing," because they were doing a lot of it now. But the idea of a fate sealed so very early was oddly *useful* in Nancy's program of benign resignation. She needed it, because if the die had been cast in the dawn of life, it was inevitable that she should work the extra month a year.

This, then, was the set of mental tricks that helped Nancy resign herself to what had at one time seemed like a "bad deal." This was how she reconciled believing one thing and living with another.

HOW MANY HOLTS?

In one key way the Holts were typical of the vast majority of two-job couples: their family life had become the shock absorber for a stalled revolution whose origin lay far outside it—in economic and cultural trends that bear very differently on men and women. Nancy was reading books, newspaper articles, and watching TV programs on the changing role of women. Evan wasn't. Nancy felt benefited by these changes; Evan didn't. In her ideals and in reality, Nancy was more different from her mother than Evan was from his father, for the culture and economy were in general pressing change faster upon women like her than upon men like Evan. Nancy had gone to college; her mother hadn't. Nancy had a professional job; her mother never had. Nancy had the idea that she should be equal with her husband; her mother hadn't been much exposed to that idea in her day. Nancy felt

she should share the job of earning money, and that Evan should share the work at home; her mother hadn't imagined that was possible. Evan went to college, his father (and the other boys in his family, though not the girls) had gone too. Work was important to Evan's identity as a man as it had been for his father before him. Indeed, Evan felt the same way about family roles as his father had felt in his day. The new job opportunities and the feminist movement of the 1960s and '70s had transformed Nancy but left Evan pretty much the same. And the friction created by this difference between them moved to the issue of second shift as metal to a magnet. By the end, Evan did less housework and childcare than most men married to working women—but not much less. Evan and Nancy were also typical of nearly 40 percent of the marriages I studied in their clash of gender ideologies and their corresponding difference in notion about what constituted a "sacrifice" and what did not. By far the most common form of mismatch was like that between Nancy, an egalitarian, and Evan, a transitional.

But for most couples, the tensions between strategies did not move so quickly and powerfully to issues of housework and childcare. Nancy pushed harder than most women to get her husband to share the work at home, and she also lost more overwhelmingly than the few other women who fought that hard. Evan pursued his strategy of passive resistance with more quiet tenacity than most men, and he allowed himself to become far more marginal to his son's life than most other fathers. The myth of the Holts' "equal" arrangement seemed slightly more odd than other family myths that encapsulated equally powerful conflicts.

Beyond their upstairs-downstairs myth, the Holts tell us a great deal about the subtle ways a couple can encapsulate the tension caused by a struggle over the second shift without resolving the problem or divorcing. Like Nancy Holt, many women struggle to avoid, suppress, obscure, or mystify a frightening conflict over the second shift. They do not struggle like this because they started off wanting to, or because such struggle is inevitable or because women inevitably lose, but because they are forced to choose between equality and marriage. And they choose marriage. When asked about "ideal" relations between men and women in general, about what they want for their daughters, about what "ideally" they'd like in their own marriage, most working mothers "wished" their men would share the work at home.

But many "wish" it instead of "want" it. Other goals—like keeping peace at home—come first. Nancy Holt did some extraordinary behind-the-scenes emotion work to prevent her ideals from clashing with her marriage. In the end, she had confined and miniaturized her ideas of equality successfully enough to do two things she badly wanted to do: feel like a feminist, and live at peace with a man who was not. Her program had "worked." Evan won on the reality of the situation, because Nancy did the second shift. Nancy won on the cover story; they would talk about it as if they shared.

Nancy wore the upstairs-downstairs myth as an ideological cloak to protect her from the contradictions in her marriage and from the cultural and economic forces that press upon it. Nancy and Evan Holt were caught on opposite sides of the gender revolution occurring all around them. Through the 1960s, 1970s, and 1980s masses of women entered the public world of work—but went only so far up the occupational ladder. They tried for "equal" marriages, but got only so far in achieving it. They married men who liked them to work at the office but who wouldn't share the extra month a year at home. When confusion about the identity of the working woman created a cultural vacuum in the 1970s and 1980s, the image of the supermom quietly glided in. She made the "stall" seem normal and happy. But beneath the happy image of the woman with the flying hair are modern marriages like the Holts', reflecting intricate webs of tension, and the huge, hidden emotional cost to women, men, and children of having to "manage" inequality. Yet on the surface, all we might see would be Nancy Holt bounding confidently out the door at 8:30 A.M., briefcase in one hand, Joey in the other. All we might hear would be Nancy's and Evan's talk about their marriage as happy, normal, even "equal"—because equality was so important to Nancy.

CHAPTER 11

Domestic Violence

The problem of violence against women in families and in other intimate settings is not new. Yet only within the last decade or two has much attention been paid to it. The feminist movement deserves much of the credit for placing violence against women on the political agenda. Even so, government responses were modest. The U.S. Congress did not pass the Violence Against Women Act until the summer of 1994, when the murder of Nicole Simpson, O. J. Simpson's wife, focused the public's attention on battered women. It can be very difficult, and even life-threatening, for a women to leave an abusive relationship with a husband or intimate partner. The following article by Katherine Ferraro describes in detail the stages battered women tend to pass through before they attempt to leave a violent partner.

Child abuse is the other major form of domestic violence. In 1995, six-year-old Elisa Izquierdo of New York City was beaten to death by her mother. After her death, it came to light that her mother had been reported seven times to local child protective authorities for suspected child abuse. Yet no action had been taken. In response, outraged legislators in New York passed strict rules aimed at requiring social service agencies to take more at-risk children from their parents and place them in foster homes.

Just two decades earlier, however, public unhappiness with the quality and cost of foster care had led to a "family preservation" movement that urged social service agencies to make greater efforts to keep potentially abusive families together by helping them increase their parenting skills and solve their other problems. In truth, public sentiment about what to do about child abuse has seesawed between family preservation and removing children from their families because neither position has solved the problem of child abuse.

There is some evidence of a rise in child abuse recently, although it is very difficult to determine how much of the apparent increase merely reflects a rise in the number of existing cases that are now reported to authorities.[1] Douglas Besharov, the first director of the U.S. National Center on Child Abuse and Neglect, tries

---

[1]See Cherlin, *Public and Private Families*, pp. 329–36.

to disentangle reporting from reality in the following article. Besharov also argues that we shouldn't treat all forms of officially noted child abuse similarly. He argues that some of the problems that are officially labeled as child abuse are more appropriately viewed as problems of poverty instead. None of this is meant to question the seriousness of the child abuse problem; rather, it suggests that social policy could be more effective if we took a closer look at the different types of cases that are often lumped together as abusive.

Battered Women: Strategies for Survival

Kathleen J. Ferraro

Women in violent intimate relationships often continue to live with abusers for many years or until the death of one partner. Over the past decade, scholarship on the battering of women has been critical of analyses that focus on the reasons women remain in violent relationships (Jones, 1994; Loseke & Cahill, 1984; Tifft, 1993; Radford & Russell, 1992). The question, "Why do battered women stay?" is misinformed and misdirected. Most women not only eventually leave their abusive partners, but they are more likely to be battered in the process of leaving or after they leave than while living with an abusive partner (Schwartz, 1988; Harlow, 1991; Barnett & LaViolette, 1993). More fundamentally, the question of why women stay implies that the battered women's behavior is problematic, rather than that of their abusive partners. The more relevant questions are "why do men batter?" and "why do they stay when women tell them to go?" (see Marano, 1993).

Over the past five years, scholars have begun recasting the image of battered women from "victim" to "survivor" (Gondolf, 1990; Hoff, 1990; Kelly, 1988; Campbell et al., 1994). This shift emphasizes the competent decision making women perform to end intimate violence. The obstacles to escape are daunting, and some women may never lead lives free of male violence. Still, many women are able, over time, to eliminate violence either through divorce or through other help-seeking efforts. Campbell and others (1994, p. 105) found that after two and a half years, 43 percent of battered women had left their abusers and two-thirds of the women were living in nonviolent situations. The researchers' interviews with women who had escaped do not suggest a simple solution to violence, but complex and persistent strategies for survival.

Although focusing on women's behavior may be a form of "victim blaming," most of our understanding of battering has come from listening to women. From women, we know that it is extremely difficult to escape from intimate violence. The contextual nature of woman battering differentiates it from other forms of interpersonal violence. One goal of this [reading] is to discuss some of the many dimensions of the context within which women who are battered develop strategies for survival. Both the context of the violence and the process women go through in their responses to battering are important issues for those concerned with women's well-being. By examining these issues, we hope to develop and implement policies that effectively respond to women's needs and desires. Battering is not a simple phenomenon, but a complex experience involving relational, institutional, and cultural contexts. Each of these contexts will be explored in this [reading] with an emphasis on the process by which women develop strategies for survival.

The analysis and examples are drawn from empirical work with women who have lived in battering relationships with husbands or lovers. Thus, the focus is on heterosexual battering, which . . . is not always identical in nature to same-sex battering. The cases are drawn from research in shelters, on police ride-alongs, with women who called the police, with battered women who killed their abusers, and with women who came to talk to me about their problems. While the interviews were conducted for separate purposes, they illuminate different aspects of the context and processes addressed here.

The [reading] outlines the stages of engagement and disengagement with the intimate relationship in which battered women participate, including ardor, accommodation, ambivalence, and terror. The factors that influence the engagement process (relational, situational, institutional, and cultural) will be examined as they support or discourage women's safety. Individual-, relational-, and institutional-level strategies will be presented for each stage, emphasizing the successful and detrimental aspects of strategies and institutional responses. The [reading] concludes with recommendations for understanding the contextual and process-oriented nature of women's responses to battering and their strategies for survival.

STAGES OF ENGAGEMENT

Ardor

Intimacy neither begins nor ends instantaneously, but follows an emotional career. Retrospective interpretations by women often identify clues that could have predicted their partners' future violence. However, the early stages of courtship are characterized by physical and emotional attractions that overshadow negative characteristics and forewarnings of danger. It is in this stage of *ardor* that individuals become bonded to the relationship and the positive feelings it generates. Most women report no experiences of physical violence during the first six months of their relationships. As described by Dobash and Dobash (1979), Walker (1979), and Kelly (1987), the first stage of a battering relationship often involves increasing isolation of the woman from her friends and family. In this stage of ardor, she usually enjoys the time alone with her partner and does not perceive his desire for social exclusivity as oppressive or abusive, but as an expression of their mutual affection. The isolation that begins to occur in this early phase, however, may establish conditions that facilitate the batterer's efforts to control his partner at a later time.

Observers, both official agents and the general public, often express surprise and sometimes disdain for women who say they love the men who have assaulted them. But this love is the dominant theme of contemporary culture, in children's films (e.g., *Beauty and the Beast*); adult literature, film, and theater; and all kinds of music and advertising. Because of the glorification of heterosexual romantic love, a high value is placed on intimate relationships; this value is socially reinforced through elaborate and expensive engagement and marital rituals. It should not be surprising that women "love" the men they live with.

At the relational level, the intense physical attraction and emotional involvement that usually are part of new intimate relationships builds ardor. Women who have been battered often discuss the deep feelings of kinship that they share with their partners; often women say that their partners are the only ones who really know and understand them. Women describe their partners as "charismatic" or "charming" and uniquely suited to meet their needs. As one woman said:

> He's all I've got. My dad's gone, and my mother disowned me when I married him. And he's really special. He understands me, and I understand him. Nobody could take his place (Ferraro & Johnson, 1983, p. 330).

Recently, Goldner and Walker have examined battered women's and their partners' perceptions that "the other knows them more profoundly and accepts them better than anyone before" (Marano, 1993, p. 49). These feelings contribute to a context in which initial violence is perceived as a profound violation of trust and intimacy, but rarely as a justification for the outright rejection of the violent man who, until then, represented her soul mate.

Accommodation

The first act of physical violence marks the beginning of the transition from ardor to the next stage of engagement—that is, *accommodation*.

It is extremely unusual for a woman to leave an abusive man after the first incidence of violence. Physical violence is so inconsistent with expectations of an intimate partner that most women perceive the first instance as an exceptional aberration. A tremendous emotional commitment is threatened by recognition of battering, and most women protect that commitment through techniques of rationalization. These techniques draw on cultural scripts, excuses by abusers, and reactions of acquaintances and institutional actors to provide these women with accounts of the battering that preserve the image of intimacy between the partners (Ferraro & Johnson, 1983). Specific techniques include appeals to the salvation ethic; denials of injury; denials of victimization; denials of who the victimizer is; denials that there are options; and appeals to higher loyalties. At the relational level, the denials related to the injury, victimization, victimizer, and options represent an internalization by the women of some of the excuses and justifications offered by batterers (Ptacek, 1988). The denial of victimization, for example, reflects the batterer's attempt to reject responsibility for his violence by focusing on the woman's behavior, which he defines as provocative or deficient. As one woman told me, "I just can't learn to keep my mouth shut. I shouldn't have asked him. I don't know why I had to ask him." These statements describe her feelings of responsibility for an incident in which her partner shattered the door of their apartment and threw her against the wall because she had asked him if he wanted to take a piece of his birthday cake to work.

The strategies of denial become intertwined with the women's diminishing sense of self-worth, which results from physical and emotional battering. Men who continually denigrate their partners, particularly when the women are isolated from other sources of nurturance, establish a definition of the situation that encourages self-blame. Women usually express feelings of bewilderment (e.g., "What did I do wrong?"),

but simultaneously they believe they must have done *something* to provoke the violence. For example, one woman commented on her feelings of responsibility for her husband's violence to others as well as to herself in the following manner:

> I blamed me, and I still feel sometimes like it was my fault that he did things to other people. What was it about me that made him want to hit me? I don't think I was the terrible person he said I was. Someone would call and get the wrong number, and just hang up, and I cannot tell you how many times I was thrown against walls for that.

This viewpoint exemplifies part of the confusion many women experience when they try to understand how they can control a batterer's violence with their own behavior, yet simultaneously see that accusations against them are not justified. It is particularly obvious to women that they are *not* having affairs with men walking down the street, at the grocery store, on the other end of a wrong telephone number, or anywhere else. When their partners beat them for these imagined infidelities, the women know they are not at fault. Still, many of these same women try to analyze why their abusers have such bizarre fantasies and what they could do to prevent future violence. They know at one level that they are not "that terrible person" their partner accuses them of being but, at the same time, believe there must be *something* wrong with them to evoke such rage.

Discussions with women who are trying to cope with battering reveal two forms of self-blame: behavioral and characterological (Manley, 1982; Barnett & LaViolette, 1993). Behavioral blame focuses on "specific controllable actions that led to the occurrence of the negative events," while characterological blame "is the identification of an enduring quality or trait that caused the hurtful events" (Barnett & LaViolette, 1993, p. 79). Behavioral blame encourages women to identify and eliminate behaviors, and it may contribute to a sense of control over their lives. While the women's behavior usually has nothing to do with their partner's violence, the perception that controlling behaviors will diminish his violence helps to maintain a sense of "internal locus of control"; that is, women maintain a sense of human dignity in which their actions matter. This may explain why Walker (1984) found that battered women were much more likely to have an internal locus of control than the general population of women. They may believe that by "walking on eggshells" they can maintain a safe environment.

Characterological blame, on the other hand, represents an internalization of the batterer's denigration of the woman's core sense of self. She begins to accept her partner's definitions, namely, that she is "a bad person," "a whore," "ugly," and undesirable to anyone but him. Characterological blame is debilitating, and it leads to depression, because there is nothing a woman can do to change. It is this form of self-blame that accompanies the feelings of "learned helplessness" described by Walker (1979). Through repeated experiences of noncontingency, a woman learns that there is nothing she can do to control the abusive context; thus, she begins to lose the ability to perceive alternatives to terror.

At the extreme end of the continuum of battering, abuse may be inflicted without any immediate prior interaction or even during a woman's sleep. The same woman quoted previously, who was beaten because of wrong telephone numbers, also said:

> He very much believed that a home is a man's castle, and he can do anything he wants there. I just found it easier not to argue. I knew there was just so far I could go, and I couldn't cross that line. Sometimes it wouldn't even matter, I wouldn't cross that line. He would wake me up in my sleep and start beatin' on me.

Batterings that occur "out of the blue" contradict the notion that men become violent when women resist their domination (see Wesson,

1994, p. 3). Once violence becomes an established pattern, there is not much a woman can do to prevent its occurrence. Nevertheless, most women try.

At the relational level, women try to control their own behavior based on their historical knowledge of their partners' violence. At the accommodation stage, women try to eliminate those conditions that have preceded violent incidents in the past, knowing that it is impossible to predict which specific behaviors will become an excuse for violence. Thus, large categories of behavior, such as talking to people or looking at strangers, are excluded from a woman's repertoire of actions. For example, one woman described how she learned not to speak or look at anyone while driving.

> It just got to the point where I don't say anything, if you say anything, he just starts yellin' at you. So I just let it be, and I just let a lot of things go . . . And then you can't even look at somebody walkin' down the street or road, and he'll get mad at you, tell you "Get your _____ eyeballs back in your eyes," you know, stuff like that, so, wherever I used to go, I used to just go to sleep . . . or just pretend to sleep, half the time until we get to where we're going.

Another woman explained how she learned not to express her own opinions.

> There's been times when we'd be sitting there having a conversation about anything, and maybe I didn't agree with him, and he'd haul off and smack me one. I got so I didn't express my opinion, I found out how he felt about it, and that's what I'd say. It was just easier.

In accommodating violence, or trying to do what is "easier" because it might diminish the violence, women relinquish both autonomy and support. Learning not to talk or express opinions may work as a temporary strategy, but it also lessens the women's sense of self-sufficiency, as well as any sense of intimacy. Similarly, eliminating contact with friends and family as a strategy for controlling the jealous partner also eliminates important sources of support and validation. In this respect, most women describe how their friends and relatives were scared away from them, and how the women themselves stopped trying to interact with others to avoid accusations of infidelity. One woman explained that her husband beat her after a visit to her family.

> When I used to go see my brothers and my family, and I used to come back and he used to accuse me.

He accused you of being with your brothers?

> And my father, and stuff like that. And he gave me certain time to go over there, and if I was so many minutes late, he would start beating up on me, hitting me around. And that was one of the reasons why I didn't go see my relatives or my family, because of the way he used to act. I just started ignoring my friends, my relatives, my family. He didn't do anything when they were there, but when we get home, he would just start hitting me, cussin' at me, and start beating me up.

Some women tell of their efforts to "do everything right," which suggests that all of their actions are oriented toward pleasing the batterer and preventing future violence. This strategy is all-consuming, and encourages women to abandon their own standards and judgments to meet those set by the batterer. In extreme cases, it is possible for the ethical perceptions of a woman to be deformed or distorted by attempts to adhere to a violent partner's criteria. One woman indicated how her efforts never really succeeded in improving the ways in which her husband treated her.

> He used to wake up in the mornings grouchy, and I used to have everything done before he gets up, so he won't start with me, start beating me and cussing me, I always wanted everything to be clean and ready for him so that he would appreciate me at least that one day. But I never got that.

The relational strategies that women develop for controlling male violence are also accompa-

nied by institutional and cultural components. At the institutional level, responses by law enforcement agencies, courts, social service agencies, and religious institutions all cooperate with or undermine techniques of rationalization. Denial of victimization, for example, is enhanced when police, under mandatory arrest policies, arrest women who have fought back, even verbally, against their batterer. In Phoenix, Arizona, in 1993, 18 percent of domestic violence arrests were of women. Norris (1994) in interviewing 10 of these women, found that all had been battered women. In terms of the effectiveness of mandatory arrest laws, one woman incarcerated for killing her abuser said:

> I've seen women in jail taken in because of defending themselves from their husbands. I wouldn't call the police, no, uh huh, who's gonna' protect me when he gets out? No one. And its gonna' be worse, I know, I been there. I think that law is crazy. They say, well, "Why didn't you call the police?" Well, what was I supposed to do, say, excuse me a minute while I go use the phone? In [country], he was so mad at me, he locked me in a trunk and left for the day. When he got back, I was so glad to get out of there, calling the police was the furthest thing from my mind.

Even when arrests of batterers do occur, unless the physical damage is severe, punishment will usually consist of a night in jail and probation. At the felony level of aggravated assault, Ferraro & Boychuk (1992) found that 16 percent of cases involving intimate partners were dismissed against the wishes of the victim. Furthermore, the vast majority of successfully prosecuted cases resulted in minor sanctions; only 11 percent of all defendants received prison sentences for violent offenses including homicide and rape. Among those cases involving violent assault by an intimate partner, severe sentences were even less common. Only in those instances involving separated couples in which severe physical injury was inflicted on the woman was a prison sentence likely to be imposed, and when administered, was usually less than two years in length (Ferraro & Boychuk, 1992). While the evidence that the incarceration of batterers is an effective deterrent of such behavior has not been convincingly demonstrated, the release of these offenders with little or no consequences is likely to send battered women the message that their abuse is not only unimportant, but that there are few options for achieving a safe haven.

Although the development of temporary restraining orders (TROs) and orders of protection was intended to provide potential victims with greater legal means for protection, the orders appear to be effective only in certain types of battering relationships. Those men who are in the early stages of battering and who are less likely to be influenced by alcohol or drugs are more likely to be deterred from harassment or stalking behavior by a court order. On the other hand, those men with long histories of dangerous and persistent violence are unlikely to be deterred from such behavior by a court order (Chaudhuri & Daly, 1992; Klein, 1996).

In addition, some women who do obtain court orders are often themselves held to be in violation of the intent of the court order by their own behavior. Thus, women who show a positive response to visits or contact by partners, when the court order required them to refrain from such behavior, are usually informed by police that they have violated the court order by allowing these individuals on their property, thereby precluding any further enforcement of the order (Ferraro, 1989). In these instances, women are given a message that it is *their* responsibility to control the violence of their partners, and *their* fault if their partners fail to do so.

Social service agencies, especially child welfare agencies, may also contribute to a woman's sense of self-blame. One woman had her children placed in foster care after she was hospitalized for three weeks because of a brutal beating; after nine months, she was unable to regain custody of her children, and may only visit them under supervised conditions. Furthermore, she has been categorized as "emotionally unstable," certainly an understandable reaction to a beating from her husband that resulted in a coma, but dubious grounds for removing children from her custody. Another woman was told by a shelter counselor during couple counseling that she had to promise not to do anything to make her partner hit her. Even when institutions intend to help, through mandatory arrest policies, laws, and the like, they often serve to reinforce the mechanisms that define the violence as appropriate and inevitable and the woman as responsible for controlling the men's behavior.

The best-trained criminal justice personnel and most sensitive legal policies depend on women who are convinced that invoking external parties is the best course of action for their families. The current cultural context is not, however, conducive to such a decision. During the administrations of Ronald Reagan and George Bush, "family values" became a focus for resolving the social problems that plagued the United States. The simplistic media portrayal of "broken families" suggested that poverty, drug abuse, teen pregnancy, HIV, and gangs were direct consequences of the breakdown in the patriarchal nuclear family. Women were bombarded with media images that inform them of the shortage of men, the perils of delayed childbearing, and the misery of choosing careers over marriage (Faludi, 1991). In *Mrs. Doubtfire,* one of the most successful 1993 films, a professional woman becomes the source of her family's downfall when she seeks divorce. Her husband, who is sympathetically portrayed as her victim, resorts to transvestism in order to be hired as his children's nanny. *Mrs. Doubtfire* reinforces the myth that divorce is disastrous to children and that women who divorce unsatisfactory men betray themselves and their children.

Battered women who are trying to survive in violent marriages at the accommodation stage must negotiate these cultural messages as they evaluate their own alternatives. Within the context of husbands' or boyfriends' accounts of victim provocation, isolation from supportive friends and family, and lack of effective intervention by criminal justice and social service agencies, these cultural scripts reinforce a woman's belief that it is her responsibility to control her partner's violence and to make the best of a bad situation.

Ambivalence

Despite the weight of forces colluding to support women's accommodation to violence, behaviors that challenge commitment may lead to the stage of *ambivalence*. The transitions in individual women's lives are impossible to predict, and some women may never move past the stage of accommodation to their partners' violence and abuse. For others, however, ambivalence about continued engagement in the relationship may be instigated by actions that are clearly at odds with intimacy and caring. These catalysts may be physical, such as a sudden increase in the severity of violence, or emotional, such as partners' flagrant affairs with other women. Sudden increases in the severity of violence may break through a woman's prior efforts at minimization and may shock a woman into realizing the potential lethality of her partner's actions. While slaps, kicks, and even beatings may be rationalized as confusing, regrettable aspects of a relationship, stabbings and threats with loaded guns are significantly more blatant violations of personal safety. As one woman said:

> It was like a pendulum. He'd swing to the extremes both ways. He'd get drunk and beat me up, then he'd get sober and treat me like a queen. One day he put a gun to my head and pulled the trigger. It wasn't loaded. But that's when I decided I'd had it. I sued for separation of property. I knew what was coming again, so I got out. I didn't want to. I still loved the guy, but I knew I had to for my own sanity (Ferraro & Johnson, 1983, p. 331).

At the emotional level, bonding to an abuser is sometimes facilitated when periods of love and contrition are interspersed with phases of tension building and battering (Walker, 1979). Dutton and Painter (1981) refer to the traumatic bonding that can occur as a consequence of intermittent violence followed by kindness. Living with "a pendulum" perpetuates hope for many women. When episodes of kindness and affection diminish or disappear, women may begin to question the nature of their relationships. The disappearance of any outward signs of emotional commitment from their partners, combined with an awareness of their partners' sexual infidelities, may lead women to reevaluate their strategies of accommodation. One woman who left her abuser to stay in a shelter said:

> At first, you know, we used to have so much fun together. He has kind've, you know, a magnetic personality; he can be really charming. But it isn't fun anymore. Since the baby came, it's changed completely. He just wants me to stay at home, while he goes out with his friends. He doesn't even talk to me, most of the time . . . No, I don't really love him anymore, not like I did.

In the stage of ambivalence, prior efforts to control behavior may give way to strategies of controlling the violence that focus less on self-blame and more on protection. One such strategy is selective fighting back. Women's violence against men has been a controversial topic in the literature, with a small group of researchers claiming parity or even greater violence by women against men (Straus & Gelles, 1990). The few detailed examinations of violence by women that do exist demonstrate that women usually use physical violence as an episodic defensive tactic, rather than a habitual offensive strategy of domination (Berke et al., 1983; Saunders, 1988; Norris, 1994; Dobash et al., 1992; Campbell et al., 1994). Selective fighting back may be used to demonstrate resistance and lack of acceptance of abuse. It is not usually effective in stopping male violence, and it may even escalate abuse.

Occasionally, however, fighting back is an effective strategy in deterring violence by male partners. One woman, in describing her perception of the police response to her call, recounted her successful use of defensive violence as follows:

> He had his arms around me and . . . and I didn't want him to get the loaded gun. So I shot him to get him to let me go and leave me alone . . . I just looked at them [the police] and I said, "I was tired of being hit. I wasn't going to be hit anymore" . . . I told him that I wasn't going to be hit again because I had been married to two other abusive husbands and I'm just, I'm tired of it.

And how is your relationship now?

> It's very, very good: quite stable. We have plans you know, going on ahead and staying married and being together . . . You couldn't ask for a happier, more content couple.

The use of defensive violence in this instance is unusual both in terms of its effectiveness and in terms of the absence of any punitive response by the criminal justice system. Both the woman and her husband received alcohol counseling and stopped drinking after the shooting incident, which had occurred after two years of wife abuse and heavy drinking by both partners.

The vast majority of women who employ defensive violence are less fortunate, however. When their response to abuse involves minor property damage or assault without injury, they are usually arrested for misdemeanor violence. When the women's response becomes lethal, they are almost always charged with homicide and later sentenced to prison.

Another strategy in the ambivalence stage is to leave the relationship. In contrast to popular views of battering, more women are battered *after* they leave a relationship than during it. According to National Crime Survey data, most victims of battering are divorced or separated from their assailants (Lehnen & Skogan, 1981). Attempts to leave a violent man are dangerous; women are more likely to be killed while trying to leave a relationship than by trying to remain in it.

While most women in violent relationships eventually attempt to leave, the first attempts do not usually result in permanent separation. Shelters for battered women report that about half their residents return to the relationships they have fled (Pagelow, 1984). Women return for a variety of reasons, including fear, continuing emotional involvement, desire to keep the family together, and lack of viable alternatives. Generally, the process of leaving begins after accommodation strategies have begun to break down. Women usually make between five and seven attempts to leave before they leave for good.

A violent man's pleas and promises are commonly cited by women as reasons for returning. Such promises are almost always never kept, however. As one woman explained:

> Every time I tried to take my kids home with me, get away from him, either he would drink and be there with my parents, he would come with his mother, and they would say, "come home" he would cry, and say he would never do it again, and I'd go home, and two days later, my other black eye would be goin' away, and he would say, "why did you tell them? why did you go to your mom, why did you have to tell them, they have nothing to do with our problems," and it just continued.

Other women try to get their abusers to leave but find that the abusers keep returning and that they beg to come back and threaten those women who refuse to take them back.

> Sometimes, you know, [it] gets so bad sometimes, I just take him to [town], and tell him to go home, and go, you know, and he won't get out until you leave him. And he'll come back, you know, bother you, call us, or he'll threaten that he's gonna' burn the house down, or lay there and shoot everybody that comes in the house, and stuff like that.

A significant factor in determining a woman's ability to leave is her economic independence. Battering crosses all classes, races, occupations, and nationalities. While celebrity status and seven-digit incomes do not protect women from battering, economic independence is an essential factor in the ability to terminate a violent relationship. In Johnson's (1992) study of 426 battered women, income and employment were found to be more important to decisions to leave violent men than psychological characteristics, such as self-esteem. Of the 85 women in her sample who were unemployed, severely abused, and whose husbands earned over $10,000, 88 percent returned to their abusers after leaving a shelter (Johnson, 1992, p. 173). As Johnson notes:

> A battered woman with few or no marketable skills or access to employment may perceive her alternatives inside the marriage as being more rewarding than alternatives outside the relationship, even though she is subjected to severe abuse. No abuser is violent 24 hours a day, and the victim may evaluate her costs and benefits and decide that it would be less costly to stay with an abuser who is financially capable of supporting her and her dependents. In such cases, the woman's economic needs may take precedence over her physical and emotional need to be free from abuse (1992, p. 175).

Women's decision making reflects relational as well as individual needs (Ferraro & Pope, 1994). When a woman's abuser is unemployed, leaving the relationship will probably not decrease her children's economic well-being. An abuser who provides a high level of income to a woman who does not work outside the home, however, poses the threat of deprivation if she tries to leave. Such men also have the means to challenge maternal custody and, according to Chesler's research (1986), usually succeed. Women who have been most obedient to traditional sex-role ideology, devoting their lives to mothering and homemaking, thus face the most difficult obstacles in achieving economic independence and freedom from abusive partners.

Many women discover that although *they* reach a point at which they no longer desire to go on with the relationship, their partners will not let them go. Beyond crying or threatening, some men employ severe violence or psychological torture when women try to leave. It is at this point that some women move beyond ambivalence to the stage of terror.

Terror

At the *terror* stage, women perceive their abusers as possessing superhuman power to control and destroy them. Constant surveillance, threats, and punishments convince these women that the men they live with pose an omnipotent and omnipresent danger. It is important to note that this terror is not mere fantasy on the women's part. It is based on experiences that would be categorized as terrorism if they involved military opponents. The perception that there is no escape from this terror is based on concrete encounters intended to demonstrate the woman's lack of alternatives. One woman who told her husband that she was going to leave him was given the following "lesson."

> He made me get in the car and drove me way out in the middle of nowhere, out in the desert, and made me get out of the car and kneel on the ground. He put the gun at the back of my head and cocked it and said, "if you ever try to leave me, I'll kill you."

Other women are exposed to the murder of pets and death threats against their children. One woman who recanted her courtroom testimony regarding her assault informed me that her partner had said that he would cut out her son's liver if she persisted with the prosecution. Prior to this threat, the husband had driven her to a remote location and bragged to her about committing a similar murder. Another woman was threatened as follows:

> "If you try to leave me, first I'll take [their daughter] and make you watch me kill her, and then I'll kill you." I didn't know it at the time, but he was saying the same thing to her.

These terrorist tactics convince most women that leaving an abuser is more dangerous for them and their children than staying. It is at this point that women enter a period of despair, characterized by use of prescription and illegal drugs and alcohol and thoughts of suicide. Physicians and psychiatrists who are untrained in the phenomenon of battering often prescribe psychotropic medication to hide the symptoms of depression and posttraumatic stress syndrome (Kurz & Stark, 1988). Many women begin to view suicide as their only alternative.

> There was one time I thought about shootin' myself, and in fact I had the gun in my mouth, and I was gonna' pull the trigger, and then I thought about [daughter] having to be raised by him, without me there, and it stopped me. Several times, I came close to doin' it, but every time, I thought about her. I thought about doin' a lot of different things. I thought about taking medication, but somethin' stopped me every time. One time in [country] I thought about driving off a mountain, but I think I just chickened out. I thought about it several times. To me, it was the only solution. But I think [daughter] would've really gotten it bad, because I wasn't there to protect her.

At this point of despair, women find that external, decisive intervention, such as police arrest, is most desired and most to be mistrusted. The distrust stems from the women's perception that such arrests will not only lead to more violence, but that the arrests will increase their vulnerability to such violence. As one woman said, "I don't think anything can help."

Homicide

Homicide is not a "strategy for survival," because it is not consciously planned. Women who resort to lethality in their struggle for survival are not strategically calculating the best method to ensure their safety. It is relevant to discuss homicide, however, since it is increasingly the outcome when other survival strategies fail. Overwhelmingly, it is an outcome that does not benefit the battered woman, whether she is sen-

tenced to prison or remains free. Homicide is not a solution that leads to peace and happiness.

. . . [M]ost homicides committed by battered women occur in the context of an immediate confrontation. These confrontations often do not meet the legal criteria for self-defense, but they exceed the battered woman's definition of "imminent danger" based on her past experiences. Over the course of a long-term battering relationship, women become adept at reading the cues that predict violent assaults. As one woman, who is currently in prison for killing her abuser, told me:

> I *lived* it, that's how I knew, I'm not ESP, not psychic. I just didn't want him to hurt me anymore. How did I know he was gonna' hurt me? I had been through it so many times [italics added].

Some women when told by their partners that they are going to be severely beaten or killed react in defensive violence that leads to death. In one such case, a woman walked in her door to find her drunk husband lying on the couch pointing a gun at her and saying, "You're gonna' die bitch." He threw the gun at her, and she shot him. She later was charged with second-degree murder. The prosecutor said that since she had the gun, she should have walked back out the door. Another woman awoke in the middle of the night to find her estranged husband pointing a gun at her. She alleged that he turned the gun around, put her hand on the trigger, and shot himself. She also was charged with second-degree murder.

The same cultural context that encourages women to remain married and denies adequate protection from abuse reacts punitively when battered women kill. When death of the abuser is the final outcome of a battering relationship, most women are sent to prison. There are approximately 2,000 women serving prison time in the United States for defending themselves against a batterer (MCTFADA, 1994, p. 4). Since the late 1970s, efforts have been initiated to educate criminal justice personnel about the impact of battering. Now a few states have laws that require judges to admit testimony about battering when it is relevant to the defense of women who kill. The National Clearinghouse on Battered Women's Self-Defense keeps records and literature on efforts to provide alternatives to incarceration. Currently, there are efforts under way in many states to require review of such cases for consideration of clemency. Most of these women pose no threat to society, and they are often separated from their children who have already lost one parent.

Even women who are not sentenced to prison for homicide continue to suffer after the death of their abusers. If they blamed themselves for being battered, they torture themselves for killing their abuser. Both their love and their fear survive the physical death of the partner. Three women who killed their abusers described their feelings as follows.

> I was screaming for help, someone to call the ambulance. It took almost an hour. They pulled me away from him. It was just like a nightmare . . . I never did hurt him, I never did try to fight back or anything, I loved him so much. . . . and when I think about it, I think to myself, I didn't do that, I didn't do that. No, at times I still do love him, sometimes I think I'm crazy, after all the things that I went through, all the pain.

> Sometimes I don't even know if I'm comin' or goin'. I try not to cry in front of the kids, it's mostly at night that I have to go through all this. Sometimes, I just get to the point that—I miss him, I miss him a lot. No matter what he put me through, I miss him. There are days where I wonder, why am I alive, stuff like that.

> Even when he's dead, he got me . . . he still has this control over me, I still catch myself saying, "Oh, I can't do that, [husband] won't let me do that." I feel like he's watching me still, I catch myself looking.

For these women, the scars of being battered and the grief of losing a partner to whom they were bonded will last for many years.

They escaped with their lives, but they remain lonely, fearful, and guilt-ridden. Their stories, however, may be helpful to women in the earlier stages of battering relationships who are looking for support.

SUCCESSFUL SURVIVAL STRATEGIES

Given the overwhelming barriers to escape, it is amazing that women do survive battering relationships. Factors that facilitate survival depend on the available resources, the current context of the relationship, and the women's stage of engagement. The most important aspect of the context is the batterer's level of dependency. Men who are extremely dependent emotionally on their partners are difficult to change or to leave. They will not accept a woman's decision to end the relationship, often responding with "If I can't have you, no one else will." They stalk, harass, threaten, and often assault or kill the women for whom they proclaim undying love. This drastic response requires drastic survival strategies, which disrupt women's lives. It is, of course, true that battered women should not be the ones to leave their homes, friends, and jobs. However, they cannot depend on their partner's fear of arrest for protection. When it is clear that men will continue to prey on their partners, regardless of the expressed wishes and efforts by women to separate, the most realistic strategy, under current law, is for women to leave and begin new lives. In fact, during the course of my research, several women with children left their communities and assumed new identities in new locations. The shelter network operates like a modern version of the Underground Railroad acting as a referral and support system for women who need to take radical steps to escape from abusers who are determined to own and control them, and who need to protect themselves and their children (Ferraro & Johnson, 1985).

In terms of social policy, a more desirable approach would be to require repetitive batterers and stalkers to leave the state in which their partner resides. Such men could be banished from the state, logged onto FBI data files, similar to those kept on federal fugitives, and arrested if they set foot in the prohibited state. Violation of banishment orders could result in lengthy prison terms. The danger of this approach is that women in other states would be unaware of the violent pasts of these men. Banishment is also inconsistent with current criminal justice policies, which prohibit punishments that infringe on an individual's right to serve a specified sentence length and then continue life as a free person. Because banishment is an unlikely prospect, women will continue to bear the burden of escape from persistently violent men.

For women involved with violent men who are not intent on keeping or killing their abusive partners, strategies that focus on the development of emotional and practical resources seem to offer the best hope of escape. Several studies, for example, have found that the major reason cited by women who leave shelters to return to abusive partners is the lack of alternative housing and income (Roy, 1977; Schechter, 1982; Johnson, 1992). Furthermore, because many women need legal assistance in obtaining child support and spousal maintenance and because attorneys usually request retainers of between $1,500 and $3,000 for contested divorce cases, many women are effectively prohibited from obtaining the legal help needed to permanently escape from an abusive relationship. Legal aid services not only are limited and involve lengthy waiting periods, but qualification for such aid is often based on family income. One result is that battered women who are married to men with above-poverty-level incomes are disqualified from receiving such assistance. Battered women who are not legally married to their abusers are usually not able to obtain any court-ordered financial assistance when they leave.

The amount of low-income housing, especially for women with children, is far from adequate. One source estimates that 50 percent of homeless women are escaping violent relationships (Schneider, 1994). Because shelters provide only temporary refuge, they cannot accommodate the large numbers of women seeking assistance. To establish a societal commitment to battered women would necessitate increasing the availability of low-income housing.

The list of resources required for survival outside of a battering relationship is lengthy. Women need day care, health care, transportation, housing, clothing, food, utility assistance, and employment. Many women need job training after having devoted themselves to bearing and rearing children and maintaining the household. In the current economic environment, women, especially older women, who have nontechnical or entry-level job skills will be noncompetitive in the job market. A basic level of income maintenance will be required for many women who are unable to obtain steady employment (Albelda et al., 1988).

While the idea that battered women need therapy has been rejected by most advocates and analysts (Dobash & Dobash, 1992; Martin, 1976), women do need advocacy, information, and support. Because of the obtuse character of the legal processes involved in filing criminal charges, obtaining orders of protection, and maintaining child custody, it is difficult to obtain the necessary information that women need for effective advocacy. Women need advocates familiar with the legal system to help make phone calls and fill out appropriate forms. While individual therapy focusing on the women's psychological issues may not be appropriate, it is important to recognize that women who have been battered have experienced both trauma and loss. These experiences create depression, confusion, and grief, so the women need emotional support in order to successfully return to a violence-free life. For some of these women therapy may be entirely appropriate.

SUMMARY

Realistically, with all the practical and emotional resources provided, some women will continue to live with violent men. For an outsider to the relationship, it is difficult to know how to be most helpful in these situations. It is important to recognize that every woman has her own complex understanding of her situation and needs that is not accessible to outsiders. The most beneficial form of assistance will depend on the woman's level of engagement with the relationship. If she is still in the stages of ardor or accommodation, any demands that she recognize and act on the danger of her situation will only increase her sense of alienation. It is especially important that agency representatives, such as law enforcement officers and social workers, respect the ability of women to interpret their situation and make choices that are best for them.

The best survival strategies for women in violent relationships cannot be divorced from the social and cultural context that supports intimate violence and the subordination of women. In this respect, it is essential that any discussion of women's experiences not overshadow the macrolevel forces that encourage male violence against women and limit the practical and emotional options available to them.

REFERENCES

Albelda, Randy, McCrate, Elaine, Melendez, Edwin, Lapidus, June, & the Center for Popular Economics. (1988). *Mink coats don't trickle down.* Boston: South End.

Barnett, Ola W., & LaViolette, Alyce D. (1993). *It could happen to anyone: Why battered women stay.* Newbury Park, CA: Sage.

Berk, R. A., Berk, S. F., Loseke, D. R., & Rauma, D. (1983). Mutual combat and other family violence myths. In D. Finkelhor, R. J. Gelles, G. T. Hotaling, & M. A. Straus (Eds.), *The dark side of families: Current family violence research.* Beverly Hills, CA: Sage.

Campbell, Jacquelyn C., Miller, Paul, & Cardwell, Mary M. (1994). Relationship status of battered women over time. *Journal of Family Violence,* 9(2): 99–111.

Chaudhuri, M., & Daly, K. (1992). Do restraining orders help? Battered women's experience with male violence and legal process. In E. S. Buzawa & C. G. Buzawa (Eds.), *Domestic violence: The changing criminal response* (pp. 227–252). Westport, CT: Auburn House.

Chesler, Phyllis. (1986). *Mothers on trial.* New York: McGraw-Hill.

Dobash, R. E., & Dobash, R. P. (1979). *Violence against wives: A case against the patriarchy.* New York: Free Press.

Dobash, R. E., & Dobash, R. P. (1992). *Women, violence, and social change.* London: Routledge.

Dobash, Russell P., Dobash, R. Emerson, Wilson, Margo, & Daly, Martin. (1992). The myth of the symmetrical nature of domestic violence. *Social Problems, 39:* 71–91.

Dutton, Donald, & Painter, Susan. (1981). Traumatic bonding: The development of emotional attachments in battered women and other relationships of intermittent abuse. *Victimology* 6(1–4): 139–155.

Faludi, Susan. (1991). *Backlash: The undeclared war against American women.* New York: Doubleday.

Ferraro, K. J. (1989a). The legal response to woman battering in the United States. In J. Hanmer, J. Radford, & E. Stanko (Eds.), *Women, policing and male violence* (pp. 155–184). London: Routledge.

———. (1989b). Policing woman battering. *Social Problems,* 6(1): 6174.

Ferraro, Kathleen, & Boychuk, Tascha. (1992). The court's response to interpersonal violence: A comparison of intimate and nonintimate assault. In E. S. Buzawa & C. G. Buzawa (Eds.). *Domestic violence: The changing criminal justice response* (pp. 209–226). Westport, CT: Auburn House.

Ferraro, Kathleen, & Johnson, John M. (1983). How women experience battering: The process of victimization, *Social Problems* 30(3): 325–339.

——— (1985). The new underground railroad. *Studies in Symbolic Interaction, 6:* 377–386.

Ferraro, Kathleen, & Pope, Lucille. (1993). Irreconcilable differences: Battered women, police, and the law. In N. Z. Hilton (Ed.). *Legal responses to wife assault* (pp. 96–123). Newbury Park, CA: Sage.

Gondolf, E. W. (1990). Battered women as survivors. Holmes Beach, FL: Learning Publications.

Harlow, C. W. (1991). *Female victims of violent crime.* Rockville, MD: U.S. Department of Justice.

Hoff, Lee A. (1990). *Battered women as survivors.* London: Routledge.

Johnson, Ida M. (1992). Economic, situational, and psychological correlates of the decision-making process of battered women. *Families in Society, 73*(3): 168–176.

———. (1994). *Next time she'll be dead: Battering and how to stop it.* Boston: Beacon Press.

Kelly, Liz. (1987). The continuum of sexual violence. In J. Hanmer & M. Maynard (Eds.), *Women, violence and social control* (pp. 46–60). Atlantic Highlands, NJ: Humanities Press.

———. (1968a). How women define their experiences of violence. In K. Yllö & M. Bograd (Eds.), *Feminist perspectives on wife abuse* (pp. 114–132). Newbury Park, CA: Sage.

Klein, A. (1994). *Recidivism in a population of court-restrained batterers after two years.* Unpublished dissertation, Northeastern University.

Kurz, Demie, & Stark, Evan. (1988). Not so benign neglect: The medical response to battering. In K. Yllö & M. Bograd (Eds.) *Feminist perspectives on wife abuse* (pp. 249–268). Newbury Park, CA: Sage.

Lehnen, R. G., & Skogan, W. G. (1981). The national crime survey. In R. G. Lehnen & W. G. Skogan (Eds.), *Working papers: Vol. 1. Current and historical perspectives.*

Loseke, Donileen R., & Spencer E. Cahill. (1984). The social construction of deviance: experts on battered women. *Social Problems, 31:* 296–310.

Manley, N. J. (1982). Battered women: The victim's perceptions. Unpublished master's thesis, California State University, Sacramento.

Marano, Hara Estroff. (1993). Inside the heart of marital violence. *Psychology Today, 26*(6): 48, 89–91.

Martin, D. (1976). *Battered wives.* San Francisco, CA: Glide Publications.

———. (1981). *Battered wives.* San Francisco, CA: Volcano Press, Inc.

MCTFADA (Maricopa County Task Force Against Domestic Abuse) (1994). Why don't batterers leave? MCTFADA Newsletter, p. 5.

Norris, Lynn. (1994). Dangerously equal or equally dangerous? An analysis of women's violence against male intimate partners. Unpublished master's thesis, Arizona State University, Tempe.

Pagelow, M. D. (1984). *Family violence.* New York: Praeger.

Ptacek, James. (1988). Why do men batter their wives? In Kersti Yllö & Michele Bograd (Eds.). *Feminist Perspectives on Wife Abuse* (Ch. 6, pp. 133–157). Newbury Park, CA: Sage.

Radford, Jill, & Russell, Diana E. H. (1992). *Femicide.* New York: Twayne.

Roy, Maria. (1977). *Battered women.* New York: Van Nostrand Reinhold.

Saunders, D. G. (1988a). Other 'Truths' about domestic violence: A reply to McNeely and Robinson-Simpson. *Social Work.* March–April, 179.

———. (1988b). Wife abuse, husband abuse or mutual combat? In K. Yllö & M. Bograd (Eds), *Feminist perspectives on wife abuse* (pp. 90–113). Newbury Park, CA: Sage.

Schechter, Susan. (1982). *Women and male violence.* New York: Macmillan.

Schneider, Elizabeth. (1994). Legal reform efforts for battered women. Cited in MCTFADA Newsletter, p. 5.

Schwartz, M. D. (1988a). Ain't got no class: Universal risk theories of battering. *Contemporary Crises, 12:* 373–392.

Schwartz, M. D. (1988b). Marital status and woman abuse theory. *Journal of Family Violence, 3:* 239–259.

Straus, M. A., & Gelles, R. (1990). How violent are American families? Estimates from the National Family Violence Resurvey and other studies. In M. A. Straus & R. J. Gelles (Eds.), *Physical violence in American families* (pp. 95–132). New Brunswick, NJ: Transaction Publishers.

Tifft, L. L. (1993). *Battering of women: The failure of intervention and the case for prevention.* Boulder, CO: Westview Press.

Walker, L. E. (1979). *The battered woman.* New York: Harper and Row.

Wesson, Mimi. (1994). Digging up the roots of violence. *Women's Review of Books, 11*(6): 1, 3.

Don't Call It Child Abuse
If It's Really Poverty

Douglas J. Besharov with Lisa A. Laumann

In 1993, about 3 million reports of suspected child abuse or child neglect were made to the police and child protective agencies. This reading argues that a large proportion of these reports—between a quarter to a half—is more properly considered a symptom of poverty, and is more appropriately handled outside the nation's child protection system. Helping these families does not require mandatory reporting laws, involuntary investigations, central registers of reports, and psychologically oriented treatment interventions.

For me, this is not an abstract issue. I prosecuted my first child abuse case 25 years ago, when the issue was far from public and professional attention. I have seen my share of brutally battered children, with open wounds and broken bones; of sexually abused children, who trembled at the touch of an adult; and of filthy, melancholy children, who received less care than a child provides to a hamster. I have spent a large part of my professional life trying to protect these children, first as a prosecutor, then as director of a state legislative committee, and, later, as the first director of the U.S. National Center on Child Abuse and Neglect.

But throughout this period, I have also seen families weakened, if not torn apart, by a system that fails to recognize the overlap between what we now label as child maltreatment and the

Douglas J. Besharov with Lisa A. Laumann, "Don't Call It Child Abuse If It's Really Poverty." Paper prepared for the conference "Social Policies for Children," Woodrow Wilson School of Public and International Affairs, Princeton University (Washington, DC: The American Enterprise Institute for Public Policy Research, 1996), pp. 1–30. Reprinted with the permission of The American Enterprise Institute for Public Policy Research, Washington, DC 20036

conditions of poverty—especially among families headed by single mothers. In this [reading], I argue that society should cease treating these disadvantaged families as if they suffer from some form of psychological deviancy and, instead, should develop intervention strategies that better address their broader problems.

This [reading] is divided into four sections: The first section summarizes what is known about the nature and extent of child abuse and neglect. The second section describes the available evidence showing the overlap between poverty and child maltreatment. The third section presents a framework for understanding different levels of government intervention and proposes an alternative to child protective intervention in poverty-related cases. The last section proposes a plan for implementation and assesses its political feasibility.

I. NATURE AND EXTENT

The first step in policy making in this area, one hopes, is understanding the nature and scope of child abuse and child neglect. But this is not such a simple matter, considering that maltreatment usually occurs in the privacy of the home. Hence, to understand the size of this problem, one must make distinctions among:

1. *Annual prevalence*—the total number of children who have been abused or neglected at least once in a particular year (whether or not reported to the authorities).[1]
2. *Reported cases*—the total number of families or children[2] reported under formal procedures to child protective agencies (usually a social service agency but sometimes a law enforcement one).
3. *Substantiated (or "indicated") reports*—the total number of reports (counted either as children or families) that were determined, after an investigation, to be supported by specific evidence. (The legal test is often "some credible evidence.")

As will be shown, each category results in a vastly different estimate of the amount of child maltreatment—but taken together, they provide a useful portrait of the situation.

Prevalence

Two major efforts have been made to estimate the total number of abused and neglected children (whether or not reported to the authorities): "The National Study of the Incidence and Severity of Child Abuse and Neglect" (1980)[3] and the "Study of National Incidence and Prevalence of Child Abuse and Neglect" (1986).[4] Both were funded by the federal government's National Center on Child Abuse and Neglect and both were conducted by Westat, Inc. (A third National Incidence Study is now being conducted, also by Westat.)

All three studies use essentially the same methodology: In a stratified sample of counties, a broadly representative sample of professionals who serve children was asked whether, during the study period, the children they had seen in their professional capacities appeared to have been abused or neglected.[5] This methodology does not allow Westat to estimate the number of children seen by nonprofessionals, such as friends, neighbors, and relatives. Thus, even if these studies had no other problems, the methodology inherently underestimates the prevalence of maltreatment because it does not count those children whose condition was either not seen or not recognized by a professional. (Complicated issues of sample frame and weighting also limit the ability of these studies to make more precise estimates of prevalence.)

Nevertheless, these two federally sponsored studies are the best source of information about unreported child abuse and neglect. Moreover, there is substantial internal consistency between the findings of the two studies, conducted six years apart, as well as between them and data about officially reported cases. Thus, it seems reasonable to use them to provide a general picture of the nature, extent, and distribution of the

various types of child maltreatment. What do they tell us?

About 1 million children were victims of child abuse or neglect in 1986. (That would be 14.8 per 1,000 children.) Both of the Westat studies had a rigorous definition of countable cases that required that the child suffer demonstrable harm that lasted at least 48 hours (e.g., bruises, emotional distress, or depression).[6] However, since child protective agencies accept cases of "threatened harm" to children, the 1986 study also employed an additional (or optional) definition which included cases where the child's "health or safety was endangered through abusive or neglectful treatment." This broader definition resulted in about 500,000 additional countable cases.

Westat examined the distribution of child maltreatment by sex, age, race, and family size. Except for sexual abuse, rates did not differ greatly between males and females. Females were, however, about three times more likely to be sexually abused than males (2.9 per 1,000 female children versus .9 per 1,000 male children).

The study found that the risk of maltreatment increased with age (2.4 per 1,000 children ages 0 to 2 versus 21.8 per 1,000 children ages 12 to 14). However, this may be an artifact of the study methodology, which relied on what professionals saw, and, since they tend to see older children who are in day care, schools, and so forth, there is a natural bias against finding maltreatment among infants and toddlers. Also, the large proportion of educational neglect cases (described in a moment), which, by definition, only involve older children, also raises the average age.

Rates of maltreatment did not differ by race, a surprising result given the relationship between reported maltreatment and poverty, discussed below. It may be that Westat's definitions are so broad that they pick up many cases of problematic child rearing among the middle class. The only difference found was that blacks were marginally more likely than whites to die as a result of abuse or neglect (.01 per 1,000 white children versus .05 per 1,000 black children). But because there were so few fatalities, this difference was not found to be statistically significant.

Family size likewise did not seem to be associated with differing rates of child maltreatment.

A relatively small proportion of maltreated children suffered battering, sexual abuse, or serious neglect. The Westat studies establish six categories of child maltreatment. The largest proportion of maltreated children experienced educational neglect (31 percent), followed by physical abuse (29 percent), physical neglect (18 percent), emotional abuse (17 percent), sexual abuse (13 percent), and emotional neglect (5 percent).[7] The majority of the maltreated children found by the study suffered from educational neglect (31 percent) and emotional maltreatment (both abuse and neglect) (22 percent)—situations of concern, certainly, but probably not what comes to mind when the public thinks of "child abuse" and "child neglect."

The vast majority of maltreated children suffered from nonserious conditions. The Westat studies establish four categories of severity: fatal, serious, moderate, or inferred.

Fatal: death as a result of child maltreatment during the study period.

Serious: a life-threatening condition, requiring treatment to prevent long-term impairment.

Moderate: injuries or impairments for which observable symptoms persisted for at least 48 hours (e.g., bruises, depression, or emotional distress).

Inferred: the nature of the maltreatment itself gives reasonable cause to assume that injuries or impairment have occurred.

By far, the greatest proportion of children suffered moderate injuries (73 percent). Only about .1 percent of maltreated children died as a result of child abuse or neglect. Fifteen percent of the children experienced serious injuries and 11 percent had injuries that were inferred.[8]

Although rating the cases by their severity is extremely helpful, some questionable classifications were made. For example, the definition of "serious" sexual abuse excluded penile penetration if the child was not considered to have suffered serious emotional trauma. As a result, only 6 percent of all sexual abuse cases were considered serious, even though over one third of them included penile penetration.[9]

Conversely, the definition of "serious" emotional neglect included the delaying or refusal of psychiatric care and the permitting of maladaptive behavior. While these conditions might be a cause for child protective concern, they are hardly the equivalent of child battering. Yet, the study labels them both "serious."

Public and professional definitions of child maltreatment seem to have expanded to include more cases of "moderate" harm to children. Although Westat counted a 49 percent increase in the prevalence of child maltreatment between its first and second studies, most of this increase was among cases of "moderate" physical abuse and neglect and educational neglect (with no corresponding increase among "fatal" or "serious" cases).[10] Hence, it seems reasonable to conclude that the level of child maltreatment did not grow nearly as much as suggested by the findings of the second incidence study. As Westat is careful to note, the increase "probably reflected an increase in the likelihood that professionals will recognize maltreatment rather than an increase in the actual occurrence of maltreatment."[11]

Awareness of possible child sexual abuse seems to have increased between 1980 and 1986. In only six years, the rate of *observed* sexual abuse cases nearly tripled, increasing from .7 per 1,000 children to 1.9 per 1,000 children (or from 44,700 to 119,200 victims).[12] It seems highly improbable that the underlying prevalence of sexual abuse could increase almost three-fold in only six years. Hence, much of this increase is probably due to greater professional awareness of this heretofore hidden problem.

The Westat statistics are for all cases of child maltreatment seen by the surveyed professionals—whether reported or not. How many of these cases are reported?

Reported Cases

Since the early 1960s, all states have passed laws that mandate designated professionals to report specified types of child maltreatment. Over the years, both the range of designated professionals and the scope of reportable conditions have been steadily expanded.

Initially, mandatory reporting laws applied only to physicians—who were only required to report "serious physical injuries" and "nonaccidental injuries." In the ensuing years, however, increased public and professional attention, sparked in part by the number of abused children revealed by these initial reporting laws, led many states to expand their reporting requirements. Now, almost all states have laws which require the reporting of all forms of suspected child maltreatment, including physical abuse, physical neglect, emotional maltreatment, and, of course, sexual abuse and exploitation.[13]

Under threat of civil and criminal penalties, these laws require most professionals who serve children to report suspected child abuse and neglect. About 20 states require all citizens to report, but in all states, any citizen is permitted to report. In addition, there have been extensive public awareness campaigns and professional education programs.

It is surprisingly difficult to get nationwide information about official reports of child maltreatment. Federal efforts to collect state data have been minimally funded,[14] and, actually, were suspended a number of times. Filling the gap have been a number of private organizations, primarily the National Committee for Prevention of Child Abuse (NCPCA) and the American Public Welfare Association (APWA).

In essence, each of these efforts uses the same methodology: a survey of state child protective agencies to determine how many reports were made in a particular year. This is not as easy as it sounds. Definitions and procedures vary sharply. For example, some states use family-based reports, while others use child-based reports. Some states collect their data on a calendar-year basis, while others use a fiscal year.[15] Compiling a national total requires a fair amount of interpretation and, thus, presents opportunity for error. Nevertheless, like the two incidence studies, there is a sufficient amount of consistency across the various studies to tell a reasonably reliable story.

In 1993, about 3 million reports of children suspected of being abused or neglected were made.[16] This is a 20-fold increase since 1963, when about 150,000 children were reported to the authorities. As we will see, however, this figure is bloated by reports that later turn out to be unfounded and by substantial double counting.

A relatively small percentage of reported cases involve serious harms to children. AHA found that, in 1986, about 10 percent of physical abuse cases (less than 3 percent of all substantiated reports) involved serious injury to the child, which is consistent with Westat's prevalence findings.[17]

Professionals still fail to report many of the children they see who have observable signs of child abuse and neglect. According to Westat, in 1986, 56 percent of apparently abused and neglected children, about 500,000 children, were not reported to the authorities. This is a decline in nonreporting from 1980, when professionals failed to report nearly two-thirds of the maltreated children they saw.[18] (The study methodology, which involved asking professionals about children they had seen in their professional capacities, did not allow Westat to estimate the number of children seen by nonprofessionals, let alone their nonreporting rate.)

Professionals seem to report most of the children they see who are suffering from serious forms of abuse and neglect. Basically, the more serious the maltreatment, the more likely a report. The surveyed professionals failed to report only 15 percent of the fatal or serious physical abuse cases they saw. They also failed to report about 28 percent of the sexually abused children they saw, and 40 percent of the moderate physical abuse cases they saw.

Nonreporting was concentrated in five types of cases: educational neglect (85 percent not reported); emotional neglect (76 percent); moderate physical neglect cases (75 percent); serious physical neglect cases (67 percent); and emotional abuse (56 percent).[19]

This means that, in 1986, about 2,000 children with observable physical injuries severe enough to require hospitalization were not reported, over 100,000 children with moderate physical injuries were also not reported, as were over 30,000 apparently sexually abused children.

These results are difficult to interpret, however, in part because of the problems with Westat's classifications of severity described above. In addition, the large proportion of unreported educational neglect cases reflects the fact that most communities do not consider them to be within the jurisdiction of child protective agencies.

Many people ask whether this vast increase in reporting signals a rise in the incidence of child maltreatment. Although some observers believe that deteriorating economic and social conditions have contributed to a rise in the level of abuse and neglect, it is impossible to tell for sure. So many maltreated children previously went unreported that earlier reporting statistics do not provide a reliable baseline against which to make comparisons. One thing is clear, however; the great bulk of reports now received by child protective agencies would not be made but for the passage of mandatory reporting laws and the media campaigns that accompanied them.

Although child protective programs still have major problems, some of which are discussed in this paper, the results of this 20-year effort to upgrade them have been unquestionably impressive. All states now have specialized child protective agencies to receive and investigate reports, and treatment services for maltreated children and their parents have been expanded substantially. Federal and state expenditures for child protective programs and associated foster care services now exceed 6 billion a year.[20]

As a result, many thousands of children have been saved from death and serious injury. The best estimate is that over the past 20 years, child abuse and neglect deaths have fallen from over 3,000 a year—and perhaps as many as 5,000—to about 1,100 a year.[21] In New York state, for example, within five years of the passage of a comprehensive reporting law which also created specialized investigative staffs, there was a 50 percent reduction in child fatalities, from about 200 a year to under 100.[22]

This is not meant to minimize the remaining problem. Even at this level, maltreatment is the sixth largest cause of death for children under 14.[23]

Substantiated Reports

After a report is made, a child protective agency is supposed to investigate it to determine whether there is reason to be concerned about the child and, if so, what action should be taken. All states make this a formal process which concludes with a determination that the report was "substantiated," "founded," or "indicated" (terminology differs) or, conversely, that the report was "unsubstantiated," "unfounded," or "not indicated."

Collecting data on state substantiation rates is even more difficult than collecting data about raw reports, partly because states do not always keep the information and partly because there can be a long delay between the making of the report and a final decision about its validity. Nevertheless, all the efforts to collect nationwide data on the subject point toward a decline in the substantiation rate in the past 20 years.

Most recently, the National Committee reported that, in 1993, only about 34 percent of the reports received by child protective agencies were substantiated. This is in sharp contrast to 1975, when about 65 percent of all reports were substantiated.[24] Thus, of the approximately

2,989,000 children reported to child protective agencies in 1993, only about 1,016,000 were actually determined to have experienced maltreatment.

But even this is an overestimation. Most states are unable to tell how many reports are repeat reports on the same child. Hence, these national estimates are based on duplicated counts—meaning that repeat reports on the same child are added to the total. In its analysis of the Illinois State Central Registry, the Chapin Hall Center for Children found that within one year about 20 percent of the founded reports were repeat reports.[25] So have other studies.[26]

Subtracting unsubstantiated cases and duplicated cases from the total number of reports reveals a vastly different picture of child abuse and neglect: The three million reports made in 1993 melt down to about 813,000 children involved in substantiated cases of child maltreatment.

This leads to a fundamental question: Since the 1986 Westat study seems to have found about 600,000 substantiated reports,[27] which was about what the American Humane Association found for the same year,[28] was there really a 200,000 increase in substantiated cases in seven years? And, if so, what seems to be driving it? The Westat study currently in progress should tell us.

But this is children—not families. If we want to see how many families are involved in substantiated cases, a better way to gauge caseloads, we need to divide the number of substantiated reports of children by the average number of children in a family. The National Center on Child Abuse and Neglect estimated that, in 1993, there were about 1.7 children per reported family.[29] This means that, if a case is a family, there were about 478,000 cases of substantiated child maltreatment that child protective agencies handled.

As mentioned above, most experts attribute the increase in reports to greater public and professional awareness. But recent increases in social problems such as out-of-wedlock births, inner-city poverty, and drug abuse, may have raised the underlying rates of child maltreat-

ment. On the other hand, a substantial portion of what we call child maltreatment is more properly considered a symptom of poverty and is more appropriately handled outside the nation's quasi-criminal child protection system. The expansion of child protective programs to cover such poverty-related cases could also explain the increase in reports.

II. THE POVERTY CONNECTION

A visit to any child welfare office would suggest a strong relationship between child maltreatment and poverty. And yet, data on income, poverty status, and welfare recipiency is rarely collected in the studies described above. What is available, however, reveals an unambiguous association between maltreatment and poverty.

Income

Across all types of maltreatment, prevalence rates are highest among low-income families. Comparing families with incomes above and below $15,000, the second national incidence study found that the rate of maltreatment was over five times higher in low-income families than high-income families (29.3 versus 5.5 per 1,000 children).[30] Two-thirds (66 percent) of all cases of maltreatment identified by the study involved families with incomes below $15,000. (No further divisions by income were made.)

These low-income families were more concentrated among particular types of maltreatment. They were nine times more likely than high-income families to be involved in cases of educational neglect and physical neglect, but only three to five times more likely across the remaining types of maltreatment.

Poor families also make up the majority of families reported to the authorities. The Virginia Department of Social Services, for example, found that 45 percent of the families reported to the child protective agencies in 1991 had incomes of less than $12,000.[31] (In 1991, the poverty rate for a family of four was $13,924.)

Similarly, in 1976, AHA found (based on incomplete data) that the median family income for reported families was only about one-third of the national median income ($5,051 versus $13,900). Almost 30 percent had incomes below $3,000.[32]

The association is even greater for AFDC (cash welfare) families. In Illinois, for example, 48 percent of the children with founded reports of child abuse or neglect also received AFDC.[33] Likewise, welfare families made up about half of all reported families. Nationwide, AHA found that 49 percent of the families reported for any type of child maltreatment received public assistance, while almost 62 percent of the families reported for neglect received assistance.[34]

Further, Pelton found that AFDC parents who maltreated their children were palpably poorer than AFDC parents who did not. They were, for example, more likely to live in crowded housing and to have to share their child's sleeping spot, and they were less likely to have a shower or a telephone in their home.[35]

Poor children also predominate in foster care. National data on the income of the families of foster children do not exist. To fill this gap, researchers look at the proportion of foster care children who are Title IV–E eligible,[36] that is, whose families received or would have been eligible for AFDC prior to the child's removal from the home. Data from APWA's Voluntary Cooperative Information System (VCIS) show that, in fiscal year 1989, between 55 and 59 percent of the national foster care caseload were Title IV–E eligible.[37] In New York, California, and Michigan, however, the proportion of AFDC children in foster care is considerably higher. In 1992, the percentages of Title IV–E eligible foster children in these states were 72 percent in California, 77 percent in Michigan, and 86 percent in New York.[38] (These three states represented 52 percent of the total foster care caseload.)

A study in Illinois found that children who received AFDC within the first five years of their life were twice as likely as children who did not to be placed in foster care during this period (2 percent versus .8 percent). Title IV–E eligible children made up over 58 percent of the state's foster care population.[39]

The level of poverty-related child protective intervention could grow even higher. Westat's second incidence study found that professionals did not report over 85 percent of the children who had been educationally neglected and 75 percent of the children with moderate cases of physical neglect. As noted earlier, poor children were particularly concentrated in these two types of maltreatment. If greater proportions of these types of "child maltreatment" were reported, an even higher proportion of child protective cases would involve the problems of poverty.

Family Demographics

This sharp connection between poverty and child maltreatment is further concentrated among families headed by single mothers, especially those who had their first babies as unwed teens.

Reported child maltreatment is many times more prevalent among single-parent families than among two-parent families. In Minnesota, for example, families headed by single parents were almost seven times more likely than two-parent families to have founded reports of maltreatment (28.7 per 1,000 children living in single-parent families versus 4.3 per 1,000 children living in two-parent families). About 57 percent of all substantiated victims lived in single-parent homes.[40] In New Jersey, this proportion was even higher (69 percent).[41]

The second Westat showed this relationship by maltreatment type. While less than 24 percent of the nation's children lived in single-parent families in 1986, 36 percent of those with substantiated reports of educational neglect lived in such homes. The proportions of single-parent families among the other maltreatment types were: physical neglect (33 percent); sexual abuse (32 percent); and physical abuse (31 percent).[42]

Reported child maltreatment is more prevalent among families headed by teen mothers than families headed by nonteen mothers. For instance, in Illinois, 7 percent of teen-headed families had founded reports of maltreatment, as compared to only 3 percent of families headed by mothers who delayed their birth until their 20s.[43]

Among mothers on welfare in Illinois, families headed by mothers under 16 years at the time of their first birth were almost twice as likely as those headed by mothers who delayed childbirth until their 20s to have founded reports of maltreatment (16 percent versus 9 percent for a four-year period). The likelihood of maltreatment decreased as the age of the mother increased. Thirteen percent of the welfare families headed by mothers who were 16 to 17 at first birth, 11 percent of those with mothers 18 to 19 at first birth, and 9 percent of those with mothers 20 or over at the time of first birth had founded reports of maltreatment.[44] (A study of foster care children in Oregon found that 83 percent of their biological mothers and 85 percent of their fathers were high school dropouts.)[45]

A strong association exists between race and reported maltreatment. Although the Westat studies found no association between the two, this was probably due to the broad definition of maltreatment that they used. The National Center on Child Abuse and Neglect found that black children were greatly overrepresented in reported cases—making up 27 percent of the substantiated reports.[46] (Blacks comprised about 12 percent of the national population in 1991.)[47] And, according to APWA, black children were even more prevalent among the foster care population: In 1989, 31 percent of the children who entered foster care were black, 54 percent were white, and 11 percent were Hispanic.[48]

A study in Illinois found that black children were almost three times as likely as white and Hispanic children to have a substantiated report of child maltreatment in their first five years of life. (The rates were 85 per 1,000 black children, 29 per 1,000 white children, and 23 per 1,000 Hispanic children).[49]

Endangering Abused Children

Ironically, this overreaction to poverty-related "child maltreatment" can endanger children who are in real jeopardy. Inconsistent as it may seem, given the overuse of child protective programs, workers and judges are deeply conscious of the hazards of foster care. Hence, they hesitate to remove children from their parents' custody except in the most extreme cases. Unfortunately, after dealing with so many cases of social deprivation, caseworkers become desensitized to the obvious warning signals of immediate and serious physical danger. Many children are left in the custody of parents who have repeatedly abused them. One study of child abuse fatalities, for example, described how: "In two of the cases, siblings of the victims had died previously . . . In one family, two siblings of the victim had died mysterious deaths that were undiagnosed. In another family, a twin had died previously of abuse."[50]

The result, all too often, is the child's tragic death. Studies in several states have shown that about 35 to 55 percent of all child fatalities attributed to abuse or neglect involve children previously reported to a child protective agency.[51] In 1993, the NCPCA reported that, of the 1,149 child maltreatment deaths, 42 percent had already been reported to the authorities.[52] Tens of thousands of other children receive serious injuries short of death while under child protective supervision.

Part of the problem is the misuse of the child protective system. Social agencies fail to protect children who need help the most—the victims of physical brutality—by not removing them from their abusive parents. At the same time, they overreact to cases of social deprivation in poor families. In fact, poor, socially deprived children are more likely to be placed in foster care than are abused children. Poor children, in no real danger of physical injury, languish for years in foster care. Living in emotionally traumatic conditions, hundreds of thousands of poor children suffer more harm than if they were simply left at home. When it comes to the plight of these children, we should remember the ancient medical maxim: *Primus, non nocere*—first, do no harm.

Given these realities, many commentators blame poverty for the parents' abusive or neglectful behavior. Certainly, "poverty exposes parents to the increased likelihood of additional stresses that may have deleterious effects upon their capacities to care adequately for their children."[53] However, lest all families be stigmatized, it is important to remember that most poor families do not abuse or neglect their children. In any one year, fewer than one in five welfare families are reported for suspected abuse or neglect.[54]

III. AN ALTERNATIVE INTERVENTION

Past Good Intentions

The harmful use of child protective programs for what is, in essence, a problem of poverty is another example of good intentions gone awry. Socially deprived children living in poor families have been known to public welfare agencies for decades. Until the mid 1970s, though, these children were the responsibility of the welfare caseworkers assigned to *each* AFDC recipient family. But then the provision of cash assistance was separated from the delivery of social services.

Besides providing a more efficient means of distributing AFDC funds, the separation of income maintenance from social services was supposed to upgrade the quality of social services for poor families. The planners had dreams of a greatly expanded network of specialized family service agencies to replace the all-purpose welfare caseworker. Unfortunately, this network of services never appeared. But the need for it remained, so cases of poverty-related maltreatment were transferred to the rapidly growing child protective system. (At the time, state child abuse reporting laws were being

amended to require the reporting of child neglect, including emotional neglect.) Thus, responsibility for AFDC children whose needs were not being met by their parents was assumed by the newly expanded child protection system.

There was a major difference, however, between how the child protection system and the welfare system handle these cases. The welfare caseworker saw the family as the client, and was inclined to view poor child-rearing as a correlate of poverty, requiring aid to the family as a unit. The child protective worker, on the other hand, rightly sees the child as the client, with poor child-rearing as a reason for coercive state intervention. And, most significantly, the two types of caseworkers had entirely different orientations to foster care and court ordered removal. Welfare caseworkers were rarely in court; they were not trained—nor deployed—toward easy access to court and court ordered removal of children from the home. Child protective workers are.

In the context of heightened concern for the "abused" child, giving child protective agencies responsibility for these poverty-related cases of social deprivation inexorably led to more poor children being placed in foster care. (In addition, federal funding for foster care, rather than for in-home services, created an added incentive to resort to foster care.)

In a paper for the U.S. Advisory Board on Child Abuse and Neglect, Leroy Pelton wrote that, ". . . the most effective way to reduce child abuse and neglect would be to raise family income."[55] If only it were that simple.

Normal A. Polansky, Regent's Professor of Social Work at the University of Georgia, is the nation's foremost expert on the relationship between poverty and child maltreatment. Through 15 years of research, he and his colleagues have concluded that the poverty/child maltreatment connection is a complex interaction: "parental personality plays a major role in determining how much income is available [to a family], as well as how it is handled."[56] Polansky's research depicts maltreating parents as

> a group of people with a modal personality: less able to love, less capable of working productively, less open about their feelings, more prone to living planlessly and impulsively, but also susceptible to psychological symptoms and to phases of passive inactivity and numb fatalism. The image is one of men and women who do not cope well with life.[57]

These parents are extremely difficult to reach, let alone successfully treat. As Polansky concludes, programs "aimed simply at increasing income will not solve the problem of child neglect."[58]

Thinking Long Term

If these families are to be helped, they will need long-term assistance. Unfortunately, child protective agencies can rarely provide intensive services over the long haul, even if that is merely defined as over 90 days. Propelled by a combination of budgetary constraints, misplaced faith in our ability to help deeply troubled clients, and single-minded prescriptions, child welfare agencies are focusing more and more on short-term services and treatment interventions.

In fact, it has even come into vogue to support short-term services like Homebuilders, the first family preservation program. There are times in people's lives when an immediate and decisive intervention can redirect their life course. Such crisis-oriented interventions can often accomplish beneficial change in family functioning more effectively—and more economically—than can long-term, intensive services. This is the essential, theoretical core of programs such as Homebuilders, and it is valid. We have a name for the process: "crisis intervention."

Many other families known to child welfare agencies, however, cannot be helped so easily and so quickly. They have more deep-seated problems, with roots in a host of social, economic, and familial troubles—and often going

back many generations. For these families, to think that sustainable change can occur in 30 days, in 60 days, or in 90 days is wishful thinking. Worse, it undermines support for the kinds of on-going efforts that must be made on behalf of these deeply troubled families.

There is an analogy here. It is unpleasant to talk about it this way, but if you accept that some of these clients have severe emotional handicaps as real as the physical disabilities that other people face, then picture a world in which we give someone a wheelchair, for 30 days or 60 days or 90 days—and then take it away. In child welfare work, this is what happens all too often.

When I was first appointed director of the National Center on Child Abuse and Neglect, I visited an inner-city multiservice treatment center. The center had a wonderful therapeutic day-care nursery and a counseling program for some relatively dysfunctional families. After the program had been set up, the staff realized that the three-room apartment over the day-care center could be used as a residential facility for severely dysfunctional families. Their plan was to place a family in the apartment and to nurture the family with services until it no longer needed their help—and then to move in another family, and then another family, and so on.

I visited this center about three years after it had opened. The same family that had moved in three years earlier was still living there. The parents were coping well, I should add, and were taking proper care of their children. But, speaking metaphorically, they were still in the wheelchair. They could have been moved out of the apartment but, and this is the point, they still would have needed sustained support and supervision.

To help families like this one—and there are more of them than any of us would like to acknowledge—we must develop an infrastructure of long-term services. There is no magic about how to do this. The answer comes from the past, from the types of services that we have let atrophy in recent years.

In most communities, for example, the public child welfare agency used to maintain a "family service" or "preventive service" unit for long-term family supervision. Never well funded, these units have shrunk considerably as agencies have responded to the often crushing burden of investigating an ever-increasing number of reports of suspected child abuse and neglect.

In-home services have likewise suffered. Homemakers, for example, were always in short supply, and many questioned how they were used. Nevertheless, most public child welfare agencies once could place homemakers with troubled families for extended periods of time. Now, budgets for homemaker services have all but withered away.

In thinking about long-term services, however, it is a mistake to think solely about what child welfare agencies can provide. At some point, child welfare agencies need to be able to turn families over to less intensive, more voluntary, community-based service programs.

As mentioned above, caseworkers used to be assigned to every AFDC family, and these caseworkers used to visit the families at home on a regular basis. There were, of course, abuses of the process: Many of us remember the notorious bed checks. Some of these workers thought their only job was to enforce the man-in-the-house rule, but many more saw themselves as helpers, as facilitators, and as encouragers of improvements in their clients' lives. Many assessed the functioning of the families on their caseloads to determine which needed on-going supervision and support. For these families, caseworkers made sure that the children got to school, even if that meant signing them up themselves; made sure that children were immunized, even if that meant going with the family to the clinic; and made sure that a host of other needs were also met.

With the separation of income maintenance and social services in the mid 1970s, this capability to provide on-going and noncategorical social services was lost. It is time to build a new and improved version of this lapsed infrastructure. Such preventive and supportive services would help families across the spectrum of social welfare programs, including AFDC, Medicaid, Food Stamps, and WIC. This is the only way to provide coherent and coordinated long-term services to disadvantaged and at-risk families.

The challenge would be to build a program that is capable of both sustaining the long-term participation of the mothers and achieving some constructive change in their behavior. Developing plans for such a program would be a major objective for the project and, although much work still needs to be done, the program's essential elements would probably include: *educational services,* including classes in cooking and housekeeping, literacy, and child development and parenting; *child care* for the mothers while they are in classes, work, or other activities; *health services* for the mothers and the children; some form of *home visitation* for families at risk of other social problems; sadly, for a large group, *drug and alcohol abuse treatment services; antismoking services;* and finally, *contraceptive services,* especially for the younger mothers. (These latter services should be voluntary in every sense of the word, but they should be provided with a clear message that, just as doing drugs is stupid, so is having another child out of wedlock.)

One important element of this service would be a modified version of a home-visitor service, an idea that C. Henry Kempe personally nurtured for many years and that was recently endorsed by the Federal Advisory Board on Child Abuse and Neglect. I say modified because I think that the home visitors should be an adjunct to the standard package of child welfare/child protective services. In addition, an attempt should be made to recruit entry-level staff who have more in common with the families they are seeking to help, that is, who share similar social and economic backgrounds as their clients.

The base for such a program could be the expanded Head Start program, which everyone seems to support. There is even a name for the revised approach, "two-generation programs," and it has three interrelated elements: (1) reaching disadvantaged children much earlier with more intensive developmental services, (2) helping low-income parents to nurture and teach their own children, and (3) encouraging unemployed parents to work or continue their education.

Finally, humility and caution should infuse any new effort to create such a service structure. The problems faced by poor families make action along the lines described in this [reading] necessary, but too many questions remain unanswered to rush headlong into radically new programs. The history of social engineering is strewn with examples of perverse and unintended consequences from even the most promising of programs.

Planning should be based on properly controlled, multiyear experiments to determine the effects of new policies. Tentative as it may seem, we should adopt a step-by-step approach, securing sound successes and avoiding overpromising and over-reaching. After all, we are tinkering with the lives of some of the most deprived and the least powerful among us.

ENDNOTES

1. As contrasted to annual "incidence," which would count the total number of "incidents." An incidence study would add five incidents to its count if a child was abused five times during a year, while a prevalence study would add just one child to its count. The difference, obviously, could result in widely different counts, which, as we will see, seems to be distorting official reporting statistics.

2. This is a substantial and confusing difference, since some states include all children in the family automatically, whether or not they have actually been abused or neglected.

3. Westat, Inc., "The National Study of the Incidence and Severity of Child Abuse and Neglect," (Washington, D.C.: National Center on Child Abuse and Neglect, 1981).

4. The original report for this study contained inaccurate information because of weighting errors by Westat. The revised report is: Andrea Sedlak, "National Incidence and Prevalence of Child Abuse and Neglect: 1988, Revised Report" (Rockville, MD: Westat, September 1991).

5. Actually, the professionals were not asked the ultimate question of whether the children appeared to be "abused" or "neglected." Instead, they were asked to identify children with certain, specified harms or conditions which were then decoded into a count of various types of child abuse and neglect.

6. See Appendix for more detailed description of the national incidence studies' definitions of maltreatment by types and levels of severity.

7. Andrea Sedlak, "Supplementary Analyses of Data on the National Incidence of Child Abuse and Neglect, Revised Report" (Rockville, MD: Westat, 1991), pp. 2–15. The percentages add to over 100, because one calculation was made for children falling within each applicable category of maltreatment and a separate one was made for the total number of maltreated children.

8. Ibid., pp. 2–15.

9. Ibid., pp. 2–7, 2–15.

10. The estimated number of maltreated children increased from 625,100 children in 1980 to 931,000 in 1986. Over 90 percent of this increase was among moderate cases. A proportion of these moderate cases, however, were cases of sexual abuse, which, for the reasons described above, might more properly be classified as "serious." Unfortunately, Westat's published report does not provide sufficient information to enable us to exclude sexual abuse cases from the increase in moderate cases. Andrea Sedlak, "National Incidence and Prevalence of Child Abuse and Neglect," p. 3–11.

11. Ibid., p. 3–12.

12. Ibid., p. 3–6.

13. *See generally,* Douglas Besharov, *Recognizing Child Abuse: A Guide for the Concerned* (New York: Free Press, 1990).

14. The two major efforts were conducted for the federal government's National Center on Child Abuse and Neglect by the American Humane Association (1974 to 1987) and Walter R. McDonald & Associates, in conjunction with Bowers

& Associates and the American Humane Association (1990 to present).

15. Walter R. McDonald & Associates, et al., "National Child Abuse and Neglect Reporting Data System: Working paper 2" (Washington, D.C.: National Center on Child Abuse and Neglect, May 1993), pp. 4–7.

16. The actual figure was 2,989,000. Deborah Daro and Karen McCurdy, "Current Trends in Child Abuse Reporting and Fatalities: The Results of the 1993 Annual Fifty State Survey" (Chicago: National Committee for the Prevention of Child Abuse, April 1994), Table 1.

17. American Association for Protecting Children, "Highlights of Official Neglect and Abuse Reporting: 1986" (Denver, CO: American Humane Association, 1988), p. 22.

18. Andrea Sedlak, "National Incidence and Prevalence of Child Abuse and Neglect," p. 6–23.

19. Andrea Sedlak, "Supplementary Analyses of Data on the National Incidence of Child Abuse and Neglect," pp. 3–19.

20. Federal expenditures for foster care, child welfare, and related services, which make up less than 50 percent of total expenditures (state and federal) for these services. In 1992, they amounted to: $273.9 million for Title IV–B child welfare services; $1,192.1 million for Title IV–E foster care maintenance; $1,017.7 million for Title IV–E foster care administration and training; $70 million for the Title IV–E independent living program; and $219.6 million for title IV–E adoption assistance, totalling $2,773.7 million. In addition, states may use a portion of the $2.8 billion federal Social Services Block Grant for such services, though detailed data on these expenditures are not available. Beginning in 1994, additional federal appropriations will fund family preservation and support services (an estimated $60 million in 1994 and $150 million in 1995). House Committee on Ways and Means *1993 Green Book* (Washington, DC: U.S. Government Printing Office, July 1993), table 2, p. 886; and *Budget of the United States Government: Appendix, Fiscal Year 1995* (Washington, DC: U.S. Government Printing Office, 1994), p. 451.

21. A. Sedlak, "Supplementary Analyses of Data on the National Incidence of Child Abuse and Neglect," 2–2, Table 2–1; Deborah Daro and Karen McCurdy, "Current Trends in Child Abuse Reporting and Fatalities: The Results of the 1993 Annual Fifty State Survey," Table 3.

22. N.Y.S. Department of Social Services, "Child Protective Services in New York State: 1979 Annual Report" (New York, 1980), Table 8.

23. Based on comparison data from "Vital Statistics of the United States for 1980: Advanced Report of Final Mortality Statistics" (Washington, D.C.: Government Printing Office, 1980).

24. American Humane Association, "National Analysis of Official Child Neglect and Abuse Reporting" (Boulder, CO: American Humane Association, 1976), p. 11.

25. A rough estimate calculated using 1990 data from the Illinois State Registry by Bong Joo Lee, Research Associate, Chapin Hall Center for Children, phone conversation with Lisa Laumann, 26 April 1994.

26. In its study, AHA found that about 25 percent of all reports to child protective agencies were repeat reports. AHA also cites a 20 percent duplication rate for official reports analyzed in Westat's second incidence study. American Association for Protecting Children, "Highlights of Official Aggregate Neglect and Abuse Reporting: 1986" (Denver, CO: American Humane Association, 1988), p. 9.

27. The second national incidence study estimated that about 26 percent of the 1.7 million official reports were founded. An additional 26 percent of the reports were still pending at the close of the study. This indicates that somewhere between 440,000 and 870,000 children were substantiated as victims of child maltreatment that year. We believe the pending cases are more likely to be determined unfounded than founded, so the most probable substantiation rate is around 35 percent, or about 600,000 substantiated victims. Andrea Sedlak, "Supplementary Analyses of Data on the National Incidence of Child Abuse and Neglect," p. 7–4.

28. Based on data from 30 states, AHA estimated that reports concerning 737,000 children were substantiated in 1986. Given a 95 percent confidence interval, however, anywhere from 603,000 to 871,000 children might have been substantiated that year. American Association for Protecting Children, "Highlights of Official Aggregate Neglect and Abuse Reporting: 1986," p. 11.

29. Walter R. McDonald & Associates, et al., "National Child Abuse and Neglect Data System: Working Paper 2," p. 21.

30. Andrea Sedlak, "National Incidence and Prevalence of Child Abuse and Neglect," pp. 5–27.

31. Virginia Child Protective Services, "Virginia Cares About its Children: 1991–1992 Annual Report" (Richmond, VA, 1992), p. 10.

32. American Humane Association, "National Analysis of Official Child Neglect and Abuse Reporting" (Boulder, CO: American Humane Association, 1976), pp. 13–14.

33. This figure refers to first-born children born in 1988. Of the children who had a founded report of maltreatment at some point in their first five years of life, 48 percent also received AFDC at some point during this time. Robert Goerge, et al., " A Longitudinal Analysis of Public Aid and Child Welfare Experiences of Illinois Families with Children" (Report prepared for the American Enterprise Institute, November 1993), p. 14.

34. American Association for Protecting Children, "Highlights of Official Child Neglect and Abuse Reporting: 1984" (Denver, CO: American Humane Association, 1986), p. 28.

35. Leroy Pelton, *For Reasons of Poverty* (New York: Praeger Press, 1989), p. 39.

36. Title IV–E funding supports the placement and maintenance of AFDC children in foster care.

37. Based on data from 25 states, at the start of FY 89, 55 percent of the foster care caseload were Title IV–E eligible. Of the children in care at the end of FY 89, 59 percent were Title IV–E eligible. Toshio Tatara, "Characteristics of Children in Substitute Care" (Washington, D.C.: American Public Welfare Association, May 1993), pp. 36–37, 40–41.

There is some evidence that states may be underestimating the number of poor children in their foster care population. In fiscal year 1990, the state of Colorado only claimed Title IV–E funds for 29 percent of their foster children, substantially lower than the national monthly average of 41 percent. A 1990 performance audit of the Colorado Department of Social Services revealed that the proportion of Title IV–E eligible foster children residing in Colorado was actually much higher, but the lack of proper identification and coding of eligible children resulted in a gross underestimation of the number. The audit found that many county department personnel were not even aware of the criteria for determining eligibility. Others thought it was not worth the paper work if the child was to be in placement for only a short time. Because of a sharpened focus on identifying Title IV–E eligible children, the proportion of Title IV–E children in Colorado foster care this year was around 54 percent. (Janet Motz, director of child protective grants, Colorado Department of Social Services, phone interview with Lisa Laumann, 20 April 1994.)

38. General Accounting Office, "Foster Care: Services to Prevent Out-of-Home Placements Are Limited by Funding Barriers" (Report to the Chairman, Subcommittee on Oversight of Government Management, Washington, D.C., June 1993), pp. 57–65.

39. This study looked at first-born children born in 1988. Robert Goerge, et al., "A Longitudinal Analysis of Public Aid and Child Welfare Experiences of Illinois Families with Children," p. 15.

40. Minnesota Department of Human Services, "Child Maltreatment Report: 1982–1991" (St. Paul, MN, 1993), pp. 48–49.

41. N.J. Department of Human Services, "Child Abuse and Neglect in New Jersey: 1992 Annual Report" (Trenton, NJ, July 1993), p. 23.

42. Andrea Sedlak, "Supplementary Analyses of Data on the National Incidence of Child Abuse and Neglect," pp. 5–2.

43. These figures represent the proportion of families that had their first child in 1988 that had founded reports of child abuse or neglect within five years of the birth of the child. Robert Goerge, et al., "A Longitudinal Analysis of Public Aid and Child Welfare Experiences of Illinois Families with Children," Table 49.

44. These figures represent the proportion of welfare families who had founded reports of child maltreatment at any time in the four-year period, 1986 to 1990. Robert Goerge, et al., "The Point-in-Time Multiple Service Use of Illinois Families with Children" (Report prepared for the American Enterprise Institute, Washington, D.C., August 1993), Table 19.

45. Leroy Pelton, *for Reasons of Poverty,* p. 63.

46. Walter R. McDonald & Associates, et al., "National Child Abuse and Neglect Reporting Data System: Working Paper 2," p. 34.

47. U.S. Census Bureau, *Statistical Abstract of the United States, 1991* (Washington, D.C., Government Printing Office, 1992), p. 46.

48. Toshio Tatara, "Characteristics of Children in Substitute Care," p. 51.

49. Robert Goerge, et al., "A Longitudinal Analysis of Public Aid and Child Welfare Experiences of Illinois Families with Children," Table 48.

50. Confidential report held by author.

51. See, e.g., Region VI Resource Center on Child Abuse, "Child Deaths in Texas," (1981), p. 26; Mayberry, "Child Protective Services in New York City: An Analysis of Case Management" (Albany, NY: Welfare Research Inc., 1979), p. 109.

52. Deborah Daro and Karen McCurdy, "Current Trends in Child Abuse Reporting and Fatalities: The Results of the 1993 Annual Fifty State Survey," Table 4.

53. Giovannoni & Billingsley, "Child Neglect Among the Poor: A Study of Parental Adequacy in Families of Three Ethnic Groups," *Child Welfare* 49 (1970): 196, 204.

54. Author's estimate based on *Social Security Bulletin* (1984) reporting that, in 1983, 3,721,000 families received AFDC.

55. Leroy Pelton, "The Role of Material Factors in Child Abuse and Neglect," in the U.S. Advisory Board on Child Abuse and Neglect Report, "Neighbors Helping Neighbors: A New National Strategy for the Protection of Children" (Washington, D.C., 1993).

56. Norman Polansky, et al., *Damaged Parents: An Anatomy of Child Neglect* (Chicago: University of Chicago Press, 1981), p. 25.

57. Ibid., p. 109.

58. Ibid., p. 25.

CHAPTER 12

Divorce

The process of adjustment to divorce has many facets. In *Public and Private Families: An Introduction,* I wrote about the emotional divorce, the legal divorce, the coparental divorce, and the economic divorce.[1] Others have written about the "community divorce," involving the loss of friends and neighbors, and the "psychic divorce," involving regaining autonomy.[2] The readings in this section focus on two of these aspects.

The first is the coparental divorce. One of the important postdivorce tasks is for the ex-spouses to work out arrangements for raising the children. Central to this task, obviously, is the physical location of the children: are they to live with the mother, the father, or split their time between both? By far the most common arrangement is for the children to live most of the time with their mothers and visit their fathers occasionally—perhaps every other weekend and during vacations. This arrangement is called maternal physical custody. Less common

is paternal physical custody, in which fathers are the primary caretakers for their children. It is still rare enough that it often signals a mother's serious problem, such as depression or alcoholism. The third arrangement is joint physical custody, in which the children spend substantial amounts of time at each parent's home. It only occurs in a minority of families in large part because it requires substantial communication and cooperation between the ex-spouses.

In *Dividing the Child: Social and Legal Dilemmas of Custody,* a northern California study of over 1,000 families that initiated divorces in 1984 and 1985, 66 percent agreed that the children would live with the mother, 8 percent agreed that the children would live with the father, and 20 percent agreed on joint physical custody. (The remaining families had other arrangements or did not specify the arrangement.) The California families were interviewed three times over a three-year period. The authors, Eleanor E. Maccoby, a developmental psychologist, and Robert H. Mnookin, a lawyer, studied a broad range of postdivorce issues. In the following excerpt, they discuss the process by which parents must adjust their child-rearing

---

[1]*Public and Private Families: An Introduction,* pp. 361–71.
[2]Paul Bohannan, "The Six Stations of Divorce," in Paul Bohannan, ed., *Divorce and After* (New York: Anchor Books, 1971), pp. 33–62.

activity from the jointly supportive style of most married couples to the individualized styles that divorced parents adopt.

The second aspect for which a reading is presented is the economic divorce. Probably no other consequence of divorce for adults has received as much attention as the sharp economic slide experienced by many women. The reasons are simple: husbands tend to earn more than their wives, and after divorce many ex-husbands pay little or no child support to their ex-wives. Some divorced wives may have done little or no work for pay while raising the couple's children. So after the breakup of their marriages, women frequently find that their standard of living plummets. Terry Arendell interviewed 60 divorced women in the San Francisco area in 1983 for her book, *Mothers and Divorce: Legal, Economic, and Social Dilemmas.* All had been divorced for at least two years (the median was four years), had custody of at least one child, and had considered themselves middle-class during their marriages. Nearly all of the women

reported sharp economic declines. Their stories are told in the excerpt reprinted here.

Keep in mind that Arendell's subjects are not representative of all divorced mothers. For one thing, she excluded women who had remarried, and remarriage is the main route out of economic decline for divorced women. So, almost by definition, her sample overrepresents divorced women with long-lasting financial problems. Also, women who shared physical custody of their children with their ex-husbands—an arrangement that typically eases the financial burdens on mothers—were underrepresented. (Only three women shared custody.) In addition, some of the women responded to advertisements, bulletin board notices, and even a newspaper article asking divorced mothers to participate in the project. It is possible that the women who replied overrepresented those with poignant stories to tell. Nevertheless, there are many divorced mothers in America with situations as moving as the ones captured by Arendell in her book.

The Parental Divorce: Coparenting Before and After Separation

Eleanor E. Maccoby and Robert H. Mnookin

While parents are dealing with the distress of the spousal divorce and the relentless pressures of the economic divorce, they must also redefine their parental roles and responsibilities. We now turn to the parental divorce, and examine in some detail the ways in which divorcing parents characteristically must modify their old patterns . . . In focusing on this central concern of our study, how divorce changes parental roles and responsibilities, we begin by considering in some detail what coparenting involves in predivorce families. Then we examine the changes in the coparental relationship that occur when parents move into separate households while each continues to see the children. From the perspective of family systems theory, we consider the implications of these changes for postseparation family organization and therapeutic approaches.

COPARENTING IN PREDIVORCE FAMILIES: THE PARENTAL ALLIANCE

In the past, most research on how parents socialize a child focused on the mother–child pair. More recently, the role of fathers in child rearing has been given more attention, and two aspects of the paternal role in the family have been emphasized: the father's role in giving support (both emotional and material) to the mother as major child rearer, and his direct interactions

Eleanor E. Maccoby and Robert H. Mnookin, "The Parental Divorce: Co-parenting Before and After Separation" from *Dividing the Child: Social and Legal Dilemmas of Custody*, pp. 24–39. Copyright © 1992 by the President and Fellows of Harvard College. Reprinted with the permission of Harvard University Press.

with the children. The interest in fathers' role in child rearing emerged partly in response to pressure for gender equality. Feminists asked why women should be the ones primarily responsible for child-care duties. Because women have traditionally occupied the primary child-rearing role in all human societies—particularly for young children—one question posed for child development researchers was whether this had to be so. In a sense, the question many studies addressed was: can men "mother" as well as women? Work by Parke and O'Leary (1976) illustrates this approach.[1] They observed fathers and mothers interacting one-on-one with infants, and found fathers to be as skillful in bottle-feeding, and as gentle and responsive, as were mothers.

Although it appears that fathers, like mothers, can successfully nurture even very young children, in most American families the two parents do not have the same functions in child rearing. When fathers are asked what it means to be a father, they are likely to mention first their role as breadwinner. Studies show that most two-parent families with young children—even those where both parents are working—adopt a division of labor such that the mother assumes more responsibility for child care and household management while the father brings in a higher portion of the family income. If either parent is to reduce the time spent in outside employment in order to care for children, many families find that it makes more economic sense for the family as a whole for the mother to be the one who does so.

Lamb and colleagues (1987), summarizing a considerable body of research, report that although there is great variation among families in the extent of the father's involvement in child rearing, fathers on the average are considerably less involved even when mothers are working. On average, fathers are "available" (that is, present and accessible) to their children for about half as much time as are mothers; mothers spend about three times as much time in face-to-face interaction with children as do fathers. And mothers are overwhelmingly more likely to be the person *responsible* for the children—the only person at home with them, the one who stays home from work with them if they are ill, the person who arranges the child care, makes medical appointments, takes the children to lessons and doctor's appointments, decides about their clothing, and so forth. In terms of the time spent as the responsible parent, mothers outweigh fathers nine to one.

When one considers the "role overload" that many women experience when they are both working outside the home and carrying the major responsibility for child care, it may come as a surprise to learn that many are not enthusiastic about their husbands' taking on a larger role with the children. Yet this is the case (Pleck, 1983), and there is evidence that when economic circumstances force a reversal of roles—with the mother as the major wage earner and the father staying home with the children—mothers express considerable dissatisfaction with the way their husbands are managing the household. It would seem that many if not most women wish to retain their dominant role in the management of household and children.

While the division of child-care labor has been extensively studied, the nature of parental cooperation in dealing with children has not been examined in as much detail. However, family systems theorists have contributed to our understanding of some of the elements of coparenting relations. They tell us, first of all, that families are indeed systems, having their own dynamic properties, boundaries, and subsystems. In well-functioning two-parent families, the strongest and most cohesive dyad is the one between the mother (wife) and father (husband) (Feldman & Gehring, 1988). Children perceive the parental pair as jointly exercising authority, and as being affectively close.

Patricia Minuchin (1985), in discussing the family, points out that much interaction between parents and children goes on when both parents are present, and the mother-father-child triad has its own dynamics in the socialization of the child. Minuchin gives an example of an interaction that was observed while the parents of a young child were being interviewed:

> The two-year-old knocks over a box of chalks and they spill out onto the carpet.
>
> Mother [soft voice]: "Brian, pick them up, please." (She turns back to adult conversation.)
>
> Father [voice raised slightly]: "Brian, put the chalks in the box." [Pause; voice stronger]: "Brian, put the chalks in the box!"
>
> Mother: "Yeah come on. Don't muck up the carpet." [Adult conversation resumes. Child is examining the chalk.]
>
> Father: "Brian, listen! You're not supposed to have the chalk on the carpet. Now pick them up. Come on."
>
> Child: "I'm doing it."
>
> Father: "You're not. You're playing. Come, pick them up first. Quickly. If I get up, you know you will. Now come on!"
>
> Adult discussion resumes. Mother glances at child, stands up and goes to him, kneeling and talking softly. As he dallies over the chalk, she says, "Don't throw them. Put away all of them." Father, seated, says "Come on," and watches as the mother tells the child he will have to sit on her lap and not play if he doesn't pick them all up. The child says, "I want to play," and gathers the chalk up more quickly. Father relaxes and mother returns to the adults. (Minuchin, 1985, p. 296)

The dynamics of this interaction are complex. Possibly, the mother sees a confrontation brewing between the father and child, and moves to forestall it. But the major feature of the interaction is that the two parents are working together in the exercise of joint authority.

A similar dynamic may be seen in the following incident, recently observed by Maccoby:

> Six-year-old girl exuberantly runs out the back door of her home, bumping into the sliding screen door and knocking it off its track. Father gets up to reset the screen, saying irritably:
>
> "Janie, that's the *third* time you've knocked that door off."
>
> Janie: "I didn't do it."
>
> Father: "Yes you did!"

Janie: "No I didn't!"

Father leaves door, goes to girl, holds her shoulders firmly, looks directly into her face, and says loudly: "Don't tell me you didn't do it. I *saw* you. You didn't mean to, but you *did* do it."

Child wails and goes to mother. Father returns to door. Mother puts arm around daughter, rubs her back, says: "It's all right, honey. You didn't mean to. But you have to be more careful. So daddy won't always have to be fixing the screen door."

Here the roles of the two parents were different—mother as comfort-giver, father as disciplinarian. Also, their momentary socialization goals were somewhat different: the father was focusing on truth telling, the mother on being considerate of another family member. Yet they were mutually supportive. In many families, instances of joint parenting such as these may be fairly rare—most of the time, only one parent at a time directly interacts with a child, although in family dinner-table conversations, three-way exchanges do occur. The point is, however, that it may not take many instances of jointly exercised parental authority for the children to form a picture of their parents as a mutually reinforcing team.

Most parental couples not only adopt a division of labor in terms of child-rearing roles and responsibilities; the father and mother may also have different characteristic styles of interaction with children. In both the vignettes, the mothers were to some extent mediating between the father and the child. That is, they softened the impact of the fathers' power-assertive style, while supporting him in his attempts to teach relevant lessons to the child. There is evidence that in most families mothers do more of the work of sustaining positive moods among family members than fathers do; fathers are observed generally to be more power-assertive in the way they speak to children (Gleason, 1987).

But fathers do much more than merely play the "heavy" role of authority figure. From the earliest period of the child's life, fathers typically spend a higher proportion of their interactive time in play than mothers do (Parke & Tinsley, 1981; Russell & Russell, 1987), and they do more joking. While father-child play involves more roughhousing, mother-child play involves more reciprocal role-taking in fantasy scripts (Maccoby & Jacklin, 1983). In addition, mothers are the primary comfort-givers for children at times of distress. Moreover, they chat more with them, and spend more time listening to what they have to say. Indeed, mothers appear to be better able to understand what a very young child is saying at a time when the child's speech can be quite unclear (Gleason, 1987). Russell and Russell (1987) report that although mothers issue more directions than fathers to school-age children (second-graders)—for example, telling the child to take a bath, come to the table, put away toys—mothers also consult the child's viewpoint more, and respond more positively than fathers do when the child makes an independent decision. Perhaps as a consequence, the children in their study expressed their feelings more freely to their mothers.

Our interpretation of the existing research is that while the affectional bonds are normally very strong between the children and each of the parents, typically there is more reciprocal give-and-take between mothers and children in the course of daily life, even though fathers may be the favorite playmates. One corollary of the maternal style is that mothers usually know more about the child's interests, friends, preferences, and goals. Adolescents report that their mothers know them better than their fathers do, even though they regard their two parents as equally important as standard-setters (Youniss & Smollar, 1985). In many households, then, the two parents play complementary roles in the lives of their children.

How a parent interacts with a child may depend, according to some research, on whether the parent is alone with the child. Per Gjerde (1986) has observed mothers and fathers interacting with their teenage children, either one-on-one or in the mother-father-child trio. He found that a parent's mode of interaction with the children does change somewhat, depending on whether the other parent is present. Fathers appeared to be somewhat inhibited in the presence of the child's mother, and when alone with the child, interacted more freely and became more relaxed and humorous. When both parents are present many fathers regard the management of the children as more in their wives' domain than their own, and they are careful about invading her territory. Mothers, on the other hand, interacted with teenage sons more comfortably and more assertively when their husbands were present. Thus, fathers may serve as "backup" authority, helping to keep children—especially sons—in line. Many a boy has heard his father say: "Young man, I don't want to hear you talking to your mother like that." Lytton (1979), in observing parents with much younger children, found that mothers were more effective in controlling their 2-year-old sons when the father was present than when he was not.

We do not have comparable information on the effect of a mother's presence on children's compliance to their fathers' demands, but suspect that her presence would not make as much difference, considering that there is evidence that fathers are usually more successful in exacting compliance even when the mother is not there. For example, in observations of mothers and fathers interacting separately with a preschool child, Hetherington and colleagues (1982) found that children complied more readily to a father's than a mother's demands, in both intact and divorced families. Furthermore, it has been reported that school-age children treat fathers as though they were more powerful than their mothers (Cowan, Drinkard, & MacGavin, 1984). Thus, mothers on the average may derive more benefit from their spouse's authority backup than do fathers.

During marriage, successful parents forge a parental alliance. When parents are closely allied, they make most decisions concerning the children jointly; or at least, they have an understanding concerning which decisions need to be discussed and which can be left to either parent acting singly. Allied parents also relieve each other of child-care duties when one parent is ill, overstressed, or subject to special demands outside the home. At such times, the other parent will step in to manage or entertain the children. When the children simply need someone to stay with them at times when no formal child care has been arranged, one parent will usually "sit" with the children so that the other can do necessary errands, or participate in out-of-home functions or recreational activities to which the children cannot be taken.

The parental alliance also involves agreeing on rules for the children, backing up the other parent's authority, and conveying an atmosphere of mutual respect and affection. Even in well-functioning families, of course, parents do not always manage to present a united front, and children become expert at finding weaknesses in the parental alliance. As they grow older, children learn which parent is more likely to soften a particular rule under particular circumstances. They try out "divide and conquer" tactics: for example, saying, "But Mom, Daddy said I could." They quickly learn whether their parents are communicating well enough so that each knows what the other has demanded or decided. Parents with a strong alliance learn, for their part, to respond to a child's demands with "We'll see" or "I'll talk to your mother (father)," so as to allow themselves time for working out a joint strategy.

In two-parent households, each parent may at times protect children from potentially damaging behavior by the other parent. Hetherington and colleagues (1982) have called this parental "buffering." Their research suggests that in intact families, one well-functioning parent can shield children from the risks entailed in exposure to a depressed, abusive, or neglectful parent. Parents know each other's behavior patterns well enough so that one parent can often anticipate a blowup on the part of the other parent, and may be able to forestall it. If one parent does become enraged or drunk or potentially abusive, the more stable parent may be able to get the children out of reach of the endangering one. In less extreme situations, if a parent has misgivings about something the other parent is doing vis-à-vis the children—for example, doing things that frighten them, or allowing too much or too little autonomy—there are opportunities for the parents to discuss the issue and perhaps influence each other's parental style.

COPARENTING AS THE PARENTAL ALLIANCE BREAKS UP

New Family Structures

In some divorcing families, the parental alliance has already begun to crumble before the couple actually separates. One parent may form an alliance with the child to exclude the other parent, thus forming what family therapists consider an unhealthy subsystem (Minuchin, 1985). Parents may also compete for the children's loyalty, and differences in their values and standards may have become evident to all family members. Recent evidence indicates that parents in conflict do not hold their children to as high standards as do parents who have a harmonious relationship (Goldberg, 1990). This research suggests that as the parental alliance weakens, the behavior standards for the children decline. If parents quarrel openly in front of the children, and show contempt for each other, the atmosphere of mutual respect that underlies their joint authority and effective coparenting is seriously weakened. In some families, however, the decision to separate is rather sudden (perhaps triggered by one parent's discovery of the other's extramarital affair), and the parental alliance may have been well maintained up to the point of separation.

When the parents do actually separate, the parental alliance must obviously be profoundly affected. For children and adults alike, the separation of spousal roles from parental roles is dif-

ficult. The mere fact of spousal divorce means that one parent (or both) no longer considers the other lovable as a spouse. Even when a mother says to a child: "I don't love your father any more, but *you* should (may) love him," the message is a mixed one. The kind of teamwork that was illustrated in the vignettes presented earlier can hardly occur when each parent is operating from a different household.

Divorce requires that the division of child-rearing responsibilities must be renegotiated. In order to understand the degree and kind of coparenting that can occur following divorce, we now consider the nature of the postdivorce family structure or structures that take the place of the predivorce structure. When therapists or mediators deal with couples who have passed the point of attempting reconciliation, a major goal is to help the couple dampen or at least manage their interpersonal conflict so that they can complete their spousal detachment from each other while still being able to do necessary business together concerning the children. Still, there are some differences among therapists concerning the kind of family structure that should be the outcome. One set of theorists suggests that so long as a child is continuing to spend time with both parents, the child is a member of a single family structure that includes both parents. The predivorce family structure continues (or can, or should continue) as a structural entity, and is merely reorganized so that the nonresident parent becomes an extended family member in the same sense that grandparents are: living in a different household, but nevertheless linked to the resident family by family ties and obligations. A contrasting viewpoint suggests that the prior nuclear family structure no longer exists, and is replaced by *two* new structures, organized within each of the two parental households. In the case of a child who spends time in both households, the child is a member of two families.

These differences in viewpoint are more than merely semantic. They affect the way mediators and family therapists define the goals of intervention. Working from the first point of view, for example, Isaacs and colleagues (1986) say:

> We place special emphasis on problem solving—parent with parent, and parent with child—that allows family members to struggle face to face with each other during the process of reorganizing the unit. We view the immediate family (mother, father and their children) as the unit of direct intervention. (Isaacs, Montalvo, & Abelsohn, 1986, p. 5)

> The unit has to maintain some subsystems, shed others, and develop new ones. In working with subsystems, we follow two elementary principles: we support those that will help the family fulfill its functions, and we attempt to limit the influence of antagonistic groupings. (p. 6)

> Separation and divorce need not herald the death of the family. For some, separation can be a transition and not an end. The well-being of parents and children can be enhanced as the family—albeit considerably changed—attempts to remain a viable, self-propelled and interprotective unit. (p. 219)

These therapists make it clear that a guiding principle of their therapeutic efforts is to prevent either parent from "abdicating"—to keep both parents involved and functioning together as coparents.

In contrast, Preston and Madison (1984), two therapists working in the Family Court of Australia, see the postdivorce family as made up of the custodial parent and children. For a child living with the mother, the mother's household is "home" for the child, even if the child visits the father. The boundary around the old system is gone, and a new boundary is formed around the mother and children. The father does not have a place within this new boundary. His visits may be experienced as intrusions, particularly if visitation is imposed against the wishes of the primary parent. Preston and Madison argue that visitation arrangements should have rules that give the new family (that is, the mother-child dyad) control over the conditions of the father's presence in their household. They say:

> Following separation, the family boundary becomes disturbed. The departure of one spouse from the family makes this boundary diffuse; it becomes more permeable and less able to provide a sense of security and containment for the members of the family. This is because of disturbance in the spousal sub-system which is responsible for maintaining the family boundary. The important task in the initial period after separation is to re-establish the boundary around the family. Disputes over access (visitation) can serve to prevent the formation of a clear family boundary. (Preston & Madison, 1984, p. 39)

In short, Preston and Madison believe that access by the father should be limited and/or clearly regulated in the interest of strengthening the boundary around a new family structure that does not include him.[2]

We are not completely satisfied with either view about the changes in family structure. Let us consider first the most common residential situation, that in which the children are living with the mother and maintaining some degree of contact with a nonresidential father. Certainly if the father is continuing to pay child support, he is joining with the mother in the enormously important function of providing food and shelter for the family. In this sense, he continues as part of the original nuclear family. Yet in other equally important respects, he is not part of this family because of the spousal divorce. He no longer has a key to the house; he cannot arrive at the house and expect to join the family for dinner; he does not share in the plans the mother and children have for their joint activities, nor in their confidences with one another. The child's family household is not the father's "home," and normally he no longer shares in the household upkeep and chores. It has been said that home is the place where "they always have to take you in." A divorced nonresident father does not have the right to be "taken in," nor to have his needs considered by other family members, and he no longer functions as a coparent in the day-to-day rearing of the children. Indeed, it may be said that a couple's decision to divorce is in effect a decision no longer to be members of the same family.

A nonresident father is not a member of an extended family, in the same sense that grandparents are. In sociological writings, the term "extended family" usually refers to a network of kin (people related by blood, marriage, or adoption) who exchange goods and services. Thus members of the extended family might baby-sit for the nuclear family, help in finding jobs for the parents or the young people as they grow into adulthood, help to provide the down payment for a house, and so on. In addition, members of an extended family usually share important symbolic occasions: birthdays, holidays, weddings, funerals. Usually, loyalty, a common identity, and pride mark an extended family. Clearly the children's father and his parents are not part of the mother's extended family as so defined. They are kin to the *child* (related by blood ties), but not kin to the extended *family* of which the child and mother are the central system.

As we see it, divorce necessarily involves the formation of at least one new family structure, having its own boundaries. When one parent simply disappears from the children's lives at the time of divorce, the family is "reconstituted" as a single-parent family. It may later be transformed in structure once more with the addition of a stepparent. When the children continue to spend time with both parents, this need not imply that mother, father, and children are now a "reconstituted" version of the original family. True, from the *child's* standpoint, both parents (and both sets of grandparents) may still be seen as members of the child's family (Funder, 1991). But when both parents remain involved in the children's lives following divorce, we believe that from a structural standpoint it is more accurate to say that a single family (both nuclear and extended) has been replaced by two family structures, and that the child may be a member of both.

Do any vestiges of the old boundary around the original family as a unit remain? This, we think, is a matter of degree, and varies from family to family. Clearly, it depends on whether, and in what way, the parental alliance is maintained. There may be no residual vestiges in circumstances where the divorced parents no longer communicate with one another concerning the children. On the other hand, there are situations in which divorced parents cooperate actively, attempting to coordinate rules for the children in the two households and jointly making decisions about the children's lives. Here, one aspect of the old family unit continues to exist, but the structure is qualitatively very different from its predecessor. The old family unit was one whose members lived together, shared many plans and activities with one another, and had unlimited access to one another. The new version of the original mother-father-child "unit" involves only a limited sharing of information and plans about the child (which can be seen as a limited overlap between the two family structures). Other aspects of the family life are separate, even in this "ideal" case of high parental cooperation. Even for those parents who succeed in the important task of developing a cooperative coparenting relationship, we see their parental unit not as a simple continuation of their old coparenting processes but as something that must be constructed anew to fit their greatly changed circumstances.

Single Parenting in Separate Households

We have seen that in intact families, mothers and fathers frequently have somewhat different roles and interactive styles where parenting is concerned. These differences, we believe, have implications for the way the two parents will function as single parents. In view of the division of labor that typically prevails in preseparation households, with mothers having the predominant role in child rearing, we may expect that there would be considerable continuity in the way mothers carry out parenting functions during the times when the children are with them following the separation. And indeed,

Hetherington and colleagues (1982) have reported that the quality of a mother's parenting after divorce can be fairly well predicted from her preseparation parenting activities. The way divorced fathers interacted with their children when the children were with them was not so predictable, however. Fathers, as single parents, or even as visiting parents, typically have more to learn than single mothers do.

Nevertheless, for mothers there are important changes. Although the mother has the advantage of greater experience in household management and day-to-day child care, she must continue to do these things when there are increasing demands on her time for other activities (for example, increased working hours outside the home). The spousal backup for her authority is largely absent. Furthermore, children tend to believe that parenting is primarily the responsibility of mothers rather than fathers. Consequently, they do not experience (or at least, do not express) any particular indebtedness to custodial mothers for their caretaking, whereas they do express such appreciation to custodial fathers, who are seen by the children as doing something beyond what might be expected (Ambert, 1982). In short, in the eyes of children, being cared for by one's mother is a right; being cared for by one's father is more a privilege. Hence, children may feel they "owe" more respect and obedience to a custodial father, and may be less responsive to a custodial mother's attempts at control. There is reason to expect, then, that custodial mothers may encounter more difficulty in maintaining discipline. Furthermore, the additional financial pressures and the lack of a partner to share household chores and child-care duties can produce sufficient stress to make the mother more irritable toward the children, less responsive, and less patient.[3] For some mothers, on the other hand, the father's departure from the household may relieve stress and simplify parenting.

Single fathers, we predict, will have a different set of problems during the times when they have responsibility for the children. Discipline should not pose any special difficulties for them. For nonresidential fathers who see the child only on brief weekend visits—particularly if the children do not stay overnight—the father may become mainly a "pal," playmate, or friend and not so much an important authority figure. But for fathers who have their children with them for any substantial portion of residential time, the "playmate" relationship must be transformed into a managerial one. As noted above, fathers may have an advantage in terms of the children's readiness to comply to parental directives. Hetherington and colleagues (Hetherington, Cox, & Cox, 1982) report that the young children in their study obeyed their divorced fathers more readily than their divorced mothers. However, all these fathers were noncustodial, and we have no information concerning how these influence patterns would work out with custodial fathers.

There is probably great variability among custodial fathers in what and how much they have to learn. A small group of fathers may have assumed primary parental management duties before the divorce, sometimes because their wives were unwilling or unable to assume them. For many fathers, however, assuming the primary parental role will be new. When the children are young, fathers who have not been especially vigilant before must learn to pay attention to small noises (or silences) that signal impending dangers or otherwise call for parental action. They must plan agendas for the children, and modify their own schedules to fit in with the children's schedules. They must monitor the whereabouts, friendships, activities, and moods of the children if they are to provide effective guidance, control, and support.

Fathers, like mothers, may experience some parental gains as well. Now they can interact directly with their children without the mother's mediation. Fathers who have taken on a major role in child rearing report that they get to know their children much better than they did in a traditional father's role, and feel closer to them (Russell, 1982). But, at least initially, their lack of familiarity with the details of the children's lives may make it more difficult to monitor the children's whereabouts and supervise their activities.

Coparenting after Separation

In some families, divorce means that one parent essentially drops out of the parental role—that is, he or she seldom sees the children, and does not participate in child care or child rearing. For such families, the question of parental cooperation hardly arises. In other families, both parents continue to be involved, and for these families important new issues emerge: What kind of agreement can the parents come to concerning the amount of time the children will spend with each parent? How will they divide responsibilities for getting the children back and forth? Should they operate independently, or should they try to achieve some form of coordination between the two households with respect to standards of behavior set for the children, discipline, chores, allowances, privileges, and so forth? When important decisions need to be made concerning the child's life (for example, what school the child should attend, medical care, religious training), should the parents plan to discuss each issue and decide jointly? What decisions should be left to the independent decision making of whichever parent has the child with him/her at the time?

It is possible for parents who are both seeing the children to carry out their parental functions almost entirely separately from each other—that is, to practice "parallel" parenting. Alternatively, parents can maintain contact with each other in connection with their joint responsibilities for the children—and this contact can be either cooperative or conflicted. Although we have argued that the parental alliance can no longer function as before, it is certainly possible for divorced parents to create a new coparental relationship that permits them to do business together concerning the children in a cooperative and mutually supportive way. Indeed, this is the goal of many mediators and family therapists

who work with divorced parents. Yet clearly, many parents are so caught up in the emotional turmoil of their spousal divorce that they cannot construct a coparental relationship.

The parental divorce is especially complex in cases of joint custody. A joint custody decree implies that parents will share responsibility for the children after divorce. Joint legal custody gives both parents the right and responsibility to be involved in decisions about the children's education, medical care, and religious training. When the decree is for joint physical custody, this suggests that the two will share in day-to-day responsibility for the upbringing of the children. Such arrangements presumably call for a considerable degree of cooperative coparenting. However, little is known about how joint-custodial parents manage their coparental functions: the extent to which they are able to cooperate, the degree of conflict, the amount of joint decision making, and the way they carry on their parental business together. In fact, we do not know how coparental functions are managed between divorced parents in *any* of the three custodial arrangements . . . Clearly, joint decision making and other forms of cooperation should be possible when both parents are eager to sustain each other's involvement with the children. But what about cases in which joint custody is ordered over the objections of one of the parents? Or cases where the parents agree to it because they can find no other solution to a serious conflict over custody? The nature of coparenting under conditions in which parents have initially been in conflict about custody has seldom been examined . . .

A final word should be said about "buffering." Hetherington and colleagues (1982) have noted that as time goes on following parental separation, the quality of children's functioning becomes more and more dependent on the quality of the residential parent's functioning, and less and less related to characteristics of the nonresidential parent. This can have either positive or negative implications—sometimes both—as far as the children are concerned. A competent residential parent can raise the children without having to worry about interference from a spouse or—in more extreme cases—about protecting the children from the other parent's endangering behavior. On the other hand, the children are left more vulnerable to the residential parent in terms of that parent's mood states, lack of parenting skills, or life style.

Parents functioning in two different households can hardly serve as effective buffers or mediators between the children and the other parent when the children are at the other parent's house. For a parent who is deeply committed to the children's welfare, this can be one of the most frustrating situations a divorced parent faces. Some parents are in the fortunate position of feeling that the former spouse is entirely reliable as a parent. But others are not; they remember all too well the former spouse's flash points and weaknesses. Indeed, they are probably more aware of these weaknesses than of the other parent's strengths. Some of their concerns will surely be unrealistic, but others will be accurate appraisals of kinds of situations that can arise between a given parent and child in the course of ordinary life situations.

ENDNOTES

1. See also Parke & Sawin (1976).
2. One sees some kinship here with the position advocated by Goldstein, Freud, & Solnit (1973).
3. See Maccoby & Martin (1983) for a review of research on the effects of stress on parent-child interaction.

REFERENCES

Ambert, A. 1982. Differences in children's behavior toward custodial mothers and custodial fathers. *Journal of Marriage and the Family 44*, 73–86.

Cowan, G., J. Drinkard, & L. MacGavin. 1984. The effects of target, age and gender on use of power strategies. *Journal of Personality and Social Psychology 47*, 1391–1398.

Feldman, S. S., & T. Gehring. 1988. Changing perceptions of family cohesion and power across adolescence. *Child Development 59*, 1034–1045.

Funder, K. 1991. Children's constructions of their post-divorce families: A family sculpture approach. In *Images of Australian families,* ed. K. Funder. Australian Institute of Family Studies. Melbourne: Longman-Cheshire.

Gjerde, P. F. 1986. The interpersonal structure of family interaction settings: Parent-adolescent relations in dyads and triads. *Developmental Psychology 22,* 297–304.

Gleason, J. B. 1987. Sex differences in parent-child interaction. In *Language, gender and sex in comparative perspective,* ed. S. U. Philips, S. Steele, and C. Tanz. Cambridge: Cambridge University Press.

Goldberg, W. A. 1990. Marital quality, parental personality, and spousal agreement about perceptions and expectations for children. *Merrill-Palmer Quarterly 36,* 531–556.

Goldstein, J., A. Freud, and A. J. Solnit. 1973. *Beyond the best interests of the child.* New York: Free Press.

Hetherington, E. M., M. Cox, & R. Cox. 1982. Effects of divorce on parents and children. In *Nontraditional families,* ed. M. E. Lamb. Hillside, N.J.: Lawrence Erlbaum Associates.

Isaacs, M. B., B. Montalvo, & D. Abelsohn. 1986. *The difficult divorce: Therapy for children and families.* New York: Basic Books.

Lamb, M. E., J. H. Pleck, E. L. Chernov, & J. A. Levine. 1987. A biosocial perspective on paternal behavior and involvement. In *Parenting across the lifespan: A biosocial perspective,* ed. J. B. Lancaster, A. Rossi, J. Altman, and L. Sherrod. New York: Aldine de Gruyter.

Lytton, H. 1979. Disciplinary encounters between young boys and their mothers: Is there a contingency system? *Developmental Psychology 15,* 256–268.

Maccoby, E. E., & C. N. Jacklin. 1983. The "person" characteristics of children and the family as environment. In *Human development: An interactional perspective,* ed. D. Magnusson and V. Allen. New York: Academic Press.

Maccoby, E. E., and J. Martin. 1983. Parent-child interaction. In *Charmichael's manual of child psychology,* vol. 4, ed. P. Mussen. New York: Wiley.

Minuchin, P. 1985. Families and individual development: Provocations from the field of family therapy. *Child Development 56,* 289–302.

Parke, R. D., & S. O'Leary. 1976. Father-mother-infant interaction in the newborn period: Some findings, some observations and some unresolved issues. In

The developing individual in a changing world, vol. 2, *Social and environmental issues*, ed. K. A. Riegel and J. Meacham. The Hague: Mouton.

Parke, R. D., and D. B. Sawin. 1976. The father's role in infancy: A re-evaluation. *The Family Coordinator* 25:365–371.

Parke, R. D., & B. R. Tinsley. 1981. The father's role in infancy: Determinants of involvement in caregiving and play. In *The role of the father in child development*, ed. M. E. Lamb, 2d ed. New York: John Wiley and Sons.

Pleck, J. 1983. Husbands' paid work and family roles: Current research issues. In *Research in the interweave of social roles*, vol. 3, *Families and jobs*. ed. H. Lopata and J. H. Pleck. Greenwich, Conn.: JAI Press.

Preston, G., & M. Madison. 1984. Access disputes in the context of the family structure after marital separation. *Australian Journal of Sex, Marriage and Family 5(1)*, 36–45.

Russell, G. 1982. Shared-caregiving families: An Australian study. In *Nontraditional families: Parenting and child development*, ed. M. E. Lamb. Hillsdale, N.J.: Lawrence Erlbaum Associates.

Russell, G., & A. Russell. 1987. Mother-child and father-child relationships in middle childhood. *Child Development 58*, 1573–1585.

Youniss, J., & J. Smollar. 1985. *Adolescent relations with mothers, fathers and friends*. Chicago: University of Chicago Press.

READING 12-2

Downward Mobility

Terry Arendell

These women had assumed that after divorce they would somehow be able to maintain a middle-class life-style for themselves and their children. Those in their 20s and 30s had been confident that they could establish themselves as

---

capable employees and find positions that would provide sufficient incomes. Most of the older women, who had been out of the work force longer, had been less confident about their earning abilities, but they had assumed that the difference between the former family income and their own earnings would be adequately compensated for by court-ordered child support and spousal support payments. In fact, virtually all of the women had assumed that family management and parenting efforts, which had kept most of them from pursuing employment and career development while they were married, would be socially valued and legally recognized in their divorce settlements. What had worried them most was not economic difficulty but the possible psychological effects of divorce on themselves and their children. Still, they had believed that they would probably recover from the emotional trauma of divorcing in a matter of months and would then be able to reorganize their lives successfully.

DRASTICALLY REDUCED INCOMES

But even the women who had worried most about how they would manage financially without their husbands' incomes had not imagined the kind of hardship they would face after divorce. All but 2 of the 60 women had to cope with a substantial loss of family income. Indeed, 90 percent of them (56 out of 60) found that divorce immediately pushed them below the poverty line, or close to it. As wives and mothers, they had been largely dependent on their husbands, who had supplied the family's primary income.* Without that source of income, they suffered a drastic reduction in standard of living—an experience not shared by

---

*According to Lee Rainwater (1984) and the U.S. Bureau of the Census (1985), the earnings of working married wives contribute only 22 percent of the average family's total income. For this reason, poverty, which occurs in only 1 of 19 husband-wife families and in only 1 of 9 families maintained by a single father, afflicts almost one of every three families headed by a woman.

their ex-husbands.[1] Like women generally, they were "declassed" by divorce.

The economic decline experienced by these 60 women, all of whom remained single parents, was not temporary.[2] With caution and careful spending, most could meet their essential monthly expenses. But few had any extra money for dealing with emergencies or unexpected demands, and some continued to fall further behind, unable even to pay their monthly bills. One of them, divorced for nearly eight years, described her experience this way:

> I've been living hand to mouth all these years, ever since the divorce. I have no savings account. The notion of having one is as foreign to me as insurance—there's no way I can afford insurance. I have an old pickup that I don't drive very often. In the summertime I don't wear nylons to work because I can cut costs there. Together the kids and I have had to struggle and struggle. Supposedly struggle builds character. Well, some things simply aren't character building. There have been times when we've scoured the shag rug to see if we could find a coin to come up with enough to buy milk so we could have cold cereal for dinner. That's not character building.

Although they had been living for a median period of over four years as divorced single parents, only 9 of these 60 women had managed to halt the economic fall prompted by divorce; four of these nine had even managed to reestablish a standard of living close to what they had had while married. Thus the remaining majority—51 women—had experienced no economic recovery. Few had any savings, and most lived from paycheck to paycheck in a state of constant uncertainty. One of them, a woman in her late 40s and divorced more than four years, told me:

> I can't go on like this. There's no way. I can manage for another year, maybe a year and a half, but no more. I don't have the stamina. It's not that I don't have a job. My problem is money, plain and simple. That's all that counts in this situation.

This group of recently divorced mothers was by no means unique. All female-headed households experience high rates of economic hardship, and the gap in median income between female-headed families and other types of families has actually widened between 1960 and 1983.* Part of the reason is obvious: certain fixed costs of maintaining a family—such as utility bills and home mortgages or rent—do not change when the family size declines by one, and many other expenses, such as food and clothing, do not change significantly. Additionally, in most cases when the mother obtained employment, it provided a low income that was substantially reduced by new expenses, such as the costs of transportation and child care.†

These women understood how their economic dependency in marriage had contributed to their present economic situation. One of them, who had been married nearly 20 years before divorcing, said:

> Money does wonders in any situation. I'm sure women with more education and better jobs don't have situations quite as desperate as mine. But I quit school when I married and stayed home to raise my children.

---

*Between 1960 and 1983, the median income of female-headed families with no husband present dropped by the following percentages: from 61 to 57 percent of the median income of male-headed families with no wife present, from 43 to 41 percent of the median income of married couples, and from 51 to 38 percent of the median income of married-couple families in which the wife was also employed. In 1983, the median income for female-headed families was $11,484; for male-headed families with no wife present, $20,140; for married-couple families, $26,019; and for married couples in which the wife was employed, $30,340 (U.S. Bureau of the Census, 1985).

†From his Michigan study, David Chambers (1979) concludes that the custodial parent needs 80 percent of the predivorce income to maintain the family's standard of living. The total income of most family units of divorced women and children falls below 50 percent of their former family income. Sweden, in fact, has determined that single-parent families actually need more income than others and provides cash supports that give them incomes comparable to those of two-parent families (Cassetty, 1983a).

Unfortunately, they arrived at such understanding the hard way, through experience. Before divorcing, they had expected to receive "reasonable" child support and had thought they could probably find jobs that paid "reasonable" wages. They had only the vaguest understanding of other women's divorce experiences. Thus two of them said:

Friends of mine had ended up divorced with children, and they would tell me some of these things. But I had no empathy at all. I might say, "Gee, that doesn't seem fair" or "Gee, that's too bad." But it never *really* hit me how serious it is until it happened to me. So I think there must be a lot of people out there who don't have the foggiest idea what it feels like.

I had no idea how *much* money it takes. You don't have the [husband's] income, but you still have your family. There's the rub.

Their experiences led them to conclude that in America today, divorced women generally must accept a reduced standard of living. And as women with children, they were keenly aware that only remarriage could offer a quick escape from economic hardship.* A mother of three told me:

I have this really close friend. She was a neighbor and often kept my daughter until I got home from school. She and her husband had two darling little kids. One day he just up and left. Surprised us all—he married his secretary eventually. My friend hadn't worked before, so I helped her get some typing skills. She worked for two weeks and said, "No more." She called me and said, "Well, I'm not going through what you did. I'm getting married." That was like a slap in the face. Gosh, did I look that bad? I started to doubt myself. Was I doing that bad a job? Should I have gone the

marriage route? Gone out and gotten a job and then married somebody? I still wonder about that. Things would have been a lot easier financially. The kids would have had a father. And I would have done what society looks at favorably. I don't know. I still don't know what to do.

Economically these women lost their middle-class status, but socially their expectations of themselves and their children remained the same. They still identified with the middle class, but their low incomes prevented them from participating in middle-class activities. This contradiction created many dilemmas and conflicts:

I went to a CETA workshop, and I started crying when all they talked about was how to get a job. A woman came after me in the hallway, and I just bawled. I'd been searching for a job for months. I had a degree and teaching credential, and here I was being told how to fill out a stupid job application. And I had three kids at home that I didn't know how I was going to feed that week and a lovely home I couldn't afford.

I moved here after the divorce because the school had a particularly good program for gifted children. Kids were classed by ability and not just by grade level. So my kid was in a really good spot for what he needed. I didn't realize at the time that I was the only single parent in that group. One reason those kids can achieve at that level is because they have a very stable home life, two parents to work with every child on the enrichment and the projects and the homework. I hate to say this, but it's all socioeconomic. Every kid in there belonged to a high socioeconomic group. Oh, they can rationalize that it's not really like that, but it's completely WASPish, all two-parent families where the mothers don't work. Mothers are available to take kids to music lessons, soccer lessons, gymnastic lessons, and all of that whenever it's needed. I had to take my son out of that class. I couldn't keep up the level of activity required of the kids and the parents. The gap was growing greater and greater. If I'd lived like this a long time, I might have known how to cope, but this was all new. And it all came down to money.

*Research supports the commonsense belief that the surest way to reverse the economic decline resulting from divorce is to remarry (Sawhill, 1976; Duncan & Morgan, 1974, 1979; Johnson & Minton, 1982). Do women remarry because they conclude, pragmatically, that being a single woman is too costly, for themselves and perhaps also for their children? Would fewer women remarry if they could successfully support themselves? The answers to such questions will have interesting political implications.

The women resented their precarious positions all the more because they knew that their former husbands had experienced no loss in class status or standard of living and could have eased their struggles to support the children.

> Five hundred dollars here or there—or taking over the orthodontist's bills—anything like that would have meant a lot. I don't see why this kid should have to live with jaw and tooth problems because I got a divorce. His jaw had to be totally realigned, so it wasn't just cosmetic. His father could easily have paid that monthly [orthodontist] bill and deducted it. That would have made a tremendous difference. But he wouldn't. By making me suffer, he made his child suffer too.

When the children retained some access to middle-class activities through involvement with their fathers, their mothers had ambivalent feelings. They were grateful that their children were not neglected by their fathers and could enjoy some enriching and entertaining activities with them; but they found their former husbands' greater financial resources a painful reminder of how little they themselves could provide. One woman, who had to let her child get free meals through the subsidized school lunch program, despite her many efforts to make more money, told me this:

> His father seldom buys him anything. But his stepmother sometimes does. She can give him all these nice things. She's given him nice books, a stereo headset. I have no idea what her motivation is, but it's a very funny feeling to know that I can't go and buy my son something he would love to have, but this perfect stranger can. And how will that affect my son ultimately? He must know how difficult things are here, and that I'm not deliberately depriving him. But it's kind of ironic—I helped establish that standard of living, but I end up with none of it, and she has full access to it.

EXPENSES AND ECONOMIZING

Living with a reduced budget was a constant challenge to most of these women because they had no cushion to fall back on if expenses exceeded their incomes. Their savings were depleted soon after they divorced; only 12 of the 60 women I talked to had enough money in savings to cover a full month's expenses. Most said they had radically cut back their spending.[3] The major expenses after divorce were housing, food, and utilities. The women with young children also had substantial child-care expenses, and several had unusually high medical bills that were not covered by health insurance.

Within a short time after their divorces, more than one-third of the women—16 women living in homes they owned and 7 living in rented places—had to move to different housing with their children in order to reduce their expenses. Two of the women had moved more than four times in the first two years after their divorces, always for financial reasons.[4] During marriage, 49 of the 60 women had lived in homes owned with their husbands. After divorce, only nine of them retained ownership of the family home. Of these nine, six were able to acquire ownership by buying out their husbands as part of the community property settlement (five of them only because they were able to get financial assistance from their parents); two retained the home by exchanging other community assets for it; and one received the home according to the dictates of the religion she and her husband shared.

Home ownership brought with it many expenses besides mortgage payments. Several women neglected upkeep and repairs for lack of money. A woman who was in her 50s reported this common dilemma:

> I owe $16,000 on this house. I could get about $135,000 for it, so I have a large equity. But it would have taken all of that to get that condominium I looked at, and my payments would still have been about $400 a month. I don't know how I'll be able to keep up the house, financially or physically. The house needs painting, and I can't keep up the yard work. I'd like to move. I'd like a fresh start. But the kids don't want to move, and I can't imagine how I'll handle all of this once

they're gone. When the alimony [spousal support] stops, there'll be no way I can manage a move. I'm stuck here now. The mortgage is really low and the interest is only 5 percent.

Two of the mothers reduced expenses by moving their children from private to public schools. Two others were able to keep their children in private schools only after administrators waived the tuition fees. Seven mothers received financial assistance for preschoolers' child care costs, five from private and two from public agencies. One of these women, who worked full-time, had this to say about her expenses:

I'm buying this house. I pay $330 a month for it. Child care for my two kids runs to almost $500 a month. Since I bring home only a little more than $900, there's no way I could make it without the child care assistance. There'd be nothing left.

About half of these women had economic situations so dire that careful budgeting was not enough, and they continued to fall further behind economically. Those living close to the margin managed by paying some bills one month and others the next. Their indebtedness increased, and opportunities for reversing the situation did not appear:

I'm so far in debt. Yes indeed. I keep thinking, why should I worry about the bills? I'll never get out of debt! All I can do is juggle. Without my charge cards, my kids would be bare-assed naked. And school is coming up again. What am I going to do for school clothes? And they've all grown fast this year . . . I probably owe $3,000 on charge cards, and I still owe rent—I haven't paid this month or last. The landlord I have has been very understanding. He's let us go along as best he can. We're been here four years, and he knows what I'm going through. Over the years, he's given me several eviction notices, but this last time he hired a lawyer and everything. I decided I'd just pitch my tent on the capitol mall in Sacramento and say, "Here I am." I've written my congressman again, because I qualify for subsidized housing. But it'll take forever to get any action on that.

For many, however, even the persistent realities of economic hardship could not extinguish middle-class hopes:

My husband liked really good food and always bought lots and the best. So when he left, it was really hard to cut the kids back. They were used to all that good eating. Now there's often no food in the house, and everybody gets really grouchy when there's no food around . . . I think I've cut back mostly on activities. I don't go to movies anymore with friends. We've lost $150 a month now because my husband reduced the support. It gets cut from activities—we've stopped doing everything that costs, and there's nowhere else to cut. My phone is shut off. I pay all the bills first and then see what there is for food . . . I grew up playing the violin, and I'd wanted my kids to have music lessons—piano would be wonderful for them. And my older two kids are very artistic. But lessons are out of the question.

Obtaining credit had been a real problem for many, for the reasons given by this woman, who had worked during the marriage while her husband attended school:

My kids and I were very poor those first years after the divorce. I had taken care of our finances during marriage. But I didn't have accounts in my own name, so I couldn't get credit. I got a job as soon as I could. I was getting $65 a month for child support and paying $175 a month for rent. Between the rent and the child care and the driving to work, I was absolutely broke. I really didn't have enough to live on. I had no benefits either, with my first job. I was living dangerously, and with children. I could barely pay the basic bills. There wasn't enough money for food lots of times. I cried many times because there wasn't enough money. I couldn't get any credit. [When I was married] my husband could get any credit he wanted, but it was on the basis of *my* job, which had the higher income. He couldn't even keep his checkbook balanced, but now I'm the one who can't get credit! It was a hard lesson to learn. Now whenever I get a chance, I tell women to start getting a credit rating.

The woman who told me this, incidentally, had managed to overcome initial impoverishment and gain a middle-class income from her job.

Some women regarded personal possessions such as jewelry, furniture, and cars as things they might sell to meet emergencies or rising indebtedness:

> I sold jewelry to have my surgery, to pay for the part that wasn't covered. I still have some silver, and I have some good furniture, which could probably bring something. That's probably what I'd do in an emergency, sell those things. What else do people do?

Teenage children helped by earning money through odd jobs and babysitting. Older teenagers changed their college plans, and several entered community colleges instead of universities. One woman's daughter was already in the Navy, pursuing her schooling in languages and working as a translator, and the daughter of another was considering military service as a way of saving money for a college education.

Most women compared their own hardship and forced economizing to the economic freedom enjoyed by their ex-husbands. For example:

> I know my ex-husband goes somewhere almost every weekend, and he usually takes a friend along. I wonder how he can do that. How can he go somewhere every weekend? The only way I could do that is find a rich man! I couldn't possibly work enough hours to pay for that much stuff. I'd be doing well to finance a [20-mile] trip to San Francisco!

There were some exceptions to the general pattern of economic decline. Nine of the 60 women had regained some latitude for discretionary spending, though only three of them had managed this economic reversal without help. These nine were a distinct subgroup; the others did not share their higher standards of living or their feelings and approaches to the future. Still, only two of these nine women had not experienced a major decline in income immediately upon divorcing (or separating). One had been living on welfare because her husband's excessive drinking and erratic behavior had prevented him from holding a job; she found employment immediately after separating from him. The other one had been the primary family wage earner during her marriage.* Four of the women whose incomes had dropped significantly had managed to stop and even reverse the economic decline very soon after divorce because they were granted temporary spousal support awards and acquired some money and assets from their community property settlement; two of them, who had been divorced after more than 20 years of marriage, also received substantial amounts of money from their parents. Although these four did not experience the degree of hardship shared by the others, they did not fully recover their formerly high income levels and therefore also had to alter their life-styles. As one of them said:

> Essentially, I took an $80,000 drop in annual income. And I had to borrow again last year. This year I finally sold the house, and that was really the only way I've made it. My change in life-style has been *tremendous*. Just my heating and electricity bill for our home was $350 a month. We just barely got by on $2,000 a month. I stopped buying household things; I stopped buying clothes for myself. And I rented out a room in the house. It was a huge house, and that helped out. I let the cleaning woman and the gardener go. I didn't paint. I let the property taxes go until I sold the house and paid them then. I quit taking trips. This house I'm in now has much lower operating expenses. My son doesn't have the same things he'd had. His grandparents buy most of his shoes and clothes now. He used to have lots and lots, so it's been a change for him.

Of the other five women who succeeded in improving their economic situations after a few

---

*A recent study by Lee Rainwater (1984, p. 84) shows how economic dependency in a previous marriage makes it difficult for a woman to recover economically from divorce: "By the fourth year that they headed their own families, women who had regular work experience before becoming female heads had family incomes equal to 80 percent of their average family income while a wife. Women who had not worked at all had incomes slightly less than half that of their last married years."

years, three did so entirely through their own work efforts, and the other two managed with help from their former husbands—one took in the child for more than a year while his ex-wife worked at several jobs, and the other accepted a shared parenting arrangement.

EMOTIONAL RESPONSES TO ECONOMIC LOSS

None of the nine women who had experienced substantial economic recovery reported suffering serious emotional changes. Forty-four of the others, however, spoke of frequent struggles with depression and despair. Every one of them attributed these intense feelings, which often seemed overwhelming, directly to the financial hardships that followed divorce. This woman spoke for many others in describing the effects that economic loss had had on her:

> I think about money a great deal. It's amazing. I used to get so bored by people who could only talk about money. Now it's all I think about. It's a perpetual thought, how to get money—not to invest, or to save, but just to live. The interesting thing is that you develop a poverty mentality. That intrigues me. I would never have thought that could happen. But if I had had money, several times in the last year I would have fought what was happening to me in a way I no longer think of fighting. You tend to accept what's coming because there's so much you *have* to accept. You get so you accept everything that comes your way. For example, I accepted at first what I was told about treating this cancer on my face: that the only surgery possible would leave my face disfigured with one side paralyzed. I knew it would ruin any possibility of my teaching if they did that to my face, but I would have just accepted it if a friend hadn't told me to go to someone else for consultation. I wouldn't have done that on my own. That's not how I would have behaved at other times in my life. I think it must happen to a lot of divorced women. It was only this year that I realized how strange this has become. I'm educated, I've come through a wealthy phase of my life, and now here I

am, being shuttled around and not even fighting. It continues to fascinate me. After a while, you develop a begging mentality in which you'd like to squeeze money out of anybody. I guess I'm somewhere in the realm of poverty. I know there are poorer people, but I'm pretty well down near the bottom. If I were to lose this job—which is always possible, there's no security to it—I'd be finished. Finished. I'd lose the house. I'd lose everything. There's no way I could survive.

The first year of divorce was traumatic for most, especially because legal uncertainties were mixed with other fears. A vicious circle was common: anxieties brought sleepless nights, and fatigue made the anxieties sharper. Although economic hardship remained, by the end of the first year most of the women had learned to control some of the anxiety surrounding it.*

Depression overtook a majority of these women at some time or other. Their feelings of despair over financial troubles were worsened by concerns for their children. One of them said:

> I thought about running away, but who would I have turned my kids over to? I also thought about suicide—especially when the youngest was still a baby and I had so much trouble with child care and it cost me so much. I kept thinking that if I were gone, it would take a major burden off of everybody.

In fact, such despair was a common experience: 26 of the 60 women volunteered that they had contemplated suicide at some time after divorce. They mentioned various contributing factors, such as emotional harassment from their husbands and uncertainty about their own abilities and identities, but all said that economic hardship

---

*Various studies argue that the first year or so after divorce is the most stressful and traumatic (Hetherington, Cox, & Cox, 1976; Wallerstein & Kelly, 1979, 1980; Weiss 1979a, 1979b). Additionally, both Pett (1982) and Buehler and Hogan (1980) found that financial concerns were among the factors that limited divorced mothers' emotional recovery from divorce. None of these studies, however, attempts to distinguish the effects of economic uncertainty from more generalized separation emotions.

was *the* primary stress that pushed them to the point of desperation.

One mother gave a very detailed account of her experience with suicidal depression, which occurred at a time when she had been barely managing for several months. She would drag herself to work and then collapse in bed when she got home. When she would get out of bed, she told me, the sight of her 10-year-old son sitting in front of the television set, alone in a cold room and eating cold cereal, would send her back to bed, where her exhaustion and despair would be exacerbated by hours of crying. She went on:

I came home to an empty house that night—it was February. I had gotten my son's father to take him that weekend so I could go to my class—the one about learning to live as a single person again. I'd hoped that by getting some encouragement, I'd be able to pull myself out of this and find a way to make a better living. About 11 o'clock, I just decided this was no way to live. I couldn't take care of this child. I'd gone to Big Brothers, and they wouldn't take him because he had a father. But his father wasn't seeing him. Family Services weren't any help. The woman there did try to help, I think. She cared. But she'd been married more than 25 years and just didn't understand. All I could do in the 50-minute appointment with her was cry. My attorney wasn't giving me any help or getting me any money. My mother was mad at me—she said it was my fault for leaving my husband.

I just couldn't see it ever being any different, so I decided to kill myself. I'm sure that's not a unique thing. It was the most logical thing in the world. I knew exactly how I was going to do it. I was going to fill the bathtub with warm water and cut my wrists. It would be fine then—that thought was the only thing that made me feel any better. Nothing was as bad as the thought of getting up the next day. So I called my son's father—he was going to bring him back the next day—and I asked him if he thought he could take care of him. I didn't think I gave any evidence [of my feelings] or anything—it wasn't a desperate call for help, or a threatening call, or anything like that, because I'd already made up my mind. I just didn't want

him to bring my son in here and find me like that. I wanted him to make some kind of arrangements to take care of him. He didn't say anything on the phone, but in about 20 minutes the doorbell rang. Two young men in blue uniforms were standing there. They wanted to take me to an emergency room. It was a crisis place, they said. They were young and scared themselves and acted like they didn't know what to do.

I guess the shock of realizing how far I'd gone was enough to snap me out of it. I'd spent those 20 minutes [after the phone call] piddling around taking care of some last-minute things, tidying up and so on. It seems that once I made the decision, it gave me such inner peace, such a perfect reconciliation. It seemed the most logical, practical thing in the world. Then their coming stopped me from doing it. I didn't go with them, but they gave me a phone number and told me there were people there who would come and get me anytime.

I've only recently put into perspective what happened. It wasn't so much my inability to cope as it was the convergence of everything in my situation. That person at Family Services did help, actually, when she pointed out that some people who've never had trouble dealing with anything don't know what else to do when they feel like they can't cope. That fit. I'd never had a crisis I couldn't deal with in some way. I'd gotten myself into bad situations before, but I could always see cause-and-effect relationships, and I'd always felt like I could make some changes right away that would change things in my life. In this case, I couldn't figure anything out. I don't even know how to tell you what I thought.

This woman had been divorced before and had not suffered depression: but she had had no child then, no one else for whom she was responsible.

These women who were new to poverty had no ideas about how to cope in their new situations, and they found little help in the society at large. Some of the most desperate were unable to afford professional counseling. One of them said:

At one point during the eviction, I was getting hysterical. I needed help. So I called a program called Women's Stress. Good thing I wasn't really suicidal, because they kept me on hold a long time. They said, "Well, this program is just for women with an alcohol or drug problem. Does that fit you?" I said, "No, but if I don't get help, it will." They said they'd send me a pamphlet, which they did. It cost twenty-five dollars to join. I never did find any help.

The worst personal pain these women suffered came from observing the effects of sudden economic hardship on their children. Here is one woman's poignant account:

I had $950 a month, and the house payment was $760, so there was hardly anything left over. So there we were: my son qualified for free lunches at school. We'd been living on over $4,000 a month, and there we were. That's so humiliating. What that does to the self-esteem of even a child is absolutely unbelievable. And it isn't hidden: everybody knows the situation. They knew at his school that he was the kid with the free lunch coupons . . . My son is real tall and growing. I reallydidn't have any money to buy him clothes, and attorneys don't think school clothes are essential. So he was wearing these sweatshirts that were too small for him. Then one day he didn't want to go to school because the kids had been calling him Frankenstein because his arms and legs were hanging out of his clothes—they were too short. That does terrible things to a kid, it really does. We just weren't equipped to cope with it.

But the need to cut costs—on food, clothing, and activities for the children—was not the only source of pain. Most of the mothers reported that their parenting approaches changed and that their emotions became more volatile, and even unstable, in periods of great financial stress. Mothers who went to work full-time resented the inevitable loss of involvement in their children's lives:

I wish I could get over the resentment. [In the first years after the divorce] I spent half the time blaming myself and the other half blaming their father. Because I was so preoccupied, I missed some really good years with them, doing things I'd

looked forward to and wanted to do. Those years are gone now.

Some of the mothers also thought the experience of economic hardship after divorce might eventually affect the society at large, as more and more women and children come to share it.[5] For example:

It's not just the mother [who's affected]. It's a whole generation of kids who don't even know how to use a knife and a fork, who don't sit at a table to eat, who don't know how to make conversation with people of different ages. There are so many awful possibilities, and it's a whole society that's affected. I'm not talking about people who have lived for years in poverty. We planned and lived one way with no idea of the other reality. Then this harsh reality hits, and everything becomes a question of survival. I think it must be different if that's all you've experienced. At least then your plans fit your possibilities—that sort of thing. You can't spend your whole day trying to survive and then care anything about what's going on in the world around you. You really can't . . . Maybe it's going to take 50 percent of the population to be in this shape before we get change. But some of us have to be salvaged, just so we can fight. We can't all be so oppressed by trying to survive that we can't do anything at all.

Although their despair was worsened by concern for their children, it was the children who gave these women their strongest incentive to continue the struggle:

Sure, I think about suicide. And I'm a smart lady who's been creative and able to do things to change our situation. But I'm tired—*tired*. And it's real hard. What keeps me alive is my kid. I may be boxed in, but if I give up, what will happen to her? She doesn't deserve that.

Most of these women also admitted to having lost a sense of the future. A 50-year-old woman, who said she wondered if she would someday become a bag lady, told me:

That's what I started to say at the beginning—*I don't have a future*. I can sit around and cry about that for a while, but then I have to move on and ask, what am I going to do about it? And there's not much I can do. What career can I start at my age? How do I retrieve all those years spent managing a family?

And another somewhat younger woman said:

The worst poverty is the poverty of the spirit that sets in when you've been economically poor too long, and it gets to the point where you can't see things turning around.

To avoid this sense of hopelessness, a majority of the 60 women tried not to think about the future and made only short-term plans:

I learned very quickly that I couldn't think too far into the future or I'd drive myself crazy. The future became, "What will I do next month?" I learned I had to go day to day and just do the best I could. That's been my major technique for coping, and I learned it right away. I've built up some retirement and Social Security through work, thank heavens. But I have to live right now. I just can't think about the future. The worst that can happen is that the state will take care of me, and I'll end up in a crappy old folks' home. But I don't think about that.

Ten of the 60 women—a unique subgroup—said they had not experienced serious depression or despair after divorce. But the reasons they gave simply reemphasize the central importance of economic loss in the lives of divorced women. Four of these 10 had various sources of income that protected them from poverty and enabled them to work actively toward improving their situation. Two of them were using income from the divorce property settlement to attend graduate school, and they hoped to regain their former standard of living by pursuing professional careers. Two were receiving financial support from their parents while they sought employment and planned for the possible sale of their homes as part of the property settlement. The remaining six said they were generally optimistic *in spite of* their poor economic positions. Like the others, they found the financial hardships imposed by divorce sur-

prising and difficult to handle; they simply found these hardships easier to cope with than the despair they had known in their marriages.

In summary, these women discovered that the most important change brought about by divorce was an immediate economic decline, which for most of them had not been reversible. Despite their economizing efforts and dramatically altered life-styles, many of them continued to lose ground financially. In addition, economic circumstances had a powerful effect on their emotional lives. Only a very few escaped feelings of despair and hopelessness. Most found that economic uncertainties fostered depression, discouragement, and despair, and nearly all said they had endured periods of intense anxiety over the inadequacy of their income and its effects on the well-being of their children. Most of them felt trapped in their present circumstances and said they had no sense of the future.

ENDNOTES

1. Glick (1983); data from U.S. Bureau of the Census (1980).
2. Duncan and Morgan (1974, 1976, 1978, 1979); M. Hill (1981).
3. U.S. Bureau of the Census (1985). There has been no significant change in the proportion of children living with a single-parent father since 1960 (U.S. Bureau of the Census, 1983c, 1985).
4. National Advisory Council of Economic Opportunity (1981:46).
5. U.S. Bureau of the Census (1985). In fact, more than half of all families in poverty are headed by women, even though female-headed households make up only about 20 percent of all households; and 55.4 percent of all children in female-headed households live in poverty; children in two-parent and male-headed families who live in poverty total 13.4 percent (U.S. Bureau of the Census, 1985).

REFERENCES

Buehler, C., & J. Hogan. 1980. "Managerial Behavior and Stress in Families Headed by Divorced Women: A Proposed Framework." *Family Relations 29(4)*, 525–532.

Cassetty, J. 1983. "Emerging Issues in Child-Support Policy and Practice." In J. Cassetty (ed.), *The Parental Child-Support Obligation.* Lexington, Mass.: Lexington Books.

Chambers, D. 1979. Making Fathers Pay: The Enforcement of Child Support. Chicago: University of Chicago Press.

Duncan, G., & J. Morgan (eds.). 1974. *Five Thousand Families,* vol. 4. Ann Arbor: University of Michigan Press.

———. 1976. *Five Thousand Families,* vol. 5. Ann Arbor: University of Michigan Press.

———. 1978. *Five Thousand Families,* vol. 6. Ann Arbor: University of Michigan Press.

———. 1979. *Five Thousand Families,* vol. 7. Ann Arbor: University of Michigan Press.

Glick, P. 1977. "Updating the Life and Cycle of the Family." *Journal of Marriage and the Family* 39:3–15.

Hetherington, E., M. Cox, & R. Cox. 1976. "Divorced Fathers." *The Family Coordinator 25,* 417–428.

Hill, M. 1981. "Some Dynamic Aspects of Poverty." In G. Duncan and J. Morgan (eds.). *Five Thousand Families,* vol. 9. Ann Arbor: University of Michigan Press.

Johnson, W., & M. Minton. 1982. "The Economic Choice in Divorce: Extended or Blended Family?" *Journal of Divorce 5(1–2),* 101–113.

Pett, M. 1982. "Predictors of Satisfactory Social Adjustment of Divorced Single Parents." *Journal of Divorce 5(3),* 1–17.

National Advisory Council on Economic Opportunity (NACEO). 1981. *The American Promise: Equal Justice and Economic Oportunity.* Washington, D.C.: NACEO.

Rainwater, L. 1984. "Mothers' Contributions to the Family Money Economy in Europe and the United States." In P. Voydanoff (ed.), *Work and Family.* Palo Alto, Calif.: Mayfield.

Sawhill, I. 1976a. "Discrimination and Poverty Among Women Who Head Families." *Signs 1,* 201–221.

———. 1976b. "Women with Low Incomes." In M. Blaxall and B. Reagan (eds.), *Women and the Workplace.* Chicago: University of Chicago Press.

U.S. Bureau of the Census. 1980. "Child Support and Alimony: 1978." In *Current Population Reports,* series P-23, no 106. Washingtion, D.C.: U.S. Government Printing Office.

———. 1983c "Households, Families, Marital Status, and Lining Arrangements." *Current Population Reports,* series P-20, no. 382. Washingtion, D.C.: U.S. Government Printing Office.

———. 1985. *Statistical Abstract of the United States, 1985. National Data Book and Guide to Sources.* Washington, D.C.: U.S. Government Printing Office.

Wallerstein, J., & J. Kelly. 1979. "Children and Divorce: A Review." *Social Work* (November): 469–475.

Weiss, R. 1979a. *Going It Alone: The Family Life and Social Situation of the Single Parent.* New York: Basic Books.

———. 1979b. "Growing Up a Little Faster: The Experience of Growing Up in a Single-Parent Household." *Journal of Social Issues 35(4),* 97–111.

CHAPTER 13

Remarriage

At current rates, about one-third of all adults can expect to marry, divorce, and remarry during their lifetimes—a far higher proportion than in previous generations. When neither spouse has children from their previous marriages, remarried life can be very similar to life in first marriages. To be sure, the spouses tend to be older, more established in their careers, and more set in their preferences about personal life, but the basic day-to-day interaction isn't all that different. When one or both partners, however, has children from previous marriages, then the remarriage creates a step-family. In past times, most stepfamilies formed after the death of a parent; today the overwhelming number form after the parent's divorce. In both types of stepfamilies, the new stepparent must adjust to the immediate presence of the children of the other spouse. This adjustment can be difficult, not just for the stepparent but for the biological parent and the stepchildren as well.

When the remarriage follows a divorce, the stepfamily often faces additional complications.[1] The stepchildren can create links to other house-holds as they go back and forth between their mothers' and their fathers' homes. Ex-spouses also play a larger role in the remarried parents' lives. For example, a remarried father whose children visit him regularly must be prepared to adjust his visitation schedule if his ex-wife is ill or otherwise unable to meet her commitments. If both remarried partners have children from previous marriages, stepfamily life can be even more complex.

In this situation, it can be difficult for the re-married couple to forge a strong, viable partner-ship because of the tugs and pulls of stepchildren, biological children, and former spouses. Most family therapists believe that the creation of a strong bond between the remarried partners is central to the long-term success of the step-family. Yet this is not an easy task. In the following excerpt from a chapter in the edited volume, *Relative Strangers: Studies of Stepfamily Processes,* Jamie K. Keshet, a family therapist, shares the stories of several couples whom she has counseled. They illustrate the diverse ways in which married couples shape their sense of themselves as a couple. She illustrates some common reasons for conflict in stepfamilies.

---

[1] *Public and Private Families: An Introduction,* pp. 386–99.

The difficulties, Keshet argues, arise not from personality defects of the couples but rather from the complex structure and history of their family lives. I argued in a 1978 article that remarriage was an "incomplete institution," by which I meant that remarried couples lack the clear-cut rules and guidelines about family life that persons in first marriages take for granted.[2] Keshet shows how stepfamily members must create their own distinctive styles in ways that depend on who has children, where they usually stay, how often they visit, how much a childless partner wants to be involved with stepchildren, and countless other factors. She discusses how the typical experiences of stepfathers differ from the typical experiences of stepmothers.

Many remarried couples, nevertheless, build successful partnerships. Keshet also analyzes the development of successful coping styles among the couples she counseled. The key, she asserts, is by "building a boundary that separates them from the rest of the family and by becoming a team in solving stepfamily problems." Building a barrier may mean deferring some of the demands of children for time and attention; but by creating a strong alliance the couple may make the family system work better for the children as well as for themselves.

Stepfamilies also can create troubling legal issues. Our laws give stepparents few rights and responsibilities. In fact, stepparents are often legally invisible in the sense that the law disregards their efforts and claims. Consider the story of Danny Henrikson, who had lived with his stepfather after his mother died when he was four. When he was seven, his biological father, who had rarely visited or kept in touch, asked the court for custody of Danny. The stepfather refused, and the biological father sued him for custody. A lower court ruled in favor of the stepfather. However, an appeals court ruled in favor of the biological father because he was a parent, whereas the stepfather was merely a "third person"; and Danny was taken to live with his father.[3]

In the following excerpt from a chapter in the edited volume *Divorce Reform at the Crossroads,* legal scholar David Chambers, who unearthed this case, comments on it and on the legal dilemma it illustrates. Should custody be based on preserving the continuity of care a child experienced or on the principle of biological relatedness? More generally, should we expand the definition of "parent" to include nonbiological caregivers or should we still restrict it to "blood" relations? Should we begin to give stepparents some of the rights and obligations that biological parents have? Questions such as these will arise ever more frequently in the years ahead as the number of stepfamilies grows.

---

[2]Andrew Cherlin, "Remarriage as an Incomplete Institution," *American Journal of Sociology 84* (1978), pp. 634–50.

[3]I discuss the case in more detail in *Public and Private Families: An Introduction,* pp. 379–80.

READING 13-1

The Remarried Couple: Stresses and Successes

Jamie K. Keshet

In every marriage there is a tension between the need for stability in the couple relationship and the desire of each member to maintain and develop an individual identity. Each relationship has different parameters of how much closeness is too much and how much separateness can be tolerated. These limits change as the couple relationship matures and in response to pressures on the couple from other family members, work, and community. In this space between ultimate oneness or union and extreme separateness and uniqueness, the drama of marriage takes place. The tension between these poles leads to creative solutions and to growth in the individual members. Along the way it can cause arguments, disappointment, and frustration. (See Askham [1984] for a description of the relationship between identity and stability in first marriages.)

A remarried family differs from a family formed by a first marriage because one or both partners have been married before and have children from that first marriage. The partners' past and present ties to their former families create special opportunities and constraints for the second marriage. This [reading] describes some of these opportunities and constraints. The emphasis is on remarriage following divorce, which is more common than remarriage following death of a spouse, and which is more likely to involve children young enough to live in the couple's home (Cherlin, 1981).

Jamie K. Keshet, "The Remarried Couple: Stresses and Successes" from William T. Beer, ed., *Relative Strangers: Studies of Stepfamily Processes* (Totowa, New Jersey: Rowman and Littlefield, 1988), pp. 29–30 and 35–53. Copyright © 1988 by Rowman & Littlefield Publishers, Inc. Reprinted with the permission of the publishers.

The material in this [reading] is based primarily on the author's experience working as a family therapist and family educator with remarried couples and stepfamilies. In this capacity I have made the acquaintance of a wide variety of families—from those experiencing mild difficulties in making the transition to a stepfamily, to those with major crises in family life. I work with a family systems perspective that influences the way in which I perceive others. A fuller description of the theoretical basis of my work can be found in Keshet (1980, 1981, 1985, and 1987). (References to available research or theories about remarriage are included in this [reading].) Even so, not nearly enough research has been done in this area to guide us.

Remarriage becomes a fact of life for a half-million couples each year (Prosen & Farmer, 1982). When people enter a second marriage they find themselves in a new and unusual situation. The remarried couple is the foundation of a stepfamily. They have brought together diverse stepfamily members and are responsible for keeping them together. Their couple relationship, however, is likely to have a shorter history and less power than the relationship between either parent and child. Nonetheless, the couple has the tremendous task of building a lasting relationship with each other at the same time that they are completing divorces from former partners, raising their children, and pursuing their careers. . .

CONCEPTS OF FAMILY

As the couple define and create their marital relationship, they are also creating a family for themselves and their children. Each brings with him concepts of what a family is and should be. These concepts are likely to need adjusting to fit the new family that is formed. Not many people envision a honeymoon with five teenagers or a home with three different last names on the mailbox.

Each person's family concept is unique and contains elements from his or her family history.

In addition, the concept of family is likely to contain two important cultural beliefs: the overriding importance of blood ties among family members (Schneider, 1980), and the superiority of the nuclear family for child rearing (Burgoyne & Clark, 1984; Duberman, 1975; Perkins, 1977). Both beliefs are challenged by the stepfamily, in which blood ties link some members and not others.

Stepfathers often have concepts of the family ideal that differ from their perceptions of their current families (Perkins, 1977; Woodruff, 1982). This difference between real and ideal families is greater for stepfathers than for fathers in nuclear families. In one study the greater the difference between real and ideal family concepts, the more dissatisfaction was expressed by stepfamily members (Woodruff, 1982). Similar studies of stepmothers have not been undertaken (Keshet, 1986). Biological parents in first families may also have ideas about family that do not fit their actual families. In a study of parents, Galinsky (1981) identified the first stage of parenthood, which takes place before the birth of the first child, as image making, becoming aware of memories and fantasies of what it means to be a parent. Part of the parent's growth process in the family is the adjustment of these old images to fit new realities.

In a stepfamily, each partner can be at a different stage of adjusting these images. A stepparent who has never had children of his own may be functioning with the kind of images of parenthood he would have if he were expecting his first child. His stepchild, however, is already a teenager. His wife has already adjusted her images and her expectations many times as she has reared her son.

One of the tasks of the remarried couple is to create a family concept, similar to the marital definition, that can help them to provide leadership for their new family. If the couple hold similar family concepts, the areas of disagreement between them are fewer and stability in their marriage is increased. Moreover, the deci-

sions they make and the ways they behave in the family will make sense to each other, because they will be founded on the same beliefs about family.

For example, a stepfather-father comes home at the end of the day. His wife is already home and has started cooking dinner. He finds the family room, dining room, and kitchen littered with the children's coats, lunchboxes, and toys. He starts to straighten up and asks his eight-year-old stepson, who is sitting nearby reading, to help him.

If this stepfather and his wife both share a family concept in which everyone pitches in to do what needs to be done, his wife will appreciate his beginning a task she has not had time to do. She will approve of his involving her son, as he, too, is a family member. If, on the other hand, she has a concept of family in which everyone has fixed roles and responsibilities, she may see her husband's action as a criticism of her housekeeping: he would not be doing her work if he thought she did it well. She may be angry that he asked her son to help, because cleaning up is not his responsibility, either.

If the stepfather had the first concept of family and the mother the second, they could become embroiled in a large conflict. His effort to help is interpreted by his wife as a criticism of her and an exploitation of her child.

Working out a mutually acceptable concept of family may be more difficult than working out a definition of marriage. The family involves many more people, who are related differently to each member of the couple; the marital relationship involves only two.

In the formation of the stepfamily, it is likely that one's former concept of family will have to be adjusted to cope with the ways in which stepfamilies differ from nuclear families. Family membership and living in the same house are not synonymous. The couple members have different commitments and different relationships with the family children. Decisions about the children may involve adults living outside the household. Children are likely to call one adult "Mom" or "Dad" and the other by a first name.

Burgoyne and Clark, who studied stepfamilies in Sheffield, England, (1984), developed a typology to describe five different ways that remarried couples reconcile their desires to be like ordinary families with the realities of their stepfamily lives.

Type 1. Not really a stepfamily. These couples did not have to change their concept of the nuclear family and the stepparent was able to function as a parent. Either the children were quite young when the remarriage took place, or they had no contact with their parents outside the stepfamily home. Many couples had children in the stepfamily fairly soon after remarriage, and these mutual children increased their similarity to nuclear families.

Type 2. Looking forward to the empty nest. These couples could not resolve the discrepancy between their ideal families and the ways in which the stepparent functioned within the current stepfamily. They avoided this dilemma by focusing on their ideal of a couple relationship that they hoped to achieve in the future. Looking forward to a time when the stepfamily would be less difficult sustained them in the present.

Type 3. The progressive stepfamily. These couples changed their family ideals so they were no longer modeled after the nuclear family. They recognized that they had a different kind of family and saw themselves as part of a historical trend. In this way, they functioned according to a new family concept that fit their daily life.

Type 4. The conscious pursuit of ordinary family life. These couples attempted to live by the nuclear family imagery. The stepparent performed the functions of parents without having blood ties to the children. In this way they reconciled their family concept and function. In doing so, however, they reduced

their allegiances to biological children who were living outside the home.

Type 5. Conscious pursuit of ordinary family life frustrated. These couples attempted to become Type 4 families but were unable to do so, largely due to the interventions of former spouses or to unresolved problems dating back to the divorce. The stepparent was unable to function as a parent, and the family did not fit the couple's concept. These couples were the most uncomfortable with their new families.

The authors point out that they had trouble placing some couples in their typology because the husband and wife did not seem to belong in the same type. These differences between husbands and wives are likely to reflect differences in family concept as well as different perceptions of the family's daily life together.

This typology illustrates how couples combine their ideas about family with such factors as the ages of the children and the amount of contact they have with former spouses to create a way of describing their families to themselves and others. Most of the couples preferred to approximate the nuclear family ideal even if that meant living in the future or breaking ties with children in other homes. Only a few were willing to restructure their view of family to suit the situation in which they found themselves.

CONFLICTS THAT RESULT FROM DIFFERENCES

In my clinical and educational work with stepfamilies I meet many couples who are in the midst of difficult struggles to resolve differences about their identity as a couple or their handling of the children. Sometimes these differences are compounded by the fact that one member of the couple is a stepparent and the other is not.

Different Definitions of the Family

When one partner in a remarriage is in a first marriage, the couple members may have particular problems in working out a definition of their marriage that works for both of them. The following incident illustrates this difficulty.

Mr. and Mrs. Abraham were attending a holiday cookout in their suburban community. Mr. Abraham, a remarried father, had joint custody of two boys, aged four and seven, who spent every other week with him. Mrs. Abraham had never been married. Most of the couples at the cookout were first-married parents of babies or young children.

When a new neighbor asked the Abrahams if they had any children, Mr. Abraham indicated his two boys. The neighbor, a new mother herself, asked Mrs. Abraham whether she had breastfed the boys. Mrs. Abraham gave her husband a dirty look for opening her up to this awkward question and replied that she was the boys' stepmother and had never breastfed anyone.

As a result, each of the Abrahams felt betrayed by the other. Mrs. Abraham was angry that Mr. Abraham did not make her role clear and opened her up to embarrassing questions. Mr. Abraham wished his wife could have kept up the illusion that these were their children.

In this example, the members of the couple, due to their different biological relationships to the children and their different marital histories, experienced the dialogue differently. They also had different ways of handling public and private realities. Mr. Abraham had chosen his new wife, in part, because she was a pediatric nurse and knew how to handle children. He wished her to be the "real mother" of his children instead of the mother they had. He took every opportunity to include the children in his new family. He would not have minded public misrepresentation that they were a fine, suburban family consisting of Mom, Dad, and two kids, and did not understand why his wife became upset by the details.

Mrs. Abraham, slightly overwhelmed by the responsibilities of caring for the two children, missed the excitement she had expected from her first marriage. When her birthday celebra-

tion, during the first year of marriage, was not a candlelit dinner in an elegant restaurant but a visit from two muddy little boys to share cake and ice cream, she spent the late-night hours crying. At the cookout, she wished she was one of the new mothers, that she knew the history of every tooth and every fever as the new mothers did. Not only had she no desire to perpetuate the illusion that she was the mother of her stepsons, she felt she would set a trap for herself if she did. How strange it would seem to the others if they called her by her first name instead of Mom.

In their private life, Mr. and Mrs. Abraham also had different ways of understanding their reality. Mr. Abraham criticized his wife for being too strict about chores, planned outings with the children without informing her, and allowed the boys to greet him with big hugs and ignore their stepmother. In other words, Mr. Abraham maintained his role as the biological parent of the children, the one they favored and the parent who had the final say in their upbringing. He already resented the amount of control he had to relinquish to the children's biological mother, and did not want to lose more control to his new wife.

In private Mrs. Abraham wanted to be treated more like a mother. She longed for the boys to give her hello hugs, good-night kisses, and homemade cards. She wanted to be part of the planning for the family and to refer to the boys as "our kids" rather than "your kids." She wanted Mr. Abraham to support her authority and let her have the control over the household, which she felt commensurate with the amount of housework she did to create a home for him and his children.

This example illustrates the difficulty this type of remarried couple (a remarried father with a wife who has not been previously married or has been married but has not had children) has in establishing a common concept of their family reality. If we ask a childless couple in a first marriage whether they have children, we will assuredly receive the same reply from both of them. If they are expecting a child, or have a child, they will also answer in the same way. Their reality around the issue of having children is the same. They may differ in their goals for having children, but they have some time and space in which to resolve those differences.

The Abraham couple actually experienced their reality around children differently. From the difference in their identities as a parent and a stepparent came many other differences in their day-to-day experiences. Within their stepfamily, Mr. Abraham received affection from his wife and his two sons; Mrs. Abraham received affection primarily from her husband. Mr. Abraham was living with a woman he chose as a partner and two children he chose to father; Mrs. Abraham was living with a man she chose as a mate and two children about whose presence she had no choice. Mr. Abraham's history with his sons dated back seven years. Mrs. Abraham had known them for two years, the same amount of time she has known Mr. Abraham. The children respected Mr. Abraham and followed his commands; they tested the authority of Mrs. Abraham. To Mr. Abraham they were "fine kids" who became rambunctious (boys will be boys). To Mrs. Abraham they often seemed disrespectful and sloppy (she demanded order and neatness, and they listened to her less often).

Every married couple has to make decisions about how to spend their money and how much they should each work as they raise children. Financial decisions created immediate differences for the Abrahams. Mr. Abraham was proud that his income supported his boys in his home and helped support them in their mother's home (the amount of child support had been worked out by Mr. Abraham, his first wife, and their lawyers, before his marriage to his second wife). Mrs. Abraham resented the money that the former Mrs. Abraham received for the boys, which improved her lifestyle as well. Mrs. Abraham also resented that she and her husband had to use her savings to have a special vacation or a new car.

These differences in family definition created communication problems. When they discussed a vacation, Mrs. Abraham pictured two adults on a deserted beach; Mr. Abraham envisioned the four of them in a camper. The same weekend with the children could be a great success for Mr. Abraham and a large disappointment for his wife.

Couples like the Abrahams are more common in counseling than in the population at large. These couples seem to have a particularly hard time when the wife takes the major responsibility for the nurturance and support of the couple relationship itself. She may feel that she looks after the couple and her husband looks after his children. She plans an evening out with him, and he has expended so much energy with his children during the day that he's too tired to enjoy their time out. She wants new furniture in the living room, and he wants to buy a climbing structure. She can easily feel abandoned if this split is too great. In a couple in which the wife is the remarried parent and the stepfather has no children, often the wife takes on the responsibility for the couple relationship as well as for the parenting. Stepfathers rarely feel they are taking prime responsibility for the couple relationship.

Different Orientations to Child-Rearing

The next example illustrates the differences that can occur between parent and stepparent about discipline.

Mr. Russell, the stepfather of a 13-year-old daughter, criticized his wife for the way she handled her daughter for coming in late the night before. "Listen, last night she came in an hour late. In my family, when I broke a rule, I got punished. Right then and there. You sweettalk her, you ask her if everything's all right, and tuck her in with a good night kiss. Why didn't you lay out a punishment last night? I think we should ground her for a month."

"Look," Mrs. Russell answered, "she's the kind of kid who will apologize and listen tomorrow. Last night we just would have had a huge argument, she would have been stubborn, I would have lost my temper, and we would all have been up for another hour fighting. This way I'll remind her how important it is for her to be in on time—she was very foolish not even to call us—and I'll cut back on her phone time for the next week."

"There you go again, being so namby-pamby. What kind of kid are you raising anyway? If she's gonna be a daughter of mine, even a step-daughter of mine, she's got to learn to obey."

The Russells illustrate another common difference in remarried couples, a difference that frequently arises in this form when a divorced or widowed mother marries a man who has never been married or has never had children of his own, but has very strong ideas about how children should be reared.

Two ways of looking at morality, a rules orientation and a response orientation, have been described by Gilligan (1982) and Lyons (1983). In the rules orientation, the priority is to fulfill one's responsibility according to an explicit code of behavior. In the response orientation, the priority is the maintenance of relationship even when that means diverging from the formal code. Most people are able to use both these orientations and use them in different settings.

Mrs. Russell expressed the response orientation and Mr. Russell the rules orientation in coping with Jennifer's misbehavior. This difference in outlook between parent and stepparent is typical for remarried couples. Mrs. Russell, as the parent, had a relationship with her child to maintain. In the context of this relationship, she could make exceptions to the rules. Mrs. Russell knew that her daughter would be apologetic and cooperative the following morning but stubborn and defiant the night of the offense. She had learned this way of handling Jennifer by trial and error over their years together. Moreover, she had a stake in handling Jennifer in a way that did not increase the emotional distance between them.

Mr. Russell, lacking this kind of intimate relationship, needed to rely on the rules to bring some order and predictability into his life. He was evaluating the child's behavior from a distance. He was also more aware and more upset by the ways in which transgressions of the rules disrupted his adult life and intruded into the private space for him and his wife. Mrs. Russell expected worry about a daughter to be part of her life; she had had 13 years to become accustomed to the strains of parenthood. Mr. Russell wanted a quiet evening, to relax, and to go to bed on time. He wanted Mrs. Russell to be attentive to him, not to listening to every footstep on the sidewalk or to look at the phone to make it ring.

This difference was also apparent in Mr. Russell's wish to return to a neat home, to walk inside without tripping over skate boards, being accosted by the blare of rock and roll, or finding books and coats piled on the dining room table. Mr. Russell interpreted these acts as a deliberate lack of consideration. To Mrs. Russell, they were minor infringements that she considered part of life with a teenager. She knew her daughter loved her; she did not interpret her messiness as disrespect or lack of caring. Mr. Russell was not sure his stepdaughter even liked him; he looked for signs of acceptance or rejection in all her behavior.

What happened in the Russells' argument is common. The conflict is likely to escalate as each one becomes more entrenched in his or her position. The more critical Mr. Russell became, the more Mrs. Russell felt she had to protect her daughter. The more Mrs. Russell defended her daughter, the more unsupported and rejected Mr. Russell felt and the angrier he became. His anger, evoked by his wife, was often displaced onto his stepdaughter so that he thought her punishment should be even greater than he did originally.

Mr. Russell is not atypical. Research on stepfather families indicates that stepfathers tend to be more authoritarian and traditional in their views about family and child-rearing than are natural fathers (Bohannon & Yahraes, 1979; Perkins, 1977; Woodruff, 1982). One reason that stepfathers express such authoritarian views may be that the family system needs more authority. Divorced mothers tend to be more permissive and less firm in disciplining their children than either mothers in intact families or mothers in stepfamilies (Hetherington, Cox & Cox, 1982; Santrock et al., 1982). When the stepfather joins the family there is a good chance that the children are behaving in ways that many adults would not accept. The mother had tolerated this behavior because she felt guilty about the divorce or because she did not have the strength to take control. Unless the stepfather is an extremely tolerant person, he is likely to be pulled into the role of bringing some order to the family. Someone needs to present the rules orientation.

A similar phenomenon does occur with stepmothers if the remarried father has been very permissive with his children. The stepmother then feels she has to establish order in the household. Her emphasis is often getting chores done, doing homework, and keeping things neat. The stepfather's concern is more often obedience to adults and showing respect. Each stepparent may enforce limits in those areas that the natural parent has let slide since the divorce. Stepmothers, however, tend to resent it when they fall into the role of "heavy" in the family. They complain that their husbands should make these demands on the children and they should not have to (an old-fashioned nuclear family model). In contrast, although stepfathers become angry at their partners for allowing the children to misbehave, they are willing to take the children on directly. They may be fulfilling what they have been taught is the masculine role—to be the authority.

These differences in orientation and the fact that the parent has gone through years of the intense experience of parenting sometimes make it hard for the couple to see eye-to-eye on these issues. Mr. Russell felt he was helping out by laying down the law and having his stepdaughter follow the rules. Mrs. Russell appreciated his strictness but at times felt he was being too harsh or did not know her daughter well enough.

Disagreement about the Former Spouse

The former spouse of one member of the remarried couple can also continue to exert an influence on that partner, which makes it more difficult for the couple to establish stability between them. The Jordan couple illustrate this problem.

Mrs. Jordan's parents had just arrived for their first visit to the new couple since the wedding. Mrs. Jordan had planned five days of sightseeing and visiting. Mr. Jordan received a phone call from his former wife, who had sprained her ankle and would not be able to drive his children to summer camp. Nor had she finished shopping for them. Mr. Jordan agreed to take the children shopping the next day and to drive them to camp the day after.

Mrs. Jordan remonstrated: "She always does this. That woman runs my life. I want to have a nice weekend with my parents and my kids and you and now this."

Mr. Jordan replied, "She didn't sprain her ankle on purpose. The kids need me to help them. I can't refuse to help my kids."

Mrs. Jordan answered, "Helping your kids hurts mine. They want their grandparents to share their new family. You're important to them, too. There's always something. Why couldn't she find a friend to drive them up? Why can't they go on a bus? Why do you always say yes to her right away.?"

The continuing relationship with a former spouse can interfere with the autonomy of the remarried couple. Many decisions cannot be made without checking with the former spouse. Events in the former spouse's life, such as this sprained ankle, affect the new couple. Sometimes both members of the new couple have the same reaction—whether anger or acceptance. When they have different reactions, additional problems arise for the couple. Mrs. Jordan saw Mr. Jordan as being manipulated by his ex-wife.

This limited her own power in the couple relationship and also lowered her respect for her husband. Mr. Jordan saw Mrs. Jordan as unsympathetic and unsupportive of his parenting of his children.

The ex-wife is frequently a character to be reckoned with. Problems seem to occur more frequently with former wives of remarried husbands than with former husbands. A former wife is more likely than a former husband to have custody of the children: she is more involved with her children's lives and may want to be in charge of the children-father relationship. Even when mothers do not have custody, they are more likely to remain involved with their children than fathers without custody (Furstenberg & Nord, 1985).

Mr. Jordan viewed his children and their mother as a unit as they were when he was married—his wife-n-kids. He helped his ex-wife pay her rent so the children would have a roof over their heads. Since he was somewhat removed from the daily care of the children, he wanted the person providing that care, his ex-wife, to do it well.

Mrs. Jordan was more likely to separate the ex-wife and the children in her thinking. She saw the children when they spent time in her home; she rarely saw the former wife. She also had a tremendous respect for the bond created between a man and a woman when they have a child together. She knew that a marriage can be ended through a divorce, but that the children, and the bonds they create, remain forever. She was jealous that the former Mrs. Jordan had this bond with her husband and she did not. Even though she knew rationally, that Mr. Jordan had no desire to return to his former wife, the new Mrs. Jordan was readily jealous of the kinds of attention, assistance, and cooperation that Mr. Jordan gave his ex-wife.

Feelings about the former spouse came between the couple members when Mr. Jordan had some direct contact with his former wife and Mrs. Jordan did not. In a long phone conversa-

tion or even in a face-to-face meeting, Mr. Jordan could express his anger and frustration at some of their dealings. At these times he could find her responsive and reasonable, and might end the conversation with an improved opinion of his former wife. Mrs. Jordan, without this outlet for her feelings and without the direct exchange with her husband's ex-wife, had no way to release her anger. She often felt abandoned by her husband when he told her that his ex-wife was trying to be reasonable.

LIVING IN THE STEPFAMILY STRUCTURE

The Abraham, Russell, and Jordan couples illustrate some characteristic conflicts in remarried couples. These problems are not caused by personality defects in the partners; they are a result of the stepfamily's complex structure and history. A look at this structure is helpful in understanding the couples' dilemmas.

The remarried couple is embedded within the larger and more complex family constellation of a stepfamily. Through their children they are tied to former spouses who may also be in stepfamilies of their own. The couple, their children, and their children's parents are all functioning within a larger system that Ahrons (1984) calls the binuclear family and Bohannon (1970) refers to as a kinship chain.

Being part of a stepfamily has a very specific influence on the couple. On the positive side, the other adults in the binuclear family may be resources for the couple when they need time without children or when the children are having difficulties. On the negative side, the couple may find their autonomy, intimacy, and power limited by the larger system. An example will illustrate:

Marge was a single parent with two children. Her mother, who lived in another state, needed surgery, and Marge wanted to spend two weeks with her after the operation. She called her former husband, Peter, to see if he could take the children for that time (Peter is a resource for her). Peter talked to his second wife, Jessica, and they agreed. (Marge's request can be seen as a disruption of their lives. They are not autonomous in planning their time.) Jessica had two children from her first marriage. She called her ex-husband, Ron, to see if he could switch his visitation weekend so it would come after Peter's kids had gone, rather than in the middle of their stay. (Ron is a potential resource for Jessica and Peter in helping them have time alone together). Ron agreed but found himself thinking, "I am expected to change my plans because my ex-wife's second husband's ex-wife's mother is ill." (His autonomy is now limited and his concept of family is being stretched). So that he could care for his children, he called the new woman in his life to reschedule a ski weekend they had planned.

This story demonstrates how the various adults can be resources for each other and how their doing so puts restraints on their own autonomy and on the intimacy of the new couples. This particular family demonstrated flexibility and cooperation. Marge, Peter, Jessica, and Ron seem to have accepted living in a kinship chain. Peter's new woman friend, Liz, is not yet a member of this system and is less likely to understand why Peter chose to agree to this change. As the newest adult in the kinship chain, she could easily feel resentful and powerless. Jessica, earlier in her marriage to Peter, might have felt the same way about Marge's request, but she has become used to changing arrangements and recognizes that an occasion may arise when she and Peter will ask Marge for a similar favor.

Peter and Jessica, because they are settled in their stepfamily and have learned to put each other first when communicating about stepfamily events, are not likely to argue about this new childcare plan. Liz and Ron, on the other hand, may have some conflict about it. Ron said yes to his ex-wife even before he consulted Liz. The Russell couple above were still experiencing conflict about similar behavior on the part of the husband toward his ex-wife.

Limits on Intimacy

Couples in remarriages usually want intimacy and closeness. Many of them have had first marriages in which they never became as intimate as they would have liked. Individuals going through the divorce process often begin to share with other people in new ways. They think about their lives, their choices, and their relationships more seriously. Some men, who care for their children after a marital separation, learn to be more attentive to feelings, more nurturant, and more responsive to others than they have been before. Couples also enter new relationships with a fear of the vulnerability they know accompanies closeness. A determination to make the relationship work despite the risks often keeps the remarried couple together as they face the hurdles of stepchildren and former spouses.

Children themselves interfere with intimacy (it is hard to hug a man who has two children on his lap). Love is not supposed to be a quantifiable entity with only so much to go around. Yet time, energy, front seats in the car, and hands to hold are finite. The romance quickly goes out of a day in the woods when two children are along. A pizza shop is not as conducive to intimacy as a candlelit café. Children often make a point of disregarding hints from the couple that they want to be alone.

Old concepts of the family often get in the way of ensuring the couple's privacy. Parents feel guilty saying no to requests their children make for help or time together. They often dislike closing or locking their bedroom doors. Stepparents feel ashamed to admit they feel jealous when their partners are loving and intimate with their children.

A parent can feel close to the new partner and the child at the same time; a stepparent rarely can. The stepfather of a six-year-old girl expressed his embarrassment when his wife would allow her daughter to come into their room while they dressed in the morning. When the stepparent experiences the child as a hindrance to couple intimacy and requests time alone, the parent often feels that the child is being rejected. When the parent can understand the motivation for the stepparent's request, the chances of resolving differences are increased.

The daily tasks of childcare can be tedious and frustrating. Preparing meals, washing dishes, doing laundry, driving the children to their lessons and appointments are not intrinsically pleasant but give parents the satisfaction of being good parents and watching their children develop. An afternoon pushing kids on swings in the park can be a meaningful, great Sunday for the visiting father and a bore for his wife. Watching a school play can be a thrill for the proud mother and a chore for her new husband. This difference in their experience, if not acknowledged, can lead to a sense of resentment and neglect on the part of the stepparent.

The former spouse can also interfere with intimacy. A phone call from an ex-husband or ex-wife interrupts an evening together far more than a call from a family member or friend. Conflicts that arise between former spouses spill over into the new marriage. The new couple may disagree about how to handle the "ex." Even when they agree, they may feel emotionally burned out from discussing the problems with a former mate. It is hard to switch gears from this kind of problem solving to intimate relations.

Reminders of the past, if they upset one member of the couple, can cause friction. The children themselves often look or behave like their other parent. A cute story about a child when he was little may include a reference to the child's mother, which sets off jealousy in the stepmother. Some stepparents hate hearing about family history that occurred before they were on the scene.

The Russell couple's dilemma is a good illustration of how the former spouse can interfere

with the couple's time together and sense of shared purpose and create disagreements between them. Although difficulties between former spouses seem to be the worst in the first years of courtship and remarriage, they may occur as long as the children are in touch with both parents. For many divorced parents, major milestones in the child's life, such as graduation or marriage, include some kind of contact with the former spouse. This contact itself may create conflict for the stepparent or differences of opinion between parent and stepparent.

Limits on Autonomy and Power of the Couple

Being a couple in a stepfamily limits the couple's power in several ways. Within their household they have to work hard for each parent's authority to be respected by all the children. The children's needs and requests often interfere with couple goals and priorities. Unless the couple take charge of the family and act as its executive team, they are not likely to feel any sense of stability and order in their marriage. When they attempt to manage the family and establish standards in their household about the kind of food served, the hours at which children are allowed to wake or sleep, or the participation of the children in family activities, they often meet resistance from children who were accustomed to another way of doing things before the marriage.

As a unit within the larger system, the remarried couple is not as autonomous as a first-married couple would be. They cannot even choose when to have their first child—the children are there already. A remarried couple often need to talk with former spouses in order to make vacation plans to go away with their own children. Many couples cannot decide to send a child to a private school, seek a therapist for a child, or move out of state without complex negotiations. Often the couple are not independent financially; a wife may be receiving child support from her former husband, while a husband is making support payments to his former wife.

Changes in the financial status of the former spouses can suddenly affect the new family's economic stability as well.

Both parents and stepparents express pain and frustration at having their hands tied in dealing with the ways the former spouses treat the children. The couple members can work together to minimize these effects, but they rarely experience the satisfaction of solving this kind of problem together. The remarried couple simple do not have the power to change the behavior of the child's other parent. They cannot, for example, make a visiting parent be responsible, be punctual, or plan appropriate activities. Sometimes when one parent remarries, the parent who is still living as a single parent puts pressure on the children to miss their visitation time and stay with her because she is alone. Although parents can go as far as the courts to enforce divorce agreements, they cannot effectively stop a parent's guilt-inducing tactics on the children.

Gender Differences

It is almost impossible to write about couple relationships without considering the effects of male and female roles and socialization. In a remarriage the gender of the stepparent (especially if he or she is not a parent already) affects the kind of differences that the couple are likely to have to work out. A stepmother's experience and a stepfather's experience are not interchangeable, primarily because being the partner of a divorced mother is different from being the partner of a divorced father.

The ways in which custody is usually awarded following divorce contributes to the ways in which the roles of stepfather and stepmother differ. These differences, in turn, create particular patterns of couple interaction.

Because most mothers are awarded custody or have joint custody following divorce (Cherlin, 1981), most stepfathers see their stepchildren regularly and share their primary household. But stepfathers vary considerably in how directly involved they are with the children. In many households the provider role is considered sufficient involvement for a stepfather or a father. The children are used to living in their mother's household. Although they have to adjust to a stepfather, he is not defined as their primary caretaker. The stepfather, by living in the custodial home of the children, shares their daily routines, sees them when they are relaxed, and has some leisure time along with his wife if the children visit their father.

Most stepmothers, who live with fathers who do not have custody of their children, see the children only at those times designated for visitation. When the children spend time with them, they seem to be a cross between family members and guests and may be particularly anxious or rebellious. Some divorced fathers feel they do not have enough time with their children and are reluctant to allow the stepmothers to become close to them. Others expect the stepmothers, as females, to take the primary responsibility for the children during their visits, especially if the stepmother is caring for children of her own or is in charge of running the household. Some stepmothers find themselves in this role because their paychecks are smaller and are more easily sacrificed when their stepchildren move in.

When fathers do have custody of their children, it is often because the mother is considered unfit or because the children have moved from the mother's home to the father's. In these cases, the children are more likely to be confused, to feel rejected, or to be lacking in basic security and social skills because of the family history. Caring for these children may be more difficult than dealing with children who are in their mother's custody. Moreover, visiting mothers are in touch with their children more frequently than visiting fathers, so the child in father custody may feel conflicted in loyalty to the two parents.

Differences in the socialization of men and women also influence the expectations they bring to the stepparent role. Both fathers and stepfathers are expected to be more distant from children than mothers. Both are expected to be out of the house a good deal of the time and to concern themselves with providing for the material needs of the family. A stepfather who is ignored by a crying child running to her mother does not often feel rejected (many biological fathers are also ignored in the dash to get comfort from Mommy). A stepfather who helps out financially, does some activities with his stepchildren on the weekend, and gives his wife comfort and support in her role can feel that he is doing a pretty good job.

A stepmother's job, on the other hand, is often closer to the role of a father than that of a mother. A father is sometimes treated as the secondary parent in the family. A stepmother is also a secondary parent, second to the father. But her ideal of a parent is usually that of a mother. She may feel like a failure when the crying child pushes past her to find Daddy's arms for comfort.

As a woman, a stepmother is also more likely to use her relationships as a measure of how her life is going. If her relationships are in good shape, other areas of her life may seem less important. Because of the structure of the visiting stepfamily and because of her unrealistic expectations of her role, it is often hard for the stepmother to feel that her steprelationships are going well. This may be true even if she has already proven to be a good mother to her biological children.

The implications of these differences between stepmothers and stepfathers are twofold. First, within each marriage they create a role and a set of role expectations for the stepmother or the stepfather. The stepparent's adjustment to this role may cause discomfort or grievances, which the couple need to resolve. Different roles for stepfathers and stepmothers also create important differences among those remarried couples that contain a stepmother and father, a stepfather and mother, or a stepmother and stepfather (the Abraham, Jordan, and Russell couples above). Disagreements between the couple members are likely to be expressed differently in each type of couple, and the particular conflicts that arise are likely to be different.

Successful Coping Patterns

Being part of a larger system puts a particular and somewhat predictable set of limits on the couple's opportunities to be intimate, powerful, and autonomous. Within these structural and historical constraints, the remarried partners work out a balance between togetherness and individuality.

The couple's sense of connection is enhanced by building a boundary that separates them from the rest of the family and by becoming a team in solving stepfamily problems. Many couples set aside time to be alone together. Planning to have a discussion about how things are going every Tuesday after dinner might seem absurd to partners in a first marriage, but it may be a necessity in a remarriage. Having time alone together increases the sense of stability, because each partner is not pulled in a different direction by his or her ties to a set of children.

The couple also learn to say no to children and former spouses on issues that interfere with their needs as a couple. Sometimes a couple with two sets of stepchildren make time for themselves by having all the children at their home some weekends and none of the children on other weekends. Although this arrangement may be less satisfactory for the children who always have to share their parents with stepsiblings, the parents find it helpful. Other activities such as entertaining friends, playing sports, and do-it-yourself projects may also be limited so the couple can be together.

The identity of each couple member is respected and encouraged by the recognition of each one's different connections to other family members. Some remarried parents find it fulfilling to spend time alone with their biological children. Honoring this desire gives the other partner a chance to be with his or her children or to pursue other interests. Some childless step-mothers find that leaving the house while the children are visiting and doing things they like by themselves or with other adults is a good antidote to feeling exploited or excluded. When they feel gratified by their own activities they are likely to be better partners in the marriage.

Remarried partners are often able to express their individual needs and interests more easily than partners in first marriages because they are more mature, have insights about themselves gained from a divorce, or have a vision of marriage that allows them to express their uniqueness. Giving up the concept of marriage as a total unity and merger of two people provides freedom for individual differences.

Remarried couples can handle their finances by pooling their resources into a common pot (Fishman, 1983) or by pooling some resources for household needs and keeping some separate for one's biological children and oneself. Fishman found that pooled resources increased family integration. Keeping some money separate can give partners a sense of independence and the freedom to spend some money without consulting the other. Each approach has some benefits.

The improved communication that happily remarried couples describe can enhance both couple stability and individual identity. Talking things over enables couples to come to agreement and to form common goals, thereby increasing the stability in the relationship. Good communication also includes listening to the other person and respecting the differences that arise. By continuing to talk together, a remarried couple can learn that differences are not always a threat to their marriage.

Stresses and Successes

Second marriages end in divorce as frequently or more frequently than first marriages (Cherlin, 1981). When one thinks about why so many remarriages are shortlived, it is important to consider both the particular stresses felt by the re-married couple and their strengths in coping with these stresses.

The stresses of the stepfamily seem to take their toll. Having stepchildren in the remarriage increases the likelihood of divorce, and having two sets of stepchildren increases it even more (White & Booth, 1985). This implies that the pressures of being a couple in the midst of a stepfamily may make some remarriages less viable. Yet the Pennsylvania couples described by Furstenberg and Spanier (1984) are living with these stresses and feel their marriages are better the second time around. They seem to represent a category of remarried couples who are well equipped to survive the difficulties of stepfamily life.

When couples in remarriages do divorce, it is likely that the difficulties of living in a stepfamily are not the only reason. Couples who divorce after a second marriage probably break up for the same reasons that their first marriages did. Many second marriages for one partner are first marriages for the other. The desire for individual gratification that is not found in the marriage may lead to divorce. Both the strengths and weaknesses of the couple relationship itself and the nature and extent of the pressures upon it are likely to influence the marriage's success or failure.

One factor that may help a remarried couple to survive is their ability to reformulate their concepts of marriage and family to fit the remarried couple and stepfamily. If they cannot do this, the frustration of trying to live up to nuclear family and first-marriage ideals may increase the tension between the partners. Not all successful remarried couples, however, give up the model of the nuclear family. Some prefer to sever ties with children in other households and treat their stepfamily as a nuclear family (Burgoyne & Clark, 1984).

Despite the similar dilemmas faced by remarried couples, there are many differences among them. There is no right way or best way for a remarried couple to achieve the balance of stability and identity that works for them. Successful stepfamilies have developed their own strategies to cope with the differences between the spouses and the differences between the parts of their stepfamily. The stepfamily can be a place for learning that differences can generate excitement and energy and that people who have different histories and different opinions can remain married and care for each other and all their children.

REFERENCES

Ahrons, C. 1984. "The Binuclear Family: Parenting Roles and Relationships." In *Parent-Child Relationships, Post-Divorce: A Seminar Report.* Copenhagen: Danish National Institute of Social Research.

Askham, J. 1984. *Identity and Stability in Marriage.* Cambridge: Cambridge University Press.

Bohannon, P. 1970. "Divorce Chains, Households of Remarriage and Multiple Chains." In Bohannon, ed., *Divorce and After: An Analysis of the Emotional and Social Problems of Divorce.* New York: Doubleday.

Bohannon, P., & H. Yahraes. 1979. "Stepfathers as Parents." In *Families Today: A Research Sampler on Families and Children,* ed. E. Corfman.

Burgoyne, J., & D. Clark. 1984. *Making a Go of It: A Study of Stepfamilies in Sheffield.* London: Routledge and Kegan Paul.

Cherlin, A. 1981. *Marriage, Divorce, Remarriage: Changing Patterns in the Post-war United States.* Cambridge: Harvard University Press.

Duberman, L. 1975. *The Reconstituted Family: A Study of Remarried Couples and Their Children.* Chicago: Nelson-Hall.

Fishman, B. 1983. "The Economic Behavior of Stepfamilies." *Family Relations 32,* pp. 359–66.

Furstenberg, F., and C. Nord. 1985. "Parenting Apart: Patterns of Childrearing after Marital Disruption." *Journal of Marriage and the Family 47,* pp. 893–904.

Furstenberg, F., and G. Spanier. 1984. *Recycling the Family: Remarriage After Divorce.* Beverly Hills, Calif.: Sage.

Galinsky, E. 1981. *Between Generations: The Six Stages of Parenthood.* New York: Times Books.

Gilligan, C. 1982. *In a Different Voice.* Cambridge: Harvard University Press.

Glick, P. 1980. "Remarriage: Some Recent Changes and Variations." *Journal of Family Issues* 1: 455–77.

Hetherington, E., M. Cox, & R. Cox. 1982. "Effects of Divorce on Parents and Children." In *Nontraditional Families: Parenting and Child Development,* ed. M. Lamb. Hillsdale, N.J.: Lawrence Erlbaum Associates.

Keshet, J. 1980. "From Separation to Stepfamily: A Subsystem Analysis." *Journal of Family Issues 1,* pp. 517–32.

————. 1981. "The Minifamily in the Stepfamily." In *Parenting After Divorce,* ed. C. Baden. Boston: Wheelock Center for Parenting Studies.

————. 1986. "The Stepparent Role: A Review of the Literature." Unpublished paper. Harvard University Graduate School of Education.

————. 1987. *Love and Power in the Stepfamily: A Practical Guide.* New York: McGraw-Hill.

Lyons, N. 1983. "Two Perspectives: On Self, Relationships, and Morality." *Harvard Educational Review 53,* pp. 125–46.

Perkins, T. 1977. *Natural-Parent Family Systems vs. Stepparent Family Systems.* Ph.D. dissertation, University of Southern California.

Prosen, S., & J. Farmer. 1982. "Understanding Stepfamilies: Issues and Implications for Counselors." *Personnel and Guidance Journal 60,* pp. 393–97.

Santrock, J., R. Warshak, C. Lindbergh, and L. Meadows. 1982. "Children's and Parents' Observed Social Behavior in Stepfather Families." *Child Development 53,* pp. 472–80.

Schneider, D. 1980. American Kinship: A Cultural Account. Chicago: Chicago University Press.

White, L., & A. Booth. 1985. "The Quality and Stability of Remarriages: The Role of Children." *American Sociological Review 50,* pp. 689–98.

Woodruff, L. 1982. "Traditionalism in Family Ideology: Effects on Adjustment and Satisfaction Comparing Biological and Stepfather Families." Ph.D. dissertation, University of Alabama.

The Law Ignores the Stepparent

David L. Chambers

How has family law conceived the stepparent relationship? The stepparent as parent? As friend? As someone in between or as someone entirely different? Family law, as a formal matter, has largely ignored the relationship. In the substantial majority of states, stepparents, even when they live with a child, have no legal obligation to contribute to the child's support; nor does a stepparent's presence in the home alter the support obligations of a noncustodial parent. The stepparent also has had no authority to make decisions about the child—no authority to approve emergency medical treatment or even to sign a permission slip for a field trip to the fire station. State law has had only one mechanism—adoption—to permit a stepparent married to the custodial parent to formalize a role with a child.

On the breakup of a marriage between a biologic parent and a stepparent, the stepparent again has been ignored by the law unless the child has been adopted. In the absence of adoption or some extraordinary circumstances noted later, the law in nearly all states imposes no continuing financial obligations on the stepparent regardless of the extent of support he or she has provided while living with the child. Similarly, except in unusual circumstances, the law has not treated the stepparent as an appropriate custodian for the child or aided the stepparent in continuing a relationship with the child through visitation. On the death of a stepparent, laws of intestate succession nearly always exclude stepchildren from the list of relations who will share in the estate. . .

David L. Chambers, "The Law Ignores the Stepparent" from Stephen D. Sugarman and Hema Hill Kay, eds., *Divorce Reform at the Crossroads*, pp. 108 and 122–125. Copyright © 1990 by Yale University. Reprinted with the permission of Yale University Press.

On occasion, courts become involved in formally adjudicating a stepparent's request for the custody of stepchildren over the objection of another parent, either after one parent's death or at the point of divorce. Probably no more than 25 appellate cases have been decided in the United States over the last two decades in which a stepparent and biologic parent have contended for custody. How many more cases have been decided by trial courts and not appealed is, as usual, impossible to say. Of course, in the United States today, relatively few parents die during their children's minority. Moreover, for at least two reasons, it is also probable that few residential stepparents seriously consider seeking custody upon divorce, let alone contesting the issue in court. First, most residential stepparents are men, and father custody after divorce, even among biologic fathers, remains much less frequent than mother custody in this country. Second and more fundamental, most stepparents themselves probably believe that the children belong with (and to) the biologic parent.

In the occasional cases in which judges must choose between stepparents and biologic parents, they face much the same ineffable choices that they do in the context of disputed stepparent adoptions. The appellate opinions recording these decisions are not a pretty sight.[1] I have read them as much to observe judges' attitudes toward stepparent-stepchild relationships and their ways of characterizing the stepparent and the biologic parent as I have to learn the developing state of the law. Whichever way one reads, it is difficult to perceive consistent patterns. The widely differing results of courts in these custody cases should not come as a surprise, however. The incoherent pattern of outcomes and the murky and inconsistent discussions of the governing rules almost certainly reflect our society's conflicting and unresolved attitudes about stepparents, even when loving, and about biologic parents, even when indifferent.

Here are some of the ways these attitudes display themselves. For dealing with custody disputes involving stepparents, only one state appears to have adopted legislation that treats them by name as potential custodians,[2] and only a few others provide general authority for courts to consider requests for custody by long-term caretakers.[3] Even the Uniform Marriage and Divorce Act, which deals at length with issues of custody on divorce, never mentions stepparents and implicitly relegates a stepparent who wishes custody to search for other sources of statutory authority for any claims. Courts in some states have thus simply held that they had no jurisdiction to consider a petition by a stepparent for custody, even after a child has lived with the stepparent as her only caretaker for many years.[4]

Most courts that find jurisdiction to resolve a claim by a stepparent for custody have to rely on legislation drafted without stepparents in particular in mind. Some state courts have taken jurisdiction by fiat, simply failing to discuss the basis for their authority to decide. Others in cases with a compelling case for placement with a stepparent have stretched, brazenly, the language of a custody statute that seemed to apply to biologic parents only.[5]

When courts have found a basis for jurisdiction, they have then had to grapple with the standard to apply. Are biologic parents and the residential stepparents competing for custody to be treated as equals or does the biologic parent stand in a preferred position before the court? Courts' opinions might have included revealing discussions about the importance of preserving biologic ties or the importance of preserving continuity of caretaking or frank discussions of the rights of biologic parents to the custody of their children regardless of children's needs. Unfortunately, nearly all the discussion is unilluminating. Courts fuss over statements of the standard without explaining what considerations are affecting their inquiry.

Consider, for example *Henrikson* v. *Gable,* a recent Michigan case involving a dispute between a residential stepfather and a biologic father after the death of the custodial mother.[6] The children, ages nine and ten, had lived in the stepfather's household since infancy and regarded the stepfather as their dad. The biologic father had rarely visited or called. A trial judge, after a long hearing, left the children with the stepfather. Wrestling with the case on appeal, the appellate court found two statutory provisions pointing in conflicting directions—one provision creating a strong preference for biologic parents and the other creating a strong preference for keeping children in "established custodial environments" under prior court orders. Then the court without anything that can generously be called reasoning held that the first section trumped the other and directed the children's return to their biologic father. The court drew on earlier state appellate decisions that make little sense either individually or as a group and at least some of which announce a different standard than the appellate court in *Henrikson* applied. Courts in some other states have candidly complained that the decisions of their own state's courts have not been wholly consistent.[7]

In a substantial number of cases, courts with a strongly sympathetic case for a stepparent simply seem to impose on the stepparent the toughest standard that that person can meet, proclaiming with vigor the rights of biologic parents and the presumptions in their favor but keeping the standard just weak enough that the stepparent can win.[8] In some cases, courts have said in one part of their opinion that there is a strong preference for biologic parents but, in the end, found that the best interests of the child controlled and placed the child with the stepparent on the basis of a standard that seemed to treat the stepparent and biologic parent as equals.[9]

Not all courts, of course, go out of their way to rule for stepparents. Forced to choose between a long-term custodial stepparent and an absent biologic parent who has regularly visited, some courts have, without much explanation, decided that children are better off returned to their biologic parent.[10] Others, dealing with cases in which the biologic parent has had little contact with the child, seem to stretch to place custody in the biologic parent.[11]

Courts also vary widely in the ways they depict the stepparents and biologic parents themselves. Appellate cases that end by ruling for a caretaking stepparent typically recite at length and with warmth the child-tending acts of the stepparent and the passive behavior of the biologic parent. The court speaks of a stepmother who treated a stepchild "as if he were her own child" or "as a member of her own family."[12] Or they refer to the stepparent with approval as the child's "psychological father"[13] or "psychological parent."[14] Not surprisingly, the highest praise for stepparents in custody cases is that they have performed in the way the court believes an ideal blood parent should behave. Courts sometimes in fact have a tone of wonder: look, they seem to be saying, at how far beyond the call of duty this stepparent went for this child.[15]

The cases in which the appellate courts rule for the biologic parent have a different tone. In these cases, the court typically says very little about the behavior of either the biologic parent or the stepparent. They say nothing about parenting acts at all and stress instead some statutory rule or presumption. When courts rely on blood, they have often found little to say.

That courts have not acted consistently and cannot explain cogently why they do what they do should not surprise us. These cases in which a stepparent and a biologic parent contend for custody are often even more difficult than they appear. The choice is not so simple as preserving blood ties versus preserving continuity, for blood ties themselves commonly offer continuity both in the sense of roots and in the sense of ties of desired affection yearned for, often by both absent parent and child, over the years. Conversely, the caretaking stepparent offers more than just continuity. In these custody cases, the stepparent has typically been living with and sharing the

bed of the biologic parent for many years. She or he has been caring for the child with the endorsement and involvement of the custodial parent. The stepparent has been "the person closest to the closest relative a child can have."[16] The stepparent may not be blood, but she has been far more than a nurse or a friend.

Katherine Bartlett, in her fine article criticizing America's absorption with parenthood as an "exclusive status," recommends dealing with cases such as *Henrikson* by fashioning rules that permit courts to order shared custody between biologic parents and long-term caretaking third persons or by ordering continued visitation between long-term caretakers and children.[17] As she points out, many courts are beginning to find authority to order visitation for stepparents and other caretakers. She has even found one court that ordered joint legal custody between a stepmother and a biologic mother upon the death of the custodial father.[18] If courts and legislatures move toward the adoption of such rules, I hope that they turn out to be ones that courts rarely impose, that they will be designed instead to set a stage for conversations and negotiations between biologic parents and caretaking stepparents (and children old enough to participate) in which all come to acknowledge the needs of the others. . .

ENDNOTES

1. Many of the cases are reviewed in Bartlett, supra note 6, and Mahoney, "Support and Custody Aspects," supra note 6. See also H. Clark, *The Law of Domestic Relations in the United States* 826 note 55 (2d ed. 1988).
2. Oreg. Rev. Stat. § 109.119.
3. See Colo. Rev. Stat. § 14–10-1236.
4. See cases in Mahoney, "Support and Custody Aspects," supra note 6 at 38, 62–65. Some trial courts have bent their divorce statutes to treat a stepchild as a "child of the marriage" for purposes of custody, but such adventurous interpretations have generally been rejected on appeal. Id. A few have held that they had no authority to

grant custody but found some sort of authority to award continuing visitation by the stepparent.

5. Consider, e.g., a Washington case in which the court found that a dedicated and loving stepmother had devoted herself to a deaf child while the biologic father stood at the sidelines "apathetic and fatalistic." The court had to cope with the fact that its divorce statute, based on the Uniform Act, seemed to provide no standing for stepparents. In seeming desperation, the court grasped onto another, purely procedural statute directing that the petition for dissolution must list "the names, ages, and addresses of any child dependent upon either or both spouses" as a reed strong enough to give it jurisdiction to determine custody. *In re* Marriage of Allen, 626 P.2d 16 (1981). See also In re *Carey,* 16 *Fam. L. Rep.* 1028 (Ill. Ct. App. 1989) (compare majority and dissenting opinions).

6. 162 Mich. App. 248, 412 N.W.2d 702 (1987).

7. E.g., In re Custody of N.M.O., 399 N.W.2d 700, 703 (Minn. App. 1987).

8. *Doe* v. *Doe,* 399 N.Y.S.2d 977 (1977); *Root* v. *Allen,* 151 Colo. 311, 377 P.2d 177 (1962); *Patrick* v. *Byerly* 325 S.E.2d 99 (Va. 1985); *Bailes* v. *Sourts,* 340 S.E.2d 824 (Va. 1986).

9. *Stanley D.* v. *Deborah D.,* 467 A.2d 249 (N.H. 1983); In re *Custody of N.M.O.,* supra note 77; *Gorman* v. *Gorman,* 400 So.2d 75 (Fla. Ct. App. 1981). See *Painter* v. *Bannister,* 258 Iowa 1390, 140 N.W.2d 152 (1966). Ironically, because of the statutes under which the cases arise, it may be easier for a stepparent to obtain custody in a divorce proceeding (even though the biologic parent has also been living with the child) than it is in a dispute with an absent parent at the time of a custodial parent's death (even though the absent parent may have lived apart from the child for many years). In the divorce case, the court is accustomed to applying a simple "best interests" test, without a presumption for either "parent."

10. See In re *Custody of Krause,* 111 Ill. App.3d 604, 444 N.E.2d 644 (1982).

11. See the appellate decisions in Henrikson, supra note 76, or in *Pape* v. *Pape,* 444 So.2d 1058 (Fla. App. 1984). See also the reported behaviors of the trial judges in In re Custody of N.M.O., supra note 77, in *Zuziak* v. *Zuziak,* 426 N.W.2d 761 (Mich. App. 1988), and in *La Croix* v. *Deyo,* 452 N.Y.S.2d 726 (App. Div. 1982).

12. *Patrick* v. *Byerly,* supra note 78.

13. In re Custody of N.M.O., supra note 77.

14. *Doe* v. *Doe,* supra note 78.

15. See, e.g., In re *Marriage of Allen;* supra note 75; *Doe* v. *Doe,* supra note 78; *Root* v. *Allen,* supra note 78.

16. B. Maddox, *The Halfparent* 20 (1975), quoted in Bartlett, supra note 6 at 912.

17. Bartlett, supra note 6 at 879.

18. *Cebryzynski* v. *Cebryzynski,* 63 Ill. App. 637, 379 N.E.2d 713 (1978).

PART FIVE

LINKS ACROSS THE GENERATIONS

CHAPTER 14

Children and Parents

How are children faring in America? This is a question that more and more observers of our society have been asking, and the answers are troubling. Nearly one in four American children lives in a family whose income is below the federal poverty line. Some of these poor children are growing up in neighborhoods where few adults work full time, the streets are infested with drugs and gangs, and killings are common occurrences. The proportion of children living in poverty declined sharply during the prosperous 1950s and 1960s but has increased since the 1970s.[1]

Many commentators have associated this increase in poverty with the changing family structure of the poor. More than one-half of all poor families were headed by single mothers in the 1990s, compared to about one-fourth in the 1960s.[2] It is alleged that children growing up in these households are not only economically disadvantaged but also receive less supervision and guidance. Defenders of these families counter that they could do just as good a job if they had more economic and child-care support.

In the political debates over welfare reform in the mid-1990s, critics of welfare maintained that open-ended economic support of poor families had created a dependent population that had lost its initiative and independence. They argued that if welfare recipients were forced to work, their self-esteem would rise, they would be better parents, and their children would have better role models. Their opponents said that welfare was the result of being poor, not the cause of it; and that cutting families off from cash assistance would hurt many more poor children than it would help.

Among children who are not poor, another large group seem to be just getting by. Their parents—like Kenny and Bonita Merten, whom you read about in Chapter 4—earn just enough to keep them above poverty but too little to support them in comfort. Some of these children will not graduate from high school and many will not graduate from college. Consequently, their jobs prospects will be limited.

Still, some children are faring well. A large group of children from middle-class homes,

---

[1]*Public and Private Families: An Introduction*, p. 430.
[2]Ibid., p. 108.

most of whom live with two parents, are comfortable, healthy, dressed in the latest styles, and headed for college. Using census data, Donald Hernandez showed that the proportion of children living in relatively prosperous families increased during the 1970s and 1980s, even as the proportion in poor families also increased.[3] In contrast, the proportion of children who were neither prosperous nor poor decreased. So for children, as for adults, inequality increased as the numbers at both extremes rose.

Pharoah and Lafeyette Rivers are two children from the poorest group. The brothers were profiled in a book, *There Are No Children Here: The Story of Two Boys Growing Up in the Other America,* by journalist Alex Kotlowitz. Pharoah, who is nine when the book begins, is an especially poignant example of the kind of child that developmental psychologists call "resilient." For reasons that experts cannot fully determine,

some children who grow up in deprived circumstances have the internal resources to successfully battle, and often triumph over, the daily trials they face. These resilient children show ingenuity and creativity in developing survival strategies. In the following excerpts, note the ways in which Pharoah is able to isolate himself from the worst of his world, gain the attention and protection of adults, and satisfy his need to learn. But note also that even a child as resourceful as Pharoah cannot avoid developing a stammer in reaction to the tension of living in his dangerous neighborhood.

The first part of this excerpt introduces Pharoah's family. The second part, which takes place a year later, describes Pharoah's hiding place. In the third part, two years later, Pharoah celebrates his birthday and recites a poem at a school assembly—always against the constant backdrop of drugs, alcohol, and violence.

---

[3]Donald J. Hernandez, *America's Children: Resources from Family, Government, and Economy* (New York: Russell Sage Foundation, 1993). See also *Public and Private Families: An Introduction,* pp. 431–36.

READING 14–1

There Are No Children Here

Alex Kotlowitz

The children called home "Hornets," or, more frequently, "the projects" or, simply, the "jects" (pronounced *jets*). Pharoah called it "the graveyard." But they never referred to it by its full name: the Governor Henry Horner Homes.

Nothing here, the children would tell you, was as it should be. Lafeyette and Pharoah lived at 1920 West Washington Boulevard, even though their high-rise sat on Lake Street. Their building had no enclosed lobby; a dark tunnel cut through the middle of the building, and the wind and strangers passed freely along it. Those tenants who received public aid had their checks sent to the local currency exchange, since the building's first-floor mailboxes had all been broken into. And since darkness engulfed the building's corridors, even in the daytime, the residents always carried flashlights, some of which had been handed out by a local politician during her campaign.

Summer, too, was never as it should be. It had become a season of duplicity.

On June 13, a couple of weeks after their peaceful afternoon on the railroad tracks, Lafeyette celebrated his 12th birthday. Under the gentle afternoon sun, yellow daisies poked through the cracks in the sidewalk as children's bright faces peered out from behind their windows. Green leaves clothed the cottonwoods, and pastel cotton shirts and shorts, which had sat for months in layaway, clothed the children. And like the fresh buds on the crabapple trees, the children's spirits blossomed with the onset of summer.

Lafeyette and his nine-year-old cousin Dede danced across the worn lawn outside their building, singing the lyrics of an L. L. Cool J rap, their small hips and spindly legs moving in rhythm. The boy and girl were on their way to a nearby shopping strip, where Lafeyette planned to buy radio headphones with $8.00 he had received as a birthday gift.

Suddenly, gunfire erupted. The frightened children fell to the ground. "Hold your head down!" Lafeyette snapped, as he covered Dede's head with her pink nylon jacket. If he hadn't physically restrained her, she might have sprinted for home, a dangerous action when the gangs started warring. "Stay down," he ordered the trembling girl.

The two lay pressed to the beaten grass for half a minute, until the shooting subsided. Lafeyette held Dede's hand as they cautiously crawled through the dirt toward home. When they finally made it inside, all but 50 cents of Lafeyette's birthday money had trickled from his pockets.

Lafeyette's summer opened the way it would close, with gunshots. For Lafeyette and Pharoah, these few months were to be a rickety bridge to adolescence.

If the brothers had one guidepost in their young lives these few months, though, it was their mother LaJoe. They depended on her; she depended on them. The boys would do anything for their mother.

A shy, soft-spoken woman, LaJoe was known for her warmth and generosity, not only to her own children but to her children's friends. Though she received Aid to Families with Dependent Children, neighbors frequently knocked on her door to borrow a can of soup or a cup of flour. She always obliged. LaJoe had often mothered children who needed advice or comforting. Many young men and women still called her "Mom." She let so many people through her apartment, sometimes just to use the bathroom, that she hid the toilet paper in the kitchen because it had often been stolen.

Alex Kotlowitz, "There Are No Children Here" from *There Are No Children Here: The Story of Two Boys Growing Up in the Other America*, pp. 8–18, 142–145, and 249–256. Copyright © 1991 by Alex Kotlowitz. Reprinted with the permission of Doubleday, a Division of Bantam Doubleday Dell Publishing Group, Inc.

But the neighborhood, which hungrily devoured its children, had taken its toll on LaJoe as well. In recent years, she had become more tired as she questioned her ability to raise her children here. She no longer fixed her kids' breakfasts every day—and there were times when the children had to wash their own clothes in the bathtub. Many of the adults had aged with the neighborhood, looking as worn and empty as the abandoned stores that lined the once-thriving Madison Street. By their mid-30s many women had become grandmothers; by their mid-40s, great-grandmothers. They nurtured and cared for their boyfriends and former boyfriends and sons and grandsons and great-grandsons.

LaJoe, in her youth, had been stunning, her smooth, light brown complexion highlighted by an open smile. When she pulled her hair back in a ponytail, she appeared almost Asian, her almond-shaped eyes gazing out from a heart-shaped face. She had been so pretty in her mid-20s that she briefly tried a modeling career. Now she was 35, and men still whistled and smiled at her on the street. Unlike many other women her age, she hadn't put on much weight, and her high-cheekboned face still had a sculptured look. But the confidence of her youth had left her. Her shoulders were often hunched. She occasionally awoke with dark circles under her eyes. And her smile was less frequent now.

LaJoe had watched and held on as the neighborhood slowly decayed, as had many urban communities like Horner over the past two decades. First, the middle-class whites fled to the suburbs. Then the middle-class blacks left for safer neighborhoods. Then businesses moved, some to the suburbs, others to the South. Over the past 10 years, the city had lost a third of its manufacturing jobs, and there were few jobs left for those who lived in Henry Horner. Unemployment was officially estimated at 19 percent; unofficially, it was probably much higher. There were neighborhoods in Chicago worse off than Horner, but the demise of this particular community was often noted because it had once been among the city's wealthiest areas.

Ashland Avenue, a six-lane boulevard just east of Henry Horner, was named for the Kentucky estate of Henry Clay. By the mid-19th century, it had become one of the city's smartest thoroughfares, lined with dwellings constructed of elegant Attic marble, fashionable churches, and exclusive clubs. "People would parade along the sidewalk to ogle at the notables and to be seen themselves; to watch the fine carriages spin along the macadam boulevard, to see the latest manifestation of changing fashion," read one newspaper account. But the neighborhood slowly changed. As immigrants, primarily German, Irish, and Eastern European Jews, settled on the west side, the city's glitter moved eastward to the lake, just north of the Loop, a strip now known as the Magnificent Mile and the Gold Coast.

The Ashland Avenue area quickly lost its luster. Jane Addams's founding of the renowned Hull House in 1889 signaled the west side's growing decline. It was one of the nation's first settlement houses, delivering various services to the poor of the area and acting as their advocate in housing, health care, and children's rights. Soon, the mansions on Ashland were transformed into headquarters for local unions or rooming houses for the transients of Skid Row. By 1906, the neighborhood had deteriorated still further, and tuberculosis claimed 5 percent of the west side's population. The Chicago Lung Association, then called the Chicago Tuberculosis Institute, opened its office on the west side, where it is still located.

The blight has continued and is particularly evident today west of Horner, a section of the city that, along with the south side, during the 1930s, 1940s, and 1950s became home to over a half-million blacks who migrated from the South, displacing the earlier immigrants. Western Avenue, now a strip of fast-food outlets, car washes, and family-run stores, borders Henry Horner to the west, though it is not a boundary of much significance, since on the other side the rubble continues. The two- and three-family tenements sag and lean like drunkards. Many of the buildings are vacant, their contents lying on the sidewalk.

To LaJoe, the neighborhood had become a black hole. She could more easily recite what wasn't there than what was. There were no banks, only currency exchanges, which charged customers up to $8.00 for every welfare check cashed. There were no public libraries, movie theaters, skating rinks, or bowling alleys to entertain the neighborhood's children. For the infirm, there were two neighborhood clinics, the Mary Thompson Hospital and the Miles Square Health Center, both of which teetered on the edge of bankruptcy and would close by the end of 1989. Yet the death rate of newborn babies exceeded infant mortality rates in a number of Third World countries, including Chile, Costa Rica, Cuba, and Turkey. And there was no rehabilitation center, though drug abuse was rampant.

According to a 1980 profile of the 27th ward—a political configuration drawn, ironically, in the shape of a gun and including Henry Horner and Rockwell Gardens, a smaller but no less forbidding public housing complex—60,110 people lived here, 88 percent of them black, 46 percent of them below the poverty level. It was an area so impoverished that when Mother Teresa visited it in 1982, she assigned nuns from her Missionaries of Charity to work at Henry Horner. They had set up a soup kitchen, a shelter for women and children, and an afterschool program. Where there used to be 13 social service agencies there were now only three: the Missionaries of Charity, the Boys Club, and the Chicago Commons Association. The latter two provided recreational activities as well as tutoring, counseling, and day care, but they had limited funds. A Chicago Commons' program called Better Days for Youth targeted children under 13 who were having problems in school or with the police, but there was money to serve only 28 children at a time.

LaJoe sometimes believed that the city had all but given up here. A local billboard warned NEEDLES KILL. There was a time when such a message read DRUGS KILL.

And despite Horner's proximity—one mile—to the city's booming downtown, LaJoe and her neighbors felt abandoned. Horner sat so close to the city's business district that from the Sears Tower observation deck tourists could have watched Lafeyette duck gunfire on his birthday. But city residents never had reason to pass the housing complex unless they attended a basketball or hockey game at the Chicago Stadium, just a block away.

Exacerbating the isolation was the fact that nearly half of the families in Henry Horner, including the Riverses, had no telephone. Residents also felt disconnected from one another; there was little sense of community at Horner, and there was even less trust. Some residents who didn't have a phone, for instance, didn't know any others in their building who would let them use theirs. Some neighbors wouldn't allow their children to go outside to play. One mother moved aside her living room furniture to make an open and safe place where her children could frolic.

But though the isolation and the physical ruin of the area's stores and homes had discouraged LaJoe, it was her family that had most let her down. Not that she could separate the two. Sometimes she blamed her children's problems on the neighborhood; at other times, she attributed the neighborhood's decline to the change in people, to the influx of drugs and violence.

Her three oldest children, to whom she felt she'd given everything she could, had all disappointed her. All had dropped out of school. All had been in jail at least once. All had been involved with drugs. The oldest, LaShawn, a slender 20-year-old, was so delicately featured some called her "China Doll." She worked as a prostitute from time to time to support her drug habit. The next oldest, 19-year-old Paul, named after his father, had served time in an Indiana prison for burglary. Terence, now 17, had been the most troublesome problem for LaJoe and, because of their extraordinary closeness, her biggest disappointment. He began selling drugs at the age of 11 and had been in and out, usually in, trouble with the law ever since.

LaJoe also had a set of four-year-old triplets: Timothy, Tiffany, and Tammie. The two girls so resembled each other that not even their father could tell them apart.

All eight children had the same father, Paul, to whom LaJoe had been married for 17 years. But the two had long ago fallen out of love. He lived at home only sporadically.

LaJoe wanted it to be different for Lafeyette and Pharoah, different from the way it had been for her three oldest children and different from the way it had been for her.

In her husband's absence, Lafeyette had become LaJoe's confidant. She relied on him. So did the younger children. Lafeyette watched after Pharoah and the triplets. He wouldn't let anything happen to them. He had been a carefree child, a bit of a ham, in fact. For a photograph taken when he was about four, he shoved a big cigar in his mouth and plopped a blue floppy hat on his small head. It was Christmastime, and Lafeyette's cousins, who in the photo were all crowded behind him, seemed amused by his antics. When he got older, around eight or nine, he'd hop on the Madison Street bus by himself to visit his grandmother, who lived in an apartment farther west. And he loved to draw, mostly pictures of superheroes. He boasted that his name appeared on all seven floors of his building. He was a boy bubbling with energy and verve.

But over the past year Lafeyette had begun to change, LaJoe thought. The past spring, he'd been caught stealing candy from a Walgreen's downtown. It was the first time he'd gotten into any kind of trouble. He had been hanging out with a youngster, Keith, who was known among the neighborhood kids for his ability to swipe expensive bottles of cologne from the display cases at downtown department stores. Lafeyette was placed in the Chicago Commons' Better Days for Youth. One of the first children in the new six-month program, Lafeyette received help with his school work as well as counseling. Keith moved out of town, and Lafeyette made friends with Chicago Commons' staff members, whom he'd periodically visit after his completion of the program.

Lafeyette still laughed and played with Pharoah and friends, but he could be bossy, ordering around his younger brother and the triplets with cockiness and the fury of a temperamental adult. He had inherited his mother's temper and could turn on the younger ones in an instant. It wasn't that Lafeyette and they didn't get along; it was that he worried about them, like a father worrying about his children. He admonished them for hanging out with the wrong people or straying too far from his sight. He cared almost too much about everything and everybody. Sometimes the strain of responsibility showed in his thin, handsome face; it would tighten, like a fist, and it seemed as if he would never smile again. He'd purse his lips and clench his jaw; his deep-set, heavy-lidded eyes would stare straight ahead. His face revealed so little, his mother thought, and yet so much.

Pharoah was different, not only from Lafeyette but from the other children, too. He didn't have many friends, except for Porkchop, who was always by his side. LaJoe had given him his name but, like his brother's name, spelled it in an unusual way. At the time, LaJoe hadn't known the story of Moses and the Pharoah, but in later years when she found out she laughed. Pharoah was anything but a king.

Pharoah clutched his childhood with the vigor of a tiger gripping his meat. He wouldn't let go. Nobody, nothing would take it away from him. When he was two, Pharoah would run around the apartment naked; sometimes he'd be wearing just small white shoes. When he was four or five, he told LaJoe that he wanted to live on a lake so that he could always feel the wind on his back. At the age of five, he had an imaginary friend, Buddy, whom he'd talk to and play with in his bedroom. Frequently, Pharoah got so lost in his daydreams that LaJoe had to shake him to bring him back from his flights of fancy. Those forays into distant lands and with other people seemed to help Pharoah fend off the ugliness around him.

Now, at the age of nine, he giggled at the slightest joke; he cried at the smallest of tragedies. He had recently developed a slight stutter, which made him seem even more vulnerable. And he listened to classical music on the radio because, he said, it relaxed him. He sensed that his playfulness delighted the adults, so he would tease them and they him. He wanted to be recognized, to know that he was wanted. At the age of eight he wrote a short letter to his Aunt LaVerne, one of LaJoe's sisters.

Jan. 1986
Pharoah Rivers

I love you do you love me. You are my best aunt verny. I love you very much. The people I love.

Verny
Grandmother
Linda
Randy
Moma
Dad
Brothers
Sisters
Cousins
Aunt

"Oh, that Pharoah," family and neighbors would say to LaJoe, recounting some enchanting incident involving the nine-year-old. They adored him.

Pharoah liked to tell people he was big-boned "like my mama," though she was, in fact, a small woman. He had LaJoe's open and generous smile, and, like his mother, who was only five feet two, he was short, so that LaJoe could, until he was nine or ten, pass him off as a five-year-old to get him on the bus without paying fare.

Where the adults found Lafeyette handsome, they found Pharoah cute. The women would josh both of them, saying that someday they'd be lady killers. The local Boys Club used a photograph of Pharoah in one of its fund-raising brochures. In the picture, Pharoah, along with four other young boys, was dressed in marching cap and cape with a drum set, almost as large as Pharoah himself, slung around his neck. As he often did, he had cocked his head to one side for the camera and grinned cheerfully, a pose he must have known made him look even cuter.

The boys got along, and for that LaJoe was grateful. The two shared a room and, on most mornings, walked to school together. Occasionally, Lafeyette played rough with Pharoah or told him off, but LaJoe knew that if Pharoah ever needed his older brother, he'd be there. Older and bigger, he offered Pharoah some protection from the tougher kids in the neighborhood.

LaJoe knew that Lafeyette and Pharoah were like millions of other children living in the nation's inner cities. She knew that she was not alone in her struggles, that other women in other cities were watching their children grow old quickly, too. She had heard of some mothers who moved their families to Milwaukee or to the suburbs, some of which were poorer than Henry Horner, in an effort to escape the neighborhood's brutality. In the end, LaJoe would almost always learn, these families were up against the same ruthless forces they had faced in Chicago.

It wouldn't happen to Lafeyette and Pharoah, she had vowed to herself. It just wouldn't happen. They would have a childhood. They would have a chance to enjoy the innocence and playfulness of youth and to appreciate the rewards of school and family. They would bring home high school diplomas. They would move out of the neighborhood. They would get jobs and raise families. She had made mistakes with the older children that she was determined not to repeat with her younger ones.

But during the summer of 1987, when drugs and the accompanying violence swept through the neighborhood, she lived in daily fear that something might happen to her young ones. Though she would never say as much, she worried that they might not make it to their 18th birthday. Too many hadn't. Already that year, 57 children had been killed in the city. Five had died in the Horner area, including two, aged eight and six, who died from smoke inhalation when firefighters had to climb the 14 stories to their apartment. Both of the building's elevators were broken. Lafeyette and Pharoah knew of more funerals than weddings.

So that summer LaJoe wanted to be prepared for the worst. She started paying $80 a month for burial insurance for Lafeyette, Pharoah, and the four-year-old triplets.

Lafeyette had promised his mother he wouldn't let anything happen to Pharoah. But for a brief moment, he thought he had lost him.

Three days after Lafeyette's birthday, gunfire once again filled the air. It was 2:30 in the afternoon; school had just let out. As Lafeyette and his mother hustled the triplets onto the floor of the apartment's narrow hallway, a drill they now followed almost instinctually, they caught glimpses through the windows of young gunmen waving their pistols about. One youth toted a submachine gun.

The dispute had started when two rival drug gangs fired at each other from one high-rise to another.

From his first-floor apartment, Lafeyette, who had left his fifth-grade class early that day, watched hopefully for Pharoah as the children poured out of the Henry Suder Elementary School, just a block away. Panicking, many of the youngsters ran directly toward the gunfire. Lafeyette and his mother screamed at the children to turn back. But they kept coming, clamoring for the shelter of their homes.

Lafeyette finally spotted his brother, first running, then walking, taking cover behind trees and fences. But then he lost sight of him. "Mama, lemme go get him. Lemme go," Lafeyette begged. He was afraid that Pharoah would run straight through the gunfire. Pharoah would later say he had learned to look both ways and that's why he'd started walking. "My mama told me when you hear the shooting, first to walk because you don't know where the bullets are coming," he explained. LaJoe refused Lafeyette's request to let him go after his brother. She couldn't even go herself. The guns kept crackling.

Lafeyette's friend James, who was cowering behind a nearby tree, sprinted for the Riverses' apartment. Pharoah saw him and ran, too. The two frantically pounded with their fists on the metal door. "Let us in!" James wailed. "Let us in! It's James and Pharoah!" James's heart was beating so hard that he could hear it above the commotion. But with all the noise, no one heard their frenzied pleas, and the two ran to a friend's apartment upstairs.

Meanwhile, the police, who at first thought they were the targets of the shooting, had taken cover in their cars and in the building's breezeway. Passersby lay motionless on the ground, protected by parked vehicles and a snow-cone vending stand. Then, as suddenly as it began, the battle ended. No one, amazingly, had been hurt. Lafeyette learned later that one errant bullet pierced a friend's third-floor window with such force that it cut through a closet door and lodged in the cinder-block wall.

The police made no arrests. And when a reporter called the police department's central headquarters the next day, he was told that there was no record of the shoot-out.

But Lafeyette knew. So did Pharoah.

* * * * *

Three blocks south of Horner sits a condominium complex called Damen Courts. Its manicured lawns and graffiti-free walls seem immaculate next to the rubble of Horner. The three-story red brick buildings look elegant and proper beside Horner's grim and worn high-rises.

Pharoah can't recall when he first discovered this small paradise, but when he did, he retreated regularly to the comfort of the lush lawns that circled the buildings. He was there when his mother returned from shopping.

The grass carpet offered a quiet resting place; it was like going to the beach. Pharoah found a shady place on the lawn and shot marbles or read a *Captain America* or *Superman* comic. Or, if the mood fit him, he just sat and daydreamed. He thought about school and next year's spelling bee. He urged on the Chicago Cubs and imagined himself a professional wrestler. It was at Damen Courts that he came up with the name for a scraggly gray cat that was now staying with the family: Useless. "He hardly don't catch no mice. He just want to freeload off our heat," he explained.

Pharoah had long sought such a refuge. For a few months last spring, he'd attended Bible classes at the First Congregational Baptist Church. Washington Boulevard was lined with churches, but most of them now served people who had since moved from the neighborhood. Churches had lost their authority in areas like Horner. Pharoah grew bored with the classes and began to question whether there was indeed a God. He often prayed to him, asking that he let them move from the projects. But, Pharoah would say, "I be praying but he don't do nothing. Maybe there ain't no God." It was as much a question as it was a statement.

At Damen Courts, Pharoah found some respite. No one knew of his discovery, not his mother, his cousin Porkchop, his friend Rickey, or Lafeyette. He wanted it that way. He wanted a place that he could escape to by himself, where nothing would interrupt his daydreaming, where no one would try to fight him, where he didn't have to worry about gunshots or firebombings. When his mother asked where he was going, he said to the corner store to play video games. He didn't want anybody to know about his hideaway.

In the weeks immediately following Jimmie Lee's conviction, an unusual calm descended over Horner. Several other gang leaders had been jailed. The drug dealing and beatings didn't stop, but they certainly slowed down in comparison with the relentless battles of the previous summer.

With fewer shootings and a reprieve from some of the family's troubles, Pharoah's stutter became less noticeable. In later months, it would recur, but never would it get so bad that it would immobilize or silence him as it had during the past year. LaJoe had taken Pharoah to the Miles Square Health Center, where a counselor urged Pharoah to slow down when he spoke. Think about what you want to say before speaking, he told Pharoah. The stuttering is partly due to nerves, he explained. Pharoah was bewildered. "What's it got to do with nerves?" he later asked his mother, who did her best to explain that when people started fighting and shooting, he got nervous and scared and would begin to stutter. It acted as a kind of warning mechanism to himself to be vigilant and cautious. Pharoah understood. He always seemed to understand—when he wanted to.

With the uneasy calm, Pharoah found other distractions in addition to Damen Courts. He and Lafeyette frequented the outdoor swimming pool in Union Park, four blocks to the east, and in this large pool filled with flailing bodies, both boys learned to swim. They also regularly visited the Boys Club to play basketball or shoot pool or to get free sandwiches, which had become endearingly known among the children as a "chokes." Or they might just hang about their building, playing basketball on the jungle gym or wading in the permanent pool created by the fire hydrant. Sometimes Red, a small man in his 50s who lived in their building, would ride around the highrise on his adult-size tricycle with presents for the neighborhood children stuffed in his basket. He found the used gifts in trash bins or behind stores. He'd give the little girls plastic necklaces and metal pendants; the little boys got tennis balls. To LaJoe and the other mothers, he presented gladioli and daisies which, in their late bloom, florists had thrown away. Over the years, Red had become like a year-round Santa to the building's kids. The triplets in particular adored him, and on his arrival on his tricycle could be heard screaming, "Red, oh, Red! What it is, Red?" as they ran up and surrounded him and gave him hugs in exchange for the presents.

Pharoah continued to badger Lafeyette and Rickey and any other older friend he could corner to take him back to the railroad tracks, which he remembered for the quiet and solace he'd found there. But no one would take him. The stories from last year of lost legs were still fresh in their minds. And now there were exaggerated children's tales of "raper mans" and other loonies hiding in the buildings by the viaduct. So, with the older boys' refusal and his own fear of what he might meet at the tracks, Pharoah spent more time at his private sanctuary.

He stayed on the lawn at Damen Courts until a security guard or janitor shooed him away, but he always left happy and satisfied. Being there for even an hour gave him a chance to catch his breath, to find the tranquillity he treasured.

On this particular afternoon, after his mother had finished putting away the groceries, Pharoah wandered through the front door, his head cocked slightly to one side. "Where you been, Pharoah?" his mother asked.

"Nowheres," he said, turning away. It was hard for him to lie, especially to his mother.

"Pharoah?"

Pharoah thought about telling her but didn't. "I been playing video games with Porkchop," he said and walked back to his room.

In later weeks, he finally confided in his mother abut his discovery. "My mind be cleared of everything there," he told her.

* * * * *

On Friday, May 19, LaJoe and Rochelle taped the last of the streamers to the walls; the narrow strips of crepe paper crisscrossed the living room like tangled vines. Balloons hung from the ceiling and bounced unfettered on the floor.

Party hats and party favors lay on the table, which was covered with a paper cloth adorned with Disney cartoon characters. A gold crown, also made of paper, sat to the side for the birthday boy. Eleven candles circled the strawberry shortcake, which read: I LOVE YOU. FROM MAMA AND ROCHELLE.

"LaJoe, here, put it up here," Rochelle urged. LaJoe pulled the last of the banners from the package. They read, "It's a Boy." LaJoe and Rochelle laughed. They hoped Pharoah wouldn't notice.

A few weeks earlier, after Pharoah had attended a birthday celebration for a friend, he mentioned to his mother that he'd never had a party. So she decided to throw him one—and to keep it a surprise. Rochelle had helped her buy the decorations and the cake. She seemed nearly as excited as LaJoe.

Since the incident the month before in which she lost control of herself, LaJoe had slowed down and tried to pull herself and her family together. With summer fast approaching, she wanted to be prepared. She did what she could to lift her spirits and her children's. She had finally made the last of the down payments on the five bunk beds, so Lafeyette, Pharoah, and the triplets now each had one. The wooden bunks were used but in good condition. LaJoe had paid $479 for them. Lafeyette and Pharoah kept the plastic covering on their mattresses. "It keeps them clean," Pharoah explained. They dreamed about what they would do now to decorate their room. Lafeyette wanted to paint it black "'cause then it won't get dirty so easy." He had taken a steel door off a vacant apartment to replace their broken wooden one, and he had installed a new lock so that only he and Pharoah could enter. They had hung a torn venetian blind over the windows, which kept the room dark but private.

LaJoe also bought a handsome wooden table and chairs from the same used-furniture dealer who had sold her the beds. The storekeeper liked LaJoe and gave her a good buy—$80 for the table and chairs—and even delivered the goods, though he refused to carry the items into the building, because he feared for his safety. Neighbors helped haul the furniture from the truck into the apartment. Pharoah particularly loved the new wooden table; he told his mother that it was the kind they had in mansions.

The triplets and Lafeyette traipsed home from school, wet from the spring downpour. Other youngsters soon arrived, mostly children the triplets' age. They awaited the birthday boy. Someone knocked on the door. The children, giggling, put their fingers to their lips. "Shh. Shh. Shh." The knocking got louder and more forceful. Lafeyette moved to the side of the door and undid its lock.

"SURPRISE!" Lafeyette slapped the back of Pharoah's head with his open palm. In all the excitement, he didn't quite know how to greet his brother. Pharoah shuffled into the living room, surprised and embarrassed by the attention. Just as he had done during the first spelling bee, he balled his hands up under the fold of his shimmery green raincoat, where he nervously played with the plastic. The children, about 10 in all, quickly scattered, many running into the kitchen for hot dogs. Pharoah stood by the door, his toothy smile lighting his face. He didn't say anything. Instead, he walked back to his room and sat on the plastic-covered mattress, trying to take it all in. Lafeyette sat with him.

"I thought you forgot it," he told his mother, who poked her head through the door. She rubbed the back of his head and gave him his present, a green shorts set. Pharoah put it on. With the suspenders and knee-length shorts, he looked quite handsome. He silently readied himself for the party: he found a new pair of white socks, and scrubbed his face and hands; he ran jell through his long, curly hair and then secured the gold paper crown on his head. And as he did almost everything, he did it all slowly and with great deliberation. The dressing and preening took him half an hour—and when he was done he wasn't fully satisfied. "I should have greased my legs," he told his brother.

"You look proper," Lafeyette told his brother. Rickey, who had been invited to the party by Lafeyette, wandered into the bedroom. With his hands in his pocket, he looked uncomfortable. He often did. "You look straight, Pharoah," he assured him. "Happy birthday."

"Thanks," Pharoah said. He didn't say much that afternoon. He mostly grinned and giggled. In Polaroid photos of the day, his smile seems to cover his face; his big grin forces his cheeks into plump balls and squeezes his eyes neatly shut. In one photo, he stands behind his seated grandmother, who has come over for the party, with his arm affectionately around her neck. In another, he sits behind the cake in one of the new chairs, his paper crown sliding off his head, looking pleased with the festivities. In yet another, LaJoe steadies Pharoah's small hands as he cuts the cake with a big kitchen knife.

Once Pharoah was dressed and had made his entrance into the party amid the screaming gaggle of kids, Lafeyette and Rickey sneaked out the door. Lafeyette told his mother he didn't want to hang around "no children's party." It was LaJoe's one disappointment. All the guests were much younger than Pharoah; no one Pharoah's age came. He didn't have many good friends, except for his cousin Porkchop. But even he wasn't there. Throughout the festivities, Pharoah asked, "Where's Porkchop?" or could be heard muttering, "I hope Porkchop comes." Porkchop showed up two hours after the party began; he'd forgotten all about it. The two, as usual, embraced. "Happy Birthday," Porkchop mumbled through his soft giggles.

The children, with half-eaten hot dogs squirting out of their hands, danced to the rap music of L. L. Cool J. Pharoah, who sat with his mother and grandmother and his Aunt LaVerne as they admired his new outfit, mouthed the words to one of his favorite songs.

When I'm alone in my room sometimes I stare at the walls
    And in the back of my mind I hear my conscience call

Telling me I need a girl that's as sweet as a dove
For the first time in my life—I see I need love
I need love.

"Keep the kids inside," a panicky voice hollered to LaJoe, distracting Pharoah from the rap music. "Keep them here. Someone's figuring to get killed at four trey." Dawn had come by with her four kids. Four trey was how everyone referred to the building next door, whose address was 1943 West Lake. LaJoe locked the door.

"Y'll stay inside, you hear," she told the children, who had momentarily stopped their dancing, knowing that something was wrong. Apparently there had been an altercation between drug dealers in the building, and Dawn was worried it might erupt into something more. Nothing, though, happened. The children resumed dancing. Dawn gave Pharoah a hug.

Just as Pharoah blew out the candles—after an off-key, half-shouted rendition of "Happy Birthday"—something heavy fell in the living room. The crash startled everyone. A relative of LaJoe's, who had passed out on the couch and had been there throughout the noisy party, had tried to get up to go to the bathroom. He didn't make it. He lay face down, urine seeping through his blue jeans onto the linoleum door.

Pharoah took Porkchop's hand and the two went outside to get away from their drunken relative and the screaming kids. As they walked out the building's back door, they stopped. A teenage girl stood there vomiting. The two boys quietly walked around her. Pharoah hadn't stopped smiling.

It was a good few weeks for Pharoah. Not only did he celebrate his birthday, but he had been picked to recite a short poem at Suder's year-end assembly. Pharoah had gotten his stammer under control. It wasn't gone entirely, but he managed it better, having learned, when necessary, to slow down before he spoke. And so this was a big honor for him; it was as if his teachers were recognizing Pharoah for conquering his stutter.

As soon as Pharoah got a copy of the rhyme he was to recite, he set it to memory. He felt so confident that he eventually threw away the crumpled piece of paper he'd been carrying around in his back pocket for weeks. He wouldn't forget it.

He wanted to look tidy for the assembly, so he had his hair shorn. He also cleaned and ironed a black-striped sport coat that his mother had bought for him two Easters ago. He didn't have many occasions to wear it. With his neatly pressed white pants and olive-green shirt buttoned at the collar, LaJoe thought, he looked very handsome.

LaJoe got to the school's gymnasium early. She was as excited as Pharoah. When she saw her son on stage, she couldn't help thinking, There's the one. There's the one. I'm going to get it back.

Lafeyette sat with his class. He too was "happy for my little brother." Ms. Barone was so proud of her former student that she took a snapshot of him in his new clothes and haircut.

Pharoah had been on this platform before for the spelling bees, so he knew what to expect. He knew that he had to speak loud and clear, and that he needed to speak deliberately so as not to stumble. But in his excitement, as he stretched to reach the microphone, he realized that he had to go to the bathroom something awful. His bladder felt ready to burst. Not here, he told himself. He locked his knees together, tensing his bladder muscles. He wasn't going to pee on himself, not in front of all these people. He tried to look relaxed.

He spotted his mother in the crowd, with her full and open grin. But he tried to avoid her eyes and fixed his stare at the back of the auditorium. That way, he'd been told, it would look as if he were talking to everyone.

"Uh-uh-uh . . . uh," Pharoah paused. He wasn't going to stutter. Not here. Not now. Slow down, he told himself. Take your time.

"Try, try, try, try, that's what special effort means." His soft, amplified voice rang through the auditorium; once he got through the first line, his confidence returned. His heart was in it. He indeed believed hard work could overcome all.

> And when you put your best foot forward, it really isn't hard as it seems.
> Success comes to those who when given a chance
> Do their very best and work hard to advance.
> The special effort award is what they've earned.
> Though it can't begin to match the things they've learned.

The applause rang in Pharoah's ears. He looked over to his mother. She winked. Lafeyette clapped so hard and long that his teacher had to ask him to stop. "Nice job," Ms. Daigre, the principal, whispered to Pharoah. He thanked her, stepped off the stage, and then sprinted for the bathroom.

That morning Pharoah received two certificates: one for placing second in the school's spelling bee, the other for special effort in math and reading. His brother Timothy got three, including the much coveted principal's list as well as one for scholastic achievement and another for excellent conduct. Tammie received one for outstanding student, another for excellent conduct. Tiffany got one for special effort in handwriting. "The only person who didn't get a ribbon was Lafie," Pharoah said later. "That made me feel bad." Along with the certificates came ribbons. LaJoe was so proud of her children's accomplishments that she pinned all eight of them to her white sweatshirt. She paraded around the neighborhood all day with a rainbow of green, purple, white, and red ribbons hanging from her chest; she looked like a decorated war hero.

After the assembly, Pharoah and his mother attended a meeting at which it was announced that Pharoah was one of 25 Suder students chosen for Project Upward Bound, a summer school designed to assist minority students in bringing up their math and reading scores. Pri-

marily a program for high school students, this Upward Bound, which operated at the University of Illinois, had in recent years begun to focus some of its efforts on sixth-, seventh-, and eighth-graders with the hope of following them through their four years of high school, working with them on Saturdays and during the summers.

The Upward Bound staff described the Summer Scholars program and then asked the assembled children what they wanted to be when they grew up. Pharoah knew. A congressman.

"I want to change a lot of rules," he told the others. "I want to change them and everybody move out of the projects. I'll pay people to build housing. Let the people who live in the projects live in other houses. Any gang member who has their hat turned, they'd go directly to jail. Stop stealing and stuff. A little kid got to come into a store with their parent or guardian or they can't come in. They'd probably steal."

He paused, then added, "If you be a congressman, there be people guarding me so you won't get hurt. I like that."

LaJoe and the children got caught up in the warmth and beauty of those first few days of summer. The children shot baskets on the jungle gym. At night, they wandered over to the stadium to watch cars and make a few dollars. Pharoah's and the triplets' awards at school had brightened the family's outlook. LaJoe displayed them on the wobbly shelves in the living room. They offered some promise of a better tomorrow. And everyone was thrilled with Pharoah for being picked to participate in the summer program. Pharoah would come back with tales of the University of Illinois campus that delighted LaJoe. He talked of the footbridges and the big glass buildings and of the students who seemed to be everywhere, always carrying books. Pharoah would tell LaJoe that he planned to attend college there. But it wasn't long before LaJoe was rudely reminded of summer's true character at Horner.

One afternoon, she and Rochelle were walking down Washington Boulevard to a corner store. She waved to two teenage boys she knew who were walking on the other side of the street; both wore red, the Vice Lords' color, in Disciples' territory. LaJoe noticed that two children, one no bigger than Pharoah, and a young man were tailing the two teens. They'd duck into alleys and behind the porches of the two-family homes on Washington. LaJoe yelled to the two teens that they were being followed. Then she watched in horror as the man handed a pistol to the little boy who reminded LaJoe of Pharoah in his small size and bobbing gait.

"Go kill the motherfucker," LaJoe overheard him say. The boy aimed the pistol, his entire body straining just to hold it straight, and opened fire on the two teens. POW. POW. LaJoe and Rochelle ducked into the corner store for cover. The two teens ran. They escaped unharmed.

The incident angered and frightened LaJoe. How did that little boy even know whom he was shooting at? All he saw was a couple of people wearing red and their hats turned to the left. From the back, they could have been girls. Later that day, LaJoe ripped the red Louisville cap off Lafeyette's head and told him he couldn't wear any hats. No earrings, either, she told him. That was that. She was putting her foot down. That could have been Lafeyette the boy was shooting at.

CHAPTER 15

The Elderly and Their Families

In 1984, Samuel Preston published an article that pointed out an emerging paradox in the well-being of children and the elderly, who constitute the two groups in society that cannot fully take care of themselves. In the article, which is reprinted here, Preston noted that the number of elderly persons had been increasing rapidly (in part due to longer life expectancy), whereas the number of children had been declining as the baby boom cohort of the 1950s gave way to the baby bust cohort of the 1970s. One would think, Preston observed, that the well-being of the elderly would be worsening because of the difficulty of caring for their vast numbers. Correspondingly, children's lot should have been improving because there were fewer of them to care for.

Yet just the opposite was occurring. On a number of indicators of health and welfare, the elderly were doing better and children were doing worse. Why was this occurring? Preston's answer was that the political power of the elderly was growing as a result of their greater numbers, compelling state and federal governments to expand Social Security, institute Medicare (the government health insurance program

for the elderly), and take other measures designed to benefit them. Moreover, Preston argued, since every nonelderly person hopes that she or he will one day be elderly, the political demands of the elderly struck a responsive chord in the general population. In contrast, children do not vote and had few effective groups advocating on their behalf. And no one anticipates being a child again.

Although more than a decade has passed since the article was published, Preston's point is still relevant. Public policy has rewarded the elderly with increased benefits; but little has been done for children. The 1996 welfare reforms cut spending for cash welfare and food stamps for families with children and subsidies to the families of disabled children.

When the baby boomers begin to retire after about 2010, it is questionable whether the nation will be able to pay for all the benefits they will be entitled to. But few politicians have the courage to confront that difficult issue now for fear of incurring the wrath of elderly voters.[1]

---

[1]*Public and Private Families: An Introduction,* pp. 454–55.

Still, critics of Preston's article have stated that there is no reason why benefits for children must fall just because their numbers are falling relative to the elderly. Our country could continue to increase benefits to both groups, the critics say. Strictly speaking, they are correct; but in practice, it is the elderly who have been accruing most of the new government benefits.

* * * * *

There is much myth about the family lives of the elderly in the past. People still have in their heads the idea that there was a golden era for the elderly—a time of large, extended families, with grandpa dispensing wisdom to the grandchildren and grandma helping mother in the kitchen. Yet we know now that there was no golden era; in many respects the lives of the elderly are better today. We know this because of an outpouring of historical research on the elderly. In the following excerpt, Tamara Hareven, a leading family historian, summarizes the research on the elderly and their families. She notes, for example, that there never was a time when most elderly people lived in three-generation families.[2]

Nevertheless, while debunking the myth of a golden age, Hareven argues that the elderly are more isolated from, and receive less assistance from, kin than in the past. In part, this change is a result of the preference of both the elderly and their children for living independently of one another. The rising affluence of the elderly—fed by the growth of Social Security—has made independent living possible on a large scale. Thus, their isolation from kin may not constitute a social problem—at least not from the perspectives of the family members who are involved. Stud-

ies show that although the elderly live apart from their children and grandchildren, they see them frequently.[3] Hareven also cites a cultural shift from seeing family relations as "instrumental," that is to say, focused on assistance and support, to viewing family ties as primarily emotional. She sees some loss to society and to the elderly in all of these changes.

Hareven applies a life-course perspective. This is an influential framework for studying change over time in individuals' lives. The life-course perspective exhorts the historian or social scientist not to study individual lives in isolation. Rather, the historical period in which their subjects lived and their subjects' relations with others (such as kin, friends, or employers) should also be considered. Being born in the period 1910–1919 and therefore being a teenager and young adult during the Great Depression, Hareven argues, provided a different outlook on life than being born in the period 1920–1929 and therefore being a teenager and young adult during World War II. Hareven uses the life course perspective to help the reader understand how the historical context of the lives of the elderly has shaped their subsequent relations with their kin.

(Hareven uses the term *family of orientation* to refer to the family in which a person grows up; whereas a *family of procreation* is the family in which a person has children. A *boarder* is someone who pays to live and eat meals in someone else's house—a common arrangement until the middle of the 20th century. A *lodger* is someone who pays to live in someone else's home but eats her or his meals elsewhere.)

---

[2]Ibid., pp. 447–57.

[3]Ibid., pp. 458–59.

Children and the Elderly in the United States

Samuel H. Preston

In the 1960s and 1970s two developments that had not been expected by demographers changed the age structure of the U.S. population in a dramatic way. The first was a decrease in the number of children. From 1960 to 1982 the number of children younger than 15 fell by 7 percent. The decline was mainly due to the drop in the birth rate that followed the "baby boom."

The second development was a rapid increase in the number of elderly people. Between 1960 and 1980 the number of people 65 or older grew by 54 percent. The increase was caused mainly by a sharp reduction in the death rate among older people, acting on a population that already was large because of the large number of babies born between 1890 and 1915. As a result, during the 1970s the elderly population of the United States increased at a higher rate than the total population of India.

One might expect such a change in age structure to help the young and hurt the old. Fewer children should mean less competition for resources in the home and greater per capita availability of social services such as public schools. More old people, on the other hand, should put great pressure on resources such as hospitals, nursing homes, and Social Security funds. I believe, however, that exactly the opposite has happened. Since the early 1960s the well-being of the elderly has improved greatly whereas that of the young has deteriorated. Demographic trends underlie these changes: in the family, in

politics and in industry the growing number of older people and the declining number of children have worked to the advantage of the group that is increasing in size.

In order to account for what has happened to children and older people in the United States it is first necessary to document the changes in living conditions among the two groups. The measures that are commonly used by social scientists to measure the well-being of large groups include levels of income, health, educational achievement, and reports of satisfaction with life.

One of the most straightforward ways to compare children with the elderly is to measure the fraction of the two groups that live in poverty. Since children generally do not have independent incomes, one cannot directly compare personal income. One can, however, measure the incomes of the families in which the children live and compare the incomes to a minimum standard of need. The Bureau of the Census uses an Economy Food Plan drawn up by the Department of Agriculture as the basis of such a standard. Families that have an income equal to an amount less than three times the cost of the food plan are said to be living in poverty.

By this standard there have been remarkable changes in the proportion of children who live in poverty compared with the corresponding proportion of the elderly. In 1970, 16 percent of those under 14 lived in poverty compared with 24 percent of those older than 65. By 1982 the situation had been reversed: 23 percent of children lived in poverty compared with 15 percent of the elderly.

Monetary income is not the only measure of material well-being. Noncash transfer payments such as food stamps and Medicare have a strong influence on the condition of society's dependents. The Census Bureau estimated that in 1982 the market value of noncash transfers was $98 billion, much of it in medical payments to the elderly. If this sum is taken into account, the disparity in poverty status between children and the elderly is increased further. The fraction of the elderly living in poverty in 1982 falls from

15 to 4 percent. The corresponding reduction for children is only from 24 to 17 percent.

An examination of public outlays as a whole reinforces the idea that the elderly have done better than children at society's hands in recent years. Mary Jo Bane of Harvard University concluded that in 1960 the average government expenditure (including federal, state and local funds) on each elderly person was about three times the expenditure on each child. Both types of spending increased rapidly in the succeeding decades; hence the ratio remained about the same through 1979. Because the expenditure on the elderly started from a higher level, however, the absolute gain for each elderly person was much larger than the gain for each child.

Since 1979 there has been a sharp break in the pattern of government expenditure that kept the ratio of per-capita outlays for the two groups roughly constant. Many public programs for children have been cut back while those for older people have been expanded. For example, the Aid to Families with Dependent Children (AFDC) program has been substantially reduced. In 1979, out of every 100 children in poverty 72 were enrolled in AFDC. By 1982 only 52 out of 100 were in the program. In comparison, Medicare outlays rose from $3.4 billion in 1967 to $57.4 billion in 1983, and it has been estimated that they will rise to $112 billion by 1988.

The Federal Office of Management and Budget has recently begun estimating the fraction of all federal benefits that are directed to those who are 65 or older. Older people got $44 billion in federal funds in 1971 and $217 billion in 1983. The 1983 figure is equivalent to about $7,700 per person who is older than 65 and is a sum larger than the total spent on national defense in that year.

Federal expenditures on children are harder to calculate, but I have attempted to do so from budget documents. The total federal outlay on the major child-oriented programs (AFDC, Head Start, food stamps, child health, child nu-

trition and aid to education) is abut $36 billion for 1984; this is about a sixth of the total spending on the elderly. Because there are more children than old people, the expenditure per child through these programs is less than a 10th the expenditure per older person. These figures are not strictly comparable to the data collected by Bane, but they do give a sense of the increasing disparity between public outlays on the young and those on the old.

The gulf in well-being that separates the old and the young has been widened still further by the fact that public spending on the young has become less effective. The largest portion of public money spent on the young goes to public schools. Many indicators suggest the quality of public schooling has declined drastically in the past two decades.

The sum of the scores on the verbal and mathematics sections of the Scholastic Aptitude Test (S.A.T.) declined by 90 points from 1963 through 1980. The Wirtz Commission, which was the most authoritative group to investigate this trend, concluded that about half of the decline was due to the fact that a wider range of students now take the test than took it in the 1960s. About half of the decline, however, represents an actual decline among students with qualifications similar to those taking the test earlier. Most of the real decline took place in the early 1970s. In addition there has been a decrease in the proportion of U.S. teen-agers who finish high school. In 1965 the fraction was 76.3 percent; by 1980 it had fallen to 73.6 percent.

Education is the principal public service for the young; health care is the principal service for the old. Some 69 percent of the medical bills of people 65 or older are paid for with public funds. The Congressional Budget Office estimates that in 1984 the Federal Government will spend an average of $2,948 on health care for each person 65 or older.

A good index of the effectiveness of public spending on health care is the mortality rate. Between 1968 and 1980 mortality rates improved in all age groups in the United States. The improvements, however, were not equally distributed between the young and the old. Demographers employ statistical standards called *model life tables* to compare the relations of death rates in different age groups with the relations that would be expected from international and historical experience. If model life tables are used to analyze the recent changes in mortality in the United States, it can be shown that the greatest improvements in the death rate have occurred in the older age groups. By normal standards of progress, children and young adults gained the least. . .

Thus according to several measures, including health, educational achievement and poverty status, the elderly appear to be doing better than the young. The elderly are not oblivious to the improvement in their welfare. A Gallup poll made in 1982 found that 71 percent of those 65 or older reported they were highly satisfied with their standard of living, by far the greatest level of satisfaction in any age group. The proportion of the elderly who scored "Very high" on a psychological scale of anxiety fell from 22 to 15 percent between 1957 and 1976, while the corresponding proportion of younger adults rose sharply. Furthermore, since 1960 there have been reductions in the suicide rate among the elderly, which also seems to suggest increased well-being.

Although suicide is rare among children, the trend appears to be upward. Other indicators also suggest that a deterioration has occurred in the mental health of children. The U.S. Health Examination Survey asked parents whether "anything had ever happened to seriously upset or disturb your child?" The fraction of parents who answered in the affirmative rose from 27 percent in 1963–65 to 37 percent in 1976.

The major reason for the increased emotional disturbance among children, as reported by parents, seems to be the intensification of marital discord. Indeed, changes in the structure of the family appear to be closely connected to what has happened to both children and the elderly in recent years.

One reason that changes in family structure can have such a strong effect on the status of dependent groups is that the family is an important vehicle for the transfer of society's resources. James N. Morgan of the University of Michigan estimated that roughly a third of the U.S. gross national product takes the form of transfers from income earners to nonearners within family groups that live together.

As a result, any change in the family's capacity to care for its dependents has powerful consequences for those who are being taken care of. These consequences are more significant for children than they are for the elderly because the family has relinquished to the state an increasing share of responsibility for elderly dependents. Hence older people are to some extent protected against changes in family structure.

The situation is very different for children. The government assumes a much smaller share of support for the young than it does for the elderly. The conjugal family is the chief source of support for children. In recent years it has begun to divest itself of its responsibility for the young, just as earlier it abandoned much of its responsibility for the elderly. Absent fathers are the main factor in this divestiture. In 1960 only 5.3 percent of births were out of wedlock. By 1980 the figure had risen to 18.4 percent. The rate of illegitimacy has a strong influence on resources available for children because in most out-of-wedlock births the father takes no lasting responsibility for his child.

Even for children born in wedlock, the situation has deteriorated. According to Larry Bumpass of the University of Wisconsin at Madison, persistence of the divorce rates that prevailed at the end of the 1970s will mean that 43 percent of the children born in wedlock will experience parental separation before they are 16. If the rate of increase in divorce of the past decade continues, the proportion could reach two-thirds. Furthermore, fathers contribute little on the average to the support of children from previous marriages. A recent study by the Census Bureau found that fewer than half of all children living with their mother after a divorce were supported by payments from their father. The immediate consequence is that the economic condition of mothers and children deteriorates after a divorce. Morgan and his colleague Greg J. Duncan conclude that in divorces occurring from 1972 through 1978, 72 percent of the affected children experienced a reduction in their family's income in relation to the minimum standard of need.

It is obvious that the economic consequences of marital disruption have much to do with the increase in the number of children who live in poverty. Census Bureau data show that 69 percent of the increase in the number of children living in poverty from 1970 through 1982 occurred in households headed by women. Evidence suggests that the instability of the nuclear family is also responsible for some of the decline in educational achievement.

The main vehicle other than the family for transferring resources to dependents is the state. In a pluralistic democracy such as that of the United States the formation of public policy is strongly influenced by the relative power of interest groups. In recent decades the old have become a far more powerful interest group, while the constituency for children has declined in power.

In exerting their political influence the elderly draw on support from three overlapping but substantial groups. The first group consists of the elderly themselves. The second consists of members of the under-65 population acting on behalf of elderly family members who are currently or potentially in need of financial assistance. The third consists of the entire under-65 population acting on behalf of themselves in their own (future) old age. The elderly, unlike some other special interests, make up a group we all expect, or at least hope, to join eventually. Most government programs for those more than 65 years old are to some extent perceived as a social contract enabling middle-aged adults to transfer resources to themselves later in life.

Children have only one of these three sources of political influence. Young people cannot vote. Furthermore, adults cannot agitate to improve conditions in their own childhood, since that is the past. Children's only remaining source of political influence is parents acting on behalf of their progeny.

Because of the imbalance between the sources of political support available to older people and the sources available to children, the change in age structure can have a "multiplier" effect on public policy. The sharp mortality decline in the older age groups has led not only to an increase in the number of voters older than 65 but also to an increase in the number of middle-aged adults who have living parents and an increase in the number of years beyond 65 that the average adult can expect to live.

The most significant of these changes is probably the increase in the number of elderly. In the past decade the increase has been combined with a high level of political participation. In the 1982 congressional elections 65 percent of those age 65 through 74 voted. This was the highest percentage of any age group and more than twice the rate among people aged 20 through 29. Once again the trend reverses earlier patterns: in the congressional elections of 1966 the voting rate for those older than 65 was lower than it was for any age group between 35 and 64.

The elderly probably have also come to exercise a stronger claim on the political allegiance of those younger than 65. I estimate that in 1980 the average 40-year-old couple had 2.59 living parents and 2.72 living children. If present fertility and mortality rates persist, however, the average 40-year-old couple would eventually have 2.88 living parents and 1.78 living children. It would not be until age 52 that the average couple would have as many living children as they would have living parents.

When parents are 52, of course, most children have left home. It turns out that under current fertility and mortality rates there is no stage in the life cycle when the average married couple will have more children under the age of 20 than they will have surviving parents. The dependency concerns of the middle-aged are thus shifting toward the elderly, at least in numerical terms.

None of this would matter if people of different ages and in different domestic circumstances saw public issues in the same light. But they do not. For example, the 1983 Gallup Poll of public attitudes toward the public schools asked whether people would vote to raise taxes for schools if asked to do so by the local school board. Those younger than 50 were evenly split; those older than 50 were opposed by 62 to 28 percent.

The foregoing discussion of politics deals only with the part of political behavior that is motivated by self-interest. What about altruism? Altruism is not a negligible motive in human affairs, particularly altruism directed toward people with whom an individual shares some corporate identity. I suspect, however, that W. Norton Grubb and Marvin Lazerson, then at the University of California at Berkeley, were at least partially correct in proposing that we have drifted toward a form of society and government based mainly on self-interest and adversarial relations between groups. Grubb and Lazerson argue that in U.S. society there has never been a strong sense of collective responsibility for other people's children. Furthermore, the wide availability of effective contraception could well have exaggerated this split between private and collective concerns. Reliable contraceptives give a married couple a high degree of control over whether they have children. Since children are now the result of a private decision rather than of chance, many people today think the parents should bear the cost of child rearing. On the other hand, we do not choose to have parents and so there is no equivalent motive for insisting that parents be privately supported.

A second factor that probably helps to suppress altruism toward other people's children is the fact that these children are increasingly from minority groups with whom the majority have trouble identifying: 24 percent of those younger than 15 are black or Hispanic, compared with only 11 percent of those older than 65. . . .

Some readers may be disturbed by the fact that in demonstrating the existence of the demographic mechanisms affecting the elderly and the young, age has been emphasized to the exclusion of other traditional demographic variables, including race. In discussing the changing status of children and the elderly in the United States, however, I see no reason to analyze the races separately. For those who think the current problems of children are confined to racial minorities it should be pointed out that there is not one trend described above that does not apply to both blacks and whites. On the contrary, in the case of some of the most significant trends, including rising illegitimacy rates and declining school achievement, the changes have been much greater among whites than they have among blacks.

In summarizing the lessons to be learned from recent demographic trends I do not want to paint the elderly as the villains of the piece. I am primarily concerned about the fate of children and in that context the elderly serve largely for comparison. Nevertheless, it is unrealistic simply to wish away the possibility that there is direct competition between the young and the old for society's resources.

Even if the young and the old are to some extent competitors, however, the elderly alone do not decide where society's resources are to be expended. That is a collective, political decision that society makes. It is certainly reasonable to ask whether such decisions in recent decades have taken us along a useful course. There is surely something to be said for a system in which conditions improve as we pass through life.

On the other hand, the failure to devote resources to children cannot be defended so easily. Whereas expenditure on the elderly can be thought of mainly as consumption, expenditure on the young is a combination of consumption and investment. The quality of education and the psychological well-being of children are crucial to the future productive capacity of the United States.

If we care about our collective future rather than simply about our futures as individuals, we are faced with the question of how best to safeguard the human and material resources represented by children. These resources have not been carefully guarded in the past two decades. Rather than assuming collective responsibility, as has been done in the case of the elderly, U.S. society has chosen to place almost exclusive responsibility for the care of children on the nuclear family. Marital instability, however, has much reduced the capacity of the family to care for its own children. Hence insisting that families alone care for the young would seem to be an evasion of collective responsibility rather than a conscious decision about the best way to provide for the future.

<hr>

READING 15-2

Family and Generational Relations in the Later Years: A Historical Perspective

Tamara K. Hareven

An understanding of the family arrangements and supports for older people in American society has been clouded by myths about the past, on the one hand, and by a narrow treatment of contemporary problems, on the other hand. A

Tamara K. Hareven, "Family and Generational Relations in Later Years: A Historical Perspective" from *Generations* (Summer 1993). Copyright © 1993 by American Society on Aging. Reprinted with the permission of the publishers, 833 Market Street, Suite 511, San Francisco, CA 94103.

historical perspective is needed, not only to understand what changes have occurred over time, but also to determine how historical events and circumstances have affected each cohort in terms of the "historical baggage" that different groups bring into old age. A life course perspective is needed in order to understand the impact of historical conditions on the life history of various cohorts and the consequences of those conditions for adaptation in the later years of life.[1]

Following a historical and life course perspective, this [reading] examines changes in demographic behavior, in family and household organization, in the timing of life course transitions, and in kin assistance of men and women as these factors affected their adaptation in the later years of life in American society since the 19th century.

MYTHS ABOUT THE PAST

Historical research has dispelled the myths about the existence of ideal three-generational families in the American past: There never was an era when coresidence of three generations in the same household was the dominant familial arrangement. The "great extended families" that became part of the folklore of modern industrial society were rarely in existence. Like families today, families in the past tended to reside in nuclear units. Early American households and families were simple in their structure and did not contain extended kin. The older generation was residing in households separate from those of their children. Given the high mortality rate, most grandparents could not have expected to overlap with their grandchildren over a significant period of their lives. It would thus be futile to argue that industrialization destroyed the great extended family of the past. In reality, such a family type rarely existed.

Nor was there a "golden age" in the family relations of older people in the American or European past. Even in the Colonial period, the aged were insecure in their familial supports, though they were more revered and accorded higher social status than today. The very fact that aging parents had to enter into contracts with their inheriting sons in order to secure supports in old age in exchange for land, suggests the potential tensions and insecurities in such arrangements (Demos, 1978; Greven, 1970; Smith, 1973). Similarly, older people were not guaranteed supports from their children in urban industrial society in the 19th and early 20th centuries. Familial supports and care for older people, as well as all other types of kin assistance, have always been voluntary, based on reciprocal relations over the life course. Kin were engaged, however, in more intensive relations of mutual assistance than today.

The rejection of the myth of the extended multigenerational family should not be misconstrued to mean that old people lived in isolation. Solitary residence was most uncommon throughout the 19th century for all age groups. The characteristic form of residence has been one where the older generation maintained separate households from those of their married children. Autonomy in old age, partly expressed in the opportunity for older people to head their own households, hinged on some form of support from an adult child living at home or on the presence of unrelated individuals in the household. The ideal was one of proximity in residence on the same land in rural areas, or in the same building or same neighborhood in urban areas. "Intimacy from a distance," the preferred mode of generational relations in contemporary American society, has been persistent since the early settlement and reaches back into the European past.

A HISTORICAL LIFE-COURSE PERSPECTIVE

The emergence of old age as a social problem can be best understood in the context of the entire life course and of the historical changes affecting people in various stages of life. In the same way, an understanding of the current problems of the family relations of older people and their supports in contemporary American society depends on a knowledge of the larger processes of change that have affected the timing of life course transitions and family and generational relations.

The adaptation of individuals and their families to the social and economic conditions they face in the later years of life is contingent on the pathways by which they reach old age (Hareven, 1981). These affect their views of family relations, their expectations of support from kin, and their ability to interact with welfare agencies and institutions. Following a historical life-course perspective, one does not view older people simply as a homogeneous group, but rather as age cohorts moving through history, each cohort with its distinct life experiences, which were shaped by the historical circumstances it encountered earlier in life (Elder, 1978). A life course perspective enables us to interpret individual and family life transitions as part of a continuous process of historical change.

DEMOGRAPHIC CHANGE

Demographic changes in American society since the late 19th century have significantly affected age configuration within the family and the timing of life course transitions and have had, therefore, a significant impact on the later years of life (Uhlenberg, 1974, 1978; Hareven, 1976). The decline in mortality has resulted in greater uniformity in the life course of American families and has dramatically increased the opportunities for intact survival of the family unit over the lifetime of its members (Uhlenberg, 1974, 1978). The chances for children to survive to adulthood and to grow up with their siblings and both parents alive have increased over time.

Similarly, the changes for women to fulfill the societal script of their family lives have increased dramatically. The culturally established life-course sequence for women—marriage, motherhood, survival with a husband through parenting, the launching of children, and widowhood—was experienced in the 19th century by only 44 percent of females born in 1870 who survived beyond age 15. The remaining 56 percent never achieved this "normal" life-course pattern, because they died young, never married, or were childless, or because their marriage was broken by the death of their husbands. As one moves into the 20th century, an increasing portion of the population has lived out its life in family units, except when disrupted by divorce (Uhlenberg, 1974).

Under the impact of demographic, economic, and cultural factors, the timing of such transitions as leaving home, entry into and exit from the labor force, marriage, parenthood, the "empty nest," and widowhood has changed considerably over the past century. In the 20th century, transitions to adulthood have become more uniform for the age cohort undergoing them, more orderly in sequence, and more rapidly timed. Timing has become more regulated according to specific age norms, rather than in relation to the needs of the family. Individual life transitions have become less closely synchronized with collective family ones, thus causing a further separation between the generations.

The 19th century pattern of transitions, which occurred more gradually and were timed less rigidly (Modell, Furstenberg, & Hershberg, 1976), allowed for a wider age spread within the family and for greater opportunity for interaction among parents and adult children. Demographic changes, combined with the increasing rapidity in the timing of the transitions to adulthood, more geographic separation between an individual's family of origin and family of procreation, and the introduction of publicly regulated transitions, such as mandatory retirement, have converged to isolate and segregate age groups in the larger society. These changes have generated new kinds of stresses on familial needs and obligations.

FAMILY TRANSITIONS INTO OLD AGE

In the 19th century, transitions to the "empty nest," to widowhood, and out of household headship followed no ordered sequence and extended over a relatively longer time period. Older women did experience more marked transitions than did men, although the continuing presence of adult children in the household meant that widowhood did not necessarily represent a dramatic transition into solitary residence (Chudacoff & Hareven, 1979; Hareven, 1981; Smith, 1979).

The most marked discontinuity in the life course has been the "empty nest" in a couple's middle age. The 20th century combination of earlier marriage and fewer children overall, with segregation of childbearing to the early stages of the family cycle and children's leaving home more uniformly earlier in their parents' lives, has resulted in a more widespread emergence of the empty nest as a characteristic of the middle and later years of life (Glick, 1977).[2] At the same time, women's tendency to live longer than men has resulted in a protracted period of widowhood in the later years. These changes have led to a separation between the generations when parents are still in middle age and to a longer period for aged couples or widowed mothers without children in the household.

By contrast, in the 19th century, later age at marriage, higher fertility, and shorter life expectancy rendered different family configurations. The parenting period, with children remaining in the household, extended over a longer time, sometimes over the parents' entire life. Most important, the nest was rarely empty, because usually one adult child was expected to remain at home while the parents were aging (Hareven, 1976, 1982).

Aging parents strove to maintain their autonomy by retaining the headship of their own households, rather than move in with relatives or with strangers. This powerful commitment to the continued autonomy of the household was clearly in conflict with the needs of people as they were aging. In the absence of adequate public and institutional supports, older people striving to maintain independent households were caught in the double bind of living separately from their children yet having to rely on their children's assistance in order to do so.

Aging parents who were unable to live alone were either joined by an adult child, who returned to live with them, or moved into a child's household. Elderly couples who had no children, or whose children had left home, took in boarders and lodgers as part of a special exchange arrangement. Boarding provided an important means of mutual exchanges between the generations even if they were not related. About one-third of the men and women in their 20s and 30s in 19th century American urban communities boarded with other families. For young men and women in a transitional stage between their departure from their parents' homes and the establishment of their own families, boarding offered surrogate familial settings. For older people, particularly for widows, it provided the extra income needed to maintain their own residence. It also helped to avert loneliness after the children had left home (Modell & Hareven, 1973). In some cases the function was reversed, and older people who could not live alone, but who had no children or relatives, boarded in other people's households. Solitary residence, a practice that has become increasingly prominent among older people today, was rarely experienced in the 19th century (Kobrin, 1976).

FAMILY STRATEGIES

The family was the most critical agent in initiating and managing life transitions. The timing of individual members' life transitions was a criti-

cal factor in the family's efforts to maintain control over its resources, especially by balancing different members' contributions to the family economy. In modern society, we are accustomed to thinking of most transitions to family roles and work careers as individual. In the past, individual members' transitions had to be synchronized with family needs and obligations. Early life transitions were bound up with later ones in a continuum of familial need and obligations. Leaving home, getting married, or setting up a separate household had to be timed in relation to one's family of origin, especially in consideration of the needs of parents as they were aging.

Under the historical conditions in which familial assistance was the almost exclusive source of security, the multiplicity of obligations that individuals incurred over life toward their relatives was more complex than in contemporary society. In addition to the ties they retained with their family of origin, individuals carried obligations toward their families of procreation and toward their spouses' family of origin. Such obligations cast individuals into various overlapping and, at times, conflicting functions over the course of their lives. The absence of institutional supports, such as welfare agencies, unemployment compensation, and Social Security, added to the pressures imposed on family members.

Families and individuals had to rely on kin assistance as their essential social base. Kin assistance was crucial in coping with critical life situations, such as unemployment, illness, or death, and with regular life-course transitions. The absence of dramatic transitions to adult life allowed for a more intensive interaction among different age groups within the family and the community, thus providing a greater sense of continuity and interdependence among people at various stages in the life course.

After the turn of the century, as greater differentiation in stages of life had begun to develop and as social and economic functions became more closely related to age, a greater segregation between age groups emerged, first in the middle class and later among the rest of society. This trend is closely related to the decline in instrumental relations among kin, with replacement by an individualistic and sentimental orientation toward family relations, and has led to an increasing isolation of the elderly (Hareven, 1982).

INTERDEPENDENCE AMONG KIN

Interdependence and mutual assistance involved extended kin as well. Kin served as the most essential resource for economic assistance and security and carried the major burden of welfare functions for individual family members. Contrary to prevailing myths, urbanization and industrialization did not break down traditional kinship ties and patterns of mutual assistance. Historical studies have documented the survival of viable functions of kin in the 19th century, especially their critical role in facilitating migration, finding jobs and housing, and assisting in critical life situations (Anderson, 1971; Hareven, 1978).

In a regime of economic severity, where kin assistance was the only constant source of support, family needs dictated that individual choices be subordinated to familial considerations. Individuals' sense of obligation to their kin was a manifestation of their family culture, a commitment to the survival, well-being, and self-reliance of the family, which took priority over individual needs and personal happiness. Autonomy of the family, essential for self-respect and good standing in the neighborhood and community, was one of the most deeply ingrained values (Hareven, 1982). Mutual assistance among kin, although involving extensive exchanges, was not strictly calculative. Rather, it expressed an overall principle of reciprocity over the life course and across generations. Individuals who subordinated their own careers and needs to those of the family as a collective unit, even if they were not cheerful about their sacrifice, did so out of a sense of responsibility,

affection, and familial obligation, rather than with the expectation of immediate gain (Hareven, 1982).

GENERATIONAL SUPPORTS OVER THE LIFE COURSE

Close contact and mutual exchanges among parents, their adult children, and other kin persisted throughout the 19th century and survived in various forms in the lives of working-class and ethnic families into the 20th century. Parents expected their grown children to support them in their old age in exchange for a variety of services they themselves had rendered their children earlier in life. Societal values rooted in their respective ethnic cultures provided an ideological reinforcement for these reciprocal relations.

Adult children's involvement with the care of their aging parents was closely related to their earlier life-course experiences, to their ethnic and cultural traditions, and to the historical context affecting their lives. Routine assistance from children to aging parents set the stage for the children's coping with subsequent crises, such as a parent's widowhood and dependence in old age. Despite a strong tradition of kin assistance among various relatives, children carried the main burden of caretaking. More distant kin provided sociability and occasional help, but the major responsibilities fell on the children, usually on one child.

The pervasive custom of the residential separation between generations in American society was modified in cases of emergency or chronic illness, handicap, or dementia among aging parents. Children, most commonly daughters, took a parent into their own household only under circumstances of extreme duress—when parents were too frail to live alone or when they needed help with their daily activities and regular care. There was no prescribed rule as to which child would become a "parent keeper." If the child was not already residing with the parent, the selection was governed by that particular child's ability and willingness to take the parent in, by the consent or support of the parent keeper's spouse, and the readiness of the parent to accept the plan. Most parent keepers evolved into that role over their life course; some were pushed into it through a sudden family crisis. Earlier life-course experience was, however, an overwhelming factor in the designation of a parent keeper. Children who had been involved in a closer day-to-day interaction with their parents during their own child-rearing years were also more likely than their siblings to take on responsibilities for caring for their parents.

Most commonly, the parent keeper was the child who continued to reside with a parent after the other siblings "bailed out." Even when both parents were alive, the common practice was to discourage the last daughter who remained at home from leaving and getting married, in order to ensure support in old age for the parents. This pattern was pervasive among various ethnic groups until World War II. Daughters remained in the parental home, postponed marriage until their middle age, or gave it up altogether. A caretaking daughter's decision to marry caused a great deal of tension. Under these circumstances, couples waited sometimes for decades until their parents died before they could marry.

Parent keepers fulfilled their responsibilities at a high price to themselves and, if they were married, to their spouses and other family members. Caretaking disrupted the daughter's work career, led to crowding in her household, often caused tension and strain in her marriage, and made her vulnerable in preparing for her own and her spouse's retirement and old age.

COHORT LOCATION IN HISTORICAL TIME

A comparison of two cohorts of adult children in an American industrial community reveals major differences in the caretaking of their aging parents. It provides a perspective on change over historical time and an understanding of the ways in which patterns of assistance of each cohort were shaped by the historical circumstances and cultural values affecting their lifetimes.

The parent generation was born before 1900 and migrated to New England to work in the Amoskeag Mills—the world's largest textile factory in Manchester, New Hampshire. The children, most of whom were born in the United States, consisted of two cohorts: the older children's cohort, born between 1910 and 1919, came of age during the Great Depression; the younger children's cohort, born between 1920 and 1929, came of age during World War II (Hareven, 1982).

The parents viewed kin as their almost exclusive source of assistance over the life course. They expected their main supports in old age to come from their own children, rather than from institutions or agencies. Their belief in the self-sufficiency of the family led them to view public assistance as demeaning. As a French Canadian man put it: "Well, they didn't have the old folks' home those days like have today. In those days it was the kids that took care of the parents. Today, the old folks . . . they place them someplace. Get rid of them! Well, the kids want their liberty a little bit more, and they don't want to be saddled with the parents that are senile or sick or whatever."

The parents' reliance on support from kin rather than from public agencies was shaped by their ethnic backgrounds. Their involvement in mutual assistance with kin represented the continuation of an earlier practice of exchange relations, as well as an ideology that shaped their expectations from each other and from the younger generation. Their ideals of kin assistance were part of their tradition and formed a survival strategy carried over from their respective premigration cultures. They modified their ideology to fit the needs, requirements, and constraints imposed by the insecurities of the industrial environment.

Both children's cohorts shared a deep involvement with the care of aging parents, which was rooted in their earlier life-course experiences and was reinforced by their ethnic traditions and family culture. They were socialized with expectations and ideals similar to those of their parents, but were faced with the challenge of implementing them under different historical circumstances. They struggled to meet the values passed on by their parents, but new pressures, their own aspirations, and the emergence of bureaucratic agencies led them to modify these ideals. Both cohorts were ambivalent toward the obligation to be the almost exclusive caretakers of their aging parents. Beyond these dilemmas they held in common, there were significant differences between the two cohorts. The older children's cohort assigned the highest priority to recovering from the Depression and to staying afloat economically. For them, survival of the family as a collective unit remained the highest goal, rather than the pursuit of individual careers. Hence, they stretched their resources in order to keep aging parents within their homes and support them as long as possible.

The younger cohort, taking advantage of the economic recovery brought about by the war and of the career training and educational benefits that the young men had gained in the military service, tried to pull themselves out from a depressed, unemployed, working-class situation into a middle-class lifestyle (Elder & Hareven, 1992). Ironically, the younger children's cohort had been coached by their own parents to aspire to occupational advancement and to develop middle-class lifestyles. As they attained these goals, the children were also less available to their parents when they needed assistance in old age.

The younger children's cohort had made the transition to a more individualistic mode of thinking. They drew firmer boundaries between the nuclear family and extended kin. Their primary energies were directed toward their children and their own futures, rather than toward their parents. They viewed themselves as separate

from their family of origin and upheld the privacy of their own nuclear family. This was also expressed in their preference for separate residence from the older generation. As Raymond Champagne (born 1926) put it: "I believe that marriage is something very sacred. It should be a husband-wife situation, nobody else . . . and I have listened when I was younger that families who took in the old people, I always felt that those people [taking in elderly parents] were not fully leading a married life . . . I just wouldn't want to be in their shoes, and I wouldn't want to put my children through it."

Members of this cohort expressed ambivalence over taking dependent elderly parents into their own homes. They helped their parents, principally by providing them with services and assistance rather than taking them in. They were more likely than the older cohort to place their physically or mentally impaired parents in nursing homes or to seek institutional help.

Neither the older nor the younger children's cohort was free, however, of the complexities involved in handling the problems of generational assistance. Both cohorts were transitional between a milieu of a deep involvement in generational assistance, reinforced by strong family and ethnic values, and the individualistic values and lifestyles that emerged in the post–World War II period. In this historical process, the older cohort's lives conformed more closely to the script of their traditional familial and ethnic cultures, while the younger cohort, as it Americanized, was being pulled in the direction of more individualistic, middle-class values.

HISTORICAL IMPLICATIONS

The difference in the experience of the two cohorts reflects major changes in attitudes toward generational assistance, kin relations, and familial values in American society. An increasing separation between the family of origin and the family of procreation over the past century, combined with a privatization of family life and especially the erosion of mutual assistance among kin, have all tended to increase insecurity and isolation as people age, especially in areas of need that are not met by public welfare programs.

While some of the intensive historical patterns of kin interaction have survived among some first-generation immigrant, black, and working-class families, there has been a gradual weakening of mutual assistance among kin over time. Gerontological studies insisting that kin assistance for older people persists in contemporary society have not documented the intensity, quality, and consistency of kin support that older people are receiving from their relatives (Sussman, 1959; Litwak, 1965; Shanas et al., 1968). Until we have more systematic evidence in this area, it would be a mistake to assume that kin are carrying or should be carrying the major responsibility for assistance to older people.

The contact that contemporary aged people have with kin, as Shanas et al. (1968) and others have found, may represent a form of behavior characteristic of certain cohorts rather than a continuing pattern (Hareven, 1978). The cohorts that are currently aged, especially the old-old, have carried over the historical attitudes and traditions of a strong reliance on kin prevalent in their youth, earlier in this century. Future cohorts, as they reach old age, might not have the same strong sense of familial interdependence, and they might not have sufficient numbers of relatives available on whom to rely. It would be a mistake, therefore, to leave kin to take care of their own at a time when the chances for people to do so effectively have considerably diminished.

Nor should the historical evidence about the continuity in kin relations be misused in support of proposals to return welfare responsibilities from the public sector to the family without basic additional supports. The historical experience reveals the high price that kin had to pay in order to assist each other without the appropriate societal supports. It thus offers a warning against romanticizing kin relations, and particularly against the attempt to transfer responsibility for the support of the elderly back to the family without adequate government assistance for caregiving relatives.

The major changes that have led to the isolation of older people in society today were rooted not so much in changes in family structure or residential arrangements, as has generally been argued, as in the transformation and redefinition of family functions. Changes in functions and values—especially the replacement of an instrumental view of the family with sentimentality and intimacy as its major cohesive forces—have led to the weakening of the role of kin assistance, in middle-class families in particular.

Over the 19th century, the family surrendered many of the functions previously concentrated within it to other social institutions. The retreat from public life and a growing commitment to the privacy of the modern middle-class family drew sharper boundaries between family and community and intensified the segregation of different age groups within and outside the family.

The transfer of social-welfare functions, once concentrated in the family, to institutions in the larger society resulted in further exacerbating the lack of needed assistance to older people. The family ceased to be the only available source of support for its dependent members, and the community—although it ceased to rely on the family as the major agency of welfare and social control—did not develop adequate substitute agencies for the care of elderly dependent people.

This shift of responsibility has generated considerable ambiguity, particularly in the expectations for support and assistance for aging relatives from their own kin. On the one hand, it is assumed that the welfare state has relieved children from the obligation of supporting their parents in old age; on the other hand, these public measures are not sufficient in the economic area, nor do they provide, in the other areas, the kind of supports and sociability that had been traditionally provided by the family. It is precisely this ambiguity and the failure of American society to consummate the historical process of the transfer of functions from the family to the public sector, and to strengthen the ability of the family to carry out its responsibilities, that has become one of the major sources of the problems currently confronting older people.

ENDNOTES

1. A cohort is an age group sharing a common historical experience.
2. Over the past decade, the empty nest has begun to fill up again with young adult children who return to the parental home, or with those who never left.

REFERENCES

Anderson, M. S., 1971. *Family Structure in Nineteenth Century Lancashire.* Cambridge, England: Cambridge University Press.

Chudacoff, H. & Hareven, T. K., 1979. "From the Empty Nest to Family Dissolution." *Journal of Family History 4(1),* pp. 69–84.

Demos, J., 1978. "Old Age in Early New England." In J. Demos and S. Boocock, eds., *Turning Points: American Journal of Sociology* 84 (Supplement).

Elder, G., 1978. "Family History and the Life Course." In T. K. Hareven, ed., *Transitions: The Family and the Life Course in Historical Perspective.* New York: Academic Press.

Elder, G. H. and Hareven, T. K., (1992). "Rising Above Life's Disadvantages: From the Great Depression to Global War." In J. Modell, G. H. Elder, Jr. and R. Parke, eds., *Children in Time and Place.* New York: Cambridge University Press.

Glick, P. C., 1977. "Updating the Life Cycle of the Family." *Journal of Marriage and the Family* (February), pp. 5–13.

Greven, P., 1970. *Four Generations: Population, Land and Family in Colonial Andover, Massachusetts.* Ithaca, N.Y.: Cornell University Press.

Hareven, T. K., 1976. "The Last Stage: Historical Adulthood and Old Age." *Daedalus American Civilization: New Perspectives 105(4),* pp. 13–17.

Hareven, T. K., 1978. "Historical Changes in the Life Course and the Family." In J. M. Vinger and S. J. Cutler, eds., *Major Social Issues: Multidisciplinary View.* New York: Free Press.

Hareven, T. K., 1981. "Historical Changes in the Timing of Family Transitions: Their Impact on Generational Relations." In J. G. March et al., eds., *Aging: Stability and Change in the Family.* New York: Academic Press.

Hareven, T. K., 1982. *Family Time and Industrial Time.* Cambridge, England: Cambridge University Press.

Hareven, T. K. and Adams, K., (1993). "The Generation in the Middle: Cohort Companies in Assistance to Aging Parents in an American Community." In T. K. Hareven, ed., *Aging and Generational Relations in Historical and Comparative Perspective: Essays from the Delaware Conference.*

Kobrin, F. E., 1976. "The Fall of Household Size and the Rise of the Primary Individual." *Demography* (February), pp. 127–38.

Litwak, E., 1965. "Extended Kin Relations in an Industrial Democratic Society." In E. Shanas and G. F. Streib, eds., *Social Structure and the Family: Generational Relations.* Englewood Cliffs, N.J.: Prentice-Hall.

Modell, J. and Hareven, T. K., 1973. "Urbanization and the Malleable Household: Boarding and Lodging in American Families." *Journal of Marriage and the Family, 35,* pp. 467–79.

Modell, J., Furstenberg, F. and Hershberg, T., 1976. "Social Change and Transitions to Adulthood in Historical Perspective." *Journal of Family History 1,* pp. 7–32.

Shanas, E. et al., 1968. *Old People in Three Industrial Societies.* New York: Atherton Press.

Smith, D. S., 1973. "Parental Power and Marriage Patterns: Analysis of Historical Trends in Hingham, Massachusetts." *Journal of Marriage and the Family, 35.*

Smith, D. S., 1979. "Life Course, Norms, and the Family System of Older Americans in 1900." *Journal of Family History 4,* pp. 285–99.

Sussman, M. B., 1959. "The Isolated Nuclear Family: Fact or Fiction?" *Social Problems 6,* pp. 333–47.

Uhlenberg, P., 1974. "Cohort Variations in Family Life Cycle Experiences of U.S. Females." *Journal of Marriage and the Family 34,* pp. 284–92.

Uhlenberg, P., 1978. "Changing Configurations of the Life Course." In T. K. Hareven, ed., *Transitions: The Family and the Life Course in Historical Perspective.* New York: Academic Press.

CHAPTER 16

Social Change and Families

Having studied the sociology of the family, you should be in a better position to evaluate the debates over its current and future state. That's not to say that you should necessarily choose a side: the issues are complex and the institution itself is always changing. It's not always clear what is the "conservative" or "liberal" or "feminist" position. If the course you are completing increases your power to critically evaluate the arguments that you will hear in the future, whether or not you sympathize with the people who are doing the arguing, then it will have been a success.

The issue on which the debates have been centered over the past few decades is how well families are caring for children. Critics ask whether the decline of life-long marriage between a father who earns the family's income and a mother who stays home and raises the children has lowered the quality of parenting that children receive today. They cite statistics that purport to show a drop in the well-being of children and link this drop to the changes in family life. Conservatives often blame the trends on a cultural drift toward greater individualism—a focus on individual growth and self-fulfillment—which is said to

have eroded the strength of social ties, including marriage.

In contrast, the defenders of contemporary families often argue that the drop in children's well-being is exaggerated and that, in any case, forces outside of the family's control are responsible for both the lowered well-being and the changes in family life. Liberals maintain that an important force is a deterioration in the job prospects for people—and especially young men—without college degrees. The worsening job market is said to have discouraged young adults from marrying and made marriages that do occur more fragile. Feminists defend the movement of married women into the work force for broadening women's lives; if, as a result, working parents are stressed and children sometimes don't receive optimal care, the solution they suggest is to provide more social support for working parents.

In the following selection, Janet Z. Giele outlines the essentials of what she sees as three different political positions in the debate about the family: conservative, liberal, and feminist. The descriptions of the conservative and liberal positions are standard ones, and the author does a good job of summarizing them. Giele's feminist position is more original—she claims that there is a coherent feminist viewpoint that is neither liberal nor conservative. Not every contributor to the debate, not even every feminist contributor, would agree with her. Giele obviously favors this third way, and you should evaluate her position as critically and thoughtfully as you would evaluate the other two.

Whether or not the family has declined, it is hard to argue against the proposition that mar-

riage plays a lesser role in family life than it did a few decades ago, when cohabitation was rare outside of the lower classes, divorce was much less common, and the vast majority of children were born to married couples. Frank F. Furstenberg, Jr., in the last selection in this reader, reviews the ways in which marriage has changed and engages in the risky business of trying to predict what will happen to marriage in the first years of the 21st century.

Decline of the Family: Conservative, Liberal, and Feminist Views

Janet Z. Giele

In the 1990s the state of American families and children became a new and urgent topic. Everyone recognized that families had changed. Divorce rates had risen dramatically. More women were in the labor force. Evidence on rising teenage suicides, high rates of teen births, and disturbing levels of addiction and violence had put children at risk.

Conservatives have held that these problems can be traced to a culture of toleration and an expanding welfare state that undercut self-reliance and community standards. They focus on the family as a caregiving institution and try to restore its strengths by changing the culture of marriage and parenthood. Liberals center on the disappearance of manual jobs that throws less educated men out of work and undercuts their status in the family as well as rising hours of work among the middle class that makes stable two-parent families more difficult to maintain. Liberals argue that structural changes are needed outside the family in the public world of employment and schools.

The feminist vision combines both the reality of human interdependence in the family and individualism of the workplace. Feminists want to protect diverse family forms that allow realization of freedom and equality while at the same time nurturing the children of the next generation.

THE CONSERVATIVE EXPLANATION: SELFISHNESS AND MORAL DECLINE

The new family advocates turn their spotlight on the breakdown in the two-parent family, saying that rising divorce, illegitimacy, and father absence have put children at greater risk of school failure, unemployment, and antisocial behavior. The remedy is to restore religious faith and family commitment as well as to cut welfare payments to unwed mothers and mother-headed families.

CONSERVATIVE MODEL

Cultural and moral weakening	→	Family breakdown, divorce, family decline	→	Father absence, school failure, poverty, crime, drug use

Cultural and Moral Weakening

To many conservatives, the modern secularization of religious practice and the decline of religious affiliation have undermined the norms of sexual abstinence before marriage and the prohibitions of adultery or divorce thereafter. Sanctions against illegitimacy or divorce have been made to seem narrow-minded and prejudiced. In addition, daytime television and the infamous example of Murphy Brown, a single mother having a child out of wedlock helped to obscure simple notions of right and wrong. Barbara Dafoe Whitehead's controversial article in the *Atlantic* entitled "Dan Quayle Was Right" is an example of this argument.[1]

Gradual changes in marriage laws have also diminished the hold of tradition. Restrictions against waiting periods, race dissimilarity, and varying degrees of consanguinity were gradually disappearing all over the United States and Europe.[2] While Mary Ann Glendon viewed the change cautiously but relativistically—as a process that waxed and waned across the centuries—others have interpreted these changes as a movement from status to contract (i.e., from attention to the particular individual's characteristics to reliance on the impersonal considerations of the marketplace). The resulting transformation lessened the family's distinctive capacity to serve as a bastion of private freedom against the leveling effect and impersonality of public bureaucracy.

Erosion of the Two-Parent Family

To conservatives, one of the most visible causes of family erosion was government welfare payments, which made fatherless families a viable option. In *Losing Ground,* Charles Murray used the rise in teenage illegitimate births as proof that government-sponsored welfare programs had actually contributed to the breakdown of marriage.[3] Statistics on rising divorce and mother-headed families appeared to provide ample proof that the two-parent family was under siege. The proportion of all households headed by married couples fell from 77 percent in 1950 to 61 percent in 1980 and 55 percent in 1993.[4] Rising cohabitation, divorce rates, and births out of wedlock all contributed to the trend. The rise in single-person households was also significant, from only 12 percent of all households in 1950 to 27 percent in 1980, a trend fed by rising affluence and the undoubling of living arrangements that occurred with the expansion of the housing supply after World War II.[5]

The growth of single-parent households, however, was the most worrisome to policy-makers because of their strong links to child poverty. . . . Of all poor children in 1959, 73 percent had two parents present and 20 percent had a mother only. By 1988, only 35 percent of children in poverty lived with two parents and 57 percent lived with a mother only. These developments were fed by rising rates of divorce and out-of-wedlock births. Between 1940 and 1990, the divorce rate rose from 8.8 to 21 per thousand married women. Out-of-wedlock births exploded from 5 percent in 1960 to 26 percent in 1990.[6]

To explain these changes, conservatives emphasize the breakdown of individual and cultural commitment to marriage and the loss of stigma for divorce and illegitimacy. They understand both trends to be the result of greater emphasis on short-term gratification and on adults' personal desires rather than on what is good for children. A young woman brings a child into the world without thinking about who will support it. A husband divorces his wife and forms another household, possibly with other children and leaves children of the earlier family behind without necessarily feeling obliged to be present in their upbringing or to provide them with financial support.

Negative Consequences for Children

To cultural conservatives there appears to be a strong connection between erosion of the two-parent family and the rise of health and social problems in children. Parental investment in children has declined—especially in the time available for supervision and companionship. Parents had roughly 10 fewer hours per week for their children in 1986 than in 1960, largely because more married women were employed (up from 24 percent in 1940 to 52 percent in 1983) and more mothers of young children (under age 6) were working (up from 12 percent in 1940 to 50 percent in 1983). By the late 1980s just over half of mothers of children under a year old were in the labor force for at least part of the year.[7] At the same time fathers were increasingly absent from the family because of desertion, divorce, or failure to marry. In 1980, 15 percent of white children, 50 percent of black children, and 27 percent of children of Hispanic origin had no father present. Today 36 percent of children are living apart from their biological fathers compared with only 17 percent in 1960.[8]

Without a parent to supervise children after school, keep them from watching television all day, or prevent them from playing in dangerous neighborhoods, many more children appear to be falling by the wayside, victims of drugs, obesity, violence, suicide, or failure in school.

During the 1960s and 1970s the suicide rate for persons aged 15 to 19 more than doubled. The proportion of obese children between the ages of 6 and 11 rose from 18 to 27 percent. Average SAT scores fell, and 25 percent of all high school students failed to graduate.[9] In 1995 the Council on Families in America reported, "Recent surveys have found that children from broken homes, when they become teenagers have 2 to 3 times more behavioral and psychological problems than do children from intact homes."[10] Father absence is blamed by the fatherhood movement for the rise in violence among young males. David Blankenhorn and others reason that the lack of a positive and productive male role model has contributed to an uncertain masculine identity which then uses violence and aggression to prove itself. Every child deserves a father and "in a good society, men prove their masculinity not by killing other people, impregnating lots of women, or amassing large fortunes, but rather by being committed fathers and loving husbands.[11]

Psychologist David Elkind, in *The Hurried Child,* suggests that parents' work and time constraints have pushed down the developmental timetable to younger ages so that small children are being expected to take care of themselves and perform at levels that are robbing them of their childhood. The consequences are depression, discouragement, and a loss of joy at learning and growing into maturity.[12]

Reinvention of Marriage

According to the conservative analysis, the solution to a breakdown in family values is to revitalize and reinstitutionalize marriage. The culture should change to give higher priority to marriage and parenting. The legal code should favor marriage and encourage parental responsibility on the part of fathers as well as mothers. Government should cut back welfare programs which have supported alternative family forms.

The cultural approach to revitalizing marriage is to raise the overall priority given to family activities relative to work, material consumption, or leisure. Marriage is seen as the basic building block of civil society, which helps to hold together the fabric of volunteer activity and mutual support that underpins any democratic society.[13] Some advocates are unapologetically judgmental toward families who fall outside the two-parent mold. According to a 1995 *Newsweek* article on "The Return of Shame," David Blankenhorn believes "a stronger sense of shame about illegitimacy and divorce would do more than any tax cut or any new governmental program to maximize the life circumstances of children." But he also adds that the ultimate goal is "to move beyond stigmatizing only teenage mothers toward an understanding of the terrible message sent by all of us when we minimize the importance of fathers or contribute to the breakup of families."[14]

Another means to marriage and family revitalization is some form of taking a "pledge." Prevention programs for teenage pregnancy affirm the ideal of chastity before marriage. Athletes for Abstinence, an organization founded by a professional basketball player, preaches that young people should "save sex for marriage." A Baptist-led national program called True Love Waits has gathered an abstinence pledge from hundreds of thousands of teenagers since it was begun in the spring of 1993. More than 2,000 school districts now offer an abstinence-based sex education curriculum entitled "Sex Respect." Parents who are desperate about their children's sexual behavior are at last seeing ways that society can resist the continued sexualization of childhood.[15]

The new fatherhood movement encourages fathers to promise that they will spend more time with their children. The National Fatherhood Initiative argues that men's roles as fathers should not simply duplicate women's roles as mothers but should teach those essential qualities which are perhaps uniquely conveyed by fathers—the ability to take risks, contain emotions, and be decisive. In addition, fathers fulfill a time-honored role of providing for children as well as teaching them.[16]

Full-time mothers have likewise formed support groups to reassure themselves that not having a job and being at home full-time for their children is an honorable choice, although it is typically undervalued and perhaps even scorned by dual-earner couples and women with careers. A 1994 *Barron's* article claimed that young people in their 20s ("generation X") were turning away from the two-paycheck family and scaling down their consumption so that young mothers could stay at home. Although Labor Department statistics show no such trend but only a flattening of the upward rise of women's employment, a variety of poll data does suggest that Americans would rather spend less time at work and more time with their families.[17] Such groups as Mothers at Home (with 15,000 members) and Mothers' Home Business Network (with 6,000 members) are trying to create a sea change that reverses the priority given to paid work outside the home relative to unpaid caregiving work inside the family.[18]

Conservatives see government cutbacks as one of the major strategies for strengthening marriage and restoring family values. In the words of Lawrence Mead, we have "taxed Peter to pay Paula."[19] According to a *Wall Street Journal* editorial, the "relinquishment of personal responsibility" among people who bring children into the world without any visible means of support is at the root of educational, health, and emotional problems of children from one-parent families, their higher accident and mortality rates, and rising crime.[20]

The new congressional solution is to cut back on the benefits to young men and women who "violate social convention by having children they cannot support."[21] Sociologist Brigitte Berger notes that the increase in children and women on welfare coincided with the explosion of federal child welfare programs—family planning, prenatal and postnatal care, child nutrition, child abuse prevention and treatment, child

health and guidance, day care, Head Start, and Aid to Families with Dependent Children (AFDC), Medicaid, and Food Stamps. The solution is to turn back the debilitating culture of welfare dependency by decentralizing the power of the federal government and restoring the role of intermediary community institutions such as the neighborhood and the church. The mechanism for change would be block grants to the states which would change the welfare culture from the ground up.[22] Robert Rector of the American Heritage Foundation explains that the states would use these funds for a wide variety of alternative programs to discourage illegitimate births and to care for children born out of wedlock, such as promoting adoption, closely supervised group homes for unmarried mothers and their children, and pregnancy prevention programs (except abortion).[23]

Government programs, however, are only one way to bring about cultural change. The Council on Families in America puts its hope in grassroots social movements to change the hearts and minds of religious and civil leaders, employers, human service professionals, courts, and the media and entertainment industry. The Council enunciates four ideals: marital permanence, childbearing confined to marriage, every child's right to have a father, and limitation of parents' total work time (60 hours per week) to permit adequate time with their families.[24] To restore the cultural ideal of the two-parent family, they would make all other types of family life less attractive and more difficult.

ECONOMIC RESTRUCTURING: LIBERAL ANALYSIS OF FAMILY CHANGE

Liberals agree that there are serious problems in America's social health and the condition of its children. But they pinpoint economic and structural changes that have placed new demands on the family without providing countervailing social supports. The economy has become ever more specialized with rapid technological change undercutting established occupations. More women have entered the labor force as their child-free years have increased due to a shorter childbearing period and longer lifespan. The family has lost economic functions to the urban workplace and socialization functions to the school. What is left is the intimate relationship between the marital couple, which, unbuffered by the traditional economic division of labor between men and women, is subject to even higher demands for emotional fulfillment and is thus more vulnerable to breakdown when it falls short of those demands.

LIBERAL MODEL

Changing economic structure → Changing family and gender roles → Diverse effects: poor v. productive children

The current family crisis thus stems from structural more than cultural change—changes in the economy, a paired-down nuclear family, and less parental time at home. Market forces have led to a new ethic of individual flexibility and autonomy. More dual-earner couples and single-parent families have broadened the variety of family forms. More single-parent families and more working mothers have decreased the time available for parenting. Loss of the father's income through separation and divorce has forced many women and children into poverty with inadequate health care, poor education, and inability to save for future economic needs. The solution that most liberals espouse is a government-sponsored safety net which will facilitate women's employment, mute the effects of poverty, and help women and children to become economically secure.

Recent Changes in the Labor Market

Liberals attribute the dramatic changes in the family to the intrusion of the money economy rather than cultural and moral decline. In a capitalist society individual behavior follows the market. Adam Smith's "invisible hand" brings together buyers and sellers who maximize their satisfaction through an exchange of resources in the marketplace. Jobs are now with an employer, not with the family business or family farm as in preindustrial times. The cash economy has, in the words of Robert Bellah, "invaded" the diffuse personal relationships of trust between family and community members and transformed them into specific impersonal transactions. In an agricultural economy husbands and wives and parents and children were bound together in relationships of exchange that served each others' mutual interests. But modern society erodes this social capital of organization, trust among individuals, and mutual obligations that enhances both productivity and parenting.[25]

The market has also eroded community by encouraging maximum mobility of goods and services. Cheaper labor in the South, lower fuel prices, and deeper tax breaks attracted first textile factories, then the shoe industry, and later automobile assembly plants which had begun in the North. Eventually, many of these jobs left the country. Loss of manufacturing jobs has had dramatic consequences for employment of young men without a college education and their capacity to support a family. In the 1970s, 68 percent of male high school graduates had a full-time, year-round job compared with only 51 percent in the 1980s. Many new jobs are located in clerical work, sales, or other service occupations traditionally associated with women. The upshot is a deteriorating employment picture for less well educated male workers at the same time that there are rising opportunities for women. Not surprisingly, ever more middle-income men and women combine forces to construct a two-paycheck family wage.[26]

Changing Family Forms

Whereas the farm economy dictated a two-parent family and several children as the most efficient work group, the market economy gives rise to a much wider variety of family forms. A woman on the frontier in the 1800s had few other options even if she were married to a drunken, violent, or improvident husband. In today's economy this woman may have enough education to get a clerical job that will support her and her children in a small apartment where the family will be able to use public schools and other public amenities.[27]

Despite its corrosive effect on family relations, the modern economy has also been a liberating force. Women could escape patriarchal domination; the young could seek their fortune without waiting for an inheritance from their elders—all a process that a century ago was aligned with a cultural shift that Fred Weinstein and Gerald Platt termed "the wish to be free."[28] Dramatic improvements took place in the status of women as they gained the right to higher education, entry into the professions, and the elective franchise.[29] Similarly, children were released from sometimes cruel and exploitive labor and became the object of deliberate parental investment and consumption.[30] Elders gained pensions for maintenance and care that made them economically independent of their adult children. All these developments could be understood as part of what William J. Goode has referred to as the "world revolution in family patterns" which resulted in liberation and equality of formerly oppressed groups.[31]

The current assessment of change in family forms is, however, mostly negative because of the consequences for children. More parental investment in work outside the family has meant less time for children. According to liberals, parents separate or divorce or have children outside of marriage because of the economic structure, not because they have become less moral or more selfish. Young women have children out of wedlock when the young men whom they might marry have few economic prospects and when the women themselves have little hope for their own education or employment.[32] Change in the family thus begins with jobs. Advocates of current government programs therefore challenge the conservatives' assertion that welfare

caused the breakup of two-parent families by supporting mothers with dependent children. According to William Julius Wilson, it is partly the lack of manual labor jobs for the would-be male breadwinner in inner-city Chicago—the scarcity of "marriageable males"—which drives up the illegitimacy rate.[33]

Among educated women, it is well known that the opportunity costs of forgone income from staying home became so high during the 1950s and 1960s that ever increasing numbers of women deserted full-time homemaking to take paid employment.[34] In the 1990s several social scientists have further noted that Richard Easterlin's prediction that women would return to the home during the 1980s never happened. Instead women continued in the labor force because of irreversible normative changes surrounding women's equality and the need for women's income to finance children's expensive college education.[35] Moreover, in light of globalization of the economy and increasing job insecurity in the face of corporate downsizing, economists and sociologists are questioning Gary Becker's thesis that the lower waged worker in a household (typically the woman) will tend to become a full-time homemaker while the higher waged partner becomes the primary breadwinner. Data from Germany and the United States on the trend toward women's multiple roles suggests that uncertainty about the future has made women invest more strongly than ever in their own careers. They know that if they drop out for very long they will have difficulty re-entering if they have to tide over the family when the main breadwinner loses his job.[36]

Consequences for Children

The ideal family in the liberal economic model, according to political philosopher Iris Young, is one which has sufficient income to support the parents and the children and "to foster in those children the emotional and intellectual capacities to acquire such well-paid, secure jobs themselves, and also sufficient to finance a retirement."[37] Dependent families do not have self-sufficient income but must rely on friends, relatives, charity, or the state to carry out their contribution to bringing up children and being good citizens.

Among liberals there is an emerging consensus that the current economic structure leads to two kinds of underinvestment in children that are implicated in their later dependency—material poverty, characteristic of the poor, and "time" poverty, characteristic of the middle class.

Thirty years ago Daniel Patrick Moynihan perceived that material poverty and job loss for a man put strain on the marriage, sometimes to the point that he would leave. His children also did less well in school.[38] Rand Conger, in his studies of Iowa families who lost their farms during the 1980s, found that economic hardship not only puts strain on the marriage but leads to harsh parenting practices and poorer outcomes for children.[39] Thus it appears possible that poverty may not just be the result of family separation, divorce, and ineffective childrearing practices; it may also be the *cause* of the irritability, quarrels, and violence which lead to marital breakdown. Material underinvestment in children is visible not just with the poor but in the changing ratio of per capita income of children and adults in U.S. society as a whole. As the proportion of households without children has doubled over the last century (from 30 to 65) percent, per capita income of children has fallen from 71 percent of adult income in 1870 to 63 percent in 1930 and 51 percent in 1983.[40]

The problem of "time" poverty used to be almost exclusively associated with mothers' employment. Numerous studies explored whether younger children did better if their mother was a full-time homemaker rather than employed outside the home but found no clear results.[41] Lately the lack of parental time for children has become much more acute because parents are working a total of 21 hours more per week than in 1970 and because there are more single-parent families. In 1965 the average child spent about 30 hours a week interacting with a parent, compared with seventeen hours in the 1980s.[42] Moreover, parents are less dependent on their children to provide support for them during old age, and children feel less obligated to do so. As skilled craftsmanship, the trades, and the family farms have disappeared, children's upbringing can no longer be easily or cheaply combined with what parents are already doing. So adults are no longer so invested in children's futures. The result is that where the social capital of group affiliations and mutual obligations is the lowest (in the form of continuity of neighborhoods, a two-parent family, or a parent's interest in higher education for her children), children are 20 percent more likely to drop out of high school.[43]

It is not that parents prefer their current feelings of being rushed, working too many hours, and having too little time with their families. Economist Juliet Schor reports that at least two-thirds of persons she surveyed about their desires for more family time versus more salary would take a cut in salary if it could mean more time with their families. Since this option is not realistically open to many, what parents appear to do is spend more money on their children as a substitute for spending more time with them.[44]

Fixing the Safety Net

Since liberals believe in a market economy with sufficient government regulation to assure justice and equality of opportunity, they support those measures which will eradicate the worst poverty and assure the healthy reproduction of the next generation.[45] What particularly worries them, however, is Charles Murray's observation that since 1970 the growth of government welfare programs has been associated with a *rise* in poverty among children. Payments to poor families with children, while not generous, have nevertheless enabled adults to be supported by attachment to their children.[46] Society is faced with a dilemma between addressing material poverty through further government subsidy and time poverty through policies on parental leave and working hours. It turns out that the United States is trying to do both.

Measures for addressing material poverty would stimulate various kinds of training and job opportunities. The Family Support Act of 1988 would move AFDC mothers off the welfare rolls by giving them job training and requiring them to join the labor force. Such action would bring their economic responsibility for supporting their children into line with their parental authority. A whole program of integrated supports for health insurance, job training, earned income tax credits for the working poor, child support by the noncustodial parent, and supported work is put forward by economist David Ellwood in *Poor Support*.[47] An opposite strategy is to consolidate authority over children with the state's economic responsibility for their care by encouraging group homes and adoption for children whose parents cannot support them economically.[48]

Means for addressing time poverty are evident in such legislative initiatives as the Family and Medical Leave Act of 1993. By encouraging employers to grant parental leave or other forms of flexible work time, government policy is recognizing the value of parents having more time with their children, but the beneficiaries of such change are largely middle-class families who can afford an unpaid parental leave.[49] Another tactic is to reform the tax law to discourage marital splitting. In a couple with two children in which the father earns $16,000 annually and the mother $9,000, joint tax filing gives them no special consideration. But if they file separately, each taking one child as a dependent, the woman will receive about $5,000 in Earned Income Tax Credit and an extra $2,000 in food stamps.[50] Changing the tax law to remove the incentives for splitting, establishing paternity of children born out of wedlock, and intensifying child support enforcement to recover economic support from fathers are all examples of state efforts to strengthen the kinship unit.

INTERDEPENDENCE: THE FEMINIST VISION OF WORK AND CAREGIVING

A feminist perspective has elements in common with both conservatives and liberals, a respect for the family as an institution (shared with the conservatives) and an appreciation of modernity (valued by the liberals). In addition, a feminist perspective grapples with the problem of women's traditionally subordinate status and how to improve it through both a "relational" and an "individualist" strategy while also sustaining family life and the healthy rearing of children.[51] At the same time feminists are skeptical of both conservative and liberal solutions. Traditionalists have so often relied on women as the exploited and underpaid caregivers in the family to enable men's activities in the public realm. Liberals are sometimes guilty of a "male" bias in focusing on the independent individual actor in the marketplace who does not realize that his so-called "independence" is possible only because he is actually *dependent* on all kinds of relationships that made possible his education and life in a stable social order.[52]

By articulating the value of caregiving along with the ideal of women's autonomy, feminists are in a position to examine modern capitalism critically for its effects on families and to offer alternative policies that place greater value on the quality of life and human relationships. They judge family strength not by their *form* (whether they have two-parents) but by their functioning (whether they promote human satisfaction and development) and whether both women and men are able to be family caregivers as well as productive workers. They attribute difficulties of children less to the absence of the two-parent family than to low-wage work of single mothers, inadequate child care, and inhospitable housing and neighborhoods.

FEMINIST MODEL

Lack of cooperation among community, family, and work	→	Families where adults are stressed and overburdened	→	Children lack sufficient care and attention from parents

Accordingly, feminists would work for reforms that build and maintain the social capital of volunteer groups, neighborhoods, and communities because a healthy civil society promotes the well-being of families and individuals as well as economic prosperity and a democratic state. They would also recognize greater role flexibility across the life cycle so that both men and women could engage in caregiving, and they would encourage education and employment among women as well as among men.

Disappearance of Community

From a feminist perspective, family values have become an issue because individualism has driven out the sense of collective responsibility in our national culture. American institutions and social policies have not properly implemented a concern for all citizens. Comparative research on family structure, teenage pregnancy, poverty, and child outcomes in other countries demonstrates that where support is generous to help *all* families and children, there are higher levels of health and general education and lower levels of violence and child deviance than in the United States.[53]

Liberal thinking and the focus on the free market have made it seem that citizens make their greatest contribution when they are self-sufficient, thereby keeping themselves off the public dole. But feminist theorist Iris Young argues that many of the activities that are basic to a healthy democratic society (such as cultural production, caretaking, political organizing, and charitable activities) will never be profitable in a private market. Yet many of the recipients of welfare and Social Security such as homemakers, single mothers, and retirees are doing important volunteer work caring for children and

helping others in their communities. Thus the social worth of a person's contribution is not just in earning a paycheck that shows economic independence but also in making a social contribution. Such caretaking of other dependent citizens and of the body politic should be regarded as honorable, not inferior, and worthy of society's support and subsidy.[54]

In fact it appears that married women's rising labor force participation from 41 percent in 1970 to 58 percent in 1990 may have been associated with their withdrawal from unpaid work in the home and community.[55] Volunteer membership in everything from the PTA to bowling leagues declined by over 25 percent between 1969 and 1993. There is now considerable concern that the very basis that Alexis de Tocqueville thought necessary to democracy is under siege.[56] To reverse this trend, social observers suggest that it will be necessary to guard time for families and leisure that is currently being sucked into the maw of paid employment. What is needed is a reorientation of priorities to give greater value to unpaid family and community work by both men and women.

National policies should also be reoriented to give universal support to children at every economic level of society, but especially to poor children. In a comparison of countries in the Organization for Economic Cooperation and Development, the United States ranks at the top in average male wages but near the bottom in its provision for disposable income for children. In comparison with the $700 per month available to children in Norway, France, or the Netherlands in 1992, U.S. children of a single nonemployed mother received only slightly under $200.[57] The discrepancy is explained by very unequal distribution of U.S. income, with the top quintile, the "fortunate fifth," gaining 47 percent of the national income while the bottom fifth receives only 3.6 percent.[58] This sharp inequality is, in turn, explained by an ideology of individualism that justifies the disproportionate gains of the few for their innovation and productivity and the meager income of the poor for their low initiative or competence. Lack of access to jobs and the low pay accruing to many contingent service occupations simply worsen the picture.

Feminists are skeptical of explanations that ascribe higher productivity to the higher paid and more successful leading actors while ignoring the efforts and contribution of the supporting cast. They know that being an invisible helper is the situation of many women. This insight is congruent with new ideas about the importance of "social capital" to the health of a society that have been put forward recently by a number of social scientists.[59] Corporations cannot be solely responsible for maintaining the web of community, although they are already being asked to serve as extended family, neighborhood support group, and national health service.

Diversity of Family Forms

Those who are concerned for strengthening the civil society immediately turn to the changing nature of the family as being a key building block. Feminists worry that seemingly sensible efforts to reverse the trend of rising divorce and single parenthood will privilege the two-parent family to the detriment of women; they propose instead that family values be understood in a broader sense as valuing the family's unique capacity for giving emotional and material support rather than implying simply a two-parent form.

The debate between conservatives, liberals, and feminists on the issue of the two-parent family has been most starkly stated by sociologist Judith Stacey and political philosopher Iris Young.[60] They regard the requirement that all women stay in a marriage as an invitation to coercion and subordination and an assault on the principles of freedom and self-determination that are at the foundation of democracy. Moreover, as Christopher Jencks and Kathryn Edin conclude from their study of several hundred welfare families, the current welfare reform rhetoric that no couple should have a child unless they can support it, does not take into ac-

count the uncertainty of life in which people who start out married or with adequate income may not always remain so. In the face of the world-wide dethronement of the two-parent family (approximately one-quarter to one-third of all families around the globe are headed by women), marriage should not be seen as the cure for child poverty. Mothers should not be seen as less than full citizens if they are not married or not employed (in 1989 there were only 16 million males between the ages of 25 and 34 who made over $12,000 compared with 20 million females of the same age who either had a child or wanted one).[61] National family policy should instead begin with a value on women's autonomy and self-determination that includes the right to bear children. Mother-citizens are helping to reproduce the next generation for the whole society, and in that responsibility they deserve at least partial support.

From a feminist perspective the goal of the family is not only to bring up a healthy and productive new generation; families also provide the intimate and supportive group of kin or fictive kin that foster the health and well-being of every person—young or old, male or female, heterosexual, homosexual, or celibate. Recognition as "family" should therefore not be confined to the traditional two-parent unit connected by blood, marriage, or adoption, but should be extended to include kin of a divorced spouse (as Stacey documented in her study of Silicon Valley families), same-sex partnerships, congregate households of retired persons, group living arrangements, and so on.[62] Twenty years ago economist Nancy Barrett noted that such diversity in family and household form was already present. Among all U.S. households in 1976, no one of the six major types constituted more than 15–20 percent: couples with and without children under 18 with the wife in the labor force (15.4 and 13.3 percent respectively); couples with or without children under 18 with the wife not in the labor force (19.1 and 17.1 percent); female- or male-headed households

(14.4 percent); and single persons living alone (20.6 percent).[63]

Such diversity both describes and informs contemporary "family values" in the United States. Each family type is numerous enough to have a legitimacy of its own, yet no single form is the dominant one. As a result the larger value system has evolved to encompass beliefs and rules that legitimate each type on the spectrum. The regressive alternative is "fundamentalism" that treats the two-parent family with children as the only legitimate form, single-parent families as unworthy of support, and the nontraditional forms as illegitimate. In 1995 the general population appears to have accepted diversity of family forms as normal. A Harris poll of 1,502 women and 460 men found that only two percent of women and one percent of men defined family as "being about the traditional nuclear family." One out of 10 women defined family values as loving, taking care of, and supporting each other, knowing right from wrong or having good values, and 9 out of 10 said society should value all types of families.[64] It appears most Americans believe that an Aunt Polly single-parent type of family for a Huck Finn that provides economic support, shelter, meals, a place to sleep and to withdraw is better than no family at all.

Amidst gradual acceptance of greater diversity in family form, the gender-role revolution is also loosening the sex-role expectations traditionally associated with breadwinning and homemaking. Feminists believe that men and women can each do both.[65] In addition, women in advanced industrial nations have by and large converged upon a new life pattern of multiple roles by which they combine work and family life. The negative outcome is an almost universal "double burden" for working women in which they spend 84 hours per week on paid and family work, married men spend 72 hours, and single persons without children spend 50 hours.[66] The positive consequence, however, appears to be improved physical and mental health for those women who, though stressed, combine work and family roles.[67] In addition, where a woman's husband helps her more with the housework, she is less likely to think of getting a divorce.[68]

The Precarious Situation of Children

The principal remedy that conservatives and liberals would apply to the problems of children is to restore the two-parent family by reducing out-of-wedlock births, increasing the presence of fathers, and encouraging couples who are having marital difficulties to avoid divorce for the sake of their children. Feminists, on the other hand, are skeptical that illegitimacy, father absence, or divorce are the principal culprits they are made out to be. . . . Arlene Skolnick and Stacey Rosencrantz cite longitudinal studies showing that most children recover from the immediate negative effects of divorce.[69]

How then, while supporting the principle that some fraction of women should be able to head families as single parents, do feminists analyze the problem of ill health, antisocial behavior, and poverty among children? Their answer focuses on the *lack of institutional supports* for the new type of dual-earner and single-parent families that are more prevalent today. Rather than attempt to force families back into the traditional mold, feminists note that divorce, lone-mother families, and women's employment are on the rise in every industrialized nation. But other countries have not seen the same devastating decline in child well-being, teen pregnancy, suicides and violent death, school failure, and a rising population of children in poverty. These other countries have four key elements of social and family policy which protect all children and their mothers: (1) work guarantees and other economic supports; (2) child care; (3) health care; and (4) housing subsidies. In the United States these benefits are scattered and uneven; those who can pay their way do so; only those who are poor or disabled receive AFDC for economic support, some help with child care, Medicaid for health care, and government-subsidized housing.

A first line of defense is to raise women's wages through raising the minimum wage, then provide them greater access to male-dominated occupations with higher wages. One-half of working women do not earn a wage adequate to support a family of four above the poverty line. Moreover, women in low-wage occupations are subject to frequent lay-offs and lack of benefits. Training to improve their human capital, provision of child care, and broadening of benefits would help raise women's capacity to support a family. Eisenberg reports that the Human Development Index of the United Nations (HDI), which ranks countries by such indicators as life expectancy, educational levels, and per capita income, places the United States fifth and Sweden sixth in the world. But when the HDI is recalculated to take into account equity of treatment of women, Sweden rises to first place and the United States falls to ninth. Therefore, one of the obvious places to begin raising children's status is to raise the economic status and earning power of their mothers.[70]

A second major benefit which is not assured to working mothers is child care. Among school-age children up to 13 years of age, one-eighth lack any kind of after-school child care. Children come to the factories where their mothers work and wait on the lawn or in the lobby until their mothers are finished working. If a child is sick, some mothers risk losing a job if they stay home. Others are latchkey kids or in unknown circumstances, such as sleeping in their parents' cars or loitering on the streets. Although 60 percent of mothers of the 22 million preschool children are working, there are only 10 million child care places available, a shortfall of one to three million slots.[71] Lack of good quality care for her children not only distracts a mother, adds to her absences from work, and makes her less productive, it also exposes the child to a lack of attention and care that leads to violent and antisocial behavior and poor performance in school.

Lack of medical benefits is a third gaping hole for poor children and lone-parent families.

Jencks and Edin analyze what happens to a Chicago-area working woman's income if she goes off welfare. Her total income in 1993 dollars on AFDC (with food stamps, unreported earnings, help from family and friends) adds up to $12,355, in addition to which she receives Medicaid and child care. At a $6 per hour full-time job, however, without AFDC, with less than half as much from food stamps, with an Earned Income Tax Credit, and help from relatives, her total income would add to $20,853. But she would have to pay for her own medical care, bringing her effective income down to $14,745 if she found free child care, and $9,801 if she had to pay for child care herself.[72]

Some housing subsidies or low-income housing are available to low-income families. But the neighborhoods and schools are frequently of poor quality and plagued by violence. To bring up children in a setting where they cannot safely play with others introduces important risk factors that cannot simply be attributed to divorce and single parenthood. Rather than being protected and being allowed to be innocent, children must learn to be competent at a very early age. The family, rather than being child-centered, must be adult-centered, not because parents are selfish or self-centered but because the institutions of the society have changed the context of family life.[73] These demands may be too much for children, and depression, violence, teen suicide, teen pregnancy, and school failure may result. But it would be myopic to think that simply restoring the two-parent family would be enough to solve all these problems. . . .

CONCLUSION

A review of the conservative, liberal, and feminist perspectives on the changing nature of the American family suggests that future policy should combine the distinctive contributions of all three. From the conservatives comes a critique of modernity that recognizes the important role of the family in maintaining child health and preventing child failure. Although their understanding of "family values" is too narrow, they deserve credit for raising the issue of family function and form to public debate. Liberals see clearly the overwhelming power of the economy to deny employment, make demands on parents as workers, and drive a wedge between employers' needs for competitiveness and families' needs for connection and community.

Surprising though it may seem, since feminists are often imagined to be "way out," the most comprehensive plan for restoring family to its rightful place is put forward by feminists who appreciate both the inherently premodern nature of the family and at the same time its inevitable interdependence with a fast-changing world economy. Feminists will not turn back to the past because they know that the traditional family was often a straightjacket for women. But they also know that family cannot be turned into a formal organization or have its functions performed by government or other public institutions that are incapable of giving needed succor to children, adults, and old people which only the family can give.

The feminist synthesis accepts both the inherent particularism and emotional nature of the family and the inevitable specialization and impersonality of the modern economy. Feminists are different from conservatives in accepting diversity of the family to respond to the needs of the modern economy. They are different from the liberals in recognizing that intimate nurturing relationships such as parenting cannot all be turned into a safety net of formal care. The most promising social policies for families and children take their direction from inclusive values that confirm the good life and the well-being of every individual as the ultimate goal of the nation. The policy challenge is to adjust the partnership between the family and its surrounding institutions so that together they combine the best of private initiative with public concern.

ENDNOTES

1. Barbara Dafoe Whitehead, "Dan Quayle Was Right," *Atlantic Monthly* (April 1993), p. 47. Her chapter in this volume on the "Story of Marriage" continues the theme of an erosion of values under the guise of tolerance for cultural diversity.

2. Mary Ann Glendon, "Marriage and the State: The Withering Away of Marriage," *Virginia Law Review 62* (May 1976), pp. 663–729.

3. Charles A. Murray, *Losing Ground: American Social Policy, 1950–1980* (New York: Basic Books, 1984). Critics point out that the rise in out-of-wedlock births continues, even though welfare payments have declined in size over the last several decades, thereby casting doubt on the perverse incentive theory of rising illegitimacy.

4. U.S. Bureau of the Census, *Statistical Abstract of the United States: 1994,* 114th ed. (Washington, DC: 1994), p. 59.

5. Suzanne M. Bianchi and Daphne Spain, *American Women in Transition* (New York: Russell Sage Foundation, 1986), p. 88.

6. Donald J. Hernandez, *America's Children: Resources from Family, Government, and the Economy* (New York: Russell Sage Foundation, 1993), pp. 284, 70; Janet Zollinger Giele, "Woman's Role Change and Adaptation, 1920–1990," in *Women's Lives through Time: Educated American Women of the Twentieth Century,* ed. K. Hulbert and D. Schuster (San Francisco: Jossey-Bass, 1993), p. 40.

7. Victor Fuchs, "Are Americans Underinvesting in Children?" in *Rebuilding the Nest,* ed. David Blankenhorn, Stephen Bayme, and Jean Bethke Elshtain (Milwaukee: Family Service America, 1990), p. 66. Bianchi and Spain, *American Women in Transition,* pp. 141, 201, 226. Janet Zollinger Giele, "Gender and Sex Roles," in *Handbook of Sociology,* ed. N. J. Smelser (Beverly Hills, CA: Sage Publications, 1988), p. 300.

8. Hernandez, *America's Children,* p. 130. Council on Families in America, *Marriage in America* (New York: Institute for American Values, 1995), p. 7.

9. Fuchs, "Are Americans Underinvesting in Children?" p. 61. Some would say, however, that the decline was due in part to a larger and more heterogeneous group taking the tests.

10. Council on Families in America, *Marriage in America,* 6. The report cites research by Nicholas Zill and Charlotte A. Schoenborn, "Developmental, Learning and Emotional Problems: Health of Our Nation's Children, United States, 1988." *Advance Data,* National Center for Health Statistics, Publication # 120, November 1990. See also, Sara McLanahan and Gary Sandefur, *Growing Up with a Single Parent* (Cambridge, MA: Harvard University Press, 1994).

11. Edward Gilbreath, "Manhood's Great Awakening," *Christianity Today* (February 6, 1995), p. 27.

12. David Elkind, *The Hurried Child: Growing Up Too Fast Too Soon* (Reading, MA: Addison-Wesley, 1981).

13. Jean Bethke Elshtain, *Democracy on Trial* (New York: Basic Books, 1995).

14. Jonathan Alter and Pat Wingert, "The Return of Shame," *Newsweek* (February 6, 1995), p. 25.

15. Tom McNichol, "The New Sex Vow: 'I won't' until 'I do'." *USA Weekend,* March 25–27, 1994, p. 4 ff. Lee Smith, "The New Wave of Illegitimacy," *Fortune* (April 18, 1994), p. 81 ff.

16. Susan Chira, "War over Role of American Fathers," *New York Times,* June 19, 1994, p. 22.

17. Juliet Schor, "Consumerism and the Decline of Family and Community: Preliminary Statistics from a Survey on Time, Money and Values," Harvard Divinity School, Seminar on Families and Family Policy, April 4, 1995.

18. Karen S. Peterson, "In Balancing Act, Scale Tips toward Family," *USA Today,* January 25, 1995.

19. Lawrence Mead, "Taxing Peter to Pay Paula," *The Wall Street Journal,* November 2, 1994.

20. Tom G. Palmer, "English Lessons: Britain Rethinks the Welfare State," *Wall Street Journal,* November 2, 1994.

21. Robert Pear, "G.O.P. Affirms Plan to Stop Money for Unwed Mothers," *New York Times,* January 21, 1995, p. 9.

22. Brigitte Berger, "Block Grants: Changing the Welfare Culture from the Ground Up," *Dialogue* (Boston: Pioneer Institute for Public Policy Research), no. 3, March 1995.

23. Robert Rector, "Welfare," *Issues '94: The Candidate's Briefing Book* (Washington, DC: American Heritage Foundation, 1994), chap. 13.

24. Council on Families in America, *Marriage in America,* pp. 13–16.

25. Robert Bellah, "Invasion of the Money World," in *Rebuilding the Nest,* ed. David Blankenhorn, Steven Bayme, and Jean Bethke Elshtain (Milwaukee: Family Service America, 1990), pp. 227–36. James Coleman, *Foundations of Social Theory* (Cambridge, MA: Harvard University Press, 1990).

26. Sylvia Nasar, "More Men in Prime of Life Spend Less Time Working," *New York Times,* December 1, 1994, p. A1.

27. John Scanzoni, *Power Politics in the American Marriage* (Englewood Cliffs, NJ: Prentice-Hall, 1972). Ruth A. Wallace and Alison Wolf, *Contemporary Sociological Theory* (Englewood Cliffs, NJ: Prentice-Hall, 1991), p. 176.

28. Fred Weinstein and Gerald M. Platt, *The Wish to Be Free: Society, Psyche, and Value Change* (Berkeley, CA: University of California Press, 1969).

29. Kingsley Davis, "Wives and Work: A Theory of the Sex-Role Revolution and Its Consequences," in *Feminism, Children, and the New Families,* ed. S. M. Dornbusch and M. H. Strober (New York: Guilford Press, 1988), pp. 67–86. Janet Zollinger Giele, *Two Paths to Women's Equality: Temperance, Suffrage, and the Origins of American Feminism* (New York: Twayne Publishers, Macmillan, 1995).

30. Vivianna A. Zelizer, *Pricing the Priceless Child: The Changing Social Value of Children* (New York: Basic Books, 1985).

31. William J. Goode, *World Revolution in Family Patterns* (New York: The Free Press, 1963).

32. Constance Willard Williams, *Black Teenage Mothers: Pregnancy and Child Rearing from Their Perspective* (Lexington, MA: Lexington Books, 1990).

33. William Julius Wilson, *The Truly Disadvantaged: The Inner City, the Underclass, and Public Policy* (Chicago: University of Chicago Press, 1987).

34. Jacob Mincer, "Labor-force Participation of Married Women: A Study of Labor Supply," in *Aspects of Labor Economics,* Report of the National Bureau of Economic Research (Princeton, NJ: Universities-National Bureau Committee of Economic Research, 1962). Glen G. Cain, *Married Women in the Labor Force: An Economic Analysis* (Chicago: University of Chicago Press, 1966).

35. Richard A. Easterlin, *Birth and Fortune: The Impact of Numbers on Personal Welfare* (New York: Basic Books, 1980). Valerie K. Oppenheimer, "Structural Sources of Economic Pressure for Wives to Work—Analytic Framework" *Journal of Family History 4,* no. 2 (1979), pp. 177–97; and Valerie K. Oppenheimer, *Work and the Family: A Study in Social Demography* (New York: Academic Press, 1982).

36. Janet Z. Giele and Rainer Pischner, "The Emergence of Multiple Role Patterns Among Women: A Comparison of Germany and the United States," *Vierteljahrshefte zur Wirtschaftsforschung* (Applied Economics Quarterly) (Heft 1–2, 1994). Alice S. Rossi, "The Future in the Making," *American Journal of Orthopsychiatry 63,* no. 2 (1993), pp. 166–76. Notburga Ott, *Intrafamily Bargaining and Household Decisions* (Berlin: Springer-Verlag, 1992).

37. Iris Young, "Mothers, Citizenship and Independence: A Critique of Pure Family Values," *Ethics 105,* no. 3 (1995), pp. 535–56. Young critiques the liberal stance of William Galston, *Liberal Purposes* (New York: Cambridge University Press, 1991).

38. Lee Rainwater and William L. Yancey, *The Moynihan Report and the Politics of Controversy* (Cambridge, MA: MIT Press, 1967).

39. Glen H. Elder, Jr., *Children of the Great Depression* (Chicago: University of Chicago Press, 1974). Rand D. Conger, Xiao-Jia Ge, and Frederick O. Lorenz, "Economic Stress and Marital Relations," in *Families in Troubled Times: Adapting to Change in Rural America,* ed. R. D. Conger and G. H. Elder, Jr. (New York: Aldine de Gruyter, 1994), pp. 187–203.

40. Coleman, *Foundations of Social Theory,* p. 590.

41. Elizabeth G. Menaghan and Toby L. Parcel, "Employed Mothers and Children's Home Environments," *Journal of Marriage and the Family 53,* no. 2 (1991), pp. 417–31. Lois Hoffman, "The Effects on Children of Maternal and Paternal Employment," in *Families and Work,* ed. Naomi Gerstel and Harriet Engel Gross (Philadelphia: Temple University Press, 1987), pp. 362–95.

42. Juliet Schor, *The Overworked American: The Unexpected Decline of Leisure* (New York: Basic Books, 1991). Robert Haveman and Barbara Wolfe, *Succeeding Generations: On the Effects of Investments in Children* (New York: Russell Sage Foundation, 1994), p. 239.

43. Coleman, *Foundations of Social Theory,* pp. 596–97.

44. Schor, "Consumerism and Decline of Family."

45. Iris Young, "Mothers, Citizenship and Independence," puts Elshtain, Etzioni, Galston, and Whitehead in this category.

46. Coleman, *Foundations of Social Theory,* pp. 597–609.

47. Sherry Wexler, "To Work and To Mother: A Comparison of the Family Support Act and the Family and Medical Leave Act" (Ph.D. diss. draft, Brandeis University, 1995). David T. Ellwood, *Poor Support: Poverty in the American Family* (New York: Basic Books, 1988).

48. Coleman, *Foundations of Social Theory,* pp. 300–321. Coleman, known for rational choice theory in sociology, put forward these theoretical possibilities in 1990, fully four years ahead of what in 1994 was voiced in the Republican Contract with America.

49. Wexler, "To Work and To Mother."

50. Robert Lerman, "Marketplace," National Public Radio, April 18, 1995.

51. Karen Offen, "Defining Feminism: A Comparative Historical Approach," *Signs 14,* no. 1 (1988), pp. 119–51.

52. Young, "Mothers, Citizenship and Independence."

53. Robert N. Bellah et al., *Habits of the Heart* (Berkeley, CA: University of California Press, 1985), pp. 250–71. Gosta Esping-Andersen, *The Three Worlds of Welfare Capitalism* (Princeton, NJ: Princeton University Press, 1990). Susan Pedersen, *Family, Dependence, and the Origins of the Welfare State: Britain and France, 1914–1945* (New York: Cambridge University Press, 1993).

54. Young, "Mothers, Citizenship and Independence."

55. Giele, "Woman's Role Change and Adaptation" presents these historical statistics.

56. Elshtain, *Democracy on Trial;* Robert N. Bellah et al., *The Good Society* (New York: Knopf, 1991), p. 210; Robert D. Putnam, "Bowling Alone: America's Declining Social Capital," *Journal of Democracy 4,* no. 1 (1995), pp. 65–78.

57. Heather McCallum, "Mind the Gap" (paper presented to the Family and Children's Policy Center colloquium, Waltham, MA, Brandeis Univer-

sity, March 23, 1995). The sum was markedly better for children of employed single mothers, around $700 per mother in the United States. But this figure corresponded with over $1,000 in 11 other countries, with only Greece and Portugal lower than the U.S. Concerning the high U.S. rates of teen pregnancy, see Planned Parenthood advertisement, "Let's Get Serious About Ending Teen Childbearing," *New York Times,* April 4, 1995, p. A25.

58. Ruth Walker, "Secretary Reich and the Disintegrating Middle Class," *Christian Science Monitor,* November 2, 1994, p. 19.

59. For reference to "social capital," see Coleman, *Foundations of Social Theory; Elshtain, Democracy on Trial;* and Putnam, "Bowling Alone." For "emotional capital," see Arlie Russell Hochschild, *The Managed Heart: The Commercialization of Human Feeling* (Berkeley, CA: University of California Press, 1983). For "cultural capital," see work by Pierre Bourdieu and Jurgen Habermas.

60. Judith Stacey, "Dan Quayle's Revenge: The New Family Values Crusaders," *The Nation,* July 25/August 1, 1994, pp. 119–22. Iris Marion Young, "Making Single Motherhood Normal," *Dissent* (winter 1994), pp. 88–93.

61. Christopher Jencks and Kathryn Edin, "Do Poor Women Have a Right to Bear Children," *The American Prospect* (winter 1995), pp. 43–52.

62. Stacey, "Dan Quayle's Revenge"; Arlene Skolnick and Stacey Rosencrantz, "The New Crusade for the Old Family," *The American Prospect* (summer 1994), pp. 59–65.

63. Nancy Smith Barrett, "Data Needs for Evaluating the Labor Market Status of Women," in *Census Bureau Conference on Federal Statistical Needs Relating to Women,* ed. Barbara B. Reagan (U.S. Bureau of the Census, 1979) Current Population Reports, Special Studies, Series P-23, no. 83, pp. 10–19. These figures belie the familiar but misleading statement that "only 7 percent" of all American families are of the traditional nuclear type because "traditional" is defined so narrowly—as husband and wife with two children under 18 where the wife is not employed outside the home. For more recent figures and a similar argument for a more universal family ethic, see Christine Winquist Nord and Nicholas Zill, "American Households in Demographic Perspective," working paper no. 5. Institute for American Values, New York, 1991.

64. Tamar Levin, "Women Are Becoming Equal Providers," *New York Times,* May 11, 1995, p. A27.

65. Marianne A. Ferber and Julie A. Nelson, *Beyond Economic Man: Feminist Theory and Economics* (Chicago: University of Chicago Press, 1993).

66. Fran Sussner Rodgers and Charles Rodgers, "Business and the Facts of Family Life," *Harvard Business Review,* no. 6 (1989), pp. 199–213, especially 206.

67. Ravenna Helson and S. Picano, "Is the Traditional Role Bad for Women?" *Journal of Personality and Social Psychology* 59 (1990), pp. 311–20. Rosalind C. Barnett, "Home-to-Work Spillover Revisited: A Study of Full-Time Employed Women in Dual-Earner Couples," *Journal of Marriage and the Family 56* (August 1994), pp. 647–56.

68. Arlie Hochschild, "The Fractured Family," *The American Prospect* (summer 1991), pp. 106–15.

69. Leon Eisenberg, "Is the Family Obsolete?" *The Key Reporter 60,* no. 3 (1995), pp. 1–5. Arlene Skolnick and Stacey Rosencrantz, "The New Crusade for the Old Family," *The American Prospect* (summer 1994), pp. 59–65.

70. Roberta M. Spalter-Roth, Heidi I. Hartmann, and Linda M. Andrews, "Mothers, Children, and Low-Wage Work: The Ability to Earn a Family Wage," in *Sociology and the Public Agenda,* ed. W. J. Wilson (Newbury Park, CA: Sage Publications, 1993), pp. 316–38.

71. Louis Uchitelle, "Lacking Child Care, Parents Take Their Children to Work," *New York Times,* December 23, 1994, p. 1.

72. Jencks and Edin, "Do Poor Women Have a Right," p. 50.

73. David Elkind, *Ties That Stress: The New Family in Balance* (Boston: Harvard University Press, 1994).

The Future of Marriage

Frank F. Furstenberg, Jr.

It's clear that the institution of family is undergoing a major overhaul. Perhaps you've recently been to a wedding where the bride and groom have invited their former spouses to join the festivities. Or maybe a family member told you that your 37-year-old unmarried cousin is pregnant by artificial insemination. Or you heard that your 75-year-old widowed grandfather just moved in with his 68-year-old woman friend. To those of us who grew up in the 1950s, the married-couple family is beginning to look like the Model T Ford.

Public concern over changes in the practice of marriage is approaching hysteria. An avalanche of books and articles declares that the American family is in a severe state of crisis. Yet little agreement exists among experts on what the crisis is about, why it has occurred, or what could be done to restore confidence in matrimony. I believe that the current situation falls somewhere between those who embrace the changes with complete sanguinity and an increasingly vocal group who see the meltdown of the so-called traditional family as an unmitigated disaster.

Social scientists agree that we have seen a startling amount of change in nuptial practices in the past half century. The shift is producing an especially striking contrast from the 1940s, because the period just after World War II was a time of remarkable domestication. The postwar period followed several decades of turbulence in marriage patterns initiated by rapid urbanization during World War I, and the Great Depression.

Frank Furstenberg, "The Future of Marriage" from *American Demographics* (June 1996). Copyright © 1996 by American Demographics, Inc. Reprinted with the permission of *American Demographics*.

Many of the complaints about family life in the 1990s sound an awful lot like those voiced in the 1950s, an era we look upon with nostalgia. We often forget that the current gold standard of family life—the family built upon an intimate marital relationship—was regarded with great suspicion when it made its debut. The middle-class nuclear family that became the norm at midcentury was a stripped-down version of the extended families of previous decades. Kingsley Davis observed that a host of social ills could be traced to this new form of family: "The family union has been reduced to its lowest common denominator—married couple and children. The family aspect of our culture has become couple-centered with only one or two children eventually entering the charmed circle," he wrote.

Ernest Burgess, one of the most respected sociologists of his generation, wrote in 1953 that urbanization, greater mobilization, individualization, increased secularization, and the emancipation of women had transformed the family from an institution based on law and custom to one based on companionship and love. Despite believing that the changes taking place in the family were largely beneficial to society, Burgess acknowledged that enormous pressure would be placed on the marital relationship to meet new expectations for intimacy. Burgess and Davis correctly predicted that divorce would rise because of the tremendous strain placed on couples to manage the growing demands for congeniality and cooperation.

Marriage is not in immediate danger of extinction, though. In 1960, 94 percent of women had been married at least once by age 45. The share in 1994 was 91 percent. In other words, the vast majority of Americans are still willing to try marriage at some point. What has changed from the 1960s is when, how, and for how long.

The median age at marriage has risen from a low of 20.3 for women and 22.8 for men in 1960, to 24.5 for women and 26.7 for men in 1994. The proportion of women never married by their late 20s tripled from a historical low of 11 percent in 1960 to a high of 33 percent in 1993. The divorce rate among ever-married women more than doubled between the early 1960s and late 1980s, although it has since leveled off.

The number of children living in married-couple families dropped from 88 percent in 1960 to 69 percent in 1994. Divorce plays a role in this decline, but much of the rise in single-parent families results from the sharp increase in non-marital childbearing. The proportion of births occurring out of wedlock jumped from 5 percent in 1960 to 31 percent in 1993. While some of these births occur among couples who are living together, the vast majority are to single parents.

The increase in single-parenthood due to divorce and out-of-wedlock births may be the most telling sign that Americans are losing confidence in marriage. Ironically, some of today's most vitriolic political rhetoric is directed toward gay couples who want the right to marry, just as the cultural legitimacy of marriage has been declining.

WHAT WE GET OUT OF MARRIAGE

What has transformed societal attitudes toward marriage so that young people delay it, older people get out of it, and some skip it altogether? Before attempting to answer these questions, a few cautions are in order. Demographers and sociologists, like climatologists, are pretty good at short-term forecasts, but have little ability to forecast into the distant future. In truth, no one can predict what marriage patterns will look like 50 years from now.

Virtually no one foresaw the "marriage rush" of the 1940s that preceded the baby boom. And few predicted the sudden decline of the institution in the 1960s. If our society alternates periods of embracing and rejecting marriage, then we could be poised on the cusp of a marriage restoration. It's doubtful, however, because most of the forces that have worked to reduce the strength of marital bonds are unlikely to reverse in the near future.

The biggest stress on marriage in the late 20th century is a transition from a clearcut gender-based division of labor to a much less focused one. For a century or more, men were assigned to the work force and women to domestic duties. This social arrangement is becoming defunct. Women are only moderately less likely than men to be gainfully employed. Even women with young children are more likely than not to be working. In 1994, 55 percent of women with children under age six were currently employed, compared with 19 percent in 1960.

Women's participation in the labor force has reduced their economic dependency on men. The traditional bargain struck between men and women—financial support in exchange for domestic services—is no longer valid. Men now expect women to help bring home the bacon. And women expect men to help cook the bacon, feed the kids, and clean up afterward. In addition, the old status order that granted men a privileged position in the family is crumbling.

These dramatic alterations in the marriage contract are widely endorsed in theory by men and women alike. The share of both who say their ideal marriage is one in which spouses share household and work responsibilities has increased since the 1970s, according to the 1995 Virginia Slims Opinion Poll. Yet in practice, moves toward gender equality have come with a price. Both men and women enter marriage with higher expectations for interpersonal communication, intimacy, and sexual gratification. If these expectations are not met, they feel freer than they once did to dissolve the relationship and seek a new partner.

Being out of marriage has its downside, too, of course. About 4 in 10 recently separated women say they are worse off financially than they were while married, according to the 1992–93 National Survey of Families and Households. This longitudinal study asked women who separated from their husbands since the previous survey in 1987–88 to evaluate several aspects of their lives. At the same time, 43 percent of separated women say their finances are better than during marriage.

Ending an unhappy marriage obviously brings about other positive changes. If it didn't, people wouldn't divorce. Being a single parent isn't easy. Yet more than half of separated women say that being a parent is better than before their split-up; 52 percent say care of children is better. Sixty-five percent say their overall home life is better, and 49 percent say their leisure time has improved. This may not mean they have more leisure time than while married, but perhaps the quality of that time is more fulfilling.

The increase in the share of women who work is not the only reason why Americans readily leave marriages that don't suit them. Legal reform and social trends have made divorce and nonmarital childbearing easier and more acceptable. Safe, affordable contraception enables couples to engage in sex outside of marriage with minimal risk of pregnancy. Women's college-enrollment rates have risen sharply in the past two decades, while public policies and societal attitudes have helped increase their involvement in politics and government. These changes have spurred women to greater autonomy. Each has affected marriage in a different way, but they have all worked in concert toward the same result: to make marriage less imperative and more discretionary.

Some Americans vigorously object to this "take-it-or-leave-it" approach to marriage on moral grounds, hoping to reverse the course of recent history by restoring "traditional" family values. Yet changes in the practice of marriage are not peculiar to the United States. The decline of marriage as it was practiced in the 1940s in the United States has occurred in virtually all Western societies.

MARRIAGE AS A LUXURY ITEM

The rise of delayed marriage, divorce, and out-of-wedlock childbearing disturbs the moral sensibilities of many observers. Others may not object on moral grounds, but they fear that the byproducts of intimate relationships—children—are no longer safeguarded by the family. Their fears are well-founded. A great deal of research shows that children are disadvantaged by our society's high level of marital flux.

A wealth of data shows that married men and women have lower incidences of alcohol-related problems and other health risks than do divorced and widowed people. Men especially seem to enjoy health benefits from marriage. Experts believe this is because wives often monitor health behavior, and because marriage provides incentives for men to avoid high-risk behaviors.

Marriage gives all parties involved an economic boost. In fact, stable marriages could be perpetuating the growing division in American society between the haves and have-nots. Marriage, quite simply, is a form of having. Children growing up with both of their biological parents are likely to be more educated, and to have better job skills and a more secure sense of themselves. Thus, they enter adulthood with greater chances of success and a greater likelihood of finding a mate with a similar profile.

This does not mean, however, that children are better off with married parents. Some think that men and women today lack the capacity to sacrifice for children as they did a generation ago. Maybe they do. But if sacrifice means remaining in a stressful, hostile, and abusive environment, it's not necessarily worth it. Even so, I doubt if failure to compromise one's own needs for the good of others is the main reason why fewer couples are getting married and staying married.

In my research on low-income families, I hear men and women talking about the virtues of marriage. Nearly all endorse the idea that children are better off when they grow up with both biological parents, although this is probably said in the context of assuming that the marriage is a "good" one.

Plenty of young people have seen "bad" marriages as they've grown up, which has given them an understandable fear of committing themselves and children to such a situation. "Most of my girlfriends, they got married when they was 20," says one woman. "Now they divorced. They got children. Fathers don't do nothing for them, so then, it was a toss-up. Either to go ahead and start out on the wrong foot or get on the right foot and then fall down." In other words, if you plan to have children, it may not matter too much whether you get married first, because you may not get anything out of the marriage, either financially or emotionally.

Although women may not depend on men's economic support as much as they used to, they still expect something out of the bargain. Young adults in low-income populations feel that they don't have the wherewithal to enter marriage. It's as if marriage has become a luxury consumer item, available only to those with the means to bring it off. Living together or single-parenthood has become the budget way to start a family. Most low-income people I talk to would prefer the luxury model. They just can't afford it.

Marriage is both a cause and a consequence of economic, cultural, and psychological stratification in American society. The recent apparent increase in income inequality in the United States means that the population may continue to sort itself between those who are eligible for marriage and a growing number who are deemed ineligible to marry.

There is little to suggest that marriage will become more accessible and enduring in the next century. The unpredictability and insecurity of the job market is likely to have an unsettling effect on marriage in the short term by making marriage a risky proposition, and in the long term by generating larger numbers of people who are the products of unstable family situations. Men are making some progress in taking on household tasks, including child care, but women still shoulder most of the burden in families, causing continued marital stress.

While this may sound unduly pessimistic, marriage may change for the better if people are committed to making the institution work, albeit in a new format. The end of the 20th century may eventually be recognized as the period when this new form of family—the symmetrical marriage—first appeared.

It's no longer noteworthy to see a man pushing a stroller or for preschoolers to be just as curious about mommy's job as daddy's. As with many social trends, well-educated couples appear to be leading the way in developing marriages based on equal sharing of economic and family responsibilities. It may be a little easier for them, too, because they are more likely to have the resources to hire people to do the things they choose not to do themselves.

The move toward symmetry may be more challenging for average Americans of more modest means. Couples who work split shifts because they can't afford child care may be sharing the economic and household load, but they don't spend much time with their spouses. Single parents who have no one with whom to share the load might have little sympathy for couples who argue about whose turn it is to do the dishes, but at least they are spared the arguing. Single people supporting themselves may feel that their finances are strapped, but when a married person loses his or her job, more than one person is adversely affected.

I am often struck by the fact that we have generous ways—both public and private—of aiding communities beset by natural disasters. Yet we do practically nothing for the same communities when a private industry abandons them, or when their young people can't find work, no matter how hard they look. Restoring marriage to an institution of enduring, compassionate relationships will require more than sanctimonious calls for traditional, communitarian, and family values. We should back up our words with resources. This includes moving toward a society that offers secure, remunerative jobs, as well as better child-care options and more flexible schedules so people can accept those jobs. Otherwise, the institution of marriage as we knew it in this century will in the 21st century become a practice of the privileged. Marriage could become a luxury item that most Americans cannot afford.